ENCYCLOPEDIA OF ASIAN-AMERICAN LITERATURE

ENCYCLOPEDIA OF ASIAN-AMERICAN LITERATURE

Seiwoong Oh

Facts On File
An imprint of Infobase Publishing

Encyclopedia of Asian-American Literature

Copyright © 2007 by Seiwoong Oh

Facts On File, Inc.
An imprint of Infobase Publishing
132 West 31st Street
New York NY 10001

Library of Congress Cataloging-in-Publication Data
Oh, Seiwoong,
    Encyclopedia of Asian-American literature / Seiwoong Oh.
        p. cm.
    Includes bibliographical references and index.
    ISBN 10:0-8160-6086-X (acid-free paper)
    ISBN 13:978-0-8160-6086-3
    1. American literature—Asian American authors—Encyclopedias. 2. American literature—Asian American authors—Bio-bibliography—Dictionaries. 3. Canadian literature—Asian authors—Encyclopedias. 4. Canadian literature—Asian authors—Bio-bibliography—Dictionaries. 5. Asian American authors—Biography—Dictionaries. 6. Asian Americans—Intellectual life—Encyclopedias. 7. Asian Americans in literature—Encyclopedias. I. Title.
    PS153.A84O37 2007
    810.9'895—dc22   2006026181

Facts On File books are available at special discounts when purchased in bulk quantities for businesses, associations, institutions, or sales promotions. Please call our Special Sales Department in New York at (212) 967-8800 or (800) 322-8755.

You can find Facts On File on the World Wide Web at http://www.factsonfile.com

Text design by Rachel Berlin
Cover design by Takeshi Takahashi

Printed in the United States of America

VB 10 9 8 7 6 5 4 3 2 1

This book is printed on acid-free paper.

TABLE OF CONTENTS

INTRODUCTION AND PREFACE

The 337 entries in this volume introduce more than 200 North American authors of Asian descent and their major literary works. Many of these authors were born and educated in the United States; some, like Ha Jin and Carlos Bulosan, are naturalized citizens or permanent residents; a few, like Ruth Prawer Jhabvala, are transnational citizens or cultural travelers whose claim to "Americanness" is limited but whose works nevertheless constitute an integral part of Asian-American culture. While the emphasis remains on authors active in the United States, Canadian authors such as Joy Kogawa are also included for their critical importance in the Asian-American literary canon. Many authors trace their roots to East Asia, many others to Southeast and South Asia, and a few to Hawaii, Afghanistan, and the Middle East.

The inclusiveness of this volume, however debatable, is forward-looking and reflective of the most recent thinking in Asian-American studies, which has constantly been redrawing and expanding its geographical and intellectual boundaries since its inception in the late 1960s on the heels of the Civil Rights movement. In the early days of the Asian-American movement, its primary aim was to claim that Asian Americans are not foreigners but legitimate American citizens whose history in America goes back more than a hundred years. To this end, participants in the movement underlined not only their American nativity and their cultural difference from Asians who came "fresh off the boat" but also their visible contributions to America's nation-building: serving in the U.S. military, building the transcontinental railroad, and participating in mining and agricultural industries.

In the late 1970s, when most Americans still insisted that Asians, wherever they were born, were alike and culturally and linguistically distinct from "real Americans," it was necessary to seek boundaries and parameters so as to advertise and establish the existence of Asian America. One of the first items of business for Asian-American activists was to do away with the term *Oriental,* which connoted an exotic, perilous, and faraway place of geishas, heathen Chinese, and opium dens. So the umbrella term *Asian-American* was popularized to help undo the stereotype, to assert American identity, and to promote solidarity among Asian Americans. Soon the hyphen in *Asian-American*—which implied a half-membership in American society—was removed to further stress the word *American.* This "strategically constructed unitary identity, a closed essence sharply dividing 'Asian

American' from 'Asian,'" explains Elaine H. Kim, "was a way to conjure up and inscribe our faces on the blank pages and screens of America's hegemonic culture" (Foreword xii).

In the 1970s and 1980s critics did not agree on the precise definition of Asian America, but nearly all of them focused on Americans of East Asian descent. In 1972, for example, when Kai-yu Hsu and Helen Palubinskas published a literary anthology titled *Asian American Authors,* the editors included, with a few exceptions, American-born authors of Chinese, Japanese, and Filipino origin. Two years later, when Frank Chin, Jeffery Paul Chan, Lawson Fusao Inada, and Shawn Wong edited *Aiiieeeee! An Anthology of Asian-American Writers,* they included only the works that they judged to show "authentic" Asian-American sensibilities free from "white supremacist" ideology (qtd. in Ling 30). When Elaine H. Kim published *Asian American Literature: An Introduction to the Writings and Their Social Context* (1982), a seminal work in the field, she defined Asian-American literature as "published creative writing in English by Americans of Chinese, Japanese, Korean and Filipino descent" and limited herself to discussing works that deal with the American experience of Asian Americans (xi).

The definition and boundaries of Asian America continued to change in the following years. While early scholars focused on authors with cultural ties to East Asia and on works that deal with American domestic issues, subsequent scholars began to expand the field to include immigrant authors and works that portray not just the United States but also their countries of origin, imagined or otherwise. Whereas early scholars and activists tried to claim America at the expense of severing ties with the ancestral cultures of Asia, later scholars attempted to empower themselves by reclaiming their ancestral cultures and embracing them.

The expansion of the field, in a sense, was closely tied to the changing global economic landscape. The economic strengths of China, South Korea, Taiwan, Singapore, and, of course, Japan had undoubtedly contributed to an improved image of Asian Americans in recent decades. Moreover, transportation between the United States and Asia became no longer a long, daunting journey but now a matter of hours and much more affordable. Immigration patterns also changed, as students, middle-class and affluent families, and professionals began flowing in and out of the country, changing the makeup of Asian America. In addition, the emergence of multinational corporations and such technological advancements as the Internet and satellite broadcasting had significantly shortened the distance between Asia and America.

The growing permeability in the boundaries between Asia and Asian America, however, created an anxiety within the Asian-American community. For example, Sau-ling Cynthia Wong, a prominent scholar, voiced caution in her 1995 essay, "Denationalization Reconsidered: Asian American Cultural Criticism at a Theoretical Crossroads." Wong poignantly argued that Asian America should remain distinct from diasporic Asia because, among other things, "collapsing the two will work to the detriment more of Asian Americans as a minority within U.S. borders than of 'Asian Asians'":

> In fact, in the age of Newt Gingrich, Rush Limbaugh, Proposition 187, and increasingly vicious attacks on affirmative action and other policies safeguarding the rights of peoples of color, there seems to me to be an even greater need for Asian Americanists to situate themselves historically. (20)

In practical terms, Wong's point was valid. After all, despite all the efforts made by many activists from the late 1960s, even a fifth-generation Asian American is likely to hear, "Where are you *really* from?" or "You speak English very well." Most scholars agree, however, that Asian-American identities are determined not solely by the American history of immigration, exclusion laws, racial discrimination, and internment but also by the ever-changing paradigm of international politics and global exchange of goods and cultures. Despite the unease expressed by Wong and others, more and more critics began to analyze Asian-American literature not just from an American domestic perspective but from a diasporic one as well.

The Asian-American movement was soon joined by Pacific Islanders and Pacific Americans. To reflect this geographical expansion, some Asian-American organizations and projects changed their names to "Asian Pacific American." This coalition, nonetheless, has been tenuous for a few reasons. First, Native Hawaiian political and community leaders were often less than enthralled with the alliance because they had a different political agenda. Unlike Asian-Americans, they wanted to have themselves recognized as an indigenous people, like Native Americans or Alaska Natives. They were also concerned with a different set of issues, such as the environment and colonization by the United States. Furthermore, Pacific and Hawaiian issues have rarely been addressed by Asian-American organizations, prompting critics like Jonathan Y. Okamura to abandon the use of the term "Asian Pacific American." According to Okamura, "its deployment is a discursive practice that constitutes a form of Asian American domination of Pacific Islanders" (187).

Despite these objections, the commonalities between the two communities have helped to maintain the coalition. Besides the geographical overlap and proximity between Asia and the Pacific Islands, many Chinese, Japanese, Korean, and Filipino Americans have their American roots in the sugar plantations of Hawaii, which became in 1959 the 50th state of the United States. Moreover, a number of canonical Asian-American authors, such as Cathy Song and Garrett Hongo, are natives of Hawaii. The increasing geopolitical and economic significance of the Pacific Rim will only strengthen the coalition between Asian America and the Pacific Islands.

Once Asian-American studies successfully began to establish itself as a vibrant field of inquiry, resulting in the founding of Asian-American studies programs or departments in several universities, other Asian ethnic groups began to join the field.

In just a few decades, the number of ethnic groups housed in Asian-American studies grew from just a few to more than 50. Southeast Asian– and South Asian–American voices became a particularly recognizable presence. Vietnamese-American authors such as Le Ly Hayslip and Jade Ngọc Quang Huy`nh, Filipino-American writers such as Cecilia Brainard and Jessica Hagedorn, and Indian writers such as Bharati Mukherjee and Meena Alexander, among many others, helped expand the Asian-American literary canon. South Asian diasporic literature, which was and remains at the center of postcolonial studies, joined Asian-American studies to focus on examining the American experience of the South Asian diaspora and on carving out its own niche within the field.

These two major developments in the field—the blurring of boundaries between Asia and Asian America and the increasing participation of Southeast and South Asian immigrants—resulted in cross-pollination between the fields of Asian-American studies and postcolonial studies. The commonalities between the two have allowed scholars to borrow ideas from one another as they grappled with questions about race, gender, identity, and representation. As if to demonstrate the cross-fertilization of the two fields, what used to be key terms in postcolonial studies—*diaspora*, *fragmentation*, *subjectivity*, *hybridity*, and *multiplicity*—are now commonly used in Asian-American studies as well. As Moustafa Bayoumi says, South and Southeast Asian-Americans have changed the "landscape of study for the discipline" of Asian–American studies ("Staying Put" 226).

In 2003 Bayoumi predicted that "it may only be a matter of time for West Asians (Arabs, Iranians, Afghans, etc.) to carve a place there" ("Staying Put" 226). Arabs are still legally defined as "white" in the United States, and West Asians have yet to wrestle with the question of a coherent group identity, if there is to be one. However, the impetus to join Asian-American studies is certainly there. As Bayoumi insists,

Arab Americans and Asian-American studies have much to learn from each other, and this has less to do with some abstract land mass long ago defined as "Asia" (which includes more than half of the Arab world) and more to do with American imperialism and domestic repression. . . . Palestine and Iraq ought now to be seen as Asian American issues. ("Our Work" 9)

This coalition is likely to become visible in the near future, as Bayoumi has predicted. I have therefore included several representative authors of Afghan and Middle-Eastern descent: Khaled Hosseini (Afghan), Samuel Hazo and Lawrence Joseph (Lebanese-Syrian), Naomi Shihab Nye (Palestinian-German), Diana Abu-Jaber (Jordanian), and Suheir Hammad (Palestinian).

HISTORY OF ASIAN-AMERICAN LITERATURE

Immigrants from Asia came to the United States in significant numbers from the 1850s. The news of the gold rush attracted thousands of people from China, who arrived in California as cheap laborers to work in the mining and agricultural industries and to complete the transcontinental railroad. From the 1880s Japanese and Koreans arrived in Hawaii to work as field hands at sugar plantations and soon found their way onto the mainland. In 1907 a large number of Punjabis who initially settled in Canada moved south to find jobs at lumber mills in Washington and agricultural fields in California. Following the two world wars, the 1965 Hart-Cellar Act, which eliminated immigration quotas based on national origins, and the end of the Vietnam War, immigrants and refugees came in the thousands and tens of thousands, making Asian Americans the fastest-growing minority group in the United States. According to the U.S. Census Bureau, 14 million people in the United States in 2004 identified themselves as Asian Americans, making up 5 percent of the total U.S. population. The bureau also predicts that the number will grow to 37.6 million by 2050, 9.3 percent of the U.S. population.

Historically speaking, Asian Americans such as Sui Sin Far (Winifred Eaton) have been writ-ing and publishing since the 19th century. In the first half of the 20th century, immigrant authors such as Younghill Kang and Carlos Bulosan wrote about life as Asian immigrants searching for a home in the United States. During and after World War II, as Americans became interested in China as a newfound ally against Japan, books such as Jade Snow Wong's *Fifth Chinese Daughter* (1950) were published to help promote the fledgling U.S.-China relationship. In the decades following World War II and the internment of Japanese Americans, Hisaye Yamamato, Milton Murayama, and John Okada explored the question of Japanese-American identity and began to show depth and maturity as literary writers.

What is now called the "Asian-American literary canon," however, had its meaningful beginning with the publication of Maxine Hong Kingston's *The Woman Warrior* in 1976, which depicts her life as a girl growing up in California. She received the National Book Critics Circle Award for the year's best work of nonfiction. A few years later, she went on to write *China Men*, which won the National Book Award in 1981. By developing a uniquely Asian-American literary voice, Kingston inspired a number of other Asian Americans to write in their own voices, and by producing a "crossover hit" in the mainstream marketplace, she paved a pathway for Asian-American writers into the book market.

Two other authors of Chinese descent followed suit. David Henry Hwang won the Tony Award for his *M. Butterfly* (1988), which was a great success on Broadway and was later made into a movie. Amy Tan's *Joy Luck Club* (1989) remained on the *New York Times* best-seller list for more than nine months and was also made into a commercial movie. As publishers began to recognize the talent and marketability of Asian-American writers, newcomers like Gish Jen, Gus Lee, Fae Myenne Ng, and Chang-rae Lee have been making successful debuts with their novels, and neglected works of the past such as those of John Okada and Richard E. Kim have resurfaced on the market. In poetry also, David Mura, Garret Hongo, Li-Young Lee, and Cathy Song made their presence conspicuous on the national scene.

The individual works by these and other writers led to several literary anthologies, allowing a choice for students and teachers. First published in 1974, *Aiiieeeee!* gave a wake-up call to the literary consciousness of Asian Americans. In 1991 the volume was reedited as *The Big Aiiieeeee!* as a more comprehensive collection. Jessica Hagedorn's *Charlie Chan Is Dead* came out in 1993, focusing on Asian-American fiction, while Garret Hongo's *The Open Boat* of the same year collected poems exclusively. As if to prove the popular demand from the public, dozens of Asian-American literary anthologies have been published in just the last decade.

In 1992 Elaine H. Kim asserted that we were witnessing the start of a "golden age of Asian American cultural production" (Foreword xi). Looking at the shelves in major bookstores now, one would agree that she was right. Moreover, as multicultural education gained momentum in school curricula, works by talented writers of South Asian background—Meena Alexander, Chitra Banerjee Divakaruni, Jhumpa Lahiri, and Bharati Mukherjee, for example—have been making regular appearances in school syllabi and academic conferences. Following the terrorist attacks against the United States on September 11, 2001, and the continuing unrest in the Middle East, public interest in works by authors of West Asian origin surged noticeably, creating another momentum for rich cultural production from Afghan- and Arab-American authors.

CHALLENGES: SOCIAL CONTEXTS AND LITERARY AESTHETICS

In her *Asian American Literature,* Elaine H. Kim cogently argues that understanding the social context of Asian-American immigration history is crucial to reading Asian-American writings, and that there are specific images, metaphors, and themes relevant to Asian-American writings. Sauling Cynthia Wong, in her *Reading Asian American Literature,* echoes this idea, although she adds that there are actually several contexts for different ethnic groups. While it is possible to enjoy a literary work without understanding its cultural background, the number-one challenge for a beginning reader is to learn about the historical and cultural contexts in which Asian-American literature has been produced.

Another challenge has to do with literary aesthetics. When Maxine Hong Kingston, Amy Tan, and David Henry Hwang were making spectacular debuts into the book market, Frank Chin claimed that they were popular mainly because they pandered to the taste of mainstream readers. According to Chin, they were the first writers of Asian ancestry to "so boldly fake the best-known works from the most universally known body of Asian literature and lore in history" (3). Chin further argued that the works of Jade Snow Wong and Maxine Hong Kingston "completely escaped the real China and Chinese America into pure white fantasy where nothing is Chinese, nothing is real, everything is born of pure imagination" (49). In response to Chin's accusations, Maxine Hong Kingston and Amy Tan insisted that myths change as people face new adventures and that early Chinese immigrants changed details of ancient Chinese myths to deal with their new realities in America. Despite the long and heated debate, this question about "authenticity" remains unresolved: Are writers responsible for representing their cultures accurately, and who is to say what is authentic and what is fake?

Another challenge facing readers of Asian-American literature is to find a proper means to evaluate each literary piece. American students who are used to reading only European or European-American literature may be tempted to dismiss any piece of Asian-American literature just because it is different or hard to understand. If a Laotian character in a short story seems impenetrable, if the symbols and metaphors used in a Korean-American poem are different from those in Shakespeare, if the historical setting used in a novel by a Pakistani-American writer seems remote and irrelevant, do we dismiss them as inferior works with no literary merit? If the issues explored in these pieces seem to have little or nothing to do with us, why should we continue to read them? To address these issues, new critical paradigms are being created, and readers are urged to develop multicultural sensibilities. In the meantime, it seems important at this point to remain open-minded and not to dismiss Asian-American or any multiethnic literature just because it is different, hard to understand, or seemingly irrelevant.

ABOUT THIS BOOK

This volume is designed for high school or college students who are beginning to read Asian-American literature in the classroom and on their own. Teachers select works that are aesthetically valuable, historically significant, teachable, and commercially available; I have therefore chosen the authors and works that meet these qualifications. Nearly every author and literary work that is likely to be taught in high school or college is included in this volume. All the canonical authors, such as Maxine Hong Kingston, Amy Tan, and David Henry Hwang, are, of course, included. Most of the authors who are frequently talked about in academic circles are also included. I have ventured to include several recent authors as well whose works are not yet tested but who promise to become prominent literary voices in the future. Also included are authors of detective fiction (Leonard Chang, Sujata Massey, and Laura Joh Rowland, for example) and young-adult literature (Linda Sue Park, Lawrence Yep, and Marie G. Lee). These authors are marginalized and rarely discussed in academic circles but nonetheless enjoyed by many readers. Although fiction, poetry, and drama make up the majority of the works included, memoirs, screenwriting, nonfiction, and experimental writings have also been included. Space is allocated for individual authors and major works according to their significance and availability of critical material. Canonical authors and their major works are treated at length; new authors and minor works are introduced briefly.

This volume is the product of a truly international collaboration. Ninety-five specialists of Asian-American literature based in the United States, Asia, and Europe have generously donated their expertise by writing entries that are uniformly packed with well-informed and updated information about each author and a brief synopsis and critical analysis of each major work. Each entry is designed to be as readable as possible and to offer enough information to get a student started on his or her own journey into the work or the author's world. To this end, lists of recommended further readings are provided wherever appropriate.

BIBLIOGRAPHY

Bayoumi, Moustafa. "Our Work Is of This World." *Amerasia Journal* 31, no. 1 (2005): 6–9.
———. "Staying Put: Aboriginal Rights, the Question of Palestine, and Asian American Studies." *Amerasia Journal* 29, no. 2 (2003): 221–228.
Cheung, King-kok, and Stan Yogi. *Asian American Literature: An Annotated Bibliography.* New York: MLA, 1988.
Chin, Frank. "Come All Ye Asian American Writers." In *The Big Aiiieeeee! An Anthology of Chinese American and Japanese American Literature,* edited by Jeffery Paul Chan, Frank Chin, Lawson Fusao Inada, and Shawn Wong, 1–92. New York: Penguin, 1991.
Chin, Frank, Jeffery Chan, Lawson Inada, and Shawn Wong, eds. *Aiiieeeee! An Anthology of Asian-American Writers.* Washington: Howard University Press, 1974.
Espiritu, Yen Le. "Asian American Studies and Ethnic Studies: About Kin Disciplines," *Amerasia Journal* 29, no. 2 (2003): 195–209.
Hsu, Kai-yu, and Helen Palubinskas. *Asian-American Authors.* Boston: Houghton, 1972.
Kim, Elaine H. *Asian American Literature: An Introduction to the Writings and Their Social Context.* Philadelphia: Temple University Press, 1982.
———. Foreword. In *Reading the Literatures of Asian America,* edited by Shirley Geok-lin Lim and Amy Ling, xi–xvii. Philadelphia: Temple University Press, 1992.
Leonard, George J. Introduction. In *The Asian Pacific American Heritage: A Companion to Literature and Arts,* edited by George J. Leonard, xxiii–xxix. New York: Garland, 1999.
Ling, Amy. "Asian American Literature: A Brief Introduction and Selected Bibliography." *ADE Bulletin* 80 (Spring 1985): 29–33.

Okamura, Jonathan Y. "Asian American Studies in the Age of Transnationalism: Diaspora, Race, Community." *Amerasia Journal* 29, no. 2 (2003): 171–193.

Palumbo-Liu, David. "The Ethnic as 'Post': Reading the Literatures of Asian America." *American Literary History* 7 (1995): 161–68.

———. "Theory and the Subject of Asian American Studies," *Amerasia Journal* 21, nos. 1 & 2 (1995): 55–65.

Takaki, Ronald. *Strangers from a Different Shore: A History of Asian Americans.* Boston: Little Brown, 1989. Reprint, New York: Penguin, 1989.

Wong, Sau-ling Cynthia. "Denationalization Reconsidered: Asian American Cultural Criticism at a Theoretical Crossroads." *Amerasia Journal* 21, nos. 1 & 2 (1995): 1–27.

———. *Reading Asian American Literature: From Necessity to Extravagance.* Princeton, N.J.: Princeton University Press, 1993.

Seiwoong Oh

A TO Z
ENTRIES

Abbasi, Talat

Born in Lucknow, India, Talat Abbasi spent her childhood in Karachi, Pakistan, and received her education in both Pakistan and England. She moved to New York in 1978 and started working for the United Nations. Her short stories on issues of class, sexuality, and gender have been published in journals, anthologies, and textbooks internationally. Abbasi's stories take an insightful yet subtle approach as she sketches incidents from everyday life. Even though most of her stories are set in Karachi, her recent stories are about immigrant Pakistanis in New York.

Bitter Gourd and Other Stories (2001) is her only collection of short stories to date. The 17 stories in the collection, written between 1988 and 2001, are very simple in plot and style. She takes everyday incidents from the lives of Pakistani women and skillfully creates climactic moments around them. In the first story of the collection, "Bitter Gourd," Miss Nilofar visits Rich Relation every first Friday of each month in order to collect a monthly remuneration promised to her mother by Rich Relation's mother. There is no proof of such a promise, but neither Rich Relation nor Miss Nilofar seems to be concerned about the truth. Miss Nilofar comes every month with the pretense of bringing a gift and goes back with the money. As the story opens,

Miss Nilofar comes to pay her monthly visit and waits for the promised money. She has brought a dish of cooked bitter gourd and leaves it in the kitchen, knowing full well that no one in that rich household is interested in her food. Miss Nilofar keeps her head high as she collects the money and leaves Rich Relation's house for that month without informing Rich Relation of her mother's death. The story has a hidden twist, almost a satirical one, as readers notice how a seemingly plain woman exploits her rich relative and learns to survive in a world which has no respect for a poor and unmarried woman. In "Granny's Portion," Abbasi deals with the issues of poverty in old age. In the story, children visit a poor relative, "a granny," to give her a portion of meat saved for poor relatives during the Muslim religious festival of Eid-ul-Azha, or "Eid Qurban." Stories like "A Piece of Cake," "Ticketless Riders," and "Swatting Flies" examine issues of poverty and child labor. Some of her stories take a different direction as they move away from simple depictions toward complex explorations of the issue of gender. In "The Birdman," for example, a poor young widow, abused by her in-laws and by her employers, dreams to build a new life with a handsome bird seller who eventually sells her to a brothel. The symbolism in the story is very dark, almost like that of Sylvia Plath.

Abbasi's most recent stories in *Bitter Gourd and Other Stories* deal with Pakistani women living in New York. These stories show how a new geographical location fails to relocate a Pakistani woman as an agent of freedom. Divorce, infidelity, and loneliness become the ultimate fate of these women, who have migrated into a new land in search of hope but end up as caged animals. "A Bear and Its Trainer" is a story about a loveless marriage of convenience between Dolly and Mr. Mirza. Like the bird seller in "The Birdman," Mr. Mirza takes pride in his power as a trainer and gladly discards his wife, "the ugly bear," after years of marriage. Yet, unlike the heroine of "The Birdman," Dolly refuses to be discarded easily. She breaks the stereotypical image of a suffering wife by creating a surprising meaning of life both for herself and her husband at the end of the story. In "Mirage," the last story of the collection and winner of the BBC World Service short-story competition in 2000, a single mother of a mentally ill child feels relieved after leaving him at an institution. The mother cleans her New York apartment and makes it look like any other normal home, getting rid of any sign of having a schizophrenic 10-year-old son. "I go to bed early," the mother says, "and sleep right through the night because the lights don't suddenly go on, off, on again at 1 a.m., the taps don't run and flood the bath at 3 and I have absolutely no fear that the stove will turn itself on" (154).

Abbasi's short stories make a patchwork of postcolonial women's lives both at home and in the diaspora. Her stories recall the style of Jane Austen as she deals with simple and delicate matters in minute detail. She also resembles Virginia Woolf in her use of the "stream of consciousness" technique. Her heroines interpret the external world in terms of disillusionment and create a secret world of their own within themselves. In their own world, these women constantly focus on their entrapment, failure, and hopelessness. The recurrent pessimistic tone in many of her stories reveals to her readers that, for a poor Muslim woman in South Asia, love and hope are nothing but a mirage.

Bibliography
Abbasi, Talat. *Bitter Gourd and Other Stories.* Karachi: Oxford University Press, 2001.
Shamsie, Muneeza, ed. *A Dragonfly in the Sun: An Anthology of Pakistani Writings in English.* Karachi: Oxford University Press, 1997.

Fayeza Hasanat

Abdullah, Shaila (1971–)

A writer and graphic designer, Shaila Abdullah was born in Karachi, Pakistan. After graduating in 1992 from the University of Karachi, with a bachelor's degree in English, she attended the Karachi School of Arts, graduating in 1993 with a diploma in graphic design. Two years later, she got married and moved to California. She currently lives in Texas, working primarily as a graphic designer.

Her career as a writer was encouraged by her father, who still serves as the first reviewer and critic of her work. She started writing at a young age, contributing to college newsletters and community magazines. She has been working as a freelance writer since 1993, publishing her articles and short stories in magazines based both in Asia and America. Her first book, a collection of short stories entitled *Beyond the Cayenne Wall* (2005), generated much critical interest and won the Jury Prize for Outstanding Fiction in the 2005 Norumbega Fiction Awards.

The collection consists of seven stories that portray female protagonists attempting to transcend the rigid gender roles imposed on them by their conservative society. "Amulet for the Caged Dove," "Moment of Reckoning," and "Ashes to Ashes, Dust to Dust" are set in Pakistan and focus on the relations of power within patriarchal households where women are deprived of their basic rights of self-definition. Although in these stories men are merely background characters, it is clear that they hold the power to make decisions that can alter women's lives. The first two stories additionally present the plight of childless women, who are invariably subjected to derision and even abuse because of their inability to produce offspring, even if their husbands are to blame for the infertility.

Other stories in the collection explore the clash between Pakistan and America, depicting female characters who are usually first-generation immigrants or temporary residents in the United States. Their encounters with the West inevitably lead to damaging consequences. The women end up uprooted, suspended between the two worlds, no longer comfortable about their home culture yet unable to assimilate into the new one. The two worlds are presented as "touching but never quite mingling." When the protagonist of "Demons of the Past" learns she is an adopted child and embarks on a literal and figurative journey to discover her roots, the knowledge she gains brings about only disillusionment and discomfort. The story suggests she would be better off not knowing her past.

In all of these stories, gender and race are pivotal constituents of the characters' hybrid identities. The only story in which the racial and cultural background does not play a significant role is "The Arrangement," an insightful analysis of a complex relationship between two childhood friends and the strength of parental love.

Abdullah is currently working on two novels depicting the lives of Pakistani women. The first one relates the experiences of a woman representing the Pakistani diaspora in the United States, whereas the latter focuses on the violation of women's rights in Pakistan.

Bibliography

Abdullah, Shaila. *Beyond the Cayenne Wall: Collection of Short Stories.* New York: iUniverse, 2005.

Shaila Abdullah. "Beyond the Cayenne Wall." Available online. URL: www.shailaabdullah.com. Downloaded on March 6, 2006.

Izabella Kimak

Abu-Jaber, Diana (1959–)

Born in Syracuse, New York, to a Jordanian father and an American mother, Diana Abu-Jaber has spent her life in between America and Jordan. Formally, her education includes an M.A. from the University of Windsor, studying under Joyce Carol Oates, and a Ph.D. in Creative Writing from SUNY Binghamton, studying under American novelist John Gardner. Informally her education comes from the experience and stories of her family. She says in a 2003 interview that "I grew up inside the shape of my father's stories. . . . These stories exerted a powerful influence on my imagination, in terms of what I chose to write about, the style of my language, and the form my own stories took" ("Author Biography").

To this point, her writing includes two novels—*ARABIAN JAZZ* (1993) and *Crescent* (2003)—and a memoir, *The Language of Baklava* (2005). In addition, she has published several essays devoted to Arab-American identity. *Crescent* is about a Lebanese chef, Sirine, who falls in love with an Iraqi professor of literature, Hanif. Set in an Arab and Persian community of Los Angeles, this novel chronicles the unusual love story of the heroine and her quest for happiness in the United States. Food, storytelling, and exile are all important subjects within the novel. In her memoir, *The Language of Baklava,* Abu-Jaber pays homage to the epicurean fascination of her childhood surrounded by food and stories. Indeed, while trying to re-create that past, she has created a loving tribute to her family members and her memories, as well as to the food that spiced the stories and characters. This memoir also contains recipes for some of the Middle Eastern dishes she remembers.

For readers her literary career provides a voice to a developing generation of Arab-American writers. As she writes, "It's a rare and lovely experience to feel like someone really has seen [and heard] you" ("Seeing Ourselves"). Abu-Jaber certainly is a writer that America will see and hear more of in the future.

Bibliography

Abu-Jaber, Diana. "Seeing Ourselves." Editorial. *Washington Post,* 21 October 2001, 807.

"BookBrowse.com. Author Biography: Diana Abu-Jaber." Available online. URL: http://www.bookbrowse.com/biographies/inex.cfin?author_number-915. Downloaded on March 15, 2006.

Matthew L. Miller

Adachi, Jiro   (?–   )

The novelist Jiro Adachi was raised in New York City by his Japanese father and Hungarian mother. His first language was not English per se but rather, as he describes it, "a form of malleable English" used in his ethnically mixed household. After receiving his B.A. from Columbia University, Adachi earned an M.F.A. in fiction from Colorado State University. After teaching at Colorado State University, the Stern College for Women, and Hunter College, Adachi is presently a faculty member at New York's New School. Besides writing several essays for the *New York Times,* Adachi drew upon his extensive experience as both a bicycle messenger in New York City and as a teacher of English as a foreign language for his critically acclaimed 2004 debut novel *The Island of Bicycle Dancers.*

The protagonist of *The Island of Bicycle Dancers* is Yurika Song, a 20-year-old half-Japanese and half-Korean woman who feels alienated in her homeland of Japan due to her mixed ethnicity. Yurika is frequently mocked by her friends for being, as they say, "half-sushi/half kim-chi," and assailed by her parents for being too rebellious for her own good. Feeling their daughter to be leading an aimless existence, Yurika's parents send her to live with her aunt and uncle in New York City, hoping that spending time in America will help rid her of her rebellious disposition. After moving to America, Yurika goes to work in her uncle's grocery store in New York City and begins to learn vernacular English from the various people she encounters both in the shop and in the city. Yurika soon becomes enthralled with the city's liveliness and multitude of cultures and languages. She is particularly intrigued by the unique underground world of the various bike messengers who frequent the store, whose apparent freedom and rebellious lifestyle she both relishes and envies. She quickly befriends a messenger named Whitey, feeling attracted to his open personality and particular gift for slang. Whitey exposes Yurika to a magical side of New York City radically different from the world she had previously experienced. He also teaches her the art of bicycle maintenance, which becomes a dominant metaphor for both trauma and healing throughout the novel. Yurika also falls in love with Bone, a Puerto Rican bicycle messenger who has a far more dangerous personality than Whitey, and who exposes her to the mysteries of sex and romantic love. A complicated and dangerous love triangle quickly forms between Yurika, Bone, and Whitey that threatens, by the end of the novel, to explode into passionate violence. Yurika's aunt, the vindictive Hyun Jeong, who feels that her husband's niece has been unfairly foisted upon her, serves as a villainous figure and a counterforce against the bicycle messengers with whom Yurika begins to discover freedom and direction. Hyun attacks every attempt Yurika makes toward self-improvement. But despite the numerous obstacles she faces, both in her family and social life, Yurika ultimately learns how to navigate her own existence through the mutually difficult terrains of family expectations and obligations, and through her American life in the multicultural environs of New York City.

Adachi's main thematic concern in *The Island of Bicycle Dancers* is not simply with presenting various cultures in ideological conflict and misunderstanding with each other, but, rather, with different cultures attempting to reconcile their differences and align themselves with one another for the purpose of mutual survival and growth. Adachi's sweeping range of dynamic characters and dramatic turns in plot recall the style of Charles Dickens. And like Dickens, Adachi's ultimate strength lies in the sheer vibrancy and verve of his prose style. His narrative voice and the manner in which his dialogue embodies each of his characters' unique cultural backgrounds and experiences are entirely distinct and original in contemporary American literature.

James R. Fleming

Ai   (1947–   )

Author of several award-winning books of poetry, Ai is foremost among controversial contemporary American poets; her work is often categorized as a critique of contemporary American society. Her volumes of poetry include *Cruelty* (1973), *Killing Floor* (1979), Lamont Poetry Selection of the Academy of American Poets), *Sin* (1986, American Book Award), *Fate* (1991), *Greed* (1993), *Vice* (2000, National Book Award for Poetry), and *Dread* (2003).

Born Florence Anthony in Tucson, Arizona, the poet Ai, whose name means *love* in Japanese, has also used the name Pelorhanke Ai Ogawa or Florence Ogawa. These names suggest the complex identity that Ai, the name she prefers to go by, possesses as a multiracial woman living in the United States. Proudly proclaiming herself to be half Japanese, an eighth Choctaw, a quarter black, and a 16th Irish, Ai does not consider herself to be a writer belonging to any single ethnicity: She states, "there is no identity for me 'out there.' I have had to step back into my own heart's cathedral and bow down before I could rise up" ("Ai" *Contemporary* 1). What Ai considers necessary for the survival of a multiracial person involves spiritual transcendence, a transcendence painfully achieved through a complex understanding of identity. The theme of transcendence beyond spiritual or bodily trauma prevails in Ai's work.

Almost all of Ai's poetry in some way pertains to trauma, usually concerning a specific historical context. The genre of choice for Ai is the dramatic monologue, and she has reinvented the poetic form to suit her content choices and stylistic purposes. These content choices and stylistic purposes are usually informed by the consideration of how to best portray and depict violence in its various forms. In *Cruelty,* Ai portrays fictional characters suffering in isolated, rural settings from violence induced by such acts as murder, sexual violence, and child abuse. Amid the trauma of violence, Ai's female characters, usually the victimized, emerge as survivors. Perhaps the best-known poem of *Cruelty* is "Cuba, 1962," in which a proletariat farmer hacks off his wife's feet as a sign of protest, simultaneously mutilating the beloved body of his wife and transcending to an abstract awareness of his social situation: "I lift the body and carry it to the wagon,/ where I load the cane to sell in the village./Whoever tastes my woman in his candy, his cake,/it is grief./ If you eat too much of it, you want more,/you can never get enough." This poem is typical of Ai's work because of its violent imagery, stark language, and desire for awareness or spiritual transcendence.

The volumes of poetry following *Cruelty* show a marked change in personas. From *Killing Floor* on, Ai invokes both fictional and historical figures, mixing fact and fiction. Some critics have faulted Ai for her departure from historical accuracy, arguing that the blurring of boundaries between fact and fiction results in irresponsible representations of reality, especially when trauma and historical circumstance are intertwined. Other critics contend that Ai renders a more artistic and poignant picture of human experience with her focus on imaginative consciousness.

In Ai's most recent work, *Dread,* characters seeking an unobtainable reconciliation with their psychological and trauma-induced wounds take center stage. The tragedy of the terrorist attacks on America on September 11, 2001, is addressed in this collection, along with childhood abuse, sexual abuse, war, and other subjects familiar to Ai's readers. While Ai's work is controversial in its violent imagery and topics, her work is significant in its contributions to a body of poetry concerning trauma.

Bibliography

Ai. "Movies, Mom, Poetry, Sex, and Death: A Self-Interview." *Onthebus,* nos. 3–4 (1991): 240–248.

"Ai." *Contemporary Literary Criticism: Excerpts from Criticism of the Works of Today's Novelists, Poets, Playwrights, Short Story Writers, Scriptwriters, and Other Creative Writers.* Vol. 69, edited by Roger Matuz, 1–18. Detroit: Gale Research, 1992.

Field, C. Renee. "Ai." *American Poets since World War II.* Vol. 120, edited by R. S. Gwynn, 10–17. Detroit: Gale Research, 1992.

Wilson, Rob. "The Will to Transcendence in Contemporary American Poet, Ai." *Canadian Review of American Studies* 17, no. 4 (Winter 1986): 437–448.

Julie Elaine Goodspeed-Chadwick

Alexander, Meena (1951–)

Born in Allahabad, India, Meena Alexander was the eldest of three sisters. Educated in India, Sudan, and Britain, Alexander received a Ph.D.

in 1973 from the University of Nottingham with a dissertation on the construction of self-image in early English romantic, symbolist and modern poetry. She returned to India and taught from 1974 to 1979 at Delhi University, Jawaharlal Nehru University (Delhi), Central Institute of English (Hyderabad), and the University of Hyderabad. She met and married an American in Hyderabad and moved to the United States in 1979. Living in New York with her husband and two children, she currently teaches at Hunter College and the Graduate Center of the City University of New York. Her work includes poetry, fiction, autobiography, and criticism. Fluent in six languages including Malayalam, Hindi, French, Arabic, and English, Alexander has written about her experiences as she moved between continents.

Alexander's poetry collections include *The Bird's Bright Ring* (1976); *I Root My Name* (1977); *Without Place* (1977); *Stone Roots* (1980); *House of a Thousand Doors* (1988); *The Storm, a Poem in Five Parts* (1989); *Night-Scene, the Garden* (1991); *River and Bridge* (1996); *Illiterate Heart* (2002); and *Raw Silk* (2004). She is also the author of two novels, NAMPALLY ROAD and *Manhattan Music*. Her prose writings include THE SHOCK OF ARRIVAL: REFLECTIONS OF POSTCOLONIAL EXPERIENCE (1996) and FAULT LINES: A MEMOIR (1991). She has also written two critical studies: *The Poetic Self: Towards a Phenomenology of Romanticism* (1979) and *Women in Romanticism: Mary Wollstonecraft, Dorothy Wordsworth and Mary Shelley* (1989). In addition to writing a one-act play, *In the Middle Earth* (1977), she has recently edited a collection of poems entitled *Indian Love Poems* (2005). Published internationally, she has also been extensively anthologized.

Alexander's novel *Manhattan Music* is set in Manhattan and outlines the life of Sandhya Rosenblum, who moves to Manhattan from Hyderabad, India, after marrying a Jewish American, Stephen Rosenblum. The novel follows Sandhya's attempts at settling into her new life as an Indian wife of an American and her fight against feelings of rootlessness and homelessness. Sandhya is very nostalgic and tries her best to belong to the new society and culture that she has adopted. Toward the end of the novel, however, she tries to commit suicide, only to be saved by her friend, Draupadi, who also serves as her alter ego. Alexander plays on the issues of exile and loss of home through the mythical character of Draupadi. The novel has interesting parallels with Alexander's life as reflected in her memoir, *The Fault Lines*.

Known as one of the most forceful South Asian postcolonial feminists, Alexander is noted for her strong sympathy for the plight of Indian women as reflected in many of her works. She rebelled against the traditions such as arranged marriage and looked for bolder roles for women in postcolonial India. Her feminist concerns highlight many of her works. Her works are also marked by a search for a homeland and a sense of belonging. Her writing is defined by her transnational migrations, and she is constantly in search of a sense of self. She writes about clashes, both internal and external, and brings the postcolonial diasporic subject to the forefront. Her narrative is lyrical and her poems are full of imagery. Postcolonial critic Homi Bhabha writes about her book *The Shock of Arrival*: "As the condition of migration and cultural displacement comes to be seen as a metaphor of our times, Meena Alexander's poignant and perceptive book is a welcome addition. Here, the postcolonial condition is addressed in its variety and its particularity: as fiction, criticism, personal reflection. This is a compelling, subtly crafted performance" (dust cover).

Focused on the issues of memory, history, diaspora, belonging, transnationalism, racism, fanaticism, language retention and identity crisis, Alexander's works are widely read in academia and are increasingly included in courses taught at universities. She has received awards from the Arts Council of England, American Council of Learned Societies, and National Council for Research on Women. Besides working as the writer-in-residence at Columbia University (1988) and National University of Singapore, she has also been a University Grants Commission fellow at Kerala University.

Bibliography

Basu, Lopamudra. "The Poet in the Public Sphere: a conversation with Meena Alexander." *Social Text* 20, no. 3 (2002): 31.

Dave, Shilpa. "The Doors to Home and History: Post-Colonial Identities in Meena Alexander and Bharati Mukherjee." *Amerasia Journal* 19, no. 3 (1993): 103–11.

Duncan, Erika. "A Portrait of Meena Alexander." *World Literature Today* 73 (1999): 23–28.

Knight, Denise. "Meena Alexander." In *Writers of Indian Diaspora,* edited by E. Nelson, 1–7. Westport, Conn.: Greenwood Press, 1993.

Asma Sayed

Ali, Agha Shahid (1949–2001)

Poet Agha Shahid Ali, a Kashmiri American born in New Delhi and raised in Kashmir, is best known for his dedication to educating the American public on a Persian form of poetry called the *ghazal.* Educated at the University of Kashmir, Srinagar, and the University of Delhi, he earned his Ph.D. from Pennsylvania State University in 1984 and his M.F.A. from the University of Arizona in 1985.

Ali received fellowships from the Pennsylvania Council on the Arts, the Bread Loaf Writers' Conference, the Ingram-Merrill Foundation, the New York Foundation for the Arts and the Guggenheim Foundation, and he was awarded a Pushcart Prize. He held teaching positions at the University of Delhi, Pennsylvania State University, SUNY Binghamton, Princeton University, Hamilton College, Baruch College, University of Utah, the M.F.A. program at Warren Wilson College and at the University of Massachusetts–Amherst.

In his poetry collections such as *The Half-Inch Himalayas* and *A Nostalgist's Map of America,* Ali revives the elegiac voice of poetry to propose that all love or pain is the same regardless of circumstances. In *Rooms Are Never Finished,* a finalist for the National Book Award in 2001 and the publication that won him the Pulitzer Prize, Ali speaks eloquently about his relationship with his mother and the grief of her death through the use of sonnets, *ghazals,* prose poems, and Sapphics. His seventh book of poetry, *The Country without a Post Office,* evokes nostalgia as Ali reminisces about his hometown of Kashmir. A posthumous collection, entitled *Call Me Ishmael Tonight,* was published by W.W. Norton in 2003.

He translated the work of Faiz Ahmed Faiz, a prominent Urdu poet and student of various traditions of classical poetry, in a book titled *The Rebel's Silhouette: Selected Poems.* Ali also edited the anthology *Ravishing DisUnities: Real Ghazals in English.* This anthology introduced the seventh-century poetic form, the *ghazal,* and Ali dedicated himself to explaining the true elements of the *ghazal* through the work of contemporary American poets such as Annie Finch, Marilyn Hacker, John Hollander, and Paul Muldoon. It was Ali's belief that attention should be paid to the traditional model of the *ghazal,* though he did appreciate many of the qualities of the Americanized version. Agha Shahid Ali died in December 2001 of brain cancer, an illness he discounted as merely an aside to his life.

Anne Marie Fowler

Ali, Samina (1969–)

Born in India, Samina Ali moved to the United States as an infant but spent childhood summers in India, learning about her Indian-Muslim heritage. This divided existence developed in Ali a sense of inverted duality, for while she was in India, she felt like an American, and while in the United States, like an Indian. When an arranged marriage took her to India, where one strife-ridden election night she and her family awaited attack by militant Hindus, Ali vowed to live her life independently, not by the dictates of parents, culture, and religion. She returned to America, changed majors, got an M.F.A. in creative writing, and became a writer.

Madras on Rainy Days (2004) is semiautobiographical and relates the experiences of Layla, a 19-year-old Indian-Muslim woman who is pressured into an arranged marriage to Sameer, a handsome, rebellious biker who is looking to exorcize the demons of class, religion, and culture by emigrating to America. Enchanted by the glamour and rituals of the elaborate marriage ceremony, Layla embraces her marriage, partly out of guilt for her sexual indiscretion with an American man, partly out of fear that she, like her mother, may be disgraced, but mostly because she finds love and acceptance in her new family. Nonetheless, despite the pornographic letters Sameer has written to her during their engagement, and in spite of all her attempts to seduce him, including clandestine trips to faith-healing *alims,* the marriage fails because Sameer is gay. Sameer assumes and assures Layla that all their problems will disappear once they are in the United States, for Sameer views America as a utopian world where sexual, religious, and class differences do not exist. However, Layla, who has lived in the United States, warns Sameer that no such utopia exists: In the United States, differences also cause discrimination and humiliation, except that the differences targeted are of a kind based on nationality and ethnicity. The rain dampens the honeymoon, and the marriage remains unconsummated, forcing each partner to confront his and her crippling secrets.

Ali writes to give voice to the Indian-Muslim experience and hopes her readers will understand the particular struggles of her characters as universal human struggles. Her novel gives readers a glimpse into the lives of aristocratic Indian-Muslim women sequestered within the walled city of old Hyderabad: their distance from, and camaraderie with, the servants they depend on and their acceptance and perpetuation of patriarchy that renders them and their needs invisible through walls and veils. *Madras on Rainy Days,* by revealing the trials and tribulations of a minority group, the Muslim community in India, functions as a parallel to Monica Ali's *Brick Lane Road,* which exposes the struggles of the minority Asian-Muslim community in England. The two novels expose different aspects of Muslim communities' struggles and their attempts to rise above the circumstances that trap them, be they of race, class, sex, or gender.

Sukanya B. Senapati

All about H. Hatterr   G. V. Desani (1948)

G. V. DESANI's only novel, *All about H. Hatterr* has become a legendary cult book—more often known about than read. Especially important, Desani's novel has influenced Indian English writers such as Amitav Ghosh and Salman Rushdie.

While *Hatterr* is Desani's only novel, he returned to it many times. In the subsequent editions, he revised the text, adding commentaries and, in the final version of 1972, a new concluding chapter. In January 2000, shortly before Desani's death, the novel was adapted for the stage in Toronto as "Damme, This Is the Oriental Scene for You!" by Rehan Ansari (Modest Productions, Theatre Passe Muraille Backspace).

Hatterr is hailed as the first Indian-English postcolonial novel. It uses the English language in a way it had not been used, bringing alive Indian-English accents and Desani's own idiosyncrasies—his personal style. For this playful relationship with language, Desani has been likened to James Joyce. In his introduction to the collection *Mirrorwork*—where a part of the novel is included—Salman Rushdie sees *Hatterr* as an Indian *Tristram Shandy*: "*Hatterr's* dazzling, puzzling, leaping prose is the first genuine effort to go beyond the Englishness of the English language" (xvi). For all its inventiveness, intertextuality, multilingual phrasing, and experimentality, it is also at times a difficult book to read.

Besides its linguistic extravaganza, the novel is a complicated story of a man of indefinite European and Oriental origin, who escapes his past and takes on the name H. Hatterr. Hatterr, as the first-person narrator, describes his path among seven sages—"the Sages of *Calcutta, Rangoon* (now resident in India), *Madras, Bombay,* and the right Honourable Sage of *Delhi,* the wholly Worshipful of *Mogalsarai-Varanasi,* and his naked Holiness Number One, the Sage of *All India* himself!" (33)—parodying the way people too easily yield to spiritual manipulation.

The chapters are divided into three parts. There is first an "Instruction," relating an encounter with one of the seven sages in which Hatterr is given more or less indecipherable instructions about how to live. In the brief "Presumption" sections, Hatterr tries to clarify the instructions for himself as well as the reader.

The main part of the narrative is in the "Life-encounter" sections of the book. These are accounts of how Hatterr actually tries to follow the instructions given by the saints. He does not succeed well in his exploits and is continuously saved from trouble by his friend Banerrji and the lawyer Sri Y. Beliram. Later Beliram becomes another sage, Sriman Y. Rambeli, whose novel is critiqued and defended by Hatterr in the concluding chapter that Desani added to the 1972 version.

Bibliography

All about G. V. Desani. "Who was G. V. Desani?" Available online. URL: www.desani.org. Accessed September 15, 2006. The Web site has begun to collect and present information on G. V. Desani and his works.

Rushdie, Salman. Introduction. In *Mirrorwork: 50 Years of Indian Writing, 1947–1997,* edited by Salman Rushdie and Elizabeth West, vii–xx. New York: Henry Holt, 1997.

Joel Kuortti

All I Asking for Is My Body Milton A. Murayama (1975)

MILTON A. MURAYAMA's award-winning *All I Asking for Is My Body* (1975) is one of the first novels written in Hawaiian local dialects. Drawing from his own experiences as a boy living in both the coastal and upcountry towns, Lahaina and Pu'ukoli'i, respectively, Murayama depicts his young protagonist Kiyoshi Oyama, who grows up before and during World War II in the fictional beach town of Pepelau and the upcountry Frontier Mill plantation camp in Kahana. *All I Asking* is the first part of a planned trilogy: the Oyama family saga continues in *Five Years on a Rock* (1994) and in *Plantation Boy* (1998).

All I Asking's plot pivots on the repayment of a $6,000 family debt that Kiyoshi, the second son of Japanese immigrants, eventually pays off. The novel is divided into three sections. The first part, "I'll Crack Your Head *Kotsun*," based on Murayama's 1959 short story, introduces the grueling demands made on individuals and families by the class-stratified Hawaiian plantation society in the 1930s and 1940s. In the second section, "The Substitute," the author illustrates how cultural traditions are remembered and revised within immigrant communities. Sometimes, as Kiyoshi finds out, some cultural practices have been modified within individual families to accommodate their new surroundings. In the final section, "All I Asking for Is My Body," Kiyoshi's childhood world of family, school, and friends becomes firmly embedded in history and global affairs with the exacerbation of race politics when Pearl Harbor is attacked.

As scholars have noted, the distinctive pidgin dialogue—an amalgamation of the English, Japanese, Spanish, Filipino, and Hawaiian languages—strikes the reader from the opening paragraphs. As Kiyoshi describes, locals "spoke four languages: good English in school, pidgin English among ourselves, good or pidgin Japanese to our parents and the other old folks" (5). The diverse ethnic composition of Hawaii provided a rich foundation for an improvised language as a means to communicate across generations and different linguistic backgrounds. Nevertheless, rather than a naïve celebration of difference, Murayama gives readers a realistic picture of the racial and economic hierarchies that divided laborers along ethnic lines, particularly when Kiyoshi describes the organization of the hillside camp. In the camp, the white overseer lives at the highest point of the hill. His home is followed by, in descending order, those of the Portuguese, Spanish, *nisei luna* (second-generation Japanese foremen), then Japanese, and finally the Filipino (96). Through the characters of Kiyoshi and his brother Toshio, Murayama shows that "American" values such as hard work, love of learning, and ambition do not necessarily guarantee equal opportunities for Japanese Americans. *All I Asking* also offers an equally scathing critique of the injustices in both the Japanese family and the plantation systems.

Although the short-story version ("I'll Crack Your Head *Kotsun*") was published in the *Arizona*

Quarterly in 1959 and well received, finding a publisher for Murayama's novel proved to be difficult. In the mid-20th century, publishers were uncertain about the profitability of books about Asian-American experiences. More specifically, they were reluctant to publish a book that was liberally sprinkled with local Hawaiian dialect. After many years of rejection, Murayama and his wife, Dawn, formed Supa Press and published the book themselves in 1975. The groundbreaking novel became a success almost immediately. Since that time it has been re-released by the University of Hawaii Press and anthologized several times, beginning with *The Spell of Hawaii* (1968) and most recently in *The Quietest Singing* (2000). The Before Columbus Foundation bestowed upon Murayama an American Book Award for his work in 1980, and the Hawai'i Literary Arts Council conferred the Hawai'i Award for Literature in 1991.

Bibliography

Murayama, Milton. *All I Asking for Is My Body*. San Francisco: Supa, 1975. Reprint, Honolulu: University of Hawaii Press, 1988.

Sumida, Stephen H. *And the View from the Shore: Literary Traditions of Hawai'i*. Seattle: University of Washington Press, 1991.

Takaki, Ronald. *A Different Mirror: A History of Multicultural America*. Boston: Little, Brown, 1993.

Hellen Lee-Keller

All over Creation   Ruth Ozeki (2003)

When retired potato farmer Lloyd Fuller ends up in the hospital, and his wife, Momoko, begins to show signs of schizophrenia, their neighbors, Cass and Will Quinn, decide they have to contact Yumi, the couple's long-estranged daughter. Yumi, or Yummy as she is often called, and Cass grew up together in the small town of Liberty Falls, Idaho, but the lives of the two women have taken different directions. At 14, the beautiful and precocious Yumi had an affair with her history teacher—a scandal that led her to flee Liberty Falls for California. While Cass stayed and eventually settled into a comfortable, yet childless, marriage to a local

potato farmer, Yumi survived life as a teenage runaway, graduated from college on her own, and gave birth to three children by three different fathers.

Although 25 years have passed since Yumi left town, an e-mail from Cass brings her back from her new home in Hawaii to care for her aging parents. This is but the first of a series of events that upsets life in the placid little town. Shortly after Yumi returns, a busload of environmental activists calling themselves the Seeds of Resistance arrive on the Fuller doorstep. Convinced that Lloyd Fuller is a prophet in the war against the genetic modification of vegetables, they decide to stay to help Lloyd and Momoko with their seed business, much to the chagrin of the local police. Then, coincidentally, Yumi's childhood seducer, Elliot Rhodes, shows up. Currently employed by a public relations firm on behalf of corporate agribusiness, Elliot's real target is the environmental activists, but his mere presence is enough to upset Yumi's precarious stability.

As in RUTH OZEKI's first novel, *MY YEAR OF MEATS*, fiction and contemporary political issues collide in *All over Creation*. In this novel about intergenerational tensions, friendship, and aging, the author revisits the issue of genetic modification. Elliot's failure to take responsibility for his actions on a personal level mirrors his compromised ethics in his career as a biotech spin doctor. Cass and Will's childlessness is linked to their experimentation in farming genetically modified potatoes, implicitly if not explicitly. Yumi's blindness to Elliot's duplicity parallels her apolitical stance on the critical issue of genetic engineering.

Some of the stylistic devices of *My Year of Meats* reappear in the second novel as well. As in the first novel, the story unfolds from multiple perspectives. Throughout the novel, Ozeki shifts her narrative focus to follow the stories of each of the main characters, including Cass, Yumi, Elliot, and the teenager Frank Perdue, a recent recruit to the Seeds's anti-biotech cause. As in the earlier work, the narrative brings together various texts including, most notably, Luther Burbank's writing on his development of the celebrated Burbank potato, Yumi's letters home, and Lloyd's newsletter to his seed customers. Much as she did in *My Year of Meats,* Ozeki returns repeatedly to a single central metaphor. In this case images of seeds, rather than meat, are pervasive and serve to underline the connections between various elements in Ozeki's complicated novel.

While some critics have expressed reservations about Ozeki's characters and some of the more unlikely turns in her novel's plot, reviewers have been intrigued by the novel's unconventional merging of politics and art. The winner of a 2004 American Book Award from the Before Columbus Foundation and the Willa Literary Award for Contemporary Fiction, *All over Creation* was a national best seller and is Ozeki's most commercially successful work to date.

Bibliography

Cohen, Judith Beth. "Bad Seeds." *Women's Review of Books* (May 2003): 6.

Dederer, Claire. Review of *All Over Creation. New York Times Book Review,* 16 March 2003, p. 30.

DiNovella, Elizabeth. "No Small Potatoes." *Progressive* (March 2003): 41.

Ozeki, Ruth. "Ruth Ozeki, Bearing Witness." Interview by Dave Weich. 18 March 2003. Available online. URL: www.powells.com/authors/ozeki.html. Downloaded on January 30, 2006.

Rachel Ihara

Aloft   Chang-rae Lee   (2004)

For Jerry Battle, Italian American, pushing 60, and protagonist of CHANG-RAE LEE's *Aloft,* the world is much more orderly when viewed from above in his private airplane. First encouraged to fly by his longtime girlfriend Rita Reyes in order to counteract his post-retirement passivity, he now uses his plane to escape from his empty house, as Rita has recently left him. However, the problems that develop throughout his extended family during the course of the novel cause Jerry to re-evaluate what his daughter calls his "preternatural lazy-heartedness."

On the surface, his grown children, Jack and Theresa, seem to be doing well. Jack is expanding the family landscaping business, Battle Brothers,

and his wife, Eunice, is furnishing a grand home in a gated development. But Jack's improvements exceed the business's real capacity, driving him and Battle Brothers toward financial ruin. Theresa has an academic career and a new fiancé, the mildly successful novelist Paul Pyun. However, she is also pregnant and suffering from non-Hodgkin's lymphoma. Although she has been advised to terminate the pregnancy in order to receive cancer treatment, she insists on carrying the child to term. In both cases a veneer of normalcy covers deep problems.

Jerry sees Rita's relationship with his nemesis, Richie Coniglio, as his most immediate problem. But his history with Rita is also entangled with one of his oldest problems, the death of his first wife, Daisy, who drowned in the backyard swimming pool during a manic-depressive episode when their children were young. Attempting an instant cure for his bereavement, Jerry filled in the pool and found Rita to help with Jack and Theresa. Rita eventually became their second mother and practically a wife to Jerry, who realizes his mistake in never formally proposing to her when Richie offers her an engagement ring.

In the novel's climactic scene, Jerry breaks his usual rule—flying only alone and in the clearest weather—in order to satisfy Theresa's sudden appetite for Maine lobster. Over their airplane headsets they finally discuss some of the family's problems, including Daisy's death and its aftermath. She suggests that he invite Paul, the baby, and the rest of the family to move in with him as well. The airplane encounters turbulence, and Theresa's water breaks much too soon. Jerry rushes her to the hospital in time to save the baby but not Theresa. Jerry finally resolves to ground himself emotionally, and at the end of the novel, Paul and his baby, Jack and Eunice and their children, and 85-year-old Pop all move into Jerry's house.

The third of Lee's novels, *Aloft* continues to address the issue of emotional distance but tackles questions of ethnicity from a new perspective, that of an assimilated Italian-American man. The novel shows the evolution of Jerry Battle's Long Island from the time when his forebears, the Battaglias, were considered exotic, to the present day in which his suburban town is populated by Koreans, Puerto Ricans, Dominicans, and blacks. His family has evolved as well, with his wife, Daisy, introducing a Korean strain into the Battaglia clan. Having known a number of Asian Americans intimately, Jerry is resistant to the usual stereotypes, and his narrating voice resists the stereotypes of working-class Italian-American men, tough and unsubtle. Instead, Jerry's thoughts come in long, musing, poetic flights. Though Jerry's voice is dominant, Lee slyly nods to his own literary reputation through the character of Paul, who "writes about The Problem with Being Sort of Himself—namely, the very conflicted and complicated state of being Asian and American and thoughtful and male."

Bibliography

Kakutani, Michiko. "Flying Instead of Feeling, but the Fantasy of Motion Is Also Risky." *New York Times,* 9 March 2004, late edition, p. E1.

Park, Ed. "Drastic Alterations." *Village Voice,* 10–16 March 2004, p. 89.

Scott, A. O. "Above It All." *New York Times,* 14 March 2004, late edition, p. 7.

Jaime Cleland

America Is in the Heart   Carlos Bulosan
(1946)

Set in the early 20th-century United States, *America Is in the Heart* tells the tale of a Filipino who leaves his homeland to move to "America," a nation inspired by the promise of freedom, equal opportunity, and justice for all. Based loosely on CARLOS BULOSAN's own life and experiences, the fictional autobiography is narrated by the protagonist "Allos," who opens the story by describing life in the colonial Philippines, highlighting economic hardships and the limitations of "free U.S. education" in the aftermath of the Philippine-American War. The remainder of the narrative depicts the protagonist's struggles against racism and class-based obstacles in the United States, where opportunities were scarce and resources limited.

Allos is an idealistic youth whose fervent belief in "the American Dream" is repeatedly tested by race

riots, vigilantism, police brutality, and hate crimes. At one point in the narrative, after having already experienced countless acts of racial violence, Allos's testicles are crushed by vigilantes. Allos's attempts to reconcile these difficult struggles with the promises of democracy constitute the central theme of the novel. The lengthy text eventually concludes with an ending that is open to conflicting interpretations. The last chapter, in particular, has been interpreted quite differently through the years by critics who disagree on the text's resolution.

Debates over whether the narrative advocates or critiques U.S. national mythologies have centered on the somewhat ambiguous final paragraphs, wherein the narrator seems to reaffirm his utopian interpretation of the United States, despite more than 300 pages of apparent evidence to the contrary. After experiencing countless acts of brutal racial violence, which prompt him to become a union organizer and social activist, Allos appears to conclude his story by simply reaffirming his faith in "the American dream": "I knew that no man could destroy my faith in America that had sprung from all our hopes and aspirations, *ever.*" Allos also cites his "defeats" among the reasons for his prevailing beliefs. Calling attention to the richness of the soil, the freedom involved in transcontinental mobility, the feeling of solidarity among the urban poor who provide "free meals in dingy gambling houses," and the transformative power of education, Allos reiterates the myths of mobility, democracy, and opportunity.

Critics have struggled to make sense of this ending, interpreting the ultimate conclusion of his narrative as, alternately, assimilation or resistance—depending on one's critical interpretation. The final paragraphs create an ambiguous space wherein readers on both sides of the debate are able to justify either interpretation with multiple textual examples. Published, significantly, in the patriotic political climate of the postwar United States (1946), the text was initially read as an affirmation of U.S. democracy, a celebration of equal opportunity and melting-pot ideology, and a patriotic tome from a racial minority perspective. Following the book's original positive reception, however, its popularity eventually declined until the text was all but erased from cultural memory. It remained out of print until the 1970s.

The book's subtitle, "A Personal History," and the numerous similarities between the narrative and the author's life helped initially to label the book an autobiography. This label remained until the 1973 republication of the text, when critics began to complicate the application of this term after discovering that the text's first-person narrator was actually constructed as a strategic rhetorical device. While all of the events described in Bulosan's "autobiography" are indeed fact-based, the text tells the story of an entire diaspora of Filipinos on the West Coast of the United States, not just Carlos Bulosan alone. For this reason, the work is more accurately described as "fictional autobiography." This unique genre was useful in allowing Bulosan to tell stories similar and related to his own—a method that reveals the systematic nature of oppression. Even as Allos's name changes to "Carlos" in America, Bulosan offers a narrative far beyond the scope of one man's self-retrospection. Once readers understand the author as separate from his narrator, we begin to appreciate the brilliance involved in structuring the nonlinear, often contradictory narrative of decolonization that is Allos's story.

Following the landmark 1972 study by Epifanio San Juan, Jr, which reintroduced Bulosan onto the intellectual scene, the University of Washington Press republished *America Is in the Heart* in 1973 with a new introduction by Carey McWilliams, the noted writer and farm workers' rights activist who had been a close personal friend of Bulosan. This republication generated a reception that posed a distinct contrast to that of the 1940s. Instead of being read as an avowal of the United States as the land of equal opportunity, the social critique woven throughout the work was now interpreted as a subversive call to action. While this new interpretation had displaced the earlier readings of the text, it certainly did not erase them. Bulosan's social critique could not be severed from his seemingly contradictory celebration of the American dream. In order to make sense of these contradictions, critics began to revisit the book's significant yet previously under-acknowledged "Part One,"

which details the narrator's experiences with colonialism during his formative years in the Philippines. Critics such as Oscar Campomanes argued for the necessity of reading Filipino-American literature as "postcolonial," or inextricably bound to its colonial past. *America Is in the Heart* began to take on new significance when read as a critique of U.S. politics, both at home and abroad.

Allos's life in the United States is marked by repeated contradictions between his fervent belief in the American dream and his growing understanding of the limitations of that dream. These contradictions are uniquely valuable, as they demonstrate the schism between his education and his awareness of his lived experience—the schism between "colonial education" and "colonial subjectivity." The disconnection between the colonial promise and Allos's inability to reap the rewards of this promise creates ambiguities in the narrative that account for the contradictions in the text. Allos, a young boy with a strong sense of idealism, believed in the promises touted by U.S. propagandists, promises that served to create a disjuncture between memory and reality. In the United States, however, he struggles to realize the difference between the real America and the America that remains only "in his heart."

In order to survive, Allos realizes he must reconcile his colonial and postcolonial memories of place and home. He therefore develops a new vision. America is no longer a land or a nation. Instead, it is now "in the hearts of men that died for freedom; it is also in the eyes of men that are building a new world. America is a prophecy of a new society of men: of a system that knows no sorrow or strife or suffering. America is a warning to those who would try to falsify the ideals of freemen" (189). In the end, *America Is in the Heart* does more than provide a collective history or a fictionalized autobiography; it challenges America to live up to its own promises.

Bibliography

Alquizola, Marilyn. "Subversion or Affirmation: The Text and Subtext of *America Is in the Heart.*" In *Asian Americans: Comparative and Global Perspectives,* edited by Shirley Hune, Hyung-Chan Kim,

Stephen S. Fugita, and Amy Ling, 199–209. Pullman: Washington State University Press, 1991.

Libretti, Tim. "*America Is in the Heart*, by Carlos Bulosan." In *A Resource Guide to Asian American Literature*, edited by Sau-ling Cynthia Wong and Stephen H. Sumida, 21–31. New York: Modern Language Association of America, 2001.

McWilliams, Carey. Introduction. In *America Is in the Heart*, vii–xxiv. New York: Harcourt, 1946. Reprint, Seattle: University Washington Press, 1973.

San Juan, Epifanio, Jr. "An Introduction to Carlos Bulosan." *Diliman Review* (Philippines) 20 (1972): 1–13.

———. *Carlos Bulosan and the Imagination of the Class Struggle*. Quezon City: University of the Philippines Press, 1972.

———. "Violence of Exile, Politics of Desire: Prologue to Carlos Bulosan." In *The Philippine Temptation: Dialectics of Philippines-U.S. Literary Relations*, 129–170. Philadelphia: Temple University Press, 1996.

Linda Pierce

American Knees Shawn Wong (1995)

Unlike other Asian-American writers, SHAWN WONG experiments with a different form and subject matter in *American Knees*. He confronts issues of gender, race, and sexuality in Hollywood style, while offering reflections beyond endless witticisms on Asian Americanness. The novel narrates a comical, touching love story about an Asian-American couple who must negotiate family traditions, racism, and sexism. Wong's intentions of writing the novel are not only to expose the falsehood of the stereotypes but also to demonstrate the diversity within Asian America. Central to the novel is the character of Raymond Ding, a 40-year-old assistant director of minority affairs at a community college, who betrays his duty of being a good Chinese son by getting divorced. Aurora Crane is a Japanese/Irish-American photographer who is confused about her mixed ethnicity. Brenda Nishitani, Aurora's best friend, does not want to date Asian men but instead goes out only with white men. Betty Nguyen is a Vietnamese refugee who was abused by her ex-husband. Raymond's father, recently widowed, wants

to marry a Chinese picture bride. In spite of their different experiences and backgrounds, all of them yearn for a sense of belonging to the family and community.

Wong shows the various ways in which Asian Americans interact with one another. Specifically, Asian-American men and women must deal with their own prejudices and stereotypes about each other. The chapter "Eye Contact" is a hilarious account of how Raymond and Aurora discover, to their discomfort, that they are the only two Asians at a party. After trying hard to avoid each other, they finally meet, only to experience further mental distress as each tries to guess the other's motivations, feelings, and phobias. After falling in love with Aurora, Raymond cannot decide whether he loves her because she is half Japanese or because she is half white. Raymond's relationship with Aurora suffers because of his insistence on seeing everything in terms of ethnic implications. He is aware that race is always a dominant factor in their relationships, both in public and private. It takes Raymond a while to recognize that true love is beyond racial and ethnic differences. After a breakup with Aurora, Raymond starts to date Betty. It is in this relationship that Raymond finally realizes his love for Aurora and what is truly important in his life.

Su-lin Yu

Among the White Moon Faces: An Asian-American Memoir of Homelands Shirley Geok-lin Lim (1996)

This memoir traces the author's life story across the continents (from Malaysia, the former British colony of Malaya, to the United States) and follows her search for a home and a previously denied feminine identity. Winner of the American Book Award for nonfiction in 1997, *Among the White Moon Faces* was also published in Singapore with the new subtitle *Memoirs of a Nonya Feminist, nonya* being a Malay word for a Chinese Malaysian woman assimilated to Malay culture.

The text is divided into four parts: the first two parts, set in Malaysia, are devoted to the first 25 years of her life until 1969, while the second two are centered on her life in the United States, from

1969 to the present. The memoir begins with the descriptions of the author's early life in Malaysia during and after British colonial rule, her education in a convent taught by strict Irish nuns, her inability to communicate in Hokkien (the language spoken in her birthplace and one of the eight most important languages of China) as opposed to her perfectly fluent English, and the xenophobic movements against Chinese Malaysians. A daughter of a Chinese father and a Malayan-born Chinese mother, SHIRLEY GEOK-LIN LIM also explores the strong influence that American culture had on Malacca, her hometown. The influence is signified by her full name, Shirley Agnes Jennifer Lim Geok-Lin, which shows the influence of Hollywood pop icons her Westernized father was fond of (for example, Shirley Temple and Jennifer Jones).

Lim's initial uneasiness with her femininity in a society where girls were seldom valued as individuals becomes more dramatic when her mother leaves for Singapore, abandoning her six children to their impoverished father. From the age of eight, therefore, the child Shirley imitates her five brothers and associates womanhood with weakness, boredom, and the absence of movement and words.

The story unfolds Lim's parallel discovery of both her femininity and her individual space through reading and writing. In her memoir, the condition of displacement, shared by many first-generation immigrants, and the dilemma of dual allegiance to the country of origin and the new land of settlement appear to be overcome through the discovery of a core identity, not as an Asian or an Asian American but as a writer. Through writing, the author reimagines and integrates, without any mutual exclusion, the lands of her life, transforming them to homelands and creating a new concept of territory without boundaries.

Elisabetta Marino

And the Soul Shall Dance Wakako Yamauchi (1974)

Originally written as a short story, *And the Soul Shall Dance* was first produced in Seattle by Northwest Asian American Theatre and later in Los Angeles, Honolulu, New York City, San Fran-

cisco, Washington, D.C., and many other U.S. cities. A play set in a California farming community in 1935, *And the Soul Shall Dance* opens with the Murata family losing their bathhouse due to a fire. Mr. and Mrs. Murata are Japanese immigrants living with their American-born daughter Masako. The neighboring farmer, Mr. Oka, an issei, comes to help the Muratas, and the dialogue between Mr. Murata and Mr. Oka reveals that Mrs. Oka is not Mr. Oka's first wife. Before Mr. Oka left Japan, he was married as a *yoshi* (a marriage arrangement for a man to marry into a woman's family to take on her family name) and has a daughter, Kiyoko, from his previous marriage back in Japan. Mr. Oka came to the United States to earn enough money to move his family to another village in Japan so as to live away from his wife's family, but his wife died soon after he left Japan, and his first wife's family tricked him into marrying her sister, Emiko. His wife's family sent Emiko over to the States to live with Mr. Oka as his wife. In the expository scene, Mr. Oka also reveals that he is getting ready to send for his daughter from his first marriage.

In the following scenes, Masako witnesses Mrs. Oka's strange behavior and Mr. Oka's abusive treatment of Mrs. Oka. Aloof and antisocial, Mrs. Oka acts as if nobody is around and starts dancing. Later, Masako learns that Mrs. Oka wants to go back to Japan, to her forbidden love. She is apparently unhappy with both her marriage to her brother-in-law and her life in America. Upon Kiyoko's arrival, Mrs. Oka's mental health further deteriorates, and in the final scene, Masako watches Mrs. Oka dance into the desert.

And the Soul Shall Dance explores the harsh realities facing Japanese immigrants who leave their homes in pursuit of their American dream. WAKAKO YAMAUCHI not only depicts the tension between the first and second generations of Japanese Americans but also examines the gender dynamics of their communities.

Kyoko Amano

Anil's Ghost Michael Ondaatje (2000)

MICHAEL ONDAATJE's first novel after his Booker Prize–winning *The English Patient* also marks his first fiction about his native Sri Lanka. Anil, a forensic anthropologist born in Sri Lanka and educated in the West, is sent to Sri Lanka by an international human rights group to investigate alleged government-sponsored killings. If she can identify the corpse known as "Sailor," and connect his death to a broader statist campaign of violence, she might spark an international intervention in Sri Lanka's cycles of bloodshed. Her task, however, proves enormously complicated, particularly as she learns that corpses are often exhumed and interred again far from their original burial sites. Convinced that her work is being undermined, she unwittingly begins a dangerous, semipublic report, using a substitute corpse for the suddenly missing Sailor. Her research is dismissed in humiliating fashion by her Sri Lankan contact, Sarath, who realizes that the only way to prevent Anil's own imminent death lies in openly renouncing not only her findings but all similar investigations. His plan succeeds: Anil safely leaves the country and discovers that Sarath hid Sailor for her ongoing investigation. Sarath, however, will be killed for his involvement in the project.

Ondaatje's latest novel did not garner the critical praise that greeted earlier efforts. Critics occasionally considered this work cold and passionless; the author's insistence that *Anil's Ghost* was "apolitical" disappointed readers who felt that the novelist should have adopted a polemic, decisive argument. But these criticisms may simply reflect theoretical issues Ondaatje is unwilling, or unable, to overcome. His choice of a principal character who assumes she can "read" both individual victims and the contemporary Sri Lankan conflict seems an unself-conscious attempt at reconciliation by a writer returning to write about an ongoing communal conflict. The novel's insistence that all groups perpetrate violence complicates Anil's own mission to isolate government-sponsored murders, which perhaps explains why Ondaatje sends her home well before the novel's conclusion. As Teresa Derrickson argues, the novel raises questions concerning the discovery of human rights abuses and the desirability of this knowledge; what the novel does not provide is a clear mandate on what "evidence" should emerge, and how. The idea

that bodies themselves contain memories and histories is fascinatingly deployed here, despite questions concerning the validity of any single body to speak for a broader collective. Perhaps Ondaatje's greatest contribution is what Antoinette Burton identifies as the central problem of the novel: how to evaluate Western notions of empirical and epistemological histories in a Sri Lankan context, where Anil's paradigms ultimately fail.

Bibliography

Burton, Antoinette. "Archive of Bones: *Anil's Ghost* and the Ends of History." *Journal of Commonwealth Literature* 38, no. 1 (2003): 39–56.

Derrickson, Teresa. "Will the 'Un-Truth' Set You Free? A Critical Look at Global Human Rights Discourse in Michael Ondaatje's *Anil's Ghost*." *LIT: Literature-Interpretation-Theory* 15, no. 2 (April–June 2004): 131–152.

Ondaatje, Michael. *Anil's Ghost*. New York: Knopf, 2000.

Scanlan, Margaret. "*Anil's Ghost* and Terrorism's Time." *Studies in the Novel* 36, no. 3 (Fall 2004): 302–317.

J. Edward Mallot

Aoki, Brenda Wong   (1953–   )

Born in Salt Lake City, Utah, and raised in Los Angeles, California, Brenda Wong Aoki is a contemporary storyteller whose solo performances challenge conventional genre categories through their eclectic combination of theater, dance, and music. Of Japanese descent on her father's side and Chinese, Spanish, and Scottish descent on her mother's side, Aoki's work draws from her unique background and consciously evokes both Eastern and Western theater traditions. In 1976, Aoki earned her B.A. in community studies from the University of California at Santa Cruz and went on to spend a decade as a community organizer working with youth groups in Long Beach and Watts, in the Los Angeles area, and with immigrants in San Francisco's Chinatown. During the 1970s and 1980s, she helped to found the Asian American Dance Collective and the Asian American Theatre

Company. She became interested in jazz, eventually cofounding the jazz performance ensemble SoundSeen with composer/musician Mark Izu. Aoki studied physical comedy with the Dell'Arte Players and, in 1978, began an apprenticeship in Noh and *Kyogen* (classical Japanese theater) in both Japan and the United States.

Since the late 1980s, Aoki has worked primarily as a playwright and solo performer, creating dramatic performance works that reflect her multiethnic heritage. In *Obake! Tales of Spirits Past and Present* (1988) and *Mermaid Meat* (1997), Aoki draws inspiration from Chinese and Japanese folklore, giving the material a new significance through her creative retellings. In *The QUEEN'S GARDEN* (1992) and *Random Acts of Kindness,* she explores aspects of her experience as a person of mixed ethnicity and as a community organizer in works that deal with contemporary issues of urban violence and crime. Other works investigate moments in Asian-American history. The multimedia piece *Last Dance* (1998) celebrates the resilience of Japanese Americans interned during World War II. In *Uncle Gunjiro's Girlfriend* (1998), Aoki reflects on her Japanese grand-uncle's love affair with, and eventual marriage to, a white woman in Seattle in 1909, an event that triggered angry protests and anti-miscegenation laws. In one of her most recent collaborative works, *Kuan Yin: Our Lady of Compassion* (2002), Aoki reaffirms the sustaining power of legend with the story of a young boy whose fears of contemporary ills, such as homelessness and terrorism, are eased when he learns of the legendary Chinese goddess of compassion.

Aoki has performed at venues throughout the United States, Canada, and Japan and has received significant recognition for her work. She received a National Endowment for the Arts Solo Theater Fellowship in 1991 and again in 1994. She is also the recipient of two Rockefeller Foundation Multi-Arts production grants in 1992 and 1993. In 1996 Aoki received a lifetime achievement award from the United States Pan Asian Chamber of Congress for being the foremost Asian Storyteller in America. In 1997 she received a Civil Liberties Public Education Fund Award from the United States Congress. Recorded versions of two of her performance works, *Dreams and Illusions: Tales of the Pacific Rim* and *The Queen's Garden,* have garnered best spoken-word album awards by the National Association of Independent Record Distributors in 1990 and 1999 respectively. In 1996 *The Queen's Garden* was included in the anthology *Contemporary Plays by Women of Color,* and in 2000 excerpts from *Random Acts* and *Mermaid Meat* appeared in *Extreme Exposure: An Anthology of Solo Performance Texts from the Twentieth Century.*

A founding faculty member of the Institute for Diversity in the Arts at Stanford University, Aoki continues to teach and perform internationally. She and her husband, composer Mark Izu, are artistic directors of First Voice, a not-for-profit organization based in San Francisco, where they live with their son, Kai Kane.

Bibliography

Aoki, Brenda Wong. "Uncle Gunjiro's Girlfriend: The True Story of the First Hapa Baby." *Nikkei Heritage* 4 (Fall 1998): 8–9.

Hurwitt, Robert. "Brenda Wong Aoki." *Extreme Exposure: An Anthology of Solo Performance Texts from the Twentieth Century,* edited by Jo Bonney, 265–266. New York: Theatre Communications Group, 2000.

———. "One Woman's Tales Paint a Portrait of a Nation." *San Francisco Chronicle,* 23 August 1998, p. D7.

Rachel Ihara

Arabian Jazz: A Novel   Diana Abu-Jaber (1993)

This novel won the Oregon Book Award and was a finalist for the PEN/Hemingway Award. DIANA ABU-JABER's most successful novel to date, *Arabian Jazz* concerns the problematic nature of Arab-American identity. The protagonist Matussem Ramoud, a Jordanian immigrant transplanted into Upstate New York, spends quite a lot of time trying to navigate the complex net of family relations that encircle him: his adult daughters Jemorah and Melvina, his sister Fatima, and his brother-in-law Zaeed. Feeling somewhat estranged from their homeland and alienated in the United States, these characters "come together in a modern regrouping, a new kind of tribal gathering" (qtd. in Shalal-Esa). As one reader notes about Ramoud's character, "Abu-Jaber centers her novel on a Jordanian American widower who loves John Coltrane, plays drums in a nightspot called the Won Ton a Go-Go, drinks when he feels like it and has a joking relationship with his two grown daughters" (Curiel). The hybrid interest of this main character speaks to the author's own struggle to merge American and Arab cultural worldviews. "Life was a constant juggling act," one interviewer summarizes, "acting Arab at home, but American in the street" (Shalal-Esa).

In what can be considered a "plotless" novel, *Arabian Jazz* presents a slice of life for the Ramoud family. The novel opens with the father, Matussem, practicing his jazz—a way for him to cope with (or grieve for) the passing of his Irish-American wife, Nora. Nora, his essential guide to America, becomes somewhat replaced by his overbearing sister Fatima, who is determined to find suitors for Matussem's daughters, particularly Jemorah. Jemorah has a few relationships with men—Gilbert Sesame, a pool shark, Ricky Ellis, a mechanic, and Nassir, a cousin—but she eventually decides to enter graduate school to investigate racial prejudice.

More than circumventing her characters' struggles, Abu-Jaber develops a theme of identity-making and journeying to find themselves in America as persons of Arab descent. While there may be a sense of loss behind each character's exile, Abu-Jaber turns this "rootlessness and solitude" into a fictional "exploration and conversation" that is redeeming through the journey itself and the humor found in the experience ("Author Biography"). Perhaps following her own philosophy of life—"You need to find a certain amount of strength or simple self-confidence in order to laugh at yourself" (qtd. in Shalal-Esa)—Abu-Jaber writes *Arabian Jazz* with a force and keen awareness of language and comedy that makes it a powerful work.

Arabian Jazz was one of the first novels to address the Arab-American struggle to belong in an America that often holds prejudices against Arabs.

The novel is significant because it becomes a way to express a silence—the unspoken plight of the Arab in America. As Abu-Jaber mentions, "[I]f there's a choice . . . between speaking and suppressing yourself . . . inevitably you have to speak" (qtd. in Shalal-Esa). Indeed, she has spoken through this profoundly moving novel.

Bibliography

BookBrowse.com. "Author Biography: Diana Abu-Jaber." Available online. URL: http://www.bookbrowse.com/biographies/index.cfm?author_number-915. Downloaded September 15, 2006.

Curiel, Jonathan. "An Arab American Writer Seeks Her Identity." *San Francisco Chronicle,* 24 May 2004. Available online. URL: http://www.sfgate.com.cgi-bin/article.cgi?f-c/a/2004/05/24/DDGM-J6PIL41.DTL&hw -abutjaber&sn-001&SC-1000. Accessed September 15, 2006.

Shalal-Esa, Andrea. "The Only Response to Silencing . . . Is to Keep Speaking." *Al Jadid* 8, no. 39 (Spring 2002). Available online by subscription. URL: http://www.dianaabujaber.com/crescent_interview.html. Accessed 28 April 2006.

Matthew L. Miller

Arranged Marriages   Chitra Banerjee Divakaruni (1995)

Arranged Marriages, CHITRA BANERJEE DIVAKARUNI's first collection of stories, explores the trials and tribulations of middle-class Indian immigrants in the United States as they experience paradigmatic shifts in cultural consciousness. Operating under their culture of arranged marriages, the characters experiment with alternative lifestyles practiced in the more sexually open culture of the United States. With these contrasting experiences comes a recognition of sexual transgressions and social ills of their old country. Divakaruni, as cofounder of MAITRI, a hotline for South-Asian domestic abuse victims, is determined to eradicate domestic violence and devotes three of her stories to spreading awareness of this issue.

"Clothes" is a beautiful story that uses saris, the traditional clothing of Indian women, to represent feelings of loss and grief and reveal the aforementioned paradigmatic shift. As the young widow in the story opts to stay in the United States and be independent, her assertion is marked by her departure from the confined role prescribed for widows in India. Her strength is physically represented as she discards colorless widowhood for a new life of color. "The Word Love," " Doors," and "Affair" explore sexual relationships more openly practiced in the United States. In "The Word Love," the pleasure and guilt of engaging in sexual relationships outside of marriage is mulled over, and the cross-cultural misinterpretations of such relationships are revealed. "Doors" examines the risks of crossing the cultural divide through the depiction of a souring marriage between an Indian woman raised in America and an Indian man raised in India. "Affair" reveals the different rates at which immigrants adapt to the culture of the new land, suggesting that arranged marriages could adapt to the concepts of love marriages. "Meeting Mrinal" explores the inability and unpreparedness Indian women experience when dealing with alien concepts such as divorce and single motherhood. In "A Perfect Life," common threads running through the two cultures are revealed. When the flawless, sanitized life of a successful, professional woman is disrupted by her intense desires to protect and nurture a homeless boy, she realizes that desires for motherhood are not culture-specific. "The Maidservant's Story" and "The Ultrasound" are set in India. The former recounts a young woman's disbelief as she recognizes how a beloved relative destroyed the life of a maid by having sex with her while his own wife was away having their child. "The Ultrasound" explores the devastating effects of a mother-in-law manipulating her traditionally sanctioned authority to force the termination of her daughter-in-law's pregnancy. Both stories reveal that the adoption of new cultural values is not the cause of ugly and unethical ways; instead, it is the willful abuse of culturally sanctioned power that causes people to behave unethically.

In "Bats" and "Silver Pavements, Golden Roofs," Divakaruni tries to understand the psyche of the victims of domestic abuse and the compelling forces that keep them locked in abusive relationship. In "Bats," domestic violence is viewed from the perspective of a child as she observes her mother's complicity in the cycle of violence from the father. As the mother repeatedly flees and returns to the cycle of abuse, the child fails to comprehend her mother's self-destructive behavior. In "Silver Pavements, Golden Roof," domestic violence is viewed from the outside. The narrator, a houseguest who has recently arrived in the United States to pursue higher education, is sickened by the sight of her high-class, sophisticated Aunt Pratima being abused by her low-class husband, Uncle Bikram. Aunt Pratima's behavior cannot simply be categorized as codependency of abuse because her compassion for her husband appears genuine and crosses stringent class-lines that are rarely transgressed in India. In "Disappearance," another story about domestic abuse, the narrator is the abuser himself. Through her deft use of irony, Divakaruni lets the abusive husband reveal his controlling behavior, his emotional and sexual abuse of his wife and his obsession with her rejection of him.

Sukanya B. Senapati

B

Bacho, Peter (1950–)

In his novels, short stories, and essays, Peter Bacho explores the often-overlooked presence and history of the *Manong* (older) generation of Filipino Americans and their children. These Filipino men came to the United States in the 1920s and 1930s, mostly from less wealthy and less educated classes in the Philippines, and worked as migrant laborers up and down the West Coast from central California's farms to Alaska's salmon canneries. Bacho draws much of his insight into the perspectives and dreams of the men in this community from his own life as the son of a *Manong*. His work relies heavily on his own experiences as a Filipino American of a particular generation and community in Seattle, centering on the assertion of masculinity, American-centered lives, a conscious reclamation of a past generation's heroism, and the complicated history of connections between the United States and the Philippines.

Bacho was born in Seattle and, after a few years of moving around the West Coast with his family, grew up in a black and Filipino-American neighborhood in Seattle where his sense of community and home still lies. He went on to graduate summa cum laude from Seattle University and also earned a law degree from the University of Washington. He has worked as an attorney, a teacher, and a journalist, mainly in Washington and California.

In his American Book Award–winning first novel, *Cebu* (1992), Bacho writes the story of Ben Lucero, a young Filipino-American priest who confronts his family's past in the turbulent history of the Philippines. The story begins with Ben's return to the island of Cebu in the Philippines to bury his mother. His trip connects him to the histories of Spanish Catholicism and colonialism, U.S. military interventions, Japanese occupation, and the various national struggles that made the Philippines the diverse nation it is today. In Cebu, Ben contacts Aunt Clara, a close friend of his mother, who relates his mother's life before she immigrated to the United States as the wife of an American soldier named Albert Lucero. When Ben returns to the United States, this newly found knowledge helps him understand his own place as a priest in his Seattle community.

In addition to essays on Filipino-American history and on boxing in various magazines and anthologies, Bacho has written a short-story cycle, *DARK BLUE SUIT AND OTHER STORIES* (1997), and another novel, *Nelson's Run* (2002).

Paul Lai

Barbarians Are Coming, The   David Wong Louie (2000)

This first novel by DAVID WONG LOUIE is a first-person narrative chronicling the experiences of a second-generation Chinese American who struggles to find a workable compromise between the old-world expectations of his parents and his own urge to assimilate into American culture. A graduate of the Culinary Institute of America, Sterling Lung is a promising young chef specializing in French cuisine. His first employment as a chef is at the Richfield Ladies' Club, an exclusive institution in the affluent Connecticut suburbs. He seems to have come a long way from the modest rooms in which he lived with his parents behind their laundry in Lynbrook, Long Island. But, of course, nothing has ever been, or ever will be, quite so perfect or easy in Sterling's life.

Sterling's parents, known to most of their family, acquaintances, and customers by their nicknames, "Genius" and "Zsa Zsa," have placed all of their hopes on their son and, in the process, have themselves assumed a curious and not entirely coherent mix of traditional Chinese and contemporary American values. They had done everything in their power to prepare Sterling for medical school and, naturally, were then quite disappointed when he chose to become a chef instead. Indeed, after he has frustrated their distinctly American fixation with having a doctor in the family, they become all the more obsessed with the idea that he should marry a traditional Chinese woman. They even go so far as to import a "catalogue" bride for him from China. As his parents are thus engaged, Sterling learns that his lover, a Jewish dental student named Bliss Sass, is pregnant. Their relationship has been so casual that he is not certain what she expects from him in this situation.

In his professional life, Sterling faces a similar conundrum. It turns out that the Richfield ladies do not have a taste for exquisite French cuisine but for pedestrian Chinese fare. Sterling very begrudgingly accommodates their tastes, and eventually he even becomes a successful Chinese "television chef" when Bliss's father, a sort of corrupt Babbitt, pulls some strings. Still, Sterling very much feels like an imposter, a sell-out, someone who has sacrificed his professional standards and a real satisfaction with his work for a shallow, material success. His parents, whose opinion matters

more to him than he is willing to admit either to them or to himself, are painfully aware that he knows next to nothing about how to prepare Chinese dishes and that he has, in fact, long disdained their efforts to interest him in this aspect of his cultural heritage.

The narrative builds to a complex crisis when "Genius" is diagnosed with terminal cancer. All of the emotional distance that has long defined the relationship between Sterling and his father must be bridged in a relatively short period or it will remain with Sterling for the rest of his life. The novel contains moments of profound pathos juxtaposed with moments of wry humor. At first, Sterling's elastic narrative voice seems to represent everything that distances him from his much more emotionally constrained father, but in the end, Sterling's voice conveys the rich ambiguities that link father and son in a family and broader cultural history, which extends well beyond their particular difficulties.

Bibliography

Gray, Paul. "Rebel Son: Assimilation's Woes in a Sprightly First Novel." *Time*, 27 March 2000, p. 97.

Lee, Don. Review of *The Barbarians Are Coming*, *Ploughshares* 26 (Fall 2000): 25.

Martin Kich

Barroga, Jeannie (1949–)

Born into a Filipino immigrant family in Milwaukee, Barroga graduated in 1972 from the University of Wisconsin at Milwaukee and moved to northern California, which since then has become a base for her career as a playwright. She has written more than 50 plays since 1979, and has taught and worked as a director, producer, and literary manager.

In 1983, Barroga founded the Playwright Forum in Palo Alto, California, and since 1985, she has worked as the literary manager and spectrum artist of TheatreWorks in Palo Alto. She has also directed and produced several plays including *Bubblegum Killers* at TheatreWorks and Il Teatro in San Francisco and *Kin* at the Asian American Theater Company in San Francisco. Due to her active participation in theatrical work, Barroga received several awards: the Maverick Award from the Los Angeles Women's Festival, the Joey Award and the Tino Award from TeleTheatre, among others.

Barroga's plays mostly explore cultural, racial, and ethnic issues. For example, *Eye of the Coconut,* produced in 1986, examines the issue of assimilation through a Filipino-American family in Milwaukee. Dad, who came from the Philippines, and his three daughters, who like to date white men, demonstrate that both Asian immigrants and their children must confront the task of adaptation although they deal with it differently. Produced in 1995, *Rita's Resources* also depicts a Filipino immigrant family who pursues the American dream. Set in the 1970s, the play especially represents the materialistic American dream harbored by Filipino immigrants through symbolic images of the Statue of Liberty, the car, and Big Bird. These objects are also sharply contrasted with the reality of the life of a seamstress, Rita. Although America appears to be a place of material success, this land for Rita signifies labor, poverty, and anxiety.

Barroga's other important play, *Walls,* premiered in 1989 and was included in Roberta Uno's *Unbroken Thread: An Anthology of Plays by Asian American Women* in 1993. In this play, Barroga examines national and racial identity. Although Maya Lin's design for the Vietnam War Memorial won the national contest, the war veterans resist the project because they think the design does not represent their patriotic ideas. While the play revolves around the conflict over the building of the memorial, it raises questions about race, ethnicity, and nationalism. In 1992, *Talk-Story* premiered and was later anthologized in *But Still, Like Air, I'll Rise: New Asian American Plays* edited by Velina Hasu Houston in 1997. The play examines Filipino immigrant history from a second-generation Filipina American's viewpoint. While recording the history of her father's and his colleagues' sufferings in the United States, Dee, a copywriter for a newspaper company, discovers her Filipino identity. The racial discrimination that Dee's father has experienced is juxtaposed with the racial prejudices of the present day faced by Dee. Ultimately, an acknowledgment and articulation of Filipino-American history empower Dee to resist racism in her society.

Barroga's plays chiefly address the struggles of Filipino Americans, problems of assimilation, lingering racial prejudices in American society, and the national identity of America in which diverse races and cultures coexist.

Bibliography

Barroga, Jeannie. *Walls*. In *Unbroken Thread: An Anthology of Plays by Asian American Women,* edited by Roberta Uno, 201–60 Amherst: University of Massachusetts Press, 1993.

———. *Talk-Story*. In *But Still, Like Air, I'll Rise: New Asian American Plays,* edited by Velina Hasu Houston, 1–47 Philadelphia: Temple University Press, 1997.

Lee, Josephine. *Performing Asian America: Race and Ethnicity on the Contemporary Stage*. Philadelphia: Temple University Press, 1997.

Hyunjoo Ki

Blu's Hanging Lois-Ann Yamanaka (1997)

LOIS-ANN YAMANAKA's second novel, *Blu's Hanging,* juxtaposes the beautiful, Edenic landscape of Hawaii against the portrait of a traumatized, deteriorated Japanese-American family. The novel introduces readers to the voice of Ivah Ogata, the 13-year-old female narrator and the eldest of the three Ogata children. Immediately, Ivah tells us about the recent death of her mother (Eleanor), the family's poverty, and her father Poppy's inability to properly care for her eight-year-old brother (Blu), and her five-year-old sister (Maisie). The mother's death is a catalyst that plunges an already hurting family into deeper sadness: Poppy longs to die so that he might join his dead wife; Blu compulsively eats to fill the gap left by his mother's death; Maisie stops talking and frequently wets her pants; and Ivah is forced to become a surrogate mother to her siblings. As a bildungsroman, the novel hinges on Ivah's maturity; she must grow up quickly, care for her family, uncover family secrets, save her brother from sexual abuse, and eventually leave her home to begin an education and embark on adulthood.

Critics praised Yamanaka for her charged portrayal of the damage caused by silence and secrets. Ivah must eventually learn, and her father must come to acknowledge, that Eleanor died from kidney failure after years of abusing medication that cured her leprosy. Ivah learns that her mother and father, when they were children, had been forcefully separated from their families and sent to live in a leper colony on Molokai. Although cured, they never returned to their homes in Honolulu, eventually married and began a family in Molokai, and buried their pain of lost youth and innocence. Eleanor's death from addiction to the medication that saved her life symbolizes the tragic effects of unhealed psychic wounds. Her loss of innocence and painful past are then inherited by her children, especially Blu, who loses his innocence when a neighbor rapes him. As the family works through the traumas of the past that continue to haunt their present lives, Yamanaka works to "retrieve and reveal the neglected voices of sexually and psychologically violated victims" (Parikh 201).

After winning a prestigious award from the Association for Asian American Studies, *Blu's Hanging* sparked controversy about the difference between ethnic studies and literary studies, and about an author's responsibility to her community. The portrayal of the rapist Filipino neighbor raised questions about the stereotypical portrayal of Filipinos as sexual deviants. However, Yamanaka and her supporters point out that the novel also portrays Japanese sexual molesters. More important, the novel raises awareness about the necessity of revealing unrecognized, untold losses in order to end the painful legacy of past trauma.

Bibliography

Shea, Renee H. "Pidgin Politics and Paradise Revised." *Poets and Writer*, 26, no. 5 (1998): 32–37.

Parikh, Crystal. "Blue Hawaii: Asian Hawaiian Cultural Production and Racial Melancholia." *JAAS* (October 2002): 199–216.

Amy Lillian Manning

Bonesetter's Daughter, The
Amy Tan (2001)

In this novel that covers both emotional and archaeological ground, AMY TAN examines the nature of memory and communication through the lives of LuLing Young, a Chinese immigrant living in California, and her daughter, Ruth Young. LuLing begins recording her life in Chinese in an effort to remember fragments of her past that had long been buried, including the name of her mother, who was the daughter of a famous bonesetter in China. Ruth, a ghostwriter in San Francisco for self-help authors, decides to translate her mother's story amid the debris of her own relatively unexamined life. Living with a man and his two daughters in San Francisco without a formal arrangement, Ruth has lost her voice each year for the past nine years for several days, always starting on August 12, and she often finds it hard to express herself. Both the mother and the daughter are searching for satisfying ways to make themselves known to each other.

The novel's prologue is in LuLing's voice and is in fact the beginning of the narrative of her life. Her story therefore encompasses the story of her daughter, which begins in part 1. As she worries about her mother's Alzheimer's disease and serves more and more as her caretaker, Ruth remembers her own past—how her mother relocated repeatedly, made her communicate with ghosts, and generally made her life difficult. As her mother begins to lose her memory, Ruth begins to read and translate her mother's memoirs given to her years before.

Part 2 of the novel is Ruth's translation of her mother's memoirs. In the first person, LuLing tells of her strained relationship with family in China, while being cared for by a disfigured woman she called Precious Auntie. Unbeknownst to LuLing, this woman is in fact her birth mother, whose identity is concealed because of her personal and cultural transgressions. The narrative mainly concerns the life of Precious Auntie, whose family made ink and lived in a village called Immortal Heart, where in nearby caves valuable "dragon bones" have been found. As Precious Auntie grew, she is described as becoming a strong-willed woman who turns down a feudal marriage proposal from a cruel man, in order to marry for love. Her husband is soon killed, however, and Precious Auntie's life is made miserable by this cruel man. Years later, when she learns that her daughter LuLing is to marry into the very family that caused her so much pain, Precious Auntie kills herself. As expected, LuLing faces a bad marriage and wartime troubles, and she finally escapes to America, all the while feeling haunted by the lack of forgiveness from her birth mother.

Part 3 of the novel concerns how Ruth is affected by her mother's narrative and how the two women, through memory and the healing power of forgiveness, are able to have a loving, close relationship. Ironically, through LuLing's loss of memory, the wrongs of the past are smoothed over and righted. The epilogue of the novel finds Ruth in full possession of her voice and happy in her own relationships on August 12, beginning to write her own story and the story of her mother and grandmother instead of ghostwriting for others.

The Bonesetter's Daughter spans three generations of women who, though intimately connected to each other, cannot at first sense the continuity of their lives. Through storytelling, however, the three lives become linked and healed. A central issue in the novel concerns the ability to speak: Precious Auntie is literally unable to speak because she has disfigured herself as a gesture of strength and anger. She is able to communicate through her daughter, who understands her sign language and shorthand. LuLing finds expression in the written word, luckily before she begins to lose her memory. She is still unable to speak to her daughter of her life, but manages to communicate nevertheless, especially through the memoirs. Ruth is paralyzed for several days each year by silence, since she is unable to voice her beliefs and opinions, even to those closest to her. When the women make an effort to respect their shared history, their lives are blessed by an easier communication and understanding. Tan is also concerned in this novel with the mystical power of memory and its real and elusive connection to actual events. Memories, however altered by our perceptions, strongly shape our

lives. Throughout the novel, Tan uses the motif of unearthing—of Peking Man from the cave, of familial history and names, and of individual emotion—to express the process of interpersonal reconciliation, so much more difficult than an archaeological excavation. Through this novel, Tan once again explores aspects of her own childhood and her mother's challenging life.

Vanessa Rasmussen

Brainard, Cecilia Manguerra   (1947–)

Born in Cebu, Brainard is best known for her internationally acclaimed novel WHEN THE RAINBOW GODDESS WEPT (1994). Having published several other collections of stories, she is now regarded as the voice of her generation in Philippine literature, working tirelessly to promote the voices of Filipino writers in the United States.

Brainard received her B.A. in communication arts from Maryknoll College in Quezon City in 1968 and in 1969 migrated to the United States to escape the oppressive political climate of the Philippines under the dictatorship of Ferdinand Marcos. She attended graduate school in film studies at UCLA. While in the United States, Brainard reestablished her friendship with Lauren Brainard, whom she had met in the Philippines when he was serving with the Peace Corps. They eventually married while Lauren was in law school in San Francisco and later moved to Santa Monica, California. Between 1969 and 1981, Cecilia Brainard worked as a scriptwriter while also being involved in fund-raising activities with a nonprofit organization. In 1981 she began a serious career in writing. Currently, Cecilia Brainard lives in Santa Monica, California, and is an adjunct professor at the University of Southern California.

Living in the United States as a Filipina provided Brainard the stimulus to grow as a writer, and from 1982 to 1988 she wrote a bimonthly column entitled *Filipina American Perspective* for the now-defunct *Philippine American News*. These essays were her first foray into writing as an exile from her home country and provided her with the perfect forum to explore both her childhood and young adulthood in the Philippines. Her essays have been collected and published as *Philippine Women in America.* Brainard continued to write short stories and essays and found different avenues to publish her writings in magazines and journals, first in the Philippines and later in the United States. Her writings can be found in such diverse publications as *Focus Philippines, Philippine Graphic, Katipunan, Amerasia Journal, Bamboo Ridge Journal, The California Examiner,* and others. Her stories have been included in anthologies, such as *Making Waves* (1989), *Forbidden Fruit* (1992), *Songs of Ourselves* (1994), and *On a Bed of Rice* (1995), bearing testimony to her varied and vast talent as a writer.

Brainard has won several awards for her writing such as the California Arts Council Artists Fellowship in Fiction in 1989, the Fortner Prize in 1985 and the Honorable Mention Award of the Philippine Arts, Letters, and Media Council in 1989. In 1997 she received the Outstanding Individual Award from the City of Cebu.

What makes Brainard's fiction compelling is her ability to integrate Filipino legends and Philippine history into her writings. In her short stories and in *When the Rainbow Goddess Wept,* Brainard reimagines the oral folktales and native traditions of her childhood into vivid contemporary characters, providing her readers with a distinctive style and voice that is Asian yet American.

In her latest novel, *Magdalena* (2002), Brainard takes the reader on another journey into the psyche of her protagonists during the time of the Japanese occupation of the Philippines. Although the book visits the traumatic terrain of war, the female protagonists, like the characters in her other stories, find love and beauty in this time of horror and destruction, refusing to capitulate in the face of insurmountable odds. Perhaps this is Brainard's own way of illustrating the timeless strength and conviction of the Filipino spirit, thus giving the reader a frame of reference for her own work and life as a writer and voice of Filipino Americans.

Bibliography

Brainard, Cecilia Manguerra. "An Interview with Cecilia Manguerra Brainard." By Dana Huebler. *Poets and Writers Magazine* (March/April 1997): 96–105.

Ty, Eleanor. "Cecilia Manguerra Brainard." In *Asian American Novelists: A Bio-Bibliographical Critical Sourcebook,* edited by Emmanuel S. Nelson, 29–33. Westport, Conn.: Greenwood Press, 2000.

Ray Chandrasekara

Brazil-Maru Karen Tei Yamashita (1992)

Brazil-Maru pieces together a fictionalized history of Esperança, an isolated Japanese community that actually existed in the deep jungles of Brazil. The nascent community of Esperança comes into being under the leadership of Kantaro Uno, who is driven by his ideal to create an egalitarian society. The story spans 50 years, beginning in 1926 with the arrival of a small group of Japanese settlers who immigrated to Brazil. The novel traces the establishment, development, maturity, and eventual decline of Esperança.

The novel is constructed of five distinct yet interconnected accounts that are *Rashomon*-like in style in that they individually reflect each narrator's unique position in relation to the commune and especially the narrators' perceptions of the community's leader, Kantaro. The first narrator, Ichiro Terada, who is also called Émile, narrates the early history of the community from 1925 to the late 1930s. He is Kantaro's loyal disciple, who closes his narrative by saying that "Kantaro's dreams were undeniably my dreams" (78). The narrator following Émile is Haru, Kantaro's wife, who outlines the period from the late 1930s to the end of World War II. Her practical voice and stark honesty in describing the disintegration of the commune expose Kantaro's less-than-perfect side in regard to his financial investments and careless relationships with women. The third narrator is Kantaro himself, as he describes the period from the end of World War II to the late 1950s. Haru's earlier description of a self-absorbed Kantaro is substantiated by his authoritarian stance and arrogant voice as he speaks of his love for Esperança but justifies his need to have a double life in São Paulo, where he conducts his alternative business. The fourth narrator is

Kantaro's nephew Genji Befu, whose cognitive limitations result in a naïve voice. His account captures the deteriorating conditions of Esperança between 1959 and 1976. The narrative ends with Genji's description of a plane crash in a forest, which kills Kantaro. In the form of an epilogue to the novel, the fifth and final narrative is told by Guilherme Kasai, son of Kantaro's business associate, Shigeshi Kasai, and the only narrator who is not a member of Esperança. Looking back, he describes the Esperança community as having been a "confined world" for its Japanese members.

What begins as a successfully self-sufficient agricultural community gradually disintegrates into a cesspool of greed, deception, and disorganization stemming from Kantaro's activities conducted for his personal financial gain rather than for that of the community. Thus, at first, *Brazil-Maru* seems to be a critique of a stagnating patriarchal society. However, more important is the underlying assertion that the hyphenated Asian is not merely a North American phenomenon. Critic Ruth Hsu poignantly emphasizes that KAREN TEI YAMASHITA's "location of the Asian immigrant experience in Brazil also frees that experience from what is, at times, an oppressive rhetoric—homegrown in the United States and Canada—on ethnicity, assimilation, and the nature of the North American nationalist identity" (190). In other words, Yamashita's text transcends a U.S.-centric perspective to a larger context in which Latin America serves as its focal point. In this way, Yamashita effectively disrupts the tendency to read Asian-American literature in relation to issues that are specific to Asian-American communities existing within North America.

Bibliography

Cheung, King-Kok, ed. *An Interethnic Companion to Asian American Literature.* New York: Cambridge University Press, 1997.

Hsu, Ruth. Review of *Brazil-Maru, Manoa: A Pacific Journal of International Writing* (1992): 188–190.

Sugano, Douglas. "Karen Tei Yamashita." In *Asian American Novelists,* edited by Emmanuel Nelson, 403–408. Westport, Conn.: Greenwood Press, 2000.

Yamashita, Karen Tei. *Brazil-Maru.* Minnesota: Coffee House Press, 1992.

———. "Karen Tei Yamashita: An Interview." By Michael S. Murashige. *Amerasia Journal* 20, no. 3 (1994): 49–59.

Eliko Kosaka

Bridegroom, The   Ha Jin (2000)

Set in Muji City, a fictitious town in northern China, this collection of 12 short stories explores everyday life in the post–Cultural Revolution period of the 1980s. This was a volatile time of social and political transition, as the old ways clashed with the new when China gradually reopened its doors to foreigners. In his characteristically simple but poetic style, Ha Jin is able to show the humanity of common people trying to live decent lives in a rapidly changing world.

The stories in *The Bridegroom* touch upon many of the dominant concerns in contemporary Chinese society. Although the Cultural Revolution ended in the late 1970s, the Maoist ideology is so pervasive that it continues to control people's minds. "Broken," for example, relates the tragic case of a female typist, who commits suicide after she is accused of being a bourgeois for having an affair with a married man. Similarly, in the title story, "The Bridegroom," the homosexual protagonist feels imprisoned because of his sexual orientation. "An Entrepreneur's Story" examines the growing phenomenon of privatization in China. It shows how, by becoming rich, an entrepreneur wins the love of a woman who had avoided him before and the respect of people who used to disdain him. "A Bad Joke" addresses the hyperinflation at the end of the 1980s, which was one of the causes of the Tiananmen Square Uprising. In "After Cowboy Chicken Came to Town," Chinese workers vent their anger at American business methods that are contrary to both their ideological and cultural beliefs. Cultural conflict is even more central to "The Woman from New York," a story about a woman who returns to her hometown after living in the United States for four years. She not only discovers that she is not accepted by her countrymen but also loses her child, husband, job, and reputation.

In *The Bridegroom* most characters are subjected to various degrees of injustice, usually at the hands of impersonal bureaucrats who pay little attention to the welfare of their fellow citizens. Often, people feel powerless and simply accept their fate. However, as "Saboteur" masterfully illustrates, they occasionally respond in unexpected ways. The story's protagonist is a mild-mannered university professor who wholeheartedly accepts the Communist Party's slogan that "all citizens [are] equal before the law." The professor is on his honeymoon with his bride and, as they eat lunch at the Muji City train station, a local police officer throws a bowl of tea in their direction, wetting their sandals. When he protests, the officer accuses him of being a "saboteur" and arrests him. The professor informs the police that he is suffering from acute hepatitis and needs urgent medical attention, but they remain unmoved. They allow his bride to go free but keep him imprisoned. With the help of a former student who has become a lawyer, the professor finally leaves the prison. Yet, before heading back to his hometown, he eats at a series of local restaurants, barely touching the food at one eatery before moving on to the next. Within a month, there is an epidemic of hepatitis in Muji City and no one knows how it started. Needless to say, the professor is not meant to be seen as a hero. Rather, he is someone who is unable to get even with his oppressors and thus, in his blindness, targets the innocent population of a whole city.

Jianwu Liu and Albert Braz

Bulosan, Carlos   (1911–1956)

Born to a large family in a small village in the Philippines, Bulosan grew into adulthood as a member of the dispossessed peasantry during the period of American occupation (1901–1946). When Bulosan migrated to the United States in 1930, he was initially seeking only a temporary stay to search for the freedom of economic opportunity advertised by the U.S. government-facilitated public education he had received in the Philippines. Only two

years after his arrival in the United States, Bulosan had already begun to establish himself as a promising literary artist. His writings appeared in numerous poetry magazines, and he was listed in *Who's Who in America.* By the 1940s Bulosan was published in several national literary journals including the *New Yorker, Harper's,* and *Current Biography.* His writings centered on the theme of what it means to be a Filipino immigrant in the United States. From his poetry and short stories to his essays and autobiography, his works were lauded for their optimistic faith in America, despite his consistent, imbedded critique of her racially inhospitable climate.

In 1943 Bulosan was selected by President Roosevelt to contribute to a popular wartime collection in the *Saturday Evening Post.* His essay, "Freedom from Want," offered his trademark hope for the nation's potential to live up to the promise of American ideals. Ironically celebrated as the epitome of the American dream, Bulosan's early literary success was initially steeped in his perceived patriotism. His popularity only continued to increase during the wartime years, as his 1944 collection of short stories, *The Laughter of My Father,* was translated into more than a dozen languages and became a national best-seller. This collection of stories employs a dark, wry humor to highlight the oppressive economic, military, and social conditions surrounding Bulosan's formative years. Once again, critics failed to grasp the underlying social critique present in Bulosan's work. When his use of ironic humor was misinterpreted as "comic," however, Bulosan himself clarified his intentions. In his 1946 essay, "I Am Not a Laughing Man," he declared, "I am mad because when my book, *The Laughter of My Father,* was published by Harcourt, Brace, and Company, the critics called me 'the pure comic spirit.' I am not a laughing man. I am an angry man. That is why I started writing."

In 1946 he published his most famous work, AMERICA IS IN THE HEART, a loosely autobiographical work detailing the Filipino immigrant experience in early 20th-century United States. With this publication, Bulosan was celebrated as one of the nation's most prominent writers. When the political tides began to change, however, so did Bulosan's public reception. As his indictment of racist institutions in a presumably egalitarian United States of America collided with "the red scare," Bulosan's popularity waned precipitously. The McCarthyism of the 1950s rendered Bulosan a blacklisted writer, and his works vanished from literary history for the next two decades. His books now out of print, Bulosan was forgotten just as quickly as he had exploded onto the intellectual scene in the United States. He died in obscurity on a Seattle street in 1956; his death, attributed to "exposure," was compounded by years of physical and psychological suffering.

In 1972 Epifanio San Juan, Jr., established himself as the premier Bulosan scholar by publishing his landmark study, *Carlos Bulosan and the Imagination of the Class Struggle.* This study became the first of many revolutionary, critical essays on Bulosan written by San Juan, and it argued for the importance of remembering (and rereading) his works. Following San Juan's study, many of Bulosan's lost writings were eventually recovered; far removed from the fear of political backlash, contemporary ethnic studies scholars were able to bring Bulosan's complex social critiques to the fore. Bulosan regained his literary notoriety posthumously, although he is celebrated today for very different reasons. Once brought to light, the complexity of his political message transformed Bulosan's legacy from a blindly optimistic patriotism to a patriotically charged social activism. What was initially viewed as a contradiction between his undying patriotism and his radical social critique is in fact a marker of his sophisticated understanding of U.S. social politics. He is remembered today as one of the early fathers of Filipino-American literature, fiercely determined to hold America accountable for her promise of greatness.

Bibliography

Bulosan, Carlos. *America Is in the Heart.* New York: Harcourt, 1946. Reprint, Seattle: University Washington Press, 1973.

———. *The Laughter of My Father.* New York: Harcourt, 1944.

———. *On Becoming Filipino: Selected Writings of Carlos Bulosan,* edited by E. San Juan, Jr. Philadelphia: Temple University Press, 1995.

———. "Writings of Carlos Bulosan." edited by E. San Juan, Jr. *Amerasia Journal* (special issue) 6, no. 1 (May 1979): 1–154.

Evangelista, Susan. *Carlos Bulosan and His Poetry: A Biography and Anthology.* Seattle: University Washington Press, 1985.

San Juan, Epifanio, Jr. *Carlos Bulosan and the Imagination of the Class Struggle.* Quezon City: University of the Philippines Press, 1972.

———. "Searching for the Heart of 'America.'" *Teaching American Ethnic Literatures: Nineteen Essays.* Edited by John R. Maitino and David R. Peck. Albuquerque: University of New Mexico Press, 1996. Available online. URL:http://www.boondocksnet. com/centennial/sctexts/bulosan.html. Posted Spring 1993.

———. "Violence of Exile, Politics of Desire: Prologue to Carlos Bulosan." *The Philippine Temptation: Dialectics of Philippines–U.S. Literary Relations,* 129–170. Philadelphia: Temple University Press, 1996.

Linda Pierce

Cao, Lan (1961–)

Born and raised in Vietnam, Cao immigrated to the United States in 1975 at the age of 13, just after the end of the Vietnam War. She graduated from Mount Holyoke College in 1983 with a B.A. in political science and from Yale School of Law in 1987 with a J.D. A talented and versatile individual, Cao distinguished herself in many ways. After earning her degrees, she held an important clerkship with Judge Constance Motley of the United States District of New York, followed by a position at the New York law firm of Paul, Weiss, Rifkind, Wharton & Garrison. Cao then taught international law at Brooklyn Law School for six years. She was also a Ford Foundation scholar for all her achievements as an academic and as a writer. In 2001 she joined the faculty of the College of William and Mary as a law professor.

Besides writing and publishing within her professional field, and reviewing film and books, she coauthored *Everything You Need to Know About Asian Americans* (1996) with Himilce Novas. As a literary writer, however, she is best known for her semiautobiographical fiction, *Monkey Bridge* (1997). Based on her own immigrant experience and family difficulties, *Monkey Bridge* is an impressive first novel about generational and cultural differences; it is also about bridging the gap between the East (war-torn Vietnam) and the West (America). Mai, the teenaged protagonist, leads the reader through a complicated and meandering narrative of political intrigues, Vietnamese ancestral myths, and traditions. The narrative attempts to reconstruct a family history during the Vietnam War from the Vietnamese immigrant perspective. The title of the novel is worthy of note because a monkey bridge in Vietnam is a uniquely Vietnamese traditional symbol of peasant life. It is often frail, built with minimum support across small rivers; thin, spindly bamboos are fastened together by ropes so that the bridge is only maneuverable with skillful and agile feet. For centuries, Vietnamese peasantry has used this bridge system for mobility. The novel's title, in this respect, is symbolic of the bridge that the protagonist and her mother have to negotiate to cross between past and present, between Vietnam and America. Crossing the bridge requires them to skillfully navigate through their past and present—to learn to live with traumatic war experiences and to reconstruct the memory of escape from their homeland so as to make it palatable in their new adoptive home in America.

At the heart of *Monkey Bridge* is the troubled relationship between the protagonist and her mother. This relationship is eloquently delineated by the author through subtle yet hauntingly meandering prose. The young protagonist wants to acculturate into the American mainstream society through school, popular media, and everyday interaction with Americans, but she also wants to obey her mother, who does not take life well in America. This desire fundamentally fluctuates with her mother's silence, secrecy, and profound sadness over her past in Vietnam. Only through time, the protagonist's love of her mother, and her familiarity with both Vietnamese and American cultures, can she understand the burdens her mother bears as she negotiates her way across the bridge between past and present, and between Vietnam and America.

Bibliography

Cao, Lan. *Monkey Bridge.* New York: Penguin Books, 1997.

Janette, Michele. "Guerrilla Irony in Lan Cao's *Monkey Bridge.*" *Contemporary Literature* 42, no. 1 (2001): 50–77.

Stocks, Claire. "Bridging the Gaps: Inescapable History in Lan Cao's *Monkey Bridge.*" *Studies in the Literary Imagination* 37, no. 1 (2004): 83–100.

Hanh Nguyen

Carbò, Nick   (1964–   )

Filipino-American poet and editor Nick Carbò was born in Legaspi, the Philippines. When he was two, he was adopted together with his younger sister by a Spanish couple. He grew up in Manila and attended the International School before completing his education in the United States. He began to write poems when he was studying at Bennington College, Vermont, in 1984–85. After receiving his Master of Fine Arts degree in creative writing from Sarah Lawrence College, New York, he has taught courses at New Jersey Institute of Technology, Bucknell University, American University in Washington D.C., University of Miami, and Columbia College in Chicago. NEA (National Endowment for the Arts) and NYFA (New York Foundation for the Arts) have awarded him grants in poetry. His poetry appeared in such magazines as *Ploughshares, Gargoyle, DisOrient,* and *Mangrove.*

Nick Carbò has published four books of poetry: *El Grupo McDonald's* (1995); *Secret Asian Man* (2000), which won the 2001 Asian American Lit-

erary Award; *Rising from Your Book* (2003), which is an e-chapbook of experimental poems; and *Andalusian Dawn* (2004), produced during his writing residency in Spain. His poems are composed in English, even though numerous Spanish and Tagalog words can be found, signifying his mixed heritage. The poems explore central issues such as colonialism, the history of the Philippines and the Filipino diaspora, cultural roots, stereotypes (such as the one according to which Asian men are supposedly emasculated). His poems are characterized by deep insights and thought-provoking and subtle irony.

Nick Carbò has also edited four poetry anthologies. *Returning a Borrowed Tongue* (1996) features Filipino and Filipino-American poets, thus aiming at recovering a sense of the Filipino poetic tradition. *Babaylan* (2000), which he coedited with Eileen Tabios, collects the works of more than 60 Filipina and Filipina-American writers of different generations from across the globe. *Sweet Jesus: Poems about the Ultimate Icon* (2002) was coedited with his wife, poet Denise Duhamel. This anthology gathers poems centered on the figure of Jesus and written from different perspectives: Asian American, Native American, gay, atheist, and others. Carbò's latest work is *Pinoy Poetics: An Anthology of Autobiographical and Critical Essays on Filipino Poetics* (2004), in which more than 40 writers of Filipino descent reflect on their poems, techniques, and sources of inspiration.

Elisabetta Marino

Cha, Theresa Hak Kyung   (1951–1982)

Even though her life was cut short by a senseless murder, Cha left a significant mark on American literature. Most of her literary and visual art works are quite autobiographical, but they also have a universal appeal since they explore, among other things, issues of gender, migration and dislocation.

Cha was born in Korea during the Korean War to parents who had been raised in Manchuria, China, as first-generation Korean exiles, and who returned to Korea after the country was emancipated in 1945 from Japanese colonial occupation. After spending her childhood in Korea during a turbulent period of political struggle, Cha moved with her family to Hawaii in 1962 and relocated to San Francisco in 1964, where she attended a Catholic school, studying French and Greco-Roman classics. She studied briefly at the University of San Francisco before transferring to the University of California, Berkeley, majoring in art and comparative literature. She was influenced by Conceptual Art, which was created during the 1960s and early 1970s and connected to the rebellious spirit of the era. She worked as an usher/cashier at the Pacific Film Archive (1974–77), where she saw numerous classical and experimental films. She started performance/visual/installation art shows around this time, and spent 1976 doing her postgraduate work in filmmaking and theory in Paris. In 1979 she made her first trip back to Korea, and then again in 1980 to begin shooting the unfinished film *White Dust from Mongolia*. She moved to New York and married Richard Barnes, a close friend since her graduate school days, in May 1982. She was murdered in November 1982, by an unknown assailant, a few days after *Dictée* was published. In 1992 the Theresa Hak Kyung Cha Memorial Foundation donated her art and archives to the Berkeley Art Museum and Pacific Film Archive.

Dictée is a complex and powerful work of art. Its nonlinear narrative, fragmented structure, pictures without captions, frequent use of the French language, and many other obscure elements make it nearly impossible for any reader to understand the work completely. Due to these experimental characteristics and an unusual blend of genres and forms, the book has not been read widely for a decade since its first publication; however, it is now rapidly being canonized in the fields of literary, feminist, film, postcolonial, and ethnic studies. The visual and spatial arrangement (for example, one section requires a separate reading of right-hand pages and left-hand pages) of the text resists a linear reading, thus appealing to the increasingly visual, multimedia-oriented young generations. In

2002 a Web site called "*Dictée* for Dummies" was created with various hyperlinks to help readers "who are having trouble with the text." Ironically, however, it is the troublesome aspects of the work that generate new meanings for readers. Cha seems to expect her readers to actively take part in creating meaning out of her text.

Dictée is composed of 10 parts, nine of which are named after the nine Muses, except that the Muse of lyric poetry, Euterpe, is changed to Elitere. The juxtaposed and seemingly unrelated fragments of each part may generate multiple meanings, depending on how readers make sense of the relationship between the classical genre of each Muse and the fragments. For example, the first part is made up of dictations (*dictée* in French) on many levels—national, political, cultural, and religious. This part, which begins with the untranslated Korean script in the frontispiece, can be seen as a text about immigration, depicting the stutters and misspellings of a second language speaker. Like Cha, who was forced to learn English and French as a teenager, Diseuse ("female speaker" in French) is very self-conscious in learning a second language. Not only does she feel the physical and mental strains of pronouncing different sounds, of remembering proper punctuation in the writing system, and of being occasionally unable to speak, but she also experiences the mental colonization involved in the acquisition of the dominant cultural language. In other words, language acquisition is not seen as a simple linguistic skill development, but as a process of brainwashing and subjugation to the national, political, cultural, and religious values of the native speakers. Cha demonstrates the ways in which the sentences in a language textbook instill in the learner a sense of national pride ("Do you know that there are about ten thousand Americans in Paris, who would quit to go to heaven?"); moral lessons ("Be industrious: The more one works, the better one succeeds"); or gender discrimination ("In the name of the Father, and of the Son, and the Holy Spirit, Amen").

Cha succeeds in transforming the passive act of dictation into a space of active cultural comment by making the reader acutely aware of the constructed nature of language. As in the overly faithful dictation on the first page, where all the directions and punctuation marks are spelled out in words, readers become aware of the narrator's resistance to cultural colonization implicit in the language acquisition process for an immigrant.

Language and memory seem to be the most poignant themes of the book. While language can be used as a tool of colonization, it can also restore buried and unspoken memories. Playing with the sound, Cha asks Diseuse to restore the dead tongue from "disuse." "Terpsichore: Choral Dance" shows the patient and slow process of voices rising from under a heavy stone in the depth of the earth. The hue-less stone emits moisture on the surface, colors appear, the stain darkens to become crimson blood, and then voices become liberated from the stone of oblivion. The last part of *Dictée* shows Cha's belief in the power of voices in our fight against the power of time and distance.

Bibliography

Kim, Elaine H., and Norman Alarcón, eds. *Writing Self, Writing Nation: A Collection of Essays on* Dictée *by Theresa Hak Kyung Cha.* Berkeley, Calif.: Third Woman Press, 1994.

Lewallen, Constance M., ed. *The Dream of the Audience: Theresa Hak Kyung Cha (1951–1982).* Berkeley: University of California Press, 2001.

Gui-woo Lee

Chai, May-lee (1967–)

Born in Redlands, California, to Winberg and Carolyn Chai, May-lee Chai took her B.A. in French and Chinese Studies from Grinnell College in 1989 and was elected to Phi Beta Kappa. In the next five years, she received an M.A. in East Asian Studies from Yale University and a second M.A. in English–Creative Writing from the University of Colorado–Boulder. Chai has taught at several universities and also worked as a journalist and editor. May-lee Chai's short fiction has been published in *North American Review, Missouri Review,* and *Grinnell Review* among others. Two of her short stories have been anthologized in *The Compact*

Bedford Introduction to Literature (2005) and in *At Our Core: Women Writing on Power* (1998).

Chai's work has gained her a solid reputation as a first-rate literary stylist as well as a careful, sensitive historian. Her first novel, *My Lucky Face* (1997), is a tightly drawn first-person narrative about cultural and personal alienation. By portraying a deteriorating marriage, Chai examines the psychological and emotional restraints in late 20th-century China. On the surface, the narrator Lin Jun's life should be pleasant. She has a good job teaching English, a husband who is an intellectual, an intelligent son away at a boarding school, and a mother-in-law with political connections. Beneath the surface, though, her introverted husband is distraught by Lin Jun's working relationship with an American woman who teaches English, and Lin Jun herself has begun to confront the early constraints on her life that led her into her marriage and career. When her husband blows up at her during dinner one day, Lin Jun decides to divorce him and pursue her individual happiness. The novel is praised for the authenticity of its background setting, its carefully developed plot and themes, the maturity and precision of its characterizations, a sardonically witty style and ingenious metaphors, and a sensitive feminist rejection of fatuous Chinese versions of Victorian gender biases.

Another of Chai's successful literary productions is a collection of short stories and essays, *Glamorous Asians* (2004). Chai uses myths, personal experiences, and a species of magical realism to lay out her perspectives on Asian-American life. "The Dancing Girl's Story," in particular, is an exquisite phantasmagorical narration that directly challenges the notion of the "melting pot." In it, Chai relates the tale of an immortalized Cambodian woman who flees westward from her ravaged native land just ahead of the arrival of the Khmer Rouge genocide. After falling into the sea, this lovely Cambodian phantasm is picked up by a passing vessel, and she eventually faces an American immigration agent who has no grasp of the cultural traditions of Southeast Asia.

The Girl from Purple Mountain (2004), coauthored with her father, Winberg Chai, is a carefully researched family epic depicting the hazards, triumphs, and distinctive personalities of the Chai clan's independent-minded intellectuals in 20th-century China and America.

Leo Mahoney

Chan, Jeffery Paul (1942–)

A third-generation Chinese American living in California, Chan earned a bachelor's and master's degrees from San Francisco State University, where he is currently professor emeritus of Asian American Studies and English. In 1973 he worked with Frank Chin, Lawson Fusao Inada, and Shawn Hsu Wong to edit the groundbreaking anthology *Aiiieeeee: An Anthology of Asian-American Writers.* In 1991 he produced an updated anthology entitled *The Big Aiiieeeee.* Chan devotes his critical attention to explaining and showing the history of Asian-American literature. Chan wants to make sure readers and critics understand the tremendous bounty and production of Chinese-American writers. For example, besides cowriting a literary history of Asian-American literature in the introduction of *Aiiieeeee,* Chan has cowritten an article in *A Literary History of the American West* on Asian-American literary production and trends. In it, he establishes the longstanding presence of Chinese-, Japanese-, and Filipino-American writings in the formation of the American West throughout the 19th century until the postwar period.

Chan's fiction has been published in various literary journals including the *Amerasia Journal* and the *Asian Pacific Journal.* His fiction typically addresses the interchanges between Chinese Americans and mainstream Americans. Most recently Chan wrote a novel entitled *Eat Everything before You Die* (2004), in which he creates the character of Christopher Columbus Wong, who "explores" the multiple countercultures of 1960s California and learns in the process what it means to be "Chinese" in America. Recently Chan has been awarded a guest editorship with *Asian Literary Journal* and divides his time between Italy and California.

Matthew L. Miller

Chang, Diana (1934–)

Writer and painter Diana Chang was born in New York City in 1934 to a Chinese father and an Amerasian mother of Chinese-Irish heritage. In 1935 the family moved to China, where Chang received her education at American schools in Beijing, Shanghai, and Nanjing. Right after World War II, Chang returned to New York City for high school and college; she majored in English at Barnard College. A prolific writer, Chang has written six novels: *The FRONTIERS OF LOVE* (1956), *A Woman of Thirty* (1959), *A Passion for Life* (1961), *The Only Game in Town* (1963), *Eye to Eye* (1974), and *A Perfect Love* (1978). Her three books of poetry include *The Horizon Is Definitely Speaking* (1982); *What Matisse Is After* (1984); and *Earth, Water, Light: Poems Celebrating the East End of Long Island* (1991). Chang's short stories and essays have also appeared in various journals and anthologies. A recipient of many literary awards (including the John Hay Whitney and Fulbright Fellowships), Chang is regarded as an important early Asian-American writer. As a painter, she has also held several exhibitions at galleries in New York. Her artistic achievements in fiction, poetry, and painting have gained Chang a special place in Asian-American culture and literature.

Raised and educated in the "between-worlds" environment, Chang reiterates in her work the salient theme of in-betweenness or, in Amy Ling's word, "bifocalness." Between her Chinese heritage and Irish identity, and between China and America, Chang inscribes the Eurasian subjectivity, a "hyphenated condition," in much of her work. For example, in *The Frontiers of Love,* Chang's most acclaimed novel, she focuses on three Eurasians' search for identity in wartime Shanghai at the close of World War II. The three young Eurasians—Sylvia Chen, Mimi Lambert, and Feng Huang—represent three responses to their hybrid identity. Despite the Eurasians' entanglement in the hyphenated condition, they choose their forms of existence in either a creative or destructive project of self-realization. In other novels, Chang extends the unhinged racial identity to a universalized existential estrangement. In *A Woman of Thirty,* the heroine, Emily Merrick, confronting the anguish she suffers from a divorce and her subsequent affair with a married man, chooses to gain a new sense of self. In *A Passion for Life,* Chang explores the between-worlds theme of freedom versus responsibility in the story of Barbara Owens, who faces the dilemma of aborting her baby after she is impregnated by a rapist. In *The Only Game in Town,* Chang features a love affair between an American Peace Corps volunteer and a Communist Chinese dancer. Chang transforms this political spoof, despite its interracial subtext, into a story whose "universal" import transcends racial and national boundaries. *Eye to Eye* hinges on the twists and turns of a visual artist's route to selfhood through his artistic creation. In her last novel, *A Perfect Love,* Chang again accentuates the feelings of estrangement in the love affair between middle-aged, married Alice Mayhew and the younger David Henderson, separated from his wife. Trapped among social imperatives and alienations, the protagonists have to confront life with resilience and resolution.

Chang's short stories and poetry also depict racial, cultural, and psychological disruptions. In the poem, "Second Nature," she writes, "I am the thin edge I sit on. I begin to gray—white and black and in between." The in-betweenness is imprinted in another poem, "Saying Yes," in which the narrator, asked whether she is Chinese or American, responds "Not neither-nor, not maybe, but both." "The Oriental Contingent," her best-known short story, delves into the psychological poignancy of the racial "neither-nor" or "both" between the two characters, Lisa Mallory and Connie Sung. The two Chinese-American women feel imperfectly "American" due to their Asian physiognomy. In most stories and poems, however, Chang works against the racial reduction and imperative determining the identity conflict. She infuses her work with a vision that life is a constant process of becoming, through which, as in paiting or writing, one can achieve self-realization and freedom.

In Asian-American literary criticism, the importance of Diana Chang and her work has been downplayed, partly because of the absence of conspicuous "Asian-American" themes in the major body of her work, and partly because of Chang's attempt to delineate universal themes in her narratives. In spite of the "universality" in her work, Chang, like other early Chinese-American women writers (for example, SUI SIN FAR and JADE SNOW WONG), explores the dual identity still nascent in the literary work of her time. It is also noteworthy that Chang's first novel was published before the Asian-American consciousness movement in the mid-1960s, when Asian-American cultural production was burgeoning, and Asian-American critics were starting to define a new literary canon. Earlier critics of Chang's novels tend to dismiss the Asian-American sensibility in her work. Benjamin Lease, for example, eulogizes Chang's "tremendous skill [of creating] the sights and sounds and smells of Shanghai" (4). Kenneth Rexroth lauds Chang's style, which is "more alive, more gripping, than even the best translation" (273). Amy Ling's critical essay, "Writer in the Hyphenated Condition: Diana Chang," is the first to point out the double consciousness in Chang's fiction and poetry. Ling's criticism serves as an important point of departure for other Asian-American critics, among them SHIRLEY GEOK-LIN LIM, Sau-ling Wong and Helena Grice, who have used Chang's texts as a touchstone for new directions of Asian-American criticism on heterogeneity, hybridity, and subjectivity.

Bibliography

Baringer, Sandra. "'The Hybrids and the Cosmopolitans': Race, Gender, and Masochism in Diana Chang's *The Frontiers of Love.*" *Essays on Mixed-Race Literature,* edited by Jonathan Brennan, 107–121. Stanford, Calif.: Stanford University Press, 2002.

Chang, Diana. "A *MELUS* Interview: Diana Chang," by Leo Hamalian. *MELUS* 20, no. 4 (1995): 29–43.

Lease, Benjamin. Review of *The Frontier of Love. Chicago Sun-Times,* 23 September 1956, sec. 2, p. 4.

Lim, Shirley Geok-lin. Introduction to *The Frontiers of Love.* Seattle: University of Washington Press, 1994, v–xxiii.

Ling, Amy. *Between Worlds: Women Writers of Chinese Ancestry.* New York: Pergamon, 1990.

———. "Writer in the Hyphenated Condition: Diana Chang." *MELUS* 7, no. 4 (1980): 69–83.

Rexroth, Kenneth. Review of *The Frontier of Love, Nation*, 29 September 1956, 271–273.

Bennett Fu

Chang, Lan Samantha (1965–)

Born and raised in Appleton, Wisconsin, Lan Samantha Chang is the third daughter of Chinese parents who immigrated to the United States because of the political upheaval in 1949 in China. Growing up in a midwestern town where very few Chinese immigrant families resided at the time, she constantly felt like an outsider. Chang received a B.A. in East Asian studies from Yale University, an M.P.A. from Harvard University and an M.F.A. in creative writing from the University of Iowa. She is the Briggs-Copeland Lecturer of Creative Writing at Harvard University. In January 2006, Chang began serving as the fifth director of the University of Iowa's Writers' Workshop, the first Asian American and woman to head this prestigious workshop.

The title of her debut work, *HUNGER: A NOVELLA AND SHORT STORIES* (1998), and her novel, *Inheritance* (2004), reflect the recurring themes of her stories. *Hunger* is not only about the desire for love, independence, and other things lacking, but, more important, about the need for understanding and dealing with the spectral persistence of the past deliberately forgotten and denied; "inheritance" is the way in which to soothe this "hunger." Chang's tendency to reach for the past in *Hunger* is more clearly seen in her account of a family history in *Inheritance*. Mainly set in China from 1925 to 1949, the story traces three generations of women whose lives are fashioned by traditional Chinese values as well as the sociopolitical turmoil in China during the first half of the 20th century. Attempts to control their fate often fail despite the power of human passion and desire. The story revolves around the love and struggle between Junan and her younger sister, Yinan. When their mother, Chanyi, commits

suicide because of her inability to produce a son, the two sisters are left to live with their gambler father. To pay his gambling debts, the father marries Junan off to the ambitious and handsome soldier Li Ang. Love blossoms between Junan and Li Ang, which leads to the birth of their two daughters, Hong and Hwa. When Li Ang is assigned to a post in Chongqing during the Sino-Japanese War, however, Junan, now possessive and controlling of others around her, sends her sister Yinan to keep an eye on him. Contrary to her plan, a true bond starts to develop between Li Ang and Yinan. Junan refuses to forgive them despite their appeal for reconciliation. The family becomes fractured when Junan and her children flee to Taiwan in 1949 and immigrate to America in the 1950s. Li Ang, Yinan, and their child stay in China and undergo hardship during the political turmoil. The spell of the past is only to be lifted with the normalization of Sino-American relations and the reconciliation of the two sisters.

In *Inheritance,* Chang's prose remains concise and subtle in unveiling the multifaceted existence of her characters. It received a PEN Beyond Margins Award in 2005. However, written from the perspective of America in the 1990s, *Inheritance* sometimes lacks precision in rendering the social and cultural milieu of China.

Yan Ying

Chang, Leonard (1968–)

A Korean-American novelist, Leonard Chang specializes in hard-boiled stories that explore the ethnic and other sources of personal identity crises. Born in New York City, Chang attended Dartmouth College but transferred to Harvard University, where he completed his B.A. in 1991, graduating cum laude. In 1994 he completed an M.F.A. at the University of California at Irvine. Since 1998 Chang has been a member of the core faculty for the M.F.A. program at Antioch University in Los Angeles, and from 2001 to 2003, he was a Distinguished Visiting Writer at Mills College in Oakland, California. His stories have been published in literary journals such as *Bamboo Ridge, Confluence, Crab Orchard Review, Crescent Review,* and *Prairie Schooner.*

Chang's first novel, *The Fruit 'n Food* (1996) received the Black Heron Press Award for social fiction. It depicts the economic, social, and cultural sources of the tensions between Korean Americans and African Americans.

For his second novel, *Dispatches from the Cold* (1998), Chang received the Outstanding Local Discovery Award for Literature from *San Francisco Bay Guardian.* The novel focuses on the entanglements in the lives of Raj Shin, a Korean-American troubleshooter for a chain of sporting-goods stores, and Farrel Gordon, an employee in one of those stores. Superficially the men are almost opposites: Shin is a workaholic, whereas Gordon is so preoccupied with his life's dissatisfactions that he has at best an intermittent interest in his work. In letters addressed to his sister Mona, Gordon pours out the details of his failing relationship with Shari, his current girlfriend, and his deepening affair with Shin's wife. But Mona has died, and the current occupant of the apartment where she had lived (the novel's narrator) finds many intersections between Gordon's letters and his own professional and personal disappointments. His decision to reveal himself to Gordon in order to prevent Gordon from channeling his despair into violence provides the novel's climax.

In his two most recent novels, *Over the Shoulder* (2000) and *Underkill* (2003), Chang focuses on Allen Choice, a Korean-American personal-security expert specializing in providing protection for corporate executives. In *Over the Shoulder,* Choice and his partner have been hired to provide security for a Silicon Valley executive. The assignment seems uneventfully routine until someone shoots Choice's partner through the head. Professional ethics compel Choice to find the killer. It is a narrative premise that has recurred frequently in hard-boiled detective fiction back to Dashiell Hammett's *The Maltese Falcon.* In the process of resolving a case that becomes much more complex and dangerous than Choice has any reason to expect, he also confronts some difficult truths about his own family background and ethnic identity. Critics lauded the novel's compelling synthesis of elements of the ethnic novel and the detective novel. Somewhat less successfully, Chang attempts the same sort of multilayered narrative in *Underkill,* as Choice attempts to find his girlfriend's missing brother while trying to sort out the truths about his own relationship with her.

Martin Kich

Chao, Patricia   (1955–   )

Although Patricia Chao has also published short stories, poems, and several children's books, she is most widely known for her novels. Her first novel, *The Monkey King* (1997), was a finalist for the Barnes and Noble Discover Great New Writers Award. That first novel and her second, *Mambo Peligroso* (2005), reflect her interest in characters seeking to come to terms with ambiguous or otherwise troubling aspects of their identities. The contexts for these exercises in self-exploration are compellingly and vibrantly multicultural.

Born in Carmel-by-the-Sea, California, Chao is the daughter of Howard S. Chao, a journalist, and Chie I. (Imaizumi) Chao, a teacher. Raised primarily in New England, Chao completed a B.A. in creative writing at Brown University and an M.A. in English at New York University. She has subsequently taught writing courses at Sarah Lawrence College and New York University. Her writing has been supported by fellowships from the MacDowell Colony, Fundacion Valparaison in Spain, and the Sacatar Foundation in Brazil.

The Monkey King draws its title from a Chinese myth and refers to the protagonist's deceased father. The novel opens in a psychiatric unit where the main character, Sally Wang, is being treated after a suicide attempt. The traumatic resurfacing of long-repressed memories of her father's molestation of her had caused Wang to begin to behave out of character. With very little previous indication of any emotional disturbance, she had suddenly left her husband, quit her job, and begun to mutilate herself. Chao convincingly links Wang's victimization with issues related to her hyphenated identity as a Chinese American. In addition, through Wang's troubled relationships with her mother and sister, Chao shows how the victimization of one family member can create acute psychological issues for every member of the family.

In contrast to the generally positive responses to *The Monkey King, Mambo Peligroso* received somewhat mixed reviews. Drawing on her own experience as a mambo dancer, Chao focuses on the experiences of a half-Japanese and half-Cuban young woman, named Catalina Ortiz Midori, who becomes obsessed with mastering the mambo. Success in this quest would provide multiple satisfactions—validating her efforts to her demanding dance teacher, strengthening the romantic attraction between them, and providing her with a much more viable sense of her cultural identity. Although reviewers thought that Chao's narrative is invested with a great deal of vivid immediacy, they did not think that she credibly integrated a subplot involving an attempted assassination of Fidel Castro. In sum, they maintained that the narrative captured the energy of Latin dance but possessed not quite enough of its controlled structure.

Martin Kich

Cheng, Terrence   (1972–)

Terrence Cheng has received wide acclaim for his first novel, *Sons of Heaven* (2002). Inspired by the Tiananmen Square Massacre in 1989 Beijing, the novel symbolically returns Cheng to the place his grandparents had once called home. Cheng's grandparents and parents moved from Beijing, China, to Taipei, Taiwan, in 1949. Born in 1972 in Taiwan, Cheng never experienced his grandparents' fear and worry while living in China during the rise of Communism. Just one year after Cheng's birth, his parents moved to New York, where he has lived ever since. Cheng's interest in politics and history was most likely encouraged by hearing of his grandmother's political activism in Beijing as a senator in the Chinese Nationalist Party before Mao Zedong and the Communist Party came to power. *Sons of Heaven* grew out of Cheng's horror as a teenager at seeing the democracy movement in Tiananmen Square crushed by a ruthless military who slaughtered numerous protesting students.

Cheng explains that he felt emotionally connected to China and the Chinese people as he watched the news footage of the massacre. He realized that he could have been one of those hurt or killed, had his grandparents not moved to Taiwan. Like many people around the world, Cheng was haunted by the widely published and now famous image of one man, probably a student, who walked in front of the Chinese military tanks and refused to move. As the tanks attempted to maneuver around, the unknown man continued to step into and block their path. Cheng's novel imagines a life and a voice for the brave, nameless young man who tried to stop a line of tanks with only his body.

Having earned an M.F.A. in fiction from the University of Miami, Cheng set out to write *Sons of Heaven* with the inspiration of his favorite authors: Don Delillo, Cormac McCarthy, Philip Roth, and HA JIN. Although the novel's backdrop is political, *Sons of Heaven* is more a story about families and individuals caught within historical contexts. Cheng explains that the nameless man became a symbol of forces in conflict: "East versus West, democracy versus communism, history clashing with the present." However, the story has also been described as a "family saga," and Cheng admits that the novel is more about individuals than about nations or politics: "I wanted to know him, his name, his family, his past, to try and understand the things in his life that had brought him to that point. What makes a man so incredibly brave, stupid, and scared—so human, and yet transcendent?"

Sons of Heaven creates a name (Xiao-Di) for the brave, proud man who stood up for his beliefs, even if it meant death. Raised by his grandparents in Beijing, Xiao-Di travels to America to study on a scholarship at Cornell University. He falls in love with an all-American blond-haired beauty, but more important, he falls in love with the American lifestyle of free thought and action. After returning to Beijing just three months before the Tiananmen Massacre, however, Xiao-Di cannot find work despite his education. In his frustration and anger with restrictive, traditional Chinese culture, he turns to the democratic student movement against the Chinese ruler, Deng Xiaoping.

At the heart of the novel, we learn the story of Xiao-Di and his brother Lu, who hold conflicting ideas about politics, protest, and loyalty to China. Lu, a Chinese soldier, is sent on a military mission to find Xiao-Di and put an end to his political protests. However, Xiao-Di's protests escalate and culminate in his final heroic action as he stands alone before the tanks in Tiananmen Square. Despite this central political conflict, Terrence Cheng has described his novel's themes with words that have little to do with politics: "family," "courage," "faith," and "love."

Bibliography

Cheng, Terrence. "Author Essay." *Meet the Writers.* Barnes & Noble: Discover Great New Writers. Available online. URL: http://www.barnesandnoble.com/writers/writer.asp?2-y&cid-969340 essay. Downloaded on September 21, 2006.

Amy Lillian Manning

Chickencoop Chinaman, The
Frank Chin (1981)

Like *The YEAR OF THE DRAGON* by the same author, *The Chickencoop Chinaman* illustrates the search for father figures and role models. The Chinese-American protagonist, Tam Lum, is a filmmaker who flies to Pittsburgh to find Charley Popcorn, the alleged African-American father of a former boxing champion, Ovaltine Jack the Dancer, for a documentary film. However, Charley Popcorn, who turns out to have been no more than the boxer's trainer, now runs a porno movie house and shows nothing but racist contempt toward "yellow people." Disappointed at being unable to find an exemplary father figure, Tam reflects on his own failed fatherhood: His children are taken away by his ex-wife, and he says of them, "I don't want them to be anything like me or know me, or remember me." Recalling his father as "a crazy old

dishwasher," Tam concludes that "Chinamans do make lousy fathers." FRANK CHIN blames America's racism for Asian-American men's loss of manhood. Tam's process of making a documentary about the life of the former light-heavyweight champion symbolizes his difficult search for an identity and a sense of manhood.

The Chickencoop Chinaman is the first work by an Asian-American playwright to be produced on a mainstream stage in New York. Despite recognitions from the *New Yorker* and *Newsweek* after the play's opening, Chin wrote in *Backtalk:* "That this play is the first play by an Asian American . . . that people should be surprised at our existence, is proof of the great success white racism has had with us. America might love us. But America's love is not good. It's racist love. I don't want it."

Bibliography

Chin, Frank. "Backtalk." *News of the American Place Theatre 4*, 4 (May 1972): 1–2.

Fu-jen Chen

Child of the Owl
Laurence Michael Yep (1977)

In this story of Casey Young, a 12-year-old Chinese American who lives with her gambler father, BARNEY, LAURENCE YEP explores the issues of isolation, alienation, and identity formation among Chinese-American children. Set in San Francisco in 1965, the story begins when Barney, beaten up by a bookie, ends up in a hospital, thus giving up the custody of his daughter, Casey, to her Americanized maternal uncle, "Phil the pill." Unable to cope with his restless niece, Phil sends Casey to live with her grandmother Paw-Paw in Chinatown, where a new, unknown world unfolds in front of the girl's eyes. Casey had always thought of herself as an American without any ethnic background; therefore, at first, life in Chinatown is rather difficult to endure, especially in her Chinese school, where she has to struggle with the Chinese language and the mockery of her fellow students and teachers.

Casey's relationship with her grandmother grows stronger when the old lady, understanding the girl's uneasiness with her Chinese side, decides to tell her the story of the jade charm that had been given to the family by the "Owl Spirit." Looking like an owl and worn by the grandmother at all times, the charm originally belonged to an owl named Jasmine, who had been induced to live in a human's body for the sake of her family, but who, thanks to her husband's love, was allowed to go back to her own community of owls. With this story, Casey begins to understand herself, her feelings of being often "trapped inside the wrong body and among the wrong people." As she starts to investigate her past, she learns about her mother from Paw-Paw and about the meaning of her Chinese name, Cheun Meih, "Taste of Spring." This name signifies a rebirth for Casey as she begins a new life as a Chinese American.

The story continues with Paw-Paw being hospitalized after trying to prevent her owl charm from being stolen by a burglar, who turns out to be Casey's father, Barney, who wanted to sell it in order to raise money for his gambling habit. The novel has a happy ending, since Paw-Paw fully recovers and mortified Barney decides to join Gamblers Anonymous.

Elisabetta Marino

Chin, Frank   (1940–   )

A novelist, essayist, playwright, editor, and short story writer, Frank Chew Chin, Jr., was born in Berkeley, California, in 1940. Describing himself as a "fifth-generation Chinaman," Frank Chin is the son of Frank Chew, an immigrant, and Lilac Bowe Yoke, a fourth-generation resident of Oakland Chinatown. After growing up in the Chinatowns of Oakland and San Francisco, he attended the University of California, Berkeley, and participated in the Program in Creative Writing at the University of Iowa. Before he received his B.A. from the University of California in Santa Barbara in 1965, he worked for the Southern Pacific Railroad for three years. Leaving the railroad company, he moved to Seattle and became a writer-producer for the television station KING-TV. Chin left Seattle to become a freelance consultant and lecturer

on Chinese America and racism at San Francisco State University, the University of California Davis, and Berkeley until 1970.

After that, he began his dramatic career. He staged his first play, The CHICKENCOOP CHINAMAN in 1972, and his second play, The YEAR OF THE DRAGON, two years later. Both were staged at The American Place Theatre. He soon founded the Asian American Theater Workshop in San Francisco and remained its director until 1977. After the success of his stage plays, Chin went on to establish his reputation as a story writer with the 1998 publication of The Chinaman Pacific & Frisco R. R. Co. His first novel, DONALD DUK, was published in 1991 and his second novel, GUNGA DIN HIGHWAY, in 1994. His collection of essays, Bulletproof Buddhists and Other Essays, was released in 1998. His most recent work, Born in the USA: A Story of Japanese America, 1889–1947, published in 2002, details Japanese-American history.

Frank Chin is regarded by some as the "Godfather" of Asian-American writing. He is the first Chinese American to rise to literary stardom; in 1970 he helped organize the first Asian-American literature curriculum at San Francisco State University; he was also the founder of the Asian-American Theater Company; most of all, he is the first Asian-American playwright to have his plays produced both by a major New York theater and on national television. Chin himself claimed that he was also "the first Chinese-American brakeman on the Southern Pacific Railroad, [and] the first Chinaman to ride the engines."

Chin is noted not only for his literary efforts but also for his role as the first editor of the groundbreaking anthology of Asian-American writings entitled Aiiieeeee!: An Anthology of Asian American Writers (1974) and its sequel The Big Aiiieeeee!: An Anthology of Chinese American and Japanese American Literature (1991). Edited by Chin and three other Californians, (JEFFERY PAUL CHAN, LAWSON FUSAO INADA, and SHAWN WONG), Aiiieeeee! acted as a catalyst for the study of Asian-American literature as a formal literary field and caused acrimonious, as well as fruitful, debates. In the context of the increasing awareness of racial and cultural identity since the era of the Vietnam War and the

Civil Rights movement of the 1960s, "What is an Asian American?" became an urgent question. The editors of *Aiiieeeee!* proposed a particular "sensibility" to unite a variety of people with different religions, languages, and cultures under the umbrella term *Asian American.* In *Aiiieeeee!* they included works written in English by American-born descendants of Asian immigrants and focused on the criterion of "Asian-American sensibility." This "sensibility" features American nativity, exclusive use of English, Asian Americans as intended audiences, participation in the Asian-American heroic tradition, and the reassertion of Asian-American manhood as an objective.

Most significant, Chin's notion of "Asian-American sensibility" serves to authenticate Asian-American writing by offering a clear distinction between "the real" and "the fake" Asian-American literary expressions. To Chin, such successful Asian-American authors as MAXINE HONG KINGSTON, AMY TAN, and DAVID HENRY HWANG are "fake" but well received by mainstream America because they feed the racist fantasy of white Americans. The "real" Asian-American writing—non-Christian, non-feminine, and non-confessional—avoids the genre of autobiography, celebrates Asian heroic heritage, restores Asian-American manhood from emasculation, and battles against white perceptions of Asian Americans. In a significant opening essay of *The Big Aiiieeeee!,* "Come All Ye Asian American Writers of the Real and the Fake," Chin delivers a 92-page harangue on the critical issue of the real and the fake, claiming that Asian-American writing is a verbal battle of the real against the fake, of authentic works against counterfeit texts. Chin insists that the real has to refute the racist assumption that "Asian culture is anti-individualistic, mystic, passive, collective, and morally and ethically opposite to Western culture." Chin's authentication of Asian-American literary expression through immigrant memories and the Asian heroic heritage became a controversial issue in early Asian-American literary studies.

Bibliography

Li, David Leiwei. "The Formation of Frank Chin and Formations of Chinese American Literature." *Asian Americans: Comparative and Global Perspectives,* edited by Amy Ling, et al., 211–224. Pullman: Washington State University Press, 1991.

McDonald, Dorothy Ritsuko. Introduction. *The Chickencoop Chinaman and the Year of the Dragon.* By Frank Chin. Seattle: University of Washington Press, 1981.

Fu-jen Chen

Chin, Marilyn Mei Ling   (1955–)

In "How I Got That Name: an essay on assimilation," the Chinese-American poet Marilyn Chin reveals the family history behind her first name. Born in Hong Kong in 1955, Chin immigrated with her family to the United States as an infant. Her father's fascination with American blond movie stars of the 1950s prompted him to rename one daughter after Marilyn Monroe and another after Jayne Mansfield. Chin grew up in Portland, Oregon, but has lived most of her adult life in California. The poet received her B.A. in ancient Chinese literature from the University of Massachusetts at Amherst in 1977. After Massachusetts, Chin entered the prestigious M.F.A. program at the University of Iowa, graduating in 1981. She completed postgraduate work at Stanford University as a Stegner Fellow in 1984–1985. In an interview with Bill Moyers for his *Language of Life* collection, Chin draws attention to her "hyphenated" identity and calls herself "a leftist radical feminist, West Coast, Pacific Rim, socialist, neo-Classical, Chinese American poet" (Moyers 67).

Marilyn Chin has been associated with San Diego State University since 1988, eventually becoming its M.F.A. program director. She has held visiting positions at several universities including UCLA, the University of Hawaii, Taiwan's National Donghwa University, and Australia's University of Technology. In 2003–2004 she was named a Radcliffe Institute Fellow. The poet has received two National Endowment for the Arts Writing Fellowships, four Pushcart Prizes, and a Mary Roberts Rinehart Award. While Chin has published translations of Chinese literature and one play, *The Love Palace* (2002), she considers herself primarily a poet. She has published individual poems in numerous journals and anthologies: *Ploughshares, The Paris Review, Parnassus, The Norton Introduction to Poetry,* and *Asian-American Poetry: The Next Generation.* Chin has published three collections of poetry: *Dwarf Bamboo* (1987), *The Phoenix Gone, The Terrace Empty* (1994), and *Rhapsody in Plain Yellow* (2002).

Since 1987, Chin's poetry has received both popular and critical attention. *Intense, angry, ironic, confrontational,* and *cynical* are the terms most commonly associated with her work. Chin's poetry erupts with emotion and intelligence. Her poems are rich with references to both ancient Chinese culture and American popular culture. Like the confessional poets of the 1960s (Robert Lowell, Sylvia Plath, and Anne Sexton), Chin mines her personal and familial history as a basis for poems about loss, betrayals of trust, and love. Furthermore, in the tradition of Gary Snyder, Adrienne Rich, and Denise Levertov (her instructor at Stanford), Chin believes that a true poet must be involved in political and community issues. To that end, Chin calls herself an activist and exercises her craft to forward her political and social concerns.

Many of Chin's poems explore the conditions of exile. The outsider persona is often, but not always, marginalized as a result of immigration. Chin's most anthologized poem, "How I Got That Name: an essay on assimilation," is composed of four sections that reflect the immigrant experience in America. Chin begins by explaining how "Mei Ling" was transliterated into "Marilyn" due to her father's obsession with beautiful white women. In the second section, she excoriates the stereotypes so-called experts disseminate about the "Model Minority." She wonders idly in the third section what her first ancestor would say about his descendants, and finds she cannot rouse herself to fight his judgment. In the last section, the author presents a final snapshot of this person called Marilyn Mei Ling Chin. In desolation she imagines her legacy after death and concludes that she was "neither cherished nor vanquished" (line 83, *The Phoenix Gone, the Terrace Empty*). The experience of the immigrant of color in America as detailed in this poem begins within the family and its assimilation of Caucasian standards of beauty and success. The immigrant must then confront the assumptions of the academy and the general public while she simultaneously defends herself against the perceived disappointment of her ancestors. In the end, the immigrant is reduced to the contents of an obituary, adrift without a firm cultural identity.

Marilyn Chin's poetry also incorporates her experiences in an extended Chinese-American family. Like the poets Lucille Clifton and JANICE MIRIKITANI, Chin was powerfully affected by her parents' marriage. In "Family Restaurant," an intense 10-line poem, Chin exposes the reality of her family life by portraying a mother in the kitchen peeling shrimp while a father coos over the phone to his current lover. Chin writes, "His daughter wide-eyed, little fists / Vows to never forgive him" (lines 7–8, *Rhapsody in Plain Yellow*). George Chin abandoned his wife, Rose, for a Caucasian woman, and his daughter returns repeatedly to this autobiographical figure to condemn the oppression and exploitation of women.

While Chin's treatment of fathers is almost universally negative and angry, her references to mothers in her poems are more varied. "Turtle Soup" from 1994 includes a mother who has labored for 12 hours to make the delicacy. The voice of the young daughter, assimilated into Western ways, mocks the mother for her unenlightened efforts. Her mother's sobbing chastises the daughter, and she prepares to honor her mother by consuming the soup. The poem ends with a question; the daughter continues to be torn between her mother's traditional Chinese culture and her own Americanized identity. In 2002's *Rhapsody in Plain Yellow* Chin mourns the passing of her mother and maternal grandmother. Both "Blues on Yellow" and "The Cock's Wife" from 2002 convey anger and resentment. The wife / mother figure is confined; her future is sacrificed while her children and husband sail through life, uncaring. The haunting "Hospital Interlude" (*Rhapsody in Plain Yellow,* 2002) describes a daughter's visit to a hospital where she is confronted only by an "empty sickroom." In stunned silence she looks out at the full moon and hears the cicadas crying. She turns to go, vowing not to forget her mother but lamenting that she "forgot to tutor me the last secret phrases" (line 13). Chin's use of mothers in her poetry is nuanced. In these references she can explore the universal tensions of the mother-daughter relationship, questions about cultural identity and loyalty, pain caused by the patriarchy, and the maternal sources of poetic inspiration. Marilyn Chin's poetry continues to evolve as she alternately draws upon Chinese literature and culture, American popular culture, the experience of immigration, and family relationships.

Bibliography

Chin, Marilyn. *Dwarf Bamboo.* New York: Greenfield Review Press, 1987.
———. *The Phoenix Gone, the Terrace Empty.* Minneapolis: Milkweed Editions, 1994.
———. *Rhapsody in Plain Yellow.* New York: Norton, 2002.
Moyers, Bill. *The Language of Life: A Festival of Poets.* New York: Broadway Books, 1995.

Ann Beebe

China Boy   Gus Lee (1991)

Thinly disguised as a novel, *China Boy* is GUS LEE's autobiography of his turbulent childhood and rites of passage in San Francisco in the 1950s. The family lives in the Panhandle, a ghetto populated with poor blacks. Kai Ting's father, T. K. Ting, once an outstanding Nationalist army officer in China, becomes an unsuccessful banker in America. His mother, beautiful and learned, dies early of cancer, leaving her two youngest children, Janie and Kai, in the cruel hands of their stepmother, Edna, a blond Philadelphia socialite who exercises an overbearing control of the family, making T. K. Ting miserable.

Deprived of love and home security, Kai, frail and once spoiled as the only son, is forced to stay in the street where he is the target of bullying. His father decides to send him to the Y.M.C.A to be trained to fight. The Y.M.C.A proves to be a transforming experience for Kai. The staff members, who come from all different ethnic backgrounds, not only provide Kai with love, care, and lessons of

life, but also train him to be a competent fighter. Kai finally beats the most feared of the bullies, Big Willie. The victory also gives him courage to stand up to his stepmother, Edna.

Named one of the *New York Times* Best 100 Books for 1991 and an American Library Association Best of the Last 50 Years, *China Boy* tackles in a humorous and compelling way such key themes in Asian-American literature as race relations, masculinity, cultural heritage, and hegemony. Lee's interweaving of these themes culminates in the question of the peculiarity and universality of Chinese-American identity; as Lee states, "My struggle on the street was really an effort to fix identity, to survive as a member of a group and even succeed as a human being." While bullying is described as brutal, the root cause of it, Lee seems to suggest, is the poverty, human tragedies, and traumatic experiences of living in the inner-city ghettoes. The Y.M.C.A is presented as an ideal place of unity of different races, where the hierarchy is determined by a fair play of physical strength and personal charisma. Ironically, Kai's inheritance of black and Y.M.C.A culture is contingent on the ruthless denial of his Chinese heritage by Edna. The assimilation she demands of the family in the form of domestic violence is in effect the blatant cultural hegemony exercised through her power as a white upper-class woman. T. K. Ting acquiescently sacrifices his masculinity in submission to the process of assimilation to the white mainstream, while Kai eventually challenges the oppression by assuming a counter-hegemonic black speech.

Bibliography

Lee, Gus. *China Boy.* London: Robert Hale, 1992.
Shen, Yichin. "The Site of Domestic Violence and the Altar of Phallic Sacrifice in Gus Lee's *China Boy.*" *College Literature* 29, no. 2 (Spring 2002): 99–113.

Yan Ying

China Men   Maxine Hong Kingston (1980)

MAXINE HONG KINGSTON's *China Men* was planned and partially drafted even before the publication of her first book, *The WOMAN WARRIOR* (1976).

While the two texts are virtually identical in tone and style, the author stated in a *New York Times* interview that she considered them two halves of "one big book." *China Men* focuses on the lives of male Chinese immigrants who performed hard labor for the railroad, farming, and laundry industries in an attempt to lay a claim to America as their own "home country."

As in *The Woman Warrior,* the stories of the men of Kingston's family are interspersed with Chinese folktales and legends. The first extended section of the book, "The Father from China," tells the story of the narrator's father, BaBa. BaBa is a favored child of his family, a precocious baby groomed to become a scholar. After his extensive education in China, BaBa travels to the United States, but his daughter-narrator has difficulty separating the "true" story of his immigration from the many versions she has heard, and the story is told twice. In the first version, BaBa is smuggled through customs in a packing crate, and in the second he is detained and interviewed extensively by immigration officials in California. He takes on the name "Edison" as part of an attempt to fashion an American identity, and enters a laundry business with three Chinese friends who have similarly renamed themselves Roosevelt, Woodrow, and Worldster. Edison is eventually driven out of the laundry partnership, and in his middle age turns brooding and churlish, muttering curse words associated with female body parts in front of his young children. Later sections, entitled "The Great-Grandfather of the Sandalwood Mountains," "The Grandfather of the Sierra Nevada Mountains" and "The Brother in Vietnam," chronicle the similar stories of multiple generations of "China men" who labored on the railroad or were called into service by the American military.

Where *The Woman Warrior* is filled with "ghosts," *China Men* is populated by "demons," the primarily Caucasian government administrators and bosses of various work sites at which groups of Chinese immigrants labor for minimal payment, sometimes under abusive circumstances. Though the book is less concerned with gender than with labor and economics, it is significant that the men do not tell their own stories. The women must preserve the men's life-narratives, and in connecting storytelling with womanhood, *China Men* is a natural extension of *The Woman Warrior.* Indeed, as the author herself has suggested, it can be considered the second half of a single long work.

China Men was included in the American Library Association's Notable Book List for 1980 and won the National Book Award for general nonfiction in 1981.

Bibliography

Buckmaster, Henrietta. Review of *China Men, Christian Science Monitor,* 11 August 1980, p. B4.

Gordon, Mary. Review of *China Men. New York Times,* 15 June 1980, sec. 7, p. 1.

Pfaff, Timothy. "Talk With Mrs. Kingston." *New York Times,* 15 June 1980, sec. 7, p. 1. Reprinted in Skenazy, Paul, and Tera Martin, eds. *Conversations with Maxine Hong Kingston,* 14–20. Literary Conversations Series. Jackson: University Press of Mississippi, 1998.

Slagter, Nicole. "Maxine Hong Kingston Under Review: The Response to *China Men.*" In Barfoot, C. C., ed. *Beyond Pug's Tour: National and Ethnic Stereotyping in Theory and Literary Practice,* 468–474. Amsterdam, Netherlands: Rodopi, 1997.

Eric G. Waggoner

Chiu, Christina   (?–   )

Largely on the basis of her one collection of short stories, *Troublemaker and Other Saints* (2001), Christina Chiu has been regarded as one of the most promising literary voices among the latest generation of Asian-American writers. Born in New York City to immigrant parents from Shanghai, Chiu was raised in suburban Westchester County. She completed a B.A. degree in East Asian studies at Bates College and an M.F.A. in creative writing at Columbia University. Chiu did not become interested in writing fiction until she participated in a creative-writing workshop during her senior year at Bates. Since graduating from Columbia, she has worked as a teacher at the Brooklyn Museum, an assistant editor at the Children's Television Workshop, a reference-book editor and then a magazine editor at Scholastic Publishing, and an associate editor for the Web site *Virtually React.* Chiu is also a cofounder of the Asian-American Writers Workshop. She has served as an editor of the literary magazine *Tin House,* and conducted workshops in creative writing at the Hudson Valley Writing Center.

Three of her books of nonfiction were published before *Troublemaker and Other Saints.* Two of these have been behavioral guides: *Eating Disorder Survivors Tell Their Stories* (1998) and *Teen Guide to Staying Sober* (1998). The third, *Notable Asian-Americans: Literature and Education* (1995), most closely complements the ethnic focus of her fiction, but the issues addressed in the other two books are also echoed in the themes of some of the stories.

Troublemaker and Other Saints, a finalist for the Asian American Literary Award and a Book-of-the-Month-Club selection, contains 11 short stories so linked by recurring settings, characters, and themes that some reviewers have asserted that the collection comes close to being a novel. The stories concern the experiences of several generations of people in the Wong family, as well as their connections to three other families—the Shengs, the Tsuis, and the Tungs. In their settings the stories range from Hong Kong and New York City to Australia. Although they treat a considerable range of themes, at a fundamental level the stories concern the issues and difficulties faced by Asian Americans in trying to assimilate into American culture.

In the title story, a young man rambunctiously flings a can of beer out into the street on the first day of the year. Unfortunately, the can hits an old man and seriously injures him. To make him confront the consequences of his impulsiveness, his mother compels him to take care of the old man during his recovery. The irony is that typically the protagonist has been a victim, not the victimizer. In particular, he has been the frequent target of his brother's physical and emotional abuse. In a further ironic turn, in caring for the old man, the protagonist begins to come to terms with his own victimization.

The abusive brother is the main character in two stories—"Trader," in which it becomes clear that his anger is rooted in a deep sense of racial inferiority, and "Gentleman," a story of multilayered ironies in which he marks the transfer of Hong Kong from Great Britain to China with a Chinese woman who, despite her obvious sexual experience, has never slept with another Chinese man. This woman's story is told more fully in "Beauty," which chronicles her attempt to subvert the stereotype of the sexually submissive Asian woman through a series of short-term relationships with Caucasian men, many of whom she meets through personal ads. She seeks to dominate these men thoroughly, even to the point of considering when it will be most painful to the man to cut off each relationship.

In "Copycat," Chiu depicts the effects of a young woman's suicide on her parents and her brother. Her father seeks refuge in her bedroom, trying to discover some psychic conduit to her spirit. Her mother becomes obsessed with transforming every feature of the landscaping of their yard, channeling her emotions into the eradication of every alteration that proves unsatisfactory, as most of them do. And her brother becomes a devout Buddhist, retreating into lengthy sessions of meditation that seem to serve not to mitigate his grief but to shield him from it.

"Doctor" concerns a young girl, suffering from an eating disorder, and her physician, incapable of maintaining an appropriate professional distance in treating the girl because she has herself suffered periodically from an eating disorder.

Martin Kich

Choi, Sook Nyul (1937–)

Born in Pyungyang, North Korea, in 1937, Sook Nyul Choi began writing poems and short stories when she was in elementary school. Choi was inspired to come to the United States during high school after reading Henry Wadsworth Longfellow's poem "I Shot an Arrow." After graduating from high school, she enrolled in Ewha University as an English major. Longing to move to the United States to study, she applied and was accepted at Manhattanville College in Purchase, New York. After passing an intensive government exam in order to obtain a visa, Choi left for the United States in September 1958. Upon graduating from college, she began teaching in the New York public school system, where she has taught literature and creative writing to high school students for more than 20 years.

In 1991, 10 years after the death of her husband, Mark, Choi wrote her first novel, *The YEAR OF IMPOSSIBLE GOODBYES*, an autobiographical novel about a young Korean girl, Sookan, and her life under the Japanese occupation of her country. *Year* won numerous awards including the Judy Lopez Book Award by the National Women's Book Association in 1992, and was selected as a Notable Book by the American Library Association. In 1993 Choi followed *The Year of Impossible Goodbyes* with a sequel, *ECHOES OF THE WHITE GIRAFFE*. The novel continues Sookan's experiences in Korea under Japanese occupation, and details the pain of a forced separation from her beloved father and older brothers. *Echoes* was placed on Tennessee's State Book Award Master Reading List as recommended reading for young adults. Choi's third novel, *GATHERING OF PEARLS*, follows the story of Sookan, who has finally realized her dream of visiting the United States. *Gathering* won the 1995 Books for the Teen Age Award from the New York Public Library.

Choi is also the author of many picture books for young children. Her first, *Halmoni and the Picnic,* was published in 1993 and is a poignant tale of young Yunmi's Korean grandmother who comes to live with Yunmi's family in America. Yunmi is embarrassed by her grandmother's Korean traditions but later recognizes their value. In 1997 Choi published *Yunmi and Halmoni's Trip,* in which Yunmi and her grandmother travel to Korea. Yunmi experiences a culture shock, which enables her to better understand her grandmother's struggles to acculturate in America. Choi's focus changed somewhat with the publication of a third picture book, *The Best Older Sister,*

which explores Sunhi's unfavorable reaction to the arrival of a new baby brother. Choi's works have been included in numerous anthologies and have been translated into five languages. Choi lives in Cambridge, Massachusetts, where she writes full time.

Debbie Clare Olson

Choi, Susan   (1969–   )

A Korean-American writer born in Indiana, Choi spent most of her childhood in Texas before attending school in the Northeast. With a B.A. from Yale University (1990) and an M.F.A. from Cornell University, Choi is currently on the editorial staff of the *New Yorker* magazine. In addition to her two published novels, *The Foreign Student* (1998) and *American Woman* (2003), Choi has published short stories in *Iowa Review* and *Epoch* and, with David Remnick, edited *Wonderful Town: New York, Stories from "The New Yorker"* (2003).

Choi's first novel, *The Foreign Student,* received critical acclaim and enjoyed commercial success. Winner of the Asian-American Literary Award for Fiction in 1998, *The Foreign Student* is set both at the University of the South in Sewanee and the war-ravaged Korean Peninsula during the 1950s. It charts the arrival of former translator Chang Ahn, a Korean national fleeing Seoul on a scholarship from the Episcopal Church Council, in Tennessee and his subsequent encounters with the xenophobia and insularity of the U.S. South and with Katherine Monroe, a wealthy and equally conflicted young woman from New Orleans.

As the novel moves constantly back and forth in time and from Korea to Tennessee, "Chang and Katherine, as they slowly fall in love, find that they—and the cultures they represent—are not that different after all, both subject to lingering issues of class, family, race, and civil war" (Lee 194). Translating not only between languages but also between cultures, in all of their manifest complexities, functions as one of the main tensions throughout the novel. As Choi writes, "Chang had done enough translation already to know that there weren't ever even exchanges" (*Foreign Student* 67). Though "even exchange" proves problematic for Chang and Katherine, their relationship demonstrates that something else, something more, can arise from the interaction between cultures and across cultural differences: Insularity remains a choice, not necessarily the only option. Chang and Katherine derive solace from each other, as their relationship facilitates a certain openness necessary to unbind their respective pasts, a task fraught with the emotional and psychological tensions of their personal histories (his experience with the Korean War and Katherine's precipitous relationship with a Sewanee professor in her youth). Taking place as it does in the American South during the 1950s, the potentialities of Chang and Katherine's interaction highlight the undercurrents of racism and class conflict that will soon come to a head during the Civil Rights era and the social upheavals occurring in the wake of the Vietnam War.

Choi's second novel, *American Woman,* fictionalizes the historical event of Patty Hearst's 1974 kidnapping at the hands of the Symbionese Liberation Army, a militant group with a radical political agenda. Nominated for the 2004 Pulitzer Prize in fiction, *American Woman* provides an intimate look at the radicalism of the 1960s and 1970s in the United States through the lens of its main characters: Jenny, a former radical in hiding from the authorities; Pauline, loosely based on Hearst; and the duo of Juan and Yvonne, lovers and the leaders of the guerrilla group. As An Hansen notes, Choi "uses these historical events as a backdrop to the development of the emotions and political motivations that drive her fictional characters, rather than keeping her storyline true to the genre of historical fiction" (34). Far from detracting from the novel, such a technique allows Choi to explore the inner lives of her characters without fully having to justify such thoughts and desires within the specifies of a rigidly historical context. In this manner, Choi investigates the intricacies of the relationships among the self-styled revolutionaries and their influence upon, and import for, American revolutionary politics during the 1970s.

More interesting for Choi is the question of how such idealistic and seemingly coherent group politics can fall apart and unravel. Jennifer Egan makes a similar point, noting that Choi "renders a lucid study of the gravitational pull of race and class in America, its ability to crush the most naively passionate fantasies of unity" (39). Taking such radicalism as a backdrop, Choi branches out to investigate issues of race, class, and gender as they play out in both group politics and citizen responsibility. By doing so, the author simultaneously presents and challenges the incitement to, and justification for, violent action. For Choi, the generation that could have benefited from the lessons learned after the horrible violence of World War II and the atomic bomb appears to have fared no better, the promise of hindsight never fully realized. Offering a meditative look at the motivations for such radicalism and violence, Choi presents the complexity of the situation to the reader without casting judgment.

When Yvonne and Juan flee after an unsuccessful and violent bank robbery, Jenny and Pauline head west to California, attempting to hide from the authorities while they develop a notably close bond, which facilitates Jenny's attempt to make sense of her own past and motivations toward political action. When Jenny and Pauline eventually come into custody, Pauline quickly repents and discards her friendship with Jenny, forcing the reader to sympathize with Jenny's position, even as she must take full possession of her past in the form of a jail sentence. Choi remains reluctant to the end to make moral pronouncements upon her characters or their problematic and sometimes ambiguous motivations; rather, as Sven Birkerts notes, "questions of right and wrong are, rightly, left to the reader"—a subtle form of interrogation that Choi's two novels share. With only two novels, Susan Choi has obtained a prominent place among contemporary American writers.

Bibliography

Birkerts. Sven. "'American Woman': Days of the Cobra." Review of *American Woman* by Susan Choi, *New York Times Book Review.* (5 October 2003) The New York Times. Available online by subscription. URL: www.nytimes.com/2003/10/05/books/review.

Choi, Susan. *The Foreign Student.* New York: Harper-Collins, 1998.

Egan, Jennifer. "La Japonaise." Review of *American Woman* by Susan Choi. *Nation* October 2003, 39–41.

Hansen, Ann. Review of *American Woman* by Susan Choi. *Herizons* 17, no. 4 (Spring 2004): 34–35.

Lee, Don. Review of *The Foreign Student* by Susan Choi. *Ploughshares* 25, no. 1 (Spring 1999): 193–194.

Skloot, Floyd. "Buried Secrets." Review of *The Foreign Student* by Susan Choi. *Sewanee Review* 107, no. 1 (Winter 1999): xx–xxii.

Zach Weir

Chong, Denise   (1952–   )

Nonfiction writer Denise Chong is best known for her award-winning The CONCUBINE'S CHILDREN (1994), a story that transcends continental and cultural borders. It is an account of her mother's and grandmother's lives in a Chinatown in Canada, and of the additional family members in China, as well as one that helps to define the extent of the evolution of the Chinese-Canadian community. She also wrote *The Girl in the Picture: The Story of Kim Phuc, the Photograph, and the Vietnam War* (2001), the story of nine-year-old Kim Phuc, whose picture, taken as she was running down a road, her body burning from napalm, made history during the Vietnam War, and was used as a propagandistic tool by her own country. It chronicles the circumstances of the little girl, the direction her life took, and the lingering effects of the event on her after the end of the war.

Chong was born in Vancouver, Canada, and raised in Prince George, British Columbia. Trained as an economist, she worked as an economic policy adviser in the Department of Finance and in the prime minister's office under Pierre Trudeau from 1980 to 1984. She left Vancouver after the publication of *The Concubine's Children* and moved with her husband and children to Ottawa.

In 2001 Chong was appointed Canada's representative to the International Board of Governors of the Vancouver-based Commonwealth of Learn-ing, which assists in expanding access to education and training through open and distance learning. She has also served on the Perinbam task force on participation of visible minorities in public service, and sits on an advisory committee to the clerk of the Privy Council of Canada on modernizing human resource management in the public service. She was also an adviser on the federal information highway advisory council.

Chong is the recipient of several awards: the Edna Staebler Award for Creative Non-Fiction (1995); the City of Vancouver Book Prize (1994); and the Van City Book Prize (1995). Her *Concubine's Children* was short-listed for the Governor General's Award and the Hubert Evans Non-Fiction Prize. The paperback edition was on *The Globe and Mail's* best seller list for more than 87 weeks.

A contributor to *Many Mouthed Birds* (1991), an anthology of contemporary Chinese Canadian writers, and *Who Speaks for Canada? Words that shape a country* (1998), Chong edited *The Penguin Anthology of Stories by Canadian Women* (1998).

Anne Marie Fowler

Chong, Ping   (1946–   )

Born in Toronto and raised in New York's Chinatown, Chong is one of the most recognized Asian-American theater directors. He studied filmmaking and graphic design at the School of Visual Arts and at the Pratt Institute. His career began in 1972 as a member of Meredith Monk's House Foundation, where he collaborated with her on several major works including *The Travelogue Series* and *The Games,* for which they shared the Outstanding Achievement in Music Theatre Award in 1986. In 1975 he established Ping Chong and Company, formerly The Fiji Theater Company, to create theatrical works for multicultural audiences nationally and internationally. Chong has created more than 50 major works for the stage. His earlier works include *Humboldt's Current* (1977), *AM/AM—The Articulated Man* (1982), *Nosferatu* (1985), *Angels of Swedenborg* (1985), *Kind Ness* (1988), and *Brightness* (1990 Bessie Award). Chong is the recipient of an Obie Award, six NEA Fellowships, a Playwrights

USA Award, a Guggenheim Fellowship, and a 1992 New York Theatre and Dance "Bessie" Award for Sustained Achievement.

Chong directed *Paris* and *Turtle Dreams* (Grand Prize Winner, Toronto Film Festival) with Meredith Monk for television. His video works include *I Will Not Be Sad in This World* (1991), *Plage Concrete* (1988), *The Absence of Memory* (1990), *A Facility for the Containment and Channeling of Undesirable Elements* (1992), and *Testimonial* (1995), which was screened at the Venice Biennale's Transcultural Show.

Undesirable Elements (1993) is an on-going series of community-specific works by Chong exploring the effects of history, culture and ethnicity on the lives of individuals in a community. The year 2002 marked the 10th anniversary of this production, celebrated in the production *UE 92/02*. *Blindness: The Irresistible Light of Encounter* (2004) explores Joseph Conrad's *The Heart of Darkness* and colonialism in the Belgian Congo. *Cathay: Three Tales of China* (2005), commissioned by the Kennedy Center, is a puppet theater work based on China's ancient history. In 2005 the Theater Communications Group published *East/West Quartets,* a collection of works dealing with East and West encounters. Through poetic dramatization of history, Chong reveals the nuances of these binaries. This collection includes *Deshima* (1990), about historical exchanges between Japan, Europe, and America; *Chinoiserie* (1995), about a clash of cultures between the West and China; *After Sorrow* (1997), about the legacy of war in Vietnam; and *Pojagi* (1999), a poetic history of Korea.

Zohra Saed

Chu, Louis Hing   (1915–1970)

Author of *Eat a Bowl of Tea* (1961), Louis Chu was born in Toishan, China, and came to the United States at the age of nine. He received his bachelor's degree in English at Upsala College in 1937. He went on to graduate study at New York University (M.A., 1940), and the New School for Social Research (1950–52). Chu also served in the U.S. Army from 1943 to 1945. He held various jobs during his lifetime: disc jockey for a radio station, 1951–61; owner of Acme Co., from 1950; director of a daycare center for New York City's Department of Welfare from 1961. Bilingual in Chinese and English, Chu was active in New York's Chinatown community, serving as executive secretary for the Soo Yuen Benevolent Association from 1954. His interest in the Chinatown community is also reflected in his master's thesis on New York's Chinese restaurants.

Like the main character in his novel, Chu went back to China to seek a wife, as was permitted by the War Brides Act of 1945. *Eat a Bowl of Tea* is set during this transitional time in the late 1940s, when discriminatory immigration laws were relaxed and male Chinese immigrants were allowed to return to their country and bring back wives and family members. Containing expressions and cultural references largely inaccessible to the average reading public, the novel did not have much public appeal when it was first published. Since its republication in 1979, however, it has been increasingly recognized as an important book about the Chinese-American experience and the Chinatown community. A movie based on the novel, directed by Wayne Wang, appeared in 1989.

Centering on the story of the marriage of Ben Loy and Mei Oi, the children of immigrant Chinese fathers, the novel explores such themes as the conflicts that arise when parents project their unfulfilled hopes onto their children, the contradictions between the idealized dream of success in America and the harsh reality of immigrant life, and the strengths as well as the restraints of the immigrant community.

Eat a Bowl of Tea is a sympathetic and realistic portrayal of a community of men who have been forced under exclusionary immigration laws to live the life of bachelors in their adopted land. Wah Gay has been married for 25 years, but he has not seen his wife after the first year of marriage. Wah Gay and most of the old men portrayed in the novel have had difficult lives as immigrant workers in America, toiling away in restaurants and laundry rooms most of their lives. They dream about returning to China and joining their families, but they have become complacently accustomed to a life of idleness and inaction. When his wife writes about their obligation to marry off their son, Wah Gay happily sets out to arrange a marriage for Ben Loy with a fellow Chinese immigrant's daughter living in China.

After getting married in China, Ben Loy returns to New York's Chinatown with Mei Oi, his young wife of 17. Despite having to live in a rundown apartment at the edge of Chinatown, they are full of hope and love. Mei Oi had dreamed about marrying a man from America and raising a family in the "Beautiful Country." What soon becomes apparent, however, is that Ben Loy is impotent, largely because he had regularly visited prostitutes and suffered several bouts of venereal disease. In many ways, Ben Loy had also lived the reckless life that the Chinatown fathers lived in their younger days in Chinatown, his impotence thus representing the hypocrisy and impotence of the bachelor society.

Ben Loy visits a doctor of Western medicine and a doctor of traditional Chinese medicine, but their prescriptions fail to cure his impotence. Disappointed and feeling lonely, Mei Oi falls prey to Ah Song's seduction and has a scandalous love affair. Soon, everyone in Chinatown finds out. Devastated when the rumors turn out to be true, Wah Gay turns to the Chinese community for intervention. When the affair continues, Wah Gay takes the situation into his own hands and attacks Ah Song, cutting off one of his ears. Although the assault charges are dropped and Ah Song is expelled from New York, Wah Gay and Mei Oi's father, Lee Gong, decide to leave New York out of shame. Ben Loy and Mei Oi also leave for San Francisco, where Mei Oi gives birth to a son fathered by Ah Song. In a departure from tradition, Ben Loy accepts the child as his own and looks forward to "a chance for a new beginning" (240). Ben Loy's impotence is also cured when he visits a Chinese herbal doctor and drinks a bitter brew of medicinal tea.

In San Francisco, Ben Loy and Mei Oi have a chance to save their marriage and make a fresh start in America without the interference of their parents or the Chinatown community. Although the ending is optimistic, the novel questions the extent to which the younger generation can succeed in America: Ben Loy and Mei Oi must still depend on their Chinatown connection for their livelihood in San Francisco. The novel is also an indictment of the historical circumstances that generated a stifling bachelor society of old married men in New York's Chinatown, who were prevented from being role models for their children.

Bibliography

Chu, Louis. *Eat a Bowl of Tea.* Seattle: University of Washington Press, 1979.

Kim, Elaine H. *Asian American Literature: An Introduction to the Writings and their Social Context.* Philadelphia: Temple University Press, 1982.

Lim, Shirley Geok-lin and Amy Ling, eds. *Reading the Literatures of Asian America.* Philadelphia: Temple University Press, 1992.

Peggy Cho

City in Which I Love You, The
Li-Young Lee (1990)

LI-YOUNG LEE's second book of poetry was the Lamont Poetry Selection for 1990. Comprising five sections, Lee's poems in *The City in Which I Love You* cycle through a physical and emotional exile to reach a personal understanding of the self in the world and to discover a deep connection with his multicultural heritage, history, and the future. Critic Zhou Xiaojing notes that "To deal with his cross-cultural experience and to show culturally conditioned ways of perception in his poetry, Lee employs and develops a major technique which relies on a central image as the organizing principle for both the subject matter and structure of the poem" (117).

The first section, which includes the seven-part poem "Furious Versions," celebrates the mysterious connections between father and son and likewise between poet and poem, attempting to trace creation through continuity. In "Furious Versions," which was collected in *The Pushcart Prize XIII*, even the knowable past is called into question, and distinct familial relationships are collapsed into one: "And did I stand/ on the train from Chicago to Pittsburgh/ so my fevered son could sleep? Or did I/ open my eyes and see my father's closed face/ rocking above me?" In this poem cycle, Lee moves back and forth between human memory—specifically the memories he has of his own parents and their exile—and natural indifference, symbolized by the sounds of water, trees, and birds. Rather than drawing a stark contrast between the world of humans and that of nature, Lee looks for continuity even in the juxtaposition: "I'll tell my human/ tale, tell it against/ the current of that vaster, that/ inhuman telling." In this introductory poem, Lee positions his work as somewhat of a harbinger, like Yeats's widening gyre: he tells the reader to listen to the poem, "a soul's/ minute chewing,/ the old poem/ birthing itself/ into the new/ and murderous century."

In the second section, composed of several shorter poems such as "The Interrogation," "This Hour and What Is Dead," "Arise, Go Down," "My Father, In Heaven, Is Reading Out Loud," "For a New Citizen of These United States," and "With Ruins," Lee deals with the difficult nature of memory as a recording instrument; the restlessness of certain memories, especially when combined with religious sentiment; the unparalleled strength of perception as a way to order the natural and spiritual world; an understanding of his father and the current that his father's life stirred in Lee's own; the sadness of forgetting and the need to preserve continuity between what seem like separate lives in different places; and the need sometimes to have a physical manifestation of an inner state in order to truly express or feel a memory. Each poem is complete in itself, yet as a group the poems serve as a transition between Lee's memory of his past and his efforts to re-create a life in the present for himself, a life that both preserves a semblance of continuity and fashions new beginnings.

The third section includes only two poems, "This Room and Everything in It" and the title poem, "The City in Which I Love You." The first poem is addressed to a loved other, and the speaker attempts to fix his memory of the moment after lovemaking by "letting this room/ and everything in it/ stand for my ideas about love/ and its difficulties." He then catalogs the visual and aural experiences he has of this woman and links each with a meaning that he wants to recall later. However, it soon becomes apparent to the speaker that trying to arrange memory in this way is artificial and ineffectual, since even moments later he cannot draw the one-to-one correspondence he had hoped would be possible: "no good . . . my idea/ has evaporated . . ." Yet even in the evaporation, the memory's essential distillation is preserved: "it had something to do/ with death . . . it had something/ to do with love." "The City in Which I Love You" begins with an inscription from the *Song of Songs,* where the speaker is searching for a loved one among city streets. Set in a ruined and rough city, the poem is a very physical and sensual account of unfulfilled longing. Garbage and dead bodies litter the way the speaker takes through the city, feeling acutely the absence of his loved one. He is led to repeatedly try to distinguish himself from the other souls in the city as it threatens to collapse his identity. As he wanders, though he does not come into contact with his loved one, the speaker is able to forge a strong identity for himself from the pieces of the past and the inviolable power of the present moment.

In the fourth section, "The Waiting" treats the intertwined relationships of mother and child, husband and wife. "A Story" traces the foresight of a father who, upon being asked for a story by his son, projects himself into the future when his son will no longer want to hear him and then back again into the present moment. "Goodnight" deals with the awkwardly symbiotic relationship between a man and his son. As the father muses over his son who is sleeping on him, he notes, "We suffer each other to have each other a while." "You Must Sing" is again about a father and son, but this time the father's age and the boy's attempts to comfort him as he confronts death are the central concerns. "Here I Am" wraps his experience with the father and son into one, focusing on their concern with visibility and presence for each other. "A Final Thing" details a memory of the speaker's wife telling their son a story that is overheard in the next room. The speaker notes the distance and closeness that link each of the three and attempts to preserve this moment in his memory. This section's poems move the speaker more into the present and into the experience of his own life as he tries to capture it in memory.

Section five, made up of one long poem, "The Cleaving," moves from concrete experiences such as observing a butcher in a butcher shop cleaving bodies of animals, to musings on how the butcher and the speaker are similarly made and how the speaker is also much like the various animals and parts of animals on display. Xiaojing points out how Lee's "singing of the world and his people must be preceded by embracing and understanding both. His singing is made possible by transformations of the self and experience; the renewal of the self is accompanied by a renewal of the traditional poetic form and language." Lee ends the poem with a long dissertation on eating: to eat is to create and to live, especially for the poet, who believes that "God is the text." By taking our experiences inside ourselves, we are able to fully know what life is, even as our ephemeral bodies pass away.

Bibliography

Lee, Li-Young. *The City in Which I Love You.* New York: BOA Editions, 1990.
Xiaojing, Zhou. "Inheritance and Invention in Li-Young Lee's Poetry." *MELUS* 21 (Spring 1996): 113–132.

Vanessa Rasmussen

Comfort Woman   Nora Okja Keller (1997)

In 1993 NORA OKJA KELLER attended a symposium on human rights at the University of Hawaii. It was there that she listened to a visiting Korean woman, Keum Ja Hwang, who spoke about her experience as a young girl during World War II, enslaved by the Japanese imperial army as a "comfort woman," or sex slave. Keller was deeply moved and haunted by the woman's story and felt compelled to contribute through her writing to the growing movement to elevate awareness about the neglected history of the comfort women.

Until recently, within the last decade or so, the plight of the comfort women had been virtually unknown on an international level and certainly not openly discussed. It has been estimated that between 100,000 and 200,000 women, primarily from Korea, which was then a Japanese colony, were forced between 1932 to 1945 to serve Japanese imperial soldiers as sex slaves in "recreation" or "comfort" stations in Japanese military camps or posts all over Asia. These women were frequently confined to separate tiny cells, forbidden to speak, sometimes bound to a bed, and raped by 30 to 40 men on an average day.

Keller's novel, *Comfort Woman,* which won the 1998 American Book Award, evolved out of her determination to work against the willingness of society to forget or exclude the history of the comfort women from the record of official, historical memory. Portraying the sufferings of Soon Hyo, a fictional former Korean comfort woman living in Honolulu, the novel focuses on the complex relationship between Soon Hyo and her adult daughter, Beccah, as they jointly attempt to come to terms with Soon Hyo's horrific past as a sex slave in a Japanese military camp.

At the age of 12, Soon Hyo is taken to a comfort camp where she is beaten, raped, and traumatized by occupying Japanese soldiers. She is assigned the name Akiko, a name that is given to all the women who have inhabited her cell in order to divest them of their individuality. Soon Hyo's resilience and ability to mentally disconnect herself from her physical circumstances allow her to survive her ordeal until she is able to escape and flee to Pyongyang, where she is taken into a Christian mission. Here she meets and marries an abusive American missionary, Richard, and decides to live with him in America. Richard remains, for the duration of their unhappy marriage, unaware of Soon Hyo's past experiences. In time, Beccah is born, Richard dies, and mother and daughter are left to fend for themselves in America.

Significantly, issues of language and the limits of representation are addressed by Keller in her depiction of Soon Hyo, not just in the comfort station in which she was enslaved, but more important, throughout her life as she is tormented by the memories of her past. Through trancelike episodes in which she returns to her past to reenact her experiences, the reader is given glimpses of the atrocities endured by the comfort women. Soon Hyo's ability to connect to the spirit world is observed by Auntie Reno, a flamboyant and eccentric friend who decides to promote her to the locals as a spirit medium and fortune-teller, thereby providing Soon Hyo with a small income. Soon Hyo's inability, however, to articulate in the "real world" the atrocities she has experienced is a mark of her psychological wound as a victim of deep trauma. She declares in one of her episodes that to survive and be a mother to Beccah, she has had to kill the part of her that was present in the comfort camp. This part of her becomes accessible only through the window of her memory, a place to which the frustrated Beccah, throughout her childhood and adolescence, cannot travel despite her desire to bear witness to her mother's trauma.

Soon Hyo finds herself deeply mistrustful of language, unable to employ mere words to express her suffering, and turns to touch as her primary means of communicating her emotions. Even an adult Beccah, who works for a newspaper, on the occasion of her mother's death, is unable to write her mother's obituary, realizing that ultimately she knows almost nothing about her mother's past, and that language is inadequate and somehow inappropriate in imagining Soon Hyo's life. It is only after Soon Hyo's death that her secret life can be revealed through a cryptic archive of memories she has stored up to share with her daughter—memories that Beccah must translate in order to piece together the truth of her mother's life. By having Soon Hyo speak in this sense only from beyond the grave, Keller is making a statement about the nature of representing the survivor of trauma. Soon Hyo's voice is a private, internal one that refuses full representation, and she goes to her death with her story intact and unresolved. While *Comfort Woman* provides a crucial site for communicating an atrocious event previously denied acknowledgment, Keller offers no easy answers or resolution to the comfort woman's pain and suffering. In so doing, she questions the capacity of language to represent the full experience of trauma, respectfully suggesting that often such experiences deny representation of any kind.

Dana Hansen

Concubine's Children, The
Denise Chong (1994)

DENISE CHONG's best-known, award-winning story, *The Concubine's Children: The Story of a Chinese Family Living on Two Sides of the Globe* (1994), tells a story that transcends continental and cultural borders. As a child, Chong suspected she might have relatives in China. It was her interest in finding out more about that extended family, and her husband's assignment to China as a journalist, that resulted in her writing *The Concubine's Children*. Appearing first as a magazine article in *Saturday Night, The Concubine's Children* grew into a book of nonfiction steeped in family traditions, transoceanic familial and marital relationships, perseverance, determination and the vestiges of gender.

This is the story of a family living on two continents and engaged in two distinctly different lives. It is the story of May-ying, who at age 17 moved to Canada to become a concubine to Chan Sam, who had earlier migrated to Canada's Gold Mountain in order to earn enough money to provide for his family back in China. May-ying, beautiful and resourceful, is forced to live with a man she does not love and is consigned to a life of hardship as a teahouse waitress in Vancouver's early Chinatown.

On the other side of the world, Chan Sam's first wife, Huangbo, endures the hardship of living without her husband and suffers under the political regime of Mao Zedong in war-torn China. As she raises the two daughters of Chan Sam and

May-ying sent from Canada, as well as her own son who suffers from a physical deformity, Huangbo witnesses the destruction of her beautiful Western-style home, built by the creativity and design of her husband, and by May-ying, who has sent her wages to China to finance its construction.

Denise Chong's mother, Hing, is May-ying's youngest daughter and one that was born and remained within the borders of Canada. Only having known of her sisters in a single picture of them, Hing leads a life of poverty and loneliness in the Chinatowns of western Canada. At various times throughout her childhood, Hing acts as a nursemaid to her mother. In 2004 *The Concubine's Children* was adapted into a stage play, directed by David Mann and produced by Nanaimo's TheatreOne and the Port Theatre, for a total of four performances.

While the story itself is concentrated in two separate countries, it deals with the sense of familial relations and the transcontinental development of Chinatowns in Canada. It also chronicles the growth of women with respect to their place in the family and community. In particular, Chong depicts the manner in which mother-daughter relationships grew intimate, especially as children helped their mothers cope with the hardships and challenges of living in a new society by acting as their eyes and ears.

Anne Marie Fowler

Crazed, The   Ha Jin (2002)

Set largely at the fictitious Shanning University, against the backdrop of the Tiananmen Square uprising of 1989, this novel is a searing exploration of political and intellectual life in post–Cultural Revolution China. Its main protagonist is Jian Wang, a promising graduate student in literature. Because of his intellectual acuity and integrity, Jian has gained the support and friendship of Professor Shenmin Yang, who is not only one of the university's most respected academics but also the father of Jian's fiancée, Meimei, a medical student studying for her exams at a university in Beijing.

The action starts when Professor Yang suffers a stroke and Jian is assigned to become one of his nurses. Although he is in the midst of preparing for the doctoral entrance exams to Beijing University so he can join Meimei in the capital, Jian willingly accepts the assignment because of his admiration for his mentor. But while Yang is supposed to have had a "cerebral thrombosis," he remains extremely articulate. In fact, he cannot seem to stop talking about the most sensitive of subjects. As he attends to his teacher, Jian learns much about Yang's life. Either through hallucination, or deliberately, Yang reveals that he was condemned as a "demon-monster" during the Cultural Revolution and sent to a labor camp for several years. More recently, he has had an affair with a female student, one of Jian's colleagues and closest friends. Because of the affair, he is now being blackmailed by the Communist Party's secretary on campus, who resents the fact Yang refused to help the secretary's nephew get admission to a Canadian university. Even more significant, after a life dedicated to scholarship, Yang has begun questioning the value of intellectual life—at least in China. Consequently, Jian decides not to take his doctoral entrance exams. After Yang dies and Meimei leaves him for the son of a prominent party functionary, he travels to Beijing with other students to attend the protests at Tiananmen Square. Deemed a counterrevolutionary, and wanted by the police, he is forced to leave the country.

Like HA JIN's other works, *The Crazed* thoroughly examines the material conditions in the society it depicts. For instance, housing is so limited that even academics feel compelled to choose their mates based on the sort of apartment they have. The novel's primary focus, though, is on people's intellectual or spiritual lives. In his nightly ramblings, the secular Professor Yang declares loudly that no one can destroy his soul. This is also what he keeps reminding Jian, not to allow anyone to quash his spirit. Furthermore, Yang confides that the only reason he was able to remain sane during his incarceration was because of the inspiration he derived from books, notably Dante's *Divine Comedy*. Another book that plays a critical role in the text is Bertolt Brecht's *Good Woman of Szechwan,* a play that the Canadian writer and theater scholar Keith Garebian says dramatizes the "main questions that lie at the heart of Ha Jin's novel: How can you be human or perfect in an inhuman and imperfect society? Can changes in society affect human nature?"

Bibliography

Garebian, Keith. "An artful reading of China's madness." (Toronto) *Globe and Mail,* 26 October 2002, D19.

Jianwu Liu and Albert Braz

Darjeeling　Bharti Kirchner　(2002)

This third novel by BHARTI KIRCHNER is much more ambitious than her first two. The story centers on two sisters, Aloka and Sujata, who are daughters of a tea planter in Darjeeling, India. Aloka is sweet, beautiful, and refined, with a love for literature. Described as "homely," Sujata is a talented businesswoman who is exceptionally knowledgeable about tea. When the novel begins in 2000, we learn that Aloka and Sujata now live in New York and Victoria, British Columbia, respectively, and that they have been summoned to Darjeeling by their grandmother, the matriarch of the family, to celebrate her birthday.

The novel then flashes back to the early 1990s, when the two sisters had had a falling-out over a man. This man, Pranab, was a tea estate manager in their father's plantation but had sympathy for the poor laborers on the plantation. When a bizarre set of events lead to his life being threatened, he marries Aloka, although he loves Sujata, and the couple flees to New York. Sujata moves to Canada and sets up a retail outlet for tea. Aloka leads a conventional immigrant wife's life until her marriage begins to dissolve. She begins working for a community newspaper and under the pseudonym Parveen writes advice columns for the newly migrated Indians. Her secret identity allows her to break out of conventional roles and to reinvent herself. The novel ends with the two sisters return-

ing to India with Pranab and reconciling their differences and establishing a happy life. They are aided in all this by their wily grandmother.

Like her other novels, this is also a romantic novel with the familiar theme of culture clash, the need for female autonomy, and the need for immigrants to balance the values of both their home culture and their new culture. The plot has impossible twists and turns that are also a hallmark of Kirchner's writing. Although the novel is set in a tea plantation and there are passing references to labor conditions, the author does little to explore these in depth. They largely remain an exotic backdrop for the plot, which is reminiscent of Indian commercial cinema with its improbable story lines and broadly drawn characters.

Nalini Iyer

Dark Blue Suit and Other Stories
Peter Bacho　(1997)

In this collection of interconnected, semi-autobiographical short stories, PETER BACHO explores the Filipino-American community of Seattle. Narrated from the perspective of Buddy, the son of a migrant worker who arrived among the first wave of Filipino immigrants in the 1920s and 1930s, the fictional stories blend the genres of oral history and personal memoir to connect the narrator's life with the deep history of Filipino community in the past. The first story, "Dark Blue Suit," sets up both the historical narrative of the elder generation of Filipinos and Buddy's personal relationship to those men. Buddy writes about "*Alaskeros,* men who went each spring to the salmon canneries of Alaska and returned each fall" (1), the powerful union built by Filipino immigrants in the 1930s, the stylish suits of these men "against the drab backdrop of cheap hotels, pool halls, card rooms, and the dull apparel of Chinatown's year-round residents" (5), and Communist union leader Chris Mensalves. He also describes the community's desires and everyday lives, the obsession with accordions, the men's relationships with female prostitutes, and their respect for local leaders. Through his childhood perspective, Buddy also introduces a number of characters like Mensalves, Leo, and Stephie featured in later stories.

Half of the stories focus on Buddy's peers whose stories reveal how individuals engage with the historical events of their time. One prominent figure is Rico, the center of both "Rico" and "Home." In "Rico," the teenaged Buddy tries to understand Rico's decision to enlist in the Vietnam War in 1967. Many poor, young Filipino men from Seattle go to war, either voluntarily or through the draft, because they have few other options. Rico is a tough character who boxes and fights as a way of life. He also asserts his masculinity at weekly dances, dancing and sleeping with women, especially "long-legged blondes" (27). In contrast, "Home" shows us Rico in the years after he returns from the war, constantly on the run from his experiences abroad. The story "August 1968" relates the end of Buddy's relationship with his childhood friend Aaron with the rise of Black Power and the drawing of racial lines. Buddy's relationships with the title characters in "Stephie" and "Dancer" give the reader a sense of how the Filipino men's liaisons with prostitutes and other women outside of marriage have created a complicated sense of family, belonging, and community.

The remaining stories in the collection provide a glimpse of Buddy's relationship with the *Manongs*—a respectful term for older men—of his community. Many of these men are bachelors, even in old age, and it is their decline as central figures in their community that spurs Buddy's need to remember their pasts. "A Life Well Lived" recounts organizer Chris Mensalves's important work in establishing the Filipino union as well as his difficulties in working as a Communist amid the anti-Red sentiment after World War II. "The Wedding" relates Uncle Leo's return to the Philippines in his old age to marry a young woman in order that he might have a family. "A Manong's Heart" tells the story of Uncle Kikoy's love of boxing as a sport that allowed Filipinos to be "men" in the United States.

As a work, this collection provides an important record of the *Manong* immigrants, their bachelor communities, and the families that descended from them. Through his personal history, Buddy is able to remember a larger community history that reveals strong links between many Filipino men in his life. What comes through most strongly is the sense of forgotten heroism that these men embodied in their struggle to get by as migrant workers and low-wage laborers in a country that barely acknowledges their presence.

Bibliography

Bacho, Peter. *Dark Blue Suit and Other Stories.* Seattle: University of Washington Press, 1997.

Paul Lai

Daswani, Kavita   (1964–   )

Kavita Daswani was born in Hong Kong and lived there for three decades. She moved to Los Angeles after her marriage but considers Mumbai (Bombay), India, her emotional home. Beginning her career as a journalist at age 17, she has been a fashion correspondent for CNN, CNBC Asia, and *Women's Wear Daily.* She has also published in the *Los Angeles Times* and the *International Herald Tribune,* and has been the fashion editor for the *South China Morning Post* in Hong Kong. Since moving to Los Angeles, she has published two novels, *For Matrimonial Purposes* (2003) and *The Village Bride of Beverly Hills* (2004). The latter novel was also published in England under the title *Everything Happens for a Reason.*

Daswani's popular novels have been described by several reviewers as "chick lit." These novels are mostly romantic comedies that focus on Indian women's experiences with love, marriage, work, and familial relationships as first-generation immigrants. Her characters struggle with cultural differences and try to balance Indian and American ways of life.

In *For Matrimonial Purposes,* Daswani tells the story of Anju, who is from an affluent family in Bombay. Since Anju does not succeed in finding a husband and is getting older, her parents become anxious about her future. Anju decides to come to New York to get an education, and her parents consent as they think that it increases Anju's chances of finding a rich, Indo-American husband. The novel traces Anju's experiences with education, American culture, her successful career in fashion, and eventually her successful romance (through the Internet) with an Indo-American man that leads to marriage. The Internet offers Anju a way to bridge the arranged marriage system of India and the American idea of romance and dating.

The Village Bride of Beverly Hills explores what happens to an Indian bride after she comes to the United States following an arranged marriage. Priya is a spunky, young woman who finds that marriage is neither romantic nor loving. Instead she becomes an unpaid cook and maid for her husband and his family in Los Angeles. By a series of coincidences, Priya begins working for a Hollywood entertainment newspaper and discovers that she has talent as a gossip columnist. She begins interviewing famous movie stars but has to keep her work life secret as its requirements in terms of clothing and lifestyle do not mesh with her role as a traditional Indian wife and daughter-in-law. Predictably, this secret unravels and causes enormous stress on her marriage, and Priya leaves her marriage and returns to her parents' home in India. Eventually, her husband realizes his mistakes and comes to India to court Priya and win her back.

Daswani's contribution to South Asian–American literature is her lighthearted look at the foibles of both Indian and American societies and her ability to provide charming narratives of cultural clash and popular feminism in which her female protagonists are able to find a middle ground between two very different sets of cultural expectations.

Bibliography

Daswani, Kavita. *For Matrimonial Purposes.* New York: G. P. Putnam, 2003.

———. *The Village Bride of Beverly Hills.* New York: G. P. Putnam, 2004.

Nalini Iyer

Daughter of the Samurai, A
Etsu (Etsuko) I. Sugimoto (1925)

A Daughter of the Samurai was first serialized in the monthly magazine called *Asia* in 1923–24 and published by Doubleday, Page & Co. in 1925. It was translated into seven languages, and the author assisted and authorized a Japanese translation by Miyo Ōiwa. Although it is often classified as autobiography, *A Daughter* is "more precisely a work of fiction filled with many autobiographical facts" (Hirakawa 397). The narrative framework of *A Daughter* is a life story of Etsu-bo, a daughter of a high-ranking samurai in the Echigo province, the northeast part of Japan. The narrative follows her life roughly in chronological order: growing up as a daughter of a samurai family amid its declining fortune; her strict education; a marriage arrangement at age 12, decided by the family; education in a Christian school; travel to America to marry Matsuo; life in American society; raising two daughters in the United States, then in Japan; and returning to the United States. In particular, the cultural practices in the early years of Meiji Japan in her childhood are described charmingly and vividly.

Inside the autobiographical framework, the narrative often digresses into episodes about Japanese customs and culture. In the preface to the Japanese translation, Etsu I. Sugimoto is quoted as saying that this book is written as an answer to many questions about Japan that she had been asked over the years. There are several detailed, colorful descriptions of annual events and festivals, including the New Year and *Ura-bon* ("A Welcome of Souls Returned" during the summer). The narrator also discusses Japanese religions, myths and legends extensively and informatively. Even some flashbacks about her father and mother are introduced as illustrations of the Way of the Samurai. The narrative often seems educational without being scholarly.

While the narrative is rife with descriptions of traditional values and practices of Japanese society, the narrator also makes observations of American society in the early 20th century. One of the recurring issues is the status of women. While Etsu-bo is sympathetic to the values that govern the lives of her mother and grandmother in Japan, she also envies the freedom and honesty of American women, whom she first encountered in a missionary school in Tokyo. Etsu also discusses the issue of reconciling her newfound Christian faith with her family religion. Overall, Etsu-bo's view of American culture and society is as positive as her view on her native practice. Etsu-bo concludes: "Hearts are the same on both sides of the world; but this is a secret that is hidden from the people of the East, and hidden from the people of the West." Because of the positive assessment of both cultures, this book is often regarded as the work of a cultural ambassador, introducing Japanese culture to an American audience and building a positive relationship between the two nations.

The stylistic elegance and flow of *A Daughter* owes much to the skillful editing of Florence Wilson (1861–1932). A daughter of the Wilson family who acted as a host when the author came to Cincinnati to marry Matsunosuke (Matsuo in *A Daughter*), Wilson encouraged Sugimoto and helped her throughout the writing process.

Almost immediately after the publication, the book was a great commercial success. In 1932 it became "the most continuously successful book of non-fiction on the Doubleday, Doran list." *A Daughter* was included in an anthology entitled *A Book of Great Autobiography* (1934), alongside the autobiographical texts by Helen Keller, Joseph Conrad, and Walt Whitman. Albert Einstein and Rabindranath Tagore wrote letters of apprecia-

tion, and Ruth Benedict's *Chrysanthemum and the Sword* quotes and refers to *A Daughter* as a source of information on Japanese culture.

Bibliography
Hirakawa, Setsuko. "Etsu I. Sugimoto's *A Daughter of the Samurai* in America." *Comparative Literature Studies,* 30, no. 4 (1993): 397–407.

Shion Kono

Dawesar, Abha (1974–)

The novelist Abha Dawesar was born in New Delhi, India, to upper-caste Brahmin parents. After graduating from Army Public School in India, she moved to the United States to study political philosophy at Harvard University, where she completed her honors thesis on the conception of human greatness in Frederick Nietzsche's *On the Genealogy of Morals.* She worked for a few years in financial services but later resigned to become a full-time novelist. She currently lives and works in New York.

Dawesar published her first novel entitled *Miniplanner* in 2000, and the event has been considered "a coming-of-age of Indian diaspora writers" since the book introduces an innovative subject matter and challenges the stereotypes of South Asian–American characters. The book was also issued in India under the title *The Three of Us.* Dawesar's next novel *Babyji* was published in 2005, winning the American Library Association's Stonewall Award for 2006, and has already been translated into Spanish and Italian. The author's third novel is *That Summer in Paris.*

The author has been noted for experimenting with various narrative voices in her fiction, invariably employing first-person narration. *Miniplanner* is written from the perspective of Andre, a 24-year-old white man for whom moving to New York to pursue a career in the banking sector leads to the exploration of his sexual identity. Andre finds himself seduced by a male top executive working for the same company and soon leads a very active sexual life, dating men and women alike. Explicit sexual scenes abound in the novel, and the protagonist ends up having to rely on the miniplanner of the title to manage his busy personal schedule. These encounters, however, leave him hollow and emotionally unstable as he grows ever more terrified of the prospect of spending a night alone. His identity crisis thus remains unresolved, and the novel evolves into what the author has termed a "sexual farce."

In *Babyji* the author adopts the point of view of a 16-year-old girl coming of age in India. Anamika, a brilliant student with a genius for quantum physics, faces some difficult questions concerning the meaning of life and her own identity, mainly pertaining to her sexuality. Far from being a simple account of the anxieties of adolescence, the novel is also a commentary on the social dynamics of contemporary Indian urban areas. Although the book is supposedly not autobiographical, its political background is factual; the novel is set in the 1990s and depicts the period of social unrest caused by the Mandal commission, an equivalent of U.S. affirmative action, according to which students of lower castes were to be given priority while applying for college admission. Precocious Anamika behaves like a boy and enters into multiple same-gender relationships with a classmate, a charming divorcee in her thirties, and a lower-caste servant; by doing so, she transcends the boundaries of gender, class, and age. Anamika has often been compared to the heroine of Nabokov's *Lolita*, yet the descriptions of Anamika's sexual exploits fit into the paradigm established by Humbert Humbert rather than Lolita. Anamika's quick mind and her close association with people representing the intellectual and economic elite of India give rise at the end of the novel to her decision to immigrate to the United States to pursue higher education there.

Dawesar's third novel, *That Summer in Paris*, published in June 2006, explores the relationship between literature and reality by depicting the experiences of a 70-year-old writer looking back at and reevaluating his life.

Bibliography

Dawesar, Abha. "Abha Dawesar: *Babyji*, A Story of Physics, Sex and Caste Politics in India." Interview by Barry Vogel. Available online. http://www.radiocurious.org/the_interviews_alpha.htm#adawesar22405. Downloaded on March 20, 2006.
———. Author's Web site. Available online. URL: http://www.abhadawesar.com. Downloaded on March 20, 2006.
———. *Babyji*. New York: Anchor Books, 2005.
———. *Miniplanner*. San Francisco: Cleis Press, 2000.
Ramakrishna, S. R. "Manhattan Masala." Hindu (8 May 2003). Available online. URL: http://www.hinduonnet.com/thehindu/mp/2003/05/08/stories/2003050800990300.htm. Accessed September 21, 2006.

Izabella Kimak

Death of a Red Heroine
Xiaolong Qiu (2000)

Nominated for the Edgar Awards, and winner of the Anthony Award, for best first novel in 2001, *Death of a Red Heroine* is Xiaolong Qiu's debut novel and the first in his Chief Inspector Chen Cao series.

The story is set in Shanghai in 1990. Chief Inspector Chen Cao, head of the special case squad, Shanghai Police Bureau, sets out to investigate a homicide case with his assistant, Inspector Yu Guangming. The female body found in a canal outside Shanghai turns out to be Guan Hongying (literally meaning "red heroine"), a national model worker. During the investigation, Chen finds out Guan lives a double life, that of a paragon Communist Party member who is selflessly dedicated to her work in Shanghai First Department Store and a closeted life of a woman with desire. The political sensitivity in this case involving a national model worker becomes more intricate when all the evidence leads to the suspect, Wu Xiaoming, the son of a high cadre. Chen is confronted with pressure and barriers from the higher power network. However, by resorting to his former girlfriend, Ling, whose father is a cadre even higher in power than Wu's father, he manages to save himself from his quandary and send Wu to trial. The irony is that the verdict for Wu in the press is not about his murder of Guan but "crime and corruption under Western bourgeois influence," a warning case that indicates the party's initiation of a political campaign.

A reflective man and a poet, Chen comes to see the similarities between himself and the object of his investigation, a theme Qiu also develops in his later novels. Behind their promising political careers are the lonely hearts craving for love. The cause of Guan's death is her desperate effort to secure a monogamous relationship with Wu, while Chen's amorous involvement with Ling is short and fruitless. The personal and the political are delicately interwoven in the social milieu of modern China.

While the plot is too transparent for a detective story, the novel offers glimpses into classic Chinese poetry beautifully translated and, though at times anachronistically depicted, of life in Shanghai. The novel is studied as a sociological text about socialism in transition.

Yan Ying

Depth Takes a Holiday: Essays from Lesser Los Angeles
Sandra Tsing Loh (1996)

In *Depth Takes a Holiday*, SANDRA TSING LOH explores the ambitions, pretensions, and obsessions of her fellow Los Angeles residents in the San Fernando Valley. This collection of humorous essays, a number of which originally appeared in her "The Valley" column in *Buzz* magazine, established Loh as a voice for her generation—specifically, for the underemployed and underinsured creative underclass coping with "genteel boho poverty" (4) in the strip-mall suburbs of L.A. Reviewers have attributed the anthology's best seller status to Loh's wit, her well-crafted prose, and her knack for satirizing her own participation in the collective neurosis.

The book begins with an apologia, a tongue-in-cheek defense of Los Angeles, "the nation's cultural scapegoat" (x). The 32 essays that follow are divided into three sections, titled "Amongst the Futon-Dwellers," "Life in Suburbia," and "Life in the City." Together, Loh's pieces paint a comic pic-

ture of hype and hope, of the struggle to secure a comfortable place in L.A.'s unstable caste system.

The futon-dwellers, as Loh reveals in the first set of essays, are late baby boomers who are in fact too late. They are highly educated young people, schooled to yuppie tastes and expectations, who find themselves in a deflated post-yuppie California economy. Those who refuse to work full time in "the pantyhose-and-tie world" (13)—including Loh, a performance artist—are reduced to imitation: buying Ikea's affordable "name-brand" furnishings and Trader Joe's Canadian Brie. They know the joys of temping, of open-mike poetry readings, of imagining glamorous alternative lives in New York City. And they follow the trends, whether in earrings or multiculturalism. In the longest essay in this section, "Is This Ethnic Enough for You?" Loh relates how, in the late 1980s and early 1990s, her biracial (Chinese-German) heritage makes her newly fashionable in artistic circles, newly eligible for "fighting over gristly little bits of grant money" (72).

The second group of essays, devoted to suburban adventures, includes pieces on Nintendo addiction, party avoidance, pseudo-camping, take-out in Van Nuys—and the respective temptations of Club Med, Tahiti, and time-share property on the "California Riviera." Loh also addresses selected suburban social interactions: attending a perky Christian church service with her brother, encountering a neighbor's pit bull, and coping with her eccentric Chinese father, who, although he is 70, insists on hitchhiking across L.A. neighborhoods because "driving is so wasteful" (139). Throughout the essay, her tone is conversational and energetic; in this section as well as the others, her narratives are peppered with snippets of wacky dialogue and twitchy stream of consciousness. Italics, exclamation points, and reiteration lend a sense of displaced drama to the ordinary and everyday: "*Sploosh!* And then: Arf, arf, arf, arf, arf! I'd continue to splash, splash, splash Joey as he ran around the pool" (133).

In the third set of essays, Loh takes on the facets of L.A. life that she has found particularly challenging: single womanhood and celebrity culture. In addition to the obligatory dating horror stories, she offers "How to Talk Dirty" and "Lesbian Pool Party," which spoof contemporary sexual fantasies and their sometimes comical manifestations. The desire for fame likewise comes in for a ribbing, especially as it leads to cheesy results: Tonya Harding's B-movie endeavors, the rise of spurious "talent" agencies, and the inane success of *Baywatch*. "Los Angeles is the best place in the country to nurture the kind of fame you make yourself," Loh declares at the start of "How to Become Famous" (198), and then provides step-by-step instructions for seizing one's own moment of notoriety.

Though its focus is regional, *Depth Takes a Holiday* is a sharp and savvy reading of popular culture and its ruling passions in American culture at large. As Loh admonishes, "Wake up, America! Admit it. 'We have seen David Hasselhoff, and he is us'" (x).

Bibliography
Loh, Sandra Tsing. *Depth Takes a Holiday: Essays from Lesser Los Angeles.* New York: Penguin, 1997.

Janis Butler Holm

Desani, G. V. (Govindas Vishnudas) (1909–2000)

Born in Nairobi, Kenya, Desani moved at the age of four with his family to the province of Sind, India (now Pakistan). During his two-year stay in England when he was a teenager, he was found to be an exceptionally talented child prodigy and gained a readership at the British Museum. Back in India, he worked as a journalist and correspondent. He continued in journalism when he returned to England at the beginning of World War II. At that time he gave numerous lectures while working for the BBC. During the war he also wrote his only novel, ALL ABOUT H. HATTERR (1948), which received immediate critical acclaim from writers such as E. M. Forster and T. S. Eliot. Besides his journalism and the novel, he published the poetic play, *Hali* (1950), short stories collected in *Hali and Collected Stories* (1991), and some nonfiction.

Very little is known about his life as he did not disclose information about himself, much like H.

Hatterr—the first-person narrator of his novel. However, Desani returned to India in 1952, and, apart from his prose poem *Hali* (1952), he kept silent, dedicating the following 10 years to studying mantra yoga. In 1962 he emerged as a columnist for *The Illustrated Weekly of India,* writing commentaries until 1967. In 1968 he was invited as a Fulbright Exchange Visitor to the University of Texas, Austin, and lectured on Eastern philosophy and religion. He was appointed professor of philosophy there in 1970, from which post he retired as a professor emeritus in 1978. Desani died in November 2000.

Desani was a nonideological critic of religion and society and an opponent of Gandhian politics. His single novel, *All about H. Hatterr,* has become a legendary cult book especially among Indian English writers such as Amitav Ghosh and Salman Rushdie, who admit the influence the novel has had on their art.

Joel Kuortti

Divakaruni, Chitra Banerjee (1956–)

Divakaruni was born in Calcutta, India, into an affluent middle-class family. After graduating from Presidency College in India, she joined the graduate program at Wright State University in Dayton, Ohio, where she met her husband, Murthy. The two moved to the San Francisco Bay area in 1979, and she earned a Ph.D. in Renaissance Literature from the University of California at Berkeley.

While she was at Berkeley, her grandfather died and she was dismayed at her inability to recall his face. To better remember her life and past, she began recording her memories in written form. She joined the Berkeley Poets Workshop and started sending her poems to *Calyx,* a women's magazine in Oregon that was so impressed by them that they republished an earlier volume of her poetry entitled *Black Candle* (1991). She has published three other volumes of poetry: *Dark Like the River* (1987), *The Reason for Nasturtiums* (1990), and *Leaving Yuba City* (1994). The last volume imagines the lives of the first wave of Indian immigrant farmers who settled in Yuba City,

California. The prose poems narrate the stories of the immigrant women's lives that were drawn from cultural artifacts such as photography, film and paintings by the American artist, Francesco Clemente. *Leaving Yuba City* won the Allen Ginsberg Poetry Prize and parts of the volume received the 1994 Pushcart Prize.

When Divakaruni realized that her poetry was becoming more narrative, she turned to fiction after taking a fiction writing class while she was teaching at Foothill College. Publication of her stories, however, was delayed by the birth of her first child and her involvement with MAITRI, a South-Asian domestic abuse victim help-line she helped create. Fortunately, an instructor of Divakaruni's, Tom Parker, took the initiative to generate interest at Anchor Publishing House. From this initiation came the acclaimed ARRANGED MARRIAGES (1995), which won the PEN Oakland Josephine Miles Prize, the Bay Area Book Reviewers Award and the American Book Award. All the stories in the collection explore women's, especially immigrant women's, desires, fears, and cultural anxieties.

Divakaruni then experimented with writing novels. Her first, *The MISTRESS OF SPICES* (1997), also explores the Indian immigrant experience, but in a fantastical way, deploying tools of magic realism and ideas of reincarnation. Her second, *Sister of My Heart* (1999), evolved from an earlier story entitled "The Ultrasound." This novel compares the divergent adult lives of two cousins who were best friends as children, growing up in an extended Indian family. Anju, one of the cousins, migrates to the United States, while Sudha, the other, stays in India. Divakaruni's third novel, The *Unknown Errors of Our Lives* (2001), continues the investigation of the Indian immigrant experience in the United States, delineating the loneliness, isolation and cultural anxiety that immigrants suffer as they struggle to carve out a niche in the new land. Her fourth novel, *The Vine of Desire* (2002), is a sequel to *Sister of My Heart* and continues examining Sudha and Anju's relationship after Sudha also immigrates to the United States. Their friendship is threat-

ened when Anju finds another vine entangling their lives—her husband's suppressed desire for her beautiful cousin and best friend Sudha. Her last novel, *Queen of Dreams* (2004), like her first, uses the paranormal to explore the lives of first-generation Indian-Americans, who are culturally all-American, and their relationships with their Indian parents. Divakaruni is currently writing children's literature and has published two popular juvenile books, *Neela: Victory Song* (2002) and *The Conch Bearer* (2003).

Sukanya B. Senapati

Dogeaters Jessica Hagedorn (1990)

Dogeaters is the first novel of JESSICA HAGEDORN, a Filipino-American poet, novelist, playwright, performance artist and musician. The novel, which takes its title from a derogatory slang term for Filipinos, depicts a wide range of characters from varied social backgrounds experiencing different forms of marginalization due to their class, gender, and sexuality, among other things. Set in Manila during the regime of dictator Ferdinand Marcos and covering the period from 1956 to the mid-1980s, it focuses on everyday lives frequently overlooked by official records.

Mixing fiction and quotations from poems, history books, and newspapers, Hagedorn presents multiple short vignettes narrated from the often contrasting perspectives of multiple characters, mostly female. There are three first-person narrators: Rio Gonzaga, Joey, and Rio's cousin Pucha. Rio is a spirited schoolgirl from an upper-middle-class background who wants to be a film director and who immigrates to the United States with her mother. Joey, a poor disc jockey, male prostitute, and drug addict, ends up joining a revolutionary group in the mountains. The open-ended novel unravels how the lives of Rio and Joey become loosely interwoven with those of a vast array of characters including relatives, film stars, star wannabes, a beauty queen, politicians, the country's First Lady, and insurgent groups. Pucha's intervention in the penultimate vignette of the novel serves as a counterpoint to Rio's narration, challenging and questioning some of her statements.

The novel is concerned with the processes through which individuals and nations construct their identities. An important factor in these processes is the characters' interactions with popular culture, from Filipino radio shows to Hollywood films. The latter symbolize both the United States's colonial legacy and neocolonial influence. Films and other forms of popular culture are simultaneously portrayed as a means of escapism, a source of pleasure, and a potential trigger for self-reflection. Hagedorn's descriptions of films, beauty contests, and sex shows also force the reader to confront the complex power dynamics between nations, social classes, and genders implicit in the acts of self-exhibition and spectatorship.

Dogeaters presents a consciously eclectic style and a fragmented narrative. Fragmentation in *Dogeaters,* however, is "not merely the sign of Hagedorn's 'virtuoso' writing skill, but an expressive tool through which the author contests absolute truths and narratives of progress" (Lee 81). References to well-established historical accounts are contrasted with the alternative discourses of popular culture and gossip. Similarly, while the main part of the narrative is presented in English, Hagedorn frequently uses Tagalog terms and refers to Filipino culture, thus positioning monolingual readers unfamiliar with the Philippines as outsiders.

Dogeaters has been celebrated for its inventiveness and uncompromising stance in the portrayal of Filipino culture and hybrid identities; it has also been accused of being a Westernized, Orientalist portrait of Filipinos. Hagedorn's controversial work makes readers question how national histories, "high" and "low" cultures, and definitions of cultural authenticity are constructed. As readers explore Hagedorn's narrative world, they have to face the myths upon which such concepts are built.

Bibliography

Davis, Rocío G, ed. *MELUS: Special Issue on Filipino American Literature* 29, no. 1 (Spring 2004).

Lee, Rachel C. *The Americas of Asian American Literature: Gendered Fictions of Nation and Transnation.* Princeton, N.J.: Princeton University Press, 1999.

Marta Vizcaya Echano

Donald Duk   Frank Chin (1991)

FRANK CHIN's male protagonists always struggle against being stereotyped by the American public as emasculated model minorities with an exotic but unthreatening culture. A wish to find a role model and to be recognized by the role model is fulfilled in *Donald Duk.*

Like the main characters in Chin's two early plays, Donald Duk, the protagonist in the novel, suffers from racial self-contempt. He hates everything about himself—his name, his looks, and his Chinese heritage. Unlike the adult characters in Chin's plays who hopelessly struggle in and out of the decaying Chinatown, Donald Duk, a 12-year-old Chinatown boy, is reared in a thriving Chinese-American community and tended by a caring father and other father figures. The novel spans the 15 days of the Chinese New Year celebration. During this period, the adolescent protagonist grows into adulthood and racial self-confidence by finding such role models as the builders of the transcontinental railroads and figures in the Chinese heroic tradition: for example, the 108 outlaws of *Water Margin* or Kwan Kung of *Romance of the Three Kingdoms.* These heroes serve as role models for the young protagonist to live up to, and his identification with the image of the role models at the level of resemblance empowers him to counter the stereotypes of Chinese taught in his history class: "The Chinese in America were made passive and nonassertive by centuries of Confucian thought and Zen mysticism. They were totally unprepared for the violently individualistic and democratic Americans" (2). Donald's self-education through his library research into early immigrant history and the Chinese heroic tradition enables him to correct his history teacher's racist teachings of Chinese culture and history. The heroes of the past become Donald's role models and inspire self-esteem. Donald's father and other fatherly figures in the community also offer a perspective through which Donald is recognized as likable and worthy of love. Donald's father and uncle are unusually caring and patient, inculcating in him a heroic tradition so that he is able to defend himself from racist attacks nonviolently. More important, they sympathize with Donald in his coming-of-age passage and recognize him as an individual with pride.

Bibliography

Chin, Frank. *Donald Duk*. Minneapolis: Coffee House Press, 1991.

Fu-jen Chen

East Goes West: The Making of an Oriental Yankee Younghill Kang (1937)

Six years after *The GRASS ROOF* (1931), YOUNGHILL KANG believed he was now prepared to write a sequel to that autobiographical novel. *East Goes West* is largely based on the author's own experiences as a struggling student during his first years in the United States.

After the annexation of Korea by Japan in 1910, the male protagonist Chungpa Han moves to New York in the 1920s to find freedom and universal truths. In his eyes, Korea, and the East in general, represents an old and dying culture, whereas the West stands for the future. Chungpa therefore adores the West and is critical of his home country and its culture. He soon realizes, however, that there is a discrepancy between the West he knows from literature and the West he experiences. His images of the United States become shattered after he faces discrimination and poverty while working as a servant, waiter, sales representative, and department store clerk.

In the end, Han remains an outsider. His unhappy love for Trip, a white American girl, can be seen as an illustration of his status as an alien. Trip is superficially interested in him and his "exoticness" but does not really care for him as a person and thus politely rejects his advances. Chungpa misinterprets her initial interest as being genuine and only later realizes that he is wrong when he finds himself in front of her door, which remains forever closed to him because she has moved without leaving her new address for him. It seems as if Chungpa unsuccessfully searches for love and a home, and as if he is trying to become an American but is not accepted as such.

More than an immigrant history, *East Goes West* is one of the rarest of literary species: a novel of ideas. Kang's great-hearted hero is a sensitive young classical scholar who arrives in America via Japan with only four dollars and a suitcase full of books, many of them on Western literature. As the title denotes, Kang regards himself as representing the East. Born into a culture in which one's obligation to others is valued more than that to oneself, Kang affirms that his sense of self is stirred by his exposure to Western knowledge. Against the stereotype of any Asian as "either a cruel and brutish heathen with horrid outlandish customs, or a subtle and crafty gentleman of inscrutable sophistication," Kang asserts that the Asian is in reality a "troubled child" who comes to the West "straight from his own antique and outmoded culture" (195).

East Goes West projects the "making of an Oriental Yankee," just as it projects his unmaking. It is a journey that ultimately leads to rebirth—or rather, what Han calls the "death of the state of exile"—and an acceptance of belonging everywhere and nowhere. As Kang's friend and mentor Thomas Wolfe wrote, Kang was "a born writer, everywhere he is free and vigorous; he has an original and poetic mind, and he loves life" (D5).

Bibliography

Kang, Younghill. *East Goes West: The Making of an Oriental Yankee.* New York: Charles Scribner's Sons, 1937. Chicago: Follett, 1965. New York: Kaya, 1997.

Lee, Sunyoung. Afterword to *East Goes West: The Making of an Oriental Yankee.* New York: Kaya, 1997.

Oh, Seiwoong. "Younghill Kang." In *Asian American Autobiographies: A Bio-Bibliographical Critical Sourcebook,* edited by Guiyou Huang. Westport, Conn.: Greenwood, 2001.

Wolfe, Thomas. "A Poetic Odyssey of the Korea That Was Crushed." *New York Evening Post,* 4 April, 1931, p. D5.

SuMee Lee

Eaton, Edith Maude   See FAR, SUI SIN.

Eaton, Winnifred   (1875–1954)

Better known under her pen name "Onoto Watanna," Winnifred Eaton was the first—and remains the most prolific—Asian-American novelist. The eighth of 16 children born to an English landscape painter, Edward Eaton, and his Chinese wife, Grace "Lotus Blossom" Trefusis, Winnifred spent her early years in Montreal, Canada, in extreme poverty that she lightened by telling stories to her younger siblings. At age 20, with no formal education, she left home for a brief stint as a journalist in Jamaica, then moved to the United States in 1896, where she spent the majority of her life, writing novels, short stories, and ultimately screenplays for Universal Studios in the early years of Hollywood.

Although Winnifred Eaton was the first Asian American to publish a sustained work of fiction, until recently scholars ignored her in favor of her older sister Edith Eaton, who wrote under the pseudonym SUI SIN FAR about the hardships Chinese Americans faced during an era of extreme discrimination. This is because Winnifred concealed her Chinese heritage in favor of what was then a more fashionable—and thus, more marketable—Japanese façade. Posing for publicity photos in kimonos, with her hair done up in a Japanese style, Winnifred wrote nearly a dozen "Japanese" romances and insisted on her false Japanese identity, claiming to be descended from a Nagasaki noblewoman. Even so, Winnifred's novels garnered scant critical attention before the late 1990s; and what little exists generally focuses on her deception. As Eve Oishi notes in an essay on Eaton's first novel, *MISS NUMÉ OF JAPAN* (1899), her ruse is problematic not merely because she capitalized on Western stereotypes of Asians but because "she was instrumental in creating them" (xxii).

The question, though, is whether this perception of Eaton as a "traitor" or "trickster" derives from the actual content of Eaton's novels or just their elaborate packaging by her publishers. Written with great rapidity—as Eaton wrote to survive—these lavishly illustrated works include *A JAPANESE NIGHTINGALE* (1901), *The Wooing of Wisteria* (1902), *The Heart of Hyacinth* (1903), *The Love of Azalea* (1904), *A Japanese Blossom* (1906), and *The Honorable Miss Moonlight* (1912). These diaphanous titles suggest that Eaton equated Asian women with birds and flowers, much like Pierre Loti in *Madame Chrysanthème* (1887) and John Luther Long in *Madame Butterfly* (1898).

Such an assessment, however, is too simplistic. Unlike the purely Japanese heroines of these earlier (and more famous) books, Eaton's central figures are often biracial, struggling to come to terms with their mixed ethnicity in an otherwise homogenous society. Indeed, in some cases such as *Tama* (1910), the Japanese-American girl suffers extreme persecution and attempted murder due to her mixed-race background. Such ethnic tension is apparent as early as in Eaton's first known story, "A Half Caste" (1899), in which the unwanted daughter of a Japanese teahouse dancer revenges herself upon her unsuspecting father. The ethnic tension remains evident all the way to her last "Japanese" novel, *Sunny-San* (1926), in which a biracial girl is literally purchased by a group of American undergraduates. As Eaton's narrator remarks in *A Japanese Nightingale,* not even the happiest of mixed marriages can prevent "the Eurasian [from being] born to a sorrowful lot," condemned to prejudice from the "pure race" people surrounding the child (90).

Surprisingly, this theme of miscegenation that runs through almost all these "Japanese" works gets short shrift in the few critical studies that have been written on Eaton's books. This is likely due to the distraction provided by the elaborate bindings, gilt-edged pages and copious illustrations that mark—and even efface—the original editions, making the pictures seem almost more important than the texts. Yet if we place this ethnic tension at the center of our reading, we may interpret Eaton's choice of Japan as providing not merely an excuse for exotica but a stage on which to enact the difficulties she and her siblings faced growing up biracial at the fin de siècle. After all, none of the Eaton children seems to have been comfortable with a Chinese-English ancestry. If Edith presented herself as all Chinese, and Winnifred as Japanese, their sister May pretended to be Mexican, while their oldest brother Edward posed as an English aristocrat, joining "whites only" clubs in Montreal.

Ultimately, Winnifred Eaton died en route to Calgary, Canada, in 1954, having published 14 novels, two thinly veiled autobiographies, almost countless articles, short stories, screenplays, and a Chinese-Japanese cookbook. She married twice: first, in 1901 to a New York journalist, Bertrand Babcock, with whom she had four children; then to a Canadian cattle rancher, Francis Fournier Reeve, in 1917, after her divorce. She witnessed her novel, *A Japanese Nightingale,* staged on Broadway and made into one of Hollywood's first silent films. By any measure, she achieved extraordinary professional success. Yet Eaton herself seems to have foreseen the difficulties her Japanese disguise would pose to future generations of Asian Americans. As her alter-ego Nora Ascough narrates in the quasi-autobiographical *Me,* "When the name of a play of mine flashed in electric letters on Broadway, and the city was papered with great posters of the play . . . I was aware only of a sense of disappointment. My success was founded upon

a cheap and popular device . . . Oh, I had sold my birthright for a mess of potage!" (153–154)

Despite her self-criticism, Eaton deserves credit for her accomplishments. Writing at a time when biracial unions were rare, Eaton posed powerful questions about what an "authentic" ethnicity entails, demonstrating through both her books and her body that race is as performative as any other aspect of human identity. In so doing, Eaton was less a trickster than a trailblazer. By exploring themes that might otherwise have been taboo if she had set her narratives in North America, she chartered new literary territories: not only as the first Asian-American novelist but as the first to investigate what it means to be Asian and Caucasian at the same time.

Bibliography

Birchall, Diana. *Onoto Watanna: The Story of Winnifred Eaton.* Chicago: University of Illinois Press, 2001.

Cole, Jean Lee. *The Literary Voices of Winnifred Eaton: Redefining Ethnicity and Authenticity.* New Brunswick, N.J.: Rutgers University Press, 2002.

Eaton, Winnifred. *A Japanese Nightingale. Two Orientalist Texts,* edited by Marguerite Honey and Jean Lee Cole, 81–171. New Brunswick, N.J.: Rutgers University Press, 2002.

———. *Me: A Book of Remembrance. With an Afterword by Linda Trinh Moser.* Jackson: University of Mississippi Press, 1997.

Ferens, Dominika. *Edith and Winnifred Eaton: Chinatown Missions and Japanese Romances.* Urbana: University of Illinois Press, 2002.

Oishi, Eve. Introduction. In *Miss Numé of Japan: A Japanese-American Romance,* xi–xxxiii. Baltimore, Md.: Johns Hopkins University Press, 1999.

Kay Chubbuck

Echoes of the White Giraffe
Sook Nyul Choi (1993)

SOOK NYUL CHOI's second novel, *Echoes of the White Giraffe* is the sequel to her autobiographical first novel, YEAR OF IMPOSSIBLE GOODBYES, the story of Sookan Bak, who, with her younger brother, escapes to the American zone in Korea during the turmoil of the Japanese occupation of Korea. It is 1950 and *Echoes* opens with 15-year-old Sookan, her mother, and her younger brother Inchun living in a refugee camp atop a mountain in Pusan, South Korea. Choi's protagonist reveals the harsh and bare existence of life as a refugee, as well as once again suffering from a forced separation from her beloved father and older brothers. *Echoes* explores the war experience through the eyes of innocent victims who attempt to flee the death and destruction and become refugees: "Famished, frostbitten, and dirty, we made our way to the base of the refugee mountain. In our tattered, filthy clothes, we stared up at the steep, jagged, red-brown mountain looming above us" (21). Sookan tries hard to come to terms with her refugee status and begins to rebuild her life amidst the ravages of a war-torn country. Sookan enters young adulthood with a brief, heartfelt, yet bittersweet romance with young Junho, a handsome young man who captures young Sookan's heart. Choi captivates the reader as Sookan and Junho talk about their dreams for the future and what they envision life to be like, free of war and hardship. The novel ends with the armistice and Sookan and her family's return to Seoul to begin rebuilding their lives. Sookan begins the steps to fulfill her dream of studying in America.

Choi's *Echoes* continues the theme of quiet defiance against repression, established in her first novel, and of the importance of family and honor in the hope for a better life. Choi's novel illuminates the repressive atmosphere of war and its effects on young people with her refreshingly honest observations. Her characters are inhabited with vitality and strength despite their circumstances, and they are a testament to the special powers of hope and courage to rise above adversity.

Bibliography

Choi, Sook Nyul. *Echoes of the White Giraffe.* New York: Houghton, Mifflin, 1993.

Debbie Clare Olson

English Patient, The
Michael Ondaatje (1992)

MICHAEL ONDAATJE's best-known novel, which shared the Booker Prize in 1992 and became the basis for a multiple–Oscar-winning film by Anthony Minghella is, in the author's words, "a book about very tentative healing. . . . It's also two or three or four versions of a love story." Much of the action takes place in a temporary hospital in an abandoned Tuscan villa in 1945. There, Canadian nurse Hana cares for her last remaining patient, a severely burned man with no apparent identity; he is ultimately revealed to be Laszlo Almasy, a Hungarian explorer, cartographer, and alleged double agent. Hana is joined by a former thief, Caravaggio, who has lost both thumbs attempting to protect his secret identity, and also by Kip, an Indian sapper, who begins a tenuous relationship with Hana. The allegedly "English" patient, however, remains the focus for the other major characters: for Hana, whose desire to heal and help now revolves exclusively around nursing the burned man; for Caravaggio, in that morphine and history carry both men to a place beyond borders and allegiances; and for Kip, whose character also interrogates the viability of single narratives to encapsulate historical truth.

The novel gradually reveals the title character's past, especially his romantic relationship with Katherine Clifton, the wife of a fellow explorer. The two share a brief but passionate relationship, and even after their affair ends, both remain emotionally tied, despite Katherine's marriage to Clifton. Clifton, however, has already learned the truth, and attempts to kill all three in a plane crash. Katherine barely survives, while Almasy's attempt to find help eventually leads him to betray his knowledge of the North African desert to the Nazis. He fails to save Katherine's life, and soon nearly perishes in his own flying accident.

Ondaatje's novel weaves past and present, fiction and history together, in a hallucinatory, postmodernist rendering of scarred bodies, lives and nations. His commitment to cosmopolitan worldviews is expressed by his eponymous character as he carries Katherine to her final rest: "We are communal histories, communal books. We are not owned or monogamous in our taste or experience. All I desired was to walk upon such an earth that had no maps." Detractors have suggested that Ondaatje's ending seems too forced, that his allegedly apolitical novel fails to represent neutrality, and that his characters seem illusory rather than real. Many of these objections, however, can be traced to Ondaatje's poetic, impressionistic style, and his determination to use literature to interrogate, rather than explain, conventional history.

Bibliography

Bierman, John. *The Secret Life of Laszlo Almasy: The Real English Patient.* London: Viking, 2004.

Ibarrola-Armendariz, Aitor. "Boundary Erasing: Postnational Characterization in Michael Ondaatje's *The English Patient.*" In *Tricks with a Glass: Writing Ethnicity in Canada,* edited by Rocio G. Davis and Rosalia Baena, 37–57. Amsterdam: Rodopi, 2000.

Ondaatje, Michael. *The English Patient.* New York: Vintage, 1993.

———. "An Interview with Michael Ondaatje." By Eleanor Wachtel. *Essays on Canadian Writing* 53 (Summer 1994): 250–261.

J. Edward Mallot

Family Devotions
David Henry Hwang (1981)

In an interview with Marty Moss-Coane, DAVID HENRY HWANG accounted for some of the origins of *Family Devotions,* a play that opened in October 1981 at the Public Theater in New York City. He explained that his own Chinese-American family had often gathered together to engage in "family devotions." At these meetings, activities pursued by historical members of the family would be lauded, their exemplary conduct cited as a model for the behavior of the present-day descendants. God would also be praised for guiding Hwang's ancestors toward a life lived justly, according to a Christian ethos. Hwang told Moss-Coane that he felt these rituals represented "a clear example of the meshing of the Christian ethic with the Confucian ancestor worship ethic." The play shows an exaggerated version of the "family devotions" that Hwang's family practiced. Because the ritual of ancestor worship based on Christianity involves traditions from both the West and the East, it can reveal the differences between the two disparate cultures. Tensions raised during the "family devotions" also reveal much about the conflicting pulls of American and Chinese cultures on Asians living in the United States.

Two elderly Chinese sisters, Ama and Po po, live in Bel Air, California, in a large family house owned by Ama's daughter, Joanne, and her Japanese-American husband, Wilbur. In this house with many rooms, a barbecue area, and a tennis court, these domineering matriarchs pontificate about the efficacies of traditional Chinese values and Christian ethics to their younger relatives, relatives who live an affluent life in America, scarcely respectful or appreciative of their extended Chinese family. Jenny, for example, a 17-year-old granddaughter of Ama, refers to an elderly relative as "some Chinese guy . . . another old relative. Another goon." During the "family devotions," Ama and Po po praise their long-deceased aunt, See-goh-poh, who, according to a family myth, brought Christianity into the family, heroically ensuring that the family (and many associates) would be forever cocooned within profound Christian morality. However, Ama and Po po are shocked when their younger brother, Di-gou, who has chosen to stay in China, visits California and shatters their illusions by revoking his Christian past and insisting that See-goh-poh was not a Christian heroine, but rather a wretched outcast. There is, then, a degree of satire against the presumptions behind ancestor worship: the figures celebrated are often legendary characters who share little with the real persons who once lived. Nevertheless, the play's more pointed humor satirizes the materialism and cultural moribundity of well-off Asian Americans who disregard any connection to their roots in Asia.

Robert, the middle-aged husband of Hannah, the daughter of Po po, perpetuates a vulgar sort of ignorant materialism. He is a first-generation Chinese American, but focuses all of his energies upon doing well under "The American Dream." The Chinese visitor, Di-gou, is particularly disturbed by Robert's willful wastefulness. Seeking to display American abundance and plenty, Robert destroys food by throwing it onto the tennis court and—as a stage direction puts it—"*stomping the guo-tieh* [dumplings] *like roaches.*" A dull banker who is obsessed with tax shelters, Robert believes so much in American capitalism that he thinks that it is a triumph to have been kidnapped. He is living the "American Dream" because he has advanced from an immigrant in "rags" to a "kidnap victim." The vacuousness of modern material consumption can be seen in the tennis-ball serving machine owned by Ama's son-in-law, Wilbur. It sends balls across the court, but when it malfunctions, it bombards Di-gou with high-speed balls. This peltering with tennis balls symbolizes the peltering of pro-capitalist propaganda with which Robert and Wilbur attack this Communist-supporting Chinese visitor.

The play also lampoons bigotry caused by ignorance of other races and long memories about historical conflicts. Ama cannot forgive the Japanese for various wars fought in the past: She despises her son-in-law, seemingly because of his Japanese origin. When a pet chicken goes missing, Ama assumes that Wilbur has killed and barbecued it: "Very bad temper. Japanese man." She also argues that classical music in an orchestra with a Japanese conductor is a dangerous occupation: Ama states, "if musicians miss one note, they must kill themself!" The irrationality of such prejudices is further underlined when Ama cites a novel explanation for why Robert missed Di-gou at the airport: "Your father trade with Japanese during war." The two sisters are also prejudiced against the non-Christian, Communist regime that flourished in China after they left. They assume that Di-gou will be brainwashed, laboring in a rice field, being remotely controlled: "wires in their heads . . . force them work all day and sing Communist songs." The two women even whip Di-gou with an electri-

cal cord, believing that his rejection of Christianity is caused by a "Communist demon" inside him. After some sensational, explosive events, Di-gou argues that it is wrong to uncritically praise ancestors who were flawed and human just like present-day people. Instead, he asserts, Americans of Asian origin must realize that their ancestors' heritage has, in part, influenced their contemporary identities, however multivalent and hybrid those identities are. Comic and rousing in its call for a greater awareness of Asian Americans' origins, *Family Devotions* reveals a serious problem of misinformation, prejudice, and disdain that exists within Asian-American families and between Asians and Asian Americans.

Bibliography

Hwang, David Henry. *Family Devotions.* In *Trying to Find Chinatown: The Selected Plays,* 89–150. New York: Theatre Communications Group, 2000.
———. Interview by Morty Moss-Coane. In Philip C. Kolin and Colby H. Kullman, eds, *Speaking on Stage: Interviews with Contemporary American Playwrights,* 277–290. Tuscaloosa: University of Alabama Press, 1996.

Kevin De Ornellas

Far, Sui Sin (Edith Maude Eaton)
(1865–1914)

Born Edith Maude Eaton in England, Sui Sin Far would become the first Asian-American fiction writer, publishing numerous short stories, essays, and articles under her adopted pen-name Sui Sin Far. Her father was a British merchant, and her mother was a Chinese missionary who had received her education in England. They met in Shanghai, were married in the early 1860s, and moved to England shortly thereafter. In 1872, when Sui Sin Far was still a child, the family left England for Canada, where Sui Sin Far would live until she was nearly 32. Sui Sin Far's early life was not easy. Although the family was culturally British, she and her siblings faced racist taunts and physical abuse because of their mixed-race status. As the eldest daughter in a family of 14 children,

Sui Sin Far was compelled to spend much of her time caring for her younger siblings. When her family's financial situation deteriorated, Sui Sin Far was obliged to abandon her formal schooling before the age of 12 in order to contribute to the family funds.

In 1883, when she was about 18 years old, Sui Sin Far went to work for the *Montreal Daily Star.* She eventually became a stenographer, a career that would provide her with a limited source of income throughout her life. In the mid-1880s she opened her own office and was able to secure employment as a freelance journalist. Although Sui Sin Far was not fluent in any language other than English and would have been forced to rely on interpreters, this work brought her into contact with Montreal's Chinese immigrant population and thus marked a crucial stage in Sui Sin Far's developing sense of her dual ethnic identity. During this time she became increasingly aware of the racist laws under which the Chinese suffered. Her reporting from this period, most of it unsigned, shows a degree of sympathy toward her Chinese subjects, absent from the writing her contemporaries produced on this topic. For instance, in an 1896 letter to the editor, "A Plea for the Chinaman," signed "E. E.," Sui Sin Far denounced the new onslaught of laws targeting the Chinese, while defending the Chinese against the racist charges used to justify the legislation.

Yet at this point in her literary career, Sui Sin Far did not deal with Chinese subject matter in fiction. Her first stories, written between 1888 and 1889 and published in the nationalistic Canadian magazine *Dominion Illustrated,* were signed "Edith Eaton" and dealt with European-American characters and themes. Sui Sin Far's first work to address Chinese-American subject matter did not appear until 1896, when several short stories on Chinese immigrants to North America appeared in the New York journal *Fly Leaf,* the Kansas City journal *Lotus,* and the Los Angeles-based *Land of Sunshine.* From this point on, Sui Sin Far would devote herself to Chinese themes, creating stories that presented the Chinese living in America in a sympathetic light and often assumed the vantage point of a Chinese-American protagonist.

In 1897 Sui Sin Far left Montreal to accept a position as a reporter for a newspaper in Kingston, Jamaica. About six months later she contracted malaria and was forced to return to Montreal, but shortly after her return she moved again, this time to the United States. Sui Sin Far arrived in San Francisco in 1898 and soon made contact with inhabitants of San Francisco's Chinatown, the oldest and largest Chinese community in North America. For the next decade, Sui Sin Far produced a number of short stories centered on the Chinese in North America, relocating several times in order to report on the Chinese communities in San Francisco, Los Angeles, and Seattle. Between 1898 and 1900, she was able to place a number of her short stories in West Coast periodicals, such as *Land of Sunshine, Overland, Monthly* and *Out West,* all edited by Charles Lummis. In 1903 a series of her articles on the Chinese in Los Angeles appeared in the *Los Angeles Express.* In 1909 the Seattle monthly *The Westerner* ran a serial by Sui Sin Far entitled "The Chinese in America."

Sui Sin Far clearly hoped to reach a national audience, but initially her efforts in this direction met with only limited success. In 1902 her story "The Coat of Many Colors" appeared in *Youth's Companion.* "A Chinese Boy-Girl" was published in *Century* in 1904. In 1905 the *Chautauquan* published the story "Aleteh." Given the prominence of *Century* among the literary periodicals of its day, Sui Sin Far's publication in this magazine marks a milestone in her literary career. Unfortunately, her repeated efforts to secure future publication in this periodical met with disappointment. There is some speculation that the absence of publications between the year 1905 and 1909 is evidence of a hiatus in Sui Sin Far's literary output, perhaps due to her frustration over repeated rejections. But it is also possible that work from this period has yet to be discovered.

In 1909 Sui Sin Far's career took a turn for the better. Her autobiographical essay, "Leaves From the Mental Portfolio of an Eurasian," appeared in 1909 in *The Independent,* an established literary periodical with a national circulation. Around 1910 she moved to Boston in order to be closer to national publishing centers, a decision that seems to have had a positive affect on her literary career. Between 1909 and 1913, Sui Sin Far was able to place stories in *Independent, Hampton's, Delineator, Good Housekeeping,* and *New England Magazine,* thereby clearly establishing herself in the literary marketplace of the East. In 1912 A. C. McClurg brought out Sui Sin Far's first book, *Mrs. Spring Fragrance,* to generally favorable reviews.

Unfortunately Sui Sin Far's career was cut short just as she was reaping the rewards of a life spent in pursuit of literary success. Shortly after the publication of *Mrs. Spring Fragrance,* Sui Sin Far disappeared from the literary scene. She died a few years later in 1914 at the age of 49, after a heart condition forced her to return to Montreal for medical treatment. Her obituary notes that she was working on a long novel when she died, but to date scholars have been unable to locate this unpublished work. Even though she was fairly well known in her own time, after her death Sui Sin Far was virtually forgotten. The revival of her literary reputation in the 1980s and 1990s is a result of the efforts of scholars of Asian-American literature such as Amy Ling and S. E. Solberg. The exhaustive research of Annette White-Parks, Sui Sin Far's contemporary biographer, and recent scholarly work on Sui Sin Far have helped to secure her place in the history of American literature.

Bibliography

Far, Sui Sin. *Mrs. Spring Fragrance and Other Writings,* edited by Amy Ling and Annette White-Parks. Urbana: University of Illinois Press, 1995.

Ferens, Dominika. *Edith and Winnifred Eaton: Chinatown Missions and Japanese Romances.* Urbana: University of Illinois Press, 2002.

Ling, Amy. "Edith Eaton: Pioneer Chinamerican Writer and Feminist." *American Literary Realism* 16 (Autumn 1893): 287–298.

Solberg, E. E. "Sui Sin Far/Edith Eaton: The First Chinese American Fictionist." *MELUS* 8 (Spring 1981): 27–37.

White-Parks, Annette. *Sui Sin Far/ Edith Maude Eaton: A Literary Biography.* Urbana: University of Illinois Press, 1995.

Rachel Ihara

Farewell to Manzanar
Jeanne Wakatsuki Houston (1973)

JEANNE WAKATSUKI HOUSTON's memoir of her family's two-and-a-half-year incarceration in the World War II internment camp at Manzanar is one of Asian-American literature's best-known books. Since its first publication, it has gone through 60 editions and sold more than 1.5 million copies. The book is assigned regularly in high school and college courses, and is excerpted in dozens of anthologies of women's and ethnic American writing.

Jeanne Wakatsuki was seven years old in 1942 when her family was interned at Manzanar, in Southern California near the Nevada border, and 10 years old when they were released. With the assistance of her husband, writer James D. Houston, Jeanne began tape-recording her recollections of that experience in the late 1960s. In the early 1970s, Jeanne and James began conducting historical research and interviews with other family members and internment survivors. Those tapes and notes provided the raw material for *Farewell to Manzanar,* which announces itself on the title page as "A true story of Japanese American experience during and after the World War II internment."

Though not the first Japanese-American autobiography to discuss the internment—MONICA SONE's 1953 *Nisei Daughter* predates it by 20 years—*Farewell to Manzanar* was the first to focus on the internment as its central dramatic event. Jeanne's memoir opens on the morning of the Pearl Harbor attack, which, she writes, "snipped [our life] off, stopped it from becoming whatever else lay ahead" (40). The book's early chapters alternately discuss the initial phases of internment, the emigration of her father, Ko, to California from Japan in 1904, and the Wakatsuki family's prewar life in California. The Wakatsukis are a close, if not particularly intimate, family, held together in large part by the strength of Ko's belligerent personality. However, Ko's arrest on false espionage charges in the days after Pearl Harbor forces his wife, Riku, and their children to adjust their family dynamics in his absence.

There are two primary narratives in *Farewell to Manzanar.* The first concerns the slow erosion of the Wakatsuki family's internal ties, as presented through confrontations between Ko and his wife and children. At Manzanar, Ko begins drinking heavily, abuses Riku, and gets into fights with other internees including, at one point, his own son Kiyo. Jeanne's older brother Woody enlists in the military, hoping that this will demonstrate his family's loyalty to the United States and speed their release, but Woody's decision enrages Ko, who tells his son that it is impossible for a soldier to fight well when he is partially invested on both sides of a war. Throughout the book, Ko's position as family patriarch slowly slips away as he alienates his family and becomes increasingly self-destructive.

The effect of the internment on Jeanne's self-image, and by extension on the self-image of all nisei (second-generation Japanese Americans), provides the book's second major narrative. Jeanne's respect for her father changes slowly to fear and resentment, and ultimately to embarrassment and shame whenever she is identified with any recognizably Asian item or practice; during a school certificate assembly following their release from Manzanar, she is mortified when her father stands and bows solemnly in front of the other parents. In school she takes up baton twirling in an attempt to make herself seem less conventionally Japanese. These attempts at hiding her ethnicity, however, ultimately fail. As Jeanne grows up, she comes to understand the internment as the moment when her family became fragmented, and the moment when her understanding of herself as a Japanese American—not simply an American—first began to develop.

Considered both as a personal and a political memoir, *Farewell to Manzanar* is one of the most significant books in Asian-American literature. In 1976 *Farewell to Manzanar* was adapted for a Universal Television film, for which Jeanne Wakatsuki Houston cowrote the screenplay.

Bibliography

Kim, Elaine H. *Asian American Literature: An Introduction to the Writings and Their Social Context.* Philadelphia: Temple University Press, 1984.

Smith, Page. *Democracy on Trial: The Japanese American Evacuation and Relocation in World War II.* New York: Simon and Schuster, 1995.

Eric G. Waggoner

Fault Lines   Meena Alexander (1993)

MEENA ALEXANDER's memoir *Fault Lines* traces her passage across different continents as she moves from India to Sudan, to England, back to India, and finally to the United States. In this enchanting narrative of her life, Alexander writes about her migration from one place to another, which left her with a feeling of homelessness. She describes herself as "a woman cracked by multiple migrations" who is "writing in search of a homeland." She depicts her childhood and adolescence in Kerela and Khartoum in Sudan, her life as an academic in Delhi and Hyderabad in India, and her life as an immigrant in the United States. She describes how she crosses cultural, geographical, and psychological boundaries as she searches for herself and a home. She has been "uprooted so many times she can connect nothing with nothing." She recounts the horror of moving to a new country as a five-year-old child and reflects upon her quest to reclaim that lost childhood. During this quest she crosses over the "fault lines" that are formed by altering loyalties to family members, languages, and cultures. The memoir was motivated by her search for a homeland and a sense of belonging.

Alexander writes about the obscurity of being in a female body in a society where gender differences are prominent. She reflects upon her culture and the expectations that are a part of being raised in a certain cultural milieu. Being a Syrian Christian born in India, she always felt that she was the "Other." This feeling does not end as she moves across countries. She records how she revives her spiritual identity through her poetry. Alexander writes about her grandfather, whose actions are motivated by the callous class system in India; her mother, who expects her to perform the traditional women's duties; her maternal grandmother, Kunju, and various other relatives and servants. Alexander also recounts that she knew six languages—Malayalam, Arabic, Hindi, Urdu, English and French—as a result of her multiple migrations.

Fault Lines reflects Alexander's struggles to come to terms with her own body, her state of homelessness amid continuous migrations, and her search for identity. Her reflections on her life also prompt her to examine larger themes of racism, arranged marriages, identity crisis, diasporic consciousness, and language retention, among others. Some of the chapters were presented as papers before they were compiled in the book, which is more of a collection of memories than a linear autobiography. Written in a sensitive style, the book is an easy read and filled with poetic expressions.

Asma Sayed

Fenkl, Heinz Insu   (1960–   )

A writer, editor, translator, and scholar of myth and folklore, Fenkl is currently the director of both the Creative Writing Program and ISIS: The Interstitial Studies Institute at State University of New York, New Paltz.

Fenkl was born in Inchun, Korea, in 1960, to a German-American father (who was a sergeant in the U.S. Army) and a Korean mother. Until he was 12 years old, Fenkl lived with his family in a camp town outside an American military base near Inchun. Following the duty stations of his father, Fenkl spent the rest of his childhood in Germany and in various parts of the United States, before his family finally settled in Castroville, California. After graduating from Vassar College, Fenkl returned to Korea as a Fulbright Scholar in 1984 to study folklore and shamanism.

Autobiographical in nature, Fenkl's first novel, *Memories of My Ghost Brother* (1996), is a bildungsroman of a young biracial boy, Insu, growing up in the destitute conditions of Korea in the late 1960s. Insu lives in a military camp town in postwar Korea among prostitutes, black marketers, and abandoned Amerasian children. According to Elaine H. Kim, the military camp town is a symbolic locus, wherein its inhabitants must "negotiate a complex and often shifting hierarchy of race, gender, class, and culture that emerges in the shadow of the American empire" (81). Insu's world is permeated with poignant stories of death, and the boundaries between the living and the dead are just as blurred as those between American soldiers and Korean locals. Cognizant of the ghost world, Insu finds himself confronting the specters of not only the Japanese occupation but also of his pregnant aunt who hangs herself after being abandoned by her G.I. lover, his friend James, whose mother kills her half-black son to attain a white husband, and his "ghost brother," whom his father sent away because he did not want to raise another man's son.

In *Memories of My Ghost Brother*, Fenkl addresses such provocative themes as Korean and American racism, neo-imperialism, military prostitution, and the interstitiality of Amerasian children. However, Fenkl seemingly tempers the political implications of such convoluted topics by employing young Insu as a naïve narrator. In tandem, numerous Korean ghost stories and traditional folktales reinforce a sense of cultural authenticity but obscure the themes of political import. Fenkl's strategic deployment of Insu as a naïve narrator achieves the very effect he had hoped for; readers appreciate the ethnic appeal of the novel, and at the same time, the details that may not befit a tale of a boy's journey into manhood are downplayed. Elided are the particular details of Insu's narrative—such as depravities of war, miscegenation, moral bankruptcy, and so forth—in favor of a universalized reading of the text as a bildungsroman.

Another critical thread that runs through the novel is the problematic relationship between Insu and his father. The uneasy tension between father and son is exacerbated by linguistic and cultural demarcations. Insu is rather aggrieved by the implications behind his father's insistence that he read Rudyard Kipling's *Kim,* a story of an Irish boy who grows up in colonized India until he is "saved" and sent to an Irish school by his father. Insu comes to recognize the disjunction between himself and his father:

> I could not imagine my voice joining my father's the way [another American's] did. I could not imagine how I would ever understand their

secret language of knowing glances and inside jokes. That was something that only yellow-haired soldiers could do. I would be forever tainted by a Koreanness.... (253–254)

Memories of My Ghost Brother was well received by both critics and readers, and was named a PEN/Hemingway finalist in 1997. Fenkl collaborated with another writer for his second novel, *Shadows Bend: A Novel of the Fantastic and Unspeakable* (2000), which was published under a pseudonym. Fenkl is the coeditor of *Kori: The Beacon Anthology of Korean American Literature* (2002) and *Century of the Tiger: One Hundred Years of Korean Culture in America* (2003). He has also published numerous short stories, translations of Korean fiction and folklore, and articles on folklore and myth. Currently, Fenkl is working on *Skull Water*—the sequel to *Memories of My Ghost Brother*—and on *Old, Old Days When Tigers Smoked Tobacco Pipes,* a book on Korean myths, legends, and folktales.

Bibliography

Fenkl, Heinz Insu. *Memories of My Ghost Brother.* New York: Dutton, 1996.
———. Heinz Insu Fenkl, Director, ISIS. *Spectator interview* by Piya Kochhar, "The Making of a Novel." Available online. URL: http://www.geocities.com/area51/rampart/2627/fenklpage.html. Accessed September 21, 2006.
Kim, Elaine H. "Myth, Memory, and Desire: Homeland and History in Contemporary Korean American Writing and Visual Art." In *Holding Their Own: Perspectives on the Multi-Ethnic Literatures of the United States,* edited by Dorothea Fischer-Hornung and Heike Raphael-Hernandez, 79–91. Tubingen, Germany: Stauffenberg-Verlag, 2000.

Hyeyurn Chung

Fifth Book of Peace, The
Maxine Hong Kingston (2003)

Like MAXINE HONG KINGSTON's first two books, *The WOMAN WARRIOR* (1976) and *CHINA MEN* (1980), *The Fifth Book of Peace* is a mix of fiction and nonfiction, autobiography and legend. The book's central topic is the potential connection between literature and nonviolence. Its first section, "Fire," chronicles the Oakland Hills Fire in October 1991, which resulted in California's largest-ever wildfire-related home loss, with more than 2,000 residences destroyed. Kingston had been working on a manuscript entitled "The Fourth Book of Peace" for nearly a decade, but when she returns to her gutted home after the fire, she finds that the entire manuscript—all print copies and backup computer files—has been reduced to ashes and melted plastic.

The second section, "Paper," presents the Chinese legend surrounding the three "Books of Peace," manuscripts produced at various times throughout Chinese history for the purpose of promoting peaceful resolutions to cultural conflicts. According to legend, the "Books of Peace" were burned by government officials who wished to perpetuate state-sponsored violence so that the pacifist teachings contained in the books would not be made available to the Chinese people. Kingston also discusses the long tradition of "the literature of war" in Asian and European cultures, and suggests that a fully developed "literature of peace" would assist cultures in developing nonmilitaristic ways of resolving conflicts.

"Water," the third section, is an attempt at reconstructing Kingston's lost manuscript. A self-contained novella, "Water" takes up the story of Wittman Ah Sing, the protagonist of *TRIPMASTER MONKEY* (1989), immediately after the ending of that novel. Ah Sing, his wife, Taña, and their son, Mario, move from California to Hawaii in an attempt to keep Wittman from being drafted and sent to Vietnam. In Hawaii, Wittman and his family find themselves at the center of a growing antiwar movement and help set up a "sanctuary" at the Church of the Crossroads. After weeks of living at the sanctuary, Wittman hears rumors that the U.S. military is preparing to raid the church and arrest the residents. The antiwar community braces for a confrontation with prowar forces, while Wittman and Taña make plans to ensure that Mario will never have to face a similar threat when he reaches draft age.

The final section, "Earth," is a long nonfiction account of Kingston's development of writing workshops for war veterans (with a large thematic emphasis on the second Iraq war, which had just begun as the book was undergoing its final revisions). Kingston suggests that by turning to writing as a way of dealing with their physical and psychological wounds, war veterans can offer some of the most eloquent voices in the construction of a "literature of peace."

Bibliography

Brickman, Julie. Review of *The Fifth Book of Peace*. *San Diego Union-Tribune,* 14 September 2003, Books Section, p. 5.

Hoong, Yong Shu. "The Fire of Peace: Chinese-American Author Maxine Hong Kingston Shares Her Views on Peace, Poetry, and Her New Book." *Straits Times* (Singapore), 10 April 2004, Life! Section.

McMillan, Alister. "Peace of the Action." *South China Morning Post,* 7 September 2003, People Section, p. 12.

Shulman, Polly. Review of *The Fifth Book of Peace*. *New York Times,* 28 September 2003, sec. 7, p. 8.

Eric G. Waggoner

Finding My Voice   Marie G. Lee (1992)

Ellen Sung is a high school senior in a small town called Arkin, Minnesota. In addition to dealing with the usual adolescent issues such as dating and wearing the right clothes on the first day of school, Ellen is under pressure from her parents to maintain straight A's and be accepted into Harvard like her perfect sister, Michelle. She ignores students who call her "chink" on the first day of school, and decides not to think about "what it means to be different" (6). Ellen struggles under her sister's shadow, preferring English to calculus, and she dates Tomper Sandel, a popular white football player. Tension escalates as Marsha, a white cheerleader and fellow gymnast, taunts Ellen with racial epithets and flirts with Tomper in an effort to steal him away. At the end of the novel, Marsha attacks Ellen in a drunken rage at a summer party, but Ellen does not press charges. Finding her voice,

she learns that she "can speak for [her]self . . . but that doesn't mean that racist people are going to go away" (207).

As the novel progresses, Ellen grows in consciousness amid the daily struggle of being a Korean American among all white students. She becomes curious to learn about her parents' past and what her Korean-American identity really means. She regrets not earlier confronting the teacher and classmates who made racist comments to her throughout the school year. Although she accepts the Harvard offer of admission that she has worked so hard for, Ellen acknowledges that in acquiescing to her parents' pressure regarding college, she is "silencing [her] own voice" (179).

MARIE G. LEE explores issues of race and identity by portraying the conflict between Ellen and Marsha, as well as the intergenerational conflict between Ellen and her parents. Ellen's growth is evident throughout the novel as she begins to acknowledge and confront racism from her classmates and teachers. Lee builds up Ellen's consciousness and ability to speak up when attacked both physically and verbally, but in the climactic finale Ellen decides not to press charges. Her decision suggests that racism, especially physically violent racism against Asian Americans, can go unpunished. She finds her voice, but she is not using it to its maximum effectiveness.

Bibliography

Lee, Marie G. *Finding My Voice*. New York: Houghton Mifflin, 1992.

Sarah Park

FOB   David Henry Hwang (1979)

DAVID HENRY HWANG himself directed *FOB* when it premiered on March 2, 1979, at the Stanford Asian American Theatre Project in Palo Alto, California. The play was also produced at the Eugene O'Neill National Playwrights Conference at Waterford, Connecticut, in July 1979. Most significant, a production of *FOB* opened at New York City's Public Theater on June 8, 1980. This off-Broadway production won an Obie Award for Best New Play.

In March 2005, the Magic Theatre of San Francisco hosted a revival directed by Mitzie Abe. *FOB* anticipates many themes and traits that characterize Hwang's subsequent plays: Asian immigrants' dilemmas about assimilation into American society; links to other, well-known literary texts; and the skillful incorporation of both naturalistic and non-naturalistic staging techniques.

At some points, the play seems like naturalistic, almost kitchen-sink family drama. At other times, the playwright's striking deployment of stage lighting, direct addresses to the audience, and the use of Chinese mythology make the play more expressionistic and anti-illusionary. Clear echoes from important Asian-American texts, like those of FRANK CHIN and MAXINE HONG KINGSTON, also underline the play's literary, non-naturalistic style. For instance, the character of Steve in Hwang's play identifies himself with Gwan Gung, a legendary Chinese warrior featured in Chin's unpublished play, *Gee, Pop!* (1974). Although the comparison between a skinny young man and a legendary warrior is laughable, it represents Steve's desire to retain his Chinese identity. Steve gets angry when other Chinese Americans do not know about the legend of Gwan Gung, and he is particularly irate when one youth prefers to follow Jesus Christ rather than Gwan Gung. Asian Americans' desire to follow Western deities (including money) rather than to maintain Chinese culture is represented in *FOB* by the character of Dale. Grace, Dale's cousin and a UCLA student, identifies herself with Fa Mu Lan, a Chinese legendary female fighter featured in Kingston's memoir, *The* WOMAN WARRIOR. Physical, practical, and intelligent, Grace pursues her own choices in life.

FOB's action takes place in one day in Los Angeles as Grace, Dale, and Steve go out to eat in a Chinese restaurant. Steve, an FOB (new immigrant, "Fresh Off the Boat") is given a hostile reception by Dale, an ABC ("American-Born Chinese"). Dale looks down on Steve, who harbors the idealistic notion that he can retain an uncomplicated Chinese identity in America. Steve, however, is given a warm welcome by Grace, who arrived in America when she was 10 years old. Both Dale and Steve are romantically attracted to Grace; indeed, their struggle for her favor mirrors their competing attitudes. As they fight over the young woman, they fight over lifestyle choices: Dale insists that every immigrant must "decide to become an American," but Steve wants to retain Asian habits. Simple moments of comedy typify this competition. For instance, Steve insists on eating large quantities of hot, Shanghai-style sauce, which appalls Dale, who calls Steve a "fucking savage" and even a "cannibal." Dale's irrational language of abuse echoes Western racist remarks about non-Europeans.

Hwang's play suggests that the gulf between assimilated Asian Americans and new immigrants is enormous. Grace remembers that she tried to be white when she was younger, even bleaching her hair, because "I figured I had a better chance of getting in with the white kids than with" Asian Americans. Although Dale is a comical figure in many ways—when he first enters, he is knocked to the ground by an alarmed Grace—Hwang does not condemn the character. Dale has had his own struggles against racism and stereotyping. He has chosen to act like a white American because he desired to be "a human being, like everyone else," not "a yellow, a slant, a gook." Although Dale loses the battle for Grace's affection and therefore becomes bitter, he accepts Grace's decision to court Steve and to choose the lifestyle of the consciously Chinese rather than the totally assimilated Asian American.

Bibliography

Hwang, David Henry. *FOB*. In His *Trying to Find Chinatown: The Selected Plays*, 1–51. New York: Theatre Communications Group, 2000.

Kevin De Ornellas

Fong-Torres, Ben (1945–)

Born in Alameda, California, Ben Fong-Torres grew up in Oakland, where his parents owned and operated a restaurant in Chinatown. His parents expected him to be part of their family business, but Fong-Torres had other plans. He graduated from San Francisco State College in 1966 with a degree in radio-television-film and worked for two years as an editor at various publications in the area, such as his day job at Pacific Telephone's employee magazine and his volunteer work at night for a bilingual paper called *East-West*. He began working full time for *Rolling Stone* magazine in May 1969. In time, Fong-Torres became something of a star writer during his time at *Rolling Stone*, winning a Deems Taylor Award for Magazine Writing in 1974 for an interview he conducted with Ray Charles. Fong-Torres eventually stayed with the magazine until 1981, interviewing artists as diverse as Bob Dylan, Stevie Wonder, Diane Keaton, Bonnie Raitt, and the Grateful Dead during his tenure there. He is also the last known person to have interviewed Jim Morrison before he left for Paris and later died in early July 1971.

The Deems Taylor Award is not his only award, nor is journalism his only field. He won a Billboard Award for Broadcast Excellence for a syndicated radio special that he wrote and narrated, called *San Francisco: What a Long, Strange Trip It's Been*. Though he is best known today as a rock journalist, Fong-Torres has actually worked extensively in radio and TV. He completed profiles of celebrity interviews on *Evening Magazine* in 1977, frequently taping the introductions to the segments from his *Rolling Stone* offices. During his time at *Rolling Stone*, Fong-Torres worked as a disc jockey on the weekends for a San Francisco radio station (1970–79); in addition, he later hosted Fog City Weekly (a weekly arts show that began in December 1994 and lasted less than a year), as well as coanchoring coverage of the Chinese New Year parades each year since 1997. Quirkily, in 1993, he "won big" on *Wheel of Fortune*, netting some $99,000 in cash and prizes. But he may be most familiar to readers as a real-life character in *Almost Famous*, the 2000 film by director-writer Cameron Crowe, in which his character was played by Terry Chen.

After leaving *Rolling Stone* in 1981, Fong-Torres worked as a screenwriter on such projects as *Cycling through China* (1982). The following year, he joined the *San Francisco Chronicle* as a feature writer and radio columnist until 1992, when he left to write his memoirs, *The Rice Room: From Number Two Son to Rock and Roll* (1994). This book details not only his life but also that of his brother Barry, who was shot to death in his San Francisco apartment in June 1972. After completing his memoirs, Fong-Torres joined the staff of a San Francisco-based trade weekly for the radio and recording industries, *Gavin*, as managing editor. He held the post until 1997 before leaving to complete his book, *The Hits Just Keep On Coming: The History of Top 40 Radio* (1998). That same year, Fong-Torres began writing the script for the nationally broadcast induction ceremonies at the Radio Hall of Fame. Widely anthologized among his pieces are *Garcia; The Rolling Stone Film Reader; The American's Search for Identity;* and *Chink!: Studies in Ethnic Prejudice*. In 1991 he published *Hickory Wind: The Life and Times of Gram Parsons*, which was nominated for the Ralph J. Gleason Book Award.

Besides contributing pieces to *The Encyclopedia of Country Music*, the CD-ROM version of the *Encyclopedia Britannica*, and *The Motown Album: The Sound of Young America*, Fong-Torres wrote the main biographies for *People* magazine's tributes to Jerry Garcia and Frank Sinatra, and his articles have appeared in a wide range of magazines including *Esquire*, *GQ* (where he was pop music columnist for three years), *Parade*, *Sports Illustrated*, *Travel & Leisure*, *American Film*, *TV Guide*, *Harper's Bazaar* and *California Business*, among others. In 1999 Miller Freeman published *Not Fade Away: A Backstage Pass to 20 Years of Rock & Roll*, a compilation of 34 articles from Fong-Torres's time at *Rolling Stone*. Fong-Torres has since worked as editorial director of myplay.com as well as vice president of Content at Collabrys, a company that does brand marketing.

As a second-generation Chinese American, Fong-Torres has long been open to speaking and giving advice about being Asian American and working in media. When he began at *Rolling Stone* more than three decades ago, there were few Asian Americans working in these fields. He has been a pioneer in this regard and continues to serve as a role model within the community, emceeing community events, writing pieces for Asianconnections.com, and becoming a curator at the Rock and Roll Hall of Fame in Cleveland. He was also named San Francisco State College's Alumnus of the Year for 2003.

Anne N. Thalheimer

Foreigner   Nahid Rachlin (1978)

Feri, a young Iranian woman, comes to America as a foreign student in a small women's college. Lonely at school, she chooses biology as her haven to acquire a sense of belonging through understanding the breaking down and building up of cells. In graduate school, she meets her future husband, a charming American. The relationship, once built on excitement over their contrasting backgrounds, descends into an empty marriage between two workaholics. After a miscarriage, infidelities on her part, and assumed but unconfirmed ones on his part, Feri returns for a short visit to her family in Iran. A small traditional family consisting of a father, stepmother, Ziba, and stepbrother, Darius, they live in a quieter and less Westernized part of Iran. Her family offers her questions rather than provides comfort to assuage her feelings of alienation. During the visit, she realizes that she has become a foreigner in her own country and even more so in her own family. On a whim, she decides to search for her long lost mother, a beautiful woman who had left her family in the middle of the night for a dashing young lover only to be abandoned by him a short time later. Left alone and unable to return to her family because she had broken with tradition, Feri's mother disappears into the outskirts of Iran, where she lives among the architectural ruins of an ancient city. Feri discovers her mother and finds a semblance of peace. It is here where she confronts her feelings about her husband and the deep fissures in her life. Interestingly enough, the only time she finds a place for herself in her motherland, which bewilders her at first, is within the ruins of her mother's home. Feri is reborn within the cavernous ruins of her mother.

Feri is stricken with a sense of living life behind a plate of glass. After her miscarriage, she seems to lock herself inside her head, unreachable by the husband she once loved. She is even diagnosed with a serious ulcer, a dull pain she becomes aware of after entering her father's home; only during her reunion with her mother is the ulcer treated. She is, in a sense, "eating" herself from the inside, embodying what psychoanalyst Julia Kristeva calls "cannibalistic solitude," a term used to describe feminine depression.

Like many of NAHID RACHLIN's protagonists in her later novels, Feri is heavily burdened with guilt for having abandoned family obligations, especially in a culture that emphasizes family over all else. Feri cannot come to peace with herself by just buying her mother a new house, giving money to a cousin to help with the wedding of her daughter, and returning to the United States. There is a discomfort in her spirit that keeps her in Iran to care for her mother. Filial obligation takes precedence over her marriage to a husband who does not understand her and looks upon her world with condescension. The novel ends with a sense of ambivalence about whether or not Feri will return to America.

Foreigner was welcomed with rave reviews for its honesty, its stark narrative style, and its deep sense of alienation; its ambience has been compared to that of Albert Camus's *The Stranger*. It continues to capture readers' imagination and is consistently taught in universities across the nation.

Zohra Saed

For Matrimonial Purposes
Kavita Daswani (2003)

This is the debut novel of the South Asian–American fashion journalist turned author, KAVITA DASWANI. The central character is Anju, a young woman who lives with her affluent parents in Mumbai, India. Anju and her parents believe that marriage and motherhood are a woman's destiny, and they frantically search for a good husband for Anju. Unfortunately, Anju does not meet her ideal husband and remains single at age 33, in contrast to many of her friends and younger cousins who are married and have children. When an astrologer predicts that Anju may have to wait awhile before she is married, she persuades her parents to let her go to New York for graduate education. Her parents agree because she will live with her relatives and because they hope she can meet eligible young Indo-American men in New York.

Anju's experience in New York is transformative as she discovers her talents in public relations and embarks on a career, much against her parents' wishes. In her quest for a husband, Anju has a brief romance with an American man, which does not work out because of the vast cultural differences between them. Her matrimonial quest becomes the subject of humor and concern for her friends both Indian and American. Eventually Anju discovers Indian matrimonial Web sites and meets a man who lives in Los Angeles. Neither Anju nor her boyfriend discloses their courtship to either's parents since they want the relationship to flourish without the influence of their respective families. They fall in love and get married at a grand ceremony in India.

The novel is a romantic comedy that humorously exposes the flaws in both Indian and American societies. Daswani's characters are funny, charming, and very human, and the novel has a dynamic plot. As a writer, Daswani takes the conventional theme of the clash of cultures and explores ways in which her heroine is able to bridge both cultures and draw upon the best in both to shape her life.

Nalini Iyer

Fox Girl   Nora Okja Keller (2002)

Nora Okja Keller followed the success of her debut novel, *Comfort Woman,* with an equally successful second novel that has confirmed Keller's capacity to illuminate dark corners in history and established her as a powerful voice. *Fox Girl,* which was long-listed for the 2003 Orange Prize, is set primarily in Korea in the mid-1960s after the Korean War and tells the story of two young Korean girls who are forced to struggle to survive by turning to the desperate world of prostitution in "America Town," a military town in southern Korea serving American GIs. Again, as in *Comfort Woman,* Keller is concerned with bringing aware-

ness to a subject too long neglected—that of the lives of "the 'throwaway' people of the postwar Korean-American towns: biracial bastard children of U.S. servicemen and the Korean prostitutes who hold onto these children as they hope for a passport to America" (Ho 118).

At the center of the narrative is the confident and cocky Hyun Jin, whose seemingly privileged and prosperous life—her parents own a store, there are regular meals, and her biggest worry is maintaining her perfect attendance record at school—is suddenly shattered. When she learns of her true parentage as the daughter of a prostitute, Hyun Jin is abandoned and reduced to making her way on her own. Sookie, her best friend, is abandoned out of necessity by her mother, Duk Hee, a former sex slave to the Japanese imperial army and now a prostitute. The two girls, confronted with extremely limited options, end up working the bars and shanties of America Town, pimped by their one-time school nemesis, Lobetto. The harsh realities of daily life for the two girls are tempered by fleeting moments of tenderness when the violence and betrayals they endure at the hands of complete strangers, and each other, give way to a deeper sense of loyalty and even love. Both Hyun Jin and Sookie manage to escape to Hawaii, but ultimately the effort to make money and stay alive takes too great a toll on the friendship and, by the novel's end, Hyun Jin and Sookie part ways, sadly confirming Sookie's assertion, "Each one of us is always alone. You can't depend on anyone" (140).

The Korean legend of the fox girl, from which the novel derives its title, offers a powerful framework for considering Keller's work. The shape-shifting creature seeking to regain something stolen from her could easily be Hyun Jin, or Sookie, or indeed any of Keller's female protagonists who are faced with the task of reclaiming what is rightfully theirs. One might even argue that Keller is herself the fox girl, attempting to restore the voice stolen from history's forgotten women—an attempt that will undoubtedly continue in her next novel.

Bibliography
Ho, Jennifer. Review of *Fox Girl* by Nora Okja Keller. *Amerasia Journal* 30, no. 2 (2004): 117–119.

Keller, Nora Okja. *Fox Girl.* New York: Penguin Books, 2002.

Dana Hansen

Frontiers of Love, The Diana Chang (1956)

The first and best-known novel of DIANA CHANG, *The Frontiers of Love* explores the issues of racial and cultural hybridity by depicting three Eurasian characters living in Shanghai in 1945 toward the end of World War II: 20-year-old Sylvia Chen (the daughter of a Chinese father, Liyi Chen, and an American mother, Helen); 19-year-old Mimi Lambert (the daughter of an Australian father and a Chinese mother); and 26-year-old Feng Huang (the son of a wealthy Chinese lawyer and an Englishwoman).

The novel opens with Sylvia's reflections on her divisiveness between her Chinese father and American mother. Sylvia, however, does not define herself through racial identity; unlike other Eurasian characters, she is able to come to grips with her life by growing up to be "Sylvia Chen"—not Chinese like nostalgic Liyi and not American like domineering Helen. In contrast, Feng abandons his English half and assumes the Chinese heritage. Resenting his aggressive, condescending English mother, he drops his English name, Farthington, for Huang. Mimi, the opposite of Feng, rejects everything Chinese and embraces her Caucasian half. After her Swiss lover, Robert Bruno, impregnates her but refuses to marry her due to her mixed racial origin, Mimi throws herself at any white man to get herself out of China. Mimi's rancor stems from the duality in herself and results in sexual promiscuity and self-loathing, which, in turn, cause her annihilation.

The tripartite perspective is juxtaposed with the viewpoints of two Chinese characters. Sixteen-year-old Peiyuan, born and raised in China, is "an untainted Chinese." Peiyuan's rustic appearance antagonizes Helen, who hates the "part savage, part leprous and totally mysterious" Chinese (48). Although he is the only character not in conflict with his identity, Peiyuan's chauvinism leads to his death in the minefield of Communist strife.

Sylvia's father, Liyi, despite his full-blooded Chineseness, is divided within himself like the three Eurasians. Liyi's Western liberal stance toward politics and his nostalgia for old China place him in a "between-worlds" condition: between the present reality and the unattainable past. At the end of the story, Liyi is able to reconcile the two halves and realize the vital force of love and responsibility. Judging from the closing of the novel, in which Liyi envisions Eurasian children as new citizens for a growing country, the author seems to suggest that self is something that one creates and constantly improvises.

It is noteworthy that vis-à-vis the inner loops of the Eurasian characters lies a metaphorical Shanghai in the narrative. Japanese-occupied Shanghai before the end of World War II stands as a geographical and cultural contact zone with the West, as a "Eurasian city" where the Chinese, Japanese, French, British, and Americans cohabit, rendering the city "both Chinese and Western, native and foreign, liberatory and oppressive, national and international" (Lim viii). Like the Eurasians, Shanghai emerges as a central symbol of hybridity and cosmopolitanism.

Bibliography

Baringer, Sandra. "'The Hybrids and the Cosmopolitans': Race, Gender, and Masochism in Diana Chang's *The Frontiers of Love.*" *Essays on Mixed-Race Literature,* edited by Jonathan Brennan, 107–121. Palo Alto, Calif.: Stanford University Press, 2002.

Lim, Shirley Geok-lin. Introduction. In *The Frontiers of Love,* v–xxiii. Seattle: University of Washington Press, 1994.

Ling, Amy. *Between Worlds: Women Writers of Chinese Ancestry.* New York: Pergamon, 1990.

Bennett Fu

Fulbeck, Kip (1965–)

The author/artist Kip Fulbeck was born in Fontana, California, to a Chinese mother and a Caucasian American father. Fulbeck's father, an English professor at California State Polytechnic University, Pomona, was also a writer and published poet, and Fulbeck counts him among his influences. As a student at South Hills High School in West Covina, California, Fulbeck excelled in swimming and at age 16 was ranked sixth in the nation. While keeping an interest in painting and drawing, he initially gravitated toward a career in medicine but eventually received an M.F.A. in Visual Arts from University of California, San Diego, in 1992. Currently a professor of art at the University of California, Santa Barbara, Fulbeck has been an artist-in-residence at Albion College in Albion, Michigan, and a visiting professor at the University of Michigan and the University of California, Berkeley.

While a graduate student, through film and the visual arts, Fulbeck began to explore the issue of mixed-race Asian identity, using the term *hapa,* which originally derived from Hawaiian slang for someone who is half Hawaiian and half white, but has now come to designate anyone who is an Asian/Pacific Islander. In 1991 he created *Banana Split,* a 37-minute short film exploring mixed race identity, which won numerous awards including first place at the Red River International Film Festival. Fulbeck was also named Best Local Filmmaker at the Santa Barbara International Film Festival. His other films include *Asian Studs Nightmare; Sex, Love & Kung Fu,* and *Lilo and Me*—a humorous video that compares Fulbeck's image to "ethnically ambiguous" characters in Disney films such as *Lilo & Stitch, Aladdin,* and *Pocahontas.* While the visual medium is an important aspect of Fulbeck's work on mixed Asian ethnicity in America, he has also contributed to the growing scholarship on this topic via the print medium.

Fulbeck is the author of *Paper Bullets: A Fictional Autobiography,* a memoir about growing up half-Chinese in a largely white community. As one of the very few memoirs dealing with the experience of being of mixed Asian race, this work contributes to the growing field of Asian-American literature by expanding its borders. In this semifictional account of his life, Fulbeck mixes reality with invention to uncover the larger truths surrounding the issues of dating and sex, family and friends, and finding one's way in the confusing landscape of contemporary America. This frank memoir muses

upon the effects of racial and ethnic stereotypes and mixes in a pastiche of popular songs, movies, TV shows, and other cultural ephemera, while exploring his growing political and personal awareness of race and ethnicity and the large part that it has played in shaping the person he has come to be.

Fulbeck has continued to explore racial identity through various performances and visual media, most notably in his photographic project entitled "The Hapa Project," a collection of photographs of self-identified mixed-race Asian/Pacific Islanders. Also included are their answers to the question, "What are you?" A book from this project, *Part Asian, 100% Hapa,* was published by Chronicle Books in 2006. Fulbeck states that the impetus behind the publishing of the Hapa Project is that he "wished a book like this had been around when I was growing up." Fulbeck's appeal and importance lie in his willingness to squarely confront and examine the ever-changing landscape of Asian America with humor, irony, and frankness.

Bibliography
Fulbeck, Kip. *Paper Bullets: A Fictional Autobiography.* Seattle: University of Washington Press, 2001.
———. *Part-Asian, 100% Hapa.* San Francisco: Chronicle Books, 2006.
Glancy, Diane, and C. W. Truesdale, eds. *Two Worlds Walking: An Anthology of Mixed Blood Writers.* Minneapolis: New Rivers Press, 1994.
Kip Fulbeck. Personal Web site focusing on the Hapa Project. Available online. URL: http://www.seaweedproductions.com. Accessed September 22, 2006.

Valerie Solar

Furutani, Dale (1946–)
Sansei author Dale Furutani was born in Hilo, Hawaii, on December 1, 1946. His grandparents emigrated from Oshima Island, just south of Hiroshima, Japan, to Hawaii, to work on sugar plantations in 1896. His grandfather later escaped plantation work to become a fisherman. At five, Furutani was adopted by John Flanagan

and moved to California, where he later received a B.A. in creative writing from California State University, Long Beach, and earned an M.B.A. from UCLA. He worked at both Mitsubishi Motors and Nissan Motors as an independent consultant and has served as CIO for Edmunds.com since leaving Nissan. Furutani has published fiction, nonfiction, and poetry. On three occasions, Furutani had been invited to speak at the U.S. Library of Congress as a mystery author and as an Asian-American author. According to the Library of Congress, Furutani has the honored distinction of being the first Asian-American author to win major mystery writing awards. He has received the Macavity Award for Best First Mystery Novel and the Anthony Award for Best First Novel in 1997 for *Death in Little Tokyo: A Ken Tanaka Mystery,* which also garnered an Agatha Award nomination.

Furutani's 1996 mystery novel, *Death in Little Tokyo,* considered "the very first Japanese-American amateur sleuth mystery written by a Japanese American," maps the eponymous Japanese-American enclave as a space that displays a political, economic, and social interconnectedness with the surrounding communities and to the larger city as a whole. In addition to the Little Tokyo area, the main character's dealings take him to geographical spaces in outlying LA suburbs, such as Silver Lake, West LA (UCLA), Pasadena, and Culver City, as well as to businesses in the Wilshire district and to the Boyle Heights area in East Los Angeles.

In this first-person point of view narrative, the protagonist, Ken Tanaka, a second-generation Japanese-American amateur detective in between jobs, becomes the filter through which readers encounter and understand aspects of Japanese-American history and culture. The novel introduces *Obon* festivals both in Hawaii and on the mainland, the internment camps, the coercive legalities regarding immigration quotas and citizenship status, and the 1970s controversy over razing parts of Little Tokyo to make way for the investment of Japanese national capital for tourism.

In *Death in Little Tokyo,* the references to and explanation of Heart Mountain and Manzanar internment camps serve to show World War II as a historical event that was not discrete. Rather,

important plot turns and character development rest upon the unconstitutionality of this government action. In the novel, the nisei and *kibei nisei* (Japanese Americans born in the United States but raised in Japan) are polarized as a result of the internment camps and the army's loyalty questionnaire. Thus, the present-day murder mystery involving *yakuza* (gangster) ties and fraudulent activities that must be solved is inextricably linked to the Japanese-American dislocation more than 50 years ago. By the novel's end, Ken Tanaka exposes a *yakuza*-based fraudulent crime scheme and ultimately discovers the true motive for the murder of a *kibei nisei* (with ties to the *yakuza*), who was hacked to death in his hotel room by the killer using a samurai-type sword. The development of this nonexotic Japanese-American detective by a Japanese-American writer delightfully subverts any stereotypical or flat qualities that may have cropped up in past novels with Asian detectives.

To date, Furutani has published five mystery novels. *The Toyotomi Blades* is a 1997 follow-up to *Death in Little Tokyo,* with Ken Tanaka visiting Tokyo due to the publicity he received for solving a crime in the previous novel. Furutani has also published a *Los Angeles Times* best-selling historical mystery trilogy involving Kaze Matsuyama, a samurai whose master has been killed: *Death at the Crossroads* (1998), *Jade Palace Vendetta* (1999), and *Kill the Shogun* (2000). This trilogy follows the protagonist's adventures as he searches for the missing daughter of his slain lord. Set in 1603 Japan, these novels give readers a strong sense of the period's atmosphere and the protagonist's physical and mental cunning as a skilled samurai.

Furutani and his wife, Sharon, spent several years living, traveling and working in Japan and presently live in the Pacific Northwest. Called "a master craftsman" by *Publishers Weekly,* Furutani is currently "working on books set in 1550 Japan and modern Los Angeles, featuring new lead characters."

Bibliography

Dale Furutani Web site. Available online. URL: http:// members.aol.com/dfurutani. Accessed April 25, 2006.

Furutani, Dale. "Furutani's Samurai Mystery Trilogy Plumbs His Ancestry." Interview by Ron Miller. 2000. Available online. URL: http://www.thecolumnists.com/miller/miller62.html. Accessed April 26, 2006.

———. Interview with Dale Furutani, by Claire E. White. January 1998. Available online. URL: http://www.writerswrite.com/journal/jan98/furutani.htm. Accessed April 22, 2006.

Suzanne K. Arakawa

Ganesan, Indira (1960–)

Born in Srirangam, India, Ganesan moved to St. Louis, Missouri, at age five. Best known for her contribution to the growing body of contemporary Indian literature, Ganesan has been compared to writers such as Arundhati Roy and CHITRA BANERJEE DIVAKARUNI. She received her bachelor of arts degree in English from Vassar College in 1982 and a master of fine arts in fiction from the University of Iowa in 1984.

Ganesan received fellowships from the Mary Ingraham Bunting Institute at Radcliffe (1997–98), the Fine Arts Work Center in Provincetown (1984–85), the MacDowell Colony, and the Paden Institute for Writers of Color in Essex, New York. She was also a Vassar College W.K. Rose Fellow. She has held teaching positions at Vassar College, Radcliffe College, the University of Missouri, the University of San Diego, and the University of California at Santa Cruz. Ganesan currently teaches in the Humanities Division at Southampton College of Long Island University, at New College of California's Writing and Consciousness Program, and is on the creative writing faculty at Lesley University. She was also a faculty mentor at the North Country Institute and Retreat for Writers of Color.

She has been a fiction editor for the literary journal *Many Mountains Moving* and wrote the introduction to the Signet Classic edition of *Nectar in a Sieve* by Kamala Markandaya. Ganesan's work has been anthologized in *Half & Half: Writers on Growing Up Biracial & Bicultural,* and she is widely published in several literary journals and women's magazines. Ganesan was also a judge for the 2003 First Words South Asian Literary Prize.

Ganesan's novels include *The JOURNEY* (1990), for which she was selected as a finalist in Granta's Best Young American Novelists Under Forty contest (1996), and *INHERITANCE* (1998), chosen as a Barnes & Noble Discover New Writers selection for Winter 1998. Her novels weave the intricacy of family with the desire to become independent. In the end, the novel's sense of family is so closely interwoven with the ability to be independent that it no longer appears to be a negative circumstance of living but rather a welcome space to reside in. Ganesan also thematizes the sense of loss, the transposition of bicultural lives, and the struggle between Indian cultural tradition and contemporary Western society.

Anne Marie Fowler

Gangster of Love, The
Jessica Hagedorn (1996)

The Gangster of Love is the second novel of Filipino-American writer and multimedia artist JESSICA HAGEDORN. It portrays the connections and divergences between Filipino and Filipino-American identities, a topic already present in Hagedorn's first novel, DOGEATERS. Spanning the period from the 1970s to the early 1990s, *The Gangster of Love* depicts the life of Rocky Rivera and her family and friends. Rocky moves to the United States as a teenager with her mother and brother in 1970, leaving her father and sister in the Philippines. Once in her new country, she forms a rock band called The Gangster of Love and witnesses the counterculture of 1970s San Francisco and Los Angeles and 1980s Manhattan. Rocky's path mirrors loosely the life of Hagedorn, who also moved from the Philippines to San Francisco after her parents' divorce, formed a rock group called The Gangster Choir, and later moved to New York.

As Rocky deals with her heterogeneous cultural background, she acknowledges her ambivalent feelings toward both the Philippines and older Filipino Americans like her mother Milagros, her uncle Marlon, and the street poet the Carabao Kid. She understands their life choices better when she becomes a mother herself in the book's second part, and even more when Milagros becomes ill and dies in the third part. The fourth part depicts Rocky's return to the Philippines to visit her father, a physical and personal journey providing an antithesis to her emigration to the United States.

Through its portrayal of Rocky Rivera's family, *The Gangster of Love* reflects on the Philippines' history of colonialism and neo-colonialism. It focuses particularly on the migration processes from the islands to the United States and vice versa, which closely reflect this history. Rocky's and Milagros's past in the Philippines and their lives in the United States merge in the vignette "Side Show," which closes the novel's second part. It depicts the trial of Imelda Marcos, the wife of President Ferdinand Marcos, whose turbulent regime lasted from 1965 until 1986. Rather than dealing with Imelda's guilt and fate, however, Hagedorn describes the feelings of Rocky's mother, aunt, and uncle during the trial.

Rocky's personal development is also intertwined with her exploration of love and sexuality. The main catalysts for her development are her musician boyfriend Elvis Chang and her artist friend Keiko Van Heller, two Asian-American characters of mixed backgrounds. Elvis and Keiko encourage Rocky to reinvent herself and not be defined primarily by her ethnic, socioeconomic, and family background. In contrast to *Dogeaters*, which investigates the relationship between identity and cinema, Rocky's search for identity is portrayed in connection with her love for rock music. Her aesthetic sense is most powerfully shaped by ethnic minorities' art forms, particularly black and Asian American, and her experiences as a Filipina in the United States strengthen her affinity with the history and image of America embodied by these artistic traditions.

Like *Dogeaters*, *The Gangster of Love* uses narrative techniques associated with postcolonial and postmodern writing, such as fragmentation, parody, and pastiche. It also blurs the boundaries between historical accounts, personal stories, and fiction. The novel questions who and what makes history, mixing historical references with gossip and interspersing the narrative with dreams, fictional script fragments, dictionary definitions, and statements by both famous historical figures and fictional characters. By doing so, *The Gangster of Love* intensely examines how personal identities are constructed across racial, ethnic, national, sociocultural, and gender categories.

Bibliography

Davis, Rocío G., ed. *MELUS: Special Issue on Filipino American Literature* 29, no. 1 (Spring 2004).

Miles, Chris, Jessica Heerwald, and Tina Avent. "Voices from the Gaps: Jessica Hagedorn." Available online. URL: http://voices.cla.umn.edu/vg/Bios/entries/hagedorn_jessica_tarahata.html. Downloaded September 23, 2006.

Sengupta, Somini. "Jessica Hagedorn: Cultivating the Art of the Melange" (December 4, 1996). Available online. URL: http://www.english.uiuc.edu/maps/poets/g_l/hagedorn/about.htm. (Reproduced from Nando Times. URL: http://somerset.nando.net/newsroom/magazine/ thirdrave/dec496/stars/1204me.html). Downloaded on July 21, 2003.

Marta Vizcaya Echano

Gangster We Are All Looking For, The
lê thi diem thúy (2003)

The partly autobiographical novel, *The Gangster We Are All Looking For,* is a series of vignettes recounting the experience of a nameless narrator. A refugee of the Vietnam War, the six-year-old narrator "stepped into the China Sea" (3) to travel to "the other side" (4) in San Diego with her father and four uncles. When the narrator and her family are taken in by Mel, the son of their sponsors, the narrator becomes obsessed with Mel's glass animal collection, specifically a brown butterfly "trapped" in a glass disc. In an effort to free the butterfly, the narrator breaks most of Mel's glass animals, resulting in the expulsion of the family.

The narrator and her father, "Ba," are eventually joined by the narrator's mother, "Ma." LÊ THI DIEM THÚY uses "Ma" to provide the most palpable response to sorrow, loss, and exile, whereas "Ba" is prone to silence, tears, and drunken rage. The marriage becomes volatile, eventually revealing Ma's lament for her past, parents, and homeland. As her sorrow over exile grows, she begins to blame her husband for her disconnection from family and home. "Ba" is the "gangster," a Buddhist man from the North who served in the South Vietnamese army, possibly a black market vendor, and a prisoner of re-education. In marrying him, the mother has defied her Catholic parents and been disinherited. The exile in America has ensured her inability to reconcile with her parents, and she seeks solace in minor things, such as a pool at their apartment. It creates a connection to her family by water, and when the landlord fills it with cement, she is greatly troubled. In the second apartment, "Ma" receives a photograph of her parents. However, the family is evicted, and Ma later realizes the photo, the only tangible connection to her parents, has been left behind, and she has betrayed them again. Her sense of loss and guilt is subtly mirrored by the narrator's longing for her dead brother. At times his absence is so overwhelming that the narrator is overcome with fear and panic.

Le's novel has been hailed for its precise and poetic prose. It is a refugee story of loss, "of youthful yearning and adult resignation," and "the tenacity of memory" (Baumann). The novel is a look into an aspect of the Vietnam War that is rarely seen: the effects of exile and immeasurable loss on the Vietnamese. A piece of the novel was originally published in *The Massachusetts Review* and later in *Best American Essays '97.*

Bibliography

Baumann, Paul. "Washing Time Away." *New York Times Book Review,* 25 May 2003, p. 26.

De Jesus, Linda. "Le Thi Diem Thuy." *Asian American Poets: A Bio-Bibliographic Critical Sourcebook,* edited by Guiyou Huang. Westport, Conn.: Greenwood Press, 2002.

Mehegan, David. "Refuge in Her Writing." Available online. URL:http://faculty.washington.edu/kendo.thuymehegan.html. Accessed September 23, 2006.

Tina Powell

Gathering of Pearls
Sook Nyul Choi (1994)

Gathering of Pearls is the third novel in SOOK NYUL CHOI's autobiographical series that begins with *YEAR OF IMPOSSIBLE GOODBYES.* In *Gathering,* the protagonist Sookan has achieved her dream of traveling to America to attend Finch College, a Catholic all-girls college. The novel is introspective and explores the many fears and cultural challenges that Sookan faces when she arrives and lives in the United States. Sookan must come to terms with trying to live up to her Korean family's extremely high expectations of her, while fulfilling her own personal desires as well. The novel opens with Sookan's meditative apprehensions about her arrival in a strange country and of the many unknowns she will face. When she arrives to find that no one is there to meet her at the airport, the realization of just how far she is from home overwhelms her: "The memory of Mother's soothing voice rang in my ears. I was glad she was not here to see me standing all alone in the big, empty airport, feeling scared and unwanted" (4). Sookan soon settles into the school, where she begins to make insightful observations on daily life and the many different aspects of Korean and American cultures.

Choi's *Gathering* does not have the suspense and action of her previous two novels, yet *Gathering* is an apt finale to Sookan's war experience. The juxtaposition between the physical hardships Sookan endured in the first two novels and the hardship she endures as a foreign student helps build the character of Sookan, whose acumen and perseverance are constantly challenged, but who has become strong enough to maintain her drive to succeed to fulfill her dreams. Part of Sookan's education is coming to terms with the high expectations placed on her by her family over in Korea. Sookan is shocked at the way her American friends seem to disrespect their elders and the wishes of their parents in favor of striving toward their personal goals. But Sookan learns to respect her family at home while allowing herself the pleasure to pursue her own dreams.

Bibliography

Choi, Sook Nyul. *Gathering of Pearls.* New York: Houghton, Mifflin, 1994.

Debbie Clare Olson

Gesture Life, A Chang-rae Lee (1999)

The affluent, reclusive New York City suburb of Bedley Run is the ideal hometown to Franklin Hata, protagonist of CHANG-RAE LEE's *A Gesture Life.* Now in his 70s and retired from his medical supply business, Hata is considered the town's ideal citizen and called "Doc Hata" by all, although he has no medical degree. As the novel unfolds, Hata tries to reconcile both his future relationship with his estranged adult daughter Sunny and his past relationship with a Korean sex slave called K, whom he cared for as a Japanese medic during World War II. Always "at the vortex of bad happenings," he attempts to atone for his past by helping others but fears that his mere presence sparks catastrophe.

On the surface Hata lives a quiet life, until he allows his fireplace to burn his family room and is hospitalized for smoke inhalation. He receives an anonymous get-well card from Sunny, now 32, a mother, and living nearby. The two begin a tentative reconciliation after 13 years apart, and Hata becomes acquainted with his six-year-old grandson Thomas. But on one disastrous day, one of Hata's friends dies in a car crash, another has a heart attack, and Thomas nearly drowns, causing Hata to question once again whether he is an angel of mercy or of death. Ultimately he decides to leave Bedley Run, removing himself from Sunny's and Thomas's lives, without any clear picture of where he will go next.

These events inspire a number of flashbacks from Hata's distant and more recent past, including Sunny's troubled adolescence. From the time he adopted her from Korea, he tiptoed around her as if she were an independent, fearsome adult, seldom disciplining her. A well-mannered child, Sunny becomes a rebellious teenager and moves away from home at 17. She returns only once, briefly, when Hata forces her to abort her nearly full-term pregnancy, personally assisting at the surgery. What he witnesses here is seared into his memory, although he had expected to be immune to the sight because of his wartime experiences. In 1944, when Hata was Lieutenant Jiro Kurohata, a medic stationed with the Japanese army in Burma, he was entrusted with the medical care of five Korean "comfort women" kidnapped to serve in the military brothel. By speaking Korean, his first language, he forges a connection to one of the women, Kkutaeh, called "K." She repeatedly asks him to save her by killing her, first as a favor to a countrywoman and later as a sign of his love. When he refuses, K murders his supervisor and is subsequently gang-raped and killed by Japanese soldiers. Kurohata, as a medic, must collect her scattered remains, discovering among them her unborn child.

A Gesture Life evolved from an earlier draft told from a comfort woman's perspective. After about two years of work Lee decided he could do the subject better justice if it were re-envisioned through the perspective of Doc Hata, focusing not on the immediate trauma but on its witnessing and aftermath. Having seen but not prevented the brutalities of war, Hata must determine how to carry on with his life and what kind of legacy he can leave. All his attempts, including the daughter he adopts, the business he founds, and the home he carefully restores, somehow go awry, and his final gesture is ambivalent. By leaving Bedley Run, he aims to protect those he loves through his very absence, while still hoping that he can remain in their memory without haunting them.

Bibliography

Chuh, Kandice. "Discomforting Knowledge, or, Korean 'Comfort Women' and Asian Americanist Critical Practice." *Journal of Asian American Studies* 6, no. 1 (2003): 5–23.

Lee, Young-Oak. "Gender, Race, and the Nation in *A Gesture Life.*" *Critique: Studies in Contemporary Fiction* 46, no. 2 (Winter 2005): 146–159.

Jaime Cleland

Ghose, Zulfikar (1935–)

Born in Pakistan, raised in India, and educated in Great Britain (B.A., University of Keele, 1959), Zulfikar Ghose has taught in the Department of English at the University of Texas since 1969 and currently resides in Austin, Texas. Before turning to academe, Ghose also wrote as a cricket correspondent for the *Observer* in London, 1960–65, and was a contractual reviewer for the *Times Literary Supplement* and *The Guardian*. A prolific novelist, poet, and critic, Ghose has published 11 novels, six collections of poetry, and seven volumes of criticism and nonfiction.

In his curious blend of poetic writing and razor-sharp prose, Ghose navigates equally well within traditional realist fiction, magical realism, and, with his later works, metafictional (postmodernist fiction that brings explicit attention to its constructedness and status as fiction) terrains. Ghose's works not only defy strict genre classification, but remain untied to any particular place or any particular national context. This type of movement, of continual travel, makes it difficult to pin down Ghose's writing to any one particular type, form, or context. As Chelva Kanaganayakam notes in the preface to his interview with Ghose, "to limit Ghose, whose sensibility is an evolving one, to a preconceived taxonomy would be both

futile and frustrating" (172). The idea of home or homeland receives continual interrogation, but the importance for Ghose lies not in answers but in the questions themselves.

Ghose's best-known novels include those comprising the *Incredible Brazilian* trilogy—*The Native* (1972), *The Beautiful Empire* (1975), and *A Different World* (1978)—which feature the protagonist Gregório Pieixoto da Silva Xavier, a character who, reincarnated through and across historical time, confronts Brazil's curious and conflicting pasts: the land of the native Brazilians, its status as a European colony, and the rise to nationhood. Sprawling and intricate, the novels together allow Ghose the space to demonstrate the overwhelming complexity of Brazil's past, which undoubtedly comes to bear on the present situation of the nation.

Ghose's later novels, in particular *Don Bueno* (1984), *Figures of Enchantment* (1986), and *The Triple Mirror of the Self* (1992), demonstrate a marked interest in the form of fiction, its possibilities and limitations. In an interview with Kanaganayakam, Ghose remarked: "As soon as you use words you are referring to reality; indeed, there is no reality outside language that can be said to have meaning; and it must follow that you cannot perceive a complex reality without creating a complex language" (176). Indeed language remains the subject of Ghose's work, just as much as, if not more than, characters, plot, history, or any element of reality outside of the work itself.

In particular, Ghose's most recent novel, *The Triple Mirror of the Self,* challenges the reader to constantly rethink genre conventions and the ways in which stories relate and mix together. Jumping from continent to continent, circling among past, present, and future, not even the characters have solid grounding. Reflecting and refracting one another, the novel's main characters—Roshan Urim, Isabel, and Jonathan Pons—meld into what Reed Way Dasenbrock refers to as "some kind of larger, composite self" (786). Such attention to form and experimentation characterizes all of Ghose's fiction, perhaps most explicitly so in this particular novel.

As an academic critic, Ghose has published works ranging from meditations on the forms and distinction of fiction to close readings of Shakespeare and T. S. Eliot. Though both his nonfiction and poetry have garnered academic critical attention, his novels have generated the most sustained criticism.

Bibliography

Dasenbrock, Reed W. Review of *The Triple Mirror of the Self* by Zulfikar Ghose. *World Literature Today* 66, no. 4 (Autumn 1992): 785–786.

Ghose, Zulfikar. "Zulfikar Ghose: An Interview," by Chelva Kanaganayakam. *Twentieth Century Literature* 32, no. 2 (Summer 1986): 169–186.

Zach Weir

Golden Child   David Henry Hwang (1998)

On one level, DAVID HENRY HWANG's two-act play, *Golden Child,* dramatizes what the playwright sees as a moment of triumphant family history: his great-grandfather's conversion to Christianity in China at the turn of the 20th century, inspiring irreversible changes for the family. In "Bringing up *Child,*" Hwang's introduction to the play in the published text, Hwang writes that the play is to an extent "an American playwright's act of ancestor worship." In the play, Hwang indeed celebrates the achievements of his family—in particular, the proto-feminist refusal of his grandmother to have her feet bound—but he also criticizes the passivity with which Chinese communities accepted the influx of Western ideas in the early 20th century.

James Lapine directed the premiere of *Golden Child* at the Public Theater/New York Shakespeare Festival on November 17, 1996. After some rewriting, the play made its way to Broadway, where it ran at the Longacre Theatre from April 2, 1998. James Lapine continued to direct the show; Julyana Soelistyo starred as Eng Ahn, the character based explicitly on Hwang's maternal grandmother. In the play, Eng Ahn is the long-suffering 10-year-old daughter of Eng Tieng-Bin, the character based on Hwang's great-grandfather. She is long-suffering because she has to endure the conflicting attentions of her father's three wives. The eldest wife, Siu-Yong, is particularly demanding, and is the

source of much of the play's satire on early 20th-century Chinese mores. She insists that Eng Ahn must have her feet kept bound in order, ironically, to become Westernized, to become as bad as the white "monkeys and devils" with whom Tieng-Bin now trades. When Eng Ahn complains about the pain and unseemly smell that the bindings are causing her, Siu-Yong replies, with an unknowing paradox, "No one ever said that feminine beauty was pretty." Siu-Yong later complains that the spirits of long-deceased family ancestors are angry because of Eng Ahn's rebellious insistence on removing her foot bindings. By then, Siu-Yong has succumbed to opium, claiming that it makes her stronger, but revealing, unwittingly, that her sexual libido has been quashed by the debilitating poppy. Discredited and ignored by the end of the first act, Siu-Yong can only watch, infuriated, as Tieng-Bin announces that his daughter—the "Golden Child"—shall be the first female member of the family not to have her feet bound: "Remove her bindings. Now!" he commands.

If the first act celebrates the discontinuation of an undesirable Chinese traditional practice, the second act is more elegiac in its depiction of a changing culture. Under the influence of a rather characterless, tea- and pastry-loving missionary, Reverend Anthony Baines, Tieng-Bin converts to Christianity, defeating the more ludicrous superstitions and reactionary repressiveness of Chinese spirit-worship. The problem is that Tieng-Bin seems to be motivated by rather earthy, practical matters. He embraces the notion of Christian monogamy to avoid the problems caused by his ever-bickering three wives. The entire family's conversion to Christianity, at his insistence, is marred with an alarming violence as well. Siu-Yong—whose adherence to old religious notions now seems principled and sincere—seeks to retain the ancestor-worshiping tradition, but Tieng-Bin smashes the picture of her parents, causing her considerable distress, and replaces it with a crucifix. While benefits have come from the cessation of certain aspects of Chinese traditions, the transition to Christianity seems hasty, all-encompassing, and rather violently enforced by the patriarchal Tieng-Bin. At the play's end, which is set in the present day, the spirit of Ahn reminds her Chinese-American grandson about her and her father's achievements in removing the negative aspects of Chinese culture from the family, but the audience may wonder if Chinese communities had to complement these changes with such a wholesale acceptance of newfangled Western characteristics.

Bibliography

Hwang, David Henry. *Golden Child.* New York: Theatre Communications Group, 1998.

———. "'Making His Muscles Work for Himself': An Interview with David Henry Hwang" by Bonnie Lyons. *Literary Review,* 42, no. 2 (1999). 230–244.

Kevin De Ornellas

Gotanda, Philip Kan   (1951–)

Widely recognized as one of the most representative Asian-American playwrights of our time, Philip Kan Gotanda is a sansei (i.e. third-generation Japanese American). During World War II, his father, Dr. Wilfred Itsuta Gotanda, was interned in a relocation camp in Rohwer, Arkansas. Upon his release and return to Stockton, California, after the war, he met and married Catherine Matsumoto, a local schoolteacher. Philip is their youngest child.

Gotanda spent his formative years playing the guitar, composing songs, and playing in bands. In 1969 he entered the University of California at Santa Cruz to study psychiatry, no doubt influenced by his physician father. He left Santa Cruz the following year to travel to his ancestral homeland of Japan to study pottery under Hisroshi Seto.

Upon his return to the States, he entered the University of California at Santa Barbara, drawn to what he termed "a particular vision of what Asian American creative expression could be." Upon his graduation in 1973, Gotanda returned for a spell to his first love, music. Gotanda formed a band with fellow playwright David Henry Hwang, with whom a friendship would be sustained throughout their writing careers. Gotanda also pursued a legal career, with a degree from Hasting College of Law in 1978. During this time, Gotanda wrote his first play, *The Avocado Kid* (1978), a musical based

on a popular Japanese children's tale "Momotaro the Peach Boy" and staged by East West Players, an Asian-American theater company in Los Angeles.

For the next decade, Gotanda continued to write exclusively for Asian-American companies; however, with the staging of *The Wash* (1985), a play about a nisei woman's efforts to come to terms with her own identity, and *Yankee Dawg You Die* (1988), a dramatic piece on the portrayal of Asians/Asian Americans in the popular media, Gotanda became a formidable presence in mainstream theaters. His plays *Ballad of Yachiyo* (1996), about Asian workers at a Hawaiian sugar cane plantation set in the early 20th century, and *Sisters Matsumoto* (1999), portraying the lives of Japanese Americans immediately following the internment, have been staged in London and Tokyo respectively.

Gotanda's other representative works include *Fish Head Soup* (1987), a narrative about generational conflicts in a Japanese-American family; *A Song of a Nisei Fisherman* (1982), the life history of a *nisei* fisherman; *Natalie Wood Is Dead* (2001), an account of two women's experiences in Hollywood; and *The Wind Cries Mary* (2003), an exploration of Asian-American identity in the tumultuous 1960s. Gotanda is also widely respected for his independent films, with no fewer than three works (*The Kiss, Drinking Tea,* and *Life Tastes Good*) featured in the Sundance Film Festival.

During his writing career, Gotanda received an impressive array of awards, including the PEN/West Award, the Rockefeller Artist Award, and the Guggenheim Award. Gotanda currently resides in San Francisco with his actress-producer wife, Diane Takei.

Kihan Lee

Grass Roof, The   Younghill Kang (1931)

Using the fictional character of Chungpa Han as the protagonist, Younghill Kang introduces Korea to Western readers in this lyrical, fictional autobiography. Set in rustic Korea, the first half describes his carefree childhood, during which he is trained by his poet uncle. His adventures in the countryside and interactions with his family and friends highlight premodern Korean culture. The second half, set in Seoul and Japan, contrasts sharply with the first half in that it depicts the protagonist's anguish and dilemma during his country's dark period under the Japanese colonial regime. After being imprisoned briefly by the Japanese for his peripheral participation in the 1919 Samil Independence March (a series of massive peaceful demonstrations protesting Japan's colonization of Korea), the protagonist renews his yearning to flee his country and come to America. Through the voice of Han, Kang concludes that the old "spiritual planet that had been [his] father's home" with its "curved lines, its brilliant colors, its haunting music, its own magic of being" was becoming a wasteland unable to sustain its young population. "In loathing of death," he is pulled as if by "natural gravity" toward the younger, more vigorous culture of the West.

Since he regards himself as a spokesperson of Korean culture and of Asian culture as well, Kang investigates in *The Grass Roof* differences between the East and the West. In depicting the tradition of arranged marriages, for example, the narrator says it is not as "barbaric" as it might seem to a Western reader. Concerning the difference between the styles of partying, he notes that "a young Western man takes to a party the kind of girl who can give him a good time, and a young Eastern man finds a trained girl when he arrives."

Despite his early attraction to Western culture, Kang is critically conscious of its disadvantages. His encounter with Western science drives him considerably away from his Confucian education, which seems to him "more and more useless." Once in the West, however, Kang becomes aware of "the moral ambiguity in which its people live, or its industrial, mechanistic trend which makes cogs of their lives." During his education in Japan, he feels trapped in a moral dilemma: "Should I try to help my nation with shrewdness and modern inventions like Japan, and thus be responsible for the suffering of millions? . . . Should I spend my life to be a missionary for the new poison gas?" Kang is also critical of the missionaries in Korea. Despite their claim to have been called to service by "the Lord," Kang suspects that they have been

truly "kicked out" of the West for "being unfit." Kang also accuses them of being unable to get a job in the West and thus drifting to the East to live cheaply and enjoy having household servants and feeling superior to the natives.

Set in the early 20th century, when Japan steadily and powerfully strove to colonize Korea, Kang's narrative also illustrates the atrocities committed by Japan. Portraying Japan as the "most unreasonable and excitable" of all nations, Kang vividly describes how his grandmother died after being roughly treated by the Japanese police and how many Koreans committed suicide to protest Japan's annexation and brutish policies.

The Grass Roof had firmly established Kang as the representative immigrant writer of his time. Valued mostly for the information it provided on Asian culture, the book nonetheless has since been praised for strong character development, descriptive language, and humor.

Bibliography

Kang, Younghill. *The Grass Roof.* New York: Charles Scribner's Sons, 1931. Chicago: Follett, 1966.

Oh, Seiwoong. "Younghill Kang." In *Asian American Autobiographies: A Bio-Bibliographical Critical Sourcebook,* edited by Guiyou Huang. Westport, Conn.: Greenwood, 2001.

SuMee Lee

Gunga Din Highway Frank Chin (1994)

According to FRANK CHIN, "We are born to fight to maintain our personal integrity. All art is martial art. Writing is fighting" ("Come" 35). He therefore continues his war against the deadening stereotypes of ethnic Americans in his second novel, *Gunga Din Highway*. The title of the novel is adapted from Rudyard Kipling's poem about a native Indian *bhisti* (water carrier) who desires to be a soldier and helps British troops against his own people. Chin employs the title to criticize contemporary Asian-American writers for eagerly seeking access and acceptance into mainstream society even at the expense of "selling out" their own people.

Told by four first-person narrators, the novel is divided into four sections. It begins with the life of an actor father, Longman Kwan. Long cast in movies as Charlie Chan's Number Four Son and as "the Chinaman who dies," Longman is obsessed with the idea of being the first Chinese actor to play Charlie Chan—the role, to the father-spokesman, as "the perfect Chinese American to lead the yellows to build the road to acceptance toward assimilation" (13). The second section is told primarily from the viewpoint of his son, Ulysses, the central character of the novel. Ulysses grows up in Oakland far from Hollywood and lives with his divorced mother. Ulysses despises his father's Hollywood roles of Asian stereotypes and wants nothing to do with him. Named after James Joyce's novel and Kwan Kung, deified as the god of war and literature, Ulysses S. Kwan undergoes a Joycean adventure, evolving into Chin's ideal Chinese-American male—an artist as well as a warrior. The rest of the novel is alternately narrated by Ulysses and his two childhood blood-brothers, Diego Chang, a musi-

cian, and Benedict Mo, a playwright. Filled with references to American pop culture, Hollywood mythology, Western literary traditions, and Chinese legend, the novel spans almost five decades from the 1940s to today and takes place all over the country.

Bibliography

Chin, Frank. "Come All Ye Asian American Writers of the Real and the Fake." *The Big Aiiieeeee!: An Anthology of Chinese American and Japanese American Literature,* edited by Frank Chin, et al., 1–92. New York: Meridian, 1991.

Ho, Wen-chin. Review of *Gunga Din Highway,* by Frank Chin. *Amerasia Journal* 22 (1996): 158–161.

Huang, Guiyou. "Frank Chin." *Asian American Novelists: A Bio-bibliographical Critical Sourcebook,* edited by Emmanuel S. Nelson, 48–55. London: Greenwood Press, 2000.

Fu-jen Chen

Habibi   Naomi Shihab Nye (1997)

Habibi is the story of Liyana Abboud, whose Palestinian father announces to the family one evening that she and her family will be moving to his hometown of Jerusalem. Though she had heard before that her parents considered moving from her home in St. Louis across the seas, Liyana is stunned and unhappy to hear the announcement. She had just shared her first kiss with a boy the day before and now she would never see him again.

Once they arrive in Jerusalem, Liyana and her family are embraced by her very interesting Palestinian relatives. She finds out quickly, however, that boys and girls cannot have relationships. Regardless, Liyana does fall in love with Omer, who happens to be Jewish. By doing so, she has crossed the invisible line drawn between Palestinians and Jews, an act that goes against all the traditions of her Palestinian relatives. During her stay, nonetheless, Liyana learns to understand her family, her heritage as an Arab, and her status in Jerusalem as an outsider. This novel, though fictional, reflects the author's own life: the family unit is constructed in the same way NAOMI SHIHAB NYE's is; the family returns to the father's native land, as did Nye's own family; and Liyana is 14 when the family moves to Jerusalem, as was the author.

At the heart of this young adult novel is the struggle between cultures, families, and traditions. Violence and destruction pervade in the background. Liyana's grandmother's home is destroyed, and violence erupts in the Jewish marketplace. Nye charts the progress of each family member's own journey into their hearts and their understanding of their identity. In Liyana's case, her gradual understanding of and appreciation for her extended family members translate into her psychological growth and identity formation. By carefully reflecting the struggles between Israel and Palestine, especially seen from the perspective of an America teenager, Nye engages her readers in the debate over cross-cultural understanding, war, peace, and tolerance.

Anne Marie Fowler

Hagedorn, Jessica Tarahata   (1949–)

Artist, playwright, poet, and novelist Jessica Hagedorn was born and raised in Manila, the capital of the Philippines, and immigrated to San Francisco with her family in her early teens. After studying for two years at the American Conservatory Theater in San Francisco, she moved to New York in 1978, where she currently lives. The wide range, thematic scope, and eclecticism of her works have made her the most prominent Filipino-American writer since CARLOS BULOSAN. Hagedorn has experimented with various media, from poetry to music and performance art; her writing, in particular, blends such genres as poetry, fiction, songs, and scripts, blurring the traditional boundaries among them. Her art is as complex as her own ancestry, which is a mixture of Filipino, Spanish, Chinese, German, Scottish, Irish, and French roots. She nevertheless defines herself primarily as Filipina mainly due to the strong connection that she feels with her Filipina grandmother. Drawing from her very diverse influences, her works show an irreverent attitude toward, and consistent efforts to dismantle, any notions of cultural, national, and racial essentialisms.

The multiple influences in Hagedorn's artistic production mirror the variety of elements shaping the history and culture of the Philippines. The Philippines were first colonized by Spain until 1896, dominated by the United States until World War II, and occupied by Japan from 1942 to 1944. Afterward it experienced the effects of U.S. neo-colonialism, a point extensively dealt with in Hagedorn's works. As her characters move between the Philippines and other multicultural nations such as the United States, Hagedorn examines how the concept of cultural authenticity is constructed, who transgresses it, and why. Displacement, cultural heterogeneity and the self-(re)definition of both individuals and communities are central themes of her writings. Her major settings, the urban areas of the Philippines and the United States, help further raise questions about power imbalances and struggles in postcolonial, class, gender and sexual contexts.

Four Young Women (1973) was the first anthology to include Hagedorn's poetry. Two years later, her first collection of poems and fiction, *Dangerous Music,* was published. In collaboration with photographer Marisa Roth, Hagedorn also published *Burning Heart* (1999), in which poems and black-and-white photographs are paired to depict the state of children in the Philippines. In 1975 she formed the experimental rock group The West Coast Gangster Choir, which lasted for a decade and was later renamed as The Gangster Choir when she moved to New York. Her theater productions include *Where the Mississipi Meets the Amazon* (1977 collaboration with Thulani Davis and Ntozake Shange), *Mango Tango* (1978), *Tene-*

ment Lover (1981), *Holy Food* (1988), *Teenytown* (1990) and a stage adaptation of her novel *Dog-EATERS* (1991). Her interest in performing arts, music, and poetry has strongly shaped her fiction, which shows an authorial concern with rhythm and speech patterns and often contains excerpts from songs, newspapers, script fragments, and quotations from real or fictional people.

Her narratives offer controversial representations of Filipino, Filipino-American and Anglo-American identities, exploring how they are constructed and reinforced through a wide range of cultural manifestations such as books, newspapers, radio and television serials, films, and rock and pop music. Hagedorn's works, concerned with the plight of marginal figures and strong female characters, attempt to destabilize any rigid boundaries between "high" and "low" culture.

Hagedorn won the American Book Award for her novella *Pet Food and Tropical Apparitions* (1981). Her first novel, *Dogeaters* (1990), earned her critical acclaim and was nominated for a National Book Award. *The GANGSTER OF LOVE* (1996), her second novel, develops further some of the themes already outlined in *Dogeaters.* Her third novel, *Dream Jungle* (2003), also studies the political and cultural relationship between the Philippines and the United States as the lives of diverse Filipino, American, and Filipino-American characters become intertwined. The two main events in the novel are based on real historical events. The discovery of a "lost" tribe in the Philippines called the Taobos is a fictionalised allusion to the historical discovery of the Tasaday, and the filming of *Napalm Sunset* is inspired by the filming of *Apocalypse Now* in the country. These plots become entangled with a portrayal of Manila from the 1970s until the late 1990s, depicting Ferdinand Marcos's regime and the neo-colonial tensions between the Philippines and the United States.

Among other projects, Hagedorn has also edited an anthology of Asian-American literature entitled *Charlie Chan Is Dead: An Anthology of Contemporary Asian American Fiction* (1993); created with John Woo the short animated series "Pink Palace," featuring a Filipina mother and her daughter living in California; and written the screenplay for the film *Fresh Kill* (1994) directed by Shu Lea Cheang.

Bibliography

Bloom, Harold, ed. *Asian-American Women Writers* Philadelphia: Chelsea House Publishers, 1997.

Gonzalez, N. V. M., and Oscar Campomanes. "Filipino American Literature," *An Interethnic Companion to Asian American Literature*, edited by King-Kok Cheung, 62–124. Cambridge: Cambridge University Press, 1997.

Miles, Chris, Jessica Heerwald, and Tina Avent. "Voices from the Gaps: Jessica Hagedorn". URL: http://voices.cla.umn.edu/vg/Bios/entries/hagedorn_jessica_tarahata.html. Downloaded September 23, 2006.

Marta Vizcaya Echano

Hahn, Kimiko (1955–)

Poet Kimiko Hahn was born in Mt. Kisco, New York, the daughter of two visual artists: the Japanese American, Maude Miyako Hamai, from Hawaii, and the German American, Walter Hahn, from Wisconsin. Her dual Eurasian parentage informs much of her poetry, grounded in the questions of racial identity she has faced throughout her life. As a child growing up in Pleasantville, New York, Hahn was never fully accepted by either the Asian-American or European-American communities. In school, her peers considered her an Asian. Similarly, while she was living with her father in Japan for a time, her schoolmates referred to her as a *gaijin,* an outsider or foreigner. Such experiences galvanized her interest in her split identity and led to her involvement, as a teenager, in New York City's growing Asian-American movement.

As an undergraduate, Hahn double-majored in English and East Asian Studies at the University of Iowa, where she later received an M.F.A. in creative writing. She also earned an M.A. in Japanese literature from Columbia University. Her extensive knowledge of cross-cultural literary traditions infuses her poetry with complex intertextual allusions and bilingual ruptures. Her first book of poetry, *Air Pocket,* published by Hanging Loose Press in 1989, established her characteristic use of varied cultural and linguistic material. In "Dance Instructions for a Young Girl," Hahn employs a double-voiced discourse to depict the strict Kabuki training geisha girls undergo, while also portraying the mental processes they employ to sublimate the acts they undertake with male clients. A longer, more complex poem that weaves together Hahn's diverse thematic strands is "Resistance: A Poem on Ikat Cloth," which acts as an appropriate capstone to her first volume. Here, Hahn emulates the highly allusive, fragmented structure of T. S. Eliot's *Waste Land* by combining Japanese ideograms with cross-cultural quotes from Murasaki Shikibu, Virginia Woolf, and Joseph Stalin. Hahn uses these to parallel the different images woven into a Japanese cloth made from resistance-dying yarn that emulates, poetically through images, the struggles of a woman living within a disorienting bicultural reality.

In 1992 Hahn began receiving critical recognition with her second book, *Earshot,* which was awarded both the Theodore Roethke Memorial Poetry Award and an Association of Asian American Studies Literature Award. Her third book, *The Unbearable Heart* (1995), won a prestigious American Book Award for Hahn's heart-wrenching confessional portrayal of how she dealt with her mother's unexpected death. The dark lyrical poems collected here often employ a childlike tone to explore the intimate yet complex relationships that existed between different generations of women within her family. In *Mosquito and Ant* (2000), Hahn resurrects the nearly extinct, millennia-old *nu shu* script—in which Chinese women held secret correspondences with one another—to present the most intimate thoughts women hold about their bodies, interpersonal relationships, and families.

Currently, Hahn lives in Manhattan with her husband and two daughters and teaches English at Queens College, City University of New York. Her most recent book, *The Artist's Daughter,* was published by Norton in 2004. True to her roots as a New Yorker, Hahn's poem "Mortal Remains" is included in *Poetry after 9/11: An Anthology of New York Poets.*

Bibliography

Xiaojing, Zhou. "Intercultural Strategies in Asian American Poetry." In *Re-placing America: Conversations and Contestations,* edited by Ruth Hsu, Cynthia Franklin, and Suzanne Kosanke, 92–108. Honolulu: University of Hawai'i and East-West Center, 2000.

———. "Kimiko Hahn (1955–   )." In *Asian American Poets: A Bio-Bibliographical Critical Sourcebook,* edited by Guiyou Huang. Westport, Conn.: Greenwood, 2002.

Shawn Holliday

Ha Jin   See JIN, HA.

Hammad, Suheir   (1973–   )

Palestinian-American poet Suheir Hammad was born in a refugee camp in Amman, Jordan, in October 1973, the same year as the Ramadan War and one year before Israel's Prime Minister Golda Meir delivered a speech in which she stated, "I cannot sleep at night knowing how many Arab babies are being born this same night." For Hammad, these events placed her birth in a context that gave her a sense that Palestinian children were a nightmare for Israel. The daughter of Palestinian refugees from Lydd and Ramleh, Hammad moved with her family to Beirut before settling in Sunset Park, Brooklyn, in 1978 when she was five years old. The eldest of five children, Hammad was raised in a home infused with poetry from the Qur'an, from Palestinian poets Fadwa Tuqan and Mahmoud Darwish, and from the melodies of singers Abdel Halim Hafiz, Om Kolthom, and Sam Cooke. In her neighborhood, she grew up with poetic influences from the burgeoning hip-hop music from groups like Public Enemy.

A self-taught poet, Hammad attended Hunter College, where she won the Audre Lorde Writing Award for her poetry in 1995. At the age of 23, she published two books: a memoir, *Drops of This Story* (1996), and a book of poems, *Born Palestinian, Born Black* (1996). Her style fuses Arab poetic rhythms with hip-hop aesthetics and builds on the politics and poetics of writers from the Black Arts Movement such as June Jordan and Audre Lorde. Poets like Jordan modeled for Hammad the importance of drawing parallels across cultural and political divides through poetry.

Hammad's poetry and autobiographical writings narrate stories of Palestinian exile by drawing parallels between the realities of the working-class, immigrant, multicultural communities of Brooklyn and the experiences of Palestinians, Arabs, and Muslims. For example, her poem "brooklyn" describes Brooklyn not only as a place that has provided her family with a sanctuary from Israeli violence, but also as a community that failed to protect Yusef Hawkins from racial violence.

Through images that show the intersections between home and exile, Hammad plays with language in her writing that reverses the dominant representations in U.S. media of Arabs and Muslims. She demands that her readers ask questions and think critically about what the media tells them. In her poems "palestinian '98" and "mike check," for example, she portrays the reality of Palestinian and Muslim experiences in the United States and the occupied territories, as a way of responding to the U.S. media's frequent representation of Palestinians as terrorists. Hammad challenges the stereotypes also by portraying the compassion of her family and her culture in poems like "daddy's song." She explores and rescues the meaning of words like "terrorist," "liberation," "freedom fighter," and "occupation" to illustrate a realistic version of Palestinians and their dispossession in 1948.

The performative and aural quality of her writing can be seen in the way she plays with language. In *"sawah,"* her inspiration comes from the music of singers like Abdel Halim Hafiz, whose Arabic songs taught her about the power of language as well as the deficiencies of English. One poem that reveals her use of language to convey parallel themes of liberation and oppression is "first writing since." This landmark poem was performed on television in HBO's *Russell Simmons Def Poetry Jam.* She has performed her work in a variety of venues, on college campuses, at spoken word poetry readings, and at rap concerts. Her libretto *Re-Orientalism,* commissioned by the Center for

Cultural Exchange, has been performed at theaters in Maine, New Hampshire, New York, Massachusetts, and Connecticut.

Bibliography

Burrell, Jocelyn, ed. *Word: On Being a Woman Writer.* New York: Feminist Press, 2004.

Danquah, Meri Nana-Ama, ed. *Becoming American: Personal Essays by First Generation Immigrant Women.* New York: Hyperion, 2000.

Hammad, Suheir. *Born Palestinian, Born Black.* New York: Harlem River Press, 1996.

———. *Drops of this Story.* New York: Harlem River Press, 1996.

———. *Zaatar Diva.* New York: Cypher, 2006.

Simmons, Danny, ed. *Russell Simmons Def Poetry Jam on Broadway and More.* New York: Atria, 2003.

Marcy Jane Knopf-Newman

Han Suyin   (1917–   )

Han Suyin is the pen name of the prolific novelist, journalist, political essayist, and biographer Chou Kuanghu (Elisabeth Rosalie Matthilde Clare Chou), whose current official name is Dr. Elisabeth Comber. She was born in Sinyang, China. Her father was a Chinese engineer who studied in Europe, and her mother was Flemish. Han Suyin has written more than 20 books in English in addition to other works in Chinese and French. Her broad oeuvre includes important works of fiction, autobiography, history, and sociopolitical essays.

Han Suyin's first published book, *Destination Chungking* (1942), is a novel that provides an idealistic account of a young couple fighting for the nationalist forces of Chiang Kai-shek. With this and other subsequent works such as ... *And the Rain My Drink* (1957), the author expresses her admiration for Chinese struggles for self-determination and her desire to make these struggles comprehensible to English-language readers. In other fictional works, Han Suyin addresses more personal issues such as interracial relationships and the intersection of cultures.

Among Han Suyin's more striking works is her multivolume autobiography, a testament published over the course of almost 30 years and consisting of *The Crippled Tree* (1965), *A Mortal Flower* (1966), *Birdless Summer* (1968), *My House Has Two Doors* (1980), *Phoenix Harvest* (1980), *A Share of Loving* (1987) and *Wind in My Sleeve* (1992). In these sweeping works, Suyin provides the reader with a portrait of Chinese history and culture, drawn from ancient history up to the present and illustrated by the stories of herself and her family.

Her most controversial works include the two-volume biography of Chairman Mao, *The Morning Deluge: Mao Tse Tung and the Chinese Revolution, 1893–1954* (1972) and *Wind in the Tower: Mao Tse Tung and the Chinese Revolution, 1949–1976* (1976), as well as her biography of Premier Zhou Enlai entitled *Eldest Son: Zhou Enlai and the Making of Modern China, 1898–1976* (1994). The latter was based largely upon materials derived from Han Suyin's numerous meetings with the premier.

All of these works, representing diverse genres, offer a broad yet richly textured picture of social, political and intellectual developments in China, especially over the dramatic and turbulent periods of the mid-20th century. Through civil wars, national liberation struggles, revolution and reconstruction, the personal yearnings of everyday people are situated in the course of world-historic events.

More than almost any other writer in English, Han Suyin has brought to life for non-Chinese readers the events and contexts underlying the Communist revolution and the specific evolution of Communism as a social and political philosophy within China. Her preference for Chinese Communism over Western capitalism, both in terms of social values and the possibilities for economic improvement for the poorest citizens, has been presented honestly and unapologetically in her works. Thus she has been viewed in the West as a controversial figure due to her unflinching criticism of imperialist powers and her willingness to challenge historians and journalists whose works seek to legitimize those powers. Western literary critics have often taken issue with her political views and outspoken criticism of Western capitalism and its value systems. She has been subjected to particularly harsh treatment among Western commentators for her sympathetic renderings of the rule of Chairman Mao. In the face of such criticism, however, Han Suyin has steadfastly maintained her allegiance and commitment to the Chinese people. Throughout her works this overriding concern with their well-being and social improvement has shone through consistently.

In *My House Has Two Doors* Han Suyin asserts that her priorities as a writer have never rested with ideologies or political systems regardless of how exultant they might be. Rather than being committed to any ideology, Han Suyin views ideologies and systems as things to shoulder and make do with. The motivating concern of her various works has been the question of whether or not specific systems or versions of systems might contribute to a step forward for the Chinese people.

Bibliography

Buss, Helen. "The Autobiographies of Han Suyin: A Female Postcolonial Subjectivity," *Canadian Review of American Studies* 23, no. 1 (1992): 107–126.

Ling, Amy. "Writers with a Cause: Sui Sin Far and Han Suyin." *Women's Studies International Forum* 9 (1986): 411–419.

Lyon, Esme. "The Writing of Han Suyin: A Survey." *World Literature Written in English* 17 (1978): 208–217.

Jeff Shantz

Hayslip, Phung Thi Le Ly (1949–)

Born in Ky La (now Xa Hoa Qui) near Danang in Vietnam, Hayslip was the seventh child of rice farmers. The Vietnam War fractured her family and village as her brothers fought on both sides; moreover, the Viet Cong, South Vietnam, and Americans alternately took and lost control of her hometown of Ky La. Hayslip's first encounter with the Viet Cong was the public execution of her teacher, Manh. After his death, Hayslip began helping the Viet Cong. Because of her Viet Cong activities, Hayslip was imprisoned and tortured by the South Vietnamese government. Her release was rumored to be attributable to her South Vietnamese allies, and the Viet Cong accused her of being a traitor. She was sentenced to death by the Viet Cong, but instead of killing her, her two executioners raped her, which shamed her and made her unmarriageble according to Vietnamese culture. Hayslip fled to Danang, then to Saigon, where she worked as a maid, black market vendor, waitress, and hospital worker.

Soon after her first son, James, was born in Vietnam, she met Ed Munro, an American GI. By the age of 20, Hayslip had two sons and had married Ed and moved to America. However, her husband became depressed and died a few years after their move to the United States. She later remarried, but her second husband, who was physically abusive, also died, leaving Hayslip to care for her three sons.

Hayslip eventually returned to Vietnam in 1986 to visit her family. Her trip inspired her to create the East Meets West Foundation in 1988, a humanitarian relief organization that focused on providing relief to Vietnam and offering comfort to American veterans. Her work inspired filmmaker Oliver Stone, Senator John Kerry, and many others, who have donated money to build a clinic for homeless children and Peace Village, a medical center for children.

Hayslip is the author of two books, *When Heaven and Earth Changed Places* (1989) and *Child of War, Woman of Peace* (1993). *When Heaven and Earth Changed Places* narrates her experiences during the war and her return in 1986 to Vietnam, and is by far the more critically acclaimed and commercially successful of the two. Its primary purpose is aimed at reconciliation, for both the Vietnamese and the Americans. It is dedicated to those who suffered, and Hayslip hopes that "anger can teach forgiveness, hate can teach us love, and war can teach us peace" (xv). The book describes the "private side" of the war and the sacrifices one must make to survive, with an emphasis on forgiveness and hope.

Praised for its blend of Western and Eastern values, *Child of War, Woman of Peace*, written with the help of her son James, details Hayslip's life in the United States from 1972 to 1986, chronicling her struggles in a foreign land and her transformation from immigrant to social activist.

Oliver Stone was so impressed with Hayslip that he developed her books into the movie *Heaven and Earth,* part of his Vietnam War series. Hayslip's work has increased the study of immigrant literature, and she has contributed significantly to our understanding of the immigrant experience and the Vietnam War.

Bibliography

Christopher, Renny. *The Viet Nam War/The American War.* Amherst: University of Massachusetts Press, 1995.

Hayslip, Phung Thi Le Ly. *When Heaven and Earth Changed Places.* New York: Doubleday, 1989.

Nguyen, Viet Thanh. *Race and Resistance: Literature and Politics in Asian America.* Oxford: Oxford University Press, 2002.

Rutledge, Paul James. *The Vietnamese Experience in America.* Bloomington: Indiana University Press, 1992.

Tina Powell

Hazo, Samuel John   (1928–   )

A prolific poet with more than 30 volumes of poetry, Dr. Samuel Hazo has also published numerous works of fiction, essays, and plays as well as translating Arabic poetry into English, notably that of the internationally acclaimed Syrian poet Adonis. Born to a Lebanese mother and an Assyrian father (from Jerusalem), Hazo believes that one's identity—ethnic, familial, political, or otherwise—is bound to have an effect on one's work, but that it should not be consciously enunciated. To do so, Hazo believes, dilutes the mystery.

He held the post of State Poet of the Commonwealth of Pennsylvania (1993–2003). In his view, a poet laureate "should strive to make poetry an expected and readily accepted part of public discourse. To this end, poetry should be an essential part of academic exercises, public events, and

newspaper op-ed pages" ("Samuel Hazo"). Hazo has put his ideas into action, giving many poetry readings throughout the United States, Europe, and the Middle East. His poetry has been translated into Arabic, Spanish, French, Russian, Polish, Turkish, Norwegian, Persian, and Bulgarian.

Hazo was born on July 19, 1928, in Pittsburgh, Pennsylvania. His mother died when he was young, and he became very close to his only brother. His aunt, who raised him, instilled a love of education in the young Hazo. He obtained a B.A. in English from the University of Notre Dame in 1948. In 1950 he served as a captain in the U.S. Marine Corps. Hazo went back to college and earned an M.A. by studying the poetry of Gerard Manley Hopkins. Between 1950 and 1957, he worked on the aesthetics of the French philosopher Jacques Maritain, earning a doctorate from the University of Pittsburgh. Since then, he has held several academic positions in universities around the United States. Between 1987 and 1996, he also worked as a commentator and narrator on National Public Radio. Hazo has been the president and director of the International Poetry Forum, which celebrated its 40th anniversary in 2006.

Hazo started writing poetry seriously at the age of 23. His early poetry followed traditional metrics. However, he discovered, when working on *Blood Rights* (1968), that "the iambic pentameter line and . . . other lines were not made for our language. These were the metrics of Greek and Roman prosody. . . . So I began to write poems in which every line contained three stressed syllables" (qtd. in Sokolowski). The themes of family, the mystery of death, the absurdity of life, and the healing power of love are recurrent in his poetry, which is also known for its musicality, resonance, vigor, and humor.

Hazo's poetry books include *Discovery and Other Poems* (1958); *The Quiet Wars* (1962); *The Holy Surprise of Right Now* (1996), selected poems from 1959–95; *As They Sail* (1999); *Just Once* (2002), recipient of the Maurice English Poetry Prize; and *A Flight to Elsewhere* (2005). His prose titles include *Seascript: A Mediterranean Logbook* (1972); *Inscripts* (1975); *Spying for God* (1999);

The Feast of Icarus: Lyrical Essays (1984); *The Wanton Summer Air* (1982); and *Stills* (1989). Hazo has written numerous essays and nonfiction books including *The Rest Is Prose* (1989) and *The Power of Less: Poetry and Public Speech* (2005). In his essays, Hazo has been very vocal in his criticism of the Bush administration in the Middle East.

Hazo has also been active as a playwright. *Until I'm Not Here Anymore* was performed at the Fulton Theater, Pittsburgh, in l992 and subsequently filmed and broadcast on PBS. Other plays include *Solos,* performed at the Carnegie Lecture Hall, Pittsburgh, in 1994; *Feather,* performed at Carnegie Lecture Hall and other venues, 1996; *Mano a Mano,* a flamenco drama written for the Carlota Santana Spanish Dance Company and performed at Duke University in 2001 and subsequently at the Joyce Theater in Manhattan. Hazo is presently working on a play called *Watching Fire, Watching Rain.*

Notable among his awards are a Phi Beta Kappa Honorary Membership (1976), the Hazlett Award for Excellence in Literature (1986), the Forbes Medal for Outstanding Cultural Contributions to Western Pennsylvania (1987), the Pittsburgh Center for the Arts Cultural Award (1995), the Maurice English Award for Poetry (2003), the Griffin Award for Creative Writing (2004), and nine honorary doctorates. Hazo continues to live with his wife, Mary Anne, and son, Samuel R. Hazo, an accomplished composer, in his hometown of Pittsburgh, where he is a Visiting Professor and McAnulty Distinguished Professor of English Emeritus at Duquesne University.

Bibliography

Poetry and Politics: Nations of the Mind. "Samuel Hazo." Available online. URL: http://www.nhwritersproject.org/poetryandpolitics/samuelhazo.htm. Accessed May 18, 2006.

Hazo, Samuel. "An Interview with Samuel Hazo" by David Sokolowski. August 5–6, 1988. Available online. URL: http://www.nd.edu/~ndr/issues/ndr8/hazo/interview.html. Accessed September 25, 2006.

Zoghby, Mary D. "The Holy Surprise of Right Now: Selected and New Poems. Samuel Hazo." *MELUS* 23, no. 4 (Winter 1998): Retrieved from the Ebsco Host, Academic Search Premier database.

Nawar Al-Hassan Golley

Heart's Desire, The   Nahid Rachlin (1995)

Jennifer and Karim Sahary, an average middle-class couple with one son, Darius, live the American dream in Ohio. After many years of a happy marriage, Karim begins to feel uncomfortable in America. A professor of urban planning at a university, he feels racism toward him pressing against his world, especially after the Iran hostage crisis. Karim begins to withdraw from his wife and wraps himself in solitude, longing for his family and life he had neglected in Iran. They return as a family to Iran, where Jennifer, a commercial artist, is at first invigorated by the colors and atmosphere of her husband's home. As their stay extends in the house of Karim's mother, Jennifer begins to feel claustrophobic and powerless within such a heavily restricted society that is both enthralled by and belligerent toward America. A move by Aziz, the matriarch of the family, to take Darius to Qom and enroll him in a religious school frightens Jennifer enough to take matters into her own hands. As an American, she has difficulty negotiating her way through Iran's streets and police to take her son back, but she manages to find her way out of Iran and back home to the States.

While sometimes compared to Betty Mahmoody's *Not without My Daughter,* a sensational story about her escape from Iran with her daughter, NAHID RACHLIN's novel offers a complex reading of post-1979 Iran from an American woman's perspective. Her nuanced understanding of both Iranian and American lifestyles gives this story an evenhanded and complex analysis of cross-cultural marriages. Jennifer's discomfort in Iran under the hierarchy of the traditional family is well noted, as well as her concern for retaining her own voice within this foreign world.

By presenting a variety of Iranian male characters, Rachlin avoids the stereotypes of hostile, rigid Iranian men. Karim, who was paralyzed by his grief and self-pity in America, becomes more and more comfortable in his home country, where he is clearly needed. As a university professor, his work in America is abstract and impersonal. In Iran, by the end of the novel, he finds more fulfilling work reconstructing villages bombed heavily during the Iraq-Iran War. Karim settles into a rewarding life in Iran although he writes his wife consistently talking of reuniting with her and Darius, their son. In the end, despite their desire for each other's company, both Jennifer and Karim seem to have made peace to live their separate lives, one in America and the other in Iran.

Zohra Saed

Him, Chanrithy (1965–)

Born in Takeo Province, Cambodia, Chanrithy Him fled with her family to the countryside when the Khmer Rouge defeated the Lol Nol army and entered Phnom Penh in 1975. Since her father, Atidsim Him, was a government bureaucrat during the post-independence Lol Nol era, her family had to live in hiding to avoid persecution by the Khmer Rouge. After just two weeks of hiding in Chanrithy's grandfather's house, however, her father and two uncles were taken away in an ox-cart by the Khmer Rouge cadres for an orientation meeting, never to be seen again. While the rest of the family was relocated several times, the children were separated and sent to different labor camps. Approximately 1.7 million to 2 million Cambodians (20 percent of the population) lost their lives to execution, forced labor, starvation, and sickness under the Khmer Rouge regime. In her family of 10, only five survived the killing fields; Him lost both parents and three siblings.

In 1979, when Vietnam invaded Cambodia, Him and her remaining siblings fled with other survivors to refugee camps at the Thai border, where she wrote to her uncle in the United States. In 1981, 16-year-old Him and her family settled in Oregon. As interpreter, Him worked for 12 years on the Khmer Adolescent Project, a federally funded study on post-traumatic stress of Cambo-

dian youths who grew up under the Khmer Rouge regime. In 1991 she graduated from the University of Oregon with a B.S.; in 1995 she postponed medical school to write her memoir. When her memoir, *When Broken Glass Floats: Growing up under the Khmer Rouge,* was published by Norton in 2000, it became, along with LOUNG UNG's *First They Killed My Father: a Daughter of Cambodia Remembers* (2000), one of the only two Cambodian-American memoirs to date by women who grew up during the Khmer Rouge regime.

When Broken Glass Floats won an Oregon Book Award in 2001 amid controversy over its authorship. In 1994 Kimber Williams, a reporter for the *Register-Guard* in Eugene, Oregon, wrote an article about Him. The two met again when Him approached Williams for assistance with her memoir. After the publication of *When Broken Glass Floats,* Williams accused Him of not crediting her contribution to the work. The case was resolved when Williams signed a legal statement relinquishing future claims to the book.

When Broken Glass Floats is written in the present tense and from a child's point of view, creating a sense of immediacy and intimacy. The memoir describes events that happened during the Khmer Rouge regime, when Him was between nine and 13 years of age. Him uses family pictures and drawings, along with maps and family trees, to document her family history. At one point, she even transcribes and translates her sister's poetry, giving voice to her dead sister, Chea. Interestingly, Him interjects newspaper articles into her personal narrative, creating a dynamic tension between official and unofficial histories, public records and personal testimonies.

As testimonial literature, *When Broken Glass Floats* is dedicated to Him's family members as well as other Cambodians who perished in the killing fields. Him introduces the memoir with her poem, "Please Give Us Voice," in which the voices of the dead plead with the living for justice: *"Please remember us. Please speak for us. Please bring us justice."* Other themes include writing and healing, the spirit of survival, oppression and resistance, history, politics, and literature. Chanrithy Him lives in Eugene, where she works as a medical interpreter, writer, researcher, and activist. She gives public lectures across the United States.

Bunkong Tuon

Hirahara, Naomi (1962–)

Born in Pasadena, California, Naomi was the first child of her parents, both of whom were affected by the 1945 Hiroshima bombing. Her father, born in California but taken to Hiroshima as a child, lived only miles away from where the bombs were dropped. He, however, survived it and was able to return to California after the war. Naomi's mother lost her father in the blast.

After receiving her bachelor's degree in international relations from Stanford University, Naomi Hirahara studied at the Inter-University Center for Advanced Japanese Language Studies in Tokyo and spent three months as a volunteer worker in Ghana, West Africa. She was a reporter and editor of *The Rafu Shimpo,* the largest Japanese-American daily newspaper, during the culmination of the redress and reparations movement for Japanese Americans who were forcibly removed from their homes during World War II. During her tenure as editor, the newspaper published a highly acclaimed interethnic-relations series after the L.A. riots. Hirahara left the newspaper in 1996 to serve as a Milton Center Fellow in creative writing at Newman University in Wichita, Kansas.

After returning to California in 1997, Hirahara began to edit, publish, and write books. She edited *Green Makers: Japanese American Gardeners in Southern California* (2000), published by Southern California Gardeners' Federation. She also authored two biographies for the Japanese American National Museum, *An American Son: The Story of George Aratani, Founder of Mikasa and Kenwood* (2000) and *A Taste for Strawberries: The Independent Journey of Nisei Farmer Manabi Hirasaki* (2003). She also compiled a reference book, *Distinguished Asian American Business Leaders* (2003), and coedited *Silent Scars of Healing Hands: Oral Histories of Japanese American Doctors in World War II Detention Camps* (2004) for the Japanese American Medical Association.

Hirahara, however, is best known for her Mas Arai mystery series. Her debut mystery novel, *Summer of the Big Bachi* (2004), introduces readers to a unique kind of literary detective—the "Japanese gardener" in a crime-solving role. The story tells of the Japanese-American gardener, Mas Arai, who spends much of his time with his friends in a sleepy Los Angeles suburb. But for more than 50 years, Mas has kept secrets about the lives of his three friends, about his youth in Hiroshima prior to the atomic bombing in 1945, and about his fears of *bachi*—the spirit of retribution. When a stranger arrives in town, a brutal homicide occurs, sending Mas on a search for long-lost truths.

The lead character, Mas Arai, is loosely based on Naomi Hirahara's issei father, who is also a survivor of the Hiroshima bombing and a Los Angeles–based gardener. *Summer of the Big Bachi,* a finalist for Barbara Kingsolver's Bellwether Prize, was also nominated for a Macavity mystery award. Naomi's second mystery, *Gasa-Gasa Girl* (2005), was on the Southern California Booksellers' Association best seller list for two weeks in 2005. Naomi's third mystery *Snakeskin Shamisen* was published in April 2006.

Monika Dix

Ho, Minfong (1951–)

An award-winning author of fiction for young readers, Minfong Ho has brought an engagingly multicultural and straightforwardly honest perspective to the subjects that she has treated in her work. Ho was born in Rangoon, Burma, to Thai parents. Her parents were well-educated professionals: her father, Rih-Hwa, was an economist, and her mother, Lienfung, a chemist. Raised largely in Thailand and Taiwan, Ho attended Tunghai University in Taichung, Taiwan, in the late 1960s. Immigrating to the United States, she attended Cornell University, completing a B.A. in history and economics in 1973 and an M.F.A. in creative writing in 1980. In 1976 she married John

Value Dennis, a soil scientist, with whom she has had three children.

In the mid-1970s, Ho worked as a journalist in Singapore and as a university instructor in Taiwan. In the early 1980s, she worked with Catholic Relief Services in the camps along the Thai-Cambodian border. She has subsequently been a writer-in-residence at Singapore University, and she has conducted writing workshops at sites around the world as well as in the K-12 schools near her current home in Ithaca, New York.

With young girls as protagonists, Ho's stories offer a realistic and sensitive view of Southeast Asia. Her first novel, *Sing to the Dawn* (1975), focuses on an ambitious girl in a rural Thai village who wins a scholarship to a prestigious urban school. Her father and brother initially try to discourage her from accepting the scholarship because they fear for her safety in the city. For this debut novel, Ho received the first prize from the Council of Interracial Books for Children. *Rice without Rain* (1986), Ho's second novel, received truly international recognition. The novel treats the coming of age of a 17-year-old Thai girl whose family becomes involved, at great cost, with reformers from an urban university who encourage the villagers to protest the disadvantageous economic conditions that have long defined their lives. The novel deals compellingly with such subjects as endemic poverty, political radicalism, and state violence. For this novel, Ho received several awards including the first prize from the National Book Development Council of Singapore and a Best Books for Young Adults citation from the American Library Association. Ho's third novel, *The Clay Marble* (1991), depicts the challenges faced by Dara, a 12-year-old Cambodian girl who flees the Khmer Rouge to a refugee camp just across the border in Thailand. The protagonist makes friends with Jantu, who creates great toys out of mud including a "magical" clay marble. When the camp is disrupted by Vietnamese bombing and Jantu later dies from friendly fire, Dara matures quickly to become assertive; when her brother wants to join the military, she persuades him to return home with the family.

In her most recent novels, *Gathering the Dew* (2003) and *The Stone Goddess* (2003), Ho chronicles the experiences of Cambodian girls whose families must confront much more directly the terrors of life under the Khmer Rouge, before finding refuge as emigrants to the United States.

Ho is also the author of the short-story collection, *Tanjong Rhu and Other Stories* (1986), and four picture books for children—*The Two Brothers* (coauthored with Saphan Ros, 1995), *Hush!: A Thai Lullaby* (1996), *Brother Rabbit: A Cambodian Tale* (also coauthored with Ros, 1997), and *Peek!: A Thai Hide-and-Seek Book* (2004). In addition, she has translated *Maples in the Mist: Children's Poems from the Tang Dynasty* (1996).

Martin Kich

Holthe, Tess Uriza (1966–)

Born to Filipino immigrant parents in San Francisco, Holthe had an atypical journey toward her impressive debut novel, *When the Elephants Dance* (2002), which was written while she was working full time as an accountant. Although Holthe grew up in a household where storytelling traditions and other aspects of Filipino national culture were an important element of her life, she did not originally consider becoming a writer. Instead, following the advice of her parents, she went to the University of California at Davis for a pre-medical degree. She dropped out of her program and returned to San Franciso to complete a degree in accounting from Golden Gate University. Always interested in writing, she once took a writing class "for fun." In this writing class, she put together a series of myths, legends, and family stories, which later became the basis for her first novel.

The book provides a detailed account of life in the Philippines during World War II, when Japanese troops invaded the country and subjected it to a brutal occupation. Much of the novel focuses on the horrors of that occupation. As Holthe writes in the opening lines, "'When the elephants dance, the chickens must be careful.' The great beasts, as they circle one another, shaking the trees and trumpeting loudly, are the Amerikanos and the Japanese as they fight. And our Philippines Islands? We are the small chickens" (3). It is this sense of national and collective vulnerability that Holthe communicates through the stories and interactions of the family, friends, and villagers who are huddling together in the cellar beneath Alejandro Karanglan's parents' house, after their own houses have been destroyed or taken over by the Japanese.

Alejandro, the primary narrator of the novel, begins with his description of life in the cellar and ends with his recollections of how his family and friends survived the occupation and returned to their shelter in the Karanglan household with the aid of the American army. In between, readers are introduced to the traumatic horrors of war. Alejandro is suspended by his thumbs from a wire in the fence, while his sister, Isabelle Karanglan, who narrates the second section of the novel, is taken to Manila, along with other women, to be used as a "comfort woman," a military sex slave. Another character, Domingo Matapang, leads a band of guerrillas and narrates the third segment of the novel. Juxtaposed against the contemporary experiences of Alejandro, Isabelle, and Domingo are the five stories of the community elders—stories that provide fascinating glimpses into the social, cultural, and political history of the Philippines, beginning with Spanish colonialism.

Resisting the temptation of turning her novel into a sociological treatise, Holthe instead explores individual human follies, pains, aspirations, and survival. These stories are rooted in social histories and realities but are never reduced to mere sociological or historical explanations. In this respect, Holthe follows in the footsteps of a specific tradition of women's writings in Asian-American literature which begins with MAXINE HONG KINGSTON and continues through writers such as LAN CAO and RUTHANNE LUM MCCUNN. These writers use folkloric narratives and cultural memory to destabilize mainstream ideas of racial, national, and historical identities. In Holthe's case, this is especially evident in the concluding chapter of the novel. Alejandro informs us, "I have my own thoughts. I keep remembering Domingo's words. He said it

is up to Roderick and me to build and teach the other children that it is better to stand together than to let other nations divide us" (368).

The novel depicts a clearly identifiable nationalist sensibility. This is not surprising given its historic context—the Philippines attained its independence in 1946, just after the events depicted in the novel. The stories, tales, and legends narrated within the novel depict a Filipino national culture that can sustain the unity of the nation even in face of foreign imperialist intervention.

Bibliography
Holthe, Tess Uriza. *When the Elephants Dance.* New York: Crown, 2002.

Nandini Dhar

Homebase　Shawn Wong　(1979)

Called a "novel" on the title page, *Homebase* can be seen as a collection of six interconnected short stories—the chapters that have appeared as separate stories in various anthologies. Rebelling against literary traditions, SHAWN WONG has experimented in various degrees of formal innovation. *Homebase* crosses the boundaries between memory, fantasy, and dream to offer a bittersweet view of Chinese-American life. He blends into the narrative real and imagined letters, essays, poetry, dialogues, and journal entries. Moreover, the settings shift constantly, defying a logical or chronological sequence of incidents. The "novel" lyrically interweaves the past and the present to chronicle the history of Chinese America.

The novel opens with the story of Rainsford, a fourth-generation Chinese American who expresses the pains of growing up as a homeless Chinese American. Orphaned at age 15, he appears restless and rootless. His family has been in America for 125 years, but he feels alienated and outcast. After the deaths of his parents, Rainsford starts a search for his identity as a Chinese-American man by way of imaginary identification with his male ancestors. He feels obliged to tell the stories about his ancestors, for the meaning of his existence lies in reconstructing the family history.

To do so, Rainsford relies on different perspectives to evoke the spirits of his father and other male ancestors. As he seeks a connection with his ancestors, the narrator employs multiple points of view, voices, and personas. The narrator either addresses his grandfather directly or assumes the persona of his great-grandfather. Sometimes the narrator becomes one of his ancestors who helped to build America by constructing the Pacific Railroad over the Sierra Nevada. By interacting with his ancestors to retell the family's story in the historical context, Rainsford not only begins to understand the sufferings and oppression of his ancestors, but also recognizes the connection: "And I knew then that I was only my father's son, that he was Grandfather's son and Grandfather was Great-Grandfather's son and that night we were all the same man" (86).

To Rainsford, the construction of his identity also depends on the relocation of places. Since the town of Rainsford, California, in which the narrator's great-grandfather first settled and after which the boy was named, does not exist anymore on the American map, he has no place to claim his identity. In an attempt to map out his identity, Rainsford tries to imagine how they endured loneliness, hardship, and violence to find a place in America. Ultimately his vision of Chinese America and his sense of home are established through his act of remembering.

Bibliography

Hsu, Ruth Y. "The Mythic West and the Discourse of Nation in Shawn Wong's *Homebase.*" *Passages: Interdisciplinary Journal of Global Studies* 2, no. 2 (2000): 221–241.

Lee, A. Robert. "Decolonizing America: The Ethnicity of Ernest Gains, Jose Antonio Villarreal, Leslie Marmon Silko and Shawn Wong." In *Shades of Empire in Colonial and Post Colonial Literatures,* edited by C. C. Barfoot and Theo D'Haen, 269–282. Amsterdam: Rodopi, 1993.

Sakurai, Patricia A. "The Politics of Possession: The Negotiation of Identity in *American in Disguise, Homebase,* and *Farewell to Manzanar.*" In *Privileging Positions: The Sites of Asian American Studies,* edited by Gary Y. Okihiro, Marilyn Alquizola, Dorothy Fujita Rony, and K. Scott Wong, 157–170. Pullman: Washington University Press, 1995.

Su-lin Yu

Hongo, Garrett Kaoru   (1951–   )

Garrett Hongo is best known for his narrative poetry, which pieces together family history and the stories of Japanese Americans to break the silence surrounding the Japanese internment camps, the destruction of Hiroshima and its aftermath, and the historically uneasy relationships between Anglo and Japanese Americans.

Hongo was born in Hawaii, but his family left the island to move to Los Angeles when the poet was six. After graduating from college in 1973, Hongo spent a year in Japan. On his return, he entered the University of Michigan's graduate program in Japanese literature but eventually left the program to work as a poet in residence for the Seattle Arts Commission. There he was the founding director of the theater group called the "Asian Exclusion Act." Influenced by other Asian-American writers such as FRANK CHIN, his work became more focused on forging a common bond among Asian Americans. In 1976 he produced his own drama, *Nisei Bar & Grill,* a play examining the postwar lives of Korean veterans, which led him to examine his growing concerns with his own identity.

Hongo's first volume of poetry, *The Buddha Bandits Down Highway 9* (1978), was written with Alan Chong Lau and LAWSON FUSAO INADA. Hongo's section of the volume, "Cruising 99," has been compared to the breezy rhythms of the beat poets, as these lines from "Cruising in the Greater Vehicle/ A Jam Session" illustrate: "I'm just laying down a bass, man,/ Just a rhythm, a scale, something to jam on, something to change, find our range, something to get us going" (26). The repetitions and parallel images in the poem also led to early comparisons to Walt Whitman.

"Cruising 99" and several other poems from *The Buddha Bandits* appear in *Yellow Light,* published in 1982, which illustrates Hongo's movement toward more introspective reflection and his use of alternate voices and perspectives. The collection combines narratives from personal and collective history as the speaker moves through the landscapes of home neighborhoods to Japan to explore the Asian-American experience. "Stepchild" is a long poem that searches for an American identity in the void created by the silence of first-generation immigrants and second-generation Japanese Americans. The speaker asks, "Where are the histories / our tragedies, our books / of fact and fiction?" The bitterness of the poem reflects Hongo's growing need to erase the shame of the Japanese relocation and to recover the lost history of Japanese Americans. Hongo has been praised for the lushness of his imagery in *Yellow Light.* Poems such as "Who Among You Knows the Essence of Garlic?" engage all the senses with beautiful evocation of details: "Flukes of giant black mushrooms / leap from their murky tubs / and strangle the toes of young carrots."

Hongo's second volume of poetry, *The River of Heaven* (1988), won the Lamont Poetry Prize and a nomination for the Pulitzer Prize in poetry. While still concerned with reconstructing the past to illuminate a culturally enforced darkness, Hongo creates specific characters to highlight the Japanese-American experience in less bitter tones. In "The Legend," a poem narrating the events surrounding the senseless death of an Asian immigrant, Hongo approaches the subject with a beautiful calm: "Let the night sky cover him as he dies. / Let the weaver girl cross the bridge of heaven / and take up his cold hands." The journey of Asian immigrants to America is continued in this dead immigrant's journey to the next world.

The journey motif is frequent in Hongo's writings, and connects his early "Cruising 99" with his later VOLCANO: A MEMOIR OF HAWAI'I (1995). *Volcano* traces Hongo's journey to his birthplace on Hawaii, near the Kilauea volcano. Hongo's family moved to Los Angeles, where he grew up in a multicultural environment that did little to encourage the poet's quest for his family history and his own identity. Hongo recounts feeling alienated from the American experience as it was taught in the California schools. Particularly frustrating to him was the exclusion of Asian-American history from the textbooks and the absence of information on the Japanese internment camps during World War II. In a 1989 interview with Bill Moyers during the making of the PBS series *The Power of the Word,* Hongo comments that traveling to Volcano, Hawai'i, provided him with an opportunity to reconnect with family and to come into his own as a writer.

Hongo is also a respected editor and has produced several collections and anthologies of Asian-American writings. *Songs My Mother Taught Me* (1994), by WAKAKO YAMAUCHI, is a collection of stories that document the lives of rural immigrants and factory workers. In 1993 he edited the influential *The Open Boat: Poems from Asian America.* In the collection's introduction, Hongo says, "It is perhaps difficult to make poetry from that emotional catch in the throat, that which compels us to speak when so much passion swells that, out of pride, the act of speaking is what we might fear the most. But our poets speak anyway" (xl). Hongo's comment highlights the primary theme of his poetry and autobiographical writings—the need to break the silence. An anthology of personal essays by Asian Americans, *Under Western Eyes,* followed in 1995. The essays use autobiography to confront the problems of racism, assimilation, and loss of identity that affect the Asian-American community.

Bibliography

Evans, Alice. "A Vicious Kind of Tenderness: An Interview with Garrett Hongo." *Poets & Writers Magazine* (September–October 1992): 37–46.

Hongo, Garrett, ed. *The Open Boat: Poems from Asian America.* New York: Anchor Books, 1993.

Hongo, Garrett, Alan Chong Lau and Lawson Fusao Inada. *The Buddha Bandits down Highway 99.* Mountain View, Calif.: Buddhead, 1978.

Slowik, Mary. "Beyond Lot's Wife: The Immigration Poems of Marilyn Chin, Garrett Hongo, Li-Young Lee, and David Mura." *MELUS* 25, nos. 3/4 (Autumn–Winter 2000): 221–242.

Uba, George. Review of *Yellow Light. The Journal of Ethnic Studies* 12, no. 4 (Winter 1985): 123–125.

Yu, Timothy. "Form and Identity in Language Poetry and Asian American Poetry." *Contemporary Literature* 41, no. 3 (Autumn 2000): 422–461.

Patricia Kennedy Bostian

Hosokawa, Kumpei William "Bill"
(1915–)

Bill Hosokawa was born and raised in Seattle. Although he began speaking English only in kindergarten, he took an early interest in reading and sports. As a teenager, he spent several summers working in Alaskan canneries. In 1933 Hosokawa entered the University of Washington to study journalism, despite being warned that no newspaper would hire a Japanese American. Soon after, he took part-time employment with a local nisei newspaper, *The Japanese-American Courier*. In 1937 Hosokawa earned his bachelor's degree. After a brief period of working for the Japanese consulate in Seattle, he moved to Singapore to found an English-language newspaper, the *Singapore Herald*. In 1940 he migrated to Shanghai, where he wrote for the *Shanghai Times* and the *Far Eastern Review*. He returned to Seattle in October 1941 and was rehired by the *Japanese-American Courier*.

In spring 1942, Hosokawa was incarcerated by the U.S. federal government with other Japanese Americans, first at Puyallup Assembly Center, then at Heart Mountain, where he was named editor of the inmate newspaper, *The Heart Mountain Sentinel*. Despite the privations of camp existence, Hosokawa enjoyed the position. In October 1943, Hosokawa resettled in Des Moines, Iowa, and was hired as copy editor by the *Des Moines Register*. Three years later, he was engaged as copy editor and reporter by the *Denver Post*. Hosokawa remained with the newspaper until 1983, serving successively as Korean War correspondent, editor of the *Post*'s Sunday magazine *Empire*, and associate editor. In 1977 Hosokawa was named the *Post*'s editorial page editor. After leaving the *Post*, Hosokawa worked for the *Rocky Mountain News*, retiring in 1992. Meanwhile, he remained active in a nisei political organization, Japanese American Citizens' League (JACL), and wrote articles and a weekly column, "From the Frying Pan," for its weekly newspaper, *The Pacific Citizen*.

In the mid-1960s, the directors of the Japanese American Research Project at UCLA persuaded Hosokawa to write a history of Japanese Americans using the materials the project had amassed. The product was Hosokawa's 1969 book, *Nisei:*

The Quiet Americans. Nisei was among the first mass-market histories of Japanese Americans, and the first written by a Nisei. Despite the book's title, the first third of the text covered issei generations, and the book was praised for its readable narrative and rich detail regarding prewar Japanese communities. While Hosokawa was later criticized for his conservative assimilationist version of history and for attributing Japanese-American success to inherited cultural factors, the book was widely adopted as a text in the new field of Asian-American studies. Meanwhile, its popular success helped bring the story of wartime incarceration to a mainstream audience. In succeeding years, Hosokawa cowrote a second history of Japanese Americans, *East to America* (1980). He meanwhile published two other books: *The Two Worlds of Jim Yoshida* (1972), the story of a nisei forced to fight for Japan in World War II, and *Thunder in the Rockies* (1976), a history of *The Denver Post*. Hosokawa also released a volume of favorite *Pacific Citizen* columns, *Thirty-Five Years in the Frying Pan* (1978). *Out of the Frying Pan: Reflections of a Japanese American*, another selection of columns coupled with a brief memoir, followed in 1998.

Hosokawa gained increased notoriety in Japanese-American circles with a pair of historical volumes, *JACL in Quest of Justice* (1982) and *They Call me Moses Masaoka* (1985). These twin works, which appeared at the height of the Japanese-American redress struggle, represented an "official history" of the JACL, and seemed designed primarily to answer criticisms of the organization's wartime actions—notably the organization's collaboration with the mass removal in 1942. The books portrayed the JACL and its leaders as civil rights heroes, and failed to treat adequately either conflicts within JACL (including those over its support of the 1952 McCarran-Walter Immigration Bill) or its contested actions. In particular, Hosokawa did not discuss the wartime draft resistance campaign of the Fair Play Committee at Heart Mountain camp or the efforts of JACL leaders to stifle it.

Hosokawa has remained active as a writer. His book, *Colorado's Japanese Americans: From 1886 to the Present* (2005), mixed a set of individual life stories with the larger history of the community. He has also continued to contribute regular columns to the Japanese-American weeklies *Rafu Shimpo* and *Rocky Mountain Jiho.*

Greg Robinson

Hosseini, Khaled   (1965–)

A novelist and practicing physician currently residing in California, Khaled Hosseini was born in northern Kabul, Afghanistan. The eldest of five children, Hosseini grew up in a family that, though not wealthy, enjoyed a comfortable life in the final years of monarchal Afghanistan. His mother was a teacher of Farsi and history at a girls' high school in Kabul, and his father was a diplomat who worked for the Afghan Foreign Ministry. In 1976, when Hosseini's father was awarded a post at the Afghan Embassy in France, the family moved to Paris, where they lived until 1980.

Hosseini has stated in interviews that his early childhood was "wonderful" and his memories of Afghanistan very happy, until the fall of the monarchy in 1973, which unseated Zahir Shah and installed Daoud Khan as president of the Republic of Afghanistan. During the time the Hosseini family was away from Afghanistan, Daoud's rule was increasingly challenged by an emerging pro-communist political movement. In 1978 Daoud was assassinated during a national communist coup; Nur Muhammed Turaki assumed the presidency, signing a friendship treaty with the Soviet Union. The Afghan guerrilla movement (mujahideen) was founded in 1978; the following year saw the assassinations of both Turaki and his successor, Hafizullah Amin. In December of 1979, the Soviet Union invaded Afghanistan.

In 1980 Hosseini's father's French diplomatic post ended. Instead of returning to Afghanistan, however, Hosseini's father requested and was granted political asylum in the United States. The family relocated to San Jose, California, in 1980. Khaled attended Santa Clara University (B.A. in biology, 1988) and later the University of California San Diego School of Medicine (M.D., 1993). He began his medical practice in 1996.

As a child, Hosseini was a fan of American films, particularly the western movies of Clint Eastwood and John Wayne. In his free time, he played a great deal of soccer and especially enjoyed "fighting kites," an activity in which kite strings are studded with glue and ground glass in an attempt to break the opponent's line, thereby cutting the kite loose. This somewhat ironic blend of innocence and aggression informs Hosseini's first novel *The Kite Runner,* published in 2003.

The book traces the friendship of two young boys: Amir, the son of a wealthy northern Kabul businessman, and Hassan, the son of Amir's father's servant. Narrated by Amir, *The Kite Runner* spans the years between the mid-1960s and December 2001. As children in the final days of the Afghan monarchy, Amir and Hassan are inseparable despite the differences in their families' backgrounds and social standings. However, an incident in which Amir fails to protect Hassan from a group of bullies raises questions about the level of Amir's faithfulness to his friend. These questions become more complicated after Hassan demonstrates his ongoing loyalty to Amir by assuming the blame for stealing money that Amir himself has stolen, thus taking the very serious shame of theft upon himself.

Amir and his father flee the country and relocate to the United States in the 1970s. In the years between the 1970s and 1990s, as rotating political factions ending with the Taliban assume control of an increasingly unstable Afghanistan, Amir establishes himself in the United States, becoming a successful novelist and starting a family. Racked with guilt over his failure to protect his friend, Amir gradually loses contact with Hassan. In the final section of the book, disturbing news—Hassan and his wife have been murdered by the Taliban, and Hassan's son Sohrab has been enslaved—moves Amir to fly back to Afghanistan in an attempt to make amends for what he sees as the cowardly acts of his childhood.

The Kite Runner was one of 2003's most visibly and highly praised novels. Many reviewers praise its timely blend of modern Middle Eastern history and examination of how cultural violence affects the lives of everyday people. *The Kite Runner* was named a *San Francisco Chronicle* "Best Book of the Year," an *Entertainment Weekly* "Top Ten Fiction Pick of the Year," and an American Library Association "Notable Book."

Bibliography

Hosseini, Khaled. "An Afghan Story: Khaled Hosseini and *The Kite Runner.*" Interview by Terry Gross. National Public Radio. Aug. 11, 2005. Available online. URL: http://www.npr.org/templates/story/story.php?storyId-4795618. Accessed April 25, 2006.

Khaled Hosseini Home Page. Available online. URL: http://www.khaledhosseini.com/index1.php?p-3.

Eric G. Waggoner

Houston, Jeanne Wakatsuki (Toyo)
(1934–)

Best known for her 1973 memoir FAREWELL TO MANZANAR, Houston is a writer and lecturer whose work deals largely with the World War II–era Japanese-American internment camps, particularly the internment's effects on families and women. Her father, born in Hiroshima, immigrated to the United States in 1904 and married Riku, a Hawaiian-born Japanese American. Jeanne, the last of 10 children, was born in Inglewood, California.

When Jeanne Wakatsuki was two, her family moved to Ocean Park, a primarily Caucasian seacoast city, where her father took up commercial fishing. Jeanne was seven years old in 1941, when Japanese bombers attacked the U.S. naval base at Pearl Harbor. On the night of the attack, her father, fearing acts of retaliation against Japanese Americans, burned the Japanese flag he had brought with him from Hiroshima, as well as any documents and papers indicating any personal connection with Japan. Despite this, two weeks after the attack, he was arrested by the FBI on false charges of supplying oil to Japanese submarines, and taken to North Dakota for questioning. Deprived of the income from Jeanne's father's fishing, the Wakatsukis moved to Terminal Island, a Japanese-American cannery community, and later to Boyle Heights, a racial ghetto in downtown Los Angeles.

In March 1942 the Wakatsukis sold or abandoned their possessions and were imprisoned near the Nevada border at Manzanar, the largest of the Japanese-American internment camps, where they were reunited with their father. The Wakatsukis would remain at Manzanar for nearly two and a half years. Upon their release in 1945, they moved to the Cabrillo Homes housing project in Long Beach.

While in junior high school at Long Beach, Jeanne won recognition from her school's journalism program for an essay she wrote about her family's preinternment life in coastal California. The response to that essay, she later recalled in her 1992 entry for the *Contemporary Authors Autobiography Series,* first made her want to become a writer. Jeanne Wakatsuki entered San Jose State University in 1952 as a journalism major, but the grim prospects for Asian-American women in that field caused her to change her major to sociology and social welfare. Throughout college she dated James D. Houston, a fellow journalism student, and on Valentine's Day 1957 Houston proposed to Jeanne. They were married a month later in Hawaii. After living abroad in England and France for nearly four years, Jeanne and James returned to California in 1961, settling first in Palo Alto and then in Santa Cruz, where they continue to live.

For many years thereafter Jeanne devoted her energies to raising their three children, but a visit from her nephew in 1971 prompted her to begin writing down her childhood memories of Manzanar and the internment experience. Published in 1973, the highly praised *Farewell to Manzanar* launched her career as a professional writer. In subsequent years she has written two more nonfiction books: *Don't Cry, It's Only Thunder* (1984, written with Paul G. Hensler), about an American soldier's experience working on behalf of Vietnamese orphans, and *Beyond Manzanar: Views of Asian-American Womanhood* (1985). She is a frequent contributor to newspapers and magazines including *Der Spiegel, Mother Jones,* and the *San Francisco Chronicle,* and she has authored several screenplays including a 1976 adaptation of *Farewell to Manzanar* for Universal/MCA-TV. In 2003 Wakatsuki Houston published her first full-length novel, *The Legend of Fire Horse Woman,* which tells the story of three generations of Japanese-American women interned together in the camps.

Bibliography

Kim, Elaine H. *Asian American Literature: An Introduction to the Writings and Their Social Context.* Philadelphia: Temple University Press, 1984.

Lim, Shirley Geok-lin, and Amy Ling. *Reading the Literatures of Asian America.* Philadelphia: Temple University Press, 1992.

Eric G. Waggoner

Houston, Velina Hasu   (1957–   )

The daughter of Lemo Houston, a mixed-race African-American and Blackfoot Indian career soldier from Alabama, and Setsuko Takechi of Matsuyama, Japan, Valina Hasu Houston was born in international waters bound for the United States. From the moment of her birth, she found herself between cultures and countries, which has become a sustaining theme of Houston's body of work for the stage.

In 1959 Houston moved to the United States with her parents, sister Hilda Rika Hatsuyo, and brother George Adam Houston, who was orphaned by World War II and adopted by Houston's family during the U.S. occupation. Houston was primarily raised in the military community of Junction City, Kansas, near the Fort Riley Army Compound. Surrounded by immigrant military wives and their children from countries such as Japan, Germany, Austria, France, and Italy, Houston's midwestern American childhood was both international and isolated. Estranged from their Japanese and American relatives alike, the Houston family found raising their biracial children in the Midwest challenging. Lemo Houston's early death further destabilized the family's already difficult settlement in American society.

Houston went on to attend Kansas State University, graduating with Phi Beta Kappa honors in 1979 with a B.A. in journalism, mass communications, and theater and with a minor in philosophy. Houston relocated permanently to California

after her mother remarried. In 1981 she completed an M.A. in theater arts with a specialization in screenwriting from the University of California, Los Angeles, and later earned a Ph.D. from the University of Southern California's School of Cinema-Television. In 1982 Houston won the Lorraine Hansberry Playwriting Award, and in both 1984 and 1987, she was appointed as a Rockefeller Foundation Playwriting Fellow. She gave birth to a son and a daughter and parented two more sons through her marriage to Peter H. Jones from Manchester, England.

Based in Los Angeles, Houston is one of the most widely produced contemporary Asian-American playwrights. Her best-known pieces, *Asa Ga Kimashita* (1981), *American Dreams* (1984) and *Tea* (1987), are based on her parents' personal history. *Asa Ga Kimashita* (Morning Has Broken) tells the story of a Japanese woman and an African-American soldier stationed in Japan who fall in love during the years just after World War II. They overcome the concerns of the woman's Japanese parents, who think the Americans occupying Japan are taking away not only their daughter but also their beloved culture and lifestyle. *American Dreams* follows this same young couple to the United States, where they attempt to begin their American lives in New York City. Moving in with the soldier's brother, the couple negotiates the complexities of racism and family relations.

Her most honored play, *Tea,* closes Houston's trilogy, and the play has found audiences in the United States and as far off as Japan and Taiwan. While mainly drawing on her mother's memories, Houston also compiled extensive interviews with Japanese women who married American military men. *Tea* follows four Japanese war brides living on a military base in Kansas. Together they reminisce while performing a tea ceremony in memory of their friend Himiko, a fellow war bride who had recently committed suicide after killing her husband.

Houston's body of work reveals her long-standing emphasis on tolerance and cultural understanding. Pieces such as *Kokoro* (True Heart) (1994) highlight the differences in Japanese and

American cultures' ideas of parental responsibility and honor. *Ikebana* ("living flowers" in Japanese) (2000) examines the elegantly beautiful, yet strictly conformist, culture imposed on Japanese women in the 1950s. Houston's later work also engages the difficult processes of identity formation. *Waiting for Tadashi* (2002), in part inspired by her brother's life, follows an Asian-American orphan through the years after World War II as he struggles with his discoveries and disillusionments about his self-identity. *Calling for Aphrodite* (2003) draws from Greek literature and modern history as it explores Hiroshima atomic bomb survivor Keiko Kimura's search for grace and beauty in a fragmented and war-tattered world.

Moving beyond the stage boards, Velina Hasu Houston's work with broadcast media also reveals her commitment to furthering an appreciation for multiculturalism and diversity. Houston's life and works were featured in the radio documentary "Don't Take The Colors Apart" (1994), part of the *Legacies: Tales From America* series. The documentary follows her on a journey back to Kansas with her mother. In *Do 2 Halves Really Make a Whole,* a 1993 video documentary produced by Martha Chono-Helsley, Houston is one of the featured subjects discussing the potential and difficulties growing up multiracial in the United States. In addition, she wrote for the PBS television children's series "The Puzzle Factory," later renamed "The Puzzle Place," which featured multiethnic puppets who teach each other about multiculturalism, decision making, and conflict resolution. Houston has also authored children's books including *Kiyoshi and the Magic Futon,* which is named for her son, and *Neapolitan Ice Cream,* which is based on her father's explanation of her own multicultural heritage.

Houston continues to contribute to American literature as an acclaimed playwright, writer, and scholar. In addition to plays, Houston has published a volume of poetry entitled *Green Tea Girl in Orange Pekoe Country* (1993) and edited *The Politics of Life: Four Plays by Asian American Women* (1993) and *But Still, Like Air, I'll Rise: New Asian American Plays* (1997). Currently a professor of theater at the University of Southern California,

Houston is the founder and director of the university's MFA program in playwriting. Her works and papers have been archived in the Velina Hasu Houston Collection at the Huntington Library and Museums in San Marino, California.

Bibliography

Do 2 Halves Really Make a Whole? Directed by Martha Chono-Helsley. Bronze Apple, National Education Media Network, 1993.

Don't Take the Colors Apart. Produced by Dmae Roberts. 1994. Available online. URL: http://www.prx.org/pieces/1260.

The Puzzle Place. Lancit Media Productions and PBS-KCET. 1994–1998.

Uno, Roberta. "Tea by Valina Hasu Houston." *A Resource Guide to Asian American Literature,* edited by Sau-ling Cynthia Wong and Stephen H. Sumida, 193–199. New York: Modern Language Association of America, 2001.

Usui, Masami, and Miles Xian Liu. "Valina Hasu Houston." *Asian American Playwrights: A Bio-Bibliographical Critical Sourcebook,* edited by Miles X. Liu, 103–111. Westport, Conn.: Greenwood, 2002.

Velina Hasu Houston. "Biography." Available online. URL: http://www.velinahasuhouston.com. Accessed September 27, 2006.

M. Gabot Fabros

Hundred Secret Senses, The Amy Tan
(1995)

At the center of AMY TAN's third novel, *The Hundred Secret Senses,* is the relationship between the half sisters Li Kwan and Olivia Bishop. They are both daughters of Jack Yee, a Chinese immigrant living in the United States. But Li Kwan was born in China to Jack's first, Chinese wife and does not immigrate to the United States until she is in her late teens, whereas Olivia Bishop was born in California to Jack's second, American wife. So, in addition to the inherent strains in their familial relationship, the half sisters are culturally very different, with Li Kwan representing a traditional Chinese outlook and Olivia exemplifying an assimilated and "hyphenated" point of view. What makes the relationship even more complex is that Olivia is a young child while Li Kwan is an adult and thus becomes something close to another maternal figure to Olivia. And yet Olivia knows intuitively how to negotiate within American society, whereas Li Kwan remains a somewhat awkward, if enthusiastic, outsider.

Although it is set primarily in the 20th century, the narrative reaches back to 19th-century China during the convulsions of the Taiping Rebellion. Li Kwan believes that she has been blessed with the ability to communicate with the "yin," the spirits of the dead, and to recall episodes from her previous reincarnations—in particular, her life as Nunumu, a servant to British missionaries who became involved in very melodramatic misadventures. When the narrative returns to the present, Olivia, now 38 years old and about to break up her marriage to Simon Bishop, agrees to travel with her husband and Li Kwan to the latter's home village in China. Once there, Olivia begins to see the validity of her half sister's incredible stories; in that peculiarly mystical atmosphere, Olivia also begins to reconcile with her husband. Ultimately, it becomes clear that, by helping Olivia and Simon stay together, Li Kwan is compensating for a lapse in judgment that she had as Nunumu.

The critical response to this novel has been more mixed than the responses to her other works. The major point of contention is Li Kwan's mystical powers. Those who accept Li Kwan's preternatural experiences as a credible aspect of the novel's milieu have praised the novel as representing, at least in some ways, a narrative and thematic advancement over Tan's first two novels. But other readers have found Li Kwan's anomalous experiences to be an elaborate gimmick that finally seems more forced than credible or even enlightening. Interestingly, both admirers and critics of the novel have asserted that the basic characterization of Li Kwan is one of the novel's greatest strengths.

Bibliography

Lee, Ken-fan. "Cultural Translation and the Exorcist: A Reading of Kingston's and Tan's Ghost Stories." *MELUS* 29 (Summer 2004): 105–127.

Ma, Sheng-mei. "'Chinese and Dogs' in Amy Tan's *The Hundred Secret Senses*: Ethnicizing the Primitive à la New Age." *MELUS* 26 (Spring 2001): 29–44.

Unali, Lina. "Americanization and Hybridization in *The Hundred Secret Senses*." *Hitting Critical Mass: A Journal of Asian American Cultural Criticism* 4 (Fall 1996): 135–144.

Zhang, Benzi. "Reading Amy Tan's Hologram: *The Hundred Secret Senses*." *International Fiction Review* 31, nos. 1–2 (2004): 13–18.

Martin Kich

Hunger: A Novella and Short Stories
Lan Samantha Chang (1998)

This collection by LAN SAMANTHA CHANG includes the title novella "Hunger" and five short stories, "Water Names," "San," "The Unforgetting," "The Eve of the Spirit Festival," and "Pipa's Story." All the stories are about Chinese immigrants and their families in America. For the immigrant parents as well as their children, the haunting memories of the past make it difficult to achieve "the forgetfulness that is essential to moving on." The alienation and estrangement of the characters become an inevitable and painful result of being unable to forget.

"Hunger" tells the story of Tian, a talented violinist who comes to America to continue his education in a music school. As a Chinese immigrant, however, he is forced to work in a Chinese restaurant. He desperately seeks to realize his dream in his two daughters, but to no avail because one daughter is tone-deaf while the other, though talented, rebels against his pressure and runs away from home. "The Eve of the Spirit Festival" is a similar story about a Chinese immigrant father's failure to be accepted into an American institution and the subsequent tension and conflict between the father and his daughters. The tugging force of the past is vividly personified in "Water Names," in which a grandmother reminds her young American granddaughters of their ancestors living by the Yangtze River. The reminder triggers a folktale about a young girl living by the Yangtze River in ancient China who is enchanted by the spirit of a drowned young man. In "Pipa's Story," set in China shortly before 1949, the past returns as a charmed stone that seeks revenge. The young girl in "San" studies mathematics hard in an attempt to understand her immigrant father, who desperately applied his mathematical skills to gambling and left the family broken.

"The Unforgetting" is the story that best illustrates Chinese Americans' dilemma of being caught between the necessity and the impossibility to forget. Ming Hwang, giving up on his dream of being a scientist, settles down with his wife and son in an isolated small town in Iowa to start a new life as a photocopier repair technician. Despite their intention and attempt to forget, Ming and his wife remain trapped in their memories and small-town life. When their son Charles decides to leave home for college, the immigrant parents realize they only have each other to keep their memories alive.

In this collection of stories, Chang explores Chinese-American experiences in a society where dreams are granted and assimilation demanded, but where neither is achievable for certain groups of immigrants. She questions the identity of Chinese Americans, both the immigrant generation of the 1950s and their children, by examining their severance from and bondage to the past.

Yan Ying

Huỳnh, Jade Ngọc Quang   (1957–)

Born in a Mekong Delta village in South Vietnam, Huỳnh was attending Saigon University in 1975 when the capital fell to the Viet Cong. He was soon sent to a re-education camp and consequently survived forced labor, starvation, torture, and war. In 1977, leaving his family behind, Huỳnh made a harrowing journey by boat to Thailand and lived in a refugee camp before he was sponsored to travel to Corinth, Tennessee. He worked at several menial jobs including as a fast-food restaurant worker, a machine operator, and a janitor, before graduating with a B.A. from Bennington College, Vermont, in 1987. He received his M.F.A. from Brown University in 1992 and a Ph.D. in 2005 from Cardiff University in the United Kingdom.

Huỳnh published his major work, *South Wind Changing*, in 1994. The memoir won several recognitions including *Time* magazine's nonfiction book of the year, and it was short-listed for the National Book Award. *South Wind Changing* is one of the early book-length narratives in English that describe civilian experiences in Vietnam after the U.S. evacuation. The book uses several tropes in describing life after the fall of Saigon: the re-education and labor camps, the persecution and execution of former government officials and intellectuals, the secret police, government corruption and abuse, and the tension between the South and the North. Throughout the narrative, however, runs the motif of nature as a transcending and eternal source of hope and inspiration. *South Wind Changing* also shares with other Southeast Asian refugee literatures (Cambodian and Hmong) such themes as war and violence, memory and trauma, hope and survival, home and family, escape and freedom.

In 2001, Huỳnh coedited with Mary Cargill *Voices of Vietnamese Boat People: Nineteen Narratives of Escape and Survival,* a collection of narratives of Vietnamese men and women, from students to professors, from entrepreneurs to doctors, who risked the dangers of starvation, pirates, and natural disasters in their escape to freedom on small make-shift boats.

In 2004, Huỳnh chose Starborn Books, a small publishing house in Wales, to publish his second major work, *The Family Wound,* a fictitious account based on his aunt's life. He wanted artistic control over his literary work rather than compromise with major publishing houses and their expectations of Hollywood adaptation of his books.

Huỳnh has taught at several colleges and universities including St. Lawrence University in New York and Appalachian State University in North Carolina.

Bibliography
Nguyen, Dinh-Hoa. Review of *South Wind Changing.* *World Literature Today* 69 (1995): 654.

Rabson, Steve. Review of *South Wind Changing.* *Journal of Asian Studies* 54 (1995): 254–256.

Truong, Monique T. D. "Vietnamese American Literature." *An Interethnic Companion to Asian Ameri-*

can *Literature,* edited by King-Kok Cheung. New York: Cambridge University Press, 1997.

Bunkong Tuon

Hwang, Caroline   (?–   )

A Korean-American writer who currently lives in New York and works as a magazine editor, Hwang graduated from the University of Pennsylvania and went on to get an M.F.A. from New York University. Her writings have appeared in *Glamour, Redbook, Self, Mademoiselle, Cosmogirl, YM,* and *Newsweek.*

In Hwang's debut novel, *In Full Bloom* (2003), Ginger Lee is a graduate school dropout who does not mind living in New York City to work as her best friend's assistant at *À la Mode* fashion magazine. Her life, however, is thrown into chaos when her mother unexpectedly arrives with a mission to get her daughter married. Conflicted with her Korean-American identity, Ginger does not date Korean-American men, a fact she is hesitant to tell her mother. Thirteen years earlier, her mother had cut off communication with George, Ginger's older brother, because he married a white woman against her wishes. Ginger staves off her mother's aggressive attempts to set her up by keeping herself busy at work; she later decides, however, that the best way to repel the blind dates is to sabotage them. To her surprise, she is forced to address her own identity issues when she goes on a blind date with a "happily-adjusted second-generation Korean American" (209). Upon reflecting on their conversation, she realizes she had been frustrated about her "Korean and American halves, trying to keep them in balance, when they all got mixed up anyway" (259).

Hwang's portrayal of Korean-American men contributes to a growing body of literature that portrays them in an unflattering light. Ginger's father turns out to be a liar about his past; her brother George marries a white woman and is disowned; the father of a potential suitor abuses his wife and blames her for their son's singleness; and the same potential suitor refuses to date Ginger while hiding his homosexuality. The novel sug-

gests that even if Korean-American women want to date Korean-American men, few are suitable or available.

Ginger's status as a single female, on the other hand, reflects a dilemma that many Korean-American women and their parents grapple with today. Hwang portrays this issue in a fresh and comical light and suggests in the conclusion that perhaps marriage is not everyone's final destination. Her protagonist realizes that "to be someone was to want to be someone more, not someone else" (252), or perhaps, not simply someone's wife.

Sarah Park

Hwang, David Henry   (1957–   )

A seminal Asian-American dramatist, Hwang is best known for his multi-award-winning Broadway sensation, *M. BUTTERFLY.* Some of his other plays have been very successful, while others have not fared well commercially or critically. Hwang has also collaborated with the acclaimed composer, Philip Glass. The 1988 collaboration between Glass and Hwang, *1,000 Airplanes on the Roof,* is a science fiction musical that celebrates a bizarre meeting between humans and aliens. Additionally, Hwang wrote the libretto for Glass's 1992 opera, *The Voyage,* which uses the theme of space travel to reflect upon the 15th-century achievements of Christopher Columbus. The work was commissioned and premiered by the Metropolitan Opera of New York. Recently, Hwang has also written screenplays including one for the David Cronenberg–directed film version of his own play, *M. Butterfly,* and others for films such as *Golden Gate* (1994) and *Possession* (2002).

In the substantial canon of his own dramatic works, Hwang often centers on Chinese-American crises of identity, portraying sympathetically the anxieties of Chinese Americans who do not feel entirely American or entirely Chinese. Taken together, Hwang's plays articulate his often-stated belief that it is limiting to be pigeon-holed as an Asian American. Identity is fluid, Hwang insists: Skin color or genetic origins should not limit choices in life. Hwang's plays also demonstrate his distaste for rigid, inflexible views about race: He deplores Western assumptions about its cultural superiority over the "Orient."

Hwang is a second-generation Chinese American. His father, Henry Hwang, came to America from Shanghai in 1940; his mother, a daughter of well-off parents who had lived in China and the Philippines, was sent to the University of South Carolina to study the piano. Henry Hwang, a dedicated businessman, established and became the first president of the East National Bank based in Los Angeles. Living in the affluent Los Angeles suburb of San Gabriel, the Hwang family spoke English and, since David's maternal grandparents had converted to Christianity, disregarded Chinese feast days.

While attending Stanford University as an English major, David Hwang became interested in playwriting. Immersed in American capitalism, however, Henry Hwang was very skeptical about his son's professional playwrighting ambitions until he was moved to tears by a performance of FOB. David Hwang married the Chinese actress Ophelia Chong in Toronto in 1984, but they were divorced in 1989. Hwang married his current wife, Kathryn Layng, in 1993.

Hwang developed a particular concern for his Chinese roots at Stanford University, an interest that developed in tandem with his interest in naturalistic and nonnaturalistic drama, particularly that of Harold Pinter and Sam Shepherd. Hwang's plays betray his interest in a wide, catholic range of dramatic genres. His plays incorporate elements of naturalism and realism (he has adapted a version of Ibsen's *Peer Gynt*), quasi-Brechtian agit-prop (one play-within-the-play in *M. Butterfly* shows Maoists staging a Party-approved, didactic play about the re-education of the bourgeoisie), and Chinese opera (Lone, a character in *The Dance and the Railroad*, is a frustrated opera performer).

Hwang's public reputation was established by the time of the award-winning run of his first play, *FOB*, at New York's Public Theater. *FOB* demonstrates a major theme in Hwang's dramatic corpus: the insistence that Asians in America do not necessarily share values of culture and identity. This disparity of experience is evident in the hostility

shown to a "fresh off the boat" Chinese, Dale, by an American-born Asian, Steve. Hwang's second play, *The Dance and the Railroad*, was first produced in 1981 at the New Federal Theatre in New York City. John Lone played the 20-year-old Lone; Tzi Ma played his naïve, 18-year-old friend, Ma. These are the only characters in the one-act, five-scene play set in 1867 as the Chinese immigrants are working on American railroads. Ma is taught some harsh lessons by Lone: His insouciant belief that he could gain instant expertise in Chinese opera is quashed, as is his pie-in-the-sky belief that working in America will bring unlimited prosperity. After uproarious comedy (Ma must pretend to be a duck and then a locust) and upbeat peaks of excitement, the play ends on a downbeat note, as Ma realizes that he must work within the realities of American, immigrant-exploiting capitalism. He and his fellow workers can negotiate with their bosses, but no Chinaman will get rich as a laborer in this ungrateful foreign land. In the drama of his unremarkable life, Ma comes to terms with being a minor player, not a Gwan Gung-like figure of heroic importance. Another play from 1981, *FAMILY DEVOTIONS*, demonstrates Hwang's discomfort with religious fanaticism. The play satirizes "born-again" Christianity with its hyperbolic depiction of two crazed, China-born sisters who set up a bizarre Californian clan. The play is a comedy of farce and misunderstanding: The sisters' uncle, an atheistic communist from China, cannot comprehend their way of living. Family ties and racial links cannot in themselves provide any common ground for these dysfunctional, mutually uncomprehending Asians.

Hwang kept busy during the 1980s, producing more full-length plays as well as shorter plays such as the two one-act works, *The House of Sleeping Beauties* and *The Sound of a Voice*. These two plays, performed together in one entertainment entitled *Sound and Beauty*, were a departure for Hwang in that the plays are set in Japan and do not feature Chinese Americans. Hwang's plays from this period, including *Rich Relations* and *As the Crow Flies* (both 1986), were performed to moderate commercial success in mid-sized theaters. *M. Butterfly* (1988) was a massive breakthrough for Hwang; he became, almost overnight, a major literary figure at the age of 30.

Both exhilarated and fatigued by the success of this Broadway hit, which ran for 777 performances, Hwang diversified into other styles of writing, including the collaborations with Glass and the 1991 one-act play, *Bondage. Bondage* draws an analogy between perceived Asian-American meekness and fantasies about erotic dominance. The play, which called for revealing costuming and explicitly sexual and even fetishistic role-playing by the actors B. D. Wong and Kathryn Layng, was produced in the Actors Theatre of Louisville, Kentucky, in 1992. In it, a man named Mark pays to be humiliated by the wise-cracking (and whip-cracking) dominatrix, Terri, at an S&M parlor in California. Hidden in their rubber masks, hoods and leather outfits, these characters play out their sexual fantasies, assuming different racial identities. When they fail to maintain their over-elaborate, constructed roles as a dominatrix and a submissive partner respectively, Terri and Mark begin to speak honestly. As their costumes and defenses are shed, their eventual abnegation of role-playing results in a physical and emotional honesty that leads to an interracial union that would have been impossible in a more normative context.

The full-length comedy *Face Value* (1992) did not survive past its Broadway previews. Hwang conceded that its mixture of sub-Orton and sub-Shakespearean confusions and farce did not provide a theatrical spectacle equal to *FOB* and *M. Butterfly*. Hwang has also conceded that the play offers a less personal, less authentic engagement with his interest in anxieties about cultural misunderstandings and ever-quarrelling families.

In *Trying to Find Chinatown* (1996), another one-act play, Hwang returned to the theme of antipathy between Asians who have had totally different experiences in America. Ronnie, a foul-mouthed New York street musician, is annoyed when Benjamin from the Midwest assumes that Ronnie will know the way to an address in Chinatown because he looks Asian. A Caucasian adopted and raised by a Chinese-American family, Benjamin has been well trained in the anthropological study of the Chinese communities in America but

does not realize the multiplicity and fluidity of identities that immigrants and descendents of immigrants have established in America.

Hwang's 1998 play, GOLDEN CHILD, was received favorably as something of a return to form. This very personal work recalls Hwang's maternal family's conversion to fundamental Christianity. It also marks the playwright's consistent insistence that the Christian lifestyles and prejudices of some Asian Americans are not necessarily better or worse than those of pre-Christian, pre-Maoist Chinese communities, but merely different.

Hwang does not write plays as prolifically as he used to, but, perhaps aware that he has produced a number of flops, he takes his time over new projects. He admits cheerfully that it is very unlikely that he will ever repeat the success of *M. Butterfly*. But because of the substantial theatrical and intellectual achievements of that work, *FOB*, and *Golden Child*, his place in the canon of Asian-American theater, and in world theater, seems guaranteed.

Bibliography

Chu, Patricia P. "David Henry Hwang." In *The Asian Pacific American Heritage: A Companion to Literature and Arts,* edited by George J. Leonard, 473–480. New York: Garland Publishing, 1998.

Kondo, Dorinne. *About Face: Performing Race in Fashion and Theater,* 211–215. New York: Routledge, 1997.

Kurahashi, Yuko. *Asian American Culture on Stage: The History of the East West Players,* 151–157, 166–167. New York: Garland. 1999.

Shin, Andrew. "Projected Bodies in David Henry Hwang's *M. Butterfly* and *Golden Gate*." MELUS 27, no. 1 (2002): 177–197.

Street, Douglas. *David Henry Hwang.* Boise, Idaho: Boise State University Press, 1989.

Kevin De Ornellas

Hyun, Peter   (Joon-Sup) (1906–1993)

Peter Hyun was not only one of the first Asian-American actors and directors, but he also wrote an autobiography in two parts. *Man Sei!* (1986)

is a personal account of Korean history during the Japanese colonial period, and it offers insight into Korean cultural traditions. *In the New World* (1991), which covers the period between 1924 and 1965, looks back on the personal triumphs and frustrations of an early Korean immigrant.

Peter Hyun was the eldest son of Soon Hyun, a descendant of Korean nobility, and Maria Hyun, the daughter of a royal physician at the Korean court. Raised with strong Confucian values, Hyun's parents were among the first converts to Christianity. In 1903 his father was hired to lead a group of Korean immigrants to Hawaii. Three years later, Peter was born on Kauai, but the family returned to Korea when he was only nine months old. In the preface to *In the New World,* David Hyun states that his brother Peter "grew up with a definite identity. He was Korean."

Man Sei! translates as "Long Live Korea!," referring to the rallying cry of the Korean independence movement. In an effort to explain the influence of colonialism, nationalism, and world history on Korean emigration, Hyun's first book focuses on the author's childhood and adolescence in Korea and China. Roughly following the chronology of historical events, it describes how Hyun attended the funeral of Korea's last king and how he witnessed the massacre following the 1919 uprising against Japanese colonial rule.

Hyun's father was involved in the organization of the uprising and consequently wanted by the police. The family managed to flee to Shanghai, a center of the Korean exile community. *Man Sei!* provides a vivid picture of the "International Settlement" and discusses the activities of the Korean Provisional Government, an organization working toward Korean independence. In 1923 Peter Hyun's father was appointed minister of the Korean Methodist Church in Honolulu. In 1924 Peter and three of his sisters went to Hawaii, and the rest of the family followed one year later. In line with the conventions of many immigrant autobiographies, the book ends by articulating the hopes and fears associated with life in the "Promised Land."

In the New World describes an odyssey toward a new "American" identity. Although it employs the concept of the self-made man as a connecting thread, the episodes of a life otherwise marked by ruptures and traumatic failures betray a sense of regret. The first chapters describe the adolescent Hyun's cultural transformation and embracing of American democratic ideals. After these initial years, Hyun left Hawaii to study philosophy and theater arts at DePauw University, Indiana. His trip across the mainland is also a rare description of the shattered Korean-American community at the time. Hyun presents himself as a strong individualist who—while maintaining his ties with the largely Christian Korean-American community—became an atheist at an early age.

Although he was critically acclaimed as an avant-garde director in New York and Boston, the many racist experiences and setbacks he suffered in the theater resulted in a serious depression. In 1937 he retired from the profession he had dedicated his life to and tried his hand at different jobs in Hawaii. In 1944 he became an officer in the U.S. Army. While he embraced this opportunity as a second chance to prove how "Americanized" he had become, he also criticized the internment of Japanese Americans and Korean POWs. His scepticism grew when at the age of 40 he returned to Korea as an army interpreter. His exchanges with the Korean elite stood in stark contrast to the racism in the U.S. Army, a realization that serves as a crucial turning point in his autobiography. As a consequence of his experiences as an American who belonged to a minority, Peter Hyun later became an activist in the Civil Rights movement. *In the New World* ends with the request that its readers "construct a world of peace and tolerance" (279).

Bibliography

Hyun Peter. *In the New World: The Making of a Korean American.* Honolulu: University of Hawai'i Press, 1995.

Kirsten Twelbeck

Iizuka, Naomi (1965–)

Naomi Iizuka did not come from a theater background and considers herself a latecomer to the art. Born in Tokyo to a Japanese banker and an American of Hispanic descent, she had a privileged and cosmopolitan upbringing in Indonesia, Holland, and Washington, D.C. She received her B.A. in classical literature from Yale University, where she also studied law for a year. Iizuka worked as a summer associate on Wall Street but soon began writing for the theater after finding inspiration and guidance from friends and mentors. She returned to school, obtaining an M.F.A. from the University of California, San Diego, in 1992. Iizuka married Bruce McKenzie, actor and cofounder of Sledgehammer Theater.

Currently, Iizuka is one of the most commissioned playwrights in contemporary American theater. Drawing from her background in classical literature, she delves into the challenges of fusing classic styles and forms to modern and contemporary voices. For example, *Polaroid Stories* (1997) sets the Greek myth of Eurydice and Orpheus among street teens in Minneapolis. A more recent work, *Anon(ymous)* (2006), is a modernization of Homer's *Odyssey,* following a young South Asian refugee's journey to his new home in the United States after surviving a shipwreck. In addition to her fascination with the classics, Iizuka is attracted to more experimental adaptations. In *Tat-*

too Girl (1994), Iizuka adapted "Perpetua," a short story by Donald Barthelme, into a serio-comedy in which the heroine, loosely based on ancient Christian martyr Perpetua, abandons her family and the comforts of her middle-class lifestyle to brave a chaotic world. In *Skin* (1995), Iizuka updates *Woyzeck,* German dramatist Georg Büchner's unfinished 19th-century play about a soldier who murders his wife, resetting this investigation of alienation and isolation on the borderland between California and Mexico. She later dramatizes the life of Orson Welles in her *War of the Worlds* (2000), which harnesses the spirit of Welles's own film *F for Fake*, as she examines the conflation of entertainment and news as well as their conflicting views of truth.

Iizuka's best-known play to date, *36 Views* (2003), draws greatly from classical Eastern influences rather than Western ones. Her acclaimed play resists the conventions of theatrical tradition and unity. By drawing inspiration from 19th-century Japanese artist Hokusai's woodblock series "36 Views of Mt. Fuji," this story of fraud and desire in the academic and art worlds is staged in 36 scenes instead of acts. The play folds together elements of traditional Japanese kabuki theater and imagistic *tableaux vivants,* which all serve to heighten the artifice of the theatrical space in which Iizuka questions issues of cultural authenticity, Orientalism, and value.

Iizuka's plays, such as *Aloha Say All the Pretty Girls* (1999), often feature travel as a central catalyst for self-transformation. However, in her other works such as *Language of Angels* (2000) set in Tennessee's cave country where a girl's disappearance continues to haunt her friends, Iizuka focuses on the intersection between voices of a community and their locale. Her *17 Reasons Why!* (2002), which borrows its title from a fragment of a neighborhood shop sign, offers a study of San Francisco's Mission District from its Gold Rush days to its present, unfolded in 17 loosely connected scenes based on its residents' oral histories. Iizuka further investigates how history is perceived and described in *At the Vanishing Point* (2004), a site-specific production staged in an abandoned warehouse and delivered through interlocking monologues. In it, the playwright employs interviews and archival research to bring to life Butchertown, a stockyard and meat-packing plant community near Louisville, Kentucky.

The hallmark of Iizuka's interests in the juncture between modern and classical voices can be found in *Hamlet: Blood in the Brain* (2006). The culmination of a three-year-long collaboration involving traditional theater organizations and the communities of Oakland, California, *Hamlet: Blood in the Brain* synthesizes residents' stories and culture with William Shakespeare's venerable tragedy to envision Hamlet's society and crises emerging from modern-day Oakland's local idioms and mythology.

Despite her brief career, Iizuka has been prolific and widely honored by institutions such as the Rockefeller Foundation, PEN Center USA, the Joyce Foundation, and the National Endowment for the Arts. Her productivity and originality portend a greater presence in the canon of American literature and theater. At present, Naomi Iizuka is a professor of dramatic arts at the University of California, Santa Barbara, and serves as the director of its playwriting program.

Bibliography

Berson, M. "Naomi Iizuka: Raising the Stakes." *American Theatre* 15, no. 7 (September 1998): 56–7.

Iizuka, Namoi. "Interview with Naomi Iizuka, playwright of *36 Views*, by Cindy Yoon." (March 29, 2002). AsiaSource: A Resource of the Asia Society. Available online. URL: http://www.asiasource.org/arts/36views.cfm Accessed Feb. 20, 2006.

Miyagawa, Chiori. "Brave, Bold, and Poetic: The New Generation of Asian American Women Playwrights." In *Women Playwrights of Diversity. A Bio-Bibliographical Sourcebook,* by Jane T. Peterson and Suzanne Bennett. Westport, Conn.: Greenwood Press, 1997.

Wren, Celia. "Navigating alien worlds," *American Theatre* 19, no. 2 (February 2002): 32.

M. Gabot Fabros

Inada, Lawson Fusao (1938–)

Born in Fresno, California, Inada is a third-generation Japanese American whose grandparents immigrated to the United States at the turn of the 20th century. Eventually settling in California's Great Central Valley region, his paternal grandparents, the Inadas, worked as sharecroppers in and around San Jose while his maternal grandparents, the Saitos, opened Fresno's first fish market. Both families believed in upward mobility and instilled a love of education in their nisei children. Subsequently, Fusaji Inada, a dentist, and Masako Saito, a schoolteacher, provided these same values to their son Lawson in a stable and warm home located on Fresno's ethnically diverse West Side.

In February 1942, two months after the Japanese attacked Pearl Harbor, President Franklin Roosevelt signed Executive Order 9066, which authorized the removal of all people of Japanese ancestry from vulnerable areas of the United States's West Coast. Forced to sell their home and to abandon most of their belongings, the Inadas were interned for three years, first in Arkansas's Jerome Camp and then in Colorado's Amache Camp. Although a small child during internment, Inada's poetic themes derive largely from this experience. Today he prefers the moniker "camp poet" to Japanese-American poet since much of his work expresses the disorienting effects of internment and its racist cause.

After their release from Amache Camp in 1945, the Inadas returned to Fresno to rebuild their life. Back in his hometown, Inada resumed his formal education at Lincoln Grammar School and, more important, began immersing himself in Fresno's large multicultural community of Asians, blacks, and Chicanos, which he later deemed a more important set of ABC's for the different sets of norms, values, and traditions he learned. Upon graduating from Edison High School in 1955, he attended Fresno State College for a year but then transferred to the University of California, Berkeley, as a sophomore. Although Inada virtually flunked out of Berkeley, his "real" education began there since he attended performances by such jazz greats as Lester Young, Miles Davis, and John Coltrane, experiences that cultivated his improvisationally based jazz aesthetic. It was after meeting singer Billie Holiday one night in San Francisco that Inada wrote his first poem, a tribute to her. After that night, he dedicated the rest of his life to writing poetry.

The following year found Inada back at Fresno State studying with poet Philip Levine, who influenced his use of colloquial diction and experimental jazz techniques. Levine helped the burgeoning poet secure a fellowship to the University of Iowa's Writer's Workshop, where he met fellow student Janet Francis. They married in 1962. After teaching at the University of New Hampshire for three years, Inada returned west to finish his M.F.A. degree at the University of Oregon in 1966. He revised much of his thesis, "The Great Bassist," for his first published book of verse, *Before the War: Poems as They Happened* (1971). A set of confessional poems that employ a geographical structure by focusing on the places Inada had traveled to in the previous 10 years, *Before the War* criticizes American society through the poet's use of scatological words, themes, and images. Although *Before the War* gained some notoriety for being the first book of poetry written by an Asian American to be published by a major New York house, it wound up in remainder bins the following year since it garnered little interest from readers or critics.

Twenty-one years elapsed before Inada published another full-length book of verse. In the meantime, he settled into his teaching job at Southern Oregon College, concentrated on writing such long poems as "Asian Brother, Asian Sister" and "Japanese Geometry," and helped FRANK CHIN, JEFFERY PAUL CHAN, and SHAWN WONG edit *Aiiieeeee!: An Anthology of Asian-American Writers* (1974), which was notable for being the first collection of Asian-American writing to be compiled and edited solely by Asian Americans. This last project began an important scholarly phase in Inada's career. With Chin, Chan, and Wong, Inada formed the Combined Asian-American Resource Project (CARP), which undertook to revive the works of such earlier Asian-American writers as JOHN OKADA and TOSHIO MORI. However, during this time, Inada did not abandon poetry. With GARRETT HONGO and Alan Chong Lau, he wrote and self-published *The Buddha Bandits down Highway 99* (1976), which contained his jazz ode to Fresno, "I Told You So."

In 1992 Inada reemerged with *Legends from Camp,* his second full-length book of poems and winner of the American Book Award for poetry in 1993. While the book's first section deals with the myths and legends about internment camp life that survive in the poet's memory, the next three sections return to such familiar places as Fresno and Oregon and to such jazz figures as Miles Davis and Billie Holiday. Especially powerful is the volume's last section, in which Inada collects his performance poetry. Included in this section are a series of haikus that he collected and composed for inscription on stone monoliths that stand at Portland's Japanese American Historical Plaza on the banks of the Willamette River.

Familiar in autobiographical theme and structure to *Legends from Camp* is *Drawing the Line,* his third full-length book of verse, published in 1997. Its difference derives from Inada's use of playful poems to highlight language's transformational nature. Throughout he runs the gamut of poetic forms from epigrams and haikus to lyric, narrative, and concrete poems. Whether Inada meant *Drawing the Line* as a capstone to his poetic career remains to be seen.

Semi-retired from teaching at Oregon State University, Inada spends most of his time today writing haikus and traveling across the country to read at colleges and universities. Because he dedicated his life to being a poet, teacher, scholar, and community leader, he is viewed as an elder statesman of American poetry, a role he is more than happy to play.

Bibliography

Chang, Juliana. "Time, Jazz, and the Racial Subject: Lawson Inada's Jazz Poetics." In *Racing and (E)Racing Language: Living with the Color of Our Words*, edited by Ellen J. Goldner and Safiya Henderson-Holmes, 134–154. Syracuse, N.Y.: Syracuse University Press, 2001.

Holliday, Shawn. *Lawson Fusao Inada*. Western Writers Series #160. Boise, Idaho: Boise State University Press, 2003.

Sato, Gayle. "Lawson Inada's Poetics of Relocation: Weathering, Nesting, Leaving the Bough." *Amerasia Journal* 26, no. 3 (2000–2001): 139–160.

Shawn Holliday

Inheritance   Indira Ganesan (1998)

Set in the mock paradise island of Pi near India—full of mango trees, monkeys, flowers, and enduring warmth—INDIRA GANESAN's *Inheritance* is a novel that defines relationships, culture, feminism, adolescence, and the discovery of self. Through its colorful characters and their personal revelations, it offers insight into family, the borders of love and hate, the angst of loss, and the healing power of acceptance.

The story revolves around 15-year-old Sonil, who, after having been raised by her aunts in mainland India, comes to the island to visit her favorite grandmother prior to attending university, and to recover from her shaky health. Her grandmother is a constant in Sonil's life and perhaps the only stabilizing force she has. As Sonil begins to recover her health, its effect spreads. Although she still avoids her mother—an eccentric, beautiful, and remarkable woman who withdrew from her when she was six—she now sneaks into her mother's room and borrows her poetry book in an attempt to understand her.

The enigma of her white American father, who left India before Sonil was born, and her mother's rejection and abandonment of her at a young age cause Sonil to search for acceptance, something she finds in Richard, an American twice her age looking for spiritual awakening in India. Their sexual relationship leads them to their own conclusions about life. Richard, on his own search for truth, eventually rejects Sonil. He has his own demons to exorcise and much like Sonil, but for different reasons, has his own set of problems in dealing with his mother, a woman who is apparently on her own quest for spirituality. Sonil, on the other hand, learns the true meaning of forgiveness and begins to look within for answers she has always searched for from the outside.

Her experiences and interactions with others throughout the story help move her from the comfortable life of her grandmother's compound into the expanse of the greater world. When her cousin Jani, afraid of arranged marriage and the pain of childbirth, enters a convent, Sonil also flees to the convent to escape the grief of being rejected by Richard. During her visit to the temple of Sita, a reincarnation of the goddess Lakshmi, after whom Sonil's mother is named, Sonil finds the path she should take. In the end, she realizes that life is a constant process and that each event only brings a new series of questions, some of which will never be answered.

Anne Marie Fowler

Innocent, The   Richard E. Kim (1968)

Revisiting characters first introduced in *The MARTYRED* (1964), RICHARD KIM's second novel—*The Innocent*—offers a thoroughly convoluted and unsentimental portrayal of the difficulties and corruption facing the nascent South Korean state in the aftermath of the Korean War. Major Lee—formerly Captain Lee in *The Martyred*—provides a first-person account of the intricate plans of the Command Group (a consort of eight officers in the Republic of South Korea Army) to stage a coup d'état in order to purge the government of corrupt officials and megalomaniacal generals betraying the ideals of the newly democratic South Korean nation. Through such diverse characters as Chaplain Koh, Lieutenant Cho, Colonels Min, Park, and Jung, and Generals Ahn, Mah, Ham, and Loon, Kim foregrounds the difficulties inherent in any attempt to centralize leadership and to remain faithful to the ideals of a nation, when so many perspectives, so many agendas and interests must first coalesce into something resembling a common good. As the plot unfolds, Kim continually probes the boundaries of innocence, consciously invoking the title to force the reader to acknowledge the impossibility of maintaining objectivity and innocence in the face of so much corruption and violence.

Serving as the conscience of the Command Group (and of the novel as a whole), Major Lee has scrutinized every detail of the planned coup so as to minimize violence and bloodshed in order to place the actions of the conspirators firmly within the ideals of their planned revamping and restructuring of a government and military establishment overrun with corruption. First on the agenda for the Command Group is the forcible removal of General Ham, the avatar of everything wrong with the present situation in South Korea, which leaves the question of what to do with him after taking control. With the exception of Major Lee, the members of the Command Group wish to execute General Ham, not to offer sanctuary abroad or a position in the new government in light of his severe abuses of power. Major Lee, very much in the Christian tradition, does not see how violence can serve as the end to violence and seriously questions the decision to murder the general.

Espionage and counterespionage abound, and the pace of the coup quickly outruns the meticulous planning of Major Lee: the bloodless revolution gives way to bloody battles between competing factions within the military, the situation further compounded by the involvement of the U.S. government and CIA in the guise of Colonel McKay. The novel's main tension between Colonel Min, the ostensible leader of the Command Group, and Major Lee comes to a head during the move to take power. Good friends before the war, Colonel Min and Major Lee have a complicated relationship, as

Colonel Min appears to need Major Lee by his side, perhaps as some form of an embodied conscience or reminder of the philosophical underpinnings of the coup. However, as the coup progresses, Colonel Min must estrange himself from Major Lee and his seemingly incorruptible—and perhaps even unrealistic—innocence.

Kim's novel captures the difficulty of building a nation in postwar South Korea: Innocent ideals must give way to the inertia of a violent and tragic history. Soon after the qualified success of the coup, Colonel Min tells Major Lee: "And that is what you have done for me—to give me one, final reminder that a man like me . . . is a simple murderer and must not be called by any other name. You have helped me . . . in this mad, maddening world, to know and to accept my own verdict" (368). Kim seems to suggest that guilt and innocence must always depend on one another for clarification and definition, a theme that runs throughout the novel and intersects with the postwar reality in South Korea.

Bibliography

Kim, Richard E. *The Innocent.* Boston: Houghton, 1968.

Zach Weir

Interpreter of Maladies: Stories
Jhumpa Lahiri (1999)

As a graduate student at Boston University, JHUMPA LAHIRI realized her passion for writing fiction and began to work intensively on crafting short stories that would later catapult her into literary superstardom. Critical and popular acclaim followed the publication of her first collection of short stories, *Interpreter of Maladies.* Prior to its publication, three of Lahiri's stories appeared in *The New Yorker* and in the same magazine's summer fiction issue of 1999, Lahiri was included as one of the "20 Best American Fiction Writers Under 40." *Interpreter of Maladies,* a collection of nine stories—three set in India and six in the United States—garnered Lahiri numerous awards and honors including the 2000 Pulitzer Prize.

Much of *Interpreter of Maladies* is concerned with examining the quotidian lives of Indian immigrants living and working in the United States, and their first generation Indian-American children. As a child herself of displaced Bengali immigrant parents, Lahiri, born in England and raised in America, is well positioned to speak about the difficulties and challenges experienced by those often compelled to live two lives—one Indian, one American. Her simple yet elegant prose weaves together themes of alienation, loss, adaptation, and the quest for belonging as her characters attempt to establish themselves in a foreign land while maintaining their vital connection to their cultural identity and heritage.

In "When Mr. Pirzada Came to Dinner," Lahiri depicts the cultural divide separating young Indian-American Lilia and her Indian-born parents. The story takes place in 1971 during the Bangladesh War and concerns a Pakistani scholar, Mr. Pirzada, who is in America on a study grant and makes regular visits to the home of Lilia's family to share meals and news of the worsening political situation in Pakistan. Lilia, who knows little to nothing about the nature of the crisis in Pakistan owing to her exclusive diet of American history at school, can only wonder at her parents' and Mr. Pirzada's solemnity and horror at the sight of the images they see of the war on the international news. To Lilia, observing from the perspective of an outsider, her parents and their visitor operate "during that time as if they were a single person, sharing a single meal, a single body, a single silence, and a single fear" (41). In much the same way that Lilia feels alienated from her parents' generation and connection to the motherland, Mrs. Sen, in "Mrs. Sen's," experiences the desperation of isolation as an Indian immigrant in America, willing but unable to transition to a new culture and deeply and detrimentally attached to aspects of her Indian life.

In the title story, "Interpreter of Maladies," Lahiri turns to India as a setting for yet another tale of cultural misunderstanding and estrangement. Mr. and Mrs. Das, children of immigrant parents living in New Jersey, travel with their children to India and hire a cab driven by Mr. Kapasi, inter-

preter and guide, to see the Sun Temple at Konarak. It becomes quickly apparent that the members of the Das family, despite being of Indian descent like Mr. Kapasi, are foreigners with whom Mr. Kapasi cannot connect on any level other than as American tourists. It is cultural and not racial difference that divides them.

Lahiri's stories deal with failed marriages, thwarted ambitions and desires, and struggles to survive in unfamiliar lands. They all underscore failed communication and missed connections between neighbors, parents and children, lovers, and strangers. Ultimately, Lahiri interprets the maladies of a variety of characters striving simply to make sense of their surroundings and themselves.

Dana Hansen

In the Pond   Ha Jin (1998)

Set in post–Cultural Revolution China, HA JIN's first novel is a hilarious political allegory about individual integrity in a highly regimented society. The protagonist is Shao Bin, a fitter at a fertilizer plant and an amateur painter and calligrapher. Bin has been working at the factory for six years and, since he is married and has a child, he expects soon to be allotted a decent apartment. When he discovers that his name has been left off the list of the people who will be given new housing, he decides to retaliate by publishing a cartoon lampooning the plant's managers as corrupt. However, instead of solving his situation, the cartoon only exacerbates it. Indeed, the cartoon initiates a series of measures and countermeasures between Bin and his antagonists, culminating, perhaps surprisingly, in his triumph.

The two top managers at the plant are Director Ma Gong and Communist Party Secretary Liu Shu. Fully aware that their workers resent the seemingly arbitrary way in which they assign apartments, they attempt to silence Bin by charging him with being a bourgeois, demanding that he produce a self-criticism, and cutting his salary. Rather than yielding, Bin files a formal complaint against the two managers to their immediate superior, Yang Chen. However, his letter is not delivered to Yang but to Ma and Liu, who blame Bin for the controversy and subject him to a series of public humiliations. Bin's fortunes finally start to change after he meets Yen, a friend of his who works at a local newspaper. Thanks to Yen, the newspaper publishes a long report on Bin, criticizing Ma, Liu, and Yang. Once again, Bin's actions do not have the desired effect, as the report not only fails to help his cause but even leads to a crackdown on the newspaper by the authorities. However, the experience binds Bin and the editorial staff in their determination to fight their common enemies and, through some relatives of the editor, Bin is eventually able to have his story published in an influential Beijing magazine. The appearance of the article leads the managers to conclude that they cannot defeat Bin, and the narrative ends with Bin's vindication, as Yang offers him a higher position where he can take advantage of his artistic talent.

In the Pond somewhat recalls the Jimmy Stewart film *Mr. Smith Goes to Washington.* Ha Jin's first and shortest novel—it is basically a novella—could have been called *Comrade Shao Bin Goes to Beijing.* Yet it already contains some of the elements that one associates with the author's more mature novels, such as WAITING and *The* CRAZED. Particularly impressive is Jin's characterization of his protagonist. Shao Bin is a very complex personage. Although he is a factory worker by profession, he has artistic talent and is obsessed with art. He is also simultaneously politically naïve and arrogant, belittling not only his leaders but also his fellow workers and, sometimes, even his wife. Likewise, for someone who perceives himself as an intellectual, he can be rather emotional. He usually acts on something first and only considers the repercussions later. Jin's most significant accomplishment in *In the Pond* is arguably his creation of Shao Bin.

Bibliography

Kinkley, Jeffrey C. Review of *In the Pond,* by Ha Jin. *World Literature Today* 73, no. 2 (1999): 390–391.

Zhang, Hang. "Bilingual Creativity in Chinese English: Ha Jin's *In the Pond.*" *World Englishes* 21, no. 2 (2002): 305–315.

Jianwu Liu and Albert Braz

Ishigaki, Ayako Tanaka (Haru Matsui) (1903–1996)

Ayako Ishigaki was born Ayako Tanaka on September 21, 1903, in Tokyo, Japan. Her mother died when she was very young, and she was brought up by her father, a university professor. Although she was educated in Western style, she had a conventional upbringing for a woman of elite background. When her elder sister was pushed into an arranged marriage, however, Ayako rebelled. During the 1920s, she asserted herself as a "new woman," took paid employment outside of the home, and became active in politics. In 1926, after being arrested and harassed by police, she agreed to her family's suggestion that she join her relatives in the United States. Once in the United States, however, she soon escaped her family and moved to New York. There she met and fell in love with a radical issei artist, Eitaro Ishigaki, whom she married despite family opposition. During the Great Depression, she worked at a variety of shop and factory jobs.

Following Japan's 1931 invasion of Manchuria, Ayako Ishigaki took a leading role in protesting Japanese aggression. Writing under various pseudonyms, she reported on Japan for such New York-based radical publications as *The New Masses* and *China Today.* In 1937 she was recruited by the American League for Peace and Democracy as an organizer on the West Coast. Upon moving to Los Angeles, she was hired as a columnist by the Japanese newspaper *Rafu Shimpo.* In her column, "Jinsei Shokan" (women's thoughts), she spoke as a housewife to other housewives, using informal, accessible language and homey metaphors to express arguments in favor of birth control and women's equality, and against militarism. Despite her column's popularity, the Little Tokyo community's overwhelming support for the Japanese invasion of China in July 1937 caused Ishigaki to give up in despair. She returned to New York in September 1937 and undertook a lecture tour in support of China. Not long after, a representative of Modern Age Books commissioned her to write the book that emerged as *Restless Wave.*

Restless Wave, published in 1940 under the pen name Haru Matsui, is one of the first English-language books written by an Asian-American woman. Mixing autobiography, fiction, and reportage, it tells the story of a young woman, Haru, and her coming of age as a feminist and political activist in Japan and the United States. *Restless Wave* is notable for the interconnections Ishigaki traces between Japanese military aggression and "feudal" attitudes within Japan that restrict the freedom of women and the poor. The author also expresses sympathy for Japanese Americans, both issei and nisei. While she criticizes Japanese immigrants for supporting Japanese militarism, she makes clear that their pro-Japanese attitude stems from their and their children's race-based isolation from mainstream American society. *Restless Wave* received numerous positive reviews and had impressive sales.

In 1942, following the outbreak of war between the United States and Japan, Ishigaki joined the Office of War Information (OWI) as a translator and writer. She worked for OWI and the War Department for the following five years. During this time, she undertook a novel about Japanese Americans, but the project was never realized. In the years following the war, Ayako and Eitaro faced increasing harassment by the U.S government due to their radical political views, including their friendship with left-wing activist Agnes Smedley. They had already planned to leave the United States when Eitaro was summarily expelled in 1951. Ayako joined him in returning to Japan.

Once in Japan, Ayako became renowned as a critic and interpreter of America, and for her feminist writings in the women's magazine *Fujyin Koron,* particularly the controversial 1955 article, "*Shufu to iu dai-in shokugyö-ron*" (Housewife: The Second Profession). In that article, Ishigaki complained that Japanese women's minds had "turned to mush" from staying at home, and she urged women to take up outside work. In later decades, Ayako Ishigaki became a familiar Japanese television personality and women's adviser, as well as the author of more than 20 Japanese-language books of memoirs, essays,

and biographies (including a Japanese translation of *Restless Wave*). Following Eitaro's death in 1958, she also dedicated her efforts to building a museum of his artwork. Ishigaki revisited the United States in 1975 and contributed to the Japanese-American literary anthology *Ayumi.* After her death in 1996, a new edition of *Restless Wave,* by then long out of print, was published in 2004. Two years later, it won a special citation as a "lost Asian American treasure" from the Association of Asian American Studies.

Greg Robinson

Itsuka   Joy Kogawa (1992)

This novel chronicles the adulthood of the protagonist Naomi Nakane in JOY KOGAWA's OBASAN from September 1983 to September 1988. She undergoes a personal and political awakening, awaiting *itsuka* ("someday" in Japanese) referring to the redress from the Canadian government for Japanese Canadians interned during World War II. The novel follows Naomi's move from the Alberta prairie to Toronto. After she gives up a frustrating teaching job and starts working for *The Bridge,* a multicultural magazine run by St. John's College, her world slowly broadens. She allows for the possibility of romance in her life with the French-Canadian Anglican priest Father Cedric and begins to attend political rallies aimed at unifying the Japanese-Canadian community and strengthening the redress movement. The novel ends with Naomi carrying banners at a rally on Parliament Hill in Ottawa. The last scene shows her at a small official ceremony during which the government officially apologizes for the injustices done to Japanese Canadians during and after World War II.

Interspersed in Naomi's first-person narrative are flashbacks to her childhood that will seem familiar to readers acquainted with *Obasan.* These scenes are aimed at clarifying Naomi's almost pathetic silence. While *Obasan* emphasizes the years spent in internment at Slocan, *Itsuka* focuses on the memories of beet farming in Granton,

Alberta, and the postwar years and early adulthood in Coaldale, where Naomi attended an evangelical church, which contribute to her feelings of exclusion and guilt.

Kogawa sensitively describes Naomi's aunt's decline after her husband's death. The accumulated clutter of things saved during a lifetime of deprivations found at the aunt's house compounds the heartbreak of having to institutionalize her and of parting from her. Equally touching are Naomi's visits to Japanese Canadians at various nursing homes to gather and document their memories.

Through Naomi's conflict with her brother Stephen, a famous violinist reticent to acknowledge his Japanese ancestry publicly, the question arises as to how to serve one's people best: through music, silence, or political action. Paralleling the Japanese Canadians' struggle, Naomi slowly emerges from her cocoon of insecurities and attains the ability to reach out to Father Cedric. This sense of connectedness also permeates Naomi's awareness of the strength of her community and distinguishes her from her brother.

While this novel is not as technically accomplished or lyrically beautiful as *Obasan,* it sheds an interesting light on the redress movement. For American readers, especially those unaware of Japanese internment during World War II, the novel may serve as a historically accurate introduction to this subject matter.

Susanna Hoeness-Krupsaw

Jaisohn, Philip (1864–1951)

Also known as Jae-pil Suh, Jaisohn was born in North Jul-la Province of Korea. The youngest person ever to pass the Korean civil service exam with top honors at the age of 18, he soon served as Minister of Defense. After a failed coup attempt, however, he became a political refugee in 1885 on his way to San Francisco. Once in the United States, he adopted the name Philip Jaisohn by rearranging the letters from his Korean name. In 1890 he became the first Korean to become a naturalized U.S. citizen. Two years later, he became the first Korean and one of the first Asians to receive a medical degree from George Washington University's Medical School. In 1894 he married Muriel Armstrong, whose father was the U.S. Postmaster General and a relative of President James Buchanan.

March 1896 saw the return of Jaisohn with his wife to Korea where he became one of the founding members of the Independence Club, an organization responsible for introducing the Western concepts of equal justice under the law, freedom of speech, and women's rights. Jaisohn published *The Independent,* the first modern newspaper in Korea, through which he actively promoted modern science and Western ideology.

Upon returning to America, he continued to publish *The Independent* and devote himself to the cause of Korean independence from Japan, orga-nizing in 1919 the first Korean Congress in Philadelphia. After studying medicine further at the University of Pennsylvania, he practiced pathology and dermatology in Media, Pennsylvania, in the 1930s. During World War II, he served in the U.S. military as a medical doctor, a position that earned him the Distinguished Service Medal. In 1947 he became senior adviser to the U.S. Military Governor of Korea, General John Hodge. Visiting Korea one last time, he helped pave the way for Korea's transition to a democratic government.

Hansu's Journey (1921), a novella published by Jaisohn under a pseudonym, "N. H. Osia," is the first known work of literary fiction in English by a Korean American. The protagonist is Hansu, a teenager from North Korea, who is unfairly imprisoned by Japanese police. Upon release from prison, Hansu attends a school run by American missionaries and later witnesses the Samil Independence Movement against Japan on March 1, 1919. He is inspired and touched by the courageous, nonviolent march of Koreans to protest the brutality of Japan. After observing the inhuman treatment of protesters by the Japanese police, Hansu moves to China and then to America to educate himself and become more valuable to his country's independence. Written to inform Americans of the sufferings of Koreans under Japanese colonial occupation, *Hansu's Journey* is the only known literary work by Jaisohn.

Bibliography

Oh, Seiwoong. "*Hansu's Journey* by Philip Jaisohn: The First Fiction in English from Korean America." *Amerasia Journal* 29, no. 3 (2003–2004): 43–55.

SuMee Lee

Japanese Nightingale, A
Winnifred Eaton (1901)

Adapted into both a play and a film in the early 1900s, WINNIFRED EATON's most successful work rewrites the "Japanese" novel of desertion made famous by Pierre Loti's *Madame Chrysanthème* (1887) and John Luther Long's *Madame Butterfly* (1898). These earlier novels portray marriages of convenience in which, Eaton notes, foreigners in Japan "for a short, happy and convenient season cheerfully take unto themselves Japanese wives, and with the same cheerfulness desert them" (90). By contrast, in *A Japanese Nightingale* the love is real, though not without its trials.

Beginning in a teahouse floating on a lake outside Tokyo, a beautiful, half-Japanese girl named Yuki entertains foreigners. There she meets Jack Bigelow, a recent college graduate who is staying in Japan on the advice of a friend, another half-Japanese named Taro Burton, whom he had met in America. Although Taro made Jack promise not to enter into a Japanese marriage, Jack is beset by brokers, called *nakodas,* and at last accepts a "look and see." The girl is Yuki. Jack struggles for several weeks because of his promise to Taro, but eventually succumbs and marries the girl because of her beauty.

The difficulty, initially, is that Jack really loves Yuki, while she seems to be doing it for the money. Just as Jack "bought" Yuki from the *nakoda,* Yuki seizes every opportunity to extract money from Jack, much like Chysanthème in Loti's novel. Unlike Chrysanthème, however, her cause is noble: She is trying to raise money for the return of her brother, who turns out to be none other than Jack's friend Taro, who is staying in America. Meanwhile, she too falls in love with Jack, but she knows Taro will be enraged by what she has done.

She tries to leave Jack before Taro's return, but her husband prevents her. Meeting Taro as soon as he returns to Tokyo, Jack brings him home, proudly displaying his Japanese wife in his arms. When Taro sees that Jack's wife is Yuki, he is so overcome by grief that he sickens and dies. Yuki runs away in shame, and Jack spends several years searching for her. He eventually finds her, accidentally, in the house they both shared, and the implication is that they will live happily ever after, rebuilding their life together.

On the surface, such a story may seem to be what Eaton herself dismissed as "a jumble of sentimental moonshine" (*Me,* 153). It is different, however, from other "Japanese" romances of the time both because it ends happily and because Eaton's heroine is of mixed race. As the Japanese teahouse proprietor declares at the start of the novel, demonstrating the prejudice people like Yuki faced, she "is but a cheap girl of Tokyo, with the blue-glass eyes of the barbarian, the yellow skin of the lower Japanese, hair of mixed color, black and red ... alien at this country, alien at your honorable country, augustly despicable—a half caste!" (89). Belonging wholly neither to East nor West, Yuki's apparent "freakishness" is highlighted by the attempts of an American circus manager to acquire her for his show of pigmies, jugglers, wizards, and dancers. To Jack, however, Yuki is "Japanese despite the hair and eyes": "There was no other country she could belong to" (93). With this statement, Eaton establishes that race is constructed socially more than biologically, a particularly apt position for a writer who pretended to be Japanese despite her Chinese blood.

As such, *A Japanese Nightingale* poses interesting questions about what truly constitutes an individual's ethnicity. Running alongside the romance between Jack and Yuki is a parallel narrative of racial belonging for both figures, with Jack promising in the final moments of the novel that the couple will settle in Japan, where they will live as Japanese and according to the principles of "the simple peasant folk" (171). In this way, Eaton posits that people can choose their race, just as they choose their clothes, putting on alternative ethnicities just as easily as donning kimonos. This theme of racial fluidity was to become the hallmark of Eaton's later work, explored perhaps most fully and provocatively in *Heart of Hyacinth* (1903), in which an English girl insists on her Japanese identity despite her Western parentage; in *A Japanese Blossom* (1906), featuring an American widow and her Caucasian children who "become" Japanese with the mother's marriage to a Japanese businessman; and in *Sunny-San* (1926), which turns the tables by having the half-Japanese girl "become" American.

Although Eaton has often been dismissed by American and Japanese critics alike as an offensive, embarrassing imposter, she is slowly coming to be viewed more positively as an avant-guarde author "on the cutting edge of what we now call race theory," as Samina Najmi has remarked (xxxvii). By demonstrating in novels like *A Japanese Nightingale* that individuals of mixed ancestry could not only be beautiful, talented, and successful but could also, in many respects, choose their race, Eaton demonstrates that ethnicity is a malleable, socially constructed concept that could be used for empowerment, rather than alienation.

Bibliography

Cole, Jean Lee. *The Literary Voices of Winnifred Eaton: Redefining Ethnicity and Authenticity.* New Brunswick, N.J.: Rutgers University Press, 2002.

Eaton, Winnifred. *A Japanese Nightingale. Two Orientalist Texts,* edited by Marguerite Honey and Jean Lee Cole, 81–171. New Brunswick, N.J.: Rutgers University Press, 2002.

———. *Me: A Book of Remembrance.* With an Afterword by Linda Trinh Moser. Jackson: University of Mississippi Press, 1997.

Najmi, Samina. Introduction. *Heart of Hyacinth,* by Winnifred Eaton, v–xlvi. Seattle: University of Washington Press, 2000.

Kay Chubbuck

Jar of Dreams, A   Yoshiko Uchida (1981)

Set in the 1930s during the Great Depression, this novel by YOSHIKO UCHIDA deals with the difficulties faced by Japanese Americans due to an increase of racism. At the center of the story is the Tsujimura family. Mama and Papa were originally born in Japan. Their three children were born in California, far away from the traditional Japanese culture and heritage. The children see themselves as American, but when they look into the mirror, they see Japanese faces.

The narrator of the story is 11-year-old Rinko Tsujimura, who wishes she was not Japanese. She wants to look like everybody else so that people would not make fun of her, or yell mean things to her, or forbid her and her best friend Tami from swimming at the Crystal Plunge swimming pool. She has straight black hair and skinny legs, and her face is that of a sweet Japanese-American girl who cannot believe in herself. Rinko's family, however, is full of dreams. Her father, Papa, dreams of becoming a mechanic. Rinko wants to be a teacher, and her big brother, Cal, studies engineering at the university. But these are only dreams to them, possibilities that rapidly turn into dissolutions. When Cal tells her that no school will hire a Japanese teacher, Rinko is disheartened because she will never be able to live her dream. In the midst of racism and hatred, the family slowly begins to lose its hopes and dreams.

Surrounding the Tsujimura family are various characters who represent different aspects of America. Wilbur J. Starr, owner of the Starr Laundry, insults Japanese-American children as they walk past his shop and makes violent threats against Mama's home laundry service. Rinko's next-door neighbor, Mrs. Sugar, always has a kind word to say and often invites Rinko into her house for tea and spice cake. Within the Japanese-American community, Uncle Kanda, Papa's best friend who came with him from Japan, spends every Sunday with the Tsujimura family. Uncle Kanda teaches the children not to give up on their dreams despite the people who are prejudiced against them. Aunt Waka, Mama's sister from Japan visiting for the summer, is not afraid to speak her mind. She shows Rinko and her mother that they need to draw upon their strength in order to fight racism and pursue their dreams. Aunt Waka also teaches Rinko that Rinko's parents are strong because they have preserved their heritage while simultaneously learning and adapting to another culture. Overcoming hardships and racism, they are still able to provide food, shelter, and love for their children and to give them every opportunity to pursue their dreams.

Anne Bahringer

Jasmine Bharati Mukherjee (1989)

Released the year following the author's National Book Critics Award–winning book *The MIDDLE-MAN AND OTHER STORIES, Jasmine* revisits aspects of the immigrant experience charted and interrogated within her critically celebrated collection of stories, though this time brought to the reader through the first-person narration of her protagonist—Jyoti/Jasmine/Jase/Jane. Jyoti, the daughter of peasant farmers in Hasnapur, Punjab, India, was born 18 years after the Partition Riots, the fifth daughter in a family of nine. Without a dowry or appreciable professional prospects, Jyoti learns English and finds solace in education. As she notes: "I couldn't marry a man who didn't speak English, or at least who didn't want to speak English. To want English was to want more than you had been given at birth, it was to want the world" (68). Thus, once her brothers bring home their friend Prakash, Jyoti finds an immediate affinity with his political progressiveness and autodidactic tendencies, especially as manifested by his ambitious plan to leave India to attend a technical university in the United States. Jyoti and Prakash marry, effectively ending the first part of her life as Jyoti when she adopts the name Jasmine, a name proposed by Prakash to symbolize her break from the social remnants of feudalism and the caste system.

However, at the time of their marriage, local religious and ethnic conflicts escalate in response to an India where "Beggars with broken bodies shoved alms bowls at suited men in automobiles" and "shacks sprouted like toadstools around high-rise office buildings" (80). In other words, Westernization provided visible competition for more traditionalist notions of religion and culture. When a homemade bomb explodes in the sari shop, killing Prakash and leaving Jasmine a widow, she then determines to set off on her own, as "Prakash had taken Jyoti and created

Jasmine, and Jasmine would complete the mission of Prakash" (97). Yet, her flight from India to the United States even further changes the 16-year-old Jasmine, as she must endure stringent racism on the European continent, slip through immigration and customs checkpoints with a fake passport and visas, and make the cross-Atlantic voyage stowed beneath tarps, largely exposed to the elements and other passengers.

Once she reaches Florida, Jasmine does not find instant safety or comfort; rather, the captain of the ship brutally rapes her, precipitating her murderous revenge with a penknife and subsequent roadside pickup by Lilian Gordon, a Floridian woman who, along with Jasmine, helps a number of immigrants and refugees to hide from the Immigration and Naturalization Service and to acclimate themselves to the United States. From Florida, Jasmine travels to New York, first staying on with an Indian immigrant family known by her late husband, then as a "caregiver" to the daughter of a Columbia University physicist, Taylor, and his wife, Wylie. With Taylor, Wylie, and their daughter Duff, Jasmine takes on the name Jase, which even further signifies the changes she has undergone as a result of her immersion in American culture and identity-in-flux. Though Jase loves both Taylor and his daughter (Wylie has left Taylor for another man), she abruptly leaves New York after seeing her husband's killer selling hot dogs in Central Park. Starting yet another life in Iowa as a bank teller and companion to Bud Ripplemeyer, Jase becomes Jane, a further permutation of self that refracts and reflects her perpetual in-betweenness as a cultural and social outsider, no matter where she finds herself geographically.

Structurally the novel shifts between past and present almost seamlessly, as the narrative voice remains constant while at the same time navigating between identities and multiple selves. The resulting narrative performs a type of fragmentary consciousness that BHARATI MUKHERJEE appears to link not only to late-20th-century American culture but also to an increasingly global world in which entire peoples and cultures interact across national boundaries. F. Timothy Ruppel makes a similar observation, remarking: "*Jasmine* is a novel that resists closure and suggests a strategy of continual transformation as a necessary and historically contingent ethic of survival" (182). As the narrator observes, farmers in Idaho can no longer maintain a profitable enterprise in response to the shifts of an increasingly global economy, just as peasant farmers in India, when rents and irrigation become unaffordable, find themselves forced to sell their land in hopes of finding some form of employment in the burgeoning and overpopulated cities. In this sense, Mukherjee challenges the reader to make any final pronouncement on the morality of Jyoti/Jasmine/Jase/Jane's decision at the end of the book to leave the paralyzed Bud while carrying his child, as no cultural values/standards appear to be absolute and unchanging; rather, they must be mitigated and deliberated within the context of a constantly shifting self and that self's relationship to increasingly destabilized notions of culture and society.

Bibliography

Carter-Sanborn, Kristin. "'We Murder Who We Were': *Jasmine* and the Violence of Identity." *American Literature* 66, no. 3 (September 1994): 573–593.

Mukherjee, Bharati. *Jasmine.* New York: Viking Penguin, 1989.

Ruppel, F. Timothy. "'Re-inventing ourselves a million times': Narrative, Desire, Identity, and Bharati Mukherjee's *Jasmine.*" *College Literature* 22, no. 1 (February 1995): 181–191.

Zach Weir

Jen, Gish (1955–)

Born Lillian Jen in New York to Shanghai immigrants, Gish Jen changed her name early in her writing career to mark the creation of a new self. The sharp, strong sound of Jen's new name matched her mission to write about subjects she calls "dangerous" and "naughty": racism, sex, power, and greed (Satz 132). The combination of dangerous topics and a tragicomic tone has earned her praise for breaking away from the established script of Asian-American experience. In fact, Jen's wildly successful writing career has been earned by pushing against and through conventional ideas about assimilation and cultural conflict. Critics point to Jen as a new kind of Asian-American writer, a writer in the post-KINGSTON era who wants to be known as an "American" writer and who insists that her books depict much more than just the so-called Asian-American experience. During a 1993 PBS interview with Bill Moyers, Jen described her multicultural writing style: "I've always been interested in my books not only just in capturing the Chinese-American experience, but the whole American experience and all the many groups jostling and intermingling and banging against each other."

Jen's parents came separately to America in the 1940s. They married, started a family, and settled in New York when the political situation in China prevented them from returning home. The family lived at first in Queens and Yonkers before moving to Scarsdale, a predominantly Jewish suburb. The second of five children, Jen distinguished herself with her passionate interest in reading literature and writing short stories. Her favorite books were Louisa May Alcott's *Little Women,* Jane Austen's *Pride and Prejudice,* Shakespeare's *King Lear,* and Tolstoy's *War and Peace.* Jen went on to receive a B.A. in English from Harvard in 1977. However, Jen felt unsure about what her future career should be. Her parents expected her to be a doctor or a lawyer, so Jen tried pre-law, pre-med, and business school. Eventually, however, she returned to writing. In 1983 she received an M.F.A from the prestigious Iowa Writer's Workshop. Her short stories from Iowa and afterward have been published in *The New Yorker, The Atlantic Monthly, Ploughshares,* and *The New Republic.* She completed her first novel, TYPICAL AMERICAN (1991), during a fellowship at Radcliffe's Bunting Institute. The novel depicts the life of Chinese immigrant Ralph Chang, whose attempts to successfully assimilate into American culture leave him emotionally and financially bankrupt.

Jen states that "dissonance" led her to pursue a writing career. No doubt Jen refers to the discord between her parents' expectations of her as a "good Chinese girl," her Catholic upbringing in a Jewish suburb, and her hyphenated existence as a Chinese American. Her short stories and novels explore acculturation, assimilation, and "outsiderness," even as she tries to write simply about what it means to be an American: "My project, like everybody's, was to define myself as an American, to define myself irrespective of my parents" (PBS interview). Keeping with her multicultural style, Jen published a sequel to *Typical American* called MONA IN THE PROMISED LAND (1996), narrated by Ralph Chang's daughter as she converts to Judaism. In 1999 she published WHO'S IRISH?, a collection of previously published and newly written short fiction. Her third novel, *The LOVE WIFE* (2004), is a shifting first-person narrative about second-generation Chinese-American Carnegie Wong and his family.

Jen's novels have been short-listed for the National Book Critics' Circle Award, and routinely named by national newspapers on "Best Books of the Year" lists. The short story "Birthmates" from *Who's Irish?* appeared in John Updike's *Best American Short Stories of the Century.* Jen acknowledges the influence of Asian-American writers who became popular in the 1970s and 1980s, but makes clear that she had to fight against the "script" of Asian-American experience popularized by MAXINE HONG KINGSTON, FRANK CHIN, and AMY TAN. The labelling of these authors as "Asian American" writers who write novels about "Asian American" experience disturbs Jen, who points out that her fiction encompasses many themes that are not necessarily, not entirely, Asian American. For example, her fiction commonly deals with abandonment, adoption, motherhood, sexuality, greed, religion, infidelity, and a host of other topics that have more to do with being human than with being American or Asian American. In an article written for *Time Asia*, Jen describes identity, ethnicity, nationality, and race as individually chosen rather than genetically determined, and more fluid than constant:

"Does identity consist of a host of daily practices that change and can be changed, some with great difficulty and some on a whim? It does seem so to me. Call me American: I came home from China [on a family trip] convinced

that we are made by culture, but that, everyday, consciously or unconsciously, we make our culture too."

Bibliography

Fedderson, R.C. "From Story to Novel and Back Again: Gish Jen's Developing Art of Short Fiction." In *Creative and Critical Approaches to the Short Story,* edited by Noel Harold Kaylor, Jr., 349–58. Lewiston, N.Y.: Mellon, 1997.

Jen, Gish. "Racial Profiling: Does Nature or Nurture Decide Who You Are?" *Time Asia: The Asian Journey Home* 18–23 August 2003. Available online. URL: http://www.time.com/time/asia/2003/journey/china_gish_jen.html. Accessed September 28, 2006.

———. Interview with Bill Moyers. *Becoming American: The Chinese Experience: A Bill Moyers Special.* Public Broadcasting Services. FFH Home Video, 2003.

Lee, Don. "About Gish Jen." *Ploughshares* 26, no. 2 (2000): 217–222.

Lee, Rachel C. "Gish Jen." In *Words Matter: Conversations with Asian American Writers,* edited by King-Kok Cheung, 215–232. Honolulu: University of Hawaii Press, 2000.

Matsukawa, Yuko. "*MELUS* Interview: Gish Jen." *MELUS* 18, no. 4 (1993–1994): 111–120.

Satz, Martha. "Writing About the Things That Are Dangerous." *Southwest Review* 78, no. 1 (1993): 132–140.

Amy Lillian Manning

Jhabvala, Ruth Prawer (1927–)

Screenwriter and novelist Ruth Prawer Jhabvala was born to Polish parents Marcus and Eleanora Prawer on May 7, 1927, in Cologne, Germany. The family immigrated to Britain in 1939, where she switched from her segregated Jewish education in German to English at the age of 12. Ten years later she acquired British citizenship. She pursued the study of English literature and received her master's degree in 1951 from London University. Around the same time, she married Cyrus Jhabvala, an Indian architect. The couple moved to India and lived there for more than 20 years with their three daughters before moving to New York, where she currently resides. She is now an American citizen.

Jhabvala's works reflect her multicultural exposure. Her early works explore an understanding of her Indian experience. In 1960 producer Ismail Merchant and director James Ivory approached her and this began her long collaboration with them and Jhabvala's entry among Hollywood's elite. Besides recognition in Hollywood as an accomplished screenwriter, Jhabvala has won numerous literary awards for her novels. In 1975 she won Britain's prestigious Booker Prize for her novel *Heat and Dust,* a love story set in India in 1923. In 1984 she won the British Academy of Film and Television Arts (BAFTA) award for Best Screenplay for the Merchant-Ivory film adaptation of *Heat and Dust.*

Gradually, Jhabvala's work began to shift away from predominantly Indian themes. In 1986 she received her first Academy Award for Best Adapted Screenplay for *A Room with a View.* This period piece adapted from E. M. Forster's novel combines a passionate romance and a study of oppression within the British class system. In 1992 Jhabvala received her second Academy Award for Best Adapted Screenplay for *Howards End.* Set in England during the early part of the century, this adaptation of E. M. Forster's novel involves the encounters of three families, each from distinct social classes whose intertwined relationships affect one another. Another adaptation by her of a story set in England was Kazuo Ishiguro's *The Remains of the Day,* which won her an Oscar nomination in 1993.

Other adaptations by Jhabvala for the Merchant-Ivory team include Henry James's novels *The Europeans, The Bostonians,* and others. Set in 1840, *The Europeans* (1979) centers on the cultural clashes that unfold when a brother and sister from Europe unexpectedly arrive at the doorstep of their American cousins. *The Bostonians* (1984) depicts the post–Civil War intellectual community of Boston in 1875, and brings to life the suffragist movement, while unfolding the life of a woman

whose journey of self-discovery leads her to make a choice that changes the lives of those around her.

Over the years Jhabvala's works continued to capture American themes, and in 1990 she won the Best Screenplay Award from the New York Film Critics Circle for *Mr. & Mrs. Bridge.* The story, originally a novel by Evan S. Conell Jr., involves a traditional middle-class family in Kansas City, Missouri, during the 1940s, caught up in the trap of repression and respectability. Her screenplay based on Kayle Jones's novel, *A Soldier's Daughter Never Cries* (1998), captures the experiences of a former American war hero, who is now a successful author living as an expatriate with his family in France. Events force the family to move back to North Carolina, where they struggle to find their true cultural identity.

Jhabvala's recent adaptation of Henry James's novel *The Golden Bowl* (2000) focuses on the tangled web of relationships between a wealthy American art collector, his wife, daughter, and son-in-law. Each character yearns to be elsewhere or with someone else, and the cracked "golden bowl" symbolically holds the plot together while tearing the family apart. Jhabvala explores similar complex familial relationships in her latest screenplay *Le Divorce* (2003), based on the novel by Diane Johnson. The story focuses on an American woman who travels to France to visit her pregnant stepsister and ends up becoming a Frenchman's mistress. Like many of her other works, this explores contemporary American and French themes.

Besides adaptations, Jhabvala's skill in handling diverse concepts and cultures is reflected in her original screenplay *Roseland* (1977). Set in contemporary America and consisting of three separate episodes, *Roseland* depicts ballroom dancing in New York, where characters attempt to find their dance partners. Similarly, Jhabvala experiments with a different plot in her screenplay *Jane Austen in Manhattan* (1980): As rival theater companies compete to produce their own versions of Jane Austen's childhood play, events during the production begin to mirror those occurring within the play itself. Another original screenplay, *Jefferson in Paris* (1995), in which Jhabvala dabbles with American history, is about America's obsession with the personal life of Thomas Jefferson in the years before he became president, especially when he went to Paris as a U.S. ambassador.

Besides screenplays, Jhabvala wrote numerous novels and short stories. Jhabvala moved to New York from India nearly 35 years ago, and her plots reflect this geographic movement. For example, in *Travelers* (1972), Jhabvala examines the odd convergence in India of four people with different psychological and cultural backgrounds: an Indian widow, an Englishman, an American woman and a young Indian student. Similarly, her collection of short stories, *How I Became a Holy Mother and other stories* (1976), includes stories about Parsees, a minority community in India, and other Western characters in search of spiritual enlightenment. Following that, her novel *In Search of Love and Beauty* (1983) explores the lives of three generations of people, their hopes and quest for idealism. In 1984, she received the MacArthur Foundation Award. Jhabvala continued her exploration across cultures in her novel *Three Continents* (1987), set in New York, London, and India. The plot circles around a fabulously wealthy young woman whose life of material privilege drives her to seek something higher. She finds her emotional peace in a fanatic religious sect, which in reality is a pious façade to raise money illegally.

In 1994 she won the Writers Guild of America's Screen Laurel Award. Two years later in *Shards of Memory* (1996), Jhabvala once again recreates an intercontinental family saga, which begins in a Manhattan townhouse and goes back in time to span four generations whose lives are knit together by an unconventional spiritual movement. Jhabvala's collection of 13 short stories, entitled *East into Upper East: Plain Tales from New York and New Delhi* (1998), explores the nature of love across two continents. Jhabvala worked on this collection for 20 years, and five of the stories appeared in *The New Yorker*.

In 2004 her nine fictional stories collected in *My Nine Lives: Chapters of a Possible Past* reflect an autobiographical tone, as the stories move between New York, London, and India. Jhabvala imagines alternative paths her life might have taken and ponders on how she never fully assimilated in any culture. Now nearly 80, Jhabvala recently wrote the novel *Refuge in London* (2003), depicting an artistic struggle in postwar London nearly half a century ago. It won the O. Henry Award in 2005.

In addition to her novels, screenplays, and short stories, Jhabvala frequently contributes to *The New Yorker*. Whether set in India, London, or New York, her works reflect her ability to experiment, adapt, challenge, provoke, and entertain.

Akhila Naik

Jin, Ha (1956–)

Born Jin Xuefei in the city of Jinzhou, Liaoning Province, China, Ha Jin had quite an eventful life in his native country. The son of a military officer, he joined the Chinese Army when he was still 13 years old. Although he took part in the Cultural Revolution of the 1960s and '70s, he was branded a counterrevolutionary and persecuted during that volatile period, since his grandfather had been a landowner. Jin left the army after five and a half years and became a telegraph operator at a railroad station, where he started to teach himself English. Following that, with the Cultural Revolution over, he earned a B.A. in English at Heilongjiang University and then an M.A. in American literature at Shangdong University.

In 1985 Jin moved to Boston to pursue a Ph.D. in English at Brandeis University. In 1990 he published his first book, *Between Silences: A Voice from China,* a volume of poetry that encapsulates many of what would become his dominant themes. In the preface, Jin declares that his main objective as a writer is to "speak for those unfortunate people who suffered, endured or perished at the bottom of life and who created the history and at the same time were fooled or ruined by it." This is something that he has continued to do in his subsequent works. In 1996, three years after earning his Ph.D., he published his second collection of poems, *Facing Shadows,* in which he relates his experience as an immigrant in the United States as well as his response to the Tiananmen Square uprising of 1989, the epochal event that barred his return to his native land. In 2001 Jin finished his third collection of poetry, *Wreckage,* which focuses mainly on China's ancient history and its impact on contemporary China.

Ocean of Words, Ha Jin's first collection of short stories, was published in 1989, the same year as *Facing Shadows.* It deals with life in the Chinese Army along the border between China and the former Soviet Union in the late 1960s and early '70s, a time when war between the two Communist countries seemed imminent. Set in a rural town during the Cultural Revolution, Jin's second collection of short stories, *Under the Red Flag,* focuses on the everyday existence of common Chinese people as they face major political and social changes. Published in 2000, Jin's third collection of stories, *The* BRIDEGROOM, concentrates on life in China in the early 1980s.

Jin's major achievement, though, is his novels. Jin is a prolific writer: Within four years, he published three novels, namely IN THE POND (1998), WAITING (1999), and *The* CRAZED (2002). In 2004 he produced his latest novel, WAR TRASH, which explores the little known history of Chinese POWs held in American and South Korean camps during the Korean War.

Ha Jin has become celebrated as one of the most prominent nonnative authors in English, which places him in the same tradition as such luminaries as Joseph Conrad and Vladimir Nabokov. Yet, while there are many similarities between him and his predecessors, there are also striking differences. For example, even though he has lived in exile for almost 20 years, Jin continues to write mainly about contemporary China. Among other things, this means that he has to translate Chinese culture for a largely non-Chinese audience. Also, despite being interested in ideas, he always underscores how people's intellectual or spiritual lives are shaped by material conditions, especially in such a regimented society as China. Because of Jin's unfailing empathy toward ordinary people and his acute sense of humor, his writings testify to the human will to persevere notwithstanding seemingly overwhelming obstacles.

Jin has been the recipient of several prestigious literary prizes, such as the PEN/Faulkner Award, the PEN/Hemingway Award, the Flannery O'Connor Award, and the National Book Award. Most of his fiction has been translated into his native language, Chinese, including *Ocean of Words, Under the Red Flag, The Bridegroom, Waiting, In the Pond,* and *The Crazed.* Almost all of those texts have been published in Taiwan, where a considerable amount of scholarship has been devoted to his work. So far, though, the only one of Jin's texts that has appeared in translation in mainland China is his novel *Waiting.*

Bibliography

Garner, Dwight. "Ha Jin's Cultural Revolution." *New York Times Magazine,* 6 February 2000, pp. 38–42.

Jin, Ha. "Ha Jin: An Interview with Liza Nelson." *Five Points: A Journal of Literature and Art* 5, no. 1 (2000): 52–67.

Zhang, Hang. "Bilingual Creativity in Chinese English: Ha Jin's *In the Pond." World Englishes* 21, no. 2 (2002): 305–315.

Jianwu Liu and Albert Braz

Joseph, Lawrence   (1948–   )

Lawrence Joseph has enjoyed two long and successful careers simultaneously since the mid-1970s: one as a highly esteemed lawyer and professor of law, with experience in labor, securities, antitrust, bankruptcy, and mergers and acquisitions; and the other as an award-winning poet and essayist. Joseph thus falls into a long line of American poets—Wallace Stevens, Edgar Lee Masters, T. S. Eliot, and James Dickey foremost among them—who have managed to balance artistic and corporate pursuits, but Joseph's high degree of success in the field of law sets him apart even from such prominent dual-career poets.

Lawrence Joseph's grandparents, who were among the first Arab immigrants to the United States, were Lebanese and Syrian Catholics. His father, Joseph Alexander, was co-owner of a grocery and liquor store; his mother, Clara Barbara Francis, was a chef. Born in Detroit, Joseph graduated Phi Beta Kappa from the University of Michigan in 1970. He thereafter attended Cambridge

University, receiving both bachelor's (1972) and master's (1976) degrees with first honours in English language and literature. In 1975 Joseph received his J.D. from the University of Michigan Law School. After serving as law clerk to Justice G. Mennen Williams of the Michigan Supreme Court, he joined the University of Detroit School of Law faculty from 1978 to 1981. In 1981 he took a litigator position in the New York firm of Shearman & Sterling; in 1987 he was hired as a professor of law at St. John's University School of Law in New York City. In 2003 Joseph was named The Reverend Joseph T. Tinnelly, C.M., Professor of Law; as of 2006, he remains on the faculty at St. John's University.

In addition to publishing and lecturing frequently on the law throughout the United States, Europe, and the Middle East, Lawrence Joseph has published five collections of poetry, as well as numerous critical articles and essays on contemporary poetry and poets. His five books are *Shouting At No One* (1983, winner of the Agnes Lunch Starrett Poetry Prize), *Curriculum Vitae* (1988), *Before Our Eyes* (1993), *Codes, Precepts, Biases, and Taboos: Poems 1973–1993* (2005), and *Into It* (2005). He is also the author of the acclaimed prose work *Lawyerland: What Lawyers Talk About When They Talk About The Law* (1997).

Like Wallace Stevens, an admitted influence, Lawrence Joseph is concerned with poetry's ability to present "things as they are"—that is, the world of experience presented in vivid and inventive language, but unfiltered by self-consciously "poetic" embellishment. Reviews of *Shouting At No One* and *Curriculum Vitae* praise the blend of cultural influences and series of strong narrative voices, such as the student narrator of "Stop Me If I've Told You" (from *CV*), who in the middle of a freezing January at Cambridge remembers a Feast of St. Elias in Lebanon, linking the rituals of religious faith with the often repetitive practices of academic study: "while Beirut's heavy moon / and tin and cardboard houses / revolved behind my eyes, / I danced one step forward / and, then, one step to the side, / knelt, rose straightbacked / upright in the beginnings / of some strange knowledge / I thought was true."

The remarkable "Sand Nigger," also from *CV*, presents the narrator's childhood in a multilingual Detroit home filled with relatives, detailing a multitude of voices in conversation and argument with each other throughout the poem. The narrator concludes by grappling with the racist slur of the title, declaring himself an amalgam of many cultures, which makes him appear strange to observers unfamiliar with the Arabic and American elements of his identity: "The name fits: I am / the light-skinned nigger / with black eyes and the look / difficult to figure ... / nice enough / to pass, Lebanese enough / to be against his brother, / with his brother against his cousin, / with cousin and brother / against the stranger." In subsequent books, Joseph's poetic devices become less narrative and more imagistic, often achieving their effect by setting tightly described, seemingly incongruous images in close proximity to each other, as in "Over Darkening Gold" (from *Before Our Eyes*), in which "The state of the state / consumes the sublime ebony of the moon," "Around us wild metallic shimmering, / history, a subject, inside the sky."

In a self-composed contribution to his biographical entry in the *Contemporary Authors* series (written in the third person), Joseph writes that "Two things remain constant throughout his poetry: a preoccupation with how a poem sounds—everything that's said in a poem is spoken by someone; voice for him is sensual—and an acute formal sense of how voice (or intonation) can be constructed." Blending the "voices" of law, religious faith, family, and multiple nations and cultures, Joseph's poetry draws attention to the diversity of voices with which Americans speak.

Joseph is the recipient of numerous awards in poetry and law, including two National Endowment for the Arts poetry fellowships, a John Simon Guggenheim Memorial Foundation fellowship, and a grant from the Employment Standards Division of the U.S. Department of Labor for his writing on workers' compensation law.

Bibliography

Contemporary Authors Online. "Lawrence Joseph." Gale, 2006. Reproduced in Biography Resource

Center. Farmington Hills, Mich.: Gale Group, 2006.

St. John's University School of Law. "Lawrence Joseph." Available online. URL: http://new.stjohns.edu/academics/graduate/law/faculty/profiles/Joseph. Accessed September 30, 2006.

Majaj, Lisa Suhair. "Arab-Americans and the Meanings of Race." In *Postcolonial Theory and the United States: Race, Ethnicity, and Literature,* edited by Amritjit Singh and Peter Schmidt, 320–327. Jackson: University of Mississippi Press, 2000.

Smith, Dinitia. "The Arab-American Writers: Uneasy in Two Worlds," *New York Times,* 19 February 2003, p. E1.

Eric G. Waggoner

Journey, The   Indira Ganesan (1990)

Novelist INDIRA GANESAN's writing revolves around the conflict between two cultures and the way her characters learn to create a fine line between traditional and contemporary society. Her first novel, *The Journey,* chronicles the actual and philosophical journey of 19-year-old Renu Krishnan. Having lived in America for 10 years while her parents pursued careers in the sciences, she finds herself returning to the mythical island of Pi with her mother and sister to attend the funeral of her favorite cousin, Rajesh. Because they were born on the same day, the families have referred to them as twins, a fact that used to bring her great joy and one that now threatens to engulf her. In spite of her already deepening sense of grief, Renu is subjected to compounded shocks.

During the funeral preparations, Renu finds herself the object of island gossip. A superstitious people, the islanders believe that since Renu's cousin, Rajesh, died by drowning, Renu will be the victim of death by fire. To add to her sense of desperation, Renu's mother attempts to get her to agree to an arranged marriage. As she retreats into herself, other events constitute the focus of the novel. Renu's sister, Manx, a very liberated 15-year-old, meets and dates an American expatriate named Freddie. Eventually Renu returns to traditional ways, much to the confusion of her sister.

This story is about journeys from many angles. It is a reflection of the challenges that confront any young female but focuses on the cultural differences of females in India and, specifically, on the way Renu deals with those differences.

Ganesan also creates interesting turns in the story, mostly secondary stories that are interwoven within the tightly defined world that belongs to Renu. Her grandfather, once a stern taskmaster for both Renu and her cousin Rajesh, is bedridden when Renu arrives. He, too, goes through his own metamorphosis and moves beyond infirmity to make a pilgrimage alone, a fact unknown to the other members of the family and one that throws them into a panic. There is also her Uncle Adda, who suffers from his memory of his beloved Spanish wife and the tragedy that befell them. Renu learns the truth about the mystery of their marriage and their boy, Kish. Renu also learns that things are not always what they seem and that sometimes choices are made because they create a world that is easier to navigate. She finds that the human heart is stronger than she could have imagined and sometimes family is not necessarily the people who share the same blood. Renu easily accepts the move back to tradition and culture, while Manx abhors the change in her sister and remains steadfast in her Americanism.

Anne Marie Fowler

Joy Luck Club, The   Amy Tan (1989)

In AMY TAN's internationally best-selling and well-reviewed first novel, the story revolves around four sets of mother-daughter pairs. The correspondences and continuities between the immigrant Chinese mothers and their first-generation American daughters overshadow the superficial differences that each pair experiences as they learn to deal with the intricacies of negotiating two very different cultures. Originally conceived by Tan as a series of short stories, the intertwined lives of the mothers and daughters form a fully fashioned novel that won critical and popular acclaim.

The novel is divided into four sections, and the stories in each section are linked thematically.

While the novel as a whole deals with Jing-Mei "June" Woo's emotional discovery of her mother's life through the stories of the women of the Joy Luck Club after her mother's death, each character in the story uncovers a closer link to her own mother or daughter through storytelling. The novel moves effortlessly from present-day California to wartime China and back again, focusing on the individual events in each woman's life to provide cohesion.

The first section of stories, "Feathers from a Thousand Li Away," includes June Woo's introduction to the ladies of the Joy Luck Club, a mah-jongg club her mother started in wartime China with three other women to create a sanctuary from the horrible conditions they endured. The club was re-created after June's mother immigrated to America, and, now that she has died, June has been called upon to take her mother's place at the game table. June's story also includes part of her mother's story about the conception of the club, the relief it brought the players, and her eventual flight from Kweilin, where they had been staying, just before the Japanese invaded. Suyuan Woo, June's mother, took only what was most valuable to her, but along the way lost nearly everything, including her twin daughters, whom she had to abandon when dysentery overtook her. Although she was rescued, she was unable to retrieve the twins, and spent the rest of her life in both China and America searching for them. The Joy Luck ladies had located Suyuan's daughters, June learns, after her death.

The mothers' stories, addressed to their daughters in hopes of explaining aspects of their lives that have remained hidden either through purposeful silence or negligence, reveal difficult and emotional formative episodes in their lives. The stories, while they relate intensely personal moments of familial duty, arranged marriages, drowned children, marital discord, and personal angst, transcend the merely personal and become emblems of women's lives throughout different eras and different cultures. The mothers, working within an intensely patriarchal system, use their own ingenuity to carve out lives for themselves, eventually reinventing themselves in a new country. Their fondest wish is that their American-born daughters, raised in a land of opportunity, would be able to appreciate the sacrifices their mothers had made for them and to live fulfilling, satisfying lives. The daughters, exposed from birth to two cultures, struggle between the dominant public American culture that informs so much of their lives and the formative private Chinese culture—incarnate in their mothers—that they feel compelled to rebel against or maintain privately. Throughout the story cycles, the mothers' and daughters' voices begin to intermingle until a continuity forms between the pairs, and the fragmented experiences that each daughter thought were unique to her becomes whole within the narrative of her mother. Each mother's strength, exhibited in the actions she took in her own life and the lessons she learned from them, spills over to ameliorate and complete her daughter's experiences.

Using eight different points of view in the novel, Tan resolves the narrative with June's reunion in China with her long-lost sisters. During the meeting, each daughter feels the presence of her mother, and several generations are united. To accomplish the unity of the novel, Tan relies on recurring symbols such as the mah-jongg table, with its four sides, four players, and four directions that hint at the multiplicity of interpretations available for each story. Other unifying devices include the difficulty each woman has with language and culture, as exemplified in several stories by the food each woman prepares and eats. As Tan links the tales and then weaves them into the whole that constitutes the novel, her poetic ability to reconcile opposites and draw meaning out of each aspect of life becomes as moving as the lives she creates.

Bibliography

Bloom, Harold. *Amy Tan's* The Joy Luck Club: *Modern Critical Interpretations.* Philadelphia: Chelsea House Publishers, 2002.

Huntley, E. D., ed. *Amy Tan: A Critical Companion: Critical Companions to Popular Contemporary Writers.* Westport, Conn.: Greenwood Press, 1998.

Vanessa Rasmussen

Kadohata, Cynthia (1956–)

Born in Chicago and raised in Arkansas, Georgia, Michigan, and California, Cynthia Kadohata spent much of her childhood on the road with her family. Her career has also been a long odyssey. She dropped out of high school, worked in department stores and fast food restaurants, and eventually graduated from the University of Southern California with a B.A. in journalism. Supporting herself with temporary work, Kadohata embarked on her writing career, and after a string of rejections, published short stories in *The New Yorker* in 1986. Despite her commitment to writing, Kadohata found life on the road more attractive, so she attended but dropped out of graduate writing programs in both the University of Pittsburgh and Columbia University. In 1989, she published her first novel, *The Floating World.*

Olivia, the 12-year-old narrator of *The Floating World,* tells of her family's experiences as they travel from the Pacific Northwest to Arkansas in search of work and a place to call home in the 1950s. The phrase "floating world," translated from *ukiyo,* a Japanese word referring to the feeling of insecurity, is associated with shuttling between gas stations and motels. However, Olivia sees the world not as just harsh but also magical and enchanting. Appropriately, Kadohata's prose reflects Olivia's sensitivity and imagination; her descriptions are at once blunt, sparse, comical, philosophical, and lyrical.

Kadohata's work often features young female protagonists who view the world as at once real and surreal, as harsh and hopeful. Francie—the 19-year-old, orphaned, mixed-race narrator of *In the Heart of the Valley of Love*—must survive in Los Angeles in the year 2052, where the polluted terrain is divided into "Richtown," where affluent whites have secluded themselves, and the slums where the "have-nots" live in hunger and disease. This second novel, with its futuristic setting, can be categorized as science fiction; however, Kadohata grounds the novel in her concerns with contemporary issues. It is no great coincidence that her novel was published in the same year as the 1992 Los Angeles riots. In an interview with *Publishers Weekly,* Kadohata remarks, "I guess I should have set the book just three years ahead."

This blending of the real and fictitious perhaps allowed Kadohata to avoid being thrust into the heated debates about self-representation in Asian-American literary circles. Because Kadohata's characters reflect aspects of the author's own life, it is tempting to read them as "authentic" representations of Kadohata's experiences as a Japanese American. However, Kadohata's stories explore universal themes and concerns, so they are not always considered ethnic-specific.

Kadohata is also the author of *The Glass Mountains,* a fantasy novel about a young woman who must travel beyond her village in search of her parents. She also wrote *Kira-Kira*, a children's book about a young Japanese-American girl who has to cope with her sister's death. Kadohata has received fellowships from the National Endowment for the Arts, the Mrs. Giles Whiting Foundation, and the Chesterfield Writer's Film Project. She lives in Los Angeles.

Catherine Fung

Kaneko, Lonny (1939–)

Born in Seattle, Washington, Kaneko is a third-generation Japanese American. At the outbreak of World War II, Kaneko and his family were sent to an assembly center in Puyallup, Washington. Later they were interned at Hunt (Minidoka) Relocation Center in Idaho. While in college, Kaneko studied under Theodore Roethke and received his M.A. in English from the University of Washington in 1963. His master's thesis was a collection of poems entitled "Catchcan of Chicken Feathers in an Old Roost." He received the National Endowment for the Arts fellowship in 1982, which enabled him to complete his manuscript for *Coming Home from Camp* (1986), a collection of poems about the internment camp and postwar experiences. He taught English at Highline Community College in Washington.

Though Kaneko considers himself primarily a teacher, then a poet, he coauthored two plays with Amy Sanbo. *Lady Is Dying* received the Henry Broderick Playwright Prize at the Pacific Northwest Writers Conference and was performed at the Asian American Theatre Workshop in 1977. He also coauthored *Benny Hana* with Amy Sanbo.

Like his poems, many of Kaneko's short stories take place in the internment camp. His masterpiece, "The Shoyu Kid" (1991), describes life in an internment camp from the young boy Masao's point of view. Along with his friends, Masao chases the title character, a boy nicknamed the Shoyu Kid after his brown, runny nose, only to find out that the Shoyu Kid receives a chocolate from an American soldier for playing with the soldier's *chimpo* (penis). The motifs of chase and trap, as well as the themes of alienation and betrayal, are prominent in this story.

Kaneko's short story "Nobody's Hero" (1996) is also set in Minidoka camp and told from Masao's point of view. In this story Masao and his friend steal candies and cigarettes from a canteen successfully, and their friends start to see Masao and his friends as their heroes because they deceived the War Relocation Authority (WRA) officers. However, their glorious days as heroes are over within a week when the WRA officers belittle Masao and his friends' deed in a camp newspaper. The theme of loyalty is central in this story: It is the loyalty among Masao and his friends that drives them to steal from the canteen and challenge the power and authority of the U.S. government represented by the characters of the WRA officers.

Kyoko Amano

Kang, Younghill (1903–1972)

Born in Hamkyung Province in North Korea, Kang was educated first in the Confucian tradition and later at Christian schools established by missionaries from North America. In 1914, against the expectations of his father, he left behind the obligations of the only son, in pursuit of higher and broader education. Kang studied in Seoul for about a year in virtual destitution, observing the modernization of Korea under the colonial rule of Japan. A year later, he continued his studies in Japan to expand his knowledge of Western science, literature, and philosophy. In 1921 Kang landed in New York.

Describing himself as "self-educated," he read English and American classics voraciously, attending classes at Harvard and Boston Universities, while working at various times as a houseboy, restaurant server, and business assistant to support himself. Between 1924 and 1927, Kang wrote in Korean and Japanese; but from 1928 he began writing in English with the help of his Wellesley-educated American wife, Frances Keeley. He found work as an editor for the *Encyclopaedia Britannica* and at the Metropolitan Museum of Art's

Department of Far Eastern Art in New York. He also obtained a position as a lecturer in the English department at New York University, where he befriended Thomas Wolfe. At the time, Kang was working on The GRASS ROOF, which describes Kang's life in Korea up to the point of his departure for the West in 1921. Wolfe read four chapters of the book and then took it to his own editor at Charles Scribner's Sons, which published it in 1931. Translated into French, German, and other languages, The Grass Roof won the French Prix Halperine Kaminsky in 1937. Between 1933 and 1935, Kang went to Germany and Italy on a Guggenheim Award in Creative Literature. The success of his first book led to the 1933 publication of The Happy Grove, a children's book based on the first part of The Grass Roof, accompanied by a number of illustrations. In 1937 Scribner's published EAST GOES WEST: THE MAKING OF AN ORIENTAL YANKEE, annals of his experiences in America.

Kang lived in genteel poverty with his wife and three children in a Long Island farmhouse overflowing with books. Always in demand as a visiting lecturer, he was nevertheless unable to obtain a stable teaching position. Instead, he traveled from one speaking engagement to another in an old Buick, astonishing Rotary Club audiences with his recitations of Hamlet's soliloquies or his lectures on Korea. He is said to have commented that it was his great misfortune that Pearl Buck's Pulitzer Prize–winning novel about China, The Good Earth, was published in the same year as The Grass Roof, eclipsing his own tale of Asia.

For a brief period after World War II, Kang served as chief of publications under the U.S. occupational forces in Korea. He received the Louis S. Weiss Memorial Prize in 1953 and an honorary doctorate in literature from Korea University in 1970. Among the 5,000 books he donated to Korea University, Kang included an unpublished play of his entitled "Kongmin Wang [King Kongmin]" (1960s), also known as "Murder in the Royal Palace," a version of which was performed in the United States in 1964. In 1970 Kang also published in Korea ill-reputed translations of Korean literature including Yongwoon Han's Meditations of the Lover. Hospitalized in New York for postoperative hemorrhaging after a massive stroke, Kang died in Florida in December 1972.

Bibliography

Kang, Younghill. *East Goes West: The Making of an Oriental Yankee.* New York: Charles Scribner's Sons, 1937. Chicago: Follett, 1965. New York: Kaya Productions, 1997.

———. *The Grass Roof.* New York: Charles Scribner's Sons, 1931. Chicago: Follett, 1966.

———. *The Happy Grove.* New York: Charles Scribner's Sons, 1933.

SuMee Lee

Keller, Nora Okja   (1965–   )

A significant voice in American literature, Keller is deeply committed to her craft and to shedding light on issues affecting women, especially women of Korean heritage, which have historically been shrouded in silence and regarded with shame.

Born in Seoul, Korea, to a Korean mother and a German-American father, Keller makes her home with her husband and two daughters in Hawaii. While issues of ethnic identity and marginalization inform Keller's literary work, her own experience of growing up was markedly different from that of her protagonists. "One of the best things about Hawaii," notes Keller, "is that the majority of people are mixed race in some way or another, so I grew up where that was the norm" (Keller, MELUS 146). Indeed, despite her diverse heritage, she declares that she "never felt singled out and looked at as a mixed-race *hapa* girl" (Keller, identity theory). Nevertheless, Keller was aware, particularly as a teenager, of her often conflicting identities, choosing to align herself more strongly with her acquired American self and rejecting most aspects of her mother's Korean heritage. It was not until she attended the University of Hawaii to study English and psychology and encountered the Asian-American literary tradition that she began to feel the need to understand and connect to her Korean-American identity.

Following the completion of her bachelor's degree, Keller attended the University of California, Santa Cruz, where she earned a master's degree in American literature, focusing largely on Asian-American literature. While Keller's interest in reading and writing dates back to her early childhood and the influence of her father's love of books and the stories she was told by her elder siblings, she did not begin to think seriously of writing fiction until she was a university student. Her early attempts were primarily works of short fiction that were, in her words, "very whitewashed" with "no ethnicity, no specific culture" (Keller, identity theory). As her familiarity with the works of writers like MAXINE HONG KINGSTON and JADE SNOW WONG grew, Keller began to consider ways to connect her own writing more meaningfully to her investigation of her heritage. The result was the beginning of her highly acclaimed first novel, COMFORT WOMAN (1997), a harrowing look at the life of a Korean woman forced into sexual slavery during the Japanese occupation of Korea in World War II. Initially Keller wrote a short story entitled "Mother Tongue," which garnered her the prestigious Pushcart Prize in 1995, and which eventually became the second chapter of the novel. When the novel was published two years later, it won the 1998 American Book Award and was long-listed for the United Kingdom's Orange Prize.

In 1999 Keller coedited an anthology of women's writing, called *Intersecting Circles: Voices of Hapa Women,* and in 2002 she produced her second novel, *FOX GIRL,* which was also long-listed for the Orange Prize (2003). A second coedited volume of writing, *YOBO: Korean Americans Writing in Hawai'i,* followed in 2003, along with a children's play, *When Tiger Smoked His Pipe,* cowritten with her 10-year-old daughter and produced by Honolulu Theatre for Youth. Keller is now working on a third novel—a sort of sequel to *Comfort Woman* and *Fox Girl*—and a collection of essays. Keller regularly participates in Hawaii's Bamboo Ridge Press literary study group and credits much of her success to the sharing of her works in progress and the feedback she receives at the monthly gatherings.

Bibliography

Keller, Nora Okja. "Interview: Nora Okja Keller," by Robert Birnbaum (29 April 2002). Identity theory. com. Available online. URL: http://www.identity-theory.com/people/birnbaum43.html. Accessed October 1, 2006.

———. "Nora Okja Keller and the Silenced Woman: An Interview," by Young-Oak Lee. *MELUS* 28, no. 4 (Winter 2003): 145–166.

Dana Hansen

Keltner, Kim Wong (1969–)

Native to the city's streets that appear with a colorful familiarity of accents, smells, and tastes in the best seller *The Dim Sum of All Things* (2004) and *Buddha Baby* (2005), Kim Wong Keltner lives in San Francisco with her husband, Rolf, and daughter Lucy. Currently completing a third novel, Keltner began her first manuscript amid her various stints as a teacher, a telephone customer service representative, and an office manager at the progressive zine *Mother Jones,* eventually redirecting her full-time working hours toward writing. Her two novels feature the witty and hilarious 20-something Lindsey Owyang, who, like the author, is an alumna of the University of California at Berkeley, has worked in humdrum retail jobs, and is a third-generation Chinese American whose *pau pau* (Cantonese for "grandma") runs a Chinatown travel agency. As both texts feature Lindsey as a working urban heroine just as savvy about pop music and television as she is male-curious and down-to-earth, they may be seen as Chinese American interventions in the emergent arena of "chick lit."

In *The Dim Sum of All Things,* Lindsey's persona is from the very start on the borderline between hybrid and paradoxical. She is a young professional who lives with her grandmother and has to deal with "her old Chinese ways"; she also loves to eat meat but happens to be the receptionist at *Vegan Warrior* magazine. With more proficiency in iambic pentameter than Cantonese, Lindsey "could not quote a single Han Dynasty proverb, but she could recite entire dialogues from numerous *Brady Bunch* episodes." Despite what seems like a lifetime of parrying "Hoarders of All Things Asian"—weird white men who unabashedly and unconditionally advance upon Asian women—and suffering failed dates with Chinese boys arranged by her *pau pau,* Lindsey is still interested in romance. She suddenly finds herself in a relationship with *Vegan Warrior* travel editor Michael Cartier, a white guy and fellow "closet meat-eater." His love of variegated foods from Twix bars to sautéed pea sprouts, like Lindsey's, knows no cultural bounds. The relationship begins tentatively, with Lindsey's anxieties of family acceptance and echoes of her cousin Brandon's scolding: "[Y]ou only like white guys. What's up with that?" Yet traveling away from San Francisco, first with her grandmother to China and then with Michael to the California town of Locke, proves to be a traveling toward herself and her family history as she learns more about her grandmother's World War II experiences and her father's western hometown. Reckoning with a new knowledge of her family's past allows Lindsey a certain stability—or a certainty in her instability—that helps her come to a decision about her relationship with Michael.

In Keltner's sequel *Buddha Baby,* clues and musings about Lindsey's family history continue on—with Lindsey's reminder that "Confucian proverbs eluded her, but she was well versed in the spunky aphorisms of great philosophers such as Fonzie and Fred Sanford." *Buddha Baby* introduces a more mature Lindsey who has left *Vegan Warrior* and now lives with her fiancé Michael. She juggles part-time work as a museum gift-shop clerk and as a teacher at St. Maude's, the Catholic school of her youth. Each job leads to a distinct adventure, revisiting the anxieties explored in *The Dim Sum of All Things:* family, racial identity, and relationships with men. At the gift shop, Lindsey runs into a childhood flame, the sweet-talking Chinese Texan, Dustin Lee. As Michael is away on business, Lindsey panders to her curiosities about dating Dustin and Chinese men in general. As it turns out, Lindsey and Dustin share similar reckonings with regard to dating and what it is to be Chinese—"authentic Chinese flavor," in Lindsey's

words—which fuels an attraction between them that could threaten her engagement to Michael. Meanwhile at St. Maude's, Lindsey wades through the bureaucracy of nuns and other cohorts to sift through the school's basement records. Shocked to discover a 1928 photograph of a girl who is her spitting image, Lindsey embarks on solving a case of mistaken identity, as Keltner reintroduces an element of gothic mystery into "chick lit" and cleverly shows how the constraints of family history always leave room for the novel individual.

Bibliography

Dong, Stella. Review of *The Dim Sum of All Things* and *Buddha Baby,* by Kim Wong Keltner. *South China Morning Post,* (Hong Kong), 25 December 2005, p. 5.

Keltner, Kim Wong. *The Dim Sum of All Things.* New York: HarperCollins, 2004.

———. *Buddha Baby.* New York: HarperCollins, 2005.

Michelle Har Kim

Kim, Myung Mi (1957–)

Award-winning, post-modern poet Myung Mi Kim was born in Seoul, South Korea. Her family immigrated to the United States when she was nine years old. Through a series of moves within the country, Kim's childhood was filled with muted struggles to learn a new language and adapt to an alien culture. Later on, such cultural and linguistic displacement and diasporic reconfiguration are traced and revisited in her poems. Kim graduated from Oberlin College in 1979, and obtained an M.A. from Johns Hopkins University in 1981. After teaching English at Stuyvesant High School, New York, from 1983 to 1984, she went on to pursue an M.F.A. and received it from the University of Iowa in 1986. After teaching at Luther College in Decorah, Iowa, and at San Francisco State University, she has been teaching poetry since 2002 at the State University of New York, Buffalo.

In 1991 Kim's first poetry collection, *Under Flag,* was published and won the 1991 Multicultural Publishers Book Award. By investigating the power of the English language and questioning the possibility of translation between cultures, Kim articulates her personal and her home country's collective memory of lost home and dislocation: "[W]e cross bridges we did not see being built." In her second collection, *The Bounty* (1996), and third collection, *Dura* (1998), Kim expresses a profound conflict with language, especially about the way it is taught and translated. In these poems, the political, historical, and ideological forces at work in language are exemplified. By juxtaposing Korean and English throughout the poems in her 2002 collection, *Commons*, Kim again draws attention to the ways in which languages compete in her daily life.

Kim's poems are framed with musical, visual, and fragmented images of languages. As critic Zhou Xiaojing maintains, Kim's poetry is more often likened to a painting of historical, cultural, political, and personal emotions toward colonization, immigration, dislocation, violent history of war, loss of the mother tongue, imperial capitalism, and rampant consumerism. As a poet "transcribing the interstices of the abbreviated, the oddly conjoined, the amalgamated recognizing," Kim defines the poem as "deciphering and embodying a 'particularizable' prosody of one's living" to bridge and reconfigure "disrupted, dilated, circulatory spaces" shaped by loss and absence ("Anacrusis").

Kim has received several awards including the Gertrude Stein Award for Innovative North American Poetry in 1993 and 1994. Kim's poems have appeared in various literary journals and anthologies such as *Conjunctions*, *Sulfur* and *Proliferations*.

Bibliography

Kim, Myung Mi. "Anacrusis." How2 Readings on the Web. Available online. URL: http://www.scc.rutgers.edu/however/v1_2_1999/current/readings/kim.html. Downloaded on Dec. 3, 2004.

———. "Generosity as Method: An Interview with Myung Mi Kim," by Yedda Morrison. Available online. URL: http://epc.buffalo.edu/authors/kim/generosity.html. Downloaded on Dec. 3, 2004.

———. "Interview with Myung Mi Kim," by James Kyung-Jin Lee. *Words Matter: Conversations with Asian American Writers*, edited by King-Kok Cheung, 92–104. Honolulu: University of Hawaii Press, 2000.

Xiaojing, Zhou. "Possibilities out of an Impossible Position: Myung Mi Kim's *Under Flag*." Available online. URL: http://epc.buffalo.edu/authors/kim/xiaojing.html. Downloaded on December 3, 2004.

Heejung Cha

Kim, Patti (1970–)

The author of *A Cab Called Reliable*, Patti Kim was born in Pusan, Korea, and immigrated to the United States in 1974 with her family. She grew up in the Washington, D.C. area and graduated from the University of Maryland at College Park with a B.A. in English in 1992 and an M.F.A. in 1996. *A Cab Called Reliable*, Kim's debut novel published in 1997, received critical acclaim and was awarded the Towson University Prize for Literature in 1997. It was included in the *New York Times*'s "new-and-noteworthy-paperbacks" list in 1998. Kim lives in Riverdale, Maryland, and is said to be working on her second book.

A Cab Called Reliable is the coming-of-age story of Ahn Joo Cho, a Korean-American immigrant girl who is left to look after her alcoholic and incompetent father at the age of nine when her mother leaves her family. The sign "reliable" she spots on the cab as the cab with her mother and younger brother speeds out of sight is etched into Ahn Joo's memory as she waits for her mother's return. In a low-income neighborhood in Arlington, Virginia, Ahn Joo struggles to find her place in a world that offers her neither comfort nor understanding. Creative writing becomes her only means of escape from the sordidness that surrounds her, as she grows up to be a strong young woman who practically runs her father's diner by the time she is in high school in Potomac. Unexpectedly finding out that the woman she believed to be her mother is not her biological mother, Ahn Joo's long wait for her mother's return comes to an end as she leaves home and her dependent father.

Jeehyun Lim

Kim, Richard E.   (1932–   )

Born in Hamhung City, Korea, Richard Kim served in the Republic of Korea Army from 1950 to 1954, where he fought in the Korean War and attained the rank of first lieutenant. Afterward, Kim traveled to the United States to attend Middlebury College, obtaining his B.A. in 1959. In addition to his M.F.A. from Iowa State University (1962), Kim holds M.A. degrees from both Johns Hopkins University (1960) and Harvard University (1963). After teaching English at Long Beach State College from 1963 to 1964, Kim held professorships at the University of Massachusetts, Amherst, San Diego State University, Syracuse University, and Seoul National University in South Korea. Best known as a novelist and author of *The MARTYRED* (1964), *The INNOCENT* (1968), and *LOST NAMES* (1970), Kim has also scripted and narrated television documentaries for KBS-TV in Seoul and published the photo essay *Lost Koreans in China and the Soviet Union* (1989). In his native Korean, Kim has published nonfiction works and written as a columnist for *The Chosun Ilbo* (1981–84).

Reflecting the devastation and tragedy of Korea during the early 20th century, Richard Kim's novels address such a conflicted past in three distinct stages. *Lost Names* takes place during the Japanese colonial occupation of the Korean peninsula and ends with the mixed blessing of liberation in 1945. His first novel, *The Martyred,* presents a particular vignette during the Korean War, and the second novel, *The Innocent,* revisits characters first introduced in *The Martyred* as they attempt to stabilize the corrupt South Korean government following the end of the war with North Korea.

This informal trilogy coincides with, though it does not claim to represent, Kim's personal experiences during the narrated events. A consistent theme that runs throughout the novels pertains to the idealism that drives each of the main characters. Though they encounter problems, setbacks, and unforeseeable pitfalls head-on, a persistent optimism pervades their thoughts and informs all of their actions. Perhaps most symbolic of this optimistic worldview in the face of its seeming contradictions, Captain Lee—the protagonist and first-person narrator of *The Martyred* and *The Innocent*—never gives up hope that a humane Korean nation can and will come of age, though he witnesses violence, atrocities, and unsympathetic governments that would appear to embody just the opposite.

Unfortunately Kim's work has not received wide critical or academic attention, aside from the publicity surrounding its initial reception. After the publication of *The Martyred,* Kim received a Guggenheim Fellowship (1964–65) to work on *The Innocent.* He has also been awarded a Ford Foundation Foreign Area Fellowship (1962–63), the First Award from the Modern Korean Literature Translation Awards (1974), and a National Endowment for the Arts Literary fellowship (1978–79). As a teacher and scholar, Kim has been distinguished as a Fulbright professor at Seoul National University during 1981–83.

Zack Weir

Kim, Ronyoung (Gloria Hahn)
(1926–1987)

Born Gloria Jane Kim in the original enclave of Koreatown in Los Angeles, California, Kim Ronyoung is best known as the author of the 1987 Pulitzer Prize–nominated novel *Clay Walls* (1986). Although Kim grew up largely acculturated to white society, she had an intimate knowledge of Korean social hierarchies reflected in her parents' backgrounds. Her mother, born into the aristocratic *yangban* class, and her father, from a rural peasant upbringing, fled Korea during the Japanese colonial occupation that began in 1910.

At the age of 19, Kim married Richard Hahn, a Korean-American medical student from the Midwest. Hahn's burgeoning career as a heart surgeon required the family to move frequently to various regions of the United States that were far from Korean communities. Consequently they brought up their four children in a principally English-speaking household while retaining some Korean language, culture, and foodways (Hahn 529). After her three daughters and one son graduated college, Kim began to pursue her own intellectual interests, primarily Asian languages, art, and art history. She became a docent at the Avery Brundage Museum (now part of the Asian Art Museum of San Francisco). Moreover she earned a B.A. in Far Eastern Art and Culture from San Francisco State University.

In 1976, at the age of 50, Kim was diagnosed with breast cancer. The disease prompted her to embark on a project that she felt would "create something of significance in her lifetime" (Hahn 530); she began writing her first and only novel, *Clay Walls*. Based loosely on the life of her mother, Haeran (Helen) Kim, who was a poet and participant in U.S.-based Korean independence activities, *Clay Walls* is the first major novel to illustrate the experiences of Korean immigrants and Korean Americans in the United States.

The story takes place primarily in Los Angeles from the 1920s to the 1940s, and it unfolds in three parts, each told from a different narrative perspective. The first part opens with the focus on the protagonist, Haesu, a mother of three children and a Korean immigrant from the *yangban* class. Her hardships represent the cultural, economic, and social difficulties of acculturation for new immigrants at the time. In particular, the problems of simple tasks, such as finding housing or jobs in the face of racial discrimination, are prominently illustrated. The middle part is dedicated to Haesu's husband, Chun, a produce merchant who comes from a tenant farming background. This section illustrates how the American dream is elusive to new immigrants from Asia, as Chun is unable to purchase a home or launch a produce wholesale business without a Caucasian intercessor. The final part closes with the attention turned to Faye, their last child and only daughter, and investigates racial and ethnic discrimination against Asian Americans. Told from Faye's perspective are stories of how children of impoverished Korean immigrants must negotiate not only their own ways through racism and elitism, but as intermediaries for their parents. In one poignant courtroom scene, Faye witnesses her older brother Harold act as a translator between his mother and the judge as the fate of their eldest brother, John, is being decided.

Major themes in *Clay Walls* portray asymmetrical gender, class, and race relations embedded in both Korean and American cultures through episodes touching upon Korean nationalism, World War II, Japanese internment, labor conditions, and immigration. For example, while Haesu's *yangban* upbringing requires her to be a submissive and obedient wife, the same upbringing allows her to feel superior to, and thus openly defy and disparage, her commoner husband. At the same time, scenes describing her employment as a housekeeper illustrate that her privileged Korean social status carries no value in the eyes of white Americans. Further, through Faye's narrative, Kim depicts the failed promises of the American dream for persons of Asian ancestry with poignant scenes capturing how Japanese Americans were interned during World War II despite generations of assimilation and hard work in the United States.

Bibliography

Hahn, Kim. "The Korean American Novel, Kim Ronyoung: A Memoir by Her Daughter." *The Asian Pacific American Heritage: A Companion to Literature and Arts,* edited by George Leonard, 527–533. New York: Garland, 1999.

Kim, Elaine H., and Laura Hyun Yi Kang, eds. *Echoes upon Echoes: New Korean American Writings.* New York: Temple University Press, 2003.

Kim, Ronyoung. *Clay Walls.* 1986. Seattle: University of Washington Press, 1990.

Takaki, Ronald. *From the Land of Morning Calm: The Koreans in America.* New York: Chelsea House, 1994.

Hellen Lee-Keller

Kim, Suki (1970–)

Born and raised in Seoul, Korea, until the age of 13, Kim moved with her affluent middle-class family to the United States in the early 1980s. In her interviews, Kim remembers her first home in New York, the upstairs of a two-family brownstone in Woodside, as dark, crammed, and ugly. As a quiet and frightened Asian girl, Kim went through a culturally nomadic childhood. This experience of being multicultural and bilingual profoundly influences her writing.

In 1992 Kim received her B.A. from Barnard College, where she majored in English and minored in East Asian literature. Right after graduation, she attended the graduate program in Korean literature and translation at the School of Oriental and African Studies, the University of London. After returning from London and going through several jobs such as editing and teaching, she came to realize that writing was what she wanted to do.

In 2003 Kim's debut novel, *The Interpreter,* was published and well received. Narrated by a young Korean-American woman, the novel revolves around the unsolved double homicide of her immigrant parents in New York five years earlier. The emotionally detached protagonist, Suzy Park, while working as a court interpreter, happens to discover that her parents' murder in their grocery store was not a random act of violence but a carefully planned act that also resulted in the sudden disappearance of her estranged sister, Grace. In searching for her missing sister, Suzy recollects fragmented memories about her dysfunctional family caught in cultural transition. She also remembers the painful loss, sacrifice, dark secrets, and social injustice through which hard-working (legal or illegal) Korean immigrants go to realize their American dreams. This dazzling, haunting mystery novel not only subverts stereotypical images of Asian Americans as the model minority but also mocks the judicial system. *The Interpreter* is the winner of the 2004 PEN Beyond Margins Award and the 2004 Gustavus Myers Outstanding Book Award.

New York Review of Books, New York Times, Boston Globe, and *Newsweek* published her prose pieces including her essays on being single in New York City and her visit to North Korea in February 2002. Kim refuses to be merely categorized as a Korean-American woman writer; instead, she wants to be recognized as an American writer. She lives in Manhattan, working on her second novel.

Heejung Cha

Kim, Yong Ik   (1920–1995)

Yong Ik Kim is among the first-generation Korean-American authors who have shown a great deal of nostalgia for their motherland. Winner of several awards, Kim published seven novels and 32 short stories, some of which were written in both English and Korean. Kim came to the United States at the age of 28 and graduated from Florida Southern College with a B.A. degree and the University of Kentucky with an M.A. degree. Kim then moved to Japan to attend Aoyama Kakuin, earning another B.A. degree. Back in Korea, he became a professor at Busan University and Korea University. In 1964 he came back to the United States to teach at Western Illinois University, Lockhaven State College, and Duquesne University.

His major works deal with Korean culture and the everyday life of Koreans before and after the Korean War. He explores the issue of class conflict in Korea in "The Wedding Shoes," one of his first short stories published in the United States. A son of a butcher, Sangdo belongs to the lowest of the social strata in Korea but has a crush on a girl whose father runs a traditional wedding-shoes store, and who therefore belongs to a class higher than Sangdo's. Sangdo's family becomes wealthy thanks to the strong demand for meat, but the girl's family becomes destitute because people now prefer Western-style weddings, which do not require the traditional wedding shoes. When Sangdo proposes a marriage to the girl's family, however, the girl's father rejects the proposal solely based on their class difference. Years later, during the Korean War, Sangdo learns of the death of the girl and her father during the war and reminisces about his first love. Known in 19 countries around the world in the form of TV programs, movies, ballets, anthologies, and other adaptations, "The Wedding Shoes" investigates the intersections of class, love, and family. It also depicts the ways in which Western culture affected modern Korea.

Kim's other well-known work is *Blue in the Seed,* a young adult novel examining the identity formation of Chun Bok, a mixed-race child growing up in Korea. Ridiculed by his peers because of his blue eyes, he decides not to go to school on the pretext that he has no shoes. His peers collect money for him to buy shoes, but Chun Bok buys sunglasses instead to cover his eyes, disappointing his schoolmates. When Chun Bok loses his ox and gets involved in a dispute with a thief over the ownership of his ox, however, it is his blue eyes that help the townspeople recognize him as the rightful owner of the ox.

The themes of his works are multifaceted: the effects of war on children (*The Shoes From Yang San Valley,* 1970); special Korean festivities and celebrations based on the lunar calendar (*Moons of Korea,* 1959); the landscape and lifestyle of Korean agricultural and fishing villages around the 1960s ("The Seed Money," 1958, and "The Sea Girl," 1978); and race issues in Korea (*Blue in the Seed*). Kim's works have been published not only in the United States and Korea but also in England, New Zealand, and India. *Blue in the Seed* was included in a Danish school textbook and read on Danish radio.

Bibliography

Jenkins, C. Esther, and Mary C. Austin. *Literature for Children about Asians and Asian Americans: Analysis and Annotated Bibliography, with Additional Reading for Adults.* New York: Greenwood Press, 1987.

Kim, Elaine H. "'These Bearers of a Homeland': An Overview of Korean American Literature, 1934–2001." *Korea Journal* 41, no. 3. (2001): 149–97.

Jinbhum Shin

Kingston, Maxine Hong (Ting Ting)
(1940–   )

Beginning with her debut, *The Woman Warrior* (1976), Chinese-American writer Maxine Hong Kingston has enjoyed a high level of critical appreciation as well as a consistently wide popular readership. Blending autobiographical and nonfiction prose with fiction, oral histories and folktales, Kingston's writing fiercely challenges the idea that Asian Americans have two essentially separate identities—the "ethnic" and the "American"—and testifies to the damaging effects such a notion can inflict on both the individual and community levels. She has also written extensively about the "silencing" of Chinese and Chinese-American women, in both nations.

Maxine was the first of six children. Her parents, Tom Hong and Chew Ling Yan, were both born and formally educated in China. Tom had been a literary scholar before he immigrated to the United States in 1924 and began to work in a New York laundry. For the next 15 years Tom regularly sent part of his salary to his wife in China, enabling her to study medicine and midwifery until she came to the United States in 1939 and also went to work in the laundry. After he was tricked out of his share in the laundry business by unscrupulous partners (a story told at length in *China Men* [1980], Kingston's second book), Tom and his wife settled in Stockton, California, where Maxine was born on October 27, 1940.

Though she was very quiet as a child—she failed kindergarten because she refused to talk out loud in class—Maxine Hong soon demonstrated a talent for writing, and by the age of nine was composing poems in English, her second language after Cantonese. Upon graduating from high school, she was awarded 11 academic scholarships. She attended the University of California, Berkeley, from which she received a B.A. in English in 1962, and in that same year married Earll Kingston, an actor and fellow Berkeley graduate. Their son Joseph was born in 1964, and in 1965 Maxine Hong Kingston began teaching high school math and English in Hayward, California.

Frustrated by America's political direction during the Vietnam era, the Kingstons planned to move to Japan in the late 1960s but settled instead in Oahu, Hawaii, where they both taught school. By the early 1970s Kingston was writing the short pieces that would eventually make up *The Woman Warrior,* and began publishing them to wide acclaim in various magazines and newspapers including the *New York Times*. When Knopf published *The Woman Warrior* as the first volume of a projected two-book set, critical response was overwhelmingly positive. *The Woman Warrior* won several awards including the National Book Critics Circle's General Nonfiction Award for 1976; *Time* magazine named it one of the top 10 nonfiction works of the decade. The attention the book received allowed Kingston the freedom to write full time. Her 1980 follow-up volume *China Men* received similar acclaim, winning the National Book Award for General Nonfiction in 1981. A short collection of essays, *Hawai'i One Summer,* appeared in 1987.

With TRIPMASTER MONKEY (1989) Kingston turned from the blend of autobiography and myth that had characterized her early work to straightforward fiction. A rollicking, wildly experimental novel, *Tripmaster Monkey* presents the escapades of a young Berkeley graduate in the late 1960s named Wittman Ah Sing, as he attempts to compose an epic drama that will bridge Chinese culture and American culture. Following *Tripmaster Monkey,* Kingston coedited *The Literature of California, Volume 1* (2000), and published a collection of lectures and poems, *To Be the Poet* (2002), which details her renewed interest in poetry and includes selections from recent work. In 2003 Kingston published *The* FIFTH BOOK OF PEACE, her longest book to date, in which she alternates sections of autobiographical prose and essays on pacifism with the continued fictional story of Wittman Ah Sing.

Throughout her writing career Kingston has held several teaching positions at various colleges and universities, and since 1990 she has been a Chancellor's Distinguished Professor at UC Berkeley.

Bibliography

Kingston, Maxine Hong. "'As Truthful as Possible': An Interview with Maxine Hong Kingston," by Eric James Schroeder. *Writing on the Edge* 7, no. 2 (Spring/Summer 1996): 83–96.

Skenazy, Paul, and Tera Martin, eds. *Conversations with Maxine Hong Kingston.* Literary Conversations Series. Jackson: University Press of Mississippi, 1998.

Eric G. Waggoner

Kirchner, Bharti   (1941?–)

Born and raised in India, Bharti Kirchner came to the United States for her graduate education and worked as a systems engineer for IBM and Bank of America before becoming a writer. The author of four acclaimed vegetarian cookbooks and four novels about India and the Indian-American experience, she also has written numerous articles for major magazines and has published several short stories.

Her debut novel, *Shiva Dancing,* tells the story of Meena, a young Rajasthani girl who is to be married at age seven to another child, Vishnu, in her village. Bandits abduct her during the ceremony, and she is rescued by an American couple who later adopt her. Meena grows up in the United States, becomes a software engineer, and gets involved with an American who is an Indophile. She searches for her roots and pines for her lost first love, her child-husband Vishnu, and returns to India.

In her second novel, *Sharmila's Book,* Kirchner writes of an Indo-American woman, Sharmila, who is disillusioned with dating and romance and returns to India to have an arranged marriage with a rich man. She discovers India and learns about herself and her fiancé. In DARJEELING, a more ambitious novel, the author traces the fortunes of two sisters who fall in love with the same man and have a fall-out when one marries him. The marriage falls apart, and the two sisters who now live in North America both return to Darjeeling to their grandmother and their tea estate. Eventually, the sisters resolve their differences and find love and happiness. In PASTRIES, Kirchner brings her passion for cooking and food into the plotline of her novel. Her protagonist, Sunya, is a Seattle baker of Indian origin who runs a small boutique bakery. She is caught up in a competitive war with a national bakery chain that threatens to put her out of business. Her stresses lead to a "baker's block," and she travels to Japan to seek healing in a Zen bakery. In Japan, she finds her confidence and resolves issues with her father, who had abandoned her as an infant. Eventually, Sunya finds peace and happiness when she saves her bakery.

Kirchner writes romantic fiction focused on the transcontinental lives of Indo-American women. Several themes inform her fiction: the clash of cultures, the importance of female autonomy in matters of the heart, the need to balance different cultural values, and the role of food in transmitting culture. Her fiction bridges the divide between mass market fiction and literary fiction. Her emphasis on Pacific Northwest locales, especially Seattle, makes her novels unique among contemporary South Asian American writings as many writers of that community set their novels in New York and California. Kirchner's writing underscores how South Asian immigrant experiences are diverse and influenced by the places where people make their new homes.

Bibliography

Bharti Kirchner. *Darjeeling.* New York: St. Martin's Press, 2002.

———. *Pastries.* New York: St. Martin's Press, 2003.

———. *Sharmila's Book.* New York: Dutton, 1999.

———. *Shiva Dancing.* New York: Dutton, 1998.

Nalini Iyer

Kitchen God's Wife, The   Amy Tan (1991)

AMY TAN's second novel is closely based on her own mother's difficult life in China. Titled after a Chinese mythological figure, *The Kitchen God's Wife* was well received and Tan began work on making it into a film, but ultimately decided to focus on her writing instead. The pair working through their thorny relationship in this novel is Pearl Louie Brandt and her mother, Winnie Louie. Both have hidden essential facts about their lives from each other—Pearl has not told her mother of her multiple sclerosis diagnosis for seven years, and Winnie has not told her daughter of her previous life in China, which includes information about Pearl's parentage. Both women are forced by family circumstances to confront each other with their own potentially devastating secret.

While the novel begins with Pearl's narrative and point of view, it is Winnie's unbelievably wrenching tale that anchors the novel. Pearl's assessment of her mother as she has known her, given in the first few chapters, pales in comparison to the vivid and sometimes shocking life that her mother had actually led before she came to America. Left by her mother at an early age, Winnie (originally Weili) was promised in marriage to Wen Fu, a cowardly wartime pilot and sadistic liar who has misrepresented himself and his family in order to gain access to Winnie's family's greater assets. During the course of their marriage, Wen Fu repeatedly rapes and abuses his wife and neglects and mistreats his three children, all of whom die in their first few years—one daughter dies through Wen Fu's deliberate refusal to send a doctor to treat his seriously ill child.

Winnie attempts to leave her husband at different times, once after a public dance where she meets her eventual second husband, Jimmy Louie. Wen Fu, enraged by their dancing together, holds a gun to his wife's head that night and forces her to sign a divorce paper. He then forces her to beg him to take her back and rapes her. Winnie endures more than eight years with this man and eventually escapes to America with Jimmy Louie, but not without one more rape from her husband. One of the secrets she reveals to Pearl is that Wen Fu is in fact her biological father. As the novel concludes, both mother and daughter are more at peace with each other, and Winnie gives her daughter a renamed Chinese idol as a gesture—once the abused and downtrodden Kitchen God's wife, she is now Lady Sorrowfree, a symbol of new beginnings for the two women.

In this novel, Tan uses the voices of mother and daughter joined in their storytelling to examine the position of women in prewar patriarchal China in feudal marriages, and in modern marriages in present-day California. The divide between mother and daughter is not merely personal; it is also cultural and linguistic. Tan weaves their lives together inextricably and forges a bond between them that is even stronger than the secrets that kept them apart.

Bibliography

Huntley, E. D., ed. *Amy Tan: A Critical Companion. Critical Companions to Popular Contemporary Writers.* Westport, Conn.: Greenwood Press, 1998.

Tan, Amy. *The Opposite of Fate: A Book of Musings.* New York: Putnam, 2003.

Vanessa Rasmussen

Kogawa, Joy (Nozomi)   (1935–   )

Born in Vancouver to Gordon Goichi and Lois Nakayama (née Yao), Kogawa is a second-generation Japanese Canadian. Her father was an Anglican minister, and her mother a kindergarten teacher. During World War II, under the War Measures Act of 1942, her family, together with 22,000 other people of Japanese ancestry, most of them Canadian nationals, were interned as enemy aliens at various inland camps, an experience she would fictionalize in her best-known novel *OBASAN* (1985).

She attended the University of Alberta in 1954, the Anglican Women's Training College and the Conservatory of Music in 1956, and the University of Saskatchewan in 1968. After working as a teacher, she was employed as staff writer for the Canadian prime minister's office from 1974 until 1976. She worked as a freelance writer and a writer in residence at the University of Ottawa (1978). She is a member of the League of Canadian Poets, the Writers' Union of Canada and the Order of Canada.

Joy married David Kogawa in May 1957 and has two children, Gordon and Deirdre. After the couple divorced in 1968, she moved to Toronto in 1970 and began working with the Japanese Citizens League. The publication of *Obasan* was instrumental in alerting a wider audience to the injustices suffered by Japanese Canadians. *Naomi's Road*, illustrated by Matt Gould, is an adaptation of *Obasan* for children. *ITSUKA* (1991), a novel conceived as a sequel to *Obasan*, focuses much more explicitly on the political struggles of the redress movement to receive official restitution from the Canadian government.

Kogawa's most recent prose piece, a short novel titled *The Rain Ascends* (1995), deals with Millicent Shelby's attempts to cope with revelations about her Anglican minister father's pedophilia.

She must deal with the chaos caused by these revelations. As in *Obasan*, Kogawa experiments with nonlinear plot development to explore how the good the Reverend Shelby has done over the years is offset by his molestation of countless boys. Kogawa remains interested in the forces of good and evil, which she often explores through the use of biblical allusions. In an interview with Ruth Hsu, she states, "The resolution was the discovery that Mercy reigns at the heart of the untellable truth. Mercy is present and unleashed into life when the journey of truth is made."

Kogawa, who currently lives and works in Toronto, began her writing career with several volumes of highly acclaimed poetry: *The Splintered Moon* (1967) was followed by *A Choice of Dreams* (1974) and *Jericho Road* (1977). Kogawa's prose benefits from her poetic expertise; moreover, thematic connections exist between her novels and her poetry. *Woman in the Woods* (1985) is a collection consisting of three sections titled "For David," "She Flees," and "In the Woods." Some of the poems have lush natural settings whereas others, mainly those in urban settings, exhibit a threatening apocalyptic tone. Some biographic references attest to the highly personal nature of these poems and echo the fears experienced by *Obasan*'s protagonist, Naomi Nakane. "In the Woods" particularly anticipates some of the walks Naomi takes with Father Cedric in *Itsuka*, and others are full of the memories and settings of Coaldale, where the family was resettled after internment.

A Song of Lilith (2000) is Kogawa's first book-length poem that combines her poetry with Lilian Broca's artwork. A testimony to Kogawa's interest in biblical stories and reminiscent of her earlier uses of biblical allusions, the poem explores the story of Adam's mythical first wife, Lilith. *A Garden of Anchors* (2003) offers a selection of previously published poems.

Bibliography

Hsu, Ruth. "A Conversation with Joy Kogawa." *Amerasia Journal* 22, no. 1 (Spring 1996): 199–216.

Susanna Hoeness-Krupsaw

Kuo, Alex (1939–)

Alex Kuo was born in Boston, where his father taught psychology at Harvard University, but grew up in wartime Chongqing and Shanghai between 1942 and 1947. When he turned eight, his family moved to the British colony of Hong Kong, where Kuo attended primary and secondary schools. In 1955 the family came back to the United States and settled in Windsor, Connecticut. Two years later, Kuo entered Knox College at Galesburg, Illinois, where, as a second-year student majoring in math and biology, he discovered his love for writing while taking a creative writing course. That experience led him to change his major to English and get a B.A. in creative writing in 1961. He then received an M.F.A. from the University of Iowa in 1963. Soon afterward, he taught creative writing and literature first at South Dakota State University and then at the University of Wisconsin at Oshkosh, but he resigned his position in 1969 to protest against the expulsion of African-American students from the university. In the following 10 years he continued teaching in several U.S. universities, but mainly at Central Washington University, where he directed the Ethnic Studies Program.

In 1971 *The Window Tree,* a collection of poems, was published in the United States, but it was paid scant attention by critics and audiences. Three years later, another collection of poetry entitled *New Letters from Hiroshima and Other Poems* came out but fared no better than the first. After interrupting his teaching career in 1979 to spend half a year working for the U.S. Forest Service, he resumed teaching at Washington State University in Pullman, Washington, where he founded the Comparative American Studies program in 1984. During this period some of his short stories were published in journals such as the *Journal of Ethnic Studies* and *The Literary Review.* Since the late 1980s he has taught in China occasionally.

In 1998 a Hong Kong publisher released *Chinese Opera,* his first novel. The story is set in China just before and during the Tiananmen Square massacre of 1989. Sissy George, a Native American jazz singer, flies to Beijing to meet her boyfriend, Sonny Ling, a Chinese-American musician temporarily teaching at the Central Conservatory. Both give extraordinary performances on the Chinese stage: Sissy playing Bizet's *Carmen* and Sonny playing Schumann, Liszt, and Beethoven in his piano recital. Written in crystalline prose, the book highlights the role of art and artists as well as intellectuals in any repressive setting, emphasizing the importance of individual artistic freedom against totalitarian regimes.

Following another volume of poetry, *This Fierce Geography* (1999), Kuo published a short-story collection *Lipstick and Other Stories* (2001). Awarded the American Book Award in 2002, this collection of 31 short stories, mostly written between 1988 and 2000, partly draws upon the author's experiences in China as a child during World War II as well as in his later life. Sometimes humorous or intensely ironic, often blurring the border between dreams, imagination, and reality, Kuo's stories focus on memory and disappearance, the horror of repression and censorship, and the complex relationships between ideology, dissidence, and everyday life.

In 2004 Kuo won a Rockfeller Foundation grant, which allowed him to travel to Italy and enter the Bellagio Program. He is currently professor of Comparative Ethnic Studies and English at Washington State University.

Manuela Vastolo

Lahiri, Jhumpa (1967–)

Born in London to Bengali parents, Lahiri was raised in South Kingstown, Rhode Island, and discovered at an early age her passion for creative writing and for documenting the complex lives of Indian immigrants and their children. Her father, a librarian at the University of Rhode Island, and her mother, a professor of Bengali, encouraged their daughter to retain her Indian identity through observing Bengali tradition, but as an adolescent, Lahiri perceived a profound divide between her parents' heritage and her own developing American identity.

Growing up in two distinct cultural worlds, Lahiri often felt there was no place to which she fully belonged. This sense of existing at the margins of all cultures permeates her fiction and motivates her characters to constantly search for places to call home. "The older I get," Lahiri declares, "the more aware I am that I have somehow inherited a sense of exile from my parents, even though in many ways—superficial ones, largely—I am so much more American than they are" (*News India Times*). Familial ties to India, particularly Calcutta, meant frequent trips to visit relatives, sometimes for months at a time during Lahiri's youth, and though she felt a connection to her parents' homeland and its people, she felt like an outsider in India: "No country is my motherland. I always find myself in exile in whichever country I travel to,

that's why I was tempted to write something about those living their lives in exile" (Jawaid). These trips abroad, however, provided her with invaluable opportunities to observe Calcutta society and culture and to later render in her fictional writings many of the fascinating individuals, places, and experiences she encountered. Crafting stories that explore questions of identity construction and cross-cultural belonging allows Lahiri to confront her own feelings of confusion and loss. "Through my characters," she says, "I can figure things out about myself" (Solan 37).

Despite her early interest in writing, Lahiri chose as a teenager to follow a scholarly path, relegating creative writing to a pastime, in the pursuit of higher education. After graduating from Barnard College with a bachelor of arts in English in 1989, she went on to Boston University to receive master of arts degrees in English, creative writing, and comparative studies in literature. She then completed her Ph.D. in Renaissance studies at Boston University. Though she excelled in her scholarship, she did not believe that her future lay in academic teaching but rather in creative writing. It was during her graduate school years that she began sincerely to write and to pursue publication, initially encountering modest success with a few literary magazines. Following the completion of her Ph.D. dissertation, she worked briefly as a research assistant at a nonprofit organization in Cambridge, Massachusetts, but the offer of a fellowship at the Fine Arts Work Center in Provincetown, Massachusetts, in 1997 proved to be a turning point in Lahiri's burgeoning literary career. In a short period of time, she secured an agent, sold her first book, and had her first story published in *The New Yorker.*

As Lahiri's confidence grew, so did her body of work. In 1999 her first collection of short stories, INTERPRETER OF MALADIES, was published. Set mainly in America, her stories portray Indian-American characters who encounter the same challenges in navigating multiple cultures as Lahiri. Her collection immediately attracted the attention of critics and readers alike. *The New Yorker* named Lahiri among the "20 Best American Fiction Writers Under 40," and she began receiving copious awards, including the PEN/Hemingway Award and the O. Henry Award for her title story, "Interpreter of Maladies." On April 10, 2000, at the age of 32, Lahiri became the youngest recipient of the prestigious Pulitzer Prize. Winning the Pulitzer for her first work overwhelmed Lahiri, who thought of the prize as "something people won when they were deep into their careers" (Solan 36). In the wake of her success with *Interpreter of Maladies,* Lahiri published her first novel, *The NAMESAKE,* in 2003 to yet more praise. The novel expands on familiar Lahirian themes of exile, displacement, loss, and cultural adaptation. It follows the growth of Gogol Ganguli, the son of Bengali immigrant parents, from infancy to his early 30s as he comes to terms with the intersection of his Bengali heritage and American identity.

Lahiri's fiction has appeared in numerous journals and magazines including the *New Yorker, Agni, Epoch, The Louisville Review, Harvard Review,* and *Story Quarterly.* In 2000 she wrote the foreword to an acclaimed collection of photographs and essays on everyday life in India titled *India Holy Song* by Xavier Zimbardo. She has taught creative writing at Boston University and the Rhode Island School of Design. An intensely private person with mixed feelings about the celebrity status of authors, Lahiri currently lives a quiet life in New York City with her husband, journalist Alberto Vourvoulias-

Bush, a Guatemalan of Greek ancestry, and their two-year-old son, Octavio. She is at work on a new collection of short stories.

Bibliography

Jawaid, Rifat. "A Home-Coming for Jhumpa Lahiri." Rediff India Abroad. Available online. URL: http://www.rediff.com/news/2001/jan/11jhum.htm. Downloaded on November 15, 2004.

Shankar, R.S. "*New Yorker* Chooses Lahiri As One of 20 Writers for 21st Century." Rediff India Abroad. Available online. URL: http://www.rediff.com/news/1999/jun/19us3.htm. Downloaded November 15, 2004.

Solan, Matthew. "Catching Up With Pulitzer Prize Winner Jhumpa Lahiri." *Poets & Writers* 31, no. 5 (September/October 2003): 36–38.

Dana Hansen

Lam, Andrew Quang   (1963–   )

A journalist, essayist, and fiction writer, Andrew Lam was born in Saigon, Vietnam, to South Vietnamese Army general Lâm Quang Thi and his wife Bich Thi. When he was 11 years old, his family fled South Vietnam on the last refugee cargo flight before a Communist attack closed the Saigon Airport. Airlifted first to Clark Air Force Base in the Philippines, Lam's family was transferred between refugee camps established on Guam and Camp Pendleton in Southern California until they resettled permanently in the San Francisco Bay area. Lam earned a B.S. in biochemistry from the University of California, Berkeley, in 1986. Lam initially worked with a cancer research laboratory after graduation, but after taking creative writing classes through the UC Berkeley extension program, he abandoned the sciences to become a writer. He returned to school and obtained an M.F.A. in creative writing from San Francisco State University in 1992.

His switch to writing and journalism proved immediately successful when he won the Society of Professional Journalists' Outstanding Young Journalist Award in 1993. In 1995 he began to report for the Pacific News Service, a newspaper wire service that specializes in news concerning the Pacific Rim. Since then his articles have appeared in major newspaper outlets such as the *New York Times, Los Angeles Times,* and the *Chicago Tribune.* In 2001 Lam was awarded with the John S. Knight Fellowship for Journalism at Stanford University. Lam contributed greatly to increasing the power of ethnic community media voices when he cofounded New California Media, which developed into New American Media, a trade association of more than 700 ethnic media organizations with offices based in San Francisco, New York, and Washington, D.C. In addition, he has lectured widely at universities in the United States and taught writing at Hong Kong University.

During his career, his short stories have been featured in literary journals such as *Amerasia Journal* and *Zyzzyva* and included in anthologies such as *The Other Side of Heaven: Post-War Fiction by Vietnamese and American Writers* (1995), *Vietnam: A Traveler's Literary Companion* (1995), and *Watermark: Vietnamese American Prose and Poetry* (1998). Collaborating with De Tran and Hai Dai Nguyen, Lam coedited the nonfiction anthology *Once Upon a Dream: The Vietnamese American Experience* (1995). In 2005 Lam published his first collection of essays, *Perfume Dreams: Reflections on the Vietnamese Diaspora,* in which he considers his difficulties as a *Viet Kieu,* a Vietnamese national who was raised and lives outside of Vietnam.

After the United States began to normalize political and economic relations with the Vietnamese government, Lam's life was featured in the PBS documentary *My Journey Home* (2004), in which a film crew journeyed with him to his birthplace. In the documentary, he returns to the sites of his once-elite and privileged childhood and attempts to reconnect with relatives and friends left behind after the Communist takeover. Finding he has to reconcile the memories of his homeland with the country's modern ambitions and troubles, he uncovers the illusiveness of home and belonging, whether in Vietnam or America.

Andrew Lam's work has been honored by the World Affairs Council for Excellence in Interna-

tional Journalism Award and the Asian American Journalists' Association. Currently, Lam is an associate editor with the Pacific News Service and a regular commentator for National Public Radio's "All Things Considered."

M. Gabot Fabros

Lau, Evelyn   (1971–)

Born in Vancouver, British Columbia, to Chinese parents, Evelyn Yee-Fun Lau has written poetry, short fiction, a novel, and two memoirs. Lau dreamed of being a writer since she was six years old and began publishing poems in her early teens. At the age of 16, Lau ran away from home, feeling stifled by the constant pressure to excel academically and her father's emotional withdrawal due to unemployment. Lau's account of her experiences, *Runaway, Diary of a Street Kid* (1989), published when she was 18, was an immediate best seller. In *Runaway,* Evelyn seeks independence from her parents while resisting the ill-fitting solutions offered by a well-meaning state bureaucracy. Featuring candid and introspective meditations on the author's drug use, prostitution, and bulimia, *Runaway* was adapted into a television movie, *The Diary of Evelyn Lau,* in 1993.

Much of Lau's work explores the experiences and perspectives of social and cultural misfits, such as prostitutes and disempowered women, and the futile search for fulfillment with older men. Drawing heavily on her own experience, Lau's fiction occupies a space between fiction and autobiography, which has sometimes been problematic: A 1997 short story based on her relationship with writer W. P. Kinsella, "Me and W. P.," led to a lawsuit for libel. Lau's poetry collections include *You Are Not Who You Claim* (1990), *Oedipal Dreams* (1992, a Governor General's Award nominee), *In the House of Slaves* (1994), and *Treble* (2005). She also published story collections, *Fresh Girls and Other Stories* (1993) and *Choose Me* (1999), and the novel *Other Women* (1995), and a second memoir, *Inside Out: Reflections on a Life So Far* (2001). Across forms and genres, Lau's searing and audacious self-explorations represent a woman constructing and revealing herself at the limits of experience.

Bibliography

Chao, Lien. "From Testimony to Erotica: The Split Subject in Evelyn Lau's Prose." In *Beyond Silence: Chinese Canadian Literature in English,* edited by Lien Chao, 156–184. Toronto: TSAR, 2001.

Alex Feerst

lê thi diem thúy   (1972–)

Pronounced *lay tee dyim twee,* lê thi diem thúy (the lower case is a preference, "lê" being the family name) was born Lê Thi Diem Trang in Phan Thiet, South Vietnam. In 1978 lê and her father fled Phan Thiet by fishing boat. Eventually they were rescued by an American naval ship and sent to a Singapore refugee camp to await resettlement. While on the U.S. ship, lê's father wrote *Thúy,* the name of her older sister, instead of *Trang* on lê's paperwork. Lê's mother quickly rectified the mistake when she joined the family two years later in San Diego. However, Thúy died during her flight from Vietnam with her mother, drowning in a Malaysian refugee camp. To honor her memory, lê kept her older sister's name. Since her older brother also died off the coast of Vietnam, lê became the oldest, but always felt the "presence" of her older siblings, a loss that is reflected in her writing.

Once lê resettled in San Diego, she picked up English quickly, using fairy tales as a means to escape and as inspiration to become a writer. In 1990, lê began college at Hampshire College in Massachusetts, a move that was partly prompted by a desire to distance herself from San Diego. At Hampshire, lê pursued her artistic desires of performance and writing while focusing her academics on cultural studies and postcolonial literature. When she returned to Hampshire after a 1993 research project in France, lê began to write various pieces, which eventually culminated in her performance of "Red Fiery Summer." In 1994 lê graduated and performed her show across the United States, portions of which culminated in her first novel, *The Gangster We Are All Looking For.*

Lê's second performance, "the bodies between us," is currently being transformed into her second novel. Lê's poetry and prose has appeared in various publications including *Watermark* and *Best American Essays 1997.*

Lê's writing has been praised for its style and content, and lê was named "Writer on the Verge" by the *Village Voice.* Her work has been called powerful and poetic in its portrayal of Vietnam beyond the war. In 1998 lê and her mother returned to Vietnam, where all of her ideas and her parents' feelings of isolation and loss came to the fore. For the first time, lê truly realized what she and her parents had lost, and she felt "profoundly sad." In 2001 lê and her mother again returned to Vietnam, and her mother, stricken with cancer, lived out her final days with her family in Phan Thiet.

Tina Powell

Lee, Chang-rae   (1965–)

Named one of the 20 best American writers under 40 by the *New Yorker* in 1999, Chang-rae Lee is the author of three critically and popularly successful novels: *Native Speaker* (1995), *A Gesture Life* (1999), and *Aloft* (2004).

Born on July 29, 1965, in Seoul, South Korea, Lee immigrated to the United States with his parents and sister in 1968. His father's white-collar career as a psychiatrist sheltered him from the kind of hardscrabble immigrant life Lee portrays in *Native Speaker,* and he experienced a comfortable upward trajectory from New York's Upper West Side to the affluent suburbs of Westchester County, then to boarding school at Philips Exeter and college at Yale. Although he was often one of only a few nonwhite children in his school or neighborhood, Lee reports having little trouble making friends, while admitting to toying briefly with the idea of Westernizing his name. After graduating from Yale, he took a job as an equities analyst but left Wall Street a year later to write full time. He earned his M.F.A. at the University of Oregon, where he wrote *Native Speaker.* This novel, published when he was 29, established him on the literary scene and was followed by appointments to the creative writing faculty at Hunter College and then at Princeton. Lee now lives in Princeton, New Jersey, with his wife and two daughters.

Each of Lee's novels concerns a protagonist who must find a way to live in the aftermath of past traumas. Henry Park of *Native Speaker* contends with the death of his son and his father as well as the estrangement of his wife and a failed assignment at work. In *A Gesture Life,* Franklin Hata's ordeals are most distant, centered on his service in World War II and the troubled adolescence of his grown daughter. In *Aloft,* Jerry Battle's family life continues to crumble years after the death of his first wife. Henry, Doc Hata, and Jerry each have a distinct narrating voice that Lee says "reflects and articulates that particular character." All the protagonists are men older than Lee, whether middle-aged, elderly, or recently retired, and none is willing or able to connect emotionally with others. These men are surrounded by equally flinty women, whether wives or daughters (mothers are seldom in the picture), making family reconciliation a challenge for the characters and an important plot thread. Ethnic identity is another important theme in Lee's novels, though his characters seldom rail against discrimination. Instead, most are accepted into the mainstream with little overt trouble and are attracted by others' racial and cultural differences. Lee's novels thus explore the challenges of inclusion, featuring mixed-race families and characters who must struggle to define their identities.

Lee's self-declared influences include James Joyce, James Agee, Jack Kerouac, Walt Whitman, Ernest Hemingway, and Yukio Mishima. He has also been compared to Kazuo Ishiguro for the passivity of his protagonists, John Cheever for his literary portrayal of New York's suburbs, and Ralph Ellison for what Tim Engles describes as their "allegorized depiction of a racial identity search." Kenneth Quan distinguishes him from the previous generation of Asian-American writers, including MAXINE HONG KINGSTON, FRANK CHIN, and AMY TAN: While they dealt with racial issues more overtly in accordance with the political issues of their day, Lee is free to handle the subject under a larger umbrella of questions of identity. Despite his different approach, the degree of critical inter-

est generated by his first three novels suggests that Lee will ultimately be regarded on a par with these classic Asian-American authors.

Bibliography

Engles, Tim. "'Visions of Me in the Whitest Raw Light': Assimilation and Doxic Whiteness in Chang-Rae Lee's *Native Speaker." Hitting Critical Mass: A Journal of Asian American Cultural Criticism* 4, no. 2 (Summer 1997): 27–48.

Garner, Dwight. "Adopted Voice," *New York Times,* 5 September 1999, late edition, sec. 7, p. 6.

McGrath, Charles. "Deep in Suburbia," *New York Times,* 29 February 2004, late edition, sec. 6, p. 44.

Quan, Kenneth. "Chang-rae Lee: Voice for a New Identity" April 23, 2004. Asia Pacific Arts. Available online. URL: http:///www.asiaarts.ucla.edu/article.asp?parentid-10559.

Jaime Cleland

Lee, C. Y. (1917–)

Born in Hunan Province, China, Chin Yang Lee moved to the United States in 1943, where he became a writer. He is best known for his novel *The Flower Drum Song* (1957), which was made into a musical by Rodgers and Hammerstein that ran on Broadway and was released as a film in 1961. The musical was revived with a new script by DAVID HENRY HWANG in 2001.

Lee began his writing career as a playwright at Yale University, where he earned his M.F.A. A New York agent cautioned him that he would not be able to sell his plays, since no play by a Chinese American had ever been produced. But she liked his writing and suggested that he switch to fiction, where he might find a market. As he worked at his fiction, he supported himself as a journalist, writing a daily column for *Chinese World* and eventually becoming an assistant editor for the paper. In 1949 his story "Forbidden Dollar" won first prize in a *Writer's Digest* short story contest, and thanks in part to this award, Lee became a U.S. citizen in 1949.

Lee's first and most famous novel, *The Flower Drum Song,* depicts an immigrant family, the

Wangs, and their struggle with two common problems in San Francisco's Chinatown: the generation gap and the imbalance between the numbers of men and women. While Old Master Wang's hobbies are gardening and coughing, younger son Wang San prefers baseball and comic books. Elder son Wang Ta's problem is more serious. He hopes to find a wife, but Caucasian women are out of the question and appropriate Chinese women are scarce. Vivacious Linda Tung turns out to be a former dancing girl with a slew of boyfriends; sisterly Helen Chao, desperate for a husband due to her pockmarked face, drowns herself when Ta rejects her. Old Master Wang and his wife's sister conspire to arrange a marriage for Ta, but he finds his own wife, May Li, a sweet and polite (yet not shy and retiring) new arrival from Peking.

Though it was the first Chinese-American novel to be published by a major publisher, *The Flower Drum Song* has not always been favored by Chinese-American critics; Frank Chin, for example, considers the novel's sensibility to be white supremacist, not Asian American. Despite being the first Broadway show starring Asian-American actors, the musical adaptation by Rodgers and Hammerstein was considered inauthentic, a representation of Chinese life by non-Chinese, and the novel was forgotten. However, the play was revised in 2001 by David Henry Hwang, who argues that *The Flower Drum Song* contains many nonstereotypical features. One of the novel's central concerns is Asian male sexuality, and neither Miss Tung, Miss Chao, nor May Li falls into the common stereotypes of Chinese women.

Lee's works in English include *The Flower Drum Song* (1957), *Lover's Point* (1958), *The Sabwa and His Secretary* (1959), *Madame Goldenflower* (1960), *Cripple Mah and the New Order* (1961), *The Virgin Market* (1964), *The Land of the Golden Mountain* (1967), *Days of the Tong Wars* (1974), *China Saga* (1987), *The Second Son of Heaven* (1990), and *Gate of Rage: A Novel of One Family Trapped by the Events at Tiananmen Square* (1991). Some are set in the United States, but many are set in China. His memoirs have been published in Chinese by *Traditional Magazine* of Taiwan; an English edition is forthcoming.

Bibliography

Shan, Te-Hsing. "Redefining Chinese American Literature from a LOWINUS Perspective: Two Recent Examples." In *Multilingual America: Transnationalism, Ethnicity, and the Languages of American Literature,* edited by Werner Sollors, 112–123. New York: New York University Press, 1998.

Shin, Andrew. "'Forty Percent Is Luck': An Interview with C. Y. (Chin Yang) Lee." *MELUS: The Journal of the Society for the Study of the Multi-Ethnic Literature of the United States* 29, no. 2 (Summer 2004): 77–104.

Jaime Cleland

Lee, Don (1959–)

A third-generation Korean American, Lee is the author of *Yellow* (2001), a collection of short stories, and the novel *Country of Origin* (2004). As the son of an officer of the U.S. State Department, Lee spent most of his childhood in Seoul and Tokyo. He graduated with a degree in English from UCLA in 1982 and received an M.F.A. from Emerson College in 1986. Since 1988 he has worked as the editor of the literary journal *Ploughshares. Yellow* has received numerous awards including the Sue Kaufman Prize for First Fiction from the American Academy of Arts and Letters. His stories have also won an O. Henry Award and a Pushcart Prize.

Yellow is a short-story cycle set in the fictional town of Rosarita Bay, California. Using a narrative strategy similar to Sherwood Anderson's *Winesburg, Ohio,* Lee creates his place by presenting independent but interdependent stories about characters who deal with being Asian in America and reflect upon issues such as race, identity, family, loyalty, and love. Each of the stories focuses on diverse issues through prose that is alternately funny, poignant, or somber. The characters in Lee's stories are as complex as the place they live in—a post-immigration Asian America, where issues of ethnic identification are complicated by social position, personal idiosyncrasy, and missed chances. Lee manages to avoid falling into stereotypical representations of Asians in America precisely because his characters are themselves painfully aware of the stereotypes that define them. The question that runs through the stories is the one Danny Kim, in the title story, struggles with as he dreams of being "exemplary, unquestionably American." Though he challenges simplistic expectations about ethnic identity, Lee's stories do not offer easy, politically correct perspectives or comfortable solutions to the problems the characters face. Rather, he critically engages the multilayered realities of contemporary life in California, laden with contradictions and ambiguities, in stories that examine notions of ethnic, personal, and professional positioning.

His novel, *Country of Origin* (2004), which won the 2005 American Book Award, centers on the disappearance of Lisa Countryman, a half-Japanese, half-black American, in Tokyo in 1980. The story's attention shifts among several main characters, including Lisa, whose disappearance is explained to the reader in the first chapter, as each character grapples with issues of identity, race, deception, loyalty, and justice. Lisa's real motives for coming to Japan eventually become clear: She is seeking the Japanese mother who gave her up for adoption. In the course of her search, she becomes involved in the world of Tokyo's sex trade and international espionage. Other characters also have to deal with racial and social identification as well as the perils of rootlessness: Tom Hurley, the embassy officer in charge of Lisa's case, identifies himself as a Hawaiian to avoid having to say he is half Korean; David Kitamura, a nisei CIA agent, functions undercover with a host of assumed names; his wife, Julia Tinsley, hides her "white trash" origins as she fights for upward mobility; Kenzo Ota, the Japanese policeman on the case, trails the Japanese-American boy he thinks is his son, dreaming of a reunion, only to realize that the boy is a cultural stranger to him. Tom and Julia have an affair; and Lisa and David Kitamura end up collaborating on one of his cases.

In this novel set in Japan, where the word *gaijin* (foreigner) appears repeatedly, these characters contest the cultural labels that might define them, giving them a sense of disconnection. The novel is written elegantly, and Lee manages to maintain the suspense of how Lisa disappears by creating a world where appearances are not what they seem

and characters are all in disguise or engaged in subterfuge. He also attends to each of the characters' weaknesses, illustrating how very often problems arise from errors that might have been avoided, or from wrong choices. The novel is sympathetic to the characters who come together at the point of tension (it is set during the Iran hostage crisis) and realize how the complex workings of history shape their individual lives.

Bibliography

Oh, Seiwoong. "Don Lee (1959–   )." In *Asian American Short Story Writers: An A-to-Z Guide,* edited by Guiyou Huang, 151–154. Westport, Conn.: Greenwood Press, 2003.

Rocío G. Davis

Lee, Gus (Augustus Samuel Mein-Sun Lee) (1946–   )

The first son and youngest of five children, Lee was born in a family who immigrated in 1944 to America from Shanghai, China. The family settled in the San Francisco Panhandle, a ghetto mainly of African Americans. The untimely death of his mother when he was five forced Lee into a turbulent childhood in a household tightly run by his white upper-class stepmother. In the street, he was bullied by tough boys. CHINA BOY (1991), Lee's debut novel, is an account of his childhood, though disguised as a novel in order not to offend his father. Lee went to West Point in 1964, the experience recounted in his second autobiographical novel, *Honor and Duty* (1994). He flunked out of the West Point due to his failure in mathematics and engineering. Lee went on to get his B.A. and L.L.B. degrees from the University of California at Davis, where he also served as the assistant dean of students for the Educational Opportunity Program and project coordinator of the Asian American Studies Program. When he rejoined the army in 1976, serving as a defense counsel and command judge advocate, Lee was sent to Korea to investigate recruits who were foreign nationals. This experience provided the basis for his third novel, a thriller, *Tiger's Tail* (1996). Upon concluding his military service, Lee returned to California to work as an attorney and legal educator. Lee and his family moved to Colorado when he decided to pursue writing as a full-time career. Lee's fourth novel, *No Physical Evidence* (1998), is a legal thriller. His fifth book, *Chasing Hepburn: A Memoir of Shanghai, Hollywood, and a Chinese Family's Fight for Freedom* (2003), is a memoir of his family.

A sequel to *China Boy, Honor and Duty* continues the story of the formation of a young Chinese American, Kai Ting, at West Point. It has been a long cherished dream of Kai's father, a former officer in the Nationalist army in China, to see his son enrolled in West Point, a move that signals an "escape from diaspora and attainment of America itself." Being Chinese American, Kai finds both familiarity and alienation at the predominantly white West Point in the 1960s. He relates the traditional Chinese teachings of morality to West Point's codes of honor and duty, which he follows in reaction to a cheating scandal at West Point. With America's escalating involvement in Vietnam, the pain is doubled when he attends the funeral of a beloved instructor from whose parents he is steered away because of his Asian face. The novel also relates the story of his fragmented family, his continuous affinity with people he got to know while in the Panhandle, and his relationship with two girls. Kai embraces the terror of his life, his stepmother, Edna, in a spirit of forgiveness on her deathbed. The story ends with the reconciliation between Kai and his father, who notes hopefully, "We climbing up American ladder!"

The protagonist of *Tiger's Tail*, Jackson Kan, is a Chinese-American West Point graduate and Vietnam veteran who works as an army lawyer in San Francisco. In 1974 Kan is sent to Korea to find a missing colleague who had been sent there earlier to investigate the malfeasance of the base commander, Colonel LeBlanc. During the investigation Kan discovers that LeBlanc, a nefarious racist and anticommunist, has an imperialist vision of a white America. With the help of two Korean shamans, Kan and his team manage to depose LeBlanc.

Deputy District Attorney Josh Jin, in *No Physical Evidence*, is the only Chinese American among the Sacramento district attorney's staff. With his daughter's death and his wife's departure, Jin is in the crisis of his personal and professional life. He is then forced to take a politically charged Chinatown rape case of a 13-year-old girl. As a Chinese American, Jin is under immense pressure from Chinatown to win the conviction. Overcoming various obstacles, the most insurmountable of which is the lack of physical evidence, Jin eventually ensures that justice is served.

Some snippets of the family history in Lee's autobiographical novels, *China Boy* and *Honor and Duty*, are expanded into a family saga of four generations, spanning a century and a half of Chinese history and two continents. *Chasing Hepburn: A Memoir of Shanghai, Hollywood, and a Chinese Family's Fight for Freedom* opens with an excruciating scene of Tzu Da-tsien's foot-binding ceremony in 1909. Her rescue by her father enables her strong feet to walk in her own path, one that eventually leads to America. It also signifies China's early 20th-century encounters with clashes between tradition and modern ideas and indicates a strong influence from the West. Despite the disapproval from both families, Da-tsien rejects an arranged marriage and marries Lee's father, Zee Zee. Both Da-tsien and Zee share an infatuation with Katharine Hepburn, an icon of independence and glamour. Zee Zee becomes a Nationalist army officer, fighting against the Japanese occupation and the Communist party. Da-tsien, resourceful and strong, preserves her family and finally joins her husband in America, where she gives birth to her long-desired son, the author.

With a strong bond to his Chinese heritage, Lee often refers to the Chinese language, culture, and tradition. His forging of a Chinese-American identity is not limited to a formula of "both/and" or "either/or"; rather, his identity is made up of multiple cultures of America. Moreover, with America's increasing involvements in Asia, Chinese-American identity, as well as American identity, is perceived in constant reconfigurations in a transnational context.

Yan Ying

Lee, Helie (1964–)

Helie Lee was born in Seoul, South Korea. When she was four years old, her family immigrated to Montreal, Canada, and then on to California a year later. She attended El Camino Real High School after her family settled in the San Fernando Valley of Southern California. Like most Asian immigrant parents, Lee's parents regarded education as the best path to a better life for their daughter. After high school, she entered the University of California, Los Angeles, and graduated with a B.A. in political science in 1986. After years of struggling to find her career path, Lee found her calling in writing. Thus far, she has published two memoirs about her family's traumatic experiences in war-torn Korea from the 1930s to 1997.

Lee often travels around the country on book tours and gives lectures on college campuses about her bicultural heritage and passion for human rights issues for North Korean refugees, the latter being the subject matter of her memoirs. In 2002 Senator Edward Kennedy invited her to testify at the Senate Subcommittee hearing on immigration based on her firsthand experience. Lee is passionate about her role as a writer and artist because she sees herself as a Korean cultural emissary to promote understanding of human rights issues in the still closed world of communist North Korea.

Lee's first book and national best seller, *Still Life with Rice* (1996), chronicles her maternal grandmother's life in North Korea until she came to America. In this work Lee introduces us to a traditional Korean family life, the ravages of war, and the partition of Korea into north and south along the 38th parallel. Lee's first book also sheds light on what it means for Asian Americans to become writers and highlights the generational gap within Asian-American immigrant families.

Lee's second book, *In the Absence of Sun* (2002), specifically deals with her family's desperate efforts to make contact with her maternal grandmother's lost son in North Korea. This gripping true account of the rescue of her uncle from North Korea was not only featured on CNN and ABC's *Nightline* but also reported by the Associated Press, the *Los Angeles Times*, and a number of other media. In this second memoir, Lee defines herself as a writer and

locates herself in the Asian-American community, especially the Korean-American community.

The overall importance of Lee's two memoirs is that the author sees her writing as a way for her to understand her Korean heritage, especially since she emigrated during her early childhood. Lee also details the difficulties and struggles for Korean-American women because of cultural gaps and generational conflicts. She especially highlights her clashes with the elders who hold that a single woman at her age should be more conventional and be married to a man, preferably in the medical profession, instead of doing something so uncertain as writing.

Hanh Nguyen

Lee, Li-Young (1957–)

Born to exiled Chinese parents in Jakarta, Indonesia, Li-Young Lee's poetry treats themes of familial and romantic love, religious convictions, and forced relocation. His family offers much fodder for his poetry, both in the deep and abiding bonds they shared and in their colorful history. Lee's paternal grandfather had been a gangster and entrepreneur in China. Lee's mother, on the other hand, came from a well-respected family; she is the granddaughter of China's first provisional president, Yuan Shikai, who was elected in 1912. The marriage was not well received in Communist China, and they were concerned about other political dangers, especially since Lee's father worked with a Nationalist general during the Chinese civil war, but later switched sides to become a personal physician to Mao Zedong. Lee's parents, therefore, led their family to exile in Indonesia. Lee's father, Lee Kuo Yuan, taught medicine and philosophy at a Christian college called Gamaliel University, which he helped found in Jakarta, Indonesia. Even in exile, the Lee family was forced to relocate again after Lee's father, who was interested in Western culture and ideas, was incarcerated in 1958 for 19 months by the then-dictator of Indonesia, Sukarno, who espoused anti-Chinese sentiments. The Lee family then traveled throughout Indochina and Southeast Asia before settling in Hong Kong, where Lee's father became a successful evangelist. The family finally settled in the United States in 1964. Once secure in the United States, Lee's father studied theology at a seminary in Pittsburgh and became a Presbyterian minister in Vandergrift, Pennsylvania.

Lee's father read both classical Chinese poetry and the Bible to him, especially the Book of Psalms, which Lee loved. Though he was instructed by his father from a young age in many subjects, Lee did not speak until he was three years old, at which point he began to speak in full sentences. When he began formal education in the United States, he again became silent, embarrassed by his limited ability to speak English. Lee attended the University of Pittsburgh, where he began to write his own poetry under the tutelage of Gerald Stern. He went on to study for an M.F.A. at the University of Arizona and the State University of New York at Brockport. He has taught at several universities including Northwestern University and the University of Iowa. Lee traveled to China and Indonesia in 1990 for a research project that resulted in a book of autobiographical prose, a memoir entitled *The Winged Seed: A Remembrance* (1995), which received an American Book Award from the Before Columbus Foundation.

Lee has written three books of poetry: *Rose* (1986), which won the 1987 Delmore Schwartz Memorial Poetry Award, *The CITY IN WHICH I LOVE YOU* (1991), and *Book of My Nights* (2001). Lee has also won a Lannan Literary Award, a 1988 Whiting Writer's Award, and a number of grants. He lives in Chicago, Illinois, with his wife, Donna, and their two sons.

Shaped by his family's exiles and immigrant experiences, Lee's poetry explores the power of memory to reconstruct a patchwork past, the forces of love and strength (especially as combined in the figure of his father) and their various permutations, and the physical and metaphysical movement that characterizes human lives throughout all times and cultures. Lee not only draws upon his own family's experiences, but also uses the Bible and classical Chinese poets such as Li Bai and Du Fu as sources of inspiration. In his poem "Furious Versions" from his second book of poetry, *The*

City in Which I Love You, Lee places these poets in Chicago and, condensing his ethnic, cultural, and linguistic history, has them say "What did you expect? Where else should we be?" Critic Zhou Xiaojing notes that as a poet, "Lee must wrestle with the limits of poetic form, and search for new possibilities of language, in order to tell his 'human tale'" (131). Lee's "human tales" in his poetry move beyond his personal and family experiences and transcend race and place to be able to speak to every human heart.

Bibliography
Lee, Li-Young. *The City in Which I Love You.* New York: BOA Editions; 1990.

Xiaojing, Zhou. "Inheritance and Invention in Li-Young Lee's Poetry." *MELUS* 21 (Spring 1996): 113–132.

Vanessa Rasmussen

Lee, Marie G. (1965–)

Marie Lee, a second-generation Korean American, was born and raised in Hibbing, Minnesota. As a pioneering author of young adult fiction featuring Korean-American characters, Lee has written seven novels that mostly deal with sensitive themes such as racial tension, ethnic identity formation, self-image, parental pressure, intergenerational conflict, and teenage problems.

Much of Lee's writing stems from her own issues of having grown up as the only Asian American in her community. Her parents immigrated to the United States in 1953, more than 10 years before the first major wave of Korean immigration to the United States. She spent much of her time in the library, partly because she loved to read and partly because she was trying to avoid the bullies at school who called her names and tried to beat her up. Lee's family enjoyed an upper-middle-class existence because her father was a doctor and her mother was a social worker. They pressured her to study and become a doctor as well, but Lee ultimately turned to writing while attending Brown University. As she grew up and realized there were no books that reflected her experiences, she chose to read other books about alienation, such as *The Outsiders* and *The Catcher in the Rye*.

Lee's novels for younger audiences include *F Is for Fabuloso, Night of the Chupacabras,* and *If It Hadn't Been For Yoon Jun. F is for Fabuloso* is the story of Jin-Ha, a junior high school student whose poor math scores cause her to tell her parents that the "F" on her math exams means "fabuloso." *Night of the Chupacabras* is about two Korean-American siblings, Mi-Sun and Ju-Won, who are invited to spend a summer in Mexico with a friend, Lupe. Some mysterious activities on the ranch lead them to conclude that there is a monster in their midst. *If It Hadn't Been For Yoon Jun* tells the story of Alice Larsen, a Korean adoptee who considers herself white. A new Korean immigrant named Yoon Jun moves to her school, and although Alice is primarily resistant, eventually they form a friendship and Alice learns more about her Korean heritage. Lee makes a significant contribution with these novels, making accessible a range of Korean-American characters and their experiences to elementary- and middle-school audiences.

Finding My Voice, Saying Goodbyes and *Necessary Roughness* are written for slightly older readers. These novels present a fresh voice speaking on behalf of young Korean Americans and their struggles in high school and college. The protagonists of these three novels are forced to negotiate their Korean-American identities as events throughout the novels cause them to learn more about their Korean roots and family histories. Each protagonist is the victim of some kind of racial altercation, to which Lee does not always bring closure. It is not always clear if the protagonist has really made the right decisions.

Besides publishing her first adult fiction, *Somebody's Daughter* (2005), Marie Lee is also an essayist whose work has been published in anthologies and newspapers such as the *New York Times*. One of her well-known pieces is "We Koreans Need an Al Sharpton," an editorial essay that calls for Korean Americans to be more politicized and to strive for leadership positions so the Korean-American community can have a public representative. She founded the Asian American Writer's Workshop, an active organization located in New York City.

Bibliography

Davidson, Cathy N., and Linda Wagner-Martin. *The Oxford Companion to Women's Writing in the United States.* New York: Oxford University Press, 1995.

Sarah Park

Lee, Mary Paik   (1900–1995)

Born Paik Kuang Sun in Pyongyang, Korea, the second of 10 children, Mary Paik Lee became the only autobiographer of early Korean experience in America by writing *Quiet Odyssey* (1990). She and her family were among the few thousand pioneers to enter the country between 1902 and 1905, the small period during which such immigration was allowed. In Korea, the Lees were an educated, influential Christian family, and Kuang Sun's paternal grandmother founded the first girls' school in Pyongyang. However, this life was interrupted by the Japanese occupation of Korea. When Kuang Sun was five, Japanese soldiers took over the Lees' house, and the extended family decided that one branch of the Lee family should leave the country to ensure that at least some of them would survive.

In 1905 Kuang Sun's family arrived in Hawaii; her father was one of more than 7,000 Koreans recruited to work on the sugar plantations. After a year, the Lees moved to the mainland, arriving in San Francisco. From there they migrated from town to town and from job to job, farming on Roberts Island and mining quicksilver in Idria. The children tried to keep up with their schooling, but that was not always possible. Kuang Sun's older brother gave up school to help support the family, while she left home to attend high school in a nearby town for a year. Feeling guilty for leaving her family, and exhausted by her housekeeping job and her studies, she dropped out of high school due to poor health, and married Hung Man Lee on January 1, 1919. Kuang Sun and her husband, known as H. M., also migrated in order to find work. For a time they grew rice as tenant farmers and later owned a fruit stand in Los Angeles; when H. M.'s health problems required them to give up the fruit stand, they returned to farming and later managed apartment buildings. The couple became citizens in 1960, when she took the name Mary Paik Lee. *Quiet Odyssey* continues into the author's old age, unique among Asian-American women's autobiographies.

Lee's family came to America at a time when few had heard of Korea. People would often take them to be "Japs," an identification Lee found offensive because of the Japanese occupation of Korea. Except for the Japanese, Lee writes of identifying closely with other minorities in America, particularly Mexicans, whom H. M. had worked with when he first came to the West and continued to hire on his farm. Her response to one man's drunken insult exemplifies her attitude. The man comes into the Lees' fruit stand, slaps her on the back, and says "Hi Mary!" a stereotypical name for any Asian woman, used by those prejudiced against Asians. Kuang Sun slaps him back and says "Hi Charlie!" calling him by the generic name he probably used for Asian men. When he asks why she calls him Charlie, she explains that not all Asians have the same name, just as black men should not be called "boy." The man takes her point, and the two become friendly. The incident shows a few essential things about the author's character: She stands up for herself in the face of discrimination, identifying with fellow minorities, but will not hold a grudge when the situation is corrected. Lee's ability to forgive relates to another important theme of *Quiet Odyssey,* the author's Christianity. When describing white Americans, she focuses more on their kindnesses than their unfairness, and writes of her admiration for family members who never complained in the face of adversity.

Bibliography

Chiu, Monica. "Constructing 'Home' in Mary Paik Lee's *Quiet Odyssey: A Pioneer Korean Woman in America.*" In *Women, America, and Movement: Narratives of Relocation,* edited by Susan L. Robertson, 121–136. Columbia: University of Missouri Press, 1998.

Jameson, Elizabeth, and Susan Armitage. *Writing the Range: Race, Class, and Culture in the Women's West.* Norman: University of Oklahoma Press, 1997.

Jaime Cleland

Leong, Russell   (1950–   )

Born and raised in San Francisco's Chinatown, Leong obtained a B.A. from San Francisco State University and went to Taiwan for graduate study at National Taiwan University. After working with the Kearny Street Workshop, a community-based organization in San Francisco that helps nurture and promote work by Asian-American writers, poets, and filmmakers, Leong earned an M.F.A. in film from the University of California, Los Angeles, where he has been teaching English and Asian American Studies, and where he has been serving as editor for *Amerasia Journal* as well as head of the Asian American Studies Center Press.

Leong's literary contributions are also marked by cultural diversity and political activism. Leong coedited a collection of essays that address dynamics of multiracial communities entitled *Los Angeles—Struggle toward Multiethnic Community: Asian American, African American, and Latino Perspectives.* His scholarly work also aims to challenge commonly held stereotypes of Asian-American sexuality. His book, *Asian American Sexualities: Dimensions of the Gay and Lesbian Experience,* aims to challenge commonly held stereotypes of Asian-American sexuality, offering a multifaceted and interdisciplinary study of sexuality and identity politics.

Leong, however, is primarily recognized for his creative work, which has been characterized as representing diasporic experiences. His characters tend to be caught in cultural exile or displacement, as individuals who either have trouble adapting to a new home, or who have to negotiate their sense of belonging in their native home. His collection of poetry, *The Country of Dreams and Dust,* includes a series of poems representing letters written between a Chinese-American man and his relatives in China. The aerogrammes show the ebbs and flows in the relationship. The family initially welcomes the speaker as a member of the family, and the speaker has a romantic idea of recapturing his ancestral past, to which the family serves as a link. As the correspondence progresses, however, the speaker struggles with defining his relationship with his distant family, as they repeatedly request his financial support and intrusively find him a potential wife. In the end, the speaker experiences disillusionment: "I wrote off filial piety / as useless, / a fallen branch." But at the same time, familial and ancestral connections play a complex and unshakable role in his feelings about his own identity, and he recognizes the pull his family will always have on him. He finds himself with "split vision," equally tied to the life his family has envisioned for him and the life he's created for himself in Los Angeles. The poem ends with the following lines: "Yet / as keenly / as the blade / of the letter opener / that falls upon my hand, / I await the arrival / of the next / immutable / aerogramme."

Because diasporic subjectivity is complicated, open, split, nomadic and hybrid, to represent it in words can be difficult. Leong aptly expresses in his poem "Threads" the complex relationship one might have with his/her identity by emphasizing that which cannot be expressed: "There is no way to show it. / No way to even break it or / Burn it or throw it away. / It is with me. / And yet / There is nothing I can say / And nothing I can do / That will make it work." The "it" in the poem is never defined, as if it were impossible to do so. And yet, Leong also goes on to describe "it" metaphorically, as a "fruit ripening on a tree." The poem illustrates diasporic consciousness as unsettling and uncomfortable, but also as having much richness and potential. Leong treats identity with ambivalence and celebration.

In Leong's work, the feeling of exile or displacement is not represented as exclusively a migrant or immigrant experience, and certainly not as an exclusively Chinese or Chinese-American experience. His characters come from a variety of ethnic and class backgrounds, genders and sexual orientations, to emphasize that feelings of loss and longing are universal. In the title story of his collection of short fiction, *Phoenix Eyes and Other Stories,* the reader catches glimpses of an international community as different people pass through Taiwan: wealthy Asian businessmen, American sinologists, and a French-Algerian student. The Chinese-American narrator, estranged from his family, comes into brief contact with several of these passers-by in erotic and passionate, but also detached and impersonal, interactions. Life seems to be only

a series of moments as the narrator blithely floats from one experience to another. However, when an old friend and lover dies of AIDS at the story's end, the weight of losing the one love in his life renders him unable to escape, unable to continue floating. And yet, coming to grips with his lover's disease has bred a different kind of isolation and exile:

Today I won't open the door and walk across the street, not even for a sixpack of beer or aspirin. I don't trust cars, pedestrians, clerks, janitors, nurses, bank tellers, not even children anymore.

The narrator, as do other characters in Leong's poems and stories, struggles to find a new way of confronting life's trials and explores Buddhism as a way of finding serenity and centeredness. The search is not always successful; Leong emphasizes that life is constantly in flux, and that human experience cannot be reduced to simple precepts and summarizations.

Appropriate to the diversity of themes and motifs in Leong's work are the sources of inspiration he has attributed to his work. Leong not only cites figures from Chinese cultural tradition, such as Lu Hsun and Mao Tun, but also Asian-American writers such as FRANK CHIN, as well as writers from various traditions, including Amiri Baraka, N. V. M. Gonzalez, Frederic Jameson, and Pablo Neruda.

Leong's work has been featured in several anthologies, including *Charlie Chan Is Dead* and *Aiiieeeee! An Anthology of Asian American Writers.* For *Phoenix Eyes and Other Stories,* Leong received the American Book Award in 2001. Leong was given the PEN Josephine Miles Literature Award in 1993 for *The Country of Dreams and Dust.*

Bibliography

Chang, Edward T., and Russell C. Leong, eds. *Los Angeles—Struggle toward Multiethnic Community: Asian American, African American, and Latino Perspectives.* Seattle: University of Washington Press, 1995.

Nomura, Gail, Russell C. Leong, Russell Endo, Stephen H. Sumida, eds. *Frontiers of Asian American*

Studies: Writing, Research, and Commentary. Pullman: Washington State University Press, 1989.

Catherine Fung

Li, Ling Ai   (1908–?)

Born in Honolulu, Li Ling Ai was nothing short of a Renaissance woman. Under the earlier tutelage of her Chinese immigrant parents—the famous doctors Tae Heong Kong Li (her mother) and Khai Fai Li (her father)—Miss Li, as she liked to be called according to one interview, learned Chinese and English and deeply respected the cultural traditions of China, Hawaii, and America. Li is best remembered now for producing *Kukan,* the 1941 Academy Award–winning documentary about the bitter struggle for Chinese independence.

Aside from this work, Li Ling Ai was an actor, dancer, playwright, writer, and teacher of dance and the theatrical arts. She was formally trained in the theater at the University of Hawaii, where she earned her B.A. degree in theater. In 1930 Li traveled to Beijing to study classical Chinese theater and dance. She later directed and wrote plays for the Fine Arts Institute in China.

Upon returning from China after the Japanese invasion prior to World War II, Li made it her personal mission to raise money and educate Americans about China's past, its philosophies, and its struggles. Miss Li became such an advocate for China's struggle that she later became the director of the Far Eastern Department of Robert Ripley's famous radio show *Believe It or Not.* Following the success of *Kukan,* Li gave lectures throughout the United States speaking on behalf of China and her Chinese-American heritage. At a time when women—and especially women of color—were not outspoken, Li was considered by many critics and observers as witty, intelligent, and entertaining.

Li considered her success to be a direct result of her upbringing by her parents. She wrote *Life Is for a Long Time: A Chinese Hawaiian Memoir* (1972) to chronicle her parents' incredible story of struggle, survival, and success both in China and the United States. In writing the book, she hoped that in today's society, "with its jagged patterns of human dissensions and disruptions, resentments and hates, perhaps the simple story of [her] parents, two Chinese in Hawaii, might help those among us who are trying to live with quiet courage—seeking to make life tolerable in an almost intolerable world." *Life Is for a Long Time* is a well-written and unique memoir of a successful Asian-American experience.

Matthew L. Miller

Lim, Shirley Geok-lin   (1944–   )

Writer, critic, university professor and activist Shirley Geok-lin Lim was born in the historic British colony of Malacca. She received her bachelor's degree from the University of Malaya, Kuala Lumpur, in 1967, and became a part-time lecturer in the same university (1967–69). In 1969 she came to the United States as a Fulbright and Wien scholar. She received her master's degree in 1971 and a Ph.D. in English and American studies in 1973, both from Brandeis University, Massachusetts.

In 1972–73 she was a teaching fellow at Queens College, City University of New York, and in 1973–76 an assistant professor at Hostos Community College, City University of New York. Between 1976 and 1990 she was an associate professor at Westchester Community College, State University of New York, before moving to California, where she has been teaching Asian American Studies, English, and Women's Studies since 1990 at the University of California, Santa Barbara. She also taught in the English Department at the University of Hong Kong (1999–2001). She has received many grants and travel awards, for example, from the British Council and National Women's Studies Association, both in 1989.

Published in 1980, Lim's first poetry collection entitled *Crossing the Peninsula and Other Poems* won the Commonwealth Poetry Prize, just after her son Gershom Kean was born from her marriage with Charles Bazerman, professor of education at the University of California, Santa Barbara. Five more poetry collections followed: *No Man's Grove and Other Poems* (1985), *Modern Secrets: New and Selected Poems* (1989), *Monsoon History:*

Selected Poems (1994), and *What the Fortune Teller Didn't Say* (1998). Her poems are often centered on the themes of migration, transculturalism, and language.

Lim has also published several collections of short stories: *Another Country and Other Stories* (1982), *Life's Mysteries* (1995), and *Two Dreams: New and Selected Stories* (1997). Divided into three sections and set in different locations ranging from Malaysia to the United States, the stories in *Two Dreams* explore the issues of cultural clashes and negotiations, especially for Asian diasporic people. They also deal with the discovery of sexuality on the part of teenage girls within the context of a patriarchal society that often responds with hostility and disgust to women's assertion of their feminine identity.

Lim is also the author of a memoir, Among the White Moon Faces (1996), which won the American Book Award, and a novel, *Joss and Gold* (2001). *Joss and Gold* highlights issues connected with cross-cultural encounters, gender roles, and the aftermath of colonialism. It is divided into three sections: "Crossing: Kuala Lumpur, 1968–1969," "Circling: Westchester County, New York, 1980," and "Landing: Singapore, 1981," mirroring the multiple settings of the plot: Malaysia, the United States, and Singapore. The main character is a Malaysian tutor of Chinese origin, Li An, who is torn between her deep love of English poetry and her allegiance to her culture, which is struggling to reinvent its own identity after the end of the British colonial rule. She aspires to promote a new ideal of independent and self-sufficient Asian women, but her life gets complicated by her marriage to Henry, a trustworthy and reliable man from her ethnic background, and her attraction toward Chester, an American Peace Corps volunteer. During an anti-Chinese riot in Kuala Lumpur in 1969, she is rescued and then seduced by Chester, who soon returns to his own country to marry an American woman, leaving Li An pregnant. After separating from Henry, Li An moves to Singapore, becomes a businesswoman, and brings up her daughter, Suyin.

Lim has coedited several anthologies including *The Forbidden Stitch: an Asian American Women's Anthology* (1989), recipient of the American Book Award, and *One World Literature: an Anthology of Contemporary Global Literature* (1993). The 1991 collection entitled *Approaches to Teaching Kingston's* The Woman Warrior (which she edited and contributed to) signifies Shirley Geok-lin Lim's parallel interest in Asian-American literature and pedagogy. Besides co-editing a 1992 collection of essays, *Reading the Literatures of Asian America: Asian American History and Culture,* she edited two other anthologies of scholarly essays: *Transnational Asia Pacific: Gender, Culture, and the Public Sphere* (1999) and *Power, Race, and Gender in Academe: Strangers in the Tower?* (2000).

Bibliography

Lim, Shirley Geok-lin. "On Being Diasporic: An Interview with Shirley Geok-lin Lim," by Elisabetta Marino. In *Transnational, National, and Personal Voices,* edited by Begona Simal and Elisabetta Marino, 241–255. Munster: Lit Verlag, 2004.

Morgan, Nina. "Locating Shirley Geok-lin Lim." *The Diasporic Imagination: Asian American Writing,* edited by Somdatta Mandal, 99—110. New Delhi: Prestige Books, 2000.

Elisabetta Marino

Liu, Aimee E. (1953–)

Born and raised in Connecticut, Liu received a B.A. from Yale University and worked as a fashion model and later a flight attendant before writing full time. She came to closely examine her Chinese heritage only later in life and through the process of writing her novels. Her childhood experiences of growing up in an interracial family living in a predominantly white neighborhood, and her sense, at the time, of being an outsider have informed her writings. Having a Chinese grandfather who married an American woman, Liu has focused on questions of interracial marriage rather than Asian-American experience per se.

Liu's first book, written when she was 23, was the memoir *Solitaire,* which documents the author's struggles with and recovery from the eating disorder anorexia nervosa. Liu attributes her success in finally overcoming anorexia, with which she was afflicted for eight years beginning at the age of 13, to the process of writing her book. Indeed her experience of writing about her eventually successful battles with anorexia led Liu to a decade-long career as a coauthor of nonfiction self-help books. Among her works from that period are *Codependency Conspiracy, False Love and Other Romantic Illusions* and *Success Trap* (all with Dr. Stan J. Katz).

Liu was moved to write her first novel, *Face,* by the Tiananmen Square massacre of prodemocracy students and workers by the Chinese government in 1989. Liu's identification with the students who assembled and died in the square forced her to examine her personal views as a woman of mixed heritage. *Face* reflected the process of that examination.

The novel centers on the character of Maibelle Chung, who, much like Liu herself, comes from a mixed Euro-American and Chinese background but has only come to examine her Chinese heritage later in life. A series of disturbing nightmares leads Chung to delve into family secrets covering three generations. The search for answers leads her from New York's Chinatown to imperial China. The novel addresses themes such as interracial marriage and the complexities of biracial identity as well as issues of community and heritage as experienced by multiracial children.

Liu returns to similar themes in her second novel, *Cloud Mountain,* a work that also addresses interracial marriage. This story, based on the relationship between the author's grandparents, Ch'eng-yu Liu and Jennie Ella Trecott, deals with the overt and violent racism in California under the antimiscegenation laws. Even after the protagonists move to Shanghai, they find that people's interactions with them are shaped by sharp prejudices against interracial marriages.

Liu's next novel, *Flash House,* departs from these themes somewhat to present a story of love and survival in India and China during World War II. At the same time, in telling the story of a 10-year-old girl, Kamla, who is rescued from a brothel in New Delhi by an American woman, Liu

further develops her concerns with relationships and family history.

In addition to her novels, Liu has deployed her writing talents as an ardent defender of human rights and civil liberties. A former president of PEN-USA West, Liu has worked in defense of imprisoned writers. When the Nigerian novelist Akinwumi Adesokan was arrested and imprisoned without charges and was denied communication with the outside world, Liu led a PEN campaign to locate his whereabouts. Following the publication in a Nigerian newspaper of an article written by Liu on his behalf, Adesokan was released.

Since the terrorist attacks on New York on September 11, 2001, Liu has devoted time to writing magazine articles that express her concerns over the imposed patriotism and curbs on personal liberties that have marked recent U.S. domestic policy. Liu has stated her opposition to the U.S. Patriot Act, which allows the government to conduct surveillance on U.S. citizens even in the absence of probable cause. She has also spoken against the deportation and/or detention of individuals without charge or trial. In opposition to mandatory flag-waving, Liu argues that the country's promise can be found in the courageous and compassionate example set by families of 9/11 victims, who visited civilian victims of the bombing of Afghanistan and who spoke out against the war in Iraq.

Jeff Shantz

Loh, Sandra Tsing   (1962–   )

A native of Los Angeles, Loh is a writer, composer, and performance artist who is best known in literary circles for her satirical essays on life in suburban Southern California—DEPTH TAKES A HOLIDAY: ESSAYS FROM LESSER LOS ANGELES (1996) and *A YEAR IN VAN NUYS* (2001). She has written, performed, and recorded in a number of media, including stage, concert, film, television, and radio. Her versatility makes categorization difficult, but Loh has said she thinks of herself as a humorist and a storyteller; she favors the monologue. In its varying genres, her work has captured the attention of a heterogeneous audience. One of her stories, "My Father's Chinese Wives," was awarded a Pushcart Prize (1995), while other publications and performances have garnered appreciative reviews in periodicals ranging from the *New York Times Book Review* to *People* magazine.

With a background in painting and piano, an undergraduate degree in physics, and graduate study in creative writing, Loh has a good sense of detail and of the nuances of everyday life—a mindfulness that served her well during her time as a columnist for *Buzz* magazine (1992–96). Writing funny, conversational pieces about living in the San Fernando Valley (some of which formed the basis for *Depth Takes a Holiday*), she offered nonfiction and fictionalized accounts of her own experience as a late Boomer of Chinese-German heritage searching for sanity on the outskirts of Hollywood culture. During this period, she continued the performance work begun in the 1980s, incorporating in her works material about growing up with immigrant parents in a troubled family environment: *Aliens in America* (1995) appeared in print in 1997. This darkly comic serial monologue addresses a disastrous family vacation to Ethiopia, problems with successive stepmothers, and the tribulations of being a teenager in an imperfect body.

After her stint with *Buzz*, Loh gave two solo performances based on material from earlier essays (*Depth Becomes Her* [1997] and *Bad Sex with Bud Kemp* [1998]). She also published a novel, *If You Lived Here, You'd Be Home by Now*, which was chosen by the *Los Angeles Times* as one of the best books of 1997. Loh's protagonist in this work of fiction is not unlike the persona of several of her essays: Bronwyn Peters is a highly trained, ambitious, imaginative young woman struggling to remain hip, productive, upwardly mobile, and ethically responsible despite the pressures of L.A. hype. Much of the book focuses on Peters's desire to move out of tract housing and into a higher-status neighborhood, into a community of the recognizably "cool." Thematically consistent with the author's shorter narratives, *If You Lived Here* lampoons the fatuous workings of celebrity culture and the frantic efforts of those seeking to make

a name for themselves. Loh manages to generate sympathy for the desperate wannabes.

As a radio commentator for public radio stations KCRW (Santa Monica, 1997–2004) and KPCC (Pasadena, 2004–present), Loh has sustained a loyal audience for her monologues, which are frequently heard on National Public Radio. Her semiautobiographical *A Year in Van Nuys* (2001), a comic rendering of her own artistic crisis, was well received; readers recognized the voice and persona as vintage Loh (as is the theme of trying to establish a satisfactory creative identity outside Tinseltown's charmed circles). Additionally, two one-woman shows have kept this artist in the public eye: *I Worry* (2002), a set of riffs on Americans' news-media-induced anxiety, and *Sugar Plum Fairy* (2003), a narrative about family holiday behavior and adolescent dreams of dancing the lead in the Nutcracker Suite.

One of our best writers of performatory prose, Loh is part social observer, part confessor, part entertainer. With Sarah Vowell, David Sedaris, and a small number of other postmodern writer-performers, she continues to redefine both story and performance.

Bibliography

Glionna, John M. "The Multi-Cult Semi-Celeb." *Los Angeles Times Magazine*, 9 April 2000, pp. 14ff.

Itagaki, Lynn M. "Sandra Tsing Loh." *Asian American Playwrights: A Bio-Bibliographical Critical Sourcebook*, edited by Miles Xian Liu, 212–217. Westport, Conn.: Greenwood Press, 2002.

Loh, Sandra Tsing. "Sandra Tsing Loh." Interview by Douglas Eby. Talent Development Resources. Available online. URL: http://www.talentdevelop.com/sloh.html. Downloaded on January 19, 2005.

Janis Butler Holm

Loh, Vyvyanne (?–)

A writer, choreographer-dancer, and physician, Vyvyane Loh was born in Ipoh, Malaysia (at the time Malaya), during British colonial rule but grew up in Singapore. She holds undergraduate and medical degrees from Boston University and graduated from the Warren Wilson College M.F.A. program in creative writing. After the publication of her first novel, *Breaking the Tongue* (2004), Loh was elected fellow at the Bread Loaf Writers' Conference in Vermont and later at the Radcliffe Institute for Advanced Study at Harvard University. Her novel was noted for the 2005 Kiriyama Prize and picked by the New York Public Library as one of the year's "Books to Remember" in 2004.

Breaking the Tongue is a historical novel set in prewar and wartime Singapore, partly drawing on Loh's childhood experience of World War II. Singapore's fall to the Japanese in 1942, a cataclysmic event in the island's history, forces its inhabitants to renegotiate their cultural identity: Having originally come from different parts of Asia to settle in Singapore, having lived so long under British colonial rule but now being faced with a Japanese military rule, the residents of Singapore are torn among British culture, Japanese culture, and their own ethnic heritage.

The novel opens with a harrowing torture scene as Claude Lim, who grew up in an Anglophilic family of Chinese origin, is interrogated by the Japanese because of his resented English-educated background and his friendship with the nurse Ling-li, who is suspected of being a Communist spy. That this allegation might only be fiction constructed out of jealousy by a female collaborator working for the Japanese at once underscores the novel's interest in understanding how cultural fiction is created; to explore this issue of cross-cultural perception and imagination, Loh uses sexual intercourse as a metaphorical vehicle. While this thematic and allegorical structure permeates the text, it is particularly overt when Claude's mother is described, through Claude's flashbacks, as having committed adultery in the past with a series of white men in order to satisfy her disconcertingly inculcated desire to please the British colonizer.

During the torturous interrogation, Claude's memories of his boyhood as part of the Paranakan culture (the English-educated Chinese diaspora in Southeast Asia), his love for Ling-li, his friendship with the Englishman Jack Winchester, and their

attempts to hide from the Japanese during the occupation can only be pieced together, or guessed at, from these disjointed flashbacks. They are juxtaposed not only with Ling-li's experience but also with extracts from a variety of sources, both historical and fictitious. This emphasis on mediation is additionally articulated by tightly linked images of different forms of linguistic practices—of movements of the tongue during mastication and sexual encounters, the switching from one language to another, and ultimately the literal and the metaphorical breaking of tongues that gives the novel its title. Thus, as Claude is tortured, his tongue is repeatedly on the point of being literally broken or twisted. This is paralleled by his increasing self-awareness of the growing number of Chinese-speaking immigrants from China after the war. Ultimately, the text itself breaks down, collapsing into a medley of English and Chinese. Claude's ethnicity is subsumed by a new understanding of homogenizing ethnic categorizations. No longer Peranakan, he is simply an English-educated Chinese who learns a new language to fit in.

Bibliography

Ban, Kah Choon and Yap Hong Kuan. *Rehearsal for War: Resistance and the Underground War against the Japanese and the Kempeitai, 1942–1945.* Singapore: Horizon Books, 2002.

Loh, Vyvyanne. *Breaking the Tongue.* New York and London: W.W. Norton, 2004.

Suryadinata, Leo. "Peranakan Chinese Identities in Singapore and Malaysia: A Re-examination." In *Ethnic Chinese in Singapore and Malaysia,* edited by Leo Suryadinata, 69–84. Singapore: Times Academic Press, 2002.

Wagner, Tamara S. *Occidentalism in Novels of Malaysia and Singapore, 1819–2004: Colonial and Postcolonial Financial Straits and Literary Style.* Lewiston, N.Y.: Edwin Mellen, 2005.

———. "Victims of Boutique Multiculturalism: Malaysian Chinese and Peranakan Women Writers and the Dangers of Self-Exoticisation." *Journal of Multicultural Discourses.* Forthcoming.

Tamara S. Wagner

Lord, Bette Bao   (1938–)

At the age of eight, Bette Bao traveled with her family to the United States when her father was sent on a business trip by the Chinese Nationalist government. When the Nationalists were defeated by the Communists in 1949, the Bao family became exiles from their homeland.

Bette Bao Lord published *In the Year of the Boar and Jackie Robinson* (1984) as a fictionalized account of her first year in the United States as a new student in Brooklyn, New York. Through the persona of Shirley Temple Wong, Lord tells her immigration story from a child's perspective and captures the hardships of adjusting to American life. Although her classmates initially welcome her, Shirley's unfamiliar habits, such as bowing, and lack of fluency in English later render her invisible to her peers. She becomes isolated from her classmates and even from her loving parents when she cannot communicate the loneliness she feels as the only Chinese girl in her school. As she learns English, however, Shirley finds that her grasp on Chinese begins to slip, and writing to cousins in China becomes more difficult. In searching for the appropriate words to describe her American experiences, such as dressing up as a turkey for a school pageant or babysitting triplets, Shirley serves as a cultural translator, bridging the gap between her old and new communities.

With no support or interference from the clan, Shirley and her family face both the obstacles and freedom of remaking themselves. The book title represents Shirley's determination to construct a multicultural American identity. Her memory of her grandfather telling folktales, combined with the voices of her ethnically diverse classmates and neighbors, enables Shirley to create a language via which she can embrace her new sense of self and home. She finds inspiration most in baseball and especially in the legendary Jackie Robinson. Baseball represents Americanism because it counts on teamwork and also encourages each player to make a significant impact individually.

Bao Lord returned to Beijing from 1985 to 1989 when her husband Winston Lord served as the American ambassador to China. She witnessed the pro-democracy student demonstrations in Tianan-men Square prior to the massacre. After returning to the United States, she published *Legacies: A Chinese Mosaic* (1990) based on many stories she collected from survivors of the Cultural Revolution. She collected some of the stories through personal interviews; other stories made their way secretly to her on audio cassettes. This book highlights the cycles of violence and violations of human rights in Communist China as each chapter presents the voice of an anonymous "I" whose identity and relationships are traumatically altered by the Cultural Revolution.

Bao Lord's other novels also explore the impact of politics on both individuals and families. *Eighth Moon: The True Story of a Young Girl's Life in Communist China* (1964) is based on the childhood of her youngest sister, Sansan, the infant who had remained in China when the Bao family embarked on what began as a business trip. When the Communists assumed power, the Bao family in the United States could not retrieve Sansan and did not see her again until 1962. *Spring Moon* (1981), a historical, romantic saga, chronicles the lives of several generations of the House of Chang during great political and cultural changes. *Middle Heart* (1996), set in contemporary China, follows a love triangle through political turmoil which tests and changes families and friendships. Bao Lord's writing and activism strive to construct cultural bridges and champion human rights by appealing to the value of family.

Bibliography

Fox, Mary Virginia. *Bette Bao Lord: Novelist and Chinese Voice for Change.* People of Distinction Series. Chicago: Children's Press, 1993.

Natov, Roni. "Living in Two Cultures: Bette Bao Lord's Stories of Chinese-American Experience." *The Lion and the Unicorn* 11, no. 1 (1987): 38–46.

Karen Li Miller

Lost Names: Scenes from a Korean Boyhood   Richard E. Kim (1970)

A work divided into seven separate yet interrelated vignettes from Richard E. Kim's childhood in

Japanese-occupied Korea, *Lost Names* blurs the boundaries between fiction and nonfiction. The narrator of the stories—unnamed, but sharing Kim's biographical background—portrays the occupation with the insight and candor of a child, though constantly moving backward and forward in time to place the events within an act of remembering. Memory, while not an easy fix or unproblematic salve for the narrator, remains the imperative that drives each of the seven distinct stories forward. What such stories reveal, and what they conceal, allows Kim to demonstrate the complexity of recapturing the past.

Ordered chronologically within the book, the seven individual stories—"Crossing," "Homecoming," "Once upon a Time, on a Sunday," "Lost Names," "An Empire for Rubber Balls," "Is Someone Dying?" and "In the Making of History—Together"—cover the latter years of the Japanese occupation and colonial domination of Korea, spanning the period from 1932 to 1945. The narrator's father, an ex-revolutionary and former prisoner of the Japanese occupiers, constantly implores his son never to forget; never to lose sight of his Korean identity; never to accept the Japanese occupation. This father-son relationship develops throughout the book, as both must confront the realities of an unacceptable present while never fully ceding their identity as Koreans.

The story from which the title of the book derives its name—"Lost Names"—captures the difficulties of maintaining a national and cultural identity under the domination of a foreign power. At the outset of World War II, at the height of Japanese imperialism, the occupying Japanese forced the Koreans to not only completely give up the teaching and learning of Korean history and language but also to give up their names. Painfully and simply, the narrator notes, "Today, I lost my name. Today, we all lost our names. February 11, 1940" (115). This act of renouncing the family name proves shameful and disgraceful to the father; the son, on the other hand, understands that the act of remembering functions to ensure that nothing remains lost for long.

While Kim sets a somber tone throughout the majority of the work, the narrator's childhood exploits and misadventures provide entertaining, hopeful, and rather upbeat moments that punctuate each individual story. Whether conspiring with his fellow student workers to puncture all the rubber balls to be collected by the school's administrators or subvert school dramatic productions to honor the Japanese emperor, the narrator reveals a worldview still fascinated by the human spirit and refuses to let the cruelties and harshness of the occupying force subdue his youthful optimism. Yet the tragic state of affairs under the Japanese occupation lurks in the shadows of even the most optimistic and carefree moments of the narrator's childhood.

The final story of the book, "In the Making of History—Together," culminates in the withdrawal of the Japanese after their unconditional surrender at the end of World War II, but the story casts an almost ambiguous tone on the developing events. Father and son discuss the liberation, yet come away with no simple answers concerning the future of the Korean nation. As J. Michael Allen remarks, "The post-liberation generation, as the concluding chapter's title suggests, must become masters of their future, making history rather than watching it happen, becoming the shapers of their destinies rather than pawns in others' power schemes." However, as Kim's earlier novels *The* MARTYRED and *The* INNOCENT demonstrate, the formation of a Korean nation requires the loss of human lives, the spread of even more violence, and an embittered struggle to define a national identity.

Bibliography

Allen, J. Michael. Review of *Lost Names: Scenes from a Korean Boyhood, Korean Studies Review* 2 (2001). Available online. URL: http://www.koreaweb.ws/ks/ksr/ksr01-02.htm. Accessed October 8, 2006.

Zach Weir

Louie, David Wong   (1954–   )

On the basis of his first two books—a collection of short fiction, *PANGS OF LOVE AND OTHER STORIES* (1991), and a novel, *The BARBARIANS ARE COMING* (2000)—David Wong Louie has established himself as one of the leading voices among Chinese-American authors of the "baby-boom" generation.

Born in Rockville Centre, New York, to parents who were laundry workers, Louie received a B.A. from Vassar College in 1977 and an M.F.A. from the University of Iowa in 1981. After working in New York City in advertising, he accepted in 1988 a visiting professorship in creative writing at the University of California at Berkeley. From 1988 to 1992, he taught writing and literature at Vassar College. Since 1992, he has taught courses in Asian-American studies and creative writing at the University of California at Los Angeles.

Pangs of Love and Other Stories is a collection of 11 unusual stories mostly treating the experiences of Chinese Americans as they attempt to adjust to American life and to their own senses of hyphenated identity. *The Barbarians Are Coming* chronicles the generational conflicts within a working-class Chinese-American family living in Long Island in the 1970s.

Louie's essays and short fiction have appeared in such notable periodicals as *Chicago Review, Fiction International, Iowa Review, New York Times Book Review, Ploughshares,* and *Zyzzyva.* In addition, his work has been included in the following anthologies: *The Best American Short Stories of 1989* (Boston: Houghton, 1989), *The Big Aiiieeeee! An Anthology of Chinese American and Japanese American Literature* (New York: Dutton, 1991), *Charlie Chan Is Dead: An Anthology of Contemporary Asian American Fiction* (New York: Viking, 1993), and *Other Sides of Silence: A Ploughshares Anthology* (New York: Faber, 1993).

Martin Kich

Love Wife, The Gish Jen (2004)

GISH JEN's inspiration for her third novel came from her own biracial family. With a husband of Irish decent, one child who looks Asian and one child who looks "American," Jen wonders about how her children experience the world differently. Strangers often ask Jen if her daughter, who looks "white" with brown hair and fair skin, is her child.

When the *Washington Post* held an online question and answer forum with Jen, she told the newspaper's readers that she started writing *The Love Wife* with these questions in mind: "What is a family? What is 'natural?'" She tackled these questions with the creation of the Wong family. Carnegie Wong, a second-generation Chinese American, marries a blonde beauty named Janie, who is renamed "Blondie" by Carnegie's mother, Mama Wong. Carnegie and Janie raise a biological son (Bailey) and two adopted Asian daughters (Lizzie, who was abandoned at a New York church, and Wendy from China). After Mama Wong dies, she continues her controlling hold on her son by willing to him a nanny named Lan from China so that her grandchildren might be raised according to their Asian ancestry. Sending for and hiring Lan are conditions of Carnegie's substantial inheritance.

Through the novel's quickly shifting first-person narrative, we hear each character's version of the family story. Jen describes the narrative as "family therapy without the therapy." The Wongs are described as "the new American family," but Carnegie worries about his multicultural family. He painfully questions if Lizzie is Chinese, like him, at all: "Was she part Japanese? Part Korean? Part Vietnamese? Was she part Chinese at all?" He also begins to feel attracted to Lan, whom Blondie believes Mama Wong has sent "from her grave, the wife [Carnegie] should have married." While Carnegie and the children develop close relationships with Lan, who cooks Asian food and tells them stories about China, Blondie feels increasingly alienated from the family: "Any passerby would have thought Lan and Carnegie the husband and wife of the family, and that I was visiting with my son, Bailey."

The Love Wife is darker and less comical than Jen's previous novels, which include more fantastical plot shifts and tragicomical family relationships. *The Love Wife,* Jen's longest novel, includes serious issues of physical abuse, emotional abandonment, and life-threatening illnesses.

Bibliography

Anshaw, Carol. "The 21st Century Family." *Women's Review of Books* 22, no. 2 (2004): 8–9.

Burns, Carole. "Off the Page: Gish Jen," Online Discussion. washingtonpost.com (30 September 2004). Available online. URL: http://www.washingtonpost.com/wp-dyn/content/discussion/2004/09/24/DI2005040307731.html.

Amy Lillian Manning

Lum, Darrell H. Y.   (1950–   )

Lum was born in Honolulu, Hawaii, where he currently lives with his family. His father, born in China, came to Hawaii at the age of six; his paternal grandfather, a former provincial government official in China and Chinese language teacher in Hawaii, maintained a lifelong interest in writing despite having to take on diverse jobs to support his family. Lum's maternal grandmother, on the other hand, moved to Hawaii as an infant and married a Chinese rice-mill manager. After graduating from McKinley High School in 1968, Lum left Hawaii to study engineering at Case Institute of Technology in Cleveland. After his freshman year, however, he transferred to the University of Hawaii at Manoa, where he studied creative writing and graphic design. In May 1972 he graduated with a B.A. in liberal studies and went on to earn a master's degree in educational communications and technology in 1976. One year later he obtained a Ph.D. in educational foundations from the same university. From 1974 he has worked as an academic adviser at the University of Hawaii Student Support Services.

Lum has written plays, children's books and short stories in which he brings to life the language and mixed heritage of the Hawaiian islands. He cofounded and is coeditor with Eric Chock of the literary magazine *Bamboo Ridge,* a nonprofit academic press promoting Hawaiian literature. In the preface to *The Quietest Singing,* a literary anthology he coedited with Joseph Stanton and Estelle Enoki, he affirms his personal commitment as a writer when he discusses "the responsibility to listen to the land, to the people, to all the voices" (2). As he writes about the varied island cultures, the themes of poverty and discrimination forcefully emerge, reflecting the dark side of an island paradise. Critic Gail Okawa argues that Lum's choice of subjects, language, and form serves a means of resistance to the dominant society's attitude towards the multiethnic population of Hawaii and its culture (179).

Many of his plays—*Oranges Are Lucky, Fighting Fire, A Little Bit Like You, My Home Is Down the Street,* and *Magic Mango*—are popular in the islands and have been produced by theatrical companies such as Kumu Kahua and Honolulu Theater for Youth. His children's books, dealing with the diversity of Asian heritage palpable in Hawaiian life, include *The Golden Slipper: A Vietnamese Legend, Hot-Pepper Kid and Iron-Mouth Chicken Capture Fire and Wind, The Rice Mystery,* and *Riding the Bullet.*

Lum has published two short-story collections, *Sun: Short Stories and Drama* (1980) and *Pass On, No Pass Back* (1990). The protagonists of these stories, very often children or adolescents, narrate events in the "language of home" (pidgin), creating a humorous and realistic tone. In addition to the stories in these books, his stories have appeared in publications such as *Manoa, Bamboo Ridge, Seattle Review, Chaminade Literary Review,* and *Hawaii Review;* some of them have also been reprinted in *Charlie Chan Is Dead* and *The Quietest Singing* (2004), both anthologies of contemporary Asian-American literature. In the latter, he presents three short stories that form a cycle about a father-son relationship. Lum's consistent use of short-story cycles emerges from what he deems natural to the island culture characterized by a tradition "of storytelling, of story-making, of retelling stories, of playing with language—a tremendous verbal fluency and expressiveness" (qtd. in Okawa 182).

Lum has received various literary awards including the 1991 Elliot Cades Award and the 1992 Outstanding Book Award in fiction from the Association for Asian American Studies. Well known and respected in the Hawaiian islands, his work has become of major interest to mainland readers and scholars.

Bibliography

Lum, Darrell H. Y., Joseph Stanton, and Estelle Enoki, eds. *The Quietest Singing.* Honolulu: Bamboo Ridge Press, 2000.

Okawa, Gail Y. "Resistance and Reclamation: Hawaii 'Pidgin English' and Autoethnography in the Short Stories of Darrell H. Y. Lum." In *Ethnicity and the American Short Story,* edited by Julie Brown, 177–196. New York: Garland, 1997.

Alice Otano

Mah, Adeline Yen (1937–)

Born Jun-ling Yen, the fifth child in an affluent family in Tianjin, China, Mah lived in Shanghai as a child and moved to Hong Kong at the age of 11. Because her mother died shortly after her birth, Mah was considered a source of bad luck to her family. Her father soon remarried a French-Chinese woman, whose tyrannical presence brought endless miseries to Mah and conflicts to the family. Although Mah found solace and love in her grandfather and aunt, she was also kept away from them. By winning the first prize at the age of 14 in a playwriting competition open to all English-speaking children, Mah convinced her father to allow her to pursue her studies in England. She graduated from University College London with a specialty in anesthesiology and moved to the United States to become a successful anesthesiologist. She now writes full time, living in California and London with her husband and two children.

Mah recounts her life experiences in her best-selling autobiography, *Falling Leaves: The True Story of an Unwanted Chinese Daughter* (1997). The success of this book led to the publication of a children's version of her autobiography, *Chinese Cinderella* (1999). Mah also wrote another book for young children, *Chinese Cinderella and the Secret Dragon* (2004). Unlike the other two, this book is a fictional story about an unwanted daughter, Ye Xian, whose training in martial arts enables her to accomplish a remarkable mission with three boys during World War II.

Mah's skill in employing Chinese idioms and proverbs and explaining Chinese culture in *Falling Leaves* is further seen in her two other books. In *A Thousand Pieces of Gold: A Memoir of China's Past through Its Proverbs* (2002), Mah renders a version of Chinese history in her explanation of Chinese proverbs. She also draws parallels between Chinese history and her personal history. In *Watching the Tree: A Chinese Daughter Reflects on Happiness, Tradition, and Spiritual Wisdom* (2001), Mah explains aspects of Chinese culture, such as Confucianism, Buddhism, Chinese food and the Chinese language, frequently illustrating them with her own experiences and reflections.

Yan Ying

Maki, John McGilvrey (1909–2006)

John Maki was born Hiroo Sugiyama in Tacoma, Washington. Since his issei parents were unable to support him, he was raised by Mr. and Mrs. Alexander McGilvrey, a white couple who legally adopted him in 1918 as John McGilvrey. With help from part-time jobs, McGilvrey (universally known as "Jack") put himself through the University of Washington (UW), graduating in 1932. Despite his unfamiliarity with Japanese-American culture, Jack joined the staff of a Seattle nisei weekly, the *Japanese American Courier,* and contributed essays and poetry to other Japanese-American newspapers.

Upon entering graduate school at UW, Jack was advised that his best career prospects, given his ancestry, were in Oriental Studies. In 1936 he and his wife Mary undertook two years of study in Tokyo on a Japanese government fellowship, and to enhance his scholarly credibility, Jack adopted the Japanese surname "Maki." In 1939 Maki was named Associate in Oriental Studies at UW and returned to America.

In May 1942 Maki was confined with other Seattle Japanese Americans in the Puyallup Assembly Center. Shortly thereafter, he was recruited as a Japan specialist by the Federal Communications Commission, and he and his wife were permitted to leave camp for Washington, D.C. In June 1943 he joined the Office of War Information (OWI) as a psychological warfare policy specialist. In the evenings Maki drafted a work on Japan in anticipation of a postwar American occupation. Maki's study, released by Knopf in May 1945 as *Japanese Militarism: Its Cause and Cure,* was the first mass-market book by a West Coast nisei. Maki argued that militarism was embedded in Japanese culture, and democratization would thus require revolutionary social change. In one passage, he recommended against executing the Japanese emperor and prophetically suggested transforming the emperor instead into a vessel for democracy. Maki's book received wide publicity, and it sold out its original run.

In 1946, after serving briefly in the American occupation of Japan, Maki enrolled at Harvard University, where two years later he became the university's first nisei Ph.D. In 1949 Maki was named assistant professor of Asian studies at UW. In succeeding years, he became a renowned expert on Japanese constitutionalism with books such as *Government and Politics in Japan* (1962). In 1966 Maki moved to the University of Massachusetts, Amherst, and served as professor and vice dean. He retired in 1980. In 2004, the nonagenarian Maki privately published a moving memoir, *A Voyage through the Twentieth Century.*

Greg Robinson

Martyred, The   Richard E. Kim   (1964)

RICHARD E. KIM's first novel, *The Martyred,* focuses on the Korean War and Korean Christianity as its two main objects of scrutiny, examining the complex interrelationships between suffering and faith, death on a massive scale and everlasting life, the needs of a country and individual interests, and honesty and guilt. Set during the latter part of the Korean War, Kim's work dissects the contradictions and irresolvable tensions between the warring military machines. Brought in to sift through sketchy evidence concerning the group murder of 12 Christian ministers in Pyongyang by the Communist army—those later consecrated as "the martyred" by the local citizenry—Captain Lee of the Republic of Korea army must discern why two ministers escaped execution, why, out of the 14 Christian ministers imprisoned, only two avoided a death sentence.

As Captain Lee progresses in his search for information, he befriends the minister Mr. Shin, who along with the mentally ill Mr. Hann, lived through their imprisonment and torture by the Northern army. Colonel Chang, Lee's commanding officer, believes that Mr. Shin knows more about the execution than he lets on and forces Lee to press Shin on this point. As Lee discovers the truth, with the aid of Chaplain Koh and his friend Park, he must confront the problem of multiple truths, each one competing on different, but equally difficult terms with regard to their likely effect on the Christians living in hunger, poverty, and despair in the war-ravaged North. Though the reader learns that Mr. Shin remained defiant until his imminent end, spitting in the face of his captors and refusing to grovel and renounce his faith, Lee also draws out the reason that Shin has remained silent about his actions and those of the 12 executed ministers: The murdered ministers each "died like dogs" (141), turning against their faith and begging for their lives before being shot one at a time by the North Korean guards. Mr. Shin bears the burden of venerating the martyrs—receiving the public outcries of "Judas! Judas!" with great stoicism (186)—as he sacrifices his own honor in order to lessen the burden of the city's Christians, providing them with an untarnished image of the martyrs so that such symbolism might help eclipse some of the daily suffering they experience due to a war over which they have no control.

As the novel progresses, Kim returns frequently to the theme of responsibility and burden. Captain Lee must perform his job to the best of his ability, while at the same time protecting his friends as much as possible. Mr. Shin must keep the absolute truth to himself in order not to demoralize the already overtaxed Christians in Pyongyang. Park must confront the death of his father (one of the martyred) and likewise his rejection of the Christian faith. Chaplain Koh must reevaluate his responsibilities to his congregation and to army intelligence.

In each case, the suffering of the civilian population effectively conveys the terrors and ravages of war upon the innocent. By the end of the novel, when the Republic of Korea army evacuates Pyongyang slightly ahead of an all-out Chinese Communist invasion, once again the innocent suffer, with no means of escape. Contrasting and eventually conflating the import of suffering for the Christian faith with the plight of the civilian citizenry, Kim forces the reader to question to which group the novel's title *The Martyred* belongs: to the 12 ministers executed on the first day of the Korean War or to the common Korean citizens sacrificed every day in the name of a war, a cause that they remain isolated from and victimized by? Arguably, for Kim, the answer would be both, along with all others indelibly marked by the devastation of war.

Bibliography

Kim, Richard E. *The Martyred.* New York: George Braziler, 1964.

Zack Weir

Massey, Sujata   (1963–)

Sujata Massey is a multicultural writer born in Sussex, the United Kingdom, of a German mother and an Indian father. Her family immigrated to the United States when Sujata Massey was five, and she grew up in Philadelphia, Berkeley, California, and St. Paul, Minnesota. She graduated from Johns Hopkins University in 1986, majoring in creative writing. She worked as a journalist for the *Baltimore Evening Sun* newspaper until 1991, when she moved to Japan for two years with her husband, who was posted there as a navy medical officer.

Back in Baltimore, Massey continued to write her first novel, which she had begun in Japan. In 1996 she won the Malice Domestic Limited grant for unpublished writers, with which she managed to complete the first book. She also signed a contract for two more detective novels. Since then Massey has published altogether eight novels, in which the main character, Rei Shimura, is multiculturally conditioned like Massey. Rei's Japanese-American roots are strongly present in the thematic development of each of the novels. Of these eight, the first four novels are set in Japan. In the next three, while still related to Japanese culture, the settings are mostly in the United States, where Rei stays for a prolonged visit. In the 2005 novel *The Typhoon Lover,* Rei returns to Japan. Massey has won the 1998 Agatha Award for the best first novel (*The Salaryman's Wife*) and the 2000 Macavity Award for the best novel (*The Flower Master*). Her other novels have been nominated for various prizes.

All the novels treat, in one way or another, issues of identity, gender, representation and cultural authenticity. In *The Salaryman's Wife* (1997), the first novel of the series, Rei Shimura is a 27-year-old teacher of English for the Japanese employees of the Nichiyu Company. She lives in Tokyo and tries to remain emotionally and economically independent. Taking a vacation in Shiroyama, however, she gets involved in the mysterious death of Setsuko Nakamura, the wife of an important Japanese businessman. In the course of the story, Rei begins an affair with Hugh Glendinning, a Scottish lawyer who is first accused of the murder. The plot centers on family honor, xenophobia, industrial espionage, the Japanese mafia known as *yakuza,* and love. A major side issue in the plot is the status of the racially hybrid children between American military servicemen and Japanese women. In the second novel, *Zen Attitude* (1998), Rei has launched her own antiques business in Tokyo and runs it from Hugh Glendinning's apartment. While searching for a specific *tansu* chest—a piece of furniture—for a client, she is enveloped in a murder mystery. The *tansu* plays a central role in the story, which also involves a depiction of Zen Buddhist practices and traditions, especially from a gendered perspective. In *The Flower Master* (1999), Hugh Glendinning leaves for Scotland, and Rei remains alone to run her business. She is enrolled in a flower arrangement class taught by her aunt, Norie Shimura. Soon there is a murder in the class and Norie is one of the suspected. The story revolves again around family honor and love, but it also deals with international environmental activism and the status of the Korean minority in Japan. In *The Floating Girl* (2000), Rei is commissioned to write about the extremely popular Japanese cartoons, the *manga,* for a Japanese magazine for foreigners. Soon a person interviewed by Rei gets murdered, and Rei is inevitably involved in the case. With her boyfriend Takeo Kayama, she tries to interpret and understand the mystery of the *manga,* especially the issue of sexuality in the *Mars Girl* series.

The setting moves to the United States in *The Bride's Kimono* (2001), in which Rei accepts a surprising and enticing offer to transport a collection of priceless antique kimonos from Japan to a museum in Washington, D.C. However, one of the kimonos—the bride's kimono—is stolen, and Rei loses her passport only to find it along with a dead Japanese woman from the group she was traveling with. She has no choice but to solve the case. She is assisted by her parents and by her former lover, Hugh Glendinning, with whom a relationship develops once more. The plot revolves around issues of prostitution, romance, and international smuggling of antiques. In *The Samurai's Daughter* (2003), Rei stays with her parents in San Francisco and researches her own family's history through the antiques they possess. When Hugh Glendinning is asked to pursue a class action lawsuit on behalf of people forced into slave labor for Japanese companies during World War II, Rei's research and Glendinning's lawsuit project become intertwined in unexpected ways. In *Pearl Diver* (2004), Rei lives in Washington, D.C., with Hugh Glendinning. Rei is asked to decorate a new Japanese restaurant in the city. Her cousin Kendall is kidnapped, and Rei manages to solve the incident, only later to be abducted herself. The novel returns to the topic of the status of the biracial children between American military servicemen and Japanese women. Having Hugh as her boyfriend is one thing, but it is another when Rei ponders marriage and motherhood.

In *The Typhoon Lover* (2005), the setting is again Japan, where Rei is acting on an undercover U.S. government assignment. A valuable ancient vessel, an ibex ewer, has been stolen from an Iraqi museum in Baghdad, and it is believed to be in Japan. The narrative is closely linked to contemporary international politics and the occupation of Iraq, and it evolves also around natural catastrophes as a severe typhoon hits Japan. The main focus is, however, on Rei and her complex, ambiguous character. Breaking up with Hugh, she meets again with her former boyfriend Takeo, who is suspected of having the stolen item in his collection. In the ninth novel in the series, *Girl in a Box* (2006), Rei works undercover as a clerk in a large department store in Tokyo. Hired again by a U.S. government agency, her task is to solve a murder and fraud case.

One intriguing aspect of these novels is that despite Massey's background as an Indo-European, or a Euro-Indian, the novels scarcely explore these cultural spheres. Whether set in Japan or the United States, the novels concentrate on Japanese culture. That Massey has chosen to write about Japan raises questions of identity, representation, and cultural authenticity common in postcolonial detective fiction. However, despite the choice of specific settings, Massey's works have a universal appeal since they examine the questions of cross-cultural identity shared by many people in the postcolonial world.

Bibliography

D'haen, Theo. "Samurai Sleuths and Detective Daughters, The American Way." In *Sleuthing Ethnicity: The Detective in Multiethnic Crime Fiction,* edited by Dorothea Fischer-Hornung and Monika

Mueller, 36–52. Madison, N.J.: Fairleigh Dickenson University Press, 2003.

Joel Kuortti

Matsueda, Pat   (1952–   )

Poet and editor Patricia Tomoko Matsueda was born on August 20, 1952, on an air force base in Kyushu, Fukuoka Prefecture, Japan. She is the author of four books of poetry and has served as editor for a range of publications including *Manoa: A Pacific Journal of International Writing,* for which she has been managing editor since 1992. Matsueda's mother was a Japanese national, and her father was a Japanese-American sergeant in the U.S. Air Force. Shortly after her parents' divorce, Matsueda, her mother, and sister settled in Honolulu, Hawaii. Matsueda received a B.A. in English from the University of Hawaii, and she continues to live in Honolulu.

Critics consider Matsueda to be an important figure in Hawaiian literature. She has been instrumental in developing Hawaiian poetry as well as in creating venues for the publication of Pacific Rim literature. Matsueda's first poem appeared in the 1978 inaugural issue of *Bamboo Ridge,* a literary journal that helped lead institutional efforts to publish Hawaiian local writing. She subsequently published three books of poetry: *The Return* (1978), *X* (1983), and *The Fish Catcher* (1985). In 1988 Matsueda received the Hawaii Literary Art Council's Elliot Cades Award for Literature. Her fourth book of poetry, *Stray,* was published in 2006.

Between 1977 and 1980, Matsueda edited the *Hawaii Literary Arts Council Newsletter,* and in 1981 she cofounded and acted as editor-in-chief for *The Paper,* an early Hawaii literary journal that published Hawaiian writing including pidgin-oriented writing, for over six years. Matsueda has also served as an editor for Houghton Mifflin's academic division. Perhaps one of her most lasting contributions to the field of Pacific Rim literature outside of her own poetry is her work with *Manoa.* Founded in 1989, *Manoa* is a biannual literary journal that publishes both Asia-Pacific and American writing. Just as *Manoa* began to pay increasing attention to works in translation or works that were relatively unfamiliar to audiences on either side of the Pacific, Matsueda became in 1992 the journal's first full-time managing editor.

Matsueda's work has received little attention in Asian-American literary criticism, probably because her work primarily explores the Hawaii-Japan connection rather than Asian-American experiences within the United States. Moreover, many of her poems have little to do with Asian-American culture as such; instead, they treat broader questions of aesthetics.

Matsueda seems interested in demonstrating the fluidity between the points of reference—whether they are body and mind, Japan and America, geography and abstraction, or other associations—and the possibility of becoming familiar with other identities and experiences. For example, a character and an object may take on completely distinct qualities, but the character's feeling or thought can be represented through that same object, or the object may take on human characteristics. This interest in materials and abstractions comes through in her poetic form, which Jared Carter describes as enlisting the visuality of poetry to interact with poetic content.

Bibliography

Carter, Jared. "Poetry Chapbooks: Back to the Basics." *Georgia Review* 40, no. 2 (Summer 1986): 532–547.

Leong, Lavonne. "Pat Matsueda." *Asian American Poets: A Bio-Bibliographical Critical Sourcebook,* edited by Guiyou Huang. Westport, Conn.: Greenwood Press, 2002.

Ronck, Ronn. "Farewell to the *Paper.*" *Literary Arts Hawaii* 83 (New Year 1987): 4–6.

Marguerite Nguyen

Matsuoka, Takashi   (1954–   )

Born in Japan, Takashi Matsuoka was raised in Hawaii. He now lives in Honolulu, where, prior to becoming a full-time writer, he was employed at a Zen Buddhist temple. He is the author of the acclaimed novel *Clouds of Sparrows* (2002), which has been translated into 15 languages, and its sequel *Autumn Bridge* (2004).

Matsuoka's first book, *Clouds of Sparrows*, echoes Asian-themed fictional adventure and spirit in the tradition of James Clavell's *Shogun* (1975). It tells of a historical adventure and a love story set amid the violence and beauty of 19th-century Japan. After two centuries of isolation, Japan has opened its doors to the West in 1861. As foreign ships threaten to destroy the shogun's castle in Edo (present-day Tokyo), a group of American missionaries—among them Emily Gibson, a woman seeking redemption from a tormented past, and Matthew Stark, a cold-eyed killer with one more death in storage—arrives at Edo Bay into a world of samurai, geishas, noblemen, and Zen monks. Shortly after, Emily meets the handsome Lord Genji of the Okumichi clan, a nobleman with a gift of prophecy who must defend his embattled family and confront his forbidden feelings for an outsider. Forced to escape from Edo and flee to his ancestral home, the Cloud of Sparrows Castle, Genji is joined by Emily and Matthew. Unaware of the dangers ahead of them, these three characters begin a harrowing journey together with Genji's uncle, the samurai Lord Shigeru, and the Lady Heiko. Matsuoka places the story at a time when traditional samurai society was about to be extinguished by the gun and the weak shogunate and began to be replaced by Western influences and modern political structures. In *Clouds of Sparrows*, Matsuoka equates the ethos of Japanese samurai (Genji's uncle Shigeru) with that of Western gunslingers (Matthew Stark), implying that somehow Japan and the West were not that different after all.

Autumn Bridge presents the revelation of the prophecy that was introduced in *Clouds of Sparrows*—linking a 14th-century event to Lord Genji's unlikely alliance with Emily in the 19th century. In 1311, while a woman in the tower of the Cloud of Sparrows Castle watches the enemies battling below and awaits her fate, she begins to write the secret history of the Okumichi clan, a gift of prophecy the clan members share, and the destiny that awaits them. Six centuries later, her writings are discovered when Emily translates the Autumn Bridge scrolls and sees common threads of her own life woven into these ancient premonitions. The strength of the novel lies in its multitude of appealing and likable characters and the complex interrelationships between them over the centuries and cultures.

Monika Dix

M. Butterfly   David Henry Hwang (1988)

With *M. Butterfly*, DAVID HENRY HWANG achieved a double success: a commercial hit on Broadway and a serious contribution to the awareness of issues affecting the relationship between the West and the Far East. *M. Butterfly* opened at the National Theatre, Washington, D. C., on February 10, 1988, and moved to Broadway within six weeks, debuting at the Eugene O'Neill Theatre on March 20. John Dexter was the director of these productions; the play's early progression onto Broadway reflected the confidence that the producers, Stuart Ostrow and David Geffen, had in the play's potential for theatrical diversion and cerebral stimulation. The play gained commercial success on Broadway for a number of reasons: the spectacular staging called for in Hwang's elaborate stage directions; the comic, innuendo-laden one-liners that are typical in Hwang's work; an extraordinary acting performance by B. D. Wong; the admirable direction of the veteran Dexter; the sumptuousness of Asian costumes; the aural effect of Puccini's opera music; and the direct, straightforward tragedy of the story. The play has also made a lasting impression on Asian-American culture because it attacks Western notions of Orientalism directly and forcefully. The play succeeds as intellectual provocation because of its merciless deconstruction of Asian stereotypes fanned by fantasies such as Puccini's opera, *Madama Butterfly*.

The plot is based very loosely on a scarcely believable real-life story about a minor French diplomat who is jailed for passing national secrets to his Chinese lover, who turns out to be a male spy for the Chinese government. In Hwang's play, set in the 1960s, 30-something Rene Gallimard, who works for the French diplomatic services in Beijing, is transfixed by a Chinese woman singing passages from Giacomo Puccini's 1904 opera,

Madama Butterfly. The woman, Song Liling—played by B. D. Wong on Broadway—tempts Gallimard into an affair. She acts coyly and submissively, reaffirming the Frenchman's lost sense of machismo and vitality—a vitality that has been missing from his dreary, childless marriage to his uninspiring, older wife, Helga, a daughter of a French ambassador. Gallimard believes that he has become another Pinkerton, the American lieutenant character in Puccini's opera who betrays a loyal, meek Japanese geisha, causing her to commit suicide. Flattered and energized, Gallimard falls for Song's act, reveling in his role as the domineering Westerner. The first act ends with Gallimard enjoying an unexpected promotion and enjoying sex with his seemingly submissive Chinese mistress, a "Butterfly" of his own.

In Act 2, it becomes apparent that Song is actually a man using his relationship with Gallimard for the purpose of gathering information about French and American intentions, particularly in Vietnam, where a catastrophic war is imminent. Song is under pressure from Chin, a functionary in the Communist Party, who has contempt for the nature of Song's relationship with the naïve Frenchman. But driven by ideology and submission to the state, Chin insists that Song continue to deceive and flatter the Frenchman who incontinently reveals sensitive information to Song and consequently to China's Communist regime. Chin even provides Song with a baby that Gallimard believes to be his. Gallimard does not suspect these layers of deception because he projects onto Song an assumption that Chinese women are indeed shy and submissive, and that it is usual for them to keep their clothes on during love-making that invariably takes place in the dark. Gallimard's blindness with regard to Song's sex is paralleled by his blindness about Asian politics. Gallimard thinks that militarily, politically, and sexually, "Orientals will always submit to a greater force." These nonsensical, racist, and sexist attitudes cause Gallimard's spectacular downfall. Because of his erroneous assumption that America will conquer Vietnam easily and entirely, and other misjudgments, he is recalled to Paris. In France, his wife leaves him, but Song—after years of hard labor under a Maoist correction scheme—finds him in Paris. Soon, though, the pair are arrested for their involvement in the passing of intelligence information out to China. Song is scheduled to be expelled to China, but Gallimard suffers ferociously. He is jailed and becomes a national laughingstock, as he refuses to acknowledge Song's maleness, even after seeing the anatomical evidence that underlines his folly.

Gallimard has loved a female Song, a female invented in a collaboration between his own fantasies about submissive Asian women and Song's masterly manipulation of Gallimard's sexual drives. Articulate in court, Song tells the judge that Gallimard is a typical Westerner because "The West has sort of an international rape mentality towards the East." Western men want Asian women to be like Madame Butterfly. In his afterword to the published text of the play, Hwang even provides anecdotal evidence of this alleged Western fetish for obedient Eastern women. In the play's stirring climax, Gallimard kills himself, having finally realized that the object of his love was after all a child of his fantasy. Gallimard has been made a fool because his combined misogyny and racism has caused him to be destroyed by a cunning Chinese actor.

David Cronenberg directed a film version of *M. Butterfly,* which was released to commercial and critical success in 1993. The film—the screenplay of which was written by Hwang—should be studied in addition to the original play, because the different genre of film necessitates many changes from the stage version. For example, whereas the narrative of the stage version progresses through flashbacks commented on by the imprisoned Gallimard, the film version moves chronologically. Cronenberg's film retains the play's thesis that Westerners project wrong-headed notions about racial and sexual submission onto Eastern women in a manner damaging to both but relegates this agit-prop to the background of a film that depicts a naturalistic, traditionally Hollywood drama about personalities. There are many minor changes to the plot as well: Gallimard has his "extra-extramarital affair" with a middle-aged Frenchwoman rather than with a young Danish student; Gallimard is berated aggressively by expense-cheating French agents; and there is a scene set in the sumptuous interior of the Paris Opera. Location work is important in the film because of its detailed construction of China during the Cultural Revolution. In the film, but not in the stage play, we see the aggression of Mao's Red Guards; a bonfire that destroys supposedly decadent remnants of bourgeois, pre-Socialist China; the hardships of the Communist labor site endured by Song; and the regime's housing of many families in living quarters once enjoyed by Song alone. The film, then, stresses the pressures faced by Song and indicates more acutely the material dangers that force him to gull Gallimard. Puccini's heroine was a mere geisha, but Hwang's Song is motivated by very real dangers, as well as a righteous insight into the assumptions and prejudices that fire Western men's libidos. In the film, Gallimard commits suicide, not alone but in front of hundreds of fellow French prisoners, thus heightening the elaborateness of the theatrical ritual that Gallimard acts out. For Puccini, such a ritual seemed appropriate for a Japanese geisha; in Hwang's and Cronenberg's visions, however, a ritualized demise is appropriate for Rene Gallimard, a proponent of unseemly Western notions of superiority and political and sexual dominance over the so-called Orient.

Bibliography

De Lauretis, Teresa. "Popular Culture, Public and Private Fantasies: Femininity and Fetishism in David Cronenberg's *M. Butterfly.*" *Signs* 24 (1999): 303–334.

Kondo, Dorinne. *About Face: Performing Race in Fashion and Theater.* New York: Routledge, 1997.

Pao, Angela. "*M. Butterfly* by David Henry Hwang." In *A Resource Guide to Asian American Litrature,* edited by Stephen H. Sumida and Sau-ling Cynthia Wong, 200–208. New York: Modern Language Association of America, 2001.

Wiegmann, Mira. *The Staging and Transformation of Gender Archetypes in* A Midsummer Night's Dream, *and* Kiss of the Spider Woman. Lewiston, N.Y.: Edwin Mellen, 2003.

Kevin De Ornellas

McCunn, Ruthanne Lum   (1947–)

Author and teacher Ruthanne Lum McCunn, known as Roxy Drysdayle when she was growing up, was born in San Francisco, across the street from the Chinatown public library. Born to a Chinese mother and a Scottish-American father and having lived in both Hong Kong and the United States, McCunn's personal identity has been intricately connected with the two cultures, a connection that is reflected in her writing.

McCunn's mother came to San Francisco from Hong Kong to attend the 1939–40 World's Fair and soon found herself unable to leave due to the breakout of World War II. She and McCunn's father, a merchant marine, met and married during the war. When McCunn was one year old, her family decided to move to Hong Kong. For the next five years, McCunn's father was away at sea, while McCunn lived in a Chinese neighborhood with her mother among her mother's extended family. McCunn's first language was Cantonese, and she attended Chinese school and played with neighborhood children, never feeling that she was not Chinese, even though she did not look like the other children. Those years of living in the Chinese neighborhood later became the source of inspiration for her writing. Her novel *The MOON PEARL,* is based on the history of the self-combers movement in southern China, in which women combed their own hair up instead of waiting for marriage, lived in communities of women, and supported themselves by working in the silk industry. McCunn acknowledges the "many spinsters, concubines, widows, and wives" who used to visit her home in Hong Kong when she was young, and who allowed her to listen as they told their stories.

McCunn had her first painful confrontation with her bicultural identity at the age of six. Her father returned home from sea, but McCunn did not recognize him. As a result, her father decided that it was time for her to attend British school. Even though she now looked like her classmates, she did not speak their language. Her classmates at the British school taunted her, calling her a "Ching Chong Chinaman." In the meantime, the children in her neighborhood had also stopped playing with her, for she was now a "white devil foreigner" to them. As McCunn's life became increasingly isolated, she turned to reading and writing for solace.

McCunn's father passed away when McCunn was 15, the same year she graduated from high school. Because prejudice against Amerasians was widespread in Hong Kong at the time, and because it was expensive to attend college there, at age 16 McCunn decided to attend college in the United States. McCunn first moved to Boise, Idaho, to live with her paternal grandmother. Feeling isolated and out of place in an area with only one Chinese family, McCunn moved to San Francisco to live with her mother's American friends in Walnut Creek. McCunn worked odd jobs as she attended Diablo Valley College. After two years, she transferred to the University of California at Berkeley. In 1964, at the end of her junior year, McCunn married Don McCunn in New York, one of the few states that permitted interracial marriage. Today, McCunn credits her mother and her husband as her biggest supporters. To honor her Chinese background, she has kept her mother's maiden name "Lum," acknowledging that everything she writes originates from that source.

By the time McCunn and her husband finally decided to settle in San Francisco for good in 1974, McCunn had been teaching as an English and bilingual teacher in public schools. After working as a teacher for another four years, McCunn left her teaching career and turned to writing full time. Since then she has taught Asian-American literature at Cornell University and the University of California at Santa Cruz for a few terms, but for the most part has dedicated her time to writing.

Writing has been a way for McCunn to channel into her creative works her experiences and feelings of living between two cultures. Although at first she did not intend to write about the Asian-American experience, her own experiences of living with racial prejudice and between two cultures motivated her to explore the themes of Asian-American immigration and survival. Another reason that inspired McCunn to write about the Chinese-American experience in particular was the lack of literature in this genre. McCunn recalled that it was not until she was in her late 20s

that she read any books about Chinese-Americans. McCunn decided to write her first book, *An Illustrated History of the Chinese,* when she was working as a bilingual teacher at a San Francisco junior high school. She wanted to write the book for her students because there was no textbook on Chinese Americans at the time. Since then, the book has been used as a college textbook, which McCunn finds "alarming" because it was intended for readers at a fifth-grade level.

Published in 1981, McCunn's second book, THOUSAND PIECES OF GOLD, was praised by MAXINE HONG KINGSTON, the Chinese-American author who wrote the critically acclaimed *The* WOMAN WARRIOR, as "a valuable book that gives Chinese Americans another true heroine." McCunn's book was adapted into a movie by independent filmmakers Nancy Kelly and Kenji Yamamoto.

McCunn's other published works include *Pie-Biter* (1983), *Sole Survivor* (1985), *Chinese American Portraits: Personal Histories 1828–1988* (1988), *Chinese Proverbs* (1991), WOODEN FISH SONGS (1995), and *The Moon Pearl* (2000). While most of these books are historical fictions with the exceptions of *Chinese American Portraits* and *Chinese Proverbs, Pie-Biter* is believed to be the first children's book that has a Chinese-American folk hero.

In an interview with the *Los Angeles Times,* McCunn said: "Writing forces you to stop and think. It has brought out all sorts of things I have repressed. I have a larger understanding of myself." McCunn's works not only allow her to explore and express her personal feelings but also to serve the Chinese-American community at large. Her books expose an English-speaking audience to the unsung tales and unrecognized contributions of Chinese/Chinese-American heroes and heroines in China and in the United States.

Bibliography

Hong, Terry. "Ruthanne Lum McCunn: Write, Teacher." In *Notable Asian Americans,* edited by Zia Helen and Susan B. Gall, 244–246. Detroit: Gale Research, 1995.

Nan Ma

Meer, Ameena (1964–)

Born in Boston to Indian parents, Ameena Meer grew up in the United States and Great Britain. *Bombay Talkie* (1994) is her only novel to date, but she has also published short stories including "I Want to Give You Devotion," about an Indian guru and ashram leader, and "Mannequin," about a wealthy Indian woman in New York who is about to enter into an arranged marriage. Meer lives in New York City with her three daughters.

Bombay Talkie questions ethnic and national identity, the tradition of arranged marriage, and homosexuality in Indian culture. The narrative focuses on Sabah, a recent college graduate who was born in America but is in conflict between her American and Muslim-Indian identities. Bibi, Sabah's mother, suggests she go to India to visit family and her childhood friend, Rani, who is having a difficult time in her marriage. Sabah thinks if she goes to India, "Maybe she'd be able to find a happy medium between what her parents wanted her to do (the good Indian girl) and what she wanted to do (the bad American girl)" (35).

During the plane ride, Sabah feels no connection with the Indian passengers. She emphasizes a Western persona, so as to not be mistaken as a native Indian woman. In India, her identity crisis is even more pronounced than in America. Sabah confuses the servants for having an Indian appearance but speaking Hindi poorly. Typical daily experiences in India are novel to Sabah, such as the Indian dinner party and palm readings. When she visits Rani, moreover, she learns that Rani's arranged marriage to Hemant is abusive and difficult. Hemant forces his wife to end her successful modeling career, and he is unfaithful to her. But Rani cannot leave the marriage unless she pays his grandfather the $60,000 dowry. Rani is miserable and lives in fear of her husband and his family. In the end, Sabah witnesses a "bride burning." Hemant and Rani enter a verbal altercation, and Hemant douses the room with alcohol and lights a match. Sabah is unable to save Rani's life from the fire.

In another part of the novel, the reader meets Sabah's wealthy uncle Jimmy, "Bombay's best known (lip-synching) singer and movie villain"

(41). Jimmy's son Adam cannot explore his identity as a homosexual while he is home in India, so he joins his boyfriend, Marc, in London. When his father joins him in London, Adam leaves again to find Marc in New York, telling only his sister Alia.

Bombay Talkie interrogates the tradition of arranged marriage from multiple perspectives. As a Westerner, Sabah learns of the common practices and atrocities of Indian marriages. She observes that a prospective wife is considered valuable in terms of her material assets judged by the size of her dowry. To an Indian, however, "Arranged marriages are so much more intelligent. . . . How stupid you Americans are, going around marrying the first person you fall in love with" (115).

Bombay Talkie also examines homosexuality. Adam's clandestine homosexuality drives him further and further away from his family. Concealed homosexuality is also shown as a major cause of Rani's failed marriage. Hemant is seen at a nightclub with an 11-year-old male prostitute, and he travels to have affairs with several other partners. However, he feels he must stay married in order to meet social expectations and to ensure his family's gain of Rani's dowry.

At the end, Sabah returns to the United States and runs into her cousin Adam in New York. The novel thus ends sadly as the two major characters seem unable to find peace with their cultural and sexual identity.

Bibliography

Meer, Ameena. *Bombay Talkie*. London: Serpent's Tail, 1994.

Alissa Appel

Mehta, Ved Parkash (1934–)

Ved Mehta was born in Lahore, India (now in Pakistan). Blinded in early childhood due to meningitis, Mehta completed his early schooling in Bombay at the Dadar School for the blind. At the age of 15, he came to the United States to attend Arkansas State School for the Blind. He got his B.A. in 1956 from Pomona College, California, another B.A. from Oxford University in 1959, and an M.A.

from Harvard University in 1961. He has lived in the United States since 1959 and is a naturalized American citizen.

Best known for his essays and autobiographical writings, Mehta is a prolific writer and has written extensively about India and the United States. He has been a staff writer for the *New Yorker* magazine since 1961 and has written more than 20 books. In *Face to Face* (1957), Mehta illustrates his childhood and the challenges he faced due to blindness. He also details at length his years in Arkansas State School for the Blind. After the triumph of *Face to Face,* he published a novel and many works of nonfiction including *Daddyji* (1972), *Mamaji* (1979), *Vedi* (1982), *The Ledge between the Streams* (1984), and *Sound-Shadows of the New World* (1986). Most of these works are autobiographical in nature and are collectively titled "Continents of Exile." In *Daddyji* and *Mamaji,* Mehta for the most part portrays his parents' lives and the childhood that he spent with them. In *The Ledge between the Streams,* Mehta writes about his youth during the 1940s. He describes at length the day-to-day pains and perils, the growing rift between the Hindus and Muslims, and the violence that overtook India during partition. Although he writes about his adolescence and his coming to terms with blindness, Mehta beautifully weaves the political struggles of his native country in the book. His latest book, *The Red Letter* (2004), which is also the 11th and concluding volume in his "Continents of Exile" series, is about his father's affair with a Nepalese young woman.

Mehta has written a satirical novel, *Delinquent Chacha* (1967), but he is best known for his observations on Indian society and for his autobiographical works that result from his early life in India and later annual trips to India. *Walking the Indian Streets* (1963), *Portrait of India* (1970), *Rajiv Gandhi and Rama's Kingdom* (1994), and *Mahatma Gandhi and his Apostles* (1977) are among his books that deal with his observations on Indian life and some of the well-known Indian figures such as Indira Gandhi, Rajiv Gandhi, and Mahatma Gandhi.

Mehta is also an outstanding essayist. His *Fly and the Fly-Bottle* (1962), *The New Theologians* (1965 collection of essays on European Christian

thinkers), and *The Ved Mehta Reader* (1998 series of essays on subjects as varied as the art of essay writing, and religion, politics, and education) are evidence of his masterly style. All in all, Mehta is an exceptional memoirist, a well-known journalist, an accomplished essayist and writer.

Asma Sayed

Middleman and Other Stories, The
Bharati Mukherjee   (1988)

In this collection of stories, BHARATI MUKHERJEE— a Calcutta-born immigrant to the United States— explores the harsh, violent, tragic, and oftentimes redemptive aspects of the immigrant experience in the later decades of the 20th century. Published to critical acclaim in 1988, *The Middleman and Other Stories* received the National Book Critics Award for Fiction, making Mukherjee the first naturalized U.S. citizen to receive the award and establishing her as a prominent writer and cartographer of an increasingly hybridized and internationalized America. Spanning several continents, shifting between male and female narrators and navigating among numerous cultures, Mukherjee's collection speaks to an increasingly cosmopolitan world, one poised to spring into full-scale globalization after the collapse of the Eastern Bloc, with all of its attendant problems, contradictions, and possibilities.

The 11 stories constituting the collection have their individually distinctive voices and tones, yet underlying their largely dissimilar narrators, plots, and characters remains a pervasive sympathy for the position of the outsider, the transient, the exile, and, more often than not, the immigrant forced to mitigate the demands of largely divergent cultures. In the collection's title story, "The Middleman," the narrator, an Iraqi Jew and naturalized American citizen in exile, serves as an unwitting accomplice and gunrunner for revolutionaries in South America, charting not only the excesses and abuses of the revolutionaries but likewise the corruption of American foreign policy in Central and South America during the 1970s and 1980s. In "A Wife's Story," Panna Bhatt narrates her tightrope walk between immersion in American culture while studying for a Ph.D. in New York and her love for and obligation to her husband when he visits from their home north of Bombay, India. These two stories address quite different concerns, but both demonstrate the author's unwavering interest in the complexity of human relations and the development of full-fledged characters capable of taking action and weighing consequences. Movement is key: While always interested in the middle position of the person caught between obligations, lovers, and cultures, Mukherjee's stories render this tenuous space as constantly in flux, for both better and worse.

In an interesting move, Mukherjee redefines the possibilities for the middle position in "Loose Ends," "Fighting for the Rebound," and "Fathering." The male narrators of these stories are all white Americans forced to re-examine their subject position in light of an American society reshaped and, arguably, driven by the expansion and vivacity of immigrant cultures and the repercussions of neo-imperialist U.S. foreign and economic policy. As the narrator in "Loose Ends," a returned Vietnam veteran and murderer-for-hire, asks: "Where did America go? I want to know. . . . Back when me and my buddies were barricading the front door, who left the back door open?" (48), Mukherjee challenges the reader to arrive at any stable definition of just what "America" is, just what makes an "American." With stories such as "Danny's Girls," the reader knows that such labels must remain expansive enough to cover not only the clichés and rhetoric of patriotism but also the exploitation of immigrants and the working poor, not to mention the thriving market for mail-order brides from Asia.

In "Orbiting," the Italian-American narrator Renata remarks upon the vastly different ways in which one can view America when its cultural logic becomes refracted by the lens of immigrant experience, in this case her Afghani boyfriend Ro: "When I'm with Ro I feel I am looking at America through the wrong end of a telescope. He makes it sound like a police state, with sudden raids, papers, detention centers, deportations, and torture and death waiting in the wings" (66). With *The Middleman and Other Stories,* Mukherjee provides the reader with just such a telescope; however, it is an instrument with both a far reach and markedly sharp focus.

Bibliography

Mukherjee, Bharati. *The Middleman and Other Stories.* New York: Grove Press, 1988.

Zach Weir

Min, Anchee   (1957–)

Born in Shanghai, China, Anchee Min was the oldest of four children. Her parents were both educators: her mother an elementary school teacher and her father an instructor of technical drawing at the Shanghai Textile Institute. In 1967 her parents were accused of being "bourgeois intellectuals" and as a result lost their apartment. By 1971 they had also lost their jobs and had turned to manual labor to support the family.

During the Cultural Revolution of China, Min threw herself wholeheartedly into the dissemination of Maoist thoughts, becoming a leader of the Little Red Guards at her elementary school. A key moment from this period, related painfully by Min in *Red Azalea,* occurred when, in order to show her commitment to the Communist Party, she denounced a favorite teacher as an enemy of Communism.

At the age of 17, Min participated in the massive movement of urban youths into the countryside to work with the peasantry. In 1974 she joined a convoy of young student-workers and moved to a farm near the East China Sea, where she spent the next two years engaged in strenuous farm labor. All of this was part of the Communist Party's plan to overcome divisions between the city and the countryside while instilling the values of manual labor in middle-class students. Min presents a poignant account of these and other experiences during the Cultural Revolution in her highly regarded memoir *Red Azalea* (1994).

In 1976 a talent scout seeking actors for one of Madame Mao's movies spotted Min and brought her to Shanghai to audition for the lead role.

While Min did not win the role, she was granted a part in the film due to her "proletarian looks." The death of Chairman Mao later that year, however, turned Min's world upside down as Madame Mao was arrested and anyone who had even slight affiliations with her, as in Min's case, was subjected to punishment. This meant that her career as an aspiring actress was over, and she returned once again to manual labor at the film studio. Once again this unfortunate series of events would provide rich material upon which Min would later draw in her writing.

The information Min gathered from her discussions with Madame Mao's friends and enemies during her time working at the film studio provided the research materials that allowed Min to write her complex historical fiction about Madame Mao's life, *Becoming Madame Mao.* This controversial work seeks to take the reader beyond the stereotypical, and even patriarchal, accounts of Madame Mao that portray her as the "White Boned Demon" and blame her for the terrible excesses of the Cultural Revolution. Instead Min argues that the responsibility for the terror and deaths that marked the period of the Cultural Revolution lies with Chairman Mao. Given this simple fact, Min asks why Mao is revered as godlike even to this day while his wife is reviled as a demon and temptress.

After eight years of working at the film studio, during which time she contracted tuberculosis, Min left China in 1984, assisted by her friend, the actress Joan Chen. Upon arrival in the United States, Min attended courses at the Art Institute of Chicago, eventually earning an M.F.A. degree. As part of her assignments for an English class, Min wrote essays about her experiences of growing up during the Cultural Revolution. These assignments eventually became her breakthrough book *Red Azalea,* which became a *New York Times* best seller and Notable Book of the Year.

In addition to *Red Azalea* and *Becoming Madame Mao,* Min's books include *Katherine* (1995), a story of an American ESL teacher in China; *Wild Ginger* (2002), a love story set in Shanghai during the Cultural Revolution; and *Empress Orchid* (2003), an account of China's last imperial ruler.

In most of her works, Min provides powerful and insightful accounts of the tragic and conflicting experiences suffered by people, in deeply personal ways, during the tumultuous period of the Cultural Revolution.

Bibliography

Jolly, Margaretta. "Coming Out of the Coming Out Story: Writing Queer Lives." *Sexualities* 4, no. 4 (2001): 474–496.

Xu, Ben. "A Face That Grows into a Mask: A Symptomatic Reading of Anchee Min's *Red Azalea.*" *MELUS* 29, no. 2 (2004): 157–181.

Xu, Wenying. "Agency via Guilt in Anchee Min's *Red Azalea*: A Critical Essay." *MELUS* 25, nos. 3–4 (2000): 203–220.

Jeff Shantz

Mirikitani, Janice   (1941–   )

Janice Mirikitani is the author of four volumes of poetry and editor of many anthologies. Since 1965, as a choreographer and director of services with the Glide Organization, founded by her husband, Cecil, she has directed programs to revitalize the Tenderloin district of San Francisco.

Mirikitani is a third-generation Japanese American whose family was interned with thousands of others during World War II. Her family spent several years in a camp in Arkansas, and among her poems are many that speak to the effects this imprisonment had on Japanese Americans and on her family. Mirikitani's poems often contain violent images as she addresses issues of taboos, incest, the Vietnam War, breaking silence, stereotypes of Asian Americans (especially women), and global events like Hiroshima or the decline of the Innu in Labrador.

Awake in the River (1978) was Mirikitani's first published volume of poetry. The theme of violence, associated with racism and global issues of U.S. imperialism and war, is central to the volume. In "For My Father," the narrator says of her father, "The desert had dried his soul." He forces strawberries to grow from a harsh landscape to sell to white Americans, denying his children even a taste of the red berries they so desire. Such inequalities of American culture are foregrounded in all of Mirikitani's poetry. The Japanese-American experience in the severe desert conditions of some internment camps is the subject of many poems, including "Tule Lake." The Vietnam War, and the atrocities perpetrated there, is explored in poems such as "Loving from Vietnam to Zimbabwe."

As a child, Mirikitani suffered sexual abuse at the hands of family members and was forced to keep silent about those traumatic events. In *Shedding Silence: Poetry and Prose* (1987), which includes 35 poems, some short stories, and a short play entitled "Shedding Silence," physical and emotional abuses of all kinds, along with the continued themes of racism, are the subjects of the work. The first section of the book focuses on racism, the second on the author's marriages (her first to a white man, her second to Cecil Williams, an African American to whom she has been married since the 1960s). Two concluding sections are more political in nature. Mirikitani's method of directly confronting taboo subjects forces readers out of any misconceptions they may have about the ability of poetry to address fiery issues. The book's first poem, "Without Tongue," explores a character who is unable to speak about her father's sexual assaults against her. She buries the knife she has stolen so that she will kill neither him nor herself. The blade of the knife is as silent as her own tongue.

In all her poems, the Japanese-American experience is the focus of her exploration of universal subjects such as assaults on women, children, disenfranchised peoples of all strands, and even the planet itself. Mirikitani's goal is to break the silence that keeps too many victims powerless: She offers a tongue to those who cannot use theirs. "Breaking Silence" focuses on the poet's mother, who, many years after her experience in the internment camps, breaks her silence before a congressional hearing.

In *We, the Dangerous: New and Selected Poems* (1995), Mirikitani continues her protest against the oppression that comes from gender inequality, stereotypes, and violence. The poems in this volume are painful to read, for they vividly capture the violation of body, mind, and soul caused by child rape, racism, and cultural degradation. A frequently anthologized poem, "Recipe" underlines the worthlessness often felt by U.S. minorities. The narrator, a young Asian-American girl, provides instructions that will ensure the creation of round Caucasian eyes from narrow Asian ones. The final instruction, "Do not cry," is especially poignant in that the narrator is willing to withstand physical pain because it is better to conform to the majority dictum of beauty than to be true to the ethnic beauty one may already have.

On March 30, 2000, Mirikitani was appointed as San Francisco's second Poet Laureate. Her inaugural address and other poems that address a wide range of subjects are included in *Love Works,* published in 2002. In an address to the congregation of Glide Church, Mirikitani said that many of the poems in the collection are about "the journey of discovering love." "Obachan's Ozoni," a poem about her grandmother's New Year's Day soup, celebrates the Japanese-American traditions that help anchor the lives of so many immigrants and their descendants. Food continues as a theme in the book, as Mirikitani commemorates a tradition that she and her husband keep: a combination of her favorite Japanese raw fish dishes and his favorite soul food. In "Bad Women," Mirikitani celebrates strong women, mothers, grandmothers, and sisters who unite to heal and help one another. The poem is a paean to the soul-nurturing feasts that these women prepare for their loved ones, even as they are resisting "violent love affairs, child abuse, and unsafe sex."

Because Mirikitani is seeking to break the cycle of violence that is set into motion by the keeping of silence, her tone is often angry and aggressive, and her subject matter harsh and unyielding. As Deirdre Lashgare says, Mirikitani's poetry challenges the reader not only to feel sorrow, rage, and horror at the violence against helpless victims, but to act upon these emotions. Mirikitani's poetry extends its boundaries to the lives of all Americans, not just Asian Americans.

Bibliography

Grotjohn, Robert. "Remapping Internment: A Postcolonial Reading of Mitsuke Yamada, Lawson Fusao

Inada, and Janice Mirikitani." *Western American Literature* 38, no. 3 (Fall 2003): 247–269.

Hong, Grace Kyungwon. "Janice Mirikitani." In *Words Matter: Conversations with Asian American Writers,* edited by King-Kok Cheung, 123–139. Honolulu, Hawaii: University of Hawaii Press, with UCLA Asian American Studies Center, 2000.

Lashgari, Deirdre. "Disrupting the Deadly Stillness: Janice Mirikitani's Poetics of Violence." In *Violence, Silence, and Anger: Women's Writing as Transgression,* edited by Deirdre Lashgari, 291–304. Charlottesville: University Press of Virginia, 1995.

Usui, Masami. "'No Hiding Place, New Speaking Space': Janice Mirikitani's Poetry of Incest and Abuse." *Chu-Shikoku Studies in American Literature* 32 (1996 June): 56–65.

Patricia Kennedy Bostian

Miss Numé of Japan: A Japanese-American Romance
Winnifred Eaton (1899)

The first known novel to be published by an Asian American, *Miss Numé of Japan* chronicles the relationships of two couples, one Japanese and one American, as they fall out of love with one another and in love with members of the other couple in an interracial romance. Central to this drama is Numé Watanabe. Betrothed since early childhood to Orito Takashima, the son of her father's closest friend, Numé has become increasingly unhappy with the match in the long years that Orito has spent pursuing his education in America. Awaiting his return, she meets the dashing young vice counsul of the American Legation in Kyoto, Arthur Sinclair, who becomes infatuated with Numé in return.

Meanwhile, Orito meets Sinclair's fiancée, Cleo Ballard, on the ship bringing them both to Japan for their marriages. Cleo is the archetypal "New Woman" of the 19th century, not unlike the Chinese-Canadian WINNIFRED EATON herself: She is brazen and flirtatious, criticized by her cousin Tom for toying mercilessly with Orito's heart as it becomes increasingly clear that the Japanese man has fallen in love with her.

Rather than allowing this match to succeed, Eaton caters to 19th-century convention by blocking a happy union between Cleo and Orito, while allowing one between Numé and Sinclair. This hesitation to subvert cultural expectation makes *Miss Numé* more cautious than Eaton's later nine novels set in Japan. In subsequent works such as *Heart of Hyacinth* (1903) and *A Japanese Blossom* (1906), for instance, Eaton does portray successful marriages between Caucasian women and Japanese men, but in *Miss Numé,* Orito commits suicide, and Cleo is paired off, unsatisfactorily, with her cousin.

Miss Numé was not only the first novel to be published by Eaton; she also used a false name, Onoto Watanna, that was accompanied by a publicity campaign to make Eaton's fabricated Japanese biography the central selling point of the book. As part of this campaign, articles profiling *Miss Numé* were accompanied by photographs of Eaton in Japanese costume, supplemented with fictional details about her Japanese background. At times, the photographs were not even of her. Yet, as Jean Lee Cole notes in *The Literary Voices of Winnifred Eaton,* this conflation of book and author was a potent fiction because it allowed readers "to indulge in erotic fantasies of possessing a geisha of their very own." By dressing in kimonos, wearing her hair in a Japanese style, and posing in front of Japanese screens, Eaton "reinforced the idea that when readers purchased her books, they were also, in a sense, purchasing *her*" (Cole 27).

Until recently literary critics have been reluctant to embrace Eaton as the first Asian-American novelist, or to accord *Miss Numé* its place within the Asian-American literary canon. "In order to fully understand Eaton's literary contribution," Eve Oishi points out in her introduction to *Miss Numé,* "scholars must first come to terms with the criteria they employ when analyzing ethnic fiction. Do we define this fiction by the author's biological identity? By her cultural identification? By the persona marketed to her audience? By the content and address of the work?" (Eaton xvii–xviii). In short, scholars have simply not known what to do with a woman who lied about her real background in order to sell her books.

Examined from a different perspective, *Miss Numé* can be viewed as a pioneering effort to question racial stereotypes at the turn of the last century. In Eaton's novel, the vivacious blond coquette does not get her man—or any man she loves, for that matter, as she winds up in a loveless marriage. Instead, genuine and lasting love is accorded only to the Japanese heroine. In this way, Eaton reverses the Orientalist trope set by fellow American author John Luther Long in *Madame Butterfly,* the publishing sensation of the previous year. In Long's novel, the American sailor chooses an American wife over the hapless geisha. By contrast, Eaton makes Numé an attractive, fiercely independent character who questions the same clichés that made Japanese women popular in this era. Unlike Butterfly, Numé is remarkable not for her weakness but for her strength. Thus we can condemn Eaton for catering to her market by making this, the first Asian-American novel, a Japanese rather than a Chinese-American romance. Nevertheless, Eaton is to be credited for paving the way for more complex definitions of ethnic heritage and for presenting strong Asian women to her audience as role models and heroines.

Bibliography

Cole, Jean Lee. *The Literary Voices of Winnifred Eaton: Redefining Ethnicity and Authenticity.* New Brunswick, N.J.: Rutgers University Press, 2002.

Eaton, Winnifred. *Miss Numé of Japan: A Japanese-American Romance. With a New Introduction by Eve Oishi.* Baltimore: Johns Hopkins University Press, 1999.

Kay Chubbuck

Mistress of Spices, The
Chitra Banerjee Divakaruni (1997)

A magical fairy tale, *The Mistress of Spices* is a blend of a gender-reversed Beauty and the Beast romance and a bildungsroman of an Indian immigrant in the United States. The unwanted and unattractive protagonist, Tillotama (Tillo), has a hybrid sense of selfhood that fluctuates between Indian and American ideas. By using magic re-alism, Divakaruni bears witness to Tillo's and the other disenfranchised characters' struggles, thereby preventing their lives from collapsing into invisibility. With the added fantastical agency, Tillo is able to construct a hybrid Indian-American self using a central tenet of Hindu philosophy: the evolution of the soul through several reincarnations for fusion with the divine. By undergoing these rebirths in varied bodily forms, the soul is able to learn from its mistakes and refine itself through pain and suffering. As the soul agonizes over its suffering, it recognizes its own culpability and is humbled by its insignificance in the larger cosmic universe.

However, for disenfranchised people, such erasure of the ego-self is politically dangerous. It is this condition of "invisibility" that allows the powerful to maintain their elevated status quo with the powerless. Thus, Tillo is forced to establish an identity that is considered useful, only to erase it in order that her soul might evolve. She must construct an illusory self so as to understand the self as a construct of sociopolitical forces. Divakaruni uses the idea of the evolving self to construct an Indian-American identity for Tillo and includes elements of the Beauty and the Beast romance to bring about her final transformation.

Tillo recounts her many incarnations from the unwanted female child, Nayan Tara, to the goddess of wealth, Bhagyavati, to the professional emotional healer, the Mistress of Spices. Tillo shuts herself within the walls of her exotic Indian grocery store, where aromatic spices work their restorative magic. The store is a safe haven for new immigrants and Tillo helps them unobtrusively; but the store also allows her to meet and fall in love with the rich and sophisticated, but lost and unanchored, Raven. The erasure of Raven's Native American identity haunts him because when he was a child his mother broke all ties with their community in an effort to distance him from the alcoholism and poverty beleaguering their kin. Raven's desire to return to his Native American identity and rekindle its spirituality is made difficult by his lack of knowledge and initiation into its lived culture. Ironically, while Tillo's mother allows her culture to dictate the rejection of her daughter, Raven's mother rejects her culture to protect her son. The unattractive Tillo with no future joins the handsome Raven with no past so that together they may have the present. Eventually, Raven's love for Tillo allows her to emerge from her isolation.

With her newfound strength, Raven ventures out of the safety of her store into the New World of her adopted land on the day it is literally fractured by an earthquake. Raven begs Tillo to discard this fractured world for the safety of the past, but Tillo chooses to straddle the gulf dividing the old and the new worlds. She chooses to extend her healing services to members of the New World and concurrently creates a sense of self in relationship with others through service in America. Tillo's final incarnation into Maya, a strong and beautiful woman, becomes possible through the fusion of her Indian self with her American milieu. Whereas her earlier stages of self-evolvement were all defined by her ability to give to others, her final evolution into Maya reflects her new humility to receive love that has been denied to her all her life.

Bibliography

Vega-Gonzalez, Susana. "Negotiating Boundaries in Divakaruni's *The Mistress of Spices*." *Comparative Literature and Culture* 5, no 2 (June 2003): Available online. URL: http://clcwebjournal.lib. purdue.edu/clcweb03-2/vega-gonzalez03.html. Downloaded on September 23, 2004.

Rajan, Gita. "Chitra Divakaruni's *The Mistress of Spices*." *Meridians: Feminism, Race, Transnationalism* 2, no. 2 (2002): 215–236.

Sukanya B. Senapati

Mochizuki, Ken (1954–)

A third-generation Japanese American, Ken Mochizuki is a Seattle native who holds a B.A. in communications from the University of Washington. Before becoming a writer of books for children and young adults, Mochizuki worked as an actor for five years and as a journalist at Seattle's *International Examiner* and *Northwest Nikkei* for 10 years.

Baseball Saved Us (1993), a picture book illustrated by Dom Lee, is written from the viewpoint of a Japanese-American boy living in an internment camp. The narrator's father sees the need to divert the internees' attention away from the terrible camp conditions, so adults and children work together to construct a baseball field. Although the narrator is not a good player, he improves as time passes, and finally hits a game-winning home run. However, upon returning from the camp, the narrator is shunned by his classmates. When baseball season arrives, he becomes acutely aware that he looks different from the other team members. With the angry crowd shouting out racial slurs, the narrator draws strength from his supportive teammates and hits another home run.

Mochizuki and Lee also collaborated on *Heroes* (1995), dedicated to the 50,000 U.S. soldiers of Asian/Pacific Islander descent who fought in World War II. Whenever young Donnie Okada plays war with his friends, he has to be the bad guy because he looks like "them." Donnie insists that his father and uncle fought for the United States in Europe and Korea, but his friends cannot believe that Asian Americans could have been part of "*our* army." Donnie races home in tears. To pick Donnie up after school the next day, Mr. Okada wears a veteran's cap with numerous medals pinned to it, and Uncle Yosh appears in full uniform with medals that look "like the top of an open crayon box." Uncle Yosh throws a football to Donnie, and the other children, deeply impressed, follow him to the field to play football.

Mochizuki and Lee's most famous effort is *Passage to Freedom: The Sugihara Story* (1997). It tells the tale of Chiune Sugihara, the so-called Japanese Schindler, through the eyes of Sugihara's five-year-old son. While serving as Japanese consul to Lithuania in 1940, the elder Sugihara, acting in defiance of his government, wrote thousands of visas for Polish Jews that enabled them to escape the Nazis. Sugihara tirelessly handwrote visas until he was reassigned, continuing to write even at a hotel and a train station. The consequences of Sugihara's actions, reported in an afterword by Sugihara's real son, Hiroki, consisted of an 18-month internment in a Soviet camp and the revocation of his diplomatic post. The book is dedicated to the Sugihara family and to "all others who place the welfare of others before themselves."

Most recently, Mochizuki has written a novel called *Beacon Hill Boys* (2002). Set in the early 1970s, it tells of the adventures of Dan Inagaki and his high school friends. Dan's problem is that his parents expect him to be the "model minority" and to live up to the image of his perfect older brother. However, Dan is upset that his high school only teaches about the mainstream culture and history, and nothing about the internment camps. Becoming an activist alongside other multicultural students, he demands a class that will discuss the camps, Cesar Chavez, and Wounded Knee. In this novel rich with the slang, pop culture, and music of the '70s, Dan and three Japanese-American friends achieve their own rebellious brand of identity, redefining what it means to be both Asian and cool.

Often dramatizing the conflict between cultures experienced by second- and third-generation immigrants, Mochizuki's works as a whole seek to celebrate heroism, to combat stereotyping, and to eradicate prejudice.

Sandra S. Hughes

Mohanraj, Mary Anne   (1971–   )

Born in Sri Lanka, Mohanraj moved to the United States when she was two years old. She has a bachelor's degree in English from the University of Chicago, an M.F.A. from Mills College, and a doctorate in creative writing from the University of Utah. A professor of South-Asian literature, creative writing and online magazine publishing at Roosevelt University, she has written an Internet erotica book, *Torn Shapes of Desire* (1997), and was the chief editor of two online magazines: the erotica magazine *Clean Sheets*, and the science fiction magazine *Strange Horizons*. In addition to founding and moderating the Internet Erotica Writers' Workshop, Mohanraj has edited two print erotica anthologies, *Aqua Erotica* (2000), and *Wet* (2002), and published two create-your-own erotic fantasy books, *Kathryn in the City* (2003)

and *The Classic Professor* (2003). For her mother as a Christmas gift, she wrote a Sri Lankan cookbook *A Taste of Serendip* (2004). She also wrote *Silence and the Word* (2004) and the mainstream novel-in-stories *Bodies in Motion* (2005). Mohanraj advocates healthy sexuality and portrays strong, consenting women as sexy and desirable and writes erotica with plausible story lines and well-defined characters.

Bodies in Motion is about multiple generations of two immigrant Sri Lankan families whose oldest members travel from Sri Lanka to Britain and then the United States to prove their exceptional brilliance to their colonizers by pursuing higher education in the first world. These characters and their progeny appear and reappear in the stories as Mohanraj nonchalantly mentions their public and professional achievements, while also delving into the intimate details of their private lives. The stories are not so much about what the characters do and achieve, but rather what they think, feel and imagine. In the first story, "Oceans Bright and Wide," the well-meaning Sister Catherine attempts to persuade Thani to send his bright and intelligent daughter, Shanthi, to study at Oxford. Sister Catherine, however, inadvertently reveals her colonial arrogance by asking Thani, "Don't you want the world to know? Don't you want us to know . . . the exceptional heights you people are capable of?" (8). Ironically, Shanthi ends up a frustrated mother of four children, teaching high school, her doctorate degree of little consequence to her, to the post-colonists, or to the first world. This power struggle between the colonizers' and the natives' culture and values, both in the past and in the present, is at the center of most of the stories. In these stories set both in the United States and Sri Lanka, Buddhists and Catholics, Tamils and Sinhalese, parents and children, men and women all battle to live according to their own particular beliefs. They remain in perpetual motion, however, since all their choices, whether they are to live by ancient Sri Lankan traditions or modern American ones, are fraught with problems. In all the stories, Mohanraj remains true to her quest of understanding the private lives and sexuality of people amid the political realities of tradition, modernism, war, violence, colonialism, race, religion, sex and gender.

Sukanya B. Senapati

Mona in the Promised Land
Gish Jen (1996)

GISH JEN's second novel continues the story of the Chang family from *TYPICAL AMERICAN,* but this time through the narration of Ralph and Helen's daughter, Mona. Set in a fictional, Jewish New York suburb called Scarshill in the late 1960s and early 1970s, the story focuses on teenager Mona's conversion to Judaism because, she tells us, "American means being whatever you want, and I happen to pick being Jewish."

While Mona diligently studies Judaism and the Torah despite her mother's disapproving eyes, her sister, Callie, immerses herself in studying her Chinese heritage and the Mandarin language at college. Jen weaves a tumultuous path for both girls. Callie causes a rift with her parents when she abandons her American name for a Chinese name (Kailan), and begins to act, dress, and eat more "Chinese-like" than they ever have. At the end of the novel, however, both girls symbolically return home for a family reunion and Mona's wedding to a Jewish American named Seth. On the wedding day, Mona decides that she, Seth, and their young daughter Io, will change their family name to 'Changowitz' to mark their Chinese-Jewish identity. This juxtaposition between Mona's cross-cultural and supposedly more mainstream path and Callie's "ethnic" path underscores questions about individuals' ability to choose cultural identity, and the resulting questions about authenticity, homogenization and assimilation. Jen is careful to show that neither girl thinks of identity as a cloak or fad that one can superficially change at whim; both girls extensively educate themselves about their chosen 'identities.'

In interviews, Jen frequently defines Americanness as "a preoccupation with identity." In a 1998 interview with *Asian Week,* Jen explains how her view of identity is different from the "very Western view in which somehow you need to resolve the tension between two things, to want things to come to a kind of conclusion." Instead, Jen believes in the idea of "fluidity": just like the idea of yin and yang, sour and sweet, "Opposites don't fight each other, but belong together and intensify each other, and are simply in the nature of the world" (Shiroishi). *Mona in the Promised Land* fulfills this vision as Mona struggles with what it means to be Chinese, American and Jewish, all at the same time. The novel is a coming-of-age story that poignantly addresses how the convergence of multiple identities complicates adolescence and maturity.

Bibliography
Gonzalez, Begoña Simal. "The (Re)Birth of Mona Changowitz: Rituals and Ceremonies of Cultural Conversion and Self-making in *Mona in the Promised Land.*" *MELUS* 26, no. 2 (2001): 225–242.

Lin, Erika T. "Mona on the Phone: The Performative Body and Racial Identity in *Mona in the Promised Land.*" *MELUS* 28, no. 2 (2003): 47–57.

Partridge, Jeffrey F. "Gish Jen's *Mona in the Promised Land.*" Vol. 2, *American Writers: Classics,* edited by Jay Parini, 215–232. New York: Scribner's, 2004.

Shiroishi, Julie. "American as Apple Pie," 27 September 1996, AsianWeek. Available online. URL: http://www.asianweek.com/092796/cover.html. Accessed October 9, 2006.

Wong, Sau-ling Cynthia. "But What in the World Is an Asian American? Culture, Class and Invented Traditions in Gish Jen's *Mona in the Promised Land.*" *EurAmerica: A Journal of European and American Studies* 32, no. 4 (2002): 641–674.

Amy Lillian Manning

Moon Pearl, The
Ruthanne Lum McCunn (2000)

By weaving together history, legends, myths, and songs, RUTHANNE LUM MCCUNN's imaginary tale offers a fictional account of the beginning of the self-combers (*sze saw*) movement in China in the 19th century. In Strongworm, a village in the Sun Duk district of China's Pearl River Delta region, three girls, Mei Ju, Rooster, and Shadow, become close friends at a girls' house where they learn weeping songs among other skills that a girl needs to possess in order to land a profitable marriage arrangement for her family. Learning from the fate of Yun Yun, whose family has been duped into contracting her into an abusive marriage, the three protagonists vow to live a life of freedom and self-reliance. In an era in which a woman's hairstyle determines her status in society—girls have two pigtails, brides require assistance to comb their hair into a bun on their wedding days, and nuns shave their hair—the spinsters create an alternative identity for themselves by combing their own hair into a single long plait, which symbolizes both their maturity and independence. Even though the three protagonists are ostracized by their families and sneered at by other villagers, they are determined to become self-sufficient. By selling their embroideries and planting their own garden, they eventually make enough money to not only support themselves but also help their families. Sneers and jeers of the villagers soon turn into praise and approval as Mei Ju and Shadow use all their savings to pay for an expensive doctor visit when Shadow's brother falls ill. The spinsters become role models for other girls in the village by creating and successfully achieving a life that does not entirely rely on marriage.

In this novel, McCunn explores the theme of individual and collective identity. Like the mythical dragon that chases after the much coveted moon pearl, the spinsters pursue their own dreams of freedom. However, they do not perform this task alone; instead, they form a nurturing and supportive female community to voice their dissent against patriarchal control. For example, when her husband's abuse becomes life-threatening, Yun Yun turns to other women for help. As the girls sing songs of Yun Yun's sorrow, the rural community becomes enraged by the cruelty of Yun Yun's husband and in-laws, and Yun Yun is able to gain better treatment. McCunn shows that a woman's identity is at once individual and communal. Through the formation of female communities, women are able to find a voice for themselves and resist patriarchal domination.

Nan Ma

Mori, Kyoko   (1957–   )

Born in Kobe, Japan, Mori studied as an exchange student in Mesa, Arizona, for one year before leaving Japan at age 16, four years after her mother's suicide. After receiving her B.A. from Rockford College, Illinois, she went on to graduate school, earning a doctorate from the University of Wisconsin, Milwaukee. She was an associate professor of English and writer-in-residence at St. Norbert College in DePere, Wisconsin. She currently serves as a Briggs Copeland lecturer in Creative Writing at Harvard. She has written six works to date, including two young adult novels, a volume of poetry, one novel, a memoir, and a book of essays.

Her first publication was a young adult novel, *Shizuka's Daughter* (1993). The following year, she published a collection of poetry, *Fall Out.* A memoir, *The Dream of Water,* and her second young adult novel, *One Bird,* were both published in 1995. An essay cycle, *Polite Lies: On Being A Woman Caught Between Cultures,* appeared in 1997, and her latest work, an adult novel, is entitled *Stone Field, True Arrow* (2000). Mori is currently at work on a new novel, tentatively entitled *The Glass Ark.*

Mori's work is autobiographical, yet she reworks events in her life creatively in order to explore larger themes including the relationship between life and art, childhood trauma, emotional scars and their effects on later relationships, and the bicultural experience of immigrants in the United States. The latter is treated in greatest detail in *Polite Lies,* in which she examines the relationship between her Japanese cultural heritage and her midwestern life, covering topics such as the role of women, language usage, and body image. She questions from a variety of angles the "advantage" that many believe comes along with being bicultural, but which for her has often made life more complicated. Her work also draws on her background in and knowledge of a variety of art forms including weaving, which figures prominently in *Stone Field, True Arrow.* This novel explores a middle-aged weaver's relationships with her mother and husband as they are influenced by her childhood departure from Japan and separation from her artist father. Similarly, Mori's interest in birding adds texture to that novel as well as to *One Bird,* in which a teenage girl's rehabilitation work with birds helps her cope with the departure of her mother. Mori's prose is uncluttered and precise. Her focus on migration, separation, and movement, however, connects her to, and establishes her affinity with, Asian-American literature and culture.

Jeanne Sokolowski

Mori, Toshio   (1910–1980)

A decade before Toshio Mori's birth, his parents had immigrated to the United States from Otake, Japan, a hamlet just outside of Hiroshima, leaving the care of their two oldest sons to the community until the couple was financially able to support them in the United States, a common practice for Japanese emigrants at the time. Toshio Mori was born in Oakland, California, on the floor of the family-owned bathhouse, making him the first U.S. citizen in the Mori family. This status played an important role in his writing since many of his stories depict the ideological split between immigrant issei adults and their American-born nisei children.

In 1913 Mori's father sold his bathhouse to open a flower nursery. Two years later, the family moved 12 miles south of Oakland to the suburb of San Leandro, the town Mori thought of as home even though he still attended school in Oakland. As a teenager, Mori could not decide whether to become an artist, a Buddhist missionary, a major-league baseball player, or a writer. After reading Sherwood Anderson's *Winesburg, Ohio,* however, he made up his mind and set himself the schedule of writing four hours a day, seven days a week, a daunting task since he worked in the family's nursery business 12 to 16 hours a day as a young adult.

Because he felt that most contemporary writers depicted Japanese Americans as caricatures, Mori strove to undo such stereotypes by placing his realistic stories in magazines geared toward "white" audiences. Although offering encouragement, editors of such periodicals as *Esquire* and *The Saturday Evening Post* rejected his work, thinking that his slice-of-life vignettes about Japanese Americans held little interest for their sophis-

ticated readers. It took Mori six years to place his first published story, "Tomorrow and Today," with a "white" magazine.

As he further honed his craft during the late 1930s, Mori's work began appearing in an increasing number of periodicals. Consequently, Caxton Printers, a small press in Idaho, agreed to publish his first collection of short fiction, *YOKOHAMA, CALIFORNIA,* in early 1942. On the brink of artistic success, however, Mori's career met with bad timing. Because of the Japanese attack on Pearl Harbor and the United States's ensuing involvement in World War II, Caxton Printers shelved Mori's book indefinitely. Moreover, along with 120,000 other Japanese Americans who lived on the country's West Coast, Mori was confined in an internment camp from mid-1942 until the end of the war in 1945. While housed in Utah's Topaz relocation camp, Mori continued to write, finding plenty of new material to invigorate his stories. His work on the camp's newspaper allowed him to master his characteristic minimalist style.

Despite praise from William Saroyan and Lewis Gannett, both the literary establishment and Japanese-American readers ignored *Yokohama, California* upon its publication in 1949. For the next three decades, Mori wrote at night and worked as a florist by day, placing his stories in magazines and anthologies of varying quality. His work did not receive much recognition until such later writers as LAWSON FUSAO INADA and SHAWN WONG, members of the Combined Asian American Resource Project, established his importance as the first Japanese-American short story writer. They encouraged the publication of his second book, *The Chauvinist and Other Stories,* in 1979 and helped to resurrect *Yokohama, California* posthumously during the mid-1980s. In 2000 Heyday Books published *Unfinished Message: Selected Works of Toshio Mori,* which illustrates Mori's growing importance as a forefather of Japanese-American literature.

Bibliography

Barnhart, Sarah Catlin. "Toshio Mori (1910–1980)." *Asian American Novelists: A Bio-Bibliographic Sourcebook,* edited by Emanuel S. Nelson, 243–249. Westport, Conn.: Greenwood, 2000.

Mayer, David R. "The Philosopher in Search of a Voice: Toshio Mori's Japanese-Influenced Narrator." *AALA Journal* 2 (1995): 12–24.

Shawn Holliday

Mukerji, Dhan Gopal   (1890–1936)

Dhan Gopal Mukerji was born into a high-class Brahmin family on July 6, 1890, in the village of Tamluk, near Calcutta in East India. His mother, a deeply religious woman, influenced him to seek a spiritual life that was later reflected in his writings. His older brother, Jadu Gopal, a freedom fighter, initially persuaded Dhan to join India's struggle for freedom, but Jadu's imprisonment caused Dhan to flee from India and British control. He escaped to Japan and then moved to California, working at menial jobs during the daytime and reading voraciously at night. He attended Berkeley and Stanford and earned a graduate degree in comparative literature from Stanford. Sensitive, moral, and intellectual, Dhan worshipped Mohandas Gandhi and had a close relationship with Jawaharlal Nehru. He categorically abhorred violence but throughout his life was suspected of being a radical political activist, causing great humiliation and moral outrage in him.

While at Stanford, Mukerji was recognized as a scholar and interpreter of Indian culture and was highly sought after as a public speaker by American and European audiences. At Stanford he launched a prodigious literary career by publishing two volumes of poetry, *Rajani: Songs of Night* (1916), *Sandhya: Songs of Twilight* (1917), and a musical play, *Layla Majnu* (1917). In the following years he published 25 volumes of poetry, drama, fiction, social commentary, and children's literature, only to commit suicide at the age of 46.

Mukerji was torn between the commercial success of writing children's literature and his personal desire to write about intellectual, ethical, and spiritual issues. The latter was buoyed by his belief that the West could learn spiritual morality from the East while the East could learn scientific rationalism from the West. His need to define a moral code for meaningful human existence enabled him

to excel in children's literature because the naive, uncorrupted voice of children provided the perfect medium for such unambiguous expression. His most popular juvenile works are *Gayneck: The Story of a Pigeon*, which won the Newberry Medal in 1927, and *Ghond: the Hunter* (1928), which was his personal favorite. With a naturalist's eye for detail, Mukerji gives vivid descriptions of the majestic landscape and jungle life in the pristine forests of India. *Gayneck* is a marvelous book about the life of a carrier pigeon, but like Benjamin Hoff's *Tao of Pooh* it is ultimately a simple moral code for people of all ages to practice.

His most famous adult books are *Caste and Outcast* (1923), *My Brother's Face* (1924), and *The Face of Silence* (1926). *Caste and Outcast* is semi-autobiographical, cataloguing the spiritual and intellectual influences on the author and describing his discovery that his purpose in life was to act as India's literary missionary. *My Brother's Face* records the highlights of Mukerji's experiences on his return to India after 14 years of living abroad. *The Face of Silence* expounds Ramakrishna's life and the message of the Vedas about the unity of all religions with one divine spirit behind all creation. Mukerji also dispelled many misunderstandings about India spread through a myopic Western gaze, the most notorious being Katherine Mayo's *Mother India* (1927). In his *A Son of Mother India Answers* (1928), Mukerji carefully exposes Mayo's superficial observations and skewed conclusions.

Sukanya B. Senapati

Mukherjee, Bharati   (1940–   )

Bharati Mukherjee, daughter of Sudhir Lal and Bina Bharrejee Mukherjee, Bengali Hindus of the Brahmin caste, was born in Calcutta on July 27, 1940. Raised in a Bengali household, Mukherjee spoke Bengali at home but also began learning English at a bilingual Protestant school before the end of British rule in India and subsequent partition in 1947. She studied English at the University of Calcutta, receiving her bachelor's degree with honors in 1959. After graduation, she attended graduate school at the University of Baroda, taking an M.A. in ancient Indian culture and English. From there, her father arranged for her to travel to the United States to enter the University of Iowa, where she later earned an M.F.A. in 1963 and a Ph.D. in English in 1969. While in Iowa, Mukherjee began writing fiction in earnest among her midwestern environs and met and married Clark Blaise, a Canadian-born novelist with whom she still resides in San Francisco. The marriage facilitated her subsequent move to Canada and the beginning of her fiction-writing career. However, due to the overt racism she experienced in Canada, where she and her husband lectured at McGill University, Mukherjee convinced Blaise to immigrate with her to the United States. After returning to the United States in 1980, Mukherjee became a naturalized U.S. citizen in 1988, the year that she would publish perhaps her best known and most critically praised work, *The MIDDLEMAN AND OTHER STORIES*. Since its publication, Mukherjee has held an appointment as a distinguished professor at the University of California at Berkeley, in addition to publishing another five books of fiction.

While lecturing at McGill University, Mukherjee published her first novel, *The Tiger's Daughter* (1972), which charts the return of a young Indian woman to her family after studying and living abroad and all of the attendant challenges she faces merging past and present and accounting for her obvious disillusionment with the discrepancy between her memories and the realities she finds. In Mukherjee's own estimation, her first novel "embodies the loneliness I felt but could not acknowledge, even to myself, as I negotiated the no man's land between the country of my past and the continent of my present. Shaped by memory, textured with nostalgia for a class and a culture I had abandoned, this novel quite naturally became an expression of the expatriate consciousness" (Mukherjee 33). Yet, this longing for the return, the longing for a lost home and culture, provides a stark contrast to Mukherjee's later works, notably darker in tone, which refuse to romanticize the experience of the expatriate or exile. As early as her second novel, *Wife* (1975), Mukherjee takes aim at traditionalist notions of culture and oppression, as the protagonist, Dimple Dasgupta, finds that one

or the other, oneself or the avatar of the oppressively dominant culture, must die: Significantly, Dimple kills her husband, not herself.

Mukherjee took a break from writing fiction between the publication of *Wife* and the release of the short-story collection *Darkness* (1985), during which she traveled to India and worked on a number of nonfiction projects including a pseudo-travel memoir, *Days and Nights in Calcutta* (1977), cowritten with her husband. However, with *Darkness,* Mukherjee initiated the phase of her writing for which she is best known, as she takes aim at the immigrant experience in both Canada and the United States, charting the trajectories of her characters with unsentimental honesty. In this phase, she not only revealed the travails and hardships faced by immersion into an oftentimes xenophobic and economically challenging environment but also developed an overriding interest in the possibilities for the immigrant experience. Her optimistic immigrant narratives have drawn the ire of certain critics. As Sharmani Gabriel comments: "One of the chief criticisms made against Mukherjee, especially by US-based India-born critics, is that her optimistic narration of the American saga of immigrant incarnations elides a consideration of the material realities impinging upon Third World immigration, namely the role of race, class and gender in the workings of identity politics in America." Yet, this take on the immigrant experience, somewhat at odds with other contemporary immigrant fiction, has arguably made Mukherjee's work central to academic and popular interest, a point perhaps most significantly demonstrated by the reception of *The Middleman and Other Stories,* which won the 1988 National Book Critics Award for Fiction.

After the publication of *The Middleman,* Mukherjee returned to novel writing, though she did not abandon her interest in the immigrant experience, especially as manifested in the stories of Eastern women. *JASMINE* (1989) deals explicitly with the realities of immigrant women in the United States, as Jyoti/Jasmine/Jase/Jane must mitigate not only economic and cultural uncertainty, but also the violence of constant remaking and constant movement. Arvindra Sant-Wade and Karen Radell argue that an interest to chart the trajectory of immigrant women's constant and necessary remaking and refashioning of the self pervades Mukherjee's later fiction, noting: "[T]he women in Mukherjee's stories are seen deep in this process of being reborn, of refashioning themselves, so deep that they can neither extricate themselves nor reverse the process, nor, once it has begun, would they wish to" (12). Mukherjee's insistence on the agency available to the immigrant to take control of her own fate, a theme echoed even in her historical novel *The Holder of the World* (1993), has encouraged John K. Hoppe to remark: "She is plainly disinterested in the preservation of cultures, the hallowing of tradition, obligations to the past. . . . Rather, her current work forwards a distinction between 'pioneers' and pitiable others for whom attachments to personal and cultural pasts foreclose possibilities" (137).

With *Leave It to Me* (1997), Mukherjee took aim at the 1960s and 1970s American counterculture, as her heroine Debby/Devil/Dee navigates natural disasters, war and the abandonment by, and search for, her parents. *Desirable Daughters* (2002) and *Tree Bride* (2004) reinforce Mukherjee's interest in the precipitous situations that occur when entrenched and vaulted cultural mores and practices come together when East meets West, most notably in marriage. Reviewing *Desirable Daughters,* Ramlal Agarwal writes: "*Desirable Daughters* deals with America and its liberties, individualism and money power and with India and its gods, ghosts, and curious social practices" (87). Juxtaposing cultures and traditions, geographic locations and socioeconomic realities, Mukherjee appears to insist upon the differences among cultures, while remaining skeptical of a blanket multiculturalism that would erase them under the banner of inclusion and hyphenated identity. Mukherjee unequivocally makes such a point, as she writes: "I choose to describe myself on my own terms, as an American, rather than as an Asian-American. . . . Rejecting hyphenation is my refusal to categorize the cultural landscape into a center and its peripheries; it is to demand that the American nation deliver the promises of its dream and its Constitution to all its citizens equally" ("American Dreamer" 34).

Thus considering herself as strictly an "American" writer, Mukherjee forces readers and critics alike to recognize the capaciousness of such a label, to recognize the multiethnic makeup of the nation and the plurality of voices that demand to be heard within its cultural space.

Bibliography

Agarwal, Ramlal. Review of Bharati Mukherjee's *Desirable Daughters. World Literature Today* 77, nos. 3–4 (2003): 86–87.

Fakrul, Alam. *Bharati Mukherjee.* New York: Twayne, 1996.

Gabriel, Sharmani P. "'Between Mosaic and Melting Pot': Negotiating Multiculturalism and Cultural Citizenship in Bharati Mukherjee's Narratives of Diaspora." May 2005. Postcolonial Text 1, no. 2. Available online. URL: http://www.pkp.ubc.ca/pocol/. Downloaded November 19, 2006.

Hoppe, John K. "The Technological Hybrid as Post American: Cross-Cultural Genetics in *Jasmine.*" *MELUS* 24, no. 4 (Winter 1999): 137–156.

Mukherjee, Bharati. "American Dreamer." *Mother Jones* 22, no. 1 (Jan/Feb. 1997): 32–35.

Nelson, Emmanuel S., ed. *Bharati Mukherjee: Critical Perspectives.* New York: Garland, 1993.

Sant-Wade, Arvindra, and Karen Marguerite Radell. "Refashioning the Self: Immigrant Women in Bharati Mukherjee's New World." *Studies in Short Fiction* 29, no. 1 (Winter 1992): 11–17.

Zach Weir

Mura, David   (1952–)

Third-generation Japanese-American poet, creative nonfiction writer, critic, playwright, and performance artist David Mura received a B.A. from Grinnell College, and later an M.F.A. in creative writing from Vermont College. He has taught at the University of Minnesota, St. Olaf College, the Loft, Hamline University and the University of Oregon. He also cofounded and served as director of the Asian American Renaissance, an Asian-American arts organization.

Mura grew up in a primarily Jewish neighborhood in Minnesota away from centers of Asian-

American culture. As in many Japanese-American families, the pain of internment and the urgings of groups like the Japanese American Citizens League caused Mura's family to assimilate by disavowing Japanese cultural heritage and adopting "Americanized" habits. Mura at first identified closely with European culture, refusing to see himself as an ethnic writer. By rediscovering his issei (first-generation Japanese-American) paternal grandfather's history, however, Mura later finds his identity and voice as a Japanese-American man.

In 1984, while working as an arts administrator for the Minnesota Writers-in-the-Schools program, Mura was given a US/Japan Creative Artist Exchange Program fellowship. On returning from Japan, Mura published his first memoir, TURNING JAPANESE: MEMOIRS OF A SANSEI (1991) detailing his experiences in Japan, which won the Oakland PEN Josephine Miles Book Award and was listed among the New York Times Notable Books of the Year.

Mura's second memoir, Where the Body Meets Memory: An Odyssey of Race, Sexuality & Identity (1996), discusses the limitations of his family's assimilation and the loss of familial history. Growing up, Mura is allowed to perform specific roles such as scholar and athlete, but racial difference prevents full access to the privileges of whiteness. The self-hatred generated by the association of beauty, desirability, and power with racial whiteness, coupled with his family's complicity with internment and racism, fuels Mura's early obsessive desire for white women expressed through pornography addiction and sexual promiscuity.

Mura's poetry deals with a broad range of subjects surrounding racial identity and desire. After We Lost Our Way (1989) was selected by Gerald Stern as a winner of the National Poetry Series. The Colors of Desire (1995) deals more specifically with racial and sexual identification through his personal battles with pornography addiction and infidelity. Conscious of recent work in postcolonial studies, Angels for the Burning (2004) is an historical investigation of the web of fatherhood and cultural memory, from immigrant experience in the late 19th century, through internment and assimilation, into contemporary Asian-American experience. Mura has also written and performed in film and stage productions, most notably with African-American writer Alexs Pate in Slowly, This, broadcast on the PBS series Alive TV.

Bibliography

Mura, David. "David Mura." Interview by Lee Rossi. Onthebus 2/3 (1990/91): 263–273.
Xiaojing, Zhou. "David Mura's Poetics of Identity," MELUS 23 (1998): 145–166.

John Pinson

Murayama, Milton A. (1923–)

Author of the ground-breaking ALL I ASKING FOR IS MY BODY (1975), Murayama was born in the coastal town of Lahaina, Maui, to Japanese immigrants from Kyushu, Japan. In the sixth grade, his family relocated upcountry to the Pioneer Mill plantation camp town in Pu'ukoli'i. His childhood experiences would provide the foundation for his novels.

After graduating from Lahainaluna High School in 1941, he enrolled at the University of Hawai'i. However, the bombing of Pearl Harbor on December 7, 1941, prompted him to enlist in the Territorial Guard, where he served briefly until he and other Japanese Americans were summarily discharged. Undeterred by this setback, Murayama volunteered in 1944 for the U.S. Army's Military Intelligence Service, for which he acted as an interpreter in China and India. After World War II, Murayama returned to the University of Hawai'i to earn a double B.A. in English and philosophy in 1947, and later an M.A. in Chinese and Japanese from Columbia University. He worked at the Armed Forces Medical Library in Washington, D.C., from 1952 to 1956, then at the U.S. Customs Office in San Francisco. He currently lives in San Francisco with his wife, Dawn.

Murayama simultaneously completed his master's thesis and a short story, which would subsequently become the first chapter of All I Asking for Is My Body, a novel that follows the struggles of a Japanese-American boy growing up in the Hawaiian plantation system during the interwar years. In 1975 he and his wife founded Supa Press and released the full-length novel, *All I Asking for Is My Body*, to critical acclaim.

Murayama has continued the saga of the Oyama family in *Five Years on a Rock* (1994) and *Plantation Boy* (1998). He has also written three plays; two have been produced by the Kumu Kahua Theatre Company in Honolulu. *Yoshitsune* (1977) premiered in 1982, and Murayama's own adaptation of *All I Asking for Is My Body* premiered in 1999.

Hellen Lee-Keller

My Year of Meats   Ruth L. Ozeki (1998)

RUTH OZEKI's first novel, *My Year of Meats* (1998), tells the story of two very different women from opposite sides of the globe whose lives become entangled due to their involvement in a Japanese television cooking show. Jane Tagaki-Little, a documentary filmmaker, is half-Japanese on her mother's side, but has inherited her Caucasian father's impressive height. At nearly six feet, with spiky dyed hair, she is fiercely independent, irreverent, and adventuresome. She would appear to have little in common with the diminutive and submissive Japanese housewife, Akiko Ueno, who meekly tolerates her loathsome and abusive husband. Yet, in the course of the novel, and over the course of a year, the lives of these two women run in parallel and then intersect, as each resists, and ultimately triumphs over, the racism, sexism, and commercialism that threaten to overwhelm their lives.

When the novel opens, Jane Tagaki-Little is unemployed, behind on the rent, and living in an unheated New York apartment. Naturally, when she gets a sudden call to work on a Japanese television series, *My American Wife!,* she jumps at the chance. Sponsored by the beef export industry, the series is unapologetically promotional, designed to encourage beef consumption in Japan through the portrayal of wholesome American wives offering up their favorite meat recipes on a weekly basis. Yet, despite the limitations inherent in such a project, Jane is confident that she can turn her work to good ends. When she is given free rein to direct the series, she immediately sets out to locate families that disrupt the stereotype of the middle-class, all-

American family: a Mexican-American immigrant family with a recipe for "Beefy Burritos"; a family from Louisiana with a slew of adopted Asian children; and a mixed-race lesbian couple, who happen to be vegetarians. This last choice almost proves too much for Jane's boss, Joichi Ueno, the advertising agency executive overseeing the series. He elicits Jane's promise to make future shows conform to company policy and she acquiesces. But when Jane begins to uncover information on the rampant use of dangerous hormones in cattle farming, she feels she must speak out by producing a damning documentary exposé of the meat industry.

As this narrative unfolds, Ozeki weaves, in a parallel plot, the story of Joichi Ueno's long-suffering wife, Akiko, who becomes empowered in the course of watching the weekly airings of *My American Wife!* Originally compelled to watch the series by her husband, who expects her to cook the meals that appear on the show and then report back to him, Akiko's response to the television series testifies to the power of culture to shape human consciousness. Profoundly moved by the lives she sees on television, particularly the segment on the lesbian couple, Akiko vows to leave her husband, to move to the United States, and to have a child on her own. Her act of quiet determination, in turn, provides Jane with the motivation necessary to complete her documentary, which is eventually picked up by major news programs in America and Japan.

In narrating the lives of these seemingly disparate women, Ozeki is able to cover significant political ground. However, even as Ozeki addresses weighty issues like domestic violence, infertility, and the rampant use of hormones in the cattle farming industry, her novel maintains an upbeat and lively tone. Frequently humorous, and often absurd, Jane's and Akiko's experiences are related as a series of narrative snapshots interspersed with a variety of other texts. Memos and faxes, excerpts from the television script, recipes for dishes like beef fudge, and selections from the 11th-century Chinese classic, the *Pillow Book* of Sei Sh nagon, coalesce into a kaleidoscope of text, resulting in an aesthetic suggestive of the cuts and transitions of film or television.

When *My Year of Meats* first appeared in 1998, critical response was generally enthusiastic. In one positive review in the *Chicago Tribune,* Jane Smiley praised Ozeki for creating "a comical-satirical-farcical-epical-tragical-romantical novel." And one *Newsweek* reviewer promised that *My Year of Meats* would leave readers "hungry for whatever Ozeki cooks up next." While Lise Funderburg suggested in her review for the *New York Times,* that Ozeki's message occasionally threatens to overshadow her fiction, the novel's merging of politics and fiction has brought it to the attention of literary scholars, leading to the publication of several recent critical essays that consider the novel's engagement with current topics such as globalization, transnationalism, and performativity.

Bibliography

Black, Shameem. "Fertile Cosmofeminism: Ruth L. Ozeki and Transnational Reproduction." *Meridians: Feminism, Race, Transnationalism* 5 (2004): 226–256.

Chiu, Monica. "Postnational Globalization and (En)Gendered Meat Production in Ruth L. Ozeki's *My Year of Meats.*" *Lit: Literature, Interpretation, Theory* 12 (April 2001): 99–128.

Cornyetz, Nina. "The Meat Manifesto: Ruth Ozeki's Performative Poetics." *Women and Performance: A Journal of Feminist Theory* 12 (2001): 207–224.

Rachel Ihara

Na, An (?–)

An Na was born in Korea and immigrated to the United States with her parents. Growing up in San Diego, she attended schools that were predominantly white and felt that she was only fully accepted at her Korean church, where all of her friends were of Korean descent. Feeling alienated from American culture and yet too embarrassed to ask questions of her parents or friends, she read authors such as Laura Ingalls Wilder, Judy Blume, and Beverly Cleary to learn about American traditions and culture. Despite her love of books, Na did not originally aspire to be a writer.

Na attended Amherst College and became a middle school English teacher. Na's career change from teacher to writer occurred when she took a children's literature course and realized that she enjoyed the process of writing. Deciding to be a writer, Na attended Vermont College, part of Norwich University, to earn her M.F.A. in children's literature. During her time as a student at Vermont College, Na began writing down her childhood memories with the intention of turning them into a novel. In her M.F.A. program, her advisers and peers workshopped her novel, and by the time she finished her M.F.A., her debut novel, *A Step From Heaven,* was accepted for publication.

Inspired by Sandra Cisneros's *The House on Mango Street,* Na's debut novel is an immigrant story that focuses on Young Ju, a Korean girl whose parents come to "Mi Gook" (the United States) to attain financial success. Despite their initial excitement and hopes, Young Ju and her family quickly realize that America is not heaven and that financial wealth is not forthcoming. A combination of menial jobs, shame, failure, and lack of financial success frustrates Young Ju's father, who becomes increasingly abusive toward his children and wife. After severely beating Young Ju's mother, her father is imprisoned and eventually leaves the family to return to Korea. It is only in his absence that the family can heal and attain financial security. In order to capture the essence of memory, Na conveys specific moments that focus on particular senses, creating a novel of vignettes. As the narrator chronicles her experiences as a young child in Korea and later as a college-bound American, she details the frustration, yearning, and longing of an immigrant. As a child, Young Ju is unclear about her identity and is frustrated by her place in two cultures; only later does she mature enough to realize her place in these two cultures.

Na's novel has been well received. It was a National Book Award Finalist in 2001 and won the American Library Association's Printz Award for teenage literature in 2002. Targeted at young adults, *A Step from Heaven* offers an understanding of the problems immigrants face and evokes empathy from the reader. Na's second novel, WAIT FOR ME (2006), signals the author's bold departure from other Korean-American young adult literature; in it, Na explores issues of interracial romance, family, religion, and sibling rivalry in ways that resist the conventional definitions of what it means to grow up a Korean American in contemporary America.

Bibliography

Choi, Yearn Hong, and Haeng-Ja Kim, eds. *Surfacing Sadness: A Centennial of Korean-American Literature 1903–2003*. Paramus, N.J.: Homa and Sekey Books, 2003.

Na, An. "Interview with Young Adult Author An Na," by Cynthia Leitich Smith. Available online. URL: http://www.cynthialeitichsmith.com/lit-resources/authors/interviews/AnNa.html. Accessed on October 9, 2006.

Tina Powell

Namesake, The   Jhumpa Lahiri (2003)

JHUMPA LAHIRI's first novel following her 2000 Pulitzer Prize–winning short story collection, *INTERPRETER OF MALADIES* (1999), charts the "string of accidents" that have determined the course of Gogol Ganguli's young life, "things for which it was impossible to prepare but which one spent a lifetime looking back at, trying to accept, interpret, comprehend" (286–287). *The Namesake* is a story of one family's desire to belong and to find the means by which to cope with the alienation of exile and the challenge of renegotiating personal and cultural identity in a foreign country.

Named for his Bengali father's favorite Russian author, Nikolai Gogol, Gogol is a first generation Bengali American growing up in a Boston suburb, caught between the oppressive expectations and traditions of his immigrant parents' extended Bengali community, and the seductive appeal of American pop culture, to which he and his younger sister, Sonia, are increasingly drawn. It is Gogol's fate, it seems, to feel like a perennial outsider, never fully belonging to or embracing one cultural identity.

As Gogol matures, he leaves the Ganguli household to study architecture at a university, eventually residing in New York, making a conscious decision to live and work at a distance from his childhood home and his cultural heritage. In order to dissociate himself from his past and reinvent himself, he changes his name to Nikhil, much to the particular dismay of his father for whom the name Gogol holds great significance, owing to his narrow survival of a train accident in West Bengal in his youth and the miraculous role a few pages torn from his beloved volume of Nikolai Gogol's short stories played in saving his life. Gogol's rejection of his name is also a dismissal of his father's traumatic history and the burdens of their complex father-son relationship.

After unfulfilling relationships with American girlfriends, the untimely death of his father, and a failed marriage to a fellow Bengali American who is equally ambivalent about her Indian identity, Gogol finds himself at the age of 32 at a turning point, reflecting on the lives of his parents, their sorrows and sacrifices, and poignantly realizing that, despite their shortcomings and idiosyncrasies, his parents valiantly fashioned a life in a foreign country for their family with a strength and optimism he fears he does not possess himself. Gogol considers with renewed appreciation the events that have shaped him and mourns for the things he has lost, observing regretfully that "[w]ithout people in the world to call him Gogol, no matter how long he himself lives, Gogol Ganguli will, once and for all, vanish from the lips of loved ones, and so, cease to exist" (289).

Lahiri's novel concludes on a somber but hopeful note with Gogol taking up a salvaged volume of Nikolai Gogol's short stories given to him years earlier by his father. He begins to read the first story, "The Overcoat," and in so doing embarks on a journey to retrieve memories of his past, his father, and ultimately himself.

Bibliography

Lahiri, Jhumpa. *The Namesake*. Boston: Houghton Mifflin, 2003.

Dana Hansen

Nampally Road   Meena Alexander (1991)

Set in Hyderabad, India, *Nampally Road* is MEENA ALEXANDER's first novel. It is narrated by Mira Kannadical, an English professor who returns to India after studying in England for four years and getting a Ph.D. on Wordsworth from Nottingham University. She felt distraught and out of place in England and decided to start anew in India. However, the India that Mira returns to is full of unrest and social disorder. She notices the poverty, misery, and pains that go with day-to-day life in India. She questions her values and realizes that what she is teaching and writing is not of much relevance to the people at large. She tries to get more involved with the society while attempting to understand the environment around her. Living on Nampally Road in the house of her landlady Durgabai (Little Mother), she observes Little Mother attending to the downtrodden people of the society. She also comes in contact with Ramu, a leftist intellectual whom she takes as a lover. Her relationship with Ramu makes her politically informed and socially mindful. Shaken by the gang rape of Rameeza Be by police, and the murder of Be's husband, Mira goes to see Rameeza Be and feels bewildered and lost. She questions her own life and the history of the nation. She endeavors to understand her past and formulate her future. She takes part in demonstrations against the chief minister, Limca Gowda, and becomes politically active. In the end, when she learns that Rameeza Be has been brought to Little Mother's house to be nursed, she finds some reconciliation.

Alexander, in *Nampally Road,* centers on various issues including feminism, cultural retention, politics, and history among others. One of the themes of the novels is obviously the portrayal of women's issues in India. By presenting women as mothers, political activists, and victims of a patriarchal society, she is bringing to attention the plight of women in a postcolonial nation. In the so-called decolonized nations, women's lives are still colonized by the patriarchs in their homes and in society at large. She describes Mira's attempts to escape an arranged marriage and her shunning of traditional values. Alexander describes the roads, crowds, shoppers, and the everyday activities on the road with minute details and observations. As Luis H. Francia puts it: "With its restless crowds, cinemas, shops, temples, mango sellers, cobblers, cafes, and bars, Nampally Road becomes a metaphor for contemporary India. Alexander has given us an unsentimental, multifaceted portrait, thankfully remote from that of the British raj." Written in a lyrical narrative style, *Nampally Road* has been received well in the literary world and was named the editor's choice in the *Village Voice* in 1991.

Bibliography

Alexander, Meena. *Nampally Road.* San Francisco: Mercury House, 1991.

Francia, Luis H. Review of *Nampally Road. Village Voice* (March 26, 1991): 74.

Perry, John Oliver. Review of Meena Alexander's *Nampally Road. World Literature Today* 65, no. 2 (1991): 364.

Asma Sayed

Narayan, Kirin   (1959–   )

Novelist and anthropologist Kirin Narayan was born Kirin Contractor in Bombay. Her father, Narayan Ramji Contractor, studied civil engineering at the University of Colorado at Boulder. He met German-American Didi Kinzinger and married her in 1950. Their fourth child, Kirin considers both of her grandmothers to be early role models who taught her to read and instilled in her a flair for storytelling. Writers such as Grace Paley, J. D. Salinger, and R. K. Narayan, meanwhile, became models for her own fiction.

After primary education in India, Kirin Narayan continued her studies in the United States, receiving a doctorate in anthropology from the University of California, Berkeley, in 1987. She teaches anthropology and South Asian studies at the University of Wisconsin. Her first book-length project, *Storytellers, Saints and Scoundrels: Folk Narratives in Hindu Religious Teaching* (1989) emerged from extensive interviews with "Swamiji," a religious teacher from her father's hometown. Narayan argues that "folk narrative is a dominant medium for the expression of Hindu insights"; her collection of Swamiji's stories collectively demonstrates "the Hindu ascetic as simpleton, charlatan, saint, and storyteller." The anthropologist seeks to understand the precise role of storytelling as an ever-changing tool used by religious ascetics for shifting purposes, revealing religious narrative as an adaptive and performative art form. Her concern with folklore extends to subsequent projects, including her coedited collection *Creativity/Anthropology* (1993) and a more recent work, *Mondays on the Dark Side of the Moon* (1997).

Narayan is most widely known for her novel *Love, Stars, and All That* (1994), a comic coming-of-age story largely set in Berkeley and New England. The protagonist, a graduate student named Gita Das, receives an astrologer's prediction that she will meet her true love in March 1984. This sparks a desperate, humorous, and occasionally heartbreaking quest. A sudden marriage to faculty member Norvin Weinstein quickly goes awry, as his fetishization of Asian women leads him to infidelity. Gita, meanwhile, moves to her first job at Whitney College, Vermont, where she will begin to mature as an adult woman. Narayan considers this section a deliberate inversion of the empty "quest narrative" of marriage that fuels so many popular conceptions of romance. Gita will ultimately embark on a relationship with Firoze Ganjifrockwala, an old acquaintance from Berkeley. Firoze himself—and his positioning within the novel—recalls the comic misadventures of Jane Austen. Narayan acknowledges early that he "wasn't exactly a strapping hero, [but] wasn't bad looking either." At the same time, while "hardly bearable on the phone, [he] was unendurable in person." The love between Firoze and Gita speaks, in part, to the protagonist's willingness to give up old, naive notions of "love, stars and all that" and to aim, instead, for a true sense of connection. According to Narayan, Gita "is free from the idea that romantic love will bring her fulfillment, and comes to understand that there are many different shades of love that can enrich life."

Narayan's novel combines academic satire, diasporic bildungsroman, and comedy of manners. It is, at some level, a novel about storytelling; family stories and fairy tales are woven together in Gita's imagination, themselves shifting over time and circumstance and, ultimately, providing her with what she needs to know about life, rather than what she wants to believe. In this sense, the novel reflects Narayan's research; she asserts that her two careers are deeply connected, symbiotically generative, and linked by her "voracious appetite for the well-told story."

Bibliography

Salgado, Minoli. "An Interview with Kirin Narayan." In *Speaking of the Short Story: Interviews with Contemporary Writers,* edited by Farhat Iftekharuddin, Mary Rohrberger and Maurice Lee. 219–228. Jackson: University Press of Mississippi, 1997.

Sharma, Maya M. "Kirin Narayan." In *Asian American Novelists: A Bio-Bibliographical Critical Sourcebook,* edited by Emmanuel S. Nelson, 257–260. Westport, Conn.: Greenwood Press, 2000.

J. Edward Mallot

Narita, Jude   (?–)

Born in the 1950s in Long Beach, California, writer and performer Jude Narita studied acting with Stella Adler in New York and with Lee Strasberg in Los Angeles. In spite of her training, Narita was frustrated by the limited roles and opportunities available to Asian-American women. In the 1980s she decided to remedy this situation by writing and performing her own work that would allow her to explore the Asian woman beyond the limiting stereotypes of dragon lady and lotus flower.

Her 1985 one-woman show *Coming Into Passion/Song for a Sansei* was a huge success, running for two years in the Los Angeles area. In the play, she is a newscaster aware of violence against Asians but unwilling to speak out or do anything about it, preferring to be a model minority American citizen. In her dreams, however, she experiences the violence that had hitherto been distanced by detachment. Among others, she becomes a nisei (second-generation Japanese-American) woman, whose childhood memories are of imprisonment in relocation camps; a prostitute in Saigon during the Vietnam War, thankful for a "good job"; a

Filipino woman being interviewed as a potential mail-order bride; a Japanese child in Hiroshima, running scared as the bombs drop. In the process, she finds herself as a sansei Japanese American, able to address her own past and to identify with members of other contemporary Asian-American communities.

In *Stories Waiting to Be Told,* Narita performs plural Asian-American identities—as Japanese, Chinese, Korean, and Cambodian women. Included among the issues addressed by these depictions of the immigrant and postimmigrant generations of Asian women living in America is the trauma of internment camps on Japanese Americans. In this play, Narita plays a daughter who catches a glimpse of her mother's psychic wounds from the camp. The daughter does not see a victim but a woman of great strength. The play also portrays a lesbian coming to terms with her sexual and ethnic identity as well as with the conflicting demands made by her community.

In *Celebrate Me Home,* Narita exposes racism perpetuated in thoughtless media images and in cultural stereotypes. This one-woman show uses comedy to address the serious issue of how to develop self-worth and pride in one's identity amid the limiting stereotypes and limited representation of Asian women (less than 1 percent) in American media and other cultural productions.

Narita takes on the media again in *Walk the Mountain* (directed by her daughter Darling Narita), focusing on the effects of the Vietnam War on women in Vietnam and Cambodia. In this play, Narita's broad project is clearly to humanize "the faceless enemy" of the United States during the war and to reveal the effects of the misinformation provided to the public by the U.S. media and Hollywood. Narita's performances are usually minimal productions, but *Walk the Mountain* shows slides of burned victims of napalm, the bombing of villages, sobering statistics, and provocative quotes.

The production of *With Darkness Behind Us, Daylight Has Come* was originally funded by the California Civil Liberties Public Education Program (CCLPEP) and the Los Angeles Cultural Affairs Department to broaden awareness of the history of Japanese Americans before, during, and

in the wake of World War II. Again Narita uses actual archival footage of the internment camp at Heart Mountain and photographs of the camp and of families in it as the backdrop to this play about the effects of internment on three generations of Japanese-American women.

Beverley Curran

Native Speaker   Chang-rae Lee (1995)

For Henry Park, the Korean-American protagonist of CHANG-RAE LEE's *Native Speaker,* identity is a central concern. His estranged wife, Lelia, labels him as a "surreptitious, B+ student of life, . . . illegal alien, emotional alien," but Henry resists clear identification, claiming that he "could be anyone, perhaps several anyones at once." This protean sense of self serves him well in his job of private investigator, in which he invents detailed personae for himself as he uncovers the personalities and motivations of his subjects. Assigned to report on a city councilman and mayoral candidate, John Kwang, who shares the same ethnic background, Henry confronts issues of identity through the lens of language in what he calls the second Babel, New York City.

Henry and his family come to New York when he is an infant. His father starts a citywide chain of grocery stores, becoming successful enough to leave Queens for the suburbs, but he still considers his job shameful because in Korea he had been trained as an industrial engineer. Henry's mother dies when he is 10 and she is replaced by a silent, anonymous Korean woman called Ahjuhma, or "aunt." As the narrative moves the Park family into the next generation, Henry marries Lelia, a WASPy speech therapist whom Henry's father loves but Ahjuhma cannot tolerate, and the two of them have a son, Mitt, who dies in an accident on his seventh birthday. The death causes tension between Henry and Lelia; she cannot hide her emotions, while he is too good at concealing his.

Henry is also on probation at work, paradoxically for becoming too personally involved on his last assignment: to infiltrate the political office of John Kwang. Kwang asks Henry to coordinate

Kwang's *ggeh*, a Korean-style private bank that pays interest to its members on a revolving basis. After a series of disasters, Kwang's mayoral campaign implodes, and the undocumented immigrants on the *ggeh* roster that Henry has turned over are taken into custody by the Immigration and Naturalization Service. In the end Henry leaves his job and finds resolution by helping Lelia teach her speech therapy classes. His job as a spy allowed him to distance himself from others, but his work with Lelia and her students shows that he is willing to connect with others and finally confront his problems.

Language is at the heart of the struggle for identity in *Native Speaker*. As an identity marker, it is used for prestige, as a weapon or as a shield in an ethnically diverse society. Ultimately, it is his language that marks Henry as foreign: although he speaks English quite well, his attentiveness to sounds and careful pronunciation keep him from perfect fluency. Identity in *Native Speaker* is conceived both racially and in broader terms. Henry's marriage to Lelia and the birth of their son raise questions of relationships in mixed-race families, while Kwang attempts to gain the support of various ethnic groups and to transcend the limiting designation of "ethnic politician." In Henry's work as a spy, he is always Asian American, but under that racial umbrella he devises a number of identities, creating and embodying diverse traits under various names, often blurring boundaries by using his real name but lying about his occupation, or by permeating an invented personality with details from his real life.

Native Speaker established Chang-rae Lee as an important young novelist. The book, his first, received a number of prizes including the Hemingway Foundation/PEN Award, and has been compared to a number of canonical American works such as Walt Whitman's *Leaves of Grass* and Ralph Ellison's *Invisible Man*.

Bibliography

Chen, Tina. "Impersonation and Other Disappearing Acts in *Native Speaker* by Chang-rae Lee." *MFS: Modern Fiction Studies* 48, no. 3 (2002 Fall): 637–667.

Dwyer, June. "Speaking and Listening: The Immigrant as Spy Who Comes in from the Cold." In *The Immigrant Experience in North American Literature: Carving Out a Niche*, edited by Katherine B. Payant and Toby Rose, 73–82. Westport, Conn.: Greenwood, 1999.

Lee, Rachel C. "Reading Contests and Contesting Reading: Chang-rae Lee's *Native Speaker* and Ethnic New York." *MELUS: The Journal of the Society for the Study of the Multi-Ethnic Literature of the United States* 29, nos. 3–4 (Fall–Winter 2004): 341–352.

Song, Min Hyoung. "A Diasporic Future? *Native Speaker* and Historical Trauma." *Lit: Literature Interpretation Theory* 12, no. 1 (April 2001): 79–98.

Jaime Cleland

Necessary Roughness   Marie G. Lee (1996)

Chan Kim, the protagonist of Lee's fourth novel, likes living in multicultural Los Angeles but his traditional Korean father thinks it is becoming too dangerous for merchants. His father moves the family to Iron River, Minnesota, a tiny town where they are the only Asian-American family. Unused to a community as homogenous as this "whiteout" and the racist remarks of their "beyond California blond" (40) classmates, Chan and his twin sister, Young, comfort each other as they adapt to their new environment. Chan is invited to join the varsity football team when their kicker is injured and is immediately liked by Coach Thorson and Mikko, the junior quarterback. The other teammates, however, are not as friendly; they call him "chink" and attack him in the locker room, but he does not tell anyone. Further complicating Chan's life is his turbulent relationship with his father, whose high expectations and stubborn narrow-mindedness make Chan's life unbearable. Young helps Chan deal with various issues, but even she is taken from him in a twisted turn of events. After his sister's death, Chan finally opens up to Coach Thorson, who makes sure the boy responsible for Chan's locker room attack is punished. Chan's uncomfortable relationship with his father escalates in intensity as Chan continues to fail to please him, but they share a moment of peace after Young's death. For the first time, the father comes to watch his son play football at the state championship game.

In a narrative as cleverly strategic as a football play, Lee steadily builds Chan's frustration with his bigoted teammates and narrow-minded father, investigating the issues of racial tolerance and intergenerational miscommunication and expectations. Lee uses Coach Thorson to contrast with Chan's father's inability to be the father that Chan desires, and this is most evident in the way Chan reacts whenever the coach puts his hand on Chan's shoulder and calls him "son." However, Chan's father regains his rightful place when they reconcile and he shows up for his son's state championship game.

It is ironic that so much violence befalls the Kim family after they leave Los Angeles for a safer life. However, all the events of the novel seem to lead to the ultimate reconciliation and mutual respect between Chan and his father. The novel suggests that perhaps the pervasive roughness that has infiltrated so many aspects of Chan's life is not so unnecessary after all.

Bibliography

Lee, Marie G. *Necessary Roughness.* New York: HarperCollins, 1996.

Sarah Park

Ng, Fae Myenne (1957–)

Born to Chinese immigrant parents, Ng grew up in San Francisco's Chinatown, spoke Cantonese, and attended the Cumberland Presbyterian Chinese school, the University of California, Berkeley, and the Columbia University School of Arts. It took Ng a decade to write her debut novel, *Bone* (1993), which won her the Pushcart Prize and a National Endowment for the Arts Award.

Bone tells the story of a family trying to find reasons for the suicide of the middle daughter, Ona. The search for answers reveals many secrets to the family's identity as both Chinese immigrants and Chinese Americans. Leila, the oldest daughter, is the product of the mother's first marriage. Abandoned by her first husband before her daughter's birth, the mother marries Leon Leong, a merchant seaman, with whom she has two more daughters, Ona and Nina.

The narrator is the oldest daughter, who works as a community relations officer at a Chinese-American school. As Leila narrates the story, we view the events that lead up to, and follow, the suicide of Ona. Though none of the family members understands Ona's reason to kill herself, they all accept blame for her death. Her mother worries that she has brought destruction upon the family because of her poor decisions in choosing men: her first husband, who abandoned her, and her boss Tommie Hong, with whom she had an illicit affair. Leong, who immigrated with false papers pretending to be a son to an old Chinese immigrant already in the U.S., believes that his failure to return his "paper" father's bones to China has resulted in Ona's suicide. Leila blames herself for failing to notice her half-sister Ona's pain. Nina, the only daughter to have left Chinatown to make a life for herself, blames everyone.

Intertwined with the search for the meaning behind Ona's suicide is the search for meaning in the family members' own lives. Born in America, attending American schools, absorbing American culture, Leila embraces individualism but wants to preserve the Chinatown culture in which she grew up. She dismisses those who are "too Chinese" or "too American." She rejects her parents' values when she perceives them as being too stereotypically Chinese; yet she also rejects her sister, Nina, who has moved to New York and is too quick to embrace American culture. Throughout *Bone,* Leila also relates the family's pursuit of the American dream, a dream that is altered beyond recognition as the Leong household faces harsh realities of immigrant life and tries to negotiate between American and Chinese cultures. In her family, Buddhism is merged with Christianity, and the capitalism of the entrepreneurial Leon is contrasted with the working class realties of his minimum-wage jobs.

Patricia Kennedy Bostian

Ngor, Haing   (ca. 1947–1996)

Born in Samrong Young, a village south of Phnom Penh, Cambodia, Ngor earned a medical degree from the national university in Phnom Penh and worked as a doctor in the government's military hospital. On April 17, 1975, he was operating on a wounded soldier when Khmer Rouge soldiers burst into the operating room ordering immediate evacuation. Ngor and staff fled the hospital and joined other Cambodians in a mass exodus to the countryside, where he later joined his wife and family.

Ngor and his schoolteacher wife, Huoy Chang, hid their identities by telling authorities he was a taxi driver and his wife a street vendor. He was interrogated about his past, tortured, and imprisoned three times by the Khmer Rouge. In 1976 his father was executed for stealing rice crumbs. In 1978 Ngor helplessly watched his wife die in childbirth, unable to intervene medically for fear of revealing his past identity. When the Vietnamese invaded Cambodia in 1979, Ngor fled to a refugee camp at the Thailand border. He arrived in the United States in 1980.

Ngor was active in the Cambodian refugee community in the United States and abroad. In 1984 he relived some of his Khmer Rouge experiences in his portrayal of Dith Pran, a Cambodian translator for Sydney H. Schanberg, a correspondent for the *New York Times*, in the movie *The Killing Fields*. In 1985 the role earned him an Academy Award, the Golden Globe, and several British Academy Awards, catapulting his acting career. Nevertheless, Ngor claimed that his greatest acting role was convincing the Khmer Rouge authorities that he was not a doctor. Using his newfound celebrity status, he cofounded groups devoted to helping international refugees. Ngor was also vocal in speaking out against the Khmer Rouge, some of whom remained in power in Cambodia. In 1996 he was shot to death outside his Los Angeles apartment by three Asian gang members. Some speculated the murder was politically motivated.

An important part of his legacy is his autobiography, *Haing Ngor: A Cambodian Odyssey* (1987), cowritten by Roger Warner, whom Ngor met in a refugee camp in 1980. One of the early Cambodian-American literary works written in the mid 1980s, the autobiography details Ngor's experiences under the Khmer Rouge regime. As a survivor's tale, the book testifies to the atrocities committed by the Khmer Rouge and bears witness to the suffering of the Cambodian people under the regime. *Haing Ngor: A Cambodian Odyssey* has been revised for several editions and adapted into plays performed in Cambodian-American communities across the United States. *Surviving The Killing Fields* is an audio-cassette publication.

Bunkong Tuon

Nieh, Hualing (Hualing Nieh Engle, Nie Hualing) (1925–)

Born in Hubei, China, Nieh lived her formative years through the unremitting Nationalist-Communist strife and the Japanese invasion and occupation of China (1937–45). In 1949 she fled with her family to Taiwan on the eve of the Communist victory. From 1949 to 1960, Nieh was the literary editor of a dissident publication in Taiwan, *The Free China Fortnightly,* which was forced to close down due to the Nationalist "White Terror." In 1964 Nieh went to the University of Iowa as a visiting artist. She has lived since in the United States and married Paul Engle, an American poet, in 1971. In her recently published memoir, *San Sheng San Shi (Three Lives)* (2004), Nieh chronicles her life in China, Taiwan, and the United States and projects sensibilities representative of the Chinese diaspora: She is a tree with "roots in China, trunk in Taiwan, and branches and leaves in the United States."

Nieh is the author of more than 20 books. Her novels, short stories, and essays are written in Chinese, some of which have been translated into other languages and anthologized. Nieh is also actively engaged in sharing literature between East and West. She wrote in English *Shen Ts'ung-wen* (1972), a critical biography of a renowned modern Chinese writer and research scholar of cultural relics. Her translations include works from English into Chinese and from Chinese into English. Among the latter category is *The Poetry of Mao Tse-tung* (with Paul Engle, 1973). Nieh is also the editor of *Literature of the Hundred Flowers* (1981), a two-volume selection and translation of the history, criticism, fiction, and poetry of 20th-century Chinese literature.

In 1967 she launched with Paul Engle the International Writing Program at the University of Iowa. For her distinguished contributions to cultural exchange, Nieh was nominated with Paul Engle for the Nobel Peace Prize in 1976, received the Award for Distinguished Service to the Arts from the Governors of the Fifty States in 1982, and also received awards from the governments of Hungary and Poland.

Narrated by a Chinese woman who suffers from schizophrenia, the full English translation of *Mulberry and Peach: Two Women of China* (1988) begins in 1945 in war-torn China when Mulberry is 16 and ends in 1970 in the United States when Mulberry becomes Peach, a totally opposite personality. The novel is divided into four parts, with each part opening with a letter to the U.S. immigration service written by Peach, an illegal alien, and closing with an excerpt from Mulberry's diary. Each excerpt of Mulberry's diary is set in a time and place saturated with historical significance: Part 1 (1945) details a journey on the Yangtze River to Chongkqing close to the end of the Japanese invasion and World War II; Part 2 (1948–49) addresses the besieged Beijing on the eve of the Communists' victory over the Nationalists; Part 3 (1957–59) takes place in an attic room in Taipei ruled by the Nationalist Party with an iron fist; Part 4 (1969–70) portrays the United States mired in the cold war and the Vietnam War. Written in a style of modernist stream-of-consciousness and postmodern pastiche, *Mulberry and Peach* is rich in allusions and images drawn from culture and classics, both Chinese and Western, and involves a diversity of themes. Among others, they consist of the struggle between a traditional society and modern colonizing powers, political turmoil, forced exile, immigration and displacement, schizophrenia, identity transformation, and the inscription of the female body with the ideologies of patriarchy and nation.

Yan Ying

Nigam, Sanjay   (?–   )

Born in India and raised in Arizona, Sanjay Nigam spent summers of his childhood with his grandparents in Delhi. A physician and medical researcher, Nigam read voraciously to relax from the demands of medical school and wrote fiction while working as a medical researcher. His works have appeared in *Story, Grand Street,* and *The Kenyon Review,* and he has been chosen by *Utne Reader* as "one of ten writers changing the face of American fiction." A sensitive and intellectual writer, Nigam sets his books both in India and the United States and writes in a distinctively different voice in each of his books. With precision, he delineates the interior landscape of Indian immigrants' surprises, compromises, and losses as they shape and shift identities, adapting to their new country without culturally abandoning their ancestral world. Fashioning identities with cultural markers of both countries, his immigrants find themselves alienated sojourners in familiar landscapes, rendered surreal by their ever-shifting consciousness.

The Non-Resident Indian and Other Stories (1996) explores the perpetual in-between world of immigrants. Deploying Indian mythical figures as frame stories in the prologue and epilogue, Nigam articulates the anguish of uncertainty and the alienation of non-resident Indians (NRIs). In the prologue is the mortal *Trishanku,* punished for entering the abode of gods, eternally stuck between heaven and earth, a spectator of souls journeying to their destinations. In the epilogue is *Ghatotkacha,* half-monster and half-human, contemplating his problematic relationship with his father, the mythical and powerful *Bhima,* again a spectator of the *Mahabharata* war, his compensation for checking his boundless power. These in-between abodes of Trishanku and the hybrid state of *Ghatotkacha* are Nigam's metaphors for the immigrant experience. The immigrants in these short stories range from doctors in "Charming," who fancy themselves descendants of kings, to math professors in "Numbers" who despite their "mathemagical" abilities cannot compute simple verbal tasks and taxes. They find their new world so unreal that they slip into either fantasy or paralysis, rendering their special talents impotent. But no matter how much their lives are in limbo, or how divided their sensibilities and allegiances are, they are dignified and noble in their search for meaning and acceptance in both worlds, even without any sense of belonging in either world.

The Snake Charmer (1998) is set in India and delves into a variety of themes, through the life, work, and art of the illiterate snake charmer, Sonalal. The novel opens at the pinnacle of artistic perfection when Sonalal plays a perfect note on his *been,* but he pays a price for such art: his beloved snake, Raju, bites him. Sonalal in fury bites the snake back. With the snake dead, this strange vengeance brings Sonalal fame and fortune, but ravaged with sorrow and impotent with guilt, he seeks out quacks, prostitutes, mad scientists and psychiatrists. Finding no cure, he returns to his village in search of a new snake and confronts Raju's widow, Rani. He wishes for an end to his pitiful, miserable life, but as he looks into Rani's eyes, he sees "the pain of all living things" (186). Finding forgiveness where he had expected vengeance, he returns to his profession with renewed vigor. When history repeats itself and the new snake bites him, with Herculean effort he refrains from biting the snake back. The novel exceeds its quaint and exotic plot by defining the nature of artistic perfection, the meaning of love, and the significance of life for even impoverished humans. It also explores the healing power of forgiving oneself and giving oneself second chances. Sonalal makes perfect music, finds love in all the wrong and right places, and understands his responsibility to his family and his art, all bound together with the gossamer dream of a perfect note.

Transplanted Man (2002) makes visible the behind-the-scene workings of the medical profession. A hospital in the middle of Little India in Manhattan attracts the best immigrants in the field, from dedicated researchers and brilliant clinicians to ward assistants, roller-coasting toward fantastic dreams. As the sanitized, taciturn professionals race through sleep-deprived frenzies to save lives, they get embroiled in the personal lives of their patients. Poised between "hypokinetic man," a catatonic, homeless man immobile as a statue, and "transplanted man," a popular Indian politician touting diversity through multiple organ transplants, is the brilliant resident, Sonny, trying to save lives both in and outside the hospital. As the neo-imperialist forces of globalization churn immigrants into sleepwalking zombies, the degrees of loss of their native identities are carefully calibrated. The precariously built identity of the immigrant accused of too much ethnicity in the United States and too little ethnicity in the homeland becomes unhinged at night as Sonny sleepwalks, exposing unnamed psychological vulnerabilities and illnesses that are by-products of immigration. The immigrant compelled to erase his/her ethnicity to fit into the new culture is thus seen as existing in a state of somnambulance. Assimilation requires the erasure of native memory, and this unconscious process exposes the immigrants' particular vulnerabilities as is revealed by Sonny's near misses with hurtling vehicles during his unconscious nightly sojourns. Thus, Nigam in all his works deftly captures facets of human consciousness, especially the vulnerable facets of the immigrant consciousness.

Bibliography
Nigam, Sanjay. *The Snake Charmer.* New York: William Morrow, 1998.

Sukanya B. Senapati

19 Varieties of Gazelle
Naomi Shihab Nye (2002)
A finalist for the National Book Award, NAOMI SHIHAB NYE's *19 Varieties of Gazelle* was writtten in response to the events that transpired in the United States on September 11, 2001. This collection of 60 new poems opens with an introduction by the author, who writes about her early life and reflects upon her desire to connect in some way to her father's family in the Middle East. The events of 9/11 hampered the efforts made by those who wished to engage in cross-cultural understanding, and Nye's book of poems introduces the Middle East in such a way as to assure the reader that her Middle East is not the Middle East of violence.

The poems portray diverse Middle Eastern characters whose voices are rich in tradition and culture, and Nye explores such topics as death, violence, the planting of a fig tree, peace, and pain. The poem "Arabic" begins by underlining cross-cultural understanding of the sufferings of Arabs. In the end, however, their pain is the threshold that connects humanity. Simple things also permeate Nye's book. In "Olive Jar," a simple fruit, the olive, becomes the focal point of the poet's depiction of an experience between the speaker and an Israeli border-crossing guard. The olive branch is a symbol of peace, and its fruit, by extension, is used in this poem as a gesture or offering of peace between the guard and the speaker. The poem also testifies to the strength of family despite the tension at the border. The speaker, after being questioned if there will be communication between family members, relates how the family will share stories, food, and laughter.

Nye's poetry creates no boundaries. Instead, it seeks to erase those made by various cultures and to explain how cultures are more similar than might be expected. Ultimately, the first stanza in "Jerusalem" makes the author's position very clear: "I'm not interested in/ who suffered the most./ I'm interested in/ getting over it."

Anne Marie Fowler

Nishikawa, Lane   (1956–   )

Born in Wahiawa, Hawaii, third-generation Japanese-American Nishikawa is a well-respected performance artist and playwright. His most significant works include his 1996 play *The Gate of Heaven* (cowritten with fellow actor Victor Talmadge), and his trilogy of one-man performance pieces about Asian-American masculinity: *Life in the Fast Lane* (1981), *I'm on a Mission from Buddha* (1990), and *Mifune and Me* (1999). Nishikawa grew up in Hawaii, San Diego, and San Francisco. He attended San Francisco State University, where he met budding theater director Marc Hayashi. Beginning in the early 1970s and throughout the next three decades, Hayashi and Nishikawa would develop a solid artistic collaboration, with Hayashi directing Nishikawa in several plays for the Asian American Theater Company (AATC). The AATC,

founded by playwright FRANK CHIN in 1973, offered Nishikawa many opportunities as an actor and director. In the early 1980s, when Asian-American theater began to approach critical mass led by the work of Chin, PHILIP KAN GOTANDA, and DAVID HENRY HWANG, Nishikawa wrote and acted in *Life in the Fast Lane.* In the play, produced by AATC, Nishikawa critiques stereotypes of Asian men and examines the struggles of Asian-American actors—two themes that he would return to in his follow-up performance piece, *I'm on a Mission from Buddha.* In both plays, Nishikawa attempts to recuperate lost chapters of Japanese-American history, especially vis-à-vis the World War II internment camps. In 1986 Nishikawa became the artistic director of AATC, where he mentored a new generation of Asian-American playwrights that included JEANNIE BARROGA and Cherylene Lee. In 1996, Nishikawa staged his play *The Gate of Heaven* at the Old Globe Theater in San Diego, California. Set in the aftermath of World War II, the play explores the historical contributions of Japanese Americans as members of the 442nd Battalion. Focusing on two friends, one a heroic soldier of Japanese descent and the other a Dachau Holocaust survivor, the play examines their attempts to negotiate the lingering after-effects of the war, including the post-traumatic stress syndrome suffered by both soldiers and survivors. As the play moves forward in time, beginning in 1945 and moving all the way to the present, Nishikawa questions the cost of sacrificing cultural identity for the sake of patriotism, demonstrating how soldiers struggled with prejudice on their return home. Nishikawa acted in the play, along with Talmadge, with playwright Hwang serving as dramaturge. In 1994 Nishikawa wrote and acted in the final piece of his trilogy, *Mifune and Me.* Inspired by the life of Japanese actor Toshiro Mifune, the play examines representations of Asian masculinity in the media, politicizing the work of such actors as Mifune, Bruce Lee, and Chow Yun Fat. Aside from his contributions as a theater artist, Nishikawa has worked in both studio and independent films. Nishikawa played a role in such Hollywood films as Wayne Wang's *Eat a Bowl of Tea* (1989), and John Carpenter's *Village of the Damned* (1995). Nishikawa has also written, directed, and acted in several independent films including *Forgotten Valor* (2001), costarring Soon-Tek Oh, and *Only the Brave* (2005), where he appeared opposite Tamlyn Tomita and Jason Scott Lee.

Samuel Park

Noguchi, Yone (Yonejiro)   (1875–1947)

Noguchi was born to a merchant family in Tsushima on the outskirts of Nagoya, Japan. Early on, Noguchi opted out of the traditional educational system but succeeded in being admitted to Keio University, one of Japan's most prestigious universities of the period. With the blessing of Keio University's founder Yukichi Fukuzawa, Noguchi left for the United States in 1893. Traveling alone by steamer ship to San Francisco at the age of 19, Noguchi supported himself in America as a reporter for a Japanese-American newspaper and by hiring himself out as domestic help.

In 1895 poet Joaquin Miller invited the young writer to his compound in the Oakland Hills, later memorialized as Joaquin Miller Park, and Noguchi resided there until 1900. Under the patronage and tutelage of California poets such as Joaquin Miller and Charles Warren Stoddard, Noguchi published the first English-language poems by a Japanese issei in the United States. His first volumes of poetry were *Seen and Unseen or, Monologues of a Homeless Snail* and *The Voice of the Valley* published by a San Francisco press in 1897.

Three years later, Noguchi left California for New York, where he met Leonie Gilmour, an American writer and teacher. Gilmour had answered Noguchi's advertisement for an English tutor, and their subsequent collaborations produced Noguchi's most successful English-language works including *American Diary of a Japanese Girl* (1902), the first Japanese-American novel. In it, Noguchi combines the diary format of traditional Japanese literature, found in Sei Shonagon's *Pillow Book* and *The Diary of Lady Murasaki,* with the American travelogues of Washington Irving's *The Sketch-Book of Geoffrey Crayon* and Jean de Crevecoeur's *Letters of an American Farmer.* Drawing heavily from his own experiences, Noguchi's novel follows the character Miss Morning Glory as she travels eastbound across the Pacific and catalogues her adventures in American society from San Francisco to New York.

After publishing *American Diary of a Japanese Girl,* Noguchi left America for England to find a sponsor for the novel's sequel, *The American Letters of a Japanese Parlor-Maid* (1905), and to promote his third book of poetry, *From the Eastern Sea* (1903), which proved to be Noguchi's most influential volume. Originally self-published by Noguchi, *From the Eastern Sea* found favor with a British publishing house and the volume circulated through literary circles in England where Noguchi's verse attracted the attention of literary elites such as Ezra Pound, W. B Yeats and Thomas Hardy. Because Noguchi was one of the first to introduce Japanese literary forms and styles to the coterie of literati residing in England, some have credited Noguchi's work as part of the body of influential Asian source material that modernists turned toward when they were reimagining the possibilities for English literature.

After his successful debut in Great Britain, Noguchi returned to New York in 1903 with a modicum of fame. Soon after his arrival, Gilmour and Noguchi married, and in the following year, Gilmour gave birth to their son Isamu Noguchi, who would become one of the leading figures of 20th-century American sculpture and design. Despite his success in England, American publishers still gave Noguchi scant attention. Noguchi returned to Japan in August 1904 and accepted a professorship in English at Keio University, the institution he left to embark on his travels in America. Noguchi had left the United States before Isamu's birth, and Gilmour and their son joined him in 1906. However, Noguchi in the meantime had remarried, and while Gilmour and their son continued to reside in Tokyo, they were estranged from Noguchi. In 1918 Isamu was sent to school in the United States, with Gilmour following in 1920 with her daughter Ailes Gilmour, who became an early member of Martha Graham's dance troupe.

Throughout his career as a poet and English professor at Keio University in Tokyo, Yone Noguchi continued to publish in English from Japan. His essay collection *Through the Torii* (1914) represents one of the earliest Asian responses in English regarding the dialogue between Eastern and Western artistic traditions. In addition to his introductions to Japanese poetry, Kyoto, and cherry blossoms, Noguchi also composed sketches about Western contemporaries such as W. B. Yeats, Oscar Wilde, and American painter James McNeill Whistler. Moreover, his two-volume poetry collection *The Pilgrimage* (1914) was well received by readers, and he eventually published his autobiography *The Story of Yone Noguchi Told by Himself* (1914).

After moving to Japan, Noguchi began to write increasingly only in his native language, and his attention turned away from literature and toward art. Noguchi's fame largely came to rest on his interpretations of Japanese culture for Western audiences in works such as *The Spirit of Japanese Art* (1915) and monographs on Japanese artists such as *Hokusai* (1925) and *Harunobu* (1927). However, during the years leading up to World War II, Noguchi's sentiments turned decidedly nationalist in works designed to rouse fervor and support among the Japanese. In 1935, capitalizing on his relationship with the Indian poet Rabindranath Tagore, the Japanese government sent Noguchi to India as an envoy of Japan to build support for Japan's East Asian expansion plans. This ambassadorial trip to India was the focus of *The Ganges Calls Me* (1938), Noguchi's final collection of poems in English.

Noguchi eventually found himself disillusioned in the aftermath of Japan's militarism. With his home destroyed by the Tokyo bombing raids and fires, Noguchi relocated to the city's outskirts, where he died of stomach cancer on July 13, 1947. He, however, had reconciled with his son before his death, and in 1950, Isamu Noguchi designed "The Noguchi Room" that looks out onto an accompanying sculpture garden at Keio University's Mita campus in honor of his father.

Bibliography

Hakutani, Yoshinobu. "Ezra Pound, Yone Noguchi, and Imagism." *Modern Philology* 90, no. 1 (August 1992): 46–69.

Noguchi, Yone. *The American Diary of a Japanese Girl.* New York: Frederick A. Stokes, 1902.

———. *Selected English Writings of Yone Noguchi: An East-West Literary Assimilation,* edited by, Yoshinobu Hakutani. London: Associated University Presses, Vol. 1, *Poetry,* 1990; Vol. 2, *Prose,* 1992.

———. *The Story of Yone Noguchi, Told by Himself.* Philadelphia: G.W. Jacobs, 1915.

Sueyoshi, Amy. "Mindful Masquerades: Que(e)rying Japanese Immigrant Dress in Turn-of-the-Century San Francisco." *Frontiers: A Journal of Women Studies.* 25, no. 3 (2004): 67–100.

M. Gabot Fabros

No-No Boy John Okada (1957)

JOHN OKADA's only novel, *No-No Boy* narrates the story of Ichiro Yamada, who is torn during World War II between his filial duty to his Japanese immigrant parents and his allegiance to the United States, his native country.

In January 1943 the U.S. War Department formed a special military unit and drafted second-generation Japanese Americans. Each man was asked to respond to the two most important questions of the required loyalty oath: Number 27—"are you willing to serve in the armed forces of the United States in combat duty wherever ordered[?]"; and number 28—"will you swear unqualified allegiance to the United States of America and faithfully defend the United States from any or all attacks of foreign or domestic forces, and forswear any form of allegiance or obedience to the Japanese Emperor, to any other foreign government, power, or organization?" Anyone who answered "no" to either of these questions was imprisoned. These reactionaries became known as the "no-no boys."

Ichiro Yamada's heartbreaking struggle centers on his inability to be either Japanese or American. Ichiro, raised in Seattle as a Japanese at home and as an American at school, cannot truly define himself. *No-No Boy* opens with the return of 25-year-old Ichiro to his parents' home. He has been gone for four years: two spent in an internment camp, and the other two in prison for saying "no" to the questions of the loyalty oath. Condemned by friends and strangers alike for being a no-no boy, Ichiro encounters people who judge and excoriate him. The narrator asks if there will ever be an answer to "the bigotry and meanness and smallness and ugliness" of people (134).

Okada's novel centers on an important question: What does it mean to be American? Raised by a mother who "breathed the air of America and yet had never lifted a foot from the land that was Japan" (11), Ichiro tries to tell his mother that the war is over, the Japanese have surrendered, and the Japan she remembers no longer exists. But he has neither the courage nor the strength to go against her, and his resentment of her builds to an explosive climax. His father, equally ineffectual in resistance to the mother's beliefs, cannot help Ichiro in this struggle.

Hoping that being with an old friend will help him ease his pain, Ichiro goes to find Freddie Akimoto, another no-no boy. Freddie, however, is coping with his own demons, and Ichiro leaves quickly. He goes next to speak with his former teacher, Professor Brown, with the idea of discussing the possibility of returning to college. This meeting leaves him unsatisfied also, because Ichiro realizes that the professor belongs to a life that Ichiro has already given up. He then meets Kenji, with whom Ichiro feels a flash of hope. Kenji was a soldier, a decorated war hero who lost his leg. The wound will not heal, and periodically more and more flesh has to be amputated from the stump. Kenji operates as a foil for Ichiro. Ichiro is hated and mistrusted; Kenji is admired. Ichiro's family is torn apart by the war; Kenji's family is brought closer together. Ichiro experiences despair for his actions, whereas Kenji receives only a death-dealing wound and horrendous physical pain. At the deaths of his mother and Freddie, Ichiro begins to see that healing can only begin with forgiveness, and that there are people in his community who are willing to cross racial barriers once the social facade is removed. Beautifully lyrical and intense, *No-No Boy* is a haunting novel of pain and healing, of suffering and redemption, of despair and hope.

Bibliography

Okada, John. *No-No Boy.* 1957. Seattle: University of Washington Press, 1976.

Mary Fakler

Nunes, Susan Miho   (1937–   )

Born to Japanese and Portuguese parents in Hilo, a small town in Hawaii, Nunes moved to Honolulu with her family when she was 22 years old and began to work as a writer and editor at the University of Hawaii. She published a series of books for children as well as some short stories. In 1982 Nunes published a collection of short stories entitled *Small Obligation and Other Stories of Hilo.* She moved to Berkeley, California, in 1991 and began to write full time. She continues to reside in California.

Nunes has won several awards, most notably for her children's stories. In 1994 her children's story *To Find the Way* was awarded the Ka Palapala Po'okela by the Hawaiian Book Academy. In 1995 her excellent children's book *The Last Dragon* was listed as one of the "Notable Books for Children" by the *Smithsonian* magazine. Nunes also writes nonfiction, much of which appeared in the *San Francisco Chronicle*.

Nunes is an important figure, particularly as a Hawaiian writer, because of her commitment to the multiethnic nature of Americans and America. Through her work, Nunes attempts to show the importance of the various strands that make up the cultural past of so many Americans. She resists privileging one part of her cultural past over another, choosing instead to maintain all of the cultures that make up her background. As she notes in an opinion piece that appeared in the *Honolulu Advertiser* (2000), "I have no quarrel with those who choose one part of their heritage over another, if that's how they see themselves. For me, though, being mixed is to be different from any single part of my multiple selves." In addition to her own biracial background, her extended family also draws on many other cultures including Jewish, Persian, African American and American Indian. Each of these cultures is reflected in her work. As a result, Nunes's works outline the possibility for a multiracial category that resists homogenizing tendencies. Her works function as a way to take back her own family history and encourage others to do the same.

It is not surprising, then, that many of the protagonists in her works are attempting to find their own identities in a world that does not always recognize the multiracial as a valid identity. In her collection of short stories entitled *A Small Obligation and Other Stories in Hilo,* the protagonist, Amy, attempts to understand her identity given her biracial ancestry—an ancestry that echoes that of the author. Her attempts at self-definition become the central theme threaded throughout the stories. Similar themes are incorporated into her children's stories. For example, in *The Last Dragon,* the main character, Peter, is sent by his parents to spend the summer with his great aunt in Chinatown. While he resists at first, Peter slowly begins to change when he spots a dilapidated dragon in a shop window. His obsession with restoring this dragon to its former glory becomes a metaphor for the importance of reclaiming one's cultural past. By the end of the story, the dancing dragon comes to represent the possibility for youth to reclaim their heritage in a meaningful way—an important theme for the young audience that this book is aimed at. Throughout her works the protagonists learn how to reclaim their pasts and keep their heritage alive.

Janet Melo-Thaiss

Nye, Naomi Shihab (1952–)

Poet, fiction writer, and children's author Naomi Shihab Nye was born in St. Louis, Missouri, to a Palestinian father and an American mother. After spending most of her childhood in St. Louis, she lived for a year in Old Jerusalem (part of Jordan at that time) when she was 14 and then returned to live in San Antonio, Texas, where she continues to live with her husband and son. Nye considers herself a "wandering poet" and is well known for highlighting the condition of Arab Americans and of the many other cultures in the United States. She received a B.A. from Trinity University in San Antonio in 1974.

Nye has received fellowships from the Lannan Foundation, the Guggenheim Foundation, and the Wittner Bynner Foundation. She has also received a Lavan Award from the Academy of American Poets, four Pushcart Prizes, and a long list of awards for her children's literature. *You & Yours,* her most recent book of poetry, won the Isabella Gardner Poetry Award for 2005, and *19 Varieties of Gazelle,* which was inspired by the events of September 11, 2001, was a finalist for the National Book Award. She was also awarded two Jane Addams Children's Book Awards and has received additional awards from the Texas Institute of Letters, the Clarity Randall prize and the International Poetry Forum. Nye is the poetry editor for *The Texas Observer.*

Nye's list of books is ever-growing and spans several genres. She writes about different cultures and their ability to connect to each other. Her most recent collections of poetry include *You and Yours* (2005); *19 Varieties of Gazelle* (2002); and *Fuel* (1998), a collection of poems about life around the poet. Also known for her young adult and children's books, Nye has recently published *Going, Going* (2005), a fictional story about a young girl's campaign against big business in favor of hometown enterprises; and *Habibi* (1997), an award-winning first novel for young adults. Nye has also written books for beginning readers, most notably *Baby Radar* (2003), *Lullaby Raft* (1997), *Benito's Dream Bottle* (1995), and *Sitti's Secrets* (1994).

Nye is also an accomplished editor. *The Flag of Childhood: Poems from the Middle East* (2002) contains 60 poems that serve to create connectivity in humanity. *The Space between Our Footsteps: Poems and Paintings from the Middle East* (1998) is an anthology of poetry and paintings that exhibit Middle Eastern culture. *This Same Sky: A Collection of Poems from around the World* (1996) investigates the natural world.

Bibliography

Howie, Mindy S. "Naomi Shihab Nye," April 9, 1999. VG: Voices from the Gaps: Women Artists and Writers of Color. Available online. URL: http://voices.cla.umn.edu/vg/Bios/entries/nye_naomi_shihab.html. Accessed on May 16, 2006.

Moyers, Bill. "Naomi Shihab Nye." *The Language of Life,* edited by James Haba. New York: Doubleday, 1995.

Steven Barclay Agency. "Naomi Shihab Nye." Available online. URL: http://www.barclayagency.com/nye.html. Accessed on May 18, 2006.

Anne Marie Fowler

Obasan **Joy Kogawa** (1985)

Narrated by Naomi Nakane, a third-generation Japanese Canadian, who in 1972 faces her uncle Isamu's death and her aunt (*Obasan*) Aya's withdrawal into nearly complete silence, this novel offers flashbacks for a polyphonic rendering of the internment experience of Japanese Canadians. Provoked by her aunt Emily's admonishments finally to remember the past and to speak out against political injustices, Naomi begins to recollect her childhood memories. She remembers the disappearance of her mother and maternal grandmother, who traveled back to Japan to assist a fatally ill great-grandmother and were prevented from returning to Canada after the bombing of Pearl Harbor by Japan and the entry of the United States and Canada into World War II.

Naomi also remembers the years spent in several internment camps, first in Slocan, British Columbia, and then in Coaldale, Alberta, where she coped with the loss of her family's home and possessions, the dispersal of her family, the death of several loved ones due to insufficient medical care, and repeated instances of blatant discrimination against Japanese Canadians. Naomi's historical trauma was compounded by the fact that just before the moment of internment, she had been sexually abused by a neighbor. Shortly thereafter, her mother disappeared. In the young girl's imagi-

nation, these events are all interrelated so that personal abuse parallels public and governmental abuse. Metaphorically speaking, desertion by the mother comes to mean abandonment by the Canadian nation.

Critics such as Patti Duncan have pointed out that Kogawa questions the transparency of both language and history when she counterpoints Naomi's silences with Emily's angry outbursts, and official historical documents with the Nakanes' personal memories and various letters and unofficial records. Duncan explains that the character of Aunt Emily is modeled on Muriel Kitagawa, a historical figure who wrote essays for the Japanese-Canadian newspaper *The New Canadian* (106). Despite Aunt Emily's continued efforts to obtain an apology from the Canadian government, all her writings and speeches are in vain.

Naomi's memories so horrify her that she represses them because she knows that the act of remembering alone does nothing to authenticate the experience of thousands and will not change official history. Naomi quickly realizes that speech is useless for the powerless (Duncan 114). Duncan explains, however, that Kogawa does not use silence to reinscribe Asian stereotypes but to articulate important truths (122). Silence can serve as a powerful statement of one's refusal to speak. As Duncan notes, "Kogawa deploys silence as a tool of unsaying the dominant historical narrative of internment," and her narrative consequently "resists the totalizing tendencies of 'master narratives' of history" (118). Indeed, Obasan's silence constitutes her refusal to reaffirm the injustices committed by the nation she deeply admires.

The novel acquires a spiritual dimension by endowing Naomi's silences with transcendent significance. Naomi often gains significant insights while communing with nature. Water imagery predominates, accentuating the maternal element. By emphasizing Naomi's sense of place, Kogawa foregrounds Naomi's identification with her Canadian home.

In several dream sequences, Naomi finds out more about her repressed memories. Dreams of dismembered women and cruel questioning by a Grand Inquisitor answer some of Naomi's unspoken questions. It is also through dreams that Naomi's mother continues to communicate with her daughter long after her death.

One passage that clearly illustrates Kogawa's lyrical, detail-oriented prose style features Naomi at Obasan's house. When Naomi and her aunt search for mementoes in the attic, Naomi notices a big spiderweb. After observing the frightening creature for some time, Naomi, already upset by the clutter of her aunt's life, begins to feel just like the spider's prey caught in the web of history.

Bibliography

Cheung, King-Kok. "Attentive Silence in Joy Kogawa's *Obasan.*" In *Listening to Silences: New Essays in Feminist Criticism,* edited by Elaine Hedges and Shelley Fisher Fishkin, 113–129. New York: Oxford University Press. 1994.

Duncan, Patti. *Tell This Silence.* Iowa City: University of Iowa Press, 2004.

Goellnicht, Donald C. "Father Land and/or Mother Tongue: The Divided Female Subject in Kogawa's *Obasan* and Hong Kingston's *The Woman Warrior.*" In *Redefining Autobiography in Twentieth-Century Women's Fiction: An Essay Collection,* edited by Janice Morgan, Colette T. Hall, Carol L. Snyder, 119–134. New York: Garland, 1991.

Susanna Hoeness-Krupsaw

Oeur, U Sam   (1936–)

U Sam Oeur (pronounced *oo samm oohr*) was born in Svay Rieng Province, Cambodia, to a large and moderately prosperous farming family when the country was a protectorate of France. As a child, Oeur herded water buffalo, tended rice paddies, and studied in the French colonial schools. In 1962, after graduating from the School of Arts and Trades in Phnom Penh, Oeur was offered the chance to study industrial arts at California State University, Los Angeles, through the U.S. Agency for International Development (AID), whose goal was to repatriate students as teachers in their respective home countries. While studying engineering, Oeur wrote poetry for fun. For a graphic arts project, he printed nine of his poems; later, the Asia Foundation sent them to Mary Gray at the University of Iowa. Impressed with his captivating melodies and skillful use of poetic structures, Gray secured Oeur a place in the Iowa Writers' Workshop, where he met his lifelong friend and translator, Kenneth McCullough, wrote *The Hunting World,* and completed his M.F.A.

In 1968 Oeur returned a very different man to a very different Cambodia. He taught for six months but left to work in a cannery after he was threatened with prison for labeling Prince Norodom Sihanouk a Communist sympathizer. Through the early 1970s, Oeur served in Lon Nol's internal security army, in the National Assembly, and as a delegate to the United Nations; he was appointed secretary general of the Khmer League for Freedom. All this time, he spoke openly about the democratic ideals of freedom and liberty that had excited him as a college student. However, Cambodia, destabilized by the U.S. invasion during the Vietnam War, fell when Nol forced Sihanouk's abdication. In retaliation, Sihanouk joined with Maoist Saloth Sar—later known as Pol Pot—and his Khmer Rouge forces. By the mid-1970s, Pol and the Khmer Rouge solidified power, forcing Phnom Penh's population into labor camps and condemning politicians, bureaucrats, and individuals deemed political dissenters. Pol eliminated an estimated 2 million Cambodians (30 percent of the country's population).

Driven out of Phnom Penh, Oeur, his pregnant wife, and their son miraculously survived six forced-labor camps over the next four years, but his twin daughters were strangled at birth by Pol's midwives. In "The Loss of My Twins" from his first book of poetry, *Sacred Vows,* Oeur retells the pain and horror:

> Cringing as if I'd entered Hell
> I took the babies in my arms
> and carried them to the banks of the Mekong River.
> Staring at the moon, I howled.

To stay alive, Oeur had to feign illiteracy and destroy his manuscripts; to stay sane, he silently recited Walt Whitman's poems, the Declaration of Independence, and Kennedy's inaugural address.

Although the Vietnamese overran Cambodia in 1978, Oeur's friends assumed that he died in Pol's killing fields. But McCullough soon learned that Oeur was alive and resumed his correspondence with Oeur although both poets knew the government read their letters. Oeur's life changed radically in 1991, when a coworker discovered one of his poems critical of the regime supported by Vietnam. Oeur was forced to resign his position as Assistant Minister of Industry. McCullough, rightly worried for his friend, sought grants—prominently one from the Lillian Hellman–Dashiell Hammett Fund for Free Expression—to sponsor Oeur's immigration to the United States as a fellow of the International Writing Program at the University of Iowa. Oeur tells how he gave a government acquaintance money for lunch; while the man was gone, Oeur illegally stamped his own visa. The courage to act, according to Oeur, came from his twin daughters' spirit: ". . . they came to me and said, 'You can't stay in this country, they will kill you.'" Even today at his home in Dallas, Texas, Oeur continues to receive death threats.

Oeur's bilingual collection of poetry, *Sacred Vows,* translated by McCullough and listed as a 1999 finalist for the Minnesota Book Award in poetry, retells Oeur's life and Cambodian history from the initial conflict with Sihanouk to 1998, the book's publication date. The poems draw heavily on Cambodian myths, stories, prophecies, and operatic language as a sharp ironical contrast to Cambodia's present-day situation. Yet while recalling the savagery that decimated Cambodia, Oeur predicts his country's imminent freedom:

> And 'out from the gloomy past'
> all Khmers shall be removed from
> misery, disdain, and at last we will
> stand 'where the white gem of our bright star
> will cast.' ("Mad Scene" from Sacred Vows)

Oeur's memoir, *Crossing Three Wildernesses,* both recounts his survival and astutely analyzes Cambodia's political fortunes. Oeur witnesses three wildernesses—death by execution, death by disease, and death by starvation—and emerges resolutely to believe in peace, freedom, and the power of literature.

Today Oeur lives in Texas with his family, where he continues to write and translate Whitman's *Song of Myself* into Khmer. He has been published in several journals including the *Iowa Review, Artful Dodge, Nebraska Humanities, Manoa,* and *Modern Poetry in Translation.* His work has been included in the anthology *Voices of Conscience: Poetry from Oppression.*

Bibliography

Brown, Sharon May. "Ambassador of the Silent World: An Interview with U Sam Oeur." *Manoa* 16, no. 1 (Summer 2004): 189–194.

———. "Sacred Vows." *Manoa* 11, no. 2 (1999): 203–206.

Cronyn, Hume, Richard McKane, and Stephen Watts, eds. *Voices of Conscience: Poetry from Oppression.* Northumberland, U.K.: Iron Press, 1995.

McCullough, Ken. "An Interview with U Sam Oeur." *Walt Whitman Quarterly Review* 13, nos. 1–2 (Summer–Fall 1995): 64–67.

———. "Translating U Sam Oeur: Notes on the Poet." *Artful Dodge* 26/27 (1994): 30–43.

———. "U Sam Oeur." *The Iowa Review* 25, no. 3 (Fall 1995): 47–57.

LynnDianne Beene

Okada, John   (1923–1971)

The eldest of three boys born to Japanese immigrant parents who owned a boardinghouse, Okada was born in Seattle, Washington, and attended Bailey Gatzert Elementary and Broadway High School. After the bombing of Pearl Harbor on December 7, 1942, when Executive Order 9066 required all citizens of Japanese origin to enter relocation and internment camps, the Okada family was relocated to Minidoka, a camp in a desolate area of Idaho. Allowed to leave the camp by volunteering for military duty, Okada entered the U.S. Air Force, serving as a sergeant. Upon his military discharge in 1946, Okada attended the University of Washington to earn a B.A. in English and library science. After receiving an M.A. in English from Columbia University, he worked at the Seattle Public Library, the Detroit Public Library, and, as a technical writer, at Chrysler Missile Operations of Sterling Township.

Okada was the first Japanese-American novelist, and has been acclaimed as one of the greatest Asian-American writers. In *No-No Boy*, his only novel (1957), Okada relates the story of Ichiro Yamada, a young second-generation Japanese American who is imprisoned for refusing to support the American war effort against the Japanese. Unable to rebel against his Japanese parents and yet wanting desperately to belong, Ichiro suffers from his inability to be either Japanese or American, and his failing search to find a way to integrate the two cultures so as to form an identity for himself.

Okada died of a heart attack in February 1971. He had been working on a second novel. After his death, his wife, Dorothy, offered his papers to the Japanese American Research Project at UCLA. According to FRANK CHIN, who met and spoke with Dorothy, the project directors refused the papers and suggested that she burn them. So she did. *No-No Boy* is his only surviving work of fiction.

Mary Fakler

Okita, Dwight   (1958–)

Poet, playwright, and screenwriter Dwight Holden Okita was born in Chicago, where he continues to live. His father, Fred, was a schoolteacher who served in World War II in the 442nd Battalion, which was made up of Japanese-American citizens. In contrast, his mother, Patsy Takeyo Okita, was interned for four years in a relocation camp when she was a teenager.

His mother's personality and experiences have been an ongoing inspiration for voices and characters in Okita's work. When Okita asked his mother about leaving for the internment camps, she could not remember leaving her high school when her family was forced to leave Fresno, California, in the wake of the bombing of Pearl Harbor. The poem "In Response to Executive Order 9066" (1982) imagines a young high school girl saying good-bye to her best friend who now sees her as an enemy. More detailed memories of his mother being interned in a camp as a teenager are the basis of "The Nice Thing about Counting Stars," found in his 1992 collection of poetry, *Crossing with the Light*.

The specific and overlapping histories of Japanese Americans and his hometown Chicago are also portrayed in Okita's poetry. "Notes for a Poem on Being Asian American" is set during a taxi ride through the city. The poet looks at his cultural identity in terms of the differences between Asian and non-Asian Americans and then attempts to find what they share. Looking into the eyes of his cab driver, the post-immigrant sansei poet can see no differences between them.

Okita's dramatic writing also investigates the intersection between Chicago's urban history and that of Asian Americans. *The Salad Bowl Dance*, commissioned by the Chicago Historical Society, looks at the aftermath of the war, when Japanese Americans were released from relocation camps and moved to Chicago in large numbers to restart their lives. Under multicultural conditions, Okita sees a crisp choreography of distinct ethnic identities tossed together, as opposed to the homogenizing notions of the melting pot or ethnic stew.

In his one-act play called *Richard Speck*, a young Chinese-American woman recalls growing up a block away from where Richard Speck killed eight female student nurses in July 1966. The brutal murder is rewritten in the comic script in which the young woman dreams that Speck visits her apartment, thinking she is the one Filipino nurse who got away from the mass murder. The one-woman play is a black comedy about a criminal milestone in Chicago history, but it foregrounds the Asian-American identity of some of the young nurses who were killed, as well as the courage, wisdom, and survival instincts of the one who escaped death. The lurid details of the brutal murder fascinated the public and drew widespread media attention. Okita's play makes a subtle comparison between the sensation caused by the Speck murders and the lack of coverage of the government's forced relocation of Japanese Americans after Pearl Harbor.

Being gay and Buddhist has also influenced Okita's writing. His play *The Rainy Season* is a multicultural gay love story in which Harry, an Asian American, meets a handsome Brazilian while waiting at a bus stop. "Flirt" is a short story about friendship between a gay man and a gay woman. As a member of Soka Gakkai International, a Buddhist network devoted to peace, Okita follows the teachings of Nichiren, a 13th-century Japanese monk who assumed a posture of utmost respect toward all others, regardless of gender, ability, or social status. In addition to his poetry, fiction, and drama, Okita has also written movie scripts and essays for the radio.

Beverley Curran

Okubo, Miné   (1912–2001)

Born in Riverside, California, Miné Okubo grew up in a family of artists including her mother, a graduate of Tokyo Art Institute, and her brother Benji Okubo, a pioneering nisei painter. Miné attended Riverside Community College and later completed an M.F.A. at the University of California, Berkeley, in 1936. In 1938 she won a Taussig fellowship, which allowed her to spend 18 months in Europe studying art. In September 1939 she returned to San Francisco and began exhibiting her art in local venues. In 1941 Okubo won an exhibition prize for her painting "Miyo and Cat," which was purchased by the Oakland Museum. Meanwhile, she assisted the famous Mexican painter Diego Rivera

in the preparation of a mural for San Francisco's Treasure Island.

The Okubo family, like 115,000 other West Coast Japanese Americans, was rounded up and moved inland by the army during 1942. Okubo's father was interned in Montana, while the children were incarcerated in different camps. Miné and one brother were confined at Tanforan Assembly Center and later sent to Topaz, where she taught art classes and helped found a literary review, *Topaz Trek,* for which she drew cover designs and illustrations. Meanwhile, Okubo undertook a series of sketches of camp life. She later explained that since inmates were not permitted cameras, such sketches were a necessary documentary record. She also publicly exhibited work depicting camp scenes. Her drawing of two military guards won critical acclaim at a show in San Francisco in spring 1943 and was reproduced in the *San Francisco Chronicle.* Encouraged by the response, the *San Francisco Chronicle* commissioned a series of camp sketches from Okubo, which soon appeared in the newspaper, along with Okubo's accompanying commentary, in August 1943.

Okubo's fame led the editors of the *Fortune* magazine to sponsor her release from camp, and in 1944 Okubo moved to New York City, where she would live the rest of her life. Hired by *Fortune* to design a special issue on Japan, she contributed several camp sketches to an article on Japanese Americans, "Issei, Nisei, Kibei." A show of her camp sketches and other art opened in New York in March 1945, followed by a national tour. Over the following months, Okubo collected her sketches into book form and drafted accompanying texts. Columbia University Press published the finished work, entitled *Citizen 13660,* in late 1946.

Citizen 13660 is a record in matched text and illustration of Okubo's camp experience, from the outbreak of war through her confinement and release. A visual as well as verbal narrator, Okubo places herself in virtually all her sketches. Her narrative depicts the hardships of camp life, including dust storms, lack of privacy, and political conflict. Although later critics have underlined the book's indictment of confinement and its subversive nature, Okubo generally presents the camp experience in comic form, as an absurd predicament. Her illustrations humanize Japanese Americans, and she praises their adjustment to their situation.

Citizen 13660 was Okubo's only published writing during her lifetime, although she wrote unpublished children's stories. In subsequent decades, she devoted herself primarily to painting and book illustration, and her art was featured in countless exhibitions. Also active in the Japanese-American redress movement, she testified in 1981 before an official government committee and presented her book as evidence. In 1983, at the height of the redress struggle, a reprint edition of *Citizen* appeared, with a new introduction by Okubo. The acclaim it received brought the book squarely into the Asian-American canon. It is also noticeable as a precursor to today's graphic novels.

Greg Robinson

Ondaatje, Michael   (1943–)

Sri Lankan–Canadian poet and novelist Philip Michael Ondaatje was born in Kegalle, Ceylon. His Dutch-Sinhala-Tamil family once owned a prosperous tea plantation; Ondaatje's father, however, having succumbed to alcoholism, had lost much of the family fortune by the time Michael arrived. When his parents were divorced in 1945, Michael remained with his mother and moved to London with her in 1952.

Toward the end of his teenage years, Ondaatje believed that a more promising life awaited him elsewhere, and he followed his older brother to Canada. There he attended Bishop's University and met Kim Jones, the wife of a professor/mentor. Jones would leave her husband and marry Ondaatje in 1964. The young student continued at the University of Toronto and Queen's University in Kingston; throughout this period Ondaatje developed his own poetry. In 1966 he was featured in a major anthology entitled *New Wave Canada,* and began to win awards for his work. The following year his first collection of poems, *The Dainty Monsters,* appeared, and Ondaatje began to teach at the University of Western Ontario.

His career soon encompassed not only poetry but performance; an actor as a young man, the writer composed *the man with seven toes* in 1969, a poetic piece intended for the stage. Cinematic efforts include *The Clinton Special* and *Carry On Crime and Punishment.* Perhaps all of his interests in various literary forms can be seen in *The Collected Works of Billy the Kid* (1970), a book that earned Ondaatje awards and higher visibility. Alternately described as fiction and poetry, this collage work includes poems, dime novels, eyewitness accounts, period photographs, and startling images both visual and verbal. *Billy the Kid* represents the work that may ultimately be remembered as the "most classically Ondaatjean," because he uses multiple narrators, genres, and registers, and because it explores many of the author's recurrent themes. Neither wholly history nor fiction, it interrogates and reshapes historical themes; the photograph that concludes the work is a picture of Ondaatje himself, dressed in Billy the Kid–like costume.

Billy the Kid coincided with public turmoil in Ondaatje's academic career, as the University of Western Ontario refused him continued employment on the grounds that he was not producing enough literary criticism—this while his book won the Governor General's Award. Ondaatje soon found a post at York University, and his writing career began to flourish. Subsequent volumes of poetry include *Elimination Dance* (1978), *There's a Trick with a Knife I'm Learning to Do* (1979), *Secular Love* (1984), and *The Cinnamon Peeler* (1991). *Secular Love* dwells on a number of painful themes for Ondaatje, who wrote it as his marriage was falling apart. By 1980 Ondaatje had met and fallen in love with writer Linda Spalding, with whom he would eventually coedit *Brick: A Journal of Reviews.*

Ondaatje's continuing prose work includes *Running in the Family* (1982), a text illustrating various events in family history. Ondaatje himself prefers to think of the work as a "gesture" rather than a memoir; the author considers memoir as "fiction . . . full of [its creator's] defences and ambitions." If anything, the book is a "gesture" of love and regret directed toward his father, whose escapades—often drunken—comprise the most touching and most humorous episodes. In fiction, Ondaatje (as in *Billy the Kid*) investigates specific historical characters with *Coming Through Slaughter* (1976), a similarly eclectic work devoted to jazz great Buddy Bolden's descent into madness. *In the Skin of a Lion* (1987) depicts the experience of immigrant workers in Canada who helped build some of the country's most prominent landmarks.

Ondaatje is best known for *The ENGLISH PATIENT* (1992), a novel that employs two of the characters from *In the Skin of a Lion*. *The English Patient* explores the complicated relationships between history and fiction, geography and identity, love and morality. The eponymous character, ironically, is not English at all; he remains enshrouded in mystery from the plane-crash injuries that leave him unidentifiable and from the emotional injuries of his relationship with Katherine. The questions he raises concern many of Ondaatje's other pieces: What does a name truly signify? Is ownership a right? How can borders be crossed, or erased entirely? To what extent is history a limiting, or liberating, force? Undoubtedly, this text has defined Ondaatje's stature, having tied for the prestigious Booker Prize in 1992. In 1996 director Anthony Minghella's cinematic adaptation of this work won multiple Academy Awards.

Ondaatje's recent novel *ANIL'S GHOST* (2000) returns his focus to his native Sri Lanka. The protagonist, a forensic anthropologist, hopes that in "reading" the corpses of violence she can spark an international intervention in the nation's ongoing cycles of bloodshed. Again, Ondaatje creates a mystery surrounding individual identity; Anil struggles to ascertain the background of a single victim christened "Sailor." While she manages to "read" a number of facts from the corpse, she is not able to mount a successful charge against government-sponsored mass-murder by the novel's conclusion.

The writer's career has been marked by dramatic and often violent imagery, such as the burned man of *The English Patient* or the starved dogs of *Billy the Kid*. He has been considered one of the so-called cosmopolitan writers, in part because of his international background and in part because of his repeated insistence that borders

and identities should be porous and flexible. The heteroglossia that marks his novels is a distinctive Ondaatje trait; he once remarked that "If you're handcuffed to a narrator for 300 pages, it seems possibly boring." Despite the generous inclusion of so many voices in single artistic works, Ondaatje has been consistently reticent about his personal life, frustrating interviewers and biographers with silence and distortion, as if he seeks a mysterious identity of his own.

Bibliography

Barbour, Douglas. *Michael Ondaatje*. New York: Twayne Publishers, 1993.

Jewinski, Ed. *Michael Ondaatje: Express Yourself Beautifully*. Toronto: ECW Press, 1994.

Michael Ondaatje in conversation with Caryl Phillips. Santa Fe, N.Mex.: Lannan Foundation, 1997. Videorecording.

Ondaatje, Michael. *Running in the Family*. New York: Vintage, 1982.

Solecki, Sam. *Ragas of Longing: The Poetry of Michael Ondaatje*. Toronto: University of Toronto Press, 2003.

J. Edward Mallot

One Hundred Million Hearts
Kerri Sakamoto (2003)

This second novel of KERRI SAKAMOTO is an innovative take on the events of World War II as they are experienced by her Japanese and Japanese-Canadian characters. Beyond merely reiterating the stories about the experience of Japanese Canadians during the war, Sakamoto raises the taboo issue of loyalty.

The protagonist of the novel is a third-generation Japanese Canadian, Miyo, who discovers only after her father's death that her Canadian nisei father left Canada to serve the emperor of Japan as a kamikaze pilot during World War II. Miyo goes to Japan on a quest to find a sister that she never knew she had. While in Japan, Miyo meets Buddy, a nisei from Vancouver who knew her father. Also a kamikaze pilot during the war, Buddy, unlike Miyo's father, did not go "home" but remained in

Japan after the war, hiding his ability to speak English and his identity as a Canadian.

The novel raises issues of "belonging" and "home," illustrating the complexities of being a Japanese-Canadian nisei, at a time when both Canada and Japan were highly xenophobic, and a nisei was not recognized as a full citizen in either country. Japanese Canadians were interned in Canada; ironically, as the novel reveals, if someone was discovered to be a nisei in wartime Japan, he or she was beaten and ostracized for being foreign-born. The extreme desire to belong and the deep betrayal felt by the nisei when the Canadian government interned them is exemplified by the ultimate sacrifice of Setsuko, the nisei second wife of Miyo's father, who decides to give up her daughter Hana for adoption in Japan in an attempt to give her daughter the one thing she and her husband never had as Canadian nisei: a sense of belonging. She wants her daughter to be Japanese, not excluded from both Canada and Japan, not lost between the two identities. However, Hana becomes obsessed with uncovering the truth about her absentee Canadian nisei father and the past. Reconstructing her version of the past through her art, she strings together traces and images of the past into a jigsaw puzzle that does not fit together.

The truth that Hana seeks is the self-same quest for truth that drives the novel. Sakamoto does something bold and political in *One Hundred Million Hearts*. She shows the complexities of loyalty to country, to ethno-cultural group, to family, to partner, and to oneself. She explores the human emotions that bind us and divide us, raising more questions than answers. Most important, she asks her readers to question stereotypes that, while creating an illusion of safety, become sources of real dangers.

This book is simultaneously a product of its time and a challenge to it. After the Japanese-Canadian community gained redress in September 1988 and produced many internment narratives, Sakamoto pushes the limits of the historical Japanese-Canadian identity. She builds on the narratives that have come before hers, introducing new identities to the pantheon of Japanese-Canadian literary and cinematic figures meant to debunk the myth of communal homogeneity and to help articulate a more nuanced Japanese-Canadian identity that transcends simplistic stereotyping and categorization. Sakamoto's rendition of history in this transgressive novel emphasizes that if people are to actually learn from history then they must understand it in all its complexities, not simply have a vague notion of the reduced versions available for easy consumption.

Sheena Wilson

Ong, Han (1968–)

Han Ong was born and raised in Manila, the Philippines, and immigrated to the United States at the age of 16. After settling briefly in Los Angeles, he moved to New York City, where he currently lives. He is the author of nearly three dozen plays, including *The L.A. Plays, The Chang Fragments, Swoony Planet, Play of Father and Junior,* and *Watcher.* Some of his plays have been produced in theaters across the country and abroad, including the Public Theater in New York City and the Almeida Theatre in London. In 1997 Ong was awarded the prestigious MacArthur "Genius" Fellowship and, at the age of 29, became one of the youngest people, as well as the first Filipino American, ever to have received the honor. He has also written two novels: *Fixer Chao* and *The Disinherited.*

While Ong has certainly accumulated acclaim from audiences and critics from within the theater community, his plays have not enjoyed any commercial success, presumably because of their experimental, avant-garde quality. Stage directions sometimes call for absolutely no set at all, and the disruptive, episodic nature of some scenes can make his plays hard to follow. Ong also sometimes inserts bizarre imagery; for example, in *Middle Finger*, a flock of birds fly out of one character's hair. Some critics would describe such a gesture as an example of magic realism, but Ong hesitates to agree with such a label, opting instead to emphasize the stark realness of the statements he wants to make in his work. Ong has addressed issues such as the economic inequality that resulted in the United States's colonization of the Philippines, and the ethnic typecasting faced by actors of color in the entertainment industry.

Ong's novels have gained wider appeal. His first, *Fixer Chao*, a *Los Angeles Times* best seller, is about William Paulinha, a Filipino street hustler who, through a plan masterminded by Shem C., an unsuccessful Jewish writer who wants to wreak revenge on the socialites who have shunned him, becomes Master Chao, a revered feng shui practitioner. Ong satirizes the upper-class society of contemporary America and provides commentary on race, class, and privilege. Not only does William pretend to know the Chinese art of creating prosperity through maneuvering one's environment, but he also turns his ethnicity into a pretense and a performance. The same patrons who claim to be appreciative of Asian cultures are also the ones who throw money at William without even realizing that he isn't Chinese, viewing all of Asia as a marketplace of commodified cultures. The same patrons who sigh with pity at the impoverishment of Third World countries also disavow any responsibility for the harm they have inflicted, both directly and indirectly, on the less privileged. Ong provides a biting and oftentimes comical look at ignorance and hypocrisy.

It should be noted, however, that *Fixer Chao* does not end with a complete triumph for William. Rather, as his plot becomes exposed, William, already a social outcast at the novel's start, finds himself thrust deeper into a state of isolation. The experience of being on the outside looking in is one that Ong captures throughout his works. Although his characters are often ostracized because of their ethnicity, class, or sexuality, Ong portrays isolation as a universal experience. *The Disinherited,* for example, features a protagonist who, despite having inherited a small fortune that he has decided to donate, is unable to feel satisfied because of his desire to give the money to the "right" cause. The search for a completely guilt-free gesture is futile.

Catherine Fung

Opposite of Fate, The   Amy Tan (2003)

AMY TAN's first nonfiction work, *The Opposite of Fate* is both educational and revealing. Organized into themed sections, Tan's book both elucidates her fiction and brings disparate aspects of her personal life into sharp focus.

In the first section, "Fate and Faith," Tan muses on the neatly packaged version of her life as presented by Cliff's Notes, her relationship with her husband, and her predilection for examining the forces of fate and faith—as well as the differences and similarities between them. Tan also includes a tribute to a murdered friend and a eulogy to her late editor. The second section, "Changing the Past," deals with the difficulty of pinning her mother's character down, and explains the process by which Tan was able to learn and record her mother's fascinating life story. It also includes a tribute to her grandmother, who, by choosing her own fate, bequeathed to her yet-unknown granddaughter a substantial source for her storytelling. She describes her writing process, discussing the links between her family history and her creativity, and corrects various misconceptions about her own life as an author.

The third section, "American Circumstances and Chinese Character," explores the novelist's own childhood experiences as she grew up negotiating the two cultures in which she was immersed. She also devotes an essay to discussing her reasons for joining the rock band "The Rock Bottom Remainders" as well as several interesting experiences she has had as a singer for the band. She then writes about a trip to China with her mother and about the difficulties inherent in being foreign and speaking a different language in her ancestral land—including negotiating cultural and culinary conventions. The last essay in the section describes both the creative and technical process involved in bringing her novel *The JOY LUCK CLUB* to the big screen.

The fourth section, "Strong Winds, Strong Influences," includes several short essays about Tan's changing relationship with her mother from early difficult childhood experiences to later-life reconciliations as her mother suffered from Alzheimer's disease. Tan also writes admiringly of Vladimir Nabokov and the lessons she has learned from reading him. The fifth section, "Luck, Chance, and a Charmed Life," discusses Tan's living arrangements, from good luck charms to ghosts, to squirrels, and to a rescue from a mudslide. The sixth section, "A Choice of Words," deals with linguistic issues, from her first award-winning essay written at age eight in appreciation of the library, to her struggle to categorize and appreciate her mother's "broken" English, and to the difficulties inherent in translating one language into another, as well as the uniqueness of each language's worldview. Also included are a speech she made to a graduating college class, where she gives five writing and living tips that concern language, a dissertation on "required" reading and the label of "ethnic" or "multicultural" literature, a description of the painstaking process of writing a second book, and an introduction to *The Best American Short Stories* of 1999 that elucidates the power of the story to affect our lives.

The last section of the book, "Hope," contains three essays. "What I Would Remember" discusses how Tan began to listen to her mother's stories after a medical scare, then promised to take her to China, and subsequently began work on *The Joy Luck Club.* "To Complain Is American" details the nature of our culture as it relates to our personal lives. "The Opposite of Fate" deals with personal trauma, medical scares, and unexpected results. Throughout the book, Tan discusses both her personal and professional lives, gleaning from each glimpses of how she was able to envision and re-envision her formative experiences and create a meaningful existence through the forces that govern us all: fate, faith, and memory.

Vanessa Rasmussen

Otsuka, Julie (1962–)

Born in Palo Alto, California, on May 15, 1962, Otsuka moved with her family to Palos Verdes at the age of nine. Her father, a first-generation Japanese American, was employed as an aerospace engineer. Her mother, a second-generation Japanese American, worked as a lab technician prior to giving birth to Otsuka and two sons. Upon graduation from high school, Otsuka attended Yale University, where she developed a passion for painting and sculpture and earned her B.A. in art in 1984. After spending several years in New Haven, Connecticut, working as a waitress and building up her portfolio, and after attending the M.F.A. program at the University of Indiana for a few months, she moved to New York to take classes at the New York Studio School of Drawing, Painting and Sculpture and to continue to pursue a career in art.

In her early 30s, however, Otsuka abandoned painting and turned to fiction. Some of her early work won her acceptance into Columbia University's prestigious M.F.A. program in creative writing in 1994. While she was a graduate student at Columbia, one of Otsuka's stories was selected for inclusion in the 1998 Scribner's *Best of the Fiction Workshops.* This story, "Evacuation Order No. 19," would become the first part of Otsuka's first novel, *When the Emperor Was Divine,* which she completed after earning her M.F.A. from Columbia in 1999. In 2002, within days of submitting the manuscript to her agent, Otsuka's novel was accepted by Knopf. It appeared in hardcover in September of that year and was released in paperback by Anchor Books in October 2003.

When the Emperor Was Divine charts the experience of one family during the World War II evacuation and internment of Japanese Americans. As one of the only recent works of fiction written by an American of Japanese descent, it marks an important milestone in the literary representation of the Japanese-American internment experience. In its unusual narrative style and innovative approach to character development, it breaks new aesthetic ground, returning public attention to a shameful moment in U.S. history, a historical moment that took on new relevance for many people after the events of September 11, 2001.

Structured as a novel in five parts, each section of Otsuka's narrative centers on a different member of an anonymous Japanese-American family. When the novel opens, the father has already been arrested and incarcerated, leaving the mother to prepare her family for the evacuation alone. The narrative then shifts to follow the daughter, who has just turned 11 when the family is forced to relocate from the temporary holding site at the Tanforan racetrack to an internment camp in the Utah desert. The third section, which centers on the son, is set in an internment camp outside Salt Lake City, where the mother and her children wait out the war. The fourth, narrated in the first person plural, documents the family's return to their home in Berkeley and eventual reunion with the father. Finally, in the brief fifth section, the father speaks in the first person, lashing out against the racism underlying this historic lapse in justice.

These shifts in narrative perspective, and Otsuka's refusal to provide names for her protagonists, paradoxically make her characters at once universal and specific. In interviews, Otsuka has acknowledged that the "bare bones" of the story derive from her family history. Like the father in the novel, her grandfather was arrested following the Japanese attack on Pearl Harbor. And, like the mother and her two children, Otsuka's grandmother, mother, and uncle were removed from California to an internment camp in Topaz, Utah, where they lived for three and a half years. Yet, in the absence of sufficient details of her relatives' experiences, Otsuka moved beyond family history, relying on research and her own imagination to flesh out the emotional lives and lived experiences of her fictional characters. In one sense, in referring to these characters simply as "the woman" or "the boy," Otsuka invites her readers to see them as prototypical victims of wartime racism and government injustice. At the same time, Otsuka's keen eye to the details that constitute each character's experience reminds her readers of the variety of ways in which specific individuals encountered and reacted to Japanese-American internment.

With the exception of the final section, Otsuka's novel is a model of restraint. Relying on spare, matter-of-fact prose, Otsuka refuses to sentimentalize her characters and resists the inherent melodrama of their situation. Even when the family returns to find their home vandalized and lives forever changed, their response is one of quiet, measured forbearance. It is only in the last section—the only one to adopt the perspective of the father and the only section related in the first person singular—that the narrative poise and restraint of the first chapters fall away, revealing a simmering outrage reminiscent of JOHN OKADA's *NO-NO BOY* (1957). This final section came under fire in Michiko Kakutani's otherwise positive review in the *New York Times Book Review.* Yet while Kakutani referred to the novel's conclusion as "a shrill diatribe" that lacks the "subtle and emotional power of the previous portions," Otsuka has expressed in interviews her certainty that this last chapter offers an appropriate conclusion to her novel.

Despite some critical misgivings about the tone of this last section, Otsuka's first novel has gone on to enjoy unexpected popularity. Recognizing parallels to the experiences of Arab Americans following the events of September 11, many high school teachers and college professors have included the book on their syllabi. The novel won the American Library Association's Alex Award, was listed as a *Booklist* Editor's Choice for Young Adults, and was a finalist for the Barnes & Noble Discover Great New Writers program. Otsuka currently lives in New York City, where she is working on a novel set in Japan and America during the first decades of the 20th century.

Bibliography

Freedman, Samuel G. "One Family's Story of Persecution Resonates in the Post-9/11 World," *New York Times,* 17 August 2005, p. B9.

Kakutani, Michiko. "War's Outcasts Dream of Small Pleasures," *New York Times,* 10 September 2002, p. E6.

Stephenson, Anne. "'Divine' Gently Drives Home History," *USA Today,* 3 October 2002, p. 8D.

Rachel Ihara

Oyabe, Jenichiro   (1867–1940)

By his own account, Jenichiro Oyabe was born in Tokyo, and his mother died early in his life. Abandoned by his father, who joined the new imperial civil service, the boy was raised by various relatives. After attending different schools, he rejoined his father, who became a judge on the northern island of Hokkaido. The young Oyabe soon became disenchanted with his father. After spending several months in an Ainu (aboriginal) village, where he adopted Ainu dress and speech, Oyabe decided to devote himself to missionary work among Ainu. Inspired by his meetings with American missionaries, he embraced Christianity and decided to travel abroad for education to uplift the Ainu.

In 1888 Oyabe sailed to the United States as a cabin boy and settled in New York, where he briefly worked as a hospital orderly. There he was recruited to study at Hampton Institute, a school for blacks and Native Americans, by its president, Samuel Chapman Armstrong. After a few years at Hampton, Oyabe enrolled at another African-American institution, Howard University, to study theology. As at Hampton, Oyabe became a favorite student of Howard's president, Jeremiah Rankin. Oyabe completed his studies at Yale University, where he obtained a doctorate in divinity in 1894. He afterward spent two years as a Christian missionary in Hawaii.

After returning to Yale, Oyabe wrote his "spiritual autobiography," presumably to raise money for further study. *A Japanese Robinson Crusoe,* published in 1898, is arguably the earliest book by a Japanese American. An account of Oyabe's curious formation as a Japanese "yankee" (as he terms himself), it can be seen as a tale of a foreigner taking on "whiteness" and absorbing the superiority of Christian culture. After the book's release, Oyabe returned to Japan, where he lectured on behalf of an Ainu aid society and served as translator and guide to American anthropologist Hiram Miller on Miller's 1901 research trip among the Ainu. Oyabe built a model Ainu school in Abuta, which he operated for the next decade. In later years, he became well known in Japan as a nationalist scholar and historian. In one work, he argued that Genghis Khan was actually Minamoto Yoshitsune, younger brother of the first Minamoto shogun. Similarly, his 1929 book *Nihon Oyobi Nihon Kokumin No Kigen (Origin of Japan and Japanese)* explored the influence of the ancient Hebrews on Japanese civilization. Despite his "yankee" self-identification, Oyabe never returned to the United States.

Greg Robinson

Ozeki, Ruth (Ruth Ozeki Lounsbury)
(1956?–)

The daughter of a Japanese mother and a Caucasian American father, Ruth Ozeki has an educational background and professional career that reflect her strong sense of her dual ethnic heritage. Born and raised in New Haven, Connecticut, Ozeki moved to Kyoto in 1976 to study Japanese literature and culture in an intensive yearlong program at Doshisha University. She returned to the United States to attend Smith College, graduating in 1980 with a double major in English and Asian studies. She then relocated once more to Japan, this time to pursue graduate research in classical Japanese literature. She would remain in Japan for the next five years, teaching English as a second language, founding an innovative language school, and teaching in the English department at Kyoto Sangyo University.

In 1985 Ozeki moved back to the United States and settled in New York City, where she began a career as a director and producer, first for low-budget horror films and then for television documentaries. She spent several years directing a series of documentary films on American culture for a Japanese television company, before deciding to pursue her own work full time. Her first film, the one-hour drama *Body of Correspondence* (1994), was shown at the San Francisco Film Festival, where it won the New Visions Award and was aired on PBS. Ozeki's second film, the autobiographical, feature-length film *Halving the Bones* (1995), has been screened at film festivals around the country including the Sundance Film Festival, the Montreal World Film Festival, and the San Francisco Asian American Film Festival.

Although Ozeki has noted in interviews that she always dreamed of being a novelist and wrote short stories throughout school and college, *MY YEAR OF MEATS* (1998) represents her first serious foray into fiction. An ambitious first novel that is, by turn, both humorous and horrific, *My Year of Meats* tells the story of a Japanese-American documentary filmmaker whose work on a series of films on American cooking shows leads her to uncover some unsavory and dangerous practices in the meat production industry. Ozeki's second novel, ALL OVER CREATION (2003), also features a Japanese-American female protagonist and again takes up issues of food, this time confronting issues of genetic modification in contemporary farming practices. Both novels, published by Viking and released in paperback by Penguin, have garnered significant critical recognition. *My Year of Meats* won the Kiriyama Pacific Rim Prize and the Imus/Barnes & Noble American Book Award. *All over Creation* received the American Book Award from the Before Columbus Foundation and the Willa Literary Award for Contemporary Fiction.

Currently vice president on the board of directors for Women Make Movies, Ozeki continues to write fiction and to lecture at colleges and universities throughout the United States. One of her short stories, "Ships in the Night," was selected for inclusion in *Charlie Chan Is Dead 2,* the follow-up to the landmark anthology of Asian-American writing edited by JESSICA HAGEDORN.

Bibliography

Ruth Ozeki. "About Ozeki." Available online. URL: http://www.ruthozeki.com. Downloaded on January 20, 2006.

Rachel Ihara

P

Pak, Gary (1952–)

Considered one of the most important Asian-Hawaiian writers of the day, Gary Pak was born and raised in Hawaii. His grandparents were among the first Koreans to immigrate to Hawaii. While Pak defines himself as a local writer whose first language is pidgin English, he acknowledges as one of the sources of his literary imagination the stories his maternal grandmother, a picture bride who immigrated to Hawaii in 1905, used to tell him about Korea. His one-year sojourn in Korea in 2002 as a Fulbright visiting lecturer at Korea University might be seen as a fulfillment of the childhood curiosity and interest raised in Pak by his Korean grandmother.

Pak completed his B.A. at Boston University and his M.A. and Ph.D. at the University of Hawaii at Manoa. His persistent interest in cultural mixing, myth-making, narrative form, and story-telling—all in the context of Hawaii's complicated history of negotiations with the West—appears in his doctoral dissertation, in which he discusses native Hawaiian historiography of the 19th century and its influence on subsequent Hawaiian literature. His first book-length publication, *The Watcher of Waipuna and Other Stories* (1992), won the 1993 National Book Award for Literature from the Association for Asian American Studies. In the short stories in this collection, Pak creates the fictional community of Kanewai, to which he later returns in his second novel, *Children of a Fireland* (2004). Just as he combines the fantastic and the realistic to represent the struggles of a colonized community, Pak incorporates what he witnessed in the lives of the first- and second-generation immigrants in these stories.

His first novel, *A Ricepaper Airplane* (1998), links the lives of two generations of men in Hawaii as the nephew, Yong Gil, is summoned to his uncle's deathbed to hear the story of his life as a laborer, revolutionary, and dreamer at a Hawaiian sugar plantation. "Uncle . . . is like a book," says the narrator, Yong Gil, early on in the novel. Indeed, the uncle's wild dream of building a ricepaper airplane that will carry him back to Korea drives this epic tale. *A Ricepaper Airplane* has been adapted for stage by John Wat and Keith Kashiwada and premiered at Kuma Kahua Theatre in Hawaii in 2002.

Pak's second novel, *Children of a Fireland* (2004), returns to the mythic community of Kanewai. Pak continues to experiment with the stream-of-consciousness technique he uses in *A Ricepaper Airplane.* The novel starts out with the characters trying to find a rational explanation for the supernatural events that take place in the community, but in the course of the narrative, the quest for a rational explanation is abandoned as the novel ultimately turns out to be a ghost story. The past and the present are brought together in the novel as Pak portrays the hold of history on the inhabitants of Kanewai and as he weaves the Hawaiian shamanic tradition with popular culture subtexts such as *The X-Files. Children of a Fireland* received honorable mention in the Association for Asian American Studies' 2004 Book Award in Prose and Poetry.

In the short stories collected in *Language of the Geckos and Other Stories* (2005), his most recent book, Pak explores the lives of local Hawaiians and their relationships to the past. Pak is presently a professor of English and creative writing at the University of Hawaii at Manoa.

Bibliography

Kim, Elaine. "Korean American Literature." In *An Interethnic Companion to Asian American Literature,* edited by King-Kok Cheung. 156–191. Cambridge: Cambridge University Press, 1997.

Kwon, Brenda. "Gary Pak." In *Words Matter: Conversations with Asian American Writers,* edited by King-Kok Cheung, 303–19. Honolulu: University of Hawaii Press, 2000.

Jeehyun Lim

Pak, Ty   (1938–   )

Ty Pak, whose Korean name is Tae-Yong Pak, was born in Korea and witnessed the Korean War between 1950 and 1953, during which his father died. He graduated from Seoul National University in 1960, and worked as a reporter for the *Korea Republic* and the *Korea Times* for the next five years. In 1965 he came to the United States for graduate study and received his Ph.D. in English from Bowling Green State University, Ohio, in 1970. He taught as a professor in the English department of the University of Hawaii.

In addition to publishing short stories in *Amerasia Journal, Hawaii Review, Bamboo Ridge, The Literary Realm,* and *The Echo,* Pak published short-story collections such as *Guilt Payment* (1983) and *Moonbay* (1999) as well as a novel, *Cry Korea Cry* (1999). His works deal with issues of survival, guilt, trauma, shame, liberation, displacement, violence, and war.

Pak shows a strong interest in mixed-blood children and racial conflict in Korea and America. *Cry Korea Cry,* for instance, depicts the life of a mixed-blood Korean war orphan, Moo Moo ("Nothing Nothing" in Korean). Born to a poor Korean prostitute and a sex-starved American soldier, Moo Moo leads a life that represents the complex history of Korea after the Korean War. After experiencing harsh racial discrimination and political disorder in Korea, he finally decides not to belong to any of the divided Koreas. Instead, he decides to live in the United States, making films to restore his life with the help of art.

Pak's writing also seeks to represent the presence of Koreans in Hawaii and other parts of America. *Moonbay* deals with the lives of Korean immigrant men who "felt penalized, castrated in subtle, invisible ways" ("A Debt" 33). The stories in *Guilt Payment* have more diverse themes: the atrocities of war, religions of Korea and America, moral ambiguity, nostalgia and patriotism. Interestingly, Pak's characters mostly suffer from a variety of psychological or physical wounds, and they sometimes assume temporal or mistaken identities. Critics such as Elaine Kim and King-Kok Cheung note Pak's misogynist tone, while other scholars like Seiwoong Oh point out his importance as an immigrant writer.

Bibliography

Cheung, King-Kok. "Fictional Re-presentation of the Los Angeles Riots: 'The Court Interpreter' by Ty Pak." *Journal of American Studies* (Seoul) 33, no. 2 (Winter 2001): 183–200.

Kim, Elaine H. "Korean American Literature." In *An Interethnic Companion to Asian American Literature,* edited by King-Kok Cheung, 156–191. Cambridge: Cambridge University Press, 1997.

Kwon, Brenda Lee. *Beyond Ke'eaumoku: Koreans, Nationalism, and Local Culture in Hawai'i.* New York: Garland, 1999.

Oh, Seiwoong. "Ty Pak." In *Asian American Short Story Writers: An A-to-Z Guide,* edited by Guiyou Huang, 251–255. New York: Greenwood Press, 2003.

Pak, Ty. "A Debt." *Moonbay: Short Stories.* New York: Woodhouse, 1999, 25–27.

Jinbhum Shin

Pangs of Love and Other Stories, The
David Wong Louie (1991)

For this, his first collection of short fiction and his first published book, DAVID WONG LOUIE received the First Fiction Award from the *Los Angeles Times Book Review* and the John C. Zacharis First Book Award from Ploughshares. The collection was also named a Notable Book by the *New York Times Book Review* and a Favorite Book by the *Village Voice Literary Supplement.* One of the stories in the collection, "Displacement," was selected for inclusion in *The Best American Short Stories of 1989.* Taken together, the 11 stories of the collection exhibit Louie's impressive capacity for invention, as well as considerable range in his topics, themes, and styles. The issues of race, gender, and class are intertwined in these stories of love, language and selfhood.

The title story is narrated by a Chinese-American man, whose mother continually and unsuccessfully urges him to find a good Chinese wife, even though he longs for a lover very different from the one his mother imagines for him. The mother, who speaks little English even though she has lived for four decades in America, is a comic-pathetic figure. In her loneliness, she develops a sense of emotional connection with late-night television host Johnny Carson, even though her very limited knowledge of English idioms leaves her incapable of understanding most of his humor.

"Displacement" is a character study of a Mrs. Chow, a woman from an aristocratic family in China who has been reduced in America to working as a domestic servant for a difficult old woman much given to uttering ethnic slurs, which Mrs. Chow pretends not to understand. In "Bottle of Beaujolais," a Chinese-American waiter in a Japanese sushi-bar becomes infatuated with a woman whom he sees repeatedly while caring for an otter kept in the window of the establishment. In "The Movers," a man takes possession of an empty home but begins to reconstruct from small clues the identity of the previous owner and then even to assume that identity. In "Disturbing the Universe," the central conceit is the supposition that the game of baseball originated in China.

Martin Kich

Park, Frances (1955–) and Park, Ginger (1962–)

Frances Park and Ginger Park are Korean-American sisters who write books for both children and young adults on universal themes such as love, loss, and war. Frances was born in Cambridge, Massachusetts, and raised in Washington, D.C.; Ginger was born and raised in Washington, D.C. They collaborate easily; one sister starts with the idea and creates a draft, which is edited by the other. While Ginger likes to write and tell stories about her Korean-American background and her parents, Frances enjoys perfecting the details and dialogue. They pass the manuscript back and forth until it is a completely polished work, never once sitting down together and discussing the manuscript.

The Park sisters' books are mostly inspired by their family's experiences. Although they knew their father was a high-ranking politician in South Korea, they did not know the details of his life, especially his youth as a poverty-stricken child. After his early death in 1979, they began researching their family's and Korea's histories. They retell their parents' experiences growing up in Korea in the love story *To Swim across the World,* which takes place before, during, and after the Korean War. *The Royal Bee* is a picture book about their maternal grandfather's determination to obtain an education despite the obstacles of poverty and class discrimination. The sisters oversaw certain aspects of the illustrations for cultural and historical accuracy. *Good-bye 382 Shin Dang Dong,* which is titled after their parents' former address in Korea, is a picture book about a little girl named Jangmi who is hesitant to leave her home in Korea for a new home in New England. Their mother's flight from North Korea, as described in *To Swim across the World,* is told for younger children in picture-book format in *My Freedom Trip.*

Frances Park is also the author of *WHEN MY SISTER WAS CLEOPATRA MOON*, a young adult novel about two Korean-American sisters and the special bond—and destruction—that ultimately shapes their destiny.

Sarah Park

Park, Linda Sue   (1960–   )

Linda Sue Park was born in Urbana, Illinois, to a computer analyst and teacher. Her mother taught her to read at an early age, and her father frequently took her to the library. A voracious reader, Park graduated from Stanford University with a B.A. in Engish and worked as a food journalist and teacher prior to writing books for children.

Park's parents were Korean immigrants, and she grew up with Korean influences in the home, but Park felt that she "knew very little about Korea itself" (Park "Newbery" 379). To rectify this gap in her life, she "learned about Korea by reading and writing about it" (Park "Newbery" 379), turning what she learned into stories for young people. She was fascinated with nuggets of information she found in her readings. For example, as a child she had read *Tales of a Korean Grandmother* by Frances Carpenter. One of the chapters contained "a reference to the fact that little girls from noble families in 17th-century Korea were never allowed to leave their homes" (Park "Newbery" 388). Park remembered this throughout her childhood and as an adult set out to explore this intriguing fact. Her findings provided the content for her first novel, *Seesaw Girl* (1999).

Since publishing her first book in 1999, Park steadily built her reputation as a children's book author. Her first three novels are historical fiction set in Korea. *Seesaw Girl* (1999) tells the story of a little girl in 17th-century Korea who is not allowed to venture outside the walls of her home. Two brothers in *The Kite Fighters* (2000) combine their talents to create and fly a beautiful kite on behalf of Korea's emperor. Park's third novel, *A Single Shard*, is set in 12th-century Korea. It tells the story of an orphan named Tree Ear who desires to be a potter. Although at the time only sons could be appren-

ticed to learning the trade, an accident provides the opportunity for Tree Ear to be an assistant for Potter Min, the greatest potter in the village. Park's last historical novel, *When My Name Was Keoko* (2002), is told through a pair of siblings. Sun-hee and her older brother Tae-yul alternately tell the story of their childhood in a Korea occupied by Japan. *Project Mulberry* (2005), Park's first contemporary Korean-American novel, is about an elementary school girl who resists the idea of raising silkworms for her Work-Grow-Give-Live project, preferring instead to do something "nice, normal, All-American, red-white-and-blue" (Park *Project* 30). *Archer's Quest* (2006) is about a Korean-American boy in New York whose world is turned upside down when Chu-mong, a Korean king from the past, shoots an arrow through his room. Kevin needs to help Chu-Mong return to the right time period so that history will not be distorted.

In addition to writing novels, Park creates picture books for younger audiences. *Mung-Mung* (2004) explores the different ways animals sound in other parts of the world. *The Firekeeper's Son* (2004) is the story about a boy who admires his father for lighting the fire that alerts the nation that all is well throughout the land. One day, when his father is injured, the boy has to decide between lighting the fire and wanting to see the soldiers who would come to defend the country if the fire is not lit. *Bee-bim Bop* (2005) is a delightfully rhyming picture book about a little girl helping her mother make *bee-bim bop,* one of Korea's most popular dishes.

Park is the first Asian-American author since DHAN GOPAL MUKERJI to win the John Newbery Medal. Although she briefly mentions the important role the Newbery Award plays in bringing visibility to a marginalized literature, Park is more concerned with the way that her stories build connections. She emphasizes the connective role of her work in bridging relationships between people and time periods. Her stories allow Korean-American children to imagine the history and culture of their parents and grandparents, while providing non-Korean Americans with the opportunity to learn about a history, culture, and time other than their own.

Bibliography

Park, Linda Sue. "Newbery Medal Acceptance." *Horn Book* (July/August 2002): 377–384.

———. *Project Mulberry*. Boston: Clarion, 2005.

Something about the Author. Vol. 127. Detroit: Gale, 2002, 166–168.

Stevenson, Dinah. "Linda Sue Park," *Horn Book* (July/August 2002): 387–391.

Sarah Park

Park, No-Yong   (1899–1976)

As a professor of Asian history, Park wrote several nonfiction books and lectured in Asian studies throughout North America. He was born in Manchuria, but his parents had emigrated from Korea during the Japanese invasion several years before his birth. Despite growing up in a small farming village, Park had the unusual luxury and privilege of being the only family member to attend school. His early schooling launched an intense search for knowledge and a truly modern education, which Park associated with the advancements and promise of the Western world.

Park's scholarly drive led him to Europe and then to America after World War I. His autobiography, *Chinaman's Chance* (1940), narrates his settlement in New York's Chinatown, where he vowed to speak English and study well so that he might break free from the limited opportunities available to Asian immigrants in America. Park writes of his educational achievements, such as his 1932 Ph.D. from Harvard, and his professional role as lecturer, but his autobiography is essentially an astute and critical look at American society in the early and mid 20th century. The autobiography begins with Park's description of his "mammoth appetite . . . without discrimination for Western culture and civilization." However, America soon teaches Park to be wary of his idealistic views of Western freedom and culture.

Throughout the book, Park combines his appreciation for American freedom and education with a sharp critique of American consumerism and waste. Despite being a "land of plenty," America reveals itself to the immigrant as a place where he cannot even have what others unquestioningly accept or wastefully discard. In a Thoreau-like manner, Park decides that he will not adopt the American drive to "keep up with the Joneses," but instead live as simply as possible. He keeps a small residence, few clothes, and spurns nonessential possessions. Even after his own professional success, Park continues to maintain a simple life without the need to mold himself into the typical American: "[After] trying the civilized ways of Western life for nearly a quarter of a century, I began to revolt against all my artificially acquired habits and traits because they did not seem to make me a better, freer, happier, or healthier human being."

In addition to his autobiography, Park published several other nonfiction books that also juxtapose and attempt to reconcile the misconceptions and misunderstandings between Eastern and Western cultures. His first book, *Making a New China* (1929), was followed by *An Oriental View of American Civilization* (1934) and *Retreat of the West: The White Man's Adventure in Eastern Asia* (1937), a collection of many of his lectures. Following the publication of his 1940 autobiography, Park published *The White Man's Peace: An Oriental View of Our Attempts at Making World Peace* (1948). As the titles of his books make explicit, Park was mainly interested in educating himself and others about the immigrant experience, the damaging divide between the West and the East, and the clash of identities and cultures that results from residence in a foreign country.

Critical reception of Park's work has been mixed. He has been criticized for historical inaccuracy and "superficial" scope. However, many critics have acknowledged Park as one of the first American writers of Korean-Chinese heritage who not only significantly contributed to the field of Asian-American studies, but also to the broad field of cultural studies.

Bibliography

Han, John Jae-Nam. "No-Yong Park: An Oriental Voice for World Peace." *Cantos: Literary and Arts Magazine* (2000): 74–79.

Huang, Guiyou, ed. *Asian American Autobiographers: A Bio-Bibliographic Sourcebook.* Westport, Conn: Greenwood Press, 2001.

Hutner, Gordon, ed. *Immigrant Voices: Twenty-Four Narratives on Becoming an American.* New York: Penguin, 1999.

Amy Lillian Manning

Pastries   Bharti Kirchner (2003)

In her fourth novel, BHARTI KIRCHNER brings together her passion for fiction writing and food to create a story focused on a young, talented baker named Sunya. Born of Indian parents, Sunya is raised in Seattle by her single mother. Her father, a graduate student at the University of Washington, mysteriously abandons the family after she is born. Her mother withstands the criticism of the small Indian community and sustains herself and her daughter by running a doughnut shop. Sunya trains in France and comes back to Seattle's Wallingford neighborhood to set up a boutique bakery that is known for its delicious desserts, notably the signature item called a "Sunya cake."

Sunya's troubles begin when a national chain plans to open a branch near her store. The chain's substandard ingredients allow them to undercut her prices, and the bakery war begins. This war is fueled by the local food critic who revels in Sunya's misery. Sunya, whose personal life is rocky because of her breakup with her Japanese boyfriend, is made further miserable by the bakery war and loses her nerve as a baker. She has a talented, if temperamental, staff that enables her to continue her business.

Sunya's personal life picks up when a filmmaker—in town to film the World Trade Organization ministerial meetings of November 1999—begins to court her and engages her ideas in developing his film. Sunya also hires a talented Japanese baker whose cheesecakes compensate for the absent "Sunya cake." Meanwhile, she receives mysterious missives from a lurking stranger inviting her to connect with the Apsara bakery in Japan. She learns from her Japanese baker that the Apsara is a Zen bakery where people go to find inner peace through baking. Upon his advice, Sunya signs up for a two-week class to rekindle her baking talents. While in Japan, she meets up with her long-lost father, who has become a monk and abandoned familial life in search of nirvana. When her father dies, she returns to Seattle, having found her baking talents. She ultimately wins the bakery war and is off to a happy life as an entrepreneur.

This romantic novel continues some of the major themes in Kirchner's writing including the clash of cultures, parent-child relationship, autonomy of women, and the need to balance the demands of multiple cultures.

Nalini Iyer

Phan, Aimee   (1977–   )

Born to Vietnamese refugee parents in Orange County, California, Phan attended the University of California, Los Angeles. During her freshman year at the university, she read and was inspired by *NO-NO BOY* by JOHN OKADA. The novel showed her the effect that Asian-American literature can have on one's perception of history and self. In college, Phan wrote for the campus newspaper and after graduation became an intern at *USA Today*. Phan, however, pursued her interest in creative writing by attending the M.F.A. program at the University of Iowa Creative Writing Workshop, where she was awarded the Maytag Fellowship. Phan currently teaches English at Washington State University.

Phan's debut novel, *We Should Never Meet*, features eight linked stories that represent the aftermath of a historical event called "Operation Babylift," the evacuation of thousands of orphans from Vietnam to the United States weeks before the fall of Saigon. The novel traces the resettlement of several of these orphans, as well as young boat refugees, as they come into adulthood in the United States. Phan's stories challenge the idea behind the operation: that these babies are destined to find a better life in the United States. The novel asks us to consider "Operation Babylift" as emblematic of the U.S.-Vietnam experience. As such, the novel poignantly highlights how even matters that seem so close to the heart—white families' adoption of Vietnamese babies—need to be contextualized within U.S. racism, U.S. intentions in Asia, and the geopolitical restructuring of the late 20th century.

Told from different perspectives, the stories relate different experiences. The title story, "We Should Never Meet," for example, introduces us to Kim, who grew up in the California foster care system. She feels anger at her society for making her feel like an outsider. "Bound" is narrated from the perspective of Bridget, a white American doctor who leaves behind her own daughter and husband in order to take care of Vietnamese orphans. "Visitors" is told by Vinh, a boat refugee orphan whose obligations to his gang force him to rob an older Vietnamese man who has shown him kindness. "Motherland" is narrated by Huan, a mixed-race orphan who returns to Vietnam with his white adoptive mother who is eager for Huan to find his roots.

Even though the novel features multiple perspectives and narrators, these eight stories are tightly woven together. For example, Kim, Mai, and Vinh, who meet while waiting to be put into foster care, are emotionally bound to one another even though they inevitably lead separate lives. By showcasing their connections within the disjunctions of their individual lives, the novel seems to suggest that the circumstances of their settlement in the United States tie them even closer to each other than to their adoptive families.

In addition to the overlapping plotlines, the novel is also held together by several themes. In particular, violence against women features prominently in several stories. In "Miss Lien," the first story of the novel, young Lien is forced to leave the safety of her family when an attack on the family farm leaves the family with no food or provisions. Lien migrates to a big city filled with potential sexual predators. As she looks for work and food, both older Vietnamese men and American soldiers see Lien as sexually available and vulnerable to their advances. The tone and imagery of the story make clear that Lien is raped and has a child; even at the end of the story, however, the identity of the father of Lien's baby remains unclear. Lien's story,

coming at the beginning of the novel, is positioned as the possible birth story for any of the orphan characters in the novel. Shrouded in sexual violence and loss, the novel portrays these babies as victims of a war that displaced traditional safety nets and social structures. In "Emancipation," orphaned Kim fears being touched and recalls being molested by her foster father. Similarly, Mai rejects intimacy, hinting at a past of solitude and rejection. Both the war and "Operation Babylift," then, are differently indicted as violence enacted on the orphans and their mothers.

The novel effortlessly moves back and forth in time and place between Orange County of the 1990s and Vietnam war-era Saigon. For example, while the first story takes place in 1970s Saigon and the last story depicts the return of several orphans to Ho Chi Mihn City of the 1990s, the novel does not privilege chronology or linear development. This fluidity of chronology positions the past as influential to the present. Similarly, the ease of movement between Vietnam and the United States situates these two farflung spaces as intimately shaping each other every day. As a whole, the novel suggests that Vietnam and the United States have inevitably and profoundly changed each other as a result of the Vietnam War.

Raised among Vietnamese immigrants, Phan was exposed to many war orphans through her mother, who, along with Phan's aunt and uncle, participated in "Operation Babylift." As a social worker in Orange County, Phan's mother worked closely with these children and adults, and Phan's observations of these orphans provided the groundwork and inspiration for *We Should Never Meet*. This debut novel won critical acclaim and was named a Notable Book by the Kiryama Prize in fiction as well as being a finalist for the 2005 Asian American Literary Awards.

Bibliography

Ciuraru, Carmela. "Vietnam's Legacy of Childhood Displacement." *Los Angeles Times Book Review*, September 24, 2004, E, p. 10.

Jinah Kim

Picture Bride   Cathy Song (1983)

Winner of the 1982 Yale Series of Younger Poets Award and the best-known collection of CATHY SONG's poetry, *Picture Bride* was published by Yale University in 1983 and was also nominated for that year's National Book Critics Circle Award. A poet who highly stresses visual body imagery in her works, Cathy Song deals with the mapping of identity by exploring the relationship of body to body and presents such imagery explicitly and symbolically. *Picture Bride* reveals the poet's corporeal interaction with animals and such people as her grandmother, mother, sister, son, father, husband, and neighbors. The book explicitly visualizes the body and its parts, such as hair, hands, eyes, and lips, and also presents the body symbolically through images of such spaces as Chinatown, Hawaii, home, the sugarcane field, and even weather.

A collection of 31 poems, divided into five sections with the subtitles named after Georgia O'Keeffe's floral paintings, *Picture Bride* begins by depicting her grandmother in its title poem, "Picture Bride." The poem dramatizes Song's grandmother at the age of 23, when she was leaving Korea to marry a man she had never seen before—a sugar-mill laborer in Waialua, Hawaii, who was 13 years her senior. Imaginatively picturing the scene of their first meeting in Hawaii, "Picture Bride" begins with the poet speaker's identification with her grandmother because of their shared appearance. Song recalls that when she wrote this poem, she was about the same age as her grandmother in the poem: "I find that incomprehensible, that she could leave willingly, forfeit all that was familiar for a place she had never seen, to marry a man she had never met" (qtd. in Solberg 544).

The collection shifts to the mother-daughter relationship in the next poem, "The Youngest Daughter," in which Song portrays moments of physical intimacy between the poet speaker and her mother: The mother massages the poet's face, and the poet in turn bathes her mother. "The Youngest Daughter," at first glance, displays a state of harmony as well as nostalgia for a physical union between mother and child. In many of the subsequent poems, Song depicts her early childhood

in the voice of a child or an adult speaker with a child's consciousness. Through the sensory organs, the child perceives the world around her as sometimes threatening and sometimes protective; the surroundings are even perceived as an extension of the body, reflecting the wholesomeness or fragmentation of the bodily identity. Heard through the voice of an adult viewer of Kitagawa Utamaro's prints and the persona of Georgia O'Keeffe, the middle part of the book reveals the oppression of a patriarchal society by meticulously depicting female body images in various paintings. The book ends with an assertion of the body as having always been ethnicized and gendered.

Bibliography

Chen, Fu-jen. "Body and Female Subjectivity in Cathy Song's *Picture Bride.*" *Women's Studies: An Interdisciplinary Journal* 33, no. 5 (2004): 577–612.

Solberg, S. E. "Cathy Song and the Korean American Experience in Poetry." In *The Asian Pacific American Heritage,* edited by George J. Leonard, 541–546. New York: Garland, 1999.

Fu-jen Chen

Picture Bride   Yoshiko Uchida (1988)

The title *Picture Bride* refers to the Japanese women who traveled to the United States in the early 20th century to join husbands whom they had never met before. Because marriage between Japanese immigrants and white Americans was strictly forbidden during this time, many Japanese men resorted to matchmakers through whom they sought to find marriage partners in Japan. Men and women would exchange photos and sometimes letters. Women who agreed to these marriages, referred to as "picture brides," then traveled to the United States to meet these men for the first time. Women like Hana Omiya, in YOSHIKO UCHIDA's *Picture Bride,* saw this as an opportunity that might not have been readily available to them in their native Japan.

Hana Omiya, a daughter of a samurai, has big dreams. She has been corresponding with a man from the San Francisco area whom she believes to be young and successful with his own business. She dreams that she will soon be married and living in the United States, the land of opportunity where dreams come true. Therefore she leaves her family and homeland for a new and strange place full of uncertainty and wonder. The story begins in 1917, when Hana, now 21 years old, is a new immigrant. Taro, her new husband, is not exactly what he said he was. He is middle-aged, and his business is not as successful as she expected. Her strength as a character shines as she learns to deal with the circumstances at hand and makes the best of it. She tries to help her headstrong and traditional husband with his failing business, while trying to raise a daughter, Mary, in the divided cultural space between traditional Japanese and contemporary American cultures. Hana encounters a world that is not so forgiving when it comes to cultural differences. Mary also struggles to live her American life while still living as a daughter of a woman who holds onto her tradition like a security blanket.

The characters are written with lifelike personalities, based on the author's personal experiences as a daughter of Japanese immigrants. *Picture Bride* takes place over a span of 26 years after Hana's arrival in California. Through the character's eyes, we watch the world through World War I and the Great Depression. As the Japanese immigration to the United States grows over these periods, anti-Asian sentiment grows at the same time. The family encounters racism at its worst after the 1941 Japanese attack on Pearl Harbor. In Uchida's story, however, hope and love prevail throughout the lives of the characters.

Anne Bahringer

Pittalwala, Iqbal   (?–)

The beginning of Iqbal Pittalwala's literary career sounds like a quirky scene from an Asian-American novel or play. Pittalwala, a native of Mumbai (Bombay), was studying for a doctorate in atmospheric science at the State University of New York at Stony Brook. Finding the writing difficult, he signed up for a writing class, not realizing that the class featured only creative writing. Compelled to take up the unexpected challenge of learning to write fiction, Pittalwala began to write stories and quickly excelled. Within a few years of accidentally taking a creative writing class, Pittalwala's stories were published in magazines such as *Confrontation, The Blue Mesa Review, Harrington Gay Men's Fiction Quarterly, The Seattle Review,* and *Trikone Magazine.* This productive period of short-story writing climaxed in 2002 with the publication of Pittalwala's first book, *Dear Paramount Pictures.*

Dear Paramount Pictures is unusual for an American literary publication because of the intensity with which it conveys the experiences of Indian people—both Indians resident on the subcontinent and Indians living in the United States. The book is also unusual because the title story, which opens the collection, is facetious and uproariously funny in complete contrast to the downbeat, serious sobriety of the rest of the collection. The title story consists of a long, rambling letter by an Indian matriarch who feels obliged to inform Hollywood studio bosses that James Dean has been reincarnated as a Muslim student from Kanpur. While this opening story is comic and digressive, the remaining stories are all direct and sometimes shocking for Westerners who are unused to detailed depictions of overcrowded Indian cities. Taken as a whole, the remaining 10 stories convey four main themes: the poverty of Indian megalopolises; cultural gaps between America and the subcontinent; parents' inability to comprehend the opinions of their children; and the misery perpetuated by loveless marriages.

Some American readers may be shocked by scenes of poverty depicted by Pittalwala in the collection. In "The Change," a 65-year-old Bombay woman's world collapses when she is abused callously on poor public transport while on a rare outing, and when a modest wedding present that she has bought is smashed, causing her great grief. A more lethal sort of poverty informs the harsh story, "A Change of Lights." A physically disabled woman, Lajwanti, begs at traffic lights, desperately seeking money for alcohol for herself and food for her weak infant. People in cars dismiss her and her child as "guttersnipes" and "filthy animals." She is made to feel no better than a starving dog that tries to ingratiate itself to her; she feels inferior even to crows who can scavenge without begging. Lajwanti considers maiming her child deliberately in the hope that a disabled infant will attract more charity than an able-bodied one. Although she does not execute this macabre plan, we are left with the impression that extreme poverty can inspire such inhumane brutality.

In "Lost in the U.S.A.," the urban middle classes are also seen to be intolerant of poor people. This time, though, the story underlines the difference in culture between America and India. Pramila, a middle-aged woman who lives in Bombay, visits her son in America. Underestimating the problems of language, Pramila attempts a foolhardy journey on a bus only to get onto a wrong vehicle and become, indeed, "Lost in the U.S.A." A middle-class couple do bring her home, but their charity is given through gritted teeth. Pramila thinks that the couple are her "new friends," but they depart from her as soon as is possible. Impromptu social gatherings may be common in Pramila's Bombay, but she must learn that friends cannot be made so easily in the individualistic milieu of America, especially not when barriers of class and race further impair the chances of sympathetic comradeship.

Several stories in *Dear Paramount Pictures* address the age-old theme of incomprehension between generations. In "Mango Season," a self-righteous old Bombay man, Aman Lal, is treated with contempt by a telephone company. His plan to bribe a relevant official runs into difficulties when it emerges that his shoddy teaching practices in the past have hindered the now bitter man's education and subsequent development. When he was teaching, Aman Lal did not comprehend the negative effects that his pedagogical inadequacies had on some children. In "Bombay Talkies," one of a number of stories that allude to India's huge movie-making industry, an ineffective, middle-aged Muslim man, Hakim Khan, fights desperately to protect the innocence of his 18-year-old daughter, Salima. Angrily, Khan attacks the "ruffians" and "swine" who deliberately bump against his daughter on a busy bus. He tells Salima that "dirty" Bombay is "far too wicked for someone

like" her. This is hugely ironic because, in fact, Salima is aroused by the attention of the men and seeks erotic pleasure from the tactile contact with insalubrious male strangers. The daughter's burgeoning sexuality is not even imagined by her uncomprehending father.

Several stories also feature loveless marriages. Arranged for other family members' convenience, these marriages result in miserable, sometimes brutally violent conjunctions between frustrated men and frustrated women. In "Ramadan," a devout Muslim woman, Bilquis, and her humiliated son, Farid, must deal with the trauma caused by her husband's regular philandering—and by his willful ignoring of sacrifices important during Islam's Ramadan period. Pittalwala is careful to paint a background here of a Bombay marred by pollution, sectarian rioting between Muslims and Hindus, and harsh working and living conditions—six taxi drivers live in a one-bedroom property. The disastrous marriage, then, becomes a microcosm of corruption and squalor throughout the city. The final story "House of Cards," features another loveless marriage, this time set in California. Here, Khalida, a woman effectively bought by her husband by mail order from Pakistan, deals with the revelation that her husband will not make love to her because he is gay—he pursues homosexual affairs, shaming her. Although Khalida's homophobic rants against her husband may cause unease for the liberal reader, her decision to leave her dishonest, unfaithful husband seems appropriate, necessary even.

Although distracted by a newfound motivation to write short stories, Pittalwala completed his Ph.D. He is an accomplished scientist and has worked as a campus communications officer for science and engineering for the University of California, Riverside. He has also acquired an M.F.A. in creative writing from the Writers' Workshop at the University of Iowa.

In 2004 Pittalwala won $1,000 in a short-story competition run by Gival Press. The winning story, "Legacy," returns to themes explored in "House of Cards." The children of Indian immigrants in California squabble over inheritance issues after their father marries his gay lover in San Francisco—a novel arrangement challenging for many Americans as well as Asians. Again in this story, Pittalwala rehearses his regular preoccupations: the gap in comprehension between parents and children; the money-obsessed, unfriendly ambience of America; the effects of a loveless marriage that causes misery even after one partner is deceased; and the conflict between duty to parents and siblings and duty to a wife. "Legacy" works well as a starting point into the serious fiction of Iqbal Pittalwala.

Presently, Pittalwala teaches creative writing for continuing education students at the University of California, Riverside Extension Center. Pittalwala has suggested that his next book may be a novel. Whether his next book is a novel or another collection of short stories, readers and scholars interested in uncompromising depictions of the Asian experience either in India or abroad in America will read it with enthusiastic interest.

Bibliography

Pittalwala, Iqbal. *Dear Paramount Pictures.* Dallas: Southern Methodist University Press, 2002.

Kevin De Ornellas

Qiu, Xiaolong (1953–)

Born in Shanghai, Qiu entered college in 1977 shortly after the Cultural Revolution and took up graduate work in Western literature at the Chinese Academy of Social Sciences. In 1988 Qiu started his Ph.D. program in comparative literature at Washington University in St. Louis, Missouri, and obtained his Ph.D. in 1995. He is currently an adjunct professor of Chinese literature at Washington University. In China Qiu had many publications in Chinese, including poetry, translations of modernist poets such as Ezra Pound and T. S. Eliot, and literary criticism. He was also a member of the Chinese Writers' Association. Best known for his detective series, *The DEATH OF A RED HEROINE* (2000), *A Loyal Character Dancer* (2002), and *When Red Is Black* (2004), Qiu also translated and edited two collections of Chinese poetry, *Lines around China* (2003) and *Treasury of Chinese Love Poems: In Chinese and English* (2003).

Written in the Western tradition of detective stories, Qiu's three novels all feature Chen Cao, chief inspector of the Shanghai Police Bureau, who investigates politically sensitive murder cases with his assistant, Detective Yu Guangming. Qiu's novels engage the reader with their revelation of the rapidly changing society of modern China in the 1990s. Despite historically and culturally inaccurate details, the stories draw a vivid portrait of Shanghai in the pleasure and pain of its dras-

tic changes deeply entangled with its past. Chen, like the author, is well versed in Chinese and English poetry, and is himself a published poet and translator of crime fiction in English. Qiu portrays Chen as a contemporary Chinese intellectual deeply rooted in traditional Chinese sensibilities but influenced by Western culture and literature. The frequent poetic allusions and creations in his novels, Qiu claims, are traditional conventions of Chinese novels. The complexity of the characterization also lies in the tension between Chen's status as a romantic individual and his delicate maneuvring to rise in the political system.

The second in the series, *A Loyal Character Dancer* (2002), examines human smuggling from China to the United States and police cooperation between the two countries. Chief Inspector Chen Cao works with Inspector Catherine Rohn of the U.S. Marshals Service to find a missing woman, Wen Liping. Wen's husband agrees to testify in a criminal trial against the Triad with which he himself is involved, but only on one condition: that his pregnant wife be allowed to join him in the United States. The tracing of Wen is also the tracing of her personal history. An enthusiastic "character dancer" who held the Chinese character for "loyal" in a performance dedicated to Chairman Mao during the Cultural Revolution, Wen was sent to the countryside in the later stage of the Cultural Revolution and suffered brutal abuse by her husband.

Hunted by the Triad, which fears her husband's testimony, she finds safety with a former suitor, who is now a successful entrepreneur.

Qiu's third book, *When Red Is Black* (2004), revolves around the murder of Yin Lige, a college teacher and author of the novel *Death of a Chinese Professor*. Yin wrote about her love affair with renowned professor Yang Bing in the cadre school during the Cultural Revolution. Yin also edits Yang's poetry translation and keeps the manuscript of Yang's novel in English, from which part of her novel is borrowed. The murder is committed purely out of greed by Yang's poor grandnephew from the countryside, who wants to seek his fortune in the royalties of Yang's works.

Yan Ying

Queen's Garden, The
Brenda Wong Aoki (1992)

The Queen's Garden, a one-woman play, is a love story and a coming-of-age tale centered on a character named Brenda Jean, a girl of mixed Japanese, Chinese, Mexican, and Scottish descent. The play opens with the narrator, an older version of Brenda Jean, recalling her childhood on Los Angeles's Westside. These reflections are interspersed with scenes from her adolescence and early adult years, as the narrator assumes various personas and voices in order to present the audience with glimpses of key moments in Brenda Jean's life: her first encounter with the neighborhood matriarch Aunti Mari, her blossoming romance with Aunti Mari's handsome surfer son, and her eventual escape from the poverty and crime of the inner city. Yet, although Brenda Jean is able to leave the Westside to attend college, her past continues to haunt her, and she is thrust back into the escalating gang violence that has enveloped the lives of her childhood sweetheart, Kali, and other friends from her past.

Partly autobiographical, *The Queen's Garden* draws on BRENDA WONG AOKI's early life and later experiences as a community organizer and teacher in Los Angeles and San Francisco. According to the artistic statement that introduces the published version of the play in *Contemporary Plays by Women of Color* (1996), *The Queen's Garden* was written in response to the Los Angeles riots of 1992 in an effort to "humanize" the experience of life in areas like South Central. By presenting her audience with sympathetic portraits of individuals whose lives might otherwise be understood only in terms of their illegal behavior, Aoki challenges pervasive views about the moral degeneracy of inner-city youth while drawing attention to the rich cultural diversity of Los Angeles. Aunti Mari's thriving rose garden in the poverty-stricken Westside suggests that beauty and human decency endure even under adverse conditions.

In October 1992, *The Queen's Garden* premiered at the Climate Theatre in San Francisco under the direction of Jael Weisman with musical accompaniment by Mark Izu. It has since been performed in theaters in Honolulu; San Diego; Washington, D.C.; Santa Monica; and New York City; and at universities across the country. In 1996 *The Queen's Garden* was included in the anthology *Contemporary Plays by Women of Color*. In 1999 a recorded version of the play was released by Asian Improv Records as a spoken-word album with music. Aoki's performance of the play garnered four Dramalogue awards and a San Diego Critics Circle Award. The recorded version went on to receive an Indie award for best spoken word recording in 1999.

Rachel Ihara

Rachlin, Nahid (1947–)

Rachlin was born in Ahvaz, a small oil-producing state in southwestern Iran, and raised in a traditional Iranian family. She came to the United States at the age of 17 to attend a small college in St. Charles, Washington, after the Iranian authorities gave her permission to leave the country on the condition that she attend an all-female college and one near her brother. Fortunately, she was able to find a small women's college close to where her brother was attending medical school. This was a dramatic move for Rachlin, who managed to sidestep the traditional expectation of an Iranian woman to enter into an arranged marriage. Instead of returning to Iran, she chose to stay in the States and marry an American.

Her early years adjusting to America as a foreign exchange student and the alienation she felt, further complicated by her own questioning of her cultural background, make up the crux of her rich novels. One of the earliest and most prolific Iranian-American authors, she has published three novels, a collection of short stories, and numerous essays. Despite the wide acclaim her books have received, her work has not been translated into Persian or distributed in Iran because of the controversial topics of her novels. True to the young rebellious girl who struggled to pave herself a new path, her works are unabashedly honest about her personal life and Iranian culture. In her personal essay, "My Observations on American-Iranian Cultural Differences," Rachlin attributes her unconventional ways and early dissatisfaction to an incident early in her childhood. Her mother, during her pregnancy with Rachlin, promised her child to a widowed aunt with no children of her own. Rachlin was raised in Tehran by this aunt in a very loving, relaxed atmosphere. This paradise between foster mother and daughter did not last. When she was nine, her father came, traumatically separating her from her foster mother/aunt, and took her back. She was immersed quickly into her father's stern household. She longed for her old life, but only once a year was she allowed to be reunited with her foster mother/aunt. This early trauma offered her, as young as she was, a comparison of two kinds of lifestyles and emotional bonds within a family. Perhaps as a result, her work lays bare the very private affairs between husbands and wives, as well as parents and children. All of this with a quiet political critique in the background makes for a deep narrative of people caught between two vastly different and, on the surface, conflicting worlds.

Her works include FOREIGNER (W.W. Norton, 1978), *Married to a Stranger* (E.P. Dutton, 1983), *Veils: Short Stories* (City Lights Press, 1992), and *The HEART'S DESIRE* (City Lights Press, 1995). Her essays have been published in *Natural History Magazine, New York Times Magazine,* and in the anthology *How I Learned to Cook and Other Writings on Complex Mother-Daughter Relationships.* Her works of short fiction have appeared in more than 50 magazines and literary journals. Awards she has received for her writing include the Bennett Cerf Award, PEN Syndicated Fiction Award, and a National Endowment for the Arts grant. Besides her latest novel, *Jumping over Fire* (2006), she also published *Persian Girls* (2006), a memoir that traces her relationship with a sister who remained in Iran and the separate paths of their lives.

In high demand as a reader, Rachlin has read in countless bookstores, schools, libraries, institutes, universities, and literary centers. She has taught at Barnard College, Yale University, and a variety of prestigious conferences across the nation. She teaches creative writing at the New School University in New York and the Unterberg Poetry Center.

Zohra Saed

Rahman, Imad   (1970–)

Imad Rahman was born and raised in Karachi, Pakistan, and educated at the Karachi Grammar School. Though he found nothing particularly inspirational or stimulating in the readings he encountered as a student in Pakistan, Rahman was quite taken by J. D. Salinger's *Catcher in the Rye* and Joseph Heller's *Catch-22* (novels which would later have an obvious influence on his own fiction) when he first discovered them at the age of 16. Rahman moved to the United States in pursuit of higher education at the age of 18 and eventually earned an M.A. in English from Ohio State University and an M.F.A. in creative writing from the University of Florida. It was during his time in college that Rahman fully developed his talent for writing fiction, feeling that fiction writing was the only thing he could do particularly well. After graduating from the University of Florida, Rahman was elected the 2001–02 James C. McReight Fiction Fellow at the Wisconsin Institute for Creative Writing. Rahman's short stories have appeared in a variety of literary publications. After teaching creative writing for several years at the University of

Wisconsin–Madison, Rahman is now an assistant professor of English at Kansas State University.

Rahman's first book, *I Dream of Microwaves* (2004), is a collection of interrelated short stories that satirize the Great American Dream. The primary narrator of the stories is a Pakistani-American actor named Kareem Abdul Jabbar, who is constantly thwarted in his pursuit of fame and success by an endless stream of absurd occurrences. Through his vast knowledge of Western culture—popular actors and movies, in particular—Kareem is ultimately able to draw inspiration and begin to cope with the numerous misadventures and follies that seem to characterize his life. In the collection's title story "I Dream of Microwaves," Kareem is fired from his job of playing a real-life Mexican fugitive on the American television show *America's Most Wanted,* leading him to comment that "I couldn't even get typecast as a criminal of Pakistani origin. Perhaps people of Pakistani origin did not commit enough heinous crimes or did not perform enough acts of extraordinary mediocrity." In an even greater twist, Kareem decides to pose as his ex-girlfriend's Bosnian refugee fiancé to help her obtain her inheritance from her dying grandmother, only to find that his ex-girlfriend has hired another actor to pose as yet another fiancé, this time a destitute African cannibal. In "Real Life, Actual Life," Kareem and his new girlfriend work for a video rental agency and are sent, in the spirit of Conrad's *Heart of Darkness,* to collect an overdue movie from a man named Mr. Patel, who also happens to be a Hollywood producer. In "Here Come the Dog People," Kareem is hired to play the role of the late comedian and actor John Belushi in a production of a play entitled *John, Ono, John,* about a fictitious love affair between Belushi and Yoko Ono.

Despite the endless absurdities that seem to surround Kareem's life, Rahman never crosses over into the realm of the truly ridiculous or trite. Even the oddest of his stories are still full of humor and, moreover, genuine pathos. Kareem's world, for all of its improbabilities and maddening happenings, is one that is quite familiar to us all. Throughout his stories, Rahman writes sensitively and insightfully of not only the Pakistani experience in America, but of the modern human experience in general, forever encountering absurdity and relentlessly striving toward ultimate success and happiness.

James R. Fleming

Rao, Raja   (1908–)

Born to a Brahmin family in Mysore in South India, Raja Rao left India in 1927 to study in France and stayed abroad for most of his life. The long stay in France and the United States was interrupted by many forays back to India, where he stayed at various ashrams, including Gandhi's in Sevagram, in search of a guru. As a writer, Rao belongs to the generation of preindependence novelists, like Mulk Raj Anand, Bhabani Bhattacharya, and G. V. DESANI, to name a few, whose writing is imbued with a strong anticolonial nationalism. Rao's writing also displays a cosmopolitan blend of Indian and Western sensibilities as a result of his having spent the impressionable years of his life in Europe. His later pieces, on the other hand, particularly the novels written after the long gap that followed *Kanthapura* (1938), is saturated with the deep mystical vision of Vedantic philosophy.

Kanthapura, Rao's only preindependence novel, has become a classic text in postcolonial studies for its foreword that functions as a manifesto on the urgent need to indigenize the English language: "One has to convey in a language that is not one's own the spirit that is one's own. . . . We cannot write like the English. We should not. . . ." Rao tackles the ambiguities and complexities arising from the use of the colonial master tongue, English, to express a cultural and historical sensibility that is far distant from it. He announces his bold attempt to forge a narrative in the oral tradition of the Puranas of Hindu tradition. But *Kanthapura* is no Purana in the religious mold; instead, it is a superb blend of the visionary and the secular, as it tells the inspiring tale of the influence of Gandhi on a remote Indian village at the height of the civil disobedience movement in the 1920s and 1930s. Rao's text idealizes the village community, even as it foregrounds the radical activism of women in the freedom movement. *Kanthapura*'s Gandhian

nationalism is tempered with a strong strain of social realism that turns an inward eye to problems endemic to Indian society, such as untouchability and superstition.

With *The Serpent and the Rope* (1960), Rao abandons the rural Indian milieu to narrate a cosmopolitan tale set across India and Europe. Semiautobiographical in inspiration, it marks a deliberate shift in his fiction from nationalist politics to metaphysical themes, as Rao rehearses the personal trajectory of the breakdown of his marriage to a French academic. The narrative traces the quest for spiritual salvation by Ramaswamy, the novel's somewhat self-absorbed protagonist, even as it explores the gap between East and West, articulated through the different world views of Ramaswamy and Madeline, his French wife. The novel explores the philosophy of Advaita Vedanta, who asserts that reality is undifferentiated, so that the serpent and the rope, which appear at odds, are really one.

The Cat and Shakespeare (1965), a companion novel to *The Serpent and the Rope* in its philosophical bent, delves even deeper into the issue of mystical self-understanding. *Comrade Kirillov* (1976), *The Chessmaster and his Moves* (1988), and his other novels continue Rao's preoccupation with metaphysical themes. Rao has also written two collections of critically acclaimed short stories: *The Cow of the Barricades, and Other Stories* (1947) and *The Policeman and the Rose* (1978). *The Ganga Ghat* (1993), a set of three interconnected stories on Benares, the holiest of Hindu cities, grapples with the question of death.

Rao's work stands out for its relentlessly philosophical focus and his consistent experimentation with generic boundaries that define the predominantly social realism of his contemporaries.

Rajender Kaur

Rizzuto, Rahna Reiko   (1963–)

Rizzuto was born in Honolulu and raised in nearby Kamuela on the big island of Hawaii. Her father was half Italian and half Irish. Her mother, a second-generation Japanese American born in

California, moved to Hawaii with her family after their release from internment during World War II. After attending Wellesley College in Massachusetts, Rizzuto transferred to Columbia University to become the first woman to graduate with a degree in astrophysics. Her writings appeared in the *Asian Pacific American Journal* and *The NuyorAsian Anthology: Asian American Writings about New York City.*

In her debut novel, *Why She Left Us*—the winner of the 1999 American Book Award for fiction from the Before Columbus Foundation—Rizzuto depicts a Japanese-American family dealing with life after World War II. Being part Japanese, Rizzuto found firsthand inspiration for the novel when she accompanied her mother and grandmother to a reunion of the Japanese-American internees held at the Amachi internment camp in Colorado. At the reunion, she learned the stories of innocent people who were stripped of their homes, lives, and civil rights. She learned the story of her grandmother and her family, who were evicted from their homes and given short notice to sell everything because they could not take anything of value into the camp. Everything they had worked for and every reason why they left Japan for a better life in America was taken from them and never given back. This was a story that she never heard as a young girl, a chapter in history that the family wanted forgotten.

The story she chose to tell is that of the Okada family as it is torn apart by its experiences during the war. The novel itself is told in a unique way. With the exception of Kaori, who speaks in the first person, Rizzuto uses a third-person narrator to allow individual family members to tell their own versions of the family history. In a nonsequential order, each of the four main characters, Kaori (Emi's mother), Mariko (Emi's daughter), Eric (Emi's son), and Jack (Emi's brother), retells the tale of how the family came together and fell apart, including vivid descriptions of Emi, the only main character who is not given a voice. The main characters explore possible reasons why Emi, whose values were drastically different from those of other Japanese Americans, left her family. The absence of Emi's perspective in the narrative makes the questions that surround Emi's leaving unanswerable, reflecting the reality of life for most of us.

Anne Bahringer

Rno, Sung   (1967–)

Sung Rno (pronounced *No*) is a playwright and poet best known for his plays *Cleveland Raining* (1995) and *wAve* (2004). Born in Minneapolis, Minnesota, Rno is the son of Jung Sik Rno, a physics professor at the University of Cincinnati, and Taewon H. Rno, a university administrator. Rno grew up in Maryland and Cincinnati, Ohio, where he attended the magnet school Walnut Hills High School. During his last two years in high school, Rno began reading the work of Tennessee Williams and Ernest Hemingway and, with the encouragement of his teachers, began to write poetry and plays. Rno went on to attend Harvard University, where he graduated with a degree in physics. At Harvard, Rno took a poetry course with the noted poet Seamus Heaney, which led him to take his own work as a poet more seriously. Upon graduation, Rno spent a year in Japan teaching English. That experience allowed him to travel to Korea and other parts of Asia, making him more aware of his own ethnicity as an American of Korean descent. When he returned to the United States, Rno enrolled in Brown University, where he earned an M.F.A. in poetry in 1991 with a thesis entitled "This Light So Quiet." At Brown, Rno studied with playwright Paula Vogel and wrote his first play, *Cleveland Raining.*

Cleveland Raining had its world premiere at Grinnell College in Ohio (1994) and was also produced by East West Players a year later in Los Angeles. The play is about two young Korean Americans who are siblings. Mari, a reluctant medical student, is haunted by memories of her parents, and her brother Jimmy, a former grocery bagger, spends his time outfitting a Volkswagen Beetle in expectation of a flood of biblical proportions. The other two characters include a mechanic and an injured motorcyclist who may or may not have broken her ankle in an accident involving Mari and Jimmy's vanished father. Told in lyrical language, the play is an examination of the trauma of assimilation and the obliterating effect of Americanization on Asian immigrants. Interestingly, the play avoids overt references to race and ethnicity. The characters, who are relatively young second-generation immigrants, see themselves as "Americans," refusing to bear the tag and possibly "burden" of their ethnicity. In this sense, the play presents a shift from a previous, more clearly militant brand of Asian-American theater. The play also posits a different model for Asian-American representation onstage: It rejects the naturalistic style common in the late 1970s and 1980s, in favor of a more fragmented, metaphorical, and postmodern approach.

After the success of *Cleveland Raining*, Rno continued to write plays and poetry. In 1998 he married Helen Yum and had their first child, a son, eight years later. In 2004 the Ma-Yi Theater Company in New York City produced Rno's second major work, *wAve. WAve* builds upon Rno's use of poetic language in *Cleveland Raining*, this time to more parodic and overtly political effect. Based on Euripides' *Medea, wAve* recasts Medea as M, a Korean-American woman who leaves her family in Korea and moves to the United States with her husband, Jason. When Jason is cast in a Hollywood film and becomes involved with a Caucasian woman (who is a genetically engineered recreation of Marilyn Monroe's DNA), M enacts revenge by killing her own son, as in the Greek tragedy. Through M, who suffers from social anxiety, Rno examines the psychological struggles of Asian-American immigrant women, whose alienation is often either neglected or pathologized. Interestingly, Rno reverses in the play the real-life dynamic of Asian women marrying outside their race, by having a Korean man involved with a Caucasian woman. As the play deconstructs the musical *Miss Saigon* (whose film adaptation Jason is starring in), Rno reconfigures commonly accepted equations of race and gender relations. Finally, as in his previous work, Rno incorporates principles from math and physics into the play, exploring how equations and laws can illuminate complex behavior and the hidden connections between things.

Rno's other plays include *Gravity Falls from Trees* (1997) and *Yi Sung Counts to Thirteen* (2000). The latter, directed by Lee Breuer of Mabou Mines, was produced in Seoul, Korea, at the Seoul Theater Festival 2000. Rno's poetry has been anthologized in *Premonitions* (1995), *Nuyorasian Anthology* (1999), and *Echoes Upon Echoes* (2003).

Samuel Park

Rosca, Ninotchka   (1946–   )

Ninotchka Rosca has been hailed as the single most eminent voice of the Filipino people. Born and raised in the Philippines, Rosca immigrated to the United States in the 1970s as a political exile after having been a political prisoner under the Marcos regime in the Philippines. Besides being a fiction writer and journalist, Rosca is also a social critic whose works are recognized worldwide. Speaking out on issues that affect women in the Third World, she has been an eloquent voice for justice and equality and is a global expert on women's and children's issues. As the founder and director of GABRIELA, an organization working against the violations of women's rights, including the mail-order bride industry, she tours around the world extensively to share her insights and expertise on women's issues.

Rosca has written novels, short stories, and essays. Her first novel, *State of War* (1988), won the National Book Award by the Manila Critics Circle in 1988, and has been translated into Dutch and published as a separate edition in Britain. *Twice Blessed* (1992), her second novel, won the American Book Award for Excellence in Literature in 1993, and is considered her most compelling work. In *Twice Blessed,* she traces the madness and grimness of Filipino politics and depicts the alienation of the people by its very own political system. She has also written two short-story collections, *Bitter Country* (1970) and *Monsoon Collection* (1983), and a work of nonfiction entitled *Endgame: The Fall of Marcos* (1987). In *Endgame*, Rosca turns to her native Philippines to write a dreamy, allegorical history of the Philippines seen through the eyes of her three main characters. In 2004 she coauthored a book with Jose Maria Sison entitled *JMS: At Home in the World,* which has been hailed as a masterpiece. This work traces the life of Jose Maria Sison and his political standing as a revolutionary leader in the Philippines. Her latest novel, *Broken Arrow,* is scheduled to be released soon.

Rosca's literary works generally focus on the plight of the Filipino people and the effect of globalization on the livelihood and culture of those who live in the Third World. Her writings pay particular attention to the lives of ordinary people and how they manage to defend and develop their humanity under difficult circumstances. She has received numerous fellowships for fiction writing, and she is the first Filipina to serve on the executive board of PEN America.

Ray Chandrasekara

Rowland, Laura Joh   (1954–   )

Mystery writer Laura Joh Rowland, a descendant of Korean and Chinese immigrants, was born and raised in Harper Woods, Michigan. Her family's emphasis on education and achievement fostered an early love of learning and a disciplined approach to academic success. She did not, however, decide to become a writer until well into adulthood, after she worked as a scientist. Artistic, ambitious, and expansively intelligent, Rowland has produced 11 books in 12 years, featuring her 17th-century samurai detective Sano Ichiro, the shogun's "Most Honorable Investigator of Events, Situations, and People."

After earning a B.S. degree in microbiology and a master's degree in public health, both from the University of Michigan, Rowland began her career as a microbiologist and chemist, working for the Environmental Protection Agency and in private industry. She moved to New Orleans in 1981 with her husband, Dr. Marty Rowland, a civil and environmental engineer, where she was a sanitary inspector for the city. Her long career as a scientist was largely spent at Lockheed Martin in New Orleans, where she worked as a quality control engineer on the NASA space shuttle's fuel tank. She describes the inception of her writing life as

a felicitous "accident." Her scientific mind was enriched and balanced by an interest in art and design. She turned her hobby into a professional opportunity and found work as a freelance illustrator. Writing was a by-product of her studious approach to learning the children's book trade: She decided to create the text for her own illustrations, took a writing class to hone her craft, and ended up enjoying writing more than drawing. Immersed in the cultural life of her city, Rowland continues to study, "workshop" her books-in-progress, and learn. She takes classes at the New Orleans Academy of Fine Art and is a member of several writing groups. She counts as a mentor and friend the late New Orleans–based science fiction writer George Alec Effinger. Though forced to leave the city for a time after Hurricane Katrina in September 2005, Rowland and her husband, like many other survivors, have returned to remake their lives in New Orleans.

Rowland turned a serendipitous discovery of talent and inclination into a lucrative and much-loved full-time job. After completing a children's book as well as two novels for adults, she set out to write compelling, marketable fiction with an Asian cast of characters. Her deliberate choice of genre and setting was born both of a reader's passion and a canny reading of the publishing market. She enjoyed detective fiction as a girl, particularly the Nancy Drew series, and was schooled on the classics: Agatha Christie, Mickey Spillane, Erle Stanley Gardner. Asian-studies classes in college and the films of Japanese master Akira Kurosawa prompted an interest in Japanese art and history.

She is not a historian, but she is an assiduous and meticulous researcher, with a keen eye for the telling detail and a reader's love of character and story. In the overwhelmingly laudatory reviews of her series, there have been some critical quibbles about her occasional lapses in historical authenticity (these, notably, center on the peculiarly modern depiction of Sano Ichiro's spirited and independent wife, Reiko, his partner in detection), but most succumb to the sweep and charm of her literary resurrection of medieval Edo (Tokyo) with its political intrigue, fascinating people and customs, and potential for violent crime. In his review of her first novel, *Shinju,* in 1994, *New York Times* critic and historian F. G. Notehelfer expresses his "crotchety" chagrin at seeing the sprinkling of historical inconsistencies that mar this "exciting" debut work and likens the feeling to "seeing wristwatches on actors in bad historical films." Despite his mild misgivings, Notehelfer celebrates Rowland's skill and talent and predicts a flourishing series. He quotes Sano, the warrior/academic who became second-in-command to the shogun: "No matter what these men thought, a tutor and history scholar had plenty of useful skills!" Certainly the reading public has agreed.

Rowland's whodunits embroil Sano and Lady Reiko in tumultuous and often grisly machinations of court politics and loyalties. Sano remains the moral center of the series, steadfast in his belief in honor, despite the ambiguities lurking in his ever-stalwart, ever-penetrating, and always dangerous quest for the truth. Medieval Edo provides a convincingly fraught social backdrop for Rowland's interlocking themes: personal and political power, love and duty, individuality and conformity, gender roles, and class. Ritual practices, court corruptions, and the rigidly ordered caste system of old Japan form the intricacies of the plots. Central to *Shinju*—which was nominated as best first novel for the prestigious Anthony Award—is the "double love suicide" of the title. *Bundori* (1996) refers to the public display of enemies' severed heads as war trophies. *The Way of the Traitor* (1997) explores *bushido,* the warrior's code, and the influence of Western contact on this closed society. Rowland makes thrilling use of obscure period details and almost Gothically charged locales: a strategically placed poisoned tattoo in *The Concubine's Tattoo* (1998); *kiai,* the scream that can kill, in *The Samurai's Wife* (2000); a mysterious sect in *Black Lotus* (2001); the world of the courtesans in *The Pillow Book of Lady Wisteria* (2002); the island haunt of the villain in *The Dragon King's Palace* (2003). *The Perfumed Sleeve* (2004) is rife with unsavory sexual exploits, and in *The Assassin's Touch* (2005), a warrior is killed by a *dim-mak,* a ritually exact wound to the head. *The Red Chrysanthemum,* published in the fall of 2006, continues Rowland's arrestingly entertaining ex-

amination of good and evil. Rowland has also contributed stories to three well-received anthologies, *Crime through Time II* (1998), *More Murder, They Wrote* (1999), and *Chronicles of Crime* (1999). Her prolific output is made possible by exceptionally disciplined work habits and an unflagging devotion to her readers, characters, and craft.

Bibliography

D'Haen, Theo. "Samurai Sleuths and Detective Daughters: The American Way." In *Sleuthing Ethnicity: The Detective in Multiethnic Crime Fiction,* edited by Dorothea Fischer-Hornung and Monika Mueller, 36–52. Madison/Teaneck, N.J.: Fairleigh Dickinson University Press, 2003.

Notehelfer, F. G. "An Old Japanese Custom: Ichiro Sano, Detective, Investigates an Apparent Joint Suicide in 17th Century Edo." *New York Times Book Review,* October 9, 1994, p. BR11.

Rowland, Laura Joh. *The Assassin's Touch.* New York: St. Martin's Minotaur, 2005.

———. *The Pillow Book of Lady Wisteria.* New York: St. Martin's Minotaur, 2002.

———. *Shinju.* New York: Random House, 1994.

———. *The Way of the Traitor.* New York: Villard Books, 1997.

Kate Falvey

Ryan, Teresa LeYung   (?–   )

Teresa LeYung Ryan is a Chinese-American fiction writer, motivational speaker, and community activist in the San Francisco Bay area. Ryan credits her encounters as a teenager with the novels of Emily Brontë and Lillian Hellman for providing her with the initial foundation for being able to appreciate the art of writing and helping her to realize her own literary ambitions. Despite her early love of literature and storytelling, it was not until she read MAXINE HONG KINGSTON's memoir *The Woman Warrior* in 1990 that Ryan truly began to develop her literary voice and undertake writing her first novel. Ryan drew from her own experiences as a woman, daughter, and Chinese American for her debut novel, *Love Made of Heart* (2002). Since the publication of *Love Made of Heart,* Ryan has taught writers' workshops at a number of colleges and writing programs. She is currently the president of the California Writers Club San Francisco/Peninsula branch.

The protagonist of *Love Made of Heart,* Ruby Lin, seems to have a perfectly fulfilling life that many would envy. She lives in a beautiful apartment in San Francisco, has an active social life, and works as a manager of special events for a major hotel. Ruby's family life, however, is hardly as balanced as her social and professional lives appear to be. After her mother's nervous breakdown and eventual hospitalization as a result of Ruby's father's physical and verbal abuse, Ruby is forced to confront, under the guidance of her wise and kindly psychotherapist, the wounds buried in not only her own past but her ancestors' as well. Despite her reservations about psychoanalysis and personal examination, Ruby embarks on a journey of self-exploration, discovering a long family history of domestic violence and loss that stretches back several generations from China to America. Ruby feels herself to be caught between two entirely different cultures, in one of which she is a successful, independent American woman; in the other she is known only as "Daughter," the fulfiller of family responsibilities. However, through

various artifacts of popular American culture, especially old television shows such as *Bewitched, Bonanza, Family Affair,* and black-and-white movies, Ruby is able to find role models for herself. While the men on *Bonanza* serve as idealized models of masculine behavior, it is the actress Joan Crawford, Ruby's film heroine, who shows her how to handle romantic relationships and rid herself of the disrespectful, brutish men in her life.

While Ryan acknowledges that much of *Love Made of Heart* is autobiographical, she insists that Ruby Lin and the details of her life are entirely fictional creations, and that Ruby's tale is meant to be a universal one capable of reaching across cultures. Ryan's primary concern in *Love Made of Heart* is with chronicling the long-term effects of abuse upon not only an individual's psyche, but upon families and whole cultures as well. Despite the dark and weighty themes she exposes and confronts throughout her novel, Ryan does not let her story, or her protagonist, fall into a state of absolute misery or despair. Instead, she provides hope by suggesting that personal healing can be found through self-exploration and reconciliation of past trauma.

James R. Fleming

S

Saiki, Patsy Sumie (1915–2005)

Writer and educator Patsy Sumie Saiki was born on March 15, 1915, on the island of Hawaii to Japanese immigrant parents from Hiroshima, Japan. Her parents were part of the first wave of contract laborers recruited to work Hawaii's sugarcane plantations. The contract labor system between the Kingdom of Hawaii, which was then a protectorate of the United States, and Asia, which had begun opening its borders to Western trade, began in 1885 and gradually came to an end by the 1910s. After concluding their three-year contract with their plantation, Saiki's parents bought a homestead with their savings on Ahualoa, Hawaii, where they raised their seven children.

In 1931 Saiki left the island of Hawaii to attend McKinley High School on the island of Oahu. Her mother died from cancer, however, before Saiki graduated. This was a formative and important event for Saiki, as memories of her mother, as well as the difficulties her parents faced as new immigrants to Hawaii, continued to influence Saiki's writing and teaching throughout her life.

In 1950, after getting married and having four children, Saiki enrolled in the University of Hawai'i at Manoa to study education. In 1952, as a junior, Saiki won the Charles Eugene Banks award for short story writing. Upon receiving a bachelor's degree in 1954 and a master's degree in education in 1959, Saiki continued to study at the University of Wisconsin on a Wall Street Journal Fellowship. In 1967, after a few years of work in education back in Oahu, she moved again to the mainland, this time to obtain a doctorate in education, with a specialization in multiethnic curriculum design, at Teachers' College of Columbia University. After teaching at the University of Hawaii, Saiki worked for the Hawaii State Department of Education.

Saiki wrote prolifically throughout her adult life. Her first book, *Sachie: A Daughter of Hawaii* (1978), explores the violence of plantation life for the Himeno family. By having a 13-year-old Sachie narrate the novel, Saiki is able to universalize the young girl's experience and highlight the pervasiveness of racism and plantation logic in structuring the everyday ethos for both immigrants and white plantation owners in the early 20th-century United States. Sachie's voice, as an American-born child of Japanese immigrants, is a particularly powerful tool for criticizing American racism; throughout the novel, Sachie experiences and elaborates the negative effects of the disparity in privilege between her and her white peers. In a different way, Sachie's sense of alienation from American culture is heightened by her parents' fear of reprisal from whites and plantation owners, which limits both their criticism of plantation life and their engagement with the broader Hawaiian society.

One of the powerful ways in which the novel engages the effects of the violence on Japanese immigrant lives is through the portrayal of Sachie's difficult negotiations with self-hatred. Even as Sachie hates the racial markers that differentiate her as Japanese and wishes that she had been born into a white family, she also recognizes that racism is what guarantees white privilege. Continually faced with these dilemmas and contradictions, Sachie tries to avoid entering adulthood and instead preoccupies herself with fairy tales that she believes more clearly discriminate between good and bad. Sachie's escape into the stories of her youth can be understood as a criticism of the social and economic structures of Hawaii that deny her fulfillment and equality in the real world. It can also be read as a commentary on how the narrative of the melting pot, which is supposed to guarantee immigrant inclusion, is in itself a fairy tale. As such, the novel poignantly develops the shaping of psychological and emotional terrains as well as material lives by racism and economic violence and how injustice based on racism remains a traumatic experience to the immigrant for a long period.

This novel is both a historical record as well as an aesthetic illustration of the lives and experiences of first- and second-generation Japanese immigrants. *Sachie* is emblematic of Saiki's works as a whole in its attention to Japanese immigrant history, Saiki's interest in the role of Hawaii in mediating the relationship between Japan and the United States, and her attempt to portray the struggles for survival by Japanese immigrants who try to make a home in a country that wants their labor but not their culture. In this work as in her future writings, Saiki uses the short-story form to weave together the overlapping, multiple, and multifaceted narratives that constitute the complex lives of early Japanese immigrants to the United States.

Her later published works, *Ganbare! An Example of Japanese Spirit* (1981), *Japanese Women in Hawaii: The First 100 Years* (1985), and *Early Japanese Immigrants in Hawaii* (1993), use different modes to narrate the themes introduced in *Sachie*. *Ganbare*, which means to heroically persevere, narrates the internment of 1,500 Japanese immigrant and

Japanese-American Hawaiians on the mainland during World War II. Her most historical narrative, *Ganbare* brings together the personal narratives of internees as well as historical documents, and focuses on how Japanese Americans were forced to see themselves as subjects of American racism when they were incarcerated by the country of their birth. While *Ganbare* is ostensibly a collection of short narratives, Saiki's privileging of chronology and multiple tellings of the aftermaths of the Pearl Harbor attack interrupt and often disturb the coherence and fluidity evident in her fictional works. *Ganbare*, however, remains a seminal work in Japanese-American studies because it is one of the few texts available in English about the internment of Japanese-American Hawaiians.

Japanese Women in Hawaii, on the other hand, portrays the particular contributions made by Japanese immigrant women to Hawaiian culture and economy. In *Early Japanese Immigrants in Hawaii*, Saiki again returns to the short-story form; this time, however, she strings together the stories of multiple families and individuals who attempt to make a home for themselves and their progeny. Painted with a sense of intimacy and immediacy, all of these later works celebrate the courage and sacrifice of the early immigrants who left a rich legacy for future generations.

Although Saiki's works have not found a great deal of critical acclaim, her works have received positive attention for her nuanced and complex portrayal of the roles of Japanese immigrants in Hawaii, and she is noted as a key figure in the multiethnic literary movement of Hawaii. Her works can often be found on school curricula, particularly on those designed to enhance secondary-school students' understanding of multiethnicity, immigration, and gender.

Bibliography

Hiura, Arnold T., Stephen H. Sumida, and Martha Webb, eds. *Talk Story: Big Island Anthology.* Honolulu: Talk Story and Bamboo Ridge Press, 1979.
Sumida, Stephen H. "Sense of Place, History, and the concept of the 'Local' in Hawaii's Asian/Pacific Literatures." In *Reading the Literatures of Asian America,* edited by Shirley Geok-lin and Amy

Ling, 215–237. Philadelphia: Temple University Press, 1992.

Jinah Kim

Sakamoto, Edward   (1940–   )

Sakamoto was born and raised in the A'ala Park neighborhood in Honolulu, Hawaii. As a ninth grader, he was assigned to revise *Treasure Island* by Robert Stevenson for extra credit, and encouraged by his teacher's comments, he became interested in writing. He attended the University of Hawaii, where he tried acting. In college, he wrote *In the Alley,* which was later included in *Kumu Kahua Plays* (1983), an anthology of plays by the Kumu Kahua Theatre. He graduated from the University of Hawaii in 1962. Discouraged by the lack of substantial, inspiring roles that Asian-American actors could play, he moved to Los Angeles in 1966 to work for the *Los Angeles Times.*

Sakamoto's relocation happened at the right time because the post–World War II generation of Asian-American actors were fighting against demeaning Asian American stereotypes in media by staging plays that accurately represent Asian Americans. In 1972 Sakamoto's second play, *Yellow Is My Favorite Color* was produced by the East West Players, and in 1980–81 by the Pan Asian Repertory Theatre in New York City. Most of Sakamoto's plays, often set in Hawaii, were staged by the East West Players at least once since then. He was awarded grants from the National Endowment for Arts and the Rockefeller Foundation. He also received two Hollywood Dramalogue Critic's awards for *Chikamatsu's Forest* and *Stew Rice* and the Hawaii Award for Literature.

Sakamoto published *Hawai'i No Ka Oi: the Kamiya Family Trilogy* (1995), which includes *The Taste of Kona Coffee, Manoa Valley,* and *The Life of the Land.* In these plays, he questions his decision to relocate to the mainland and expresses his doubts through his characters. His plays often present a contrast between Hawaii and the mainland, Japanese values and American values, and the old and the new, often dealing with the meaning of "home" as their central theme. For example, in *The Taste of Kona Coffee* and *The Life of the Land,* characters like Jiro and Spencer relocate to the mainland only to become alienated from family members and friends. Sakamoto's Hawaiian characters also face difficulties in assimilating to the mainstream culture when they move away from their island home. For example, in *Stew Rice,* a play included in *Aloha Las Vegas and Other Plays* (2000) along with *A'ala Park* and *Aloha Las Vegas,* Russell becomes keenly aware of the differences between haoles and himself.

Sakamoto's plays received positive reviews from theater reviewers and public audiences, particularly for his effective use of Hawaiian pidgin English in the dialogues.

Bibliography

Amano, Kyoko. "Edward Sakamoto (1940–   )." *Encyclopedia of Ethnic American Writers.* Westport, Conn.: Greenwood Press, 2005.

Huot, Nikolas. "Edward Sakamoto (1940–   )." *Asian American Playwrights: A Bio-Bibliographical Critical Sourcebook,* edited by Miles Xian Liu. Westport, Conn.: Greenwood Press, 2002.

Kyoko Amano

Sakamoto, Kerri   (1959–   )

Born in Toronto, Sakamoto grew up in Etibicoke during the 1960s and 1970s. The racism of her childhood and her struggle with her identity as a Japanese Canadian are reflected in her short stories, novels, and screenplays.

As an adult Sakamoto lived in New York for six years, working as a writer for an art gallery. While in New York, Sakamoto published two short stories, both in 1993: "View from the Edge of the World" was published in *Harbour: Magazine of Art & Everyday Life* and "Walk-In Closet" in *Charlie Chan Is Dead: An Anthology of Contemporary Asian American Fiction* edited by JESSICA HAGEDORN. The only other Canadian to be included in the anthology is the renowned poet and novelist JOY KOGAWA.

Kerri Sakamoto returned to Canada and finished her first novel, *The Electrical Field,* which she had begun in New York. Published in 1998, the novel made a huge impression on the Canadian literary scene and was nominated for numerous awards: the Governor General's Award, the Kiriyama Pacific Rim Book Prize, and the IMPAC Dublin Literary Award. It won the Commonwealth Writers' Prize for Best First Book and the Canada-Japan Literary Award. Since then, Kerri Sakamoto has continued to write, publishing another short story in 2001 entitled "Ghost-town" in *Interlope 6: the first criticism issue,* edited by Alvin Lu. Her second novel, ONE HUNDRED MILLION HEARTS, was published in 2003.

Kerri Sakamoto has also written several screenplays for independent films, including Helen Lee's 1992 film *My Niagara* (with the earlier working title *Little Baka Girl*), a made-for-television film for which Sakamoto was both cowriter and associate producer. She has also worked closely with the American filmmaker Rea Tajiri: Tajiri acted as the mother in the film *My Niagara,* and Sakamoto later cowrote the screenplay for the 1997 film *The Strawberry Fields* with Rea Tajiri, which Tajiri directed. Tajiri and Sakamoto are presently collaborating on a film version of Sakamoto's first novel, *The Electrical Field,* for which Kerri Sakamoto is the screenplay writer, with Tajiri as the director.

The leitmotifs of Sakamoto's creative writing deal predominantly with the struggle to reclaim history—personal, communal, and national—which in her writing is always affected by the fallibility of memory. Strongly linked to her fascination with history is the haunting effect the past has on the identity of individuals and of communities. Through an eclectic ensemble of characters of both genders, Sakamoto explores their personal struggles to accept their marginalized identity as Japanese Canadian/Americans, and to come to terms with the historical fracture of Japanese-Canadian/American families and communities. Through her cast of characters, the author provokes readers to reflect on history: both the events that constitute history, and the various tellings and retellings of it.

Sheena Wilson

Samurai of Gold Hill
Yoshiko Uchida (1972)

In 1969, 100 years after its establishment, the Wakamatsu Colony of California was named an official landmark by the California Historical Landmark Society. The novel *Samurai of Gold Hill* narrates the history of the brave Japanese men and women who left their homeland after a civil war to establish the Wakamatsu Colony in 1869. Named after the town in Japan they had come from, the colony consisted of many samurai warriors and their families who served under the lordship of Matsudaira. Because Lord Matsudaira and his warriors lost the war, they no longer felt welcome in their homeland with their enemies in control of the government. Lord Matsudaira decided to send his loyal followers to the United States, where they were to join other Japanese immigrants to start a new colony and establish a new life in exile.

In the novel, Koichi is a 12-year-old boy in Japan who is studying to become a samurai like his father and older brother. Unfortunately, his brother dies in the civil war, and Koichi wants to honor his brother's memory by following in his footsteps. His father has been entrusted with Lord Matsudaira's plans to start a colony in California. Even though Koichi is scared to go to a new country, he must obey his father. When they arrive at Gold Hill, they find that the land is dry and dusty, unlike Japan where there is lush vegetation and dark, moist soil in the countryside. They quickly find out that their traditional farming techniques do not work here. With the help of their neighbors, farmers Thomas and Kate Whitlow, they learn how to irrigate their fields by using a small nearby stream. The Japanese colonists also become acquainted with Native Americans and learn that they too have a culture rich in tradition and ritual. Native Americans also sympathize with the Japanese colonists since both groups are marginalized by the white settlers and prospectors mining for gold in the area.

Koichi is often assigned to work with Toyoko, a nine-year-old girl who is half Japanese and half German. Displaced by two different cultural worlds, Koichi and Toyoko need to find their place in society. Koichi was an outcast in Japan because of its political turmoil; he is considered alien in America because he is not white. Toyoko was seen as an outsider in Japan because her father is German; in America, she does not feel welcomed because she is only half white. Even in the colony she is treated differently, not just because she is only half Japanese, but because she is a girl. Women in traditional Japanese society are expected to obey men without question and are left out of the decision-making process concerning the colony. Toyoko sees her situation as a challenge to prove herself to the others as a useful member of the colony. She works hard, and by doing so she gains self-respect and the respect of Koichi, who watches her take care of the silkworms and other tasks with competence and without complaint.

The racism from the white settlers eventually causes the downfall of the colony. The white settlers find a way to block the stream that the colonists rely on to irrigate their fields. Even though the colony fails, Koichi is given the opportunity to mature by learning about different cultures and people. He learns that some people are willing to look past racial and gender differences and some are not. More important, he learns how to be open-minded and more tolerant of other people.

Anne Bahringer

Santos, Bienvenido N.   (1911–1996)

The poet, novelist, short-story writer, and essayist Bienvenido N. Santos was born in Tondo, Manila, to Pampango parents from Lubao. His childhood and first literary experiences were influenced by the three languages that surrounded his life: Pampango at home, Tagalog in the streets, and English at school.

When he left for America in 1941 to study for a master's degree at the University of Illinois, he was already an established short-story writer in his country. But when World War II broke out and the Philippines was invaded by Japan, he was forced to stay in the United States while his wife and three daughters remained in the Philippines. This sep-

aration was crucial in his life and influenced his writing, as exile became a central theme to his fiction. During the war, he studied at Columbia and Harvard Universities and served the Philippine government in exile in Washington, D.C.

Santos went back to the Philippines in 1946 and stayed there until 1958, when he returned to the United States with his wife. In 1961, he again returned to the Philippines to take a position as dean and vice president of the University of Nueva Caceres. In 1965 he received the most prestigious literary award in that country, the Republic Cultural Heritage Award in Literature. Returning to the United States in 1965, he attended the Writers' Workshop at the University of Iowa. From 1973 to 1982, Santos was Distinguished Writer-in-Residence at Wichita State University and in 1976 he became a U.S. citizen.

His first two novels, *Villa Magdalena* and *The Volcano,* were published in Manila in 1965, followed by a serialized novel, *The Praying Man.* While these first three novels deal with the political situation and anti-American sentiments in the Philippines, his next works deal with the experiences of Filipino immigrants in the United States, especially as they move between their homeland and the adopted land. As the characters look for a place to call home, they are forced to negotiate their feelings of isolation and ambivalence not only in their adopted land but also in their homeland. In America, they miss living in the Philippines; in the Philippines, they miss living in the United States.

The maturity of his writing and literary experimentation is shown in texts such as "Immigration Blues," which won the Best Fiction Award given by *New Letters* magazine in 1977. To examine the ways in which immigration affects people's lives, Santos creates the character of Alpino, who is asked to marry a fellow countrywoman to allow her to stay in the United States. In *Scent of Apples,* a book of short stories published in 1980 by the University of Washington and winner of the 1981 American Book Award from the Before Columbus Foundation, Santos again explores the cross sections between culture and identity, between their senses of isolation and belonging. In most of these stories, the Filipino characters seem to idealize their homeland in order to find comfort in the new land, where they are marginalized.

Covadonga Lamar Prieto

Saving Fish from Drowning
Amy Tan (2005)

Bibi Chen, purportedly a well-known San Francisco art dealer and socialite who perished mysteriously in her store, narrates the events that occur after her death when the tour group she was supposed to lead is abducted in Myanmar (Burma) by the Karen, a minority ethnic group persecuted by the military regime. Reminiscent of AMY TAN's earlier novels, the main plot is interspersed with Bibi's recollections of her youth in China, a conflicted relationship with her stepmother Sweet Ma, and her eventual immigration to the United States. As in *A HUNDRED SECRET SENSES*, elements of magical realism abound: the deceased narrator, for instance, can visit the other characters in their dreams. In an interview, Tan says that Bibi has "no counterpart in real life" ("Discussion"); however, Tan's preface claims that the novel was inspired by documents retrieved from the Manhattan archives of the American Society for Psychical Research.

Tan's novel emphasizes "the tensions of living between worlds" (Huntley 137). Bibi does not know, for instance, how long she must remain in limbo before she is allowed to move on to her final destination. In the borderlands between China and Myanmar, evidence of cultural hybridity proliferates in art, religion, and social customs. The members of the tour group must spend an unplanned vacation at No Name Place, the Karens' exile, where they undergo transformation.

This aspect of the novel displays strong Jungian overtones. The members of the group receive a call to adventure when they enter the strange and exotic world of Myanmar, their entry into the jungle marking their descent into the subconscious, where they will have to face their own private fears. For Benny, the inept tour-guide who replaced Bibi, this means admitting his weaknesses to the others

and even experiencing a seizure right in front of them. For Heidi, who has lived in a state of terror ever since she found her murdered roommate, it is realizing that she is not alone in her plight, that the others are also afraid. Moff and Harry overcome their respective midlife crises by finding new partners.

It is not surprising that this quest story should feature strong mystic components such as Bibi's numerous explanations of Buddhist practices. She is particularly eager to point out differences between the native populations' beliefs and trendy San Francisco variations thereof. Faith and magic converge when the Karen interpret Rupert's card trick as a sign of their spiritual leader Younger White Brother's reincarnation. The tourists' admission that miracles can occur eventually becomes a liberating experience that results in a moment of transcendental ecstasy revealing the power of love to the group. Tan seems to embrace the Chinese mysticism promoted by her immigrant mother figures in previous novels but rejected by the Chinese-American daughter protagonists.

Since the tour group is evenly split between males and females, Tan is able to develop male characters more fully than she did in the past. Ben, Moff, and Harry are believably created middle-aged men whose fears and hopes Tan explores compassionately, albeit humorously. This approach also gives Tan the opportunity to explore gender roles and gender stereotypes. While Harry prides himself on his dog-training aptitude, Bibi describes his advances toward Marlene in terms of an elaborate mating ritual. Readers hear many different voices, a concept Tan derives from the *Canterbury Tales* ("Discussion").

Among these interpersonal relationships, Tan's exploration of various forms of excess stands out. The theme is first introduced through the loss of Bibi's mother to what Sweet Ma describes as excessive behaviors. By urinating in a sacred grotto, Harry's ignorance invites the wrath of the gods. In their desire to assist the Karen, the tourists inadvertently inflict grave injury. In this manner, Tan's investigation of "disturbing questions about intentions" ("Discussion") ties the novel's plot to the Buddhist proverb she uses as its title.

Bibliography

Ho, Wendy. *In Her Mother's House: The Politics of Mother-Daughter Writing.* Walnut Creek, Calif.: Altamira Press, 1999.

Huntley, E. D., ed. *Amy Tan: A Critical Companion.* Westport, Conn.: Greenwood Press, 1998.

Tan, Amy. *Saving Fish from Drowning.* New York: Putnam's, 2005.

———. "A Discussion with Amy Tan." Available online. URL: http://amytan.net/InterviewWithAmy-Tan.aspx. Accessed 17 March 2006.

Susanna Hoeness-Krupsaw

Saying Goodbye   Marie G. Lee   (1994)

In this sequel to the author's Finding My Voice, Ellen Sung is a new freshman at Harvard University. Following in her perfect sister's footsteps, Ellen enrolls as a pre-med student, but her heart is still with writing. She easily slips into college life, becoming close with her new roommate Leecia, an African-American student, maturing through her writing class, and dating Jae, a Korean American from Los Angeles. As she starts meeting more Korean-American college students, she begins to think critically about her own Korean-American identity. Sensitized by her new peers of the ongoing Korean-black conflict that exploded in the Los Angeles riots of 1992, Ellen's political consciousness is raised when the African American Students Alliance invites a rap artist whose lyrics advocate violence against Korean-American small-business owners. When the Korean American Students of Harvard asks Ellen to help protest, she realizes she has the power to sabotage the artist's event. Ellen and Leecia's differences explode in the midst of the protest and are televised to the entire nation. Ellen tries to restore her relationship with Leecia, but the damage is done; her participation in the protest has destroyed their friendship.

Riding on the tension in the wake of the Los Angeles riots, Lee educates readers about the conflicts between Korean small-business owners and black customers through the sometimes stereotypical dialogue among Ellen, Tae, Leecia and other students. Unfortunately, this novel suggests that pursuing resolution of the Korean-black conflict is hopeless. Leecia and Ellen are ultimately torn apart along color lines, and their irreconcilability is manifested in a physical line made of masking tape bisecting their dormitory.

In this sequel, Lee continues to develop Ellen's sense of identity. Jae's character serves as a foil to show how Ellen moves along a continuum toward a more politicized social conscience. Harvard, home to Korean Americans from different parts of the nation, is an appropriate setting for Ellen to nurture her desire to learn more about her Korean roots and contemporary issues facing Korean Americans. This story does not end in physical violence in the tradition of Lee's other novels, yet the finale is highly charged with anger, betrayal, and a strong sense of social justice.

Sarah Park

See, Lisa Lenine   (1955–   )

See was born in Paris, France, to Carolyn Laws (best known as Carolyn See), a successful writer, and Richard See, a fourth-generation Chinese-American anthropologist. After her parents' divorce when she was four, she lived in Los Angeles with her mother, who was then a struggling writer, changing residence and schools many times between the second and fourth grades. Nonetheless, her ties with her father's side of the family did not weaken, and See spent a long time with her relatives in Los Angeles's Chinatown, where she experienced the dynamic nature of life in a Chinese family.

In the mid-1970s, while traveling through Europe, she realized that the unstructured life of the writer was what she wanted. She returned to Loyola Marymount College in 1976, where she obtained a B.A. degree in modern Greek studies in 1979. Her freelance writing started in 1979 with an assignment from *TV Guide;* since then, she has been a freelance contributor to several publications such as the *Los Angeles Times, USA Today,* and *LA Weekly.* From 1983 to 1996, she worked as the West Coast correspondent for *Publishers Weekly,* writing articles about the West Coast literary and publishing world. She wrote commentaries on book fairs and the latest trends for ethnic literature; she also conducted several interviews with famous novelists such as Michael Chabon, Cynthia Kadohata, and others. Her work as a journalist turned out to be crucial to her writing career.

Between 1983 and 1988, with her mother and her collaborator John Espey (under the joint pseudonym of Monica Highland), Lisa See published *Lotus Land, 110 Shanghai Road* and *Greetings from Southern California.* It was in 1995 that See's first full-length solo project, *On Gold Mountain: The One Hundred Year Odyssey of My Chinese-American Family,* was published to widespread critical acclaim. It became a national best seller and a New York Times Notable Book. This comprehensive family portrait chronicles the life of See's Chinese-American family from the 1860s to the present. It starts with Fong Dun, See's great-great-grandfather, leaving China to work on the transcontinental railroad in California, and traces the struggles of four generations of Chinese Americans founding businesses, dealing in art, antiques and furniture, marrying Caucasians and looking for social acceptance in frequently hostile Los Angeles. The book is the result of exhaustive archival research and five years of interviews with nearly 100 relatives. It mixes elements of personal reminiscence with the social history of the Chinese experience in the United States. U.S. journalists have praised See's research and her insight into both the American and Chinese cultural backgrounds of her family, while pointing out the apparent contradiction between her long account of her Chinese past and claim to a Chinese identity, on the one hand, and her Caucasian appearance on the other.

In 1997 See published *Flower Net,* her first murder mystery featuring Chinese inspector Liu Hulan and American attorney David Stark. Set in the United States and China, the thriller begins with the discovery of an American corpse in China and a Chinese corpse in the United States. To solve the mystery, the detectives have to trust their cultural knowledge more than their forensic education. Two other mysteries featuring the same characters were released in 1999 and in 2003: *The Interior* and *Dragon Bones.* Great commercial successes, these novels sometimes manage to challenge some ste-

reotypical views held by Americans about China and by Chinese about America. See lives in Los Angeles with her husband, Richard Becker Kendall, an attorney, and their two sons.

Bibliography
Liu, Xian. "Lisa Lenine See." In *Asian American Novelists: A Bio-Bibliographical Critical Sourcebook,* edited by Emmanuel S. Nelson, 323–331. Westport, Conn.: Greenwood, 2000.
See, Lisa. "Lisa See." Beatrice interview by Ron Hogan (1996). Available online. URL: http://www.beatrice.com/interviews/lisasee/. Accessed October 16, 2006.

Manuela Vastolo

Seth, Vikram   (1952–   )

Born in Calcutta, India, to an upper-middle-class family, Seth is among the foremost Indians writing in English today. More versatile, perhaps, than his contemporaries, Amitav Ghosh and Salman Rushdie, Seth's creative oeuvre consists of a host of well-received, critically acclaimed works of fiction, carefully crafted collections of poetry, an award-winning travelogue, a collection of short stories from around the world for children, and a libretto for the English National Opera that he was specially commissioned to write. Widely traveled, Seth has studied at Oxford, Stanford, and Nanjing Universities, in the United Kingdom, the United States, and China, respectively. He abandoned his doctorate in Economics at Stanford, after the publication of *The Golden Gate* in 1982, to concentrate his energies on being a creative writer.

In 1980 Seth published *Mappings,* a collection of poetry that includes translations of poems in Hindi, Chinese, and German. In 1983 came a travelogue, *From Heaven Lake: Travels through Sinkiang and Tibet,* which won the Thomas Cook Award for the best travel book. It tells of his hitchhiking trip through China to Lhasa in Tibet, and a subsequent journey through Nepal. Written with an observant eye for local color and the character eccentricities of the various people he met, it describes a journey born out of serendipitous circumstances that allowed Seth, while he was studying at Nanjing University in China, to travel to restricted areas where few non-Chinese tourists had been. *The Humble Administrator's Garden* (1985), which won him the Commonwealth Poetry Prize (Asia), *All You Who Sleep Tonight* (1990), and *Three Chinese Poets* (1992) are his other books of verse. *Beastly Tales from Here to There* (1992) offers yet another example of Seth's metrical propensities.

Seth first gained literary prominence in 1986 with the publication of *The Golden Gate,* his first novel in verse based on Pushkin's *Eugene Onegin.* Consisting of 690 exact tetrameter verses, it has been hailed by Norman Mailer as "the Great California novel." *The Golden Gate* tells of the lives and loves of a group of friends in San Francisco, immersed in the typically yuppie routines of the latest foodie, yoga, and music trends.

Seth won the Commonwealth Writer's Prize, and the W. H. Smith Literary Award for *A SUITABLE BOY* (1993). Organized around the fates and fortunes of four families, it tells of the search for a suitable boy for Lata Mehra and is an allegorical narrative of the aims and aspirations of a postcolonial India.

The passion and knowledge of music that led Seth to write the libretto *Arion and the Dolphin* (1994) can also be seen in his novel *An Equal Music* (1999). Set in Venice and London, it is a first-person narrative about the life of a string quartet and an intensely psychological study of an obsessive and somewhat unstable character. In his most recent work, *Two Lives* (2005), a memoir of the marriage of his great uncle and aunt, Seth returns to the familial terrain that was the inspiration for *A Suitable Boy.*

Rajender Kaur

Seventeen Syllables and Other Stories
Hisaye Yamamoto [DeSoto] (1998)

Many of the stories in *Seventeen Syllables* explore the intersections between race and family. The fathers in HISAYE YAMAMOTO's stories are frequently stubborn and distant from their children and wives, made so in some cases by terrible situations involving poverty, gender roles, internment, and racism. Sometimes they are so entrenched in the customs of where they lived before that their behavior seems unthinkable to modern readers. The mothers in these pieces often fare far worse; if they survive childbirth, their marriages are rarely happy, and they must make their own peace with the situation. Often the stories are told from the perspective of a young girl who is unaware of the complexities of adult lives.

The most widely anthologized story of this collection, "Seventeen Syllables" (1949), tells the heart-wrenching story of an anguished issei mother trapped in a loveless marriage, juxtaposed with the bittersweet sexual awakening of her teenage daughter, Rosie. Rosie's mother wins the first prize in a haiku-writing contest sponsored by a Japanese-American newspaper, but in a fit of jealousy, Rosie's father destroys the prize, a beautiful woodblock print by a famous Japanese artist. Infuriated, Rosie's mother tells Rosie that she only married Rosie's father as an alternative to suicide after the birth of a stillborn son conceived out of wedlock, about which her husband does not know. She also makes Rosie swear to never marry.

"The Legend of Miss Sasagawara" (1950) is one of a handful of stories Yamamoto wrote about life in an internment camp, drawing on her own experience. It is the story of a woman, Miss Sasagawara, who was once a dancer but is driven insane by life at a camp and by her distant, religious father.

"Yoneko's Earthquake" (1951), on the other hand, tells the story of 10-year-old Yoneko Hosoume, who waits for God to answer her prayers to end the aftershocks of an earthquake. She does not fully understand all of what is happening around her, but the careful reader can piece together the family's tragic history. Her father is initially made distant by circumstance, as he was nearly electrocuted while driving during the earthquake, but he becomes increasingly unpleasant as the story progresses headlong into tragedy. Marpo, a Filipino worker at the family farm, disappears one day without saying goodbye to Yoneko and her little brother, Seigo. What Yoneko does not know is that her mother and Marpo had an affair, which resulted in an aborted pregnancy. Not long after,

Seigo becomes ill from being in the fields and later dies. Yoneko's mother pointedly tells her, "Never kill a person, Yoneko, because if you do, God will take from you someone you love" (56).

In "A Day in Little Tokyo" (1986), the protagonist is a 13-year-old girl, Chisato, who spends the day wandering in Little Tokyo after her father and younger brother elect to attend a wrestling match in the city instead of going to the beach as they had originally planned. While her father is not cruel, he is inattentive; he and her brother both believe she has sat in the car all day while they were at the wrestling match. On the way back home, her father accidentally runs the car into a streetlamp, for which they are later billed. Everything is fine, including the car, but there is small satisfaction for Chisato when her father ruefully admits that they should have gone to the beach.

Yamamoto's own life frequently informs her work; some of her pieces go so far as to indicate in their titles that they are memoirs. "Life among the Oil Fields: A Memoir" (1979), for example, recounts her memories of being a child in California. There are not always direct autobiographical parallels; more often, it is as if her own memories and experiences resonate in those of her characters.

Marriage in Yamamoto's stories is often presented as a matter of contract or duty, with little or no pleasure involved. For example, in "The Brown House" (1951), Mrs. Hattori leaves her gambling, lying, and abusive husband and takes two of her five children with her to stay with her sister. When he promises to quit gambling, she returns to him for the sake of her children, only to see him resume his gambling habit. In "Epithalamium" (1960), Yuki Tsumagari from San Francisco stays in Staten Island to work for a Catholic rehabilitation center. She is due to return home but, against the advice of her supervisors and her own better judgment, she marries an alcoholic sailor, who remains drunk throughout their wedding ceremony. Interestingly, in "Reading and Writing" (1987), marriage is what sparks the unlikely friendship between two women, Kazuko and Hallie, who meet only through their husbands. Their marriages seem happy enough, but, more important, the story is about female friendship, something missing from earlier stories.

Fathers do not always appear as simply stubborn and malicious. "Morning Rain" (1952) is a story in which a daughter realizes that the two men in her life—her husband and her father—cannot communicate, partly because of the language barrier but also because her father is becoming deaf. It is one of the rare stories where the father is a sympathetic character, for more than any other in Yamamoto's stories. "Las Vegas Charley" (1961) also presents a sympathetic male character. The Charlie of the title has two sons, left behind by his young wife who died while giving birth to the second. His sons were raised in Japan by their grandfather, while he worked in the States. When his father dies, his sons come to the United States only to see the outbreak of World War II and their own internment at a relocation camp. Charley's first son, Isamu, enlists and is killed (like Yamamoto's own brother). The second son, Noriyuki, plans to return to Japan but falls in love, marries his sweetheart, has children, and settles. The story resolves around Noriyuki finding some small compassion for his father in a mire of frustration and shame after his father dies from cancer. "My Father Can Beat Muhammad Ali" (1986) recounts the story of a father, Henry Kusomoto, whose two sons, Dirk and Curt, mock his boastful claims of athletic prowess and provoke him to attempt to prove his impossible claims.

Yamamoto's work also frequently addresses issues of racism and cultural difference. "Wilshire Bus" (1950) tells the story of a Japanese-American woman visiting her World War II–veteran husband at a hospital and hearing anti-Asian racist remarks from a drunken man on the bus on the way there. "Underground Lady" (1986) is a first-person narrative about a 63-year-old Japanese-American woman who meets the Underground Lady, a homeless woman who speaks of living underground after her Japanese neighbors burned down her house. The most meditative story on these issues may be "The Eskimo Connection" (1983), which recounts the unlikely correspondence between an Eskimo inmate at a federal prison and Emiko Toyama, an old second-generation Japanese-American woman living in Los Angeles.

Bibliography

Cheung, King-Kok. Introduction. *Seventeen Syllables and Other Stories.* New Brunswick, N.J.: Rutgers University Press, 1998.

Cheung, King-Kok, and Stan Yogi. *Asian American Literature: An Annotated Bibliography.* New York: Modern Language Association, 1988.

Yamamoto [DeSoto], Hisaye. *Seventeen Syllables and Other Stories.* Latham, N.Y.: Kitchen Table— Women of Color Press, 1988.

Anne N. Thalheimer

Shock of Arrival, The
Meena Alexander (1996)

The Shock of Arrival: Reflections on Postcolonial Experience is a collection of prose and poetry that rise out of various moments in the author's life. MEENA ALEXANDER takes her readers on a journey through her childhood in India to her life as an immigrant in America, highlighting the "shock of arrival" that accompanied such a journey. As a way of illustrating the experiences that influenced her life and writing, she depicts physical, mental, and emotional tearing that she went through as she moved from one continent to the other. According to Alexander, postcolonial experiences are much different and more painful for women, who are considered the carriers of culture and values. She writes that "the shock of arrival is multifold— what was borne in the mind is jarred, tossed into new shapes, an exciting exfoliation of sense." Alexander records how she lost her language, Malayalam, while she picked up other languages as she migrated from one place to another.

The book is divided into several sections: "Overture," "Piecemeal Shelters," "Translating Violence," "Making Up Memory," "Skin with Fire Inside: Indian Women Writers," and "Coda." Each section comprises prose as well as poetry. Mostly independent from one another, the sections deal with the themes of diaspora, culture, identity, hybridity, language, dislocation, and relocation. In "Piecemeal Shelters," she writes about her act of writing, which is "more or less governed by the strictures of colonialism": She notes that even in the era of decolonization, her memory is marked by the impact of colonialism. In "Making Up Memory," she illustrates her experiences as a woman of color in America; in the section titled "Skin with Fire Inside," she recalls Indian women writers such as Sarojini Naidu, Nalapat Balamaniamma, and Lalithambika Antherjanam. Alexander speaks at length about the idea of "home" and the sense of homelessness that she feels in America. She battles emotionally and psychologically to settle in a new home where she has to deal with racism and alienation. The combination of fictional and nonfictional works in the book brilliantly depicts the challenges faced by an immigrant. In her words, the sections "braid together difficult truths of body and language."

The Shock of Arrival has been received with great enthusiasm in postcolonial literary circles. It has received accolades from writers such as Homi Bhabha, Adrienne Rich, and Gayatri Chakravorty Spivak.

Bibliography

Alexander, Meena. *The Shock of Arrival: Reflections of Postcolonial Experience.* Boston: South End Press, 1996.

Malieckal, Bindu. Review of *The Shock of Arrival: Reflections of Postcolonial Experience. MELUS* 24 (1990): 192.

Shankar, Lavina Dhingra. "Postcolonial Diasporics 'Writing in Search of a Homeland': Meena Alexander's *Manhattan Music, Fault Lines,* and *The Shock of Arrival." Literature Interpretation Theory* 12, no. 2 (2001): 285–312.

Asma Sayed

Sidhwa, Bapsi   (1938–   )

Set in both Pakistan, her native country, and the United States, her adopted country, Bapsi Sidhwa's novels and stories explore the cultural constraints that make it difficult for South Asian women to lead satisfying lives. More specifically, Sidhwa focuses on the Parsi minority, the contemporary adherents to the Zoroastrian faith. In effect, she emphasizes the experiences of a largely disenfranchised segment of an already marginalized community.

Born in Karachi, Pakistan, Sidhwa suffered from polio when she was a child. After receiving her B.A. from Kinnaird College for Women in 1956, she traveled widely throughout Asia, Europe, and North America. In 1983 she immigrated to the United States and became a U.S. citizen in 1992. She has taught at St. Thomas University in Texas, Rice University, the University of Houston, and Columbia University. Since 1990 she has been a writer-in-residence at Mount Holyoke College.

Sidhwa's first novel, *The Crow Eaters* (1978), is a comic satire set in British India. The novel focuses on a Parsi family's decision to relocate from a village in central India to the city of Lahore. In the city, the family's patriarch shrewdly pursues prosperity without much regard for business ethics. But his single-minded attention to his own success brings him repeatedly into conflict with his mother-in-law, whom he cannot outmaneuver as easily as his business rivals.

For *The Bride* (1982), Sidhwa received the National Award for English Literature from the Pakistan Academy. Very different in tone from *The Crow Eaters,* the novel focuses on Zaitoon, a young woman from the plains who is orphaned during the violence related to the partition of India and Pakistan. Adopted by a man from a more mountainous region but raised in Lahore, Zaitoon is unprepared for the marriage that her adoptive father arranges for her with a man from his native region. The mountains overwhelm her emotionally, and her new husband soon becomes abusive, in part because he has been conditioned by his upbringing to permit no dissent from his wife. Juxtaposed with Zaitoon's crisis over her unhappy marriage is an account of an American woman's sometimes difficult adjustments to life in India.

For *Cracking India* (1988), published as *Ice-Candy Man* in the United Kingdom, Sidhwa received Germany's LiBeraturepreis. The novel was also named a "Notable Book of the Year" by the *New York Times Book Review* and by the American Library Association. Told from the perspective of a young Parsi girl who is being home-schooled because she has been afflicted with polio, the novel juxtaposes her gradual coming of age with the historical trauma of the partition of India and

Pakistan. The Parsi community is not as directly affected by the partition as the Hindus and Muslims, but the Parsis are nonetheless affected by the tumult of economic, political, and cultural tensions that are brought to the surface during the forced relocations of their neighbors.

An American Brat (1993), Sidhwa's fourth novel, focuses on a Parsi woman who is sent by her parents to the United States to be educated away from the increasing Islamic fundamentalism in Pakistan. But when she transfers from the Mormon university in which they have enrolled her to the much more liberal atmosphere of a public university, her parents become very concerned. When she falls in love with a Jewish-American student, their concern devolves into something between outrage and panic.

Sidhwa's short stories and essays have appeared in such publications as *Femina, Houston Chronicle, New York Times Book Review, Pakistan Times,* and *Radcliffe Quarterly.*

Bibliography

Allen, Diane S. "Reading the Body Politic in Bapsi Sidhwa's Novels: *The Crow-Eaters, Ice-Candy Man* and *An American Brat.*" *South Asian Review* 18 (Dec. 1994): 69–80.

Didur, Jill. "Cracking the Nation: Gender, Minorities, and Agency in Bapsi Sidhwa's *Cracking India.*" *ARIEL* 29 (July 1998): 43–64.

Hai, Ambreen. "Border Work, Border Trouble: Postcolonial Feminism and the Ayah in Bapsi Sidhwa's *Cracking India.*" *Modern Fiction Studies* 46 (Summer 2000): 379–426.

Montenegro, David. "Bapsi Sidhwa: An Interview." *Massachusetts Review* 31 (Winter 1990): 513–533.

Martin Kich

Somebody's Daughter
Marie Myung-Ok Lee (2005)

Sarah Thorson, adopted at birth from Korea into a Caucasian family in Minnesota, shocks her family by dropping out of college and enrolling in a Motherland Program in Korea. Unfortunately, she is the least experienced Korean speaker in the lowest-level Korean language class at Chosun University and is treated as an outcast by her fellow Korean-American classmates. Lonely for companionship, Sarah befriends Doug Henderson, who is also shunned because he is half Korean and half white—the son of a Korean prostitute and an American GI. Sarah observes her Korean-American classmates with their seemingly simple lives and thinks she is not "Korean-hyphen anything, for what was Korean in [her] had become vestigial, useless" through adoption (20). When Sarah visits the Little Angels Orphanage, from which she was adopted, she finds out that the story of her birthparents' death from a car accident was not true, and this sends her on a mission to find her Korean birth mother.

Meanwhile, MARIE LEE weaves Sarah's birth mother's story into the novel. Kyung-sook is a country girl with a head for education and a heart for music. So she moves to Seoul for better education, only to find herself among spoiled girls and boring classes. She runs away and takes a job as a serving girl at a dumpling house, where she meets a foreigner named David who eventually becomes her lover. Seduced by David's extravagant taste and her own hopes for their new life together in "A-me-ri-ca" (155), Kyung-sook soon finds herself carrying his child. David, however, tells her to get an abortion and then abandons her. Kyung-sook returns to her native village and gives birth but decides she cannot keep the baby.

This novel marks a new direction for Marie Lee, who had previously written primarily for younger audiences. She uses irony by creating characters whose lives overlap and intertwine; Doug's mother is Kyung-sook's childhood friend, and Kyung-sook almost runs into Sarah and Doug in the subway. Lee also gives Sarah a name that sounds like "child for purchase"—"Sal-Ah"—in Korean (27). Although the novel contributes to a growing interest in Korean adoptee experiences, *Somebody's Daughter* lacks the inward complexity and sensibility commonly found in memoirs written by those who have actually lived the experience. Still, Sarah and Kyung-sook's stories are intriguing and shed light on international adoption and racial hybridity from multiple perspectives.

Bibliography

Lee, Maria Myung-Ok. *Somebody's Daughter*. Boston: Beacon, 2005.

Sarah Park

Son, Diana (1965–)

Born in Philadelphia to Korean-American parents, Diana Son started to write plays in 1987 and has been actively involved in writing and teaching drama. She has received several awards including the 1999 GLAAD (Gay and Lesbian Alliance Against Defamation) Media Award with *Stop Kiss* and the Berilla Kerr Award for Playwriting.

While Son was growing up in Dover, Delaware, two major incidents played a crucial role in her decision to become a playwright. First, in fourth grade, her essay was chosen as the best and was posted for the entire class, which allowed her to perceive herself as an independent person. Second, in 12th grade, she went on a field trip to New York City, during which she saw Joseph Papp's famous production of *Hamlet*. The encounter with the play inspired her to become a playwright. She entered New York University in 1983, majoring in drama. As a senior in college, she interned at La Mama Experimental Theatre Club, where her play, *Wrecked on Brecht*, was performed in June 1987.

After graduating from New York University in 1987, Son started to establish herself as a professional playwright. After attending the Playwrights Horizons Theatre School in New York City in 1991 and 1992, she went on to study at the Iowa Playwrights Workshop at the University of Iowa in 1993. Back in New York, Son joined the Asian American Playwrights Lab at the Public Theater, where she wrote *R.A.W. ('Cause I'm a Woman)*, which examines issues of race and gender via four Asian-American women characters. In her second full-length play, *Boy*, written in 1996, Son extends the issue of identity especially in terms of sex and gender. Directed by Michael Greif, the artistic director of La Jolla Playhouse in California, *Boy* questions the idea of identity as constructed in accordance with social environments. Mama and Papa Uber Alles, who desperately want to have a boy, name their fourth daughter "Boy" and raise her as a son. With humor, the play explores how time and place affect the ways in which concepts of gender and sex are constructed. Son's interest in identity politics is further articulated in another full-length play, *Stop Kiss,* which was written in 1997 and premiered in 1998 at the Public Theater. In this love story, two heterosexual women, Callie and Sara, find themselves falling in love with each other. When Callie kisses Sara at the Greenwich Village Park, however, a homophobic person attacks the two women, causing Sara to become disabled. While the play focuses on love, it also delves into the process of self-discovery. In 1999 Son worked as a staff writer for NBC-TV's drama series *The West Wing,* but she left the TV show in 2000. Overall, Son's works examine the quest for self-discovery. Even though some of her characters are Asian Americans, her themes address the general concerns of humanity.

Bibliography

Kim, Esther S. "Diana Son." In *Asian American Playwrights: A Bio-Bibliographical Critical Sourcebook,* edited by Miles Xian Liu. Westport, Conn.: Greenwood Press, 2000.

Tanaka, Jennifer. "Only Connect: An Interview with the Playwright." *American Theatre* 16, no. 6 (July/ Aug. 1999): 26–27.

Hyunjoo Ki

Sone, Monica (1919–)

Born Kuzuko Monica Itoi in Seattle, Washington, Monica Sone is best known for her autobiographical work, *Nisei Daughter* (1953). This book tells the story of a second (*ni*) generation (*sei*) Japanese-American girl in the 1930s and early 1940s. Monica, the second of four children, was raised in Seattle, where her parents managed a small hotel. Her father immigrated in 1904 with hopes of resuming his legal studies, but he eventually took over the hotel. Her mother, an amateur poet, was the daughter of a Japanese Christian minister and arrived in the United States two years before Monica's birth. Sone contracted tuberculosis as a teen-

ager, but a nine-month stay in a sanitarium cured her of the disease.

During World War II, her family was incarcerated briefly at Camp Harmony before they were transferred to Camp Minidoka in Idaho. Monica and her remaining siblings (Henry and Sumiko) were eventually permitted to leave the camp; she later entered Hanover College. Her parents, however, remained in the camp until the war's end. Monica's father died in 1948, but her mother was finally permitted to become an American citizen after the Naturalization Act of 1952. Monica studied clinical psychology at Case Western Reserve University and practiced for 38 years. She married Geary Sone, a nisei World War II veteran, and raised four children. She contributed a new preface to the reprint of *Nisei Daughter* (1979) that called for the American government to apologize for its wrongful imprisonment of Japanese Americans during the war.

Nisei Daughter, dedicated to her parents, began as a series of letters Sone wrote to her friend Betty McDonald during the war. A groundbreaking work, it is the first in a series of autobiographies by second-generation Japanese-American women, including FAREWELL TO MANZANAR (1973, JEANNE WAKATSUKI HOUSTON); *Through Harsh Winters* (1981, Akemi Kikumura); OBASAN (1981, JOY KOGAWA); and *Desert Exile* (1982, YOSHIKO UCHIDA). Decades later, David Guterson used Sone's text as a source for his popular novel *Snow Falling on Cedars* (1994).

In some ways, *Nisei Daughter* is a typical American bildungsroman, a story of initiation and identity formation. The central character's growth in this novel is complicated by her conflicted sense of Japanese and American identities. *Nisei Daughter* is also a typical immigrant's story from early 20th-century America that centers on issues of language, education, and wealth. The tension surrounding these assimilation issues is heightened by the dual loyalties of the central character during the war. Lastly, *Nisei Daughter* is a story of generational conflict. The children in the novel keenly feel the generational gap; in particular, the female narrator exhibits a teenager's angst in her relationship with her mother. The generational gap is even more complicated since the narrator is growing up at a time when the general public and media are telling her to fear or hate everything she associates with her immigrant parents.

Later critics who feel the author should have been more overtly political in her denunciation of the government's treatment of Japanese Americans during World War II have criticized *Nisei Daughter*'s humorous tone. However, Sone's tone and carefully worded anecdotes are measured to allow her access to a 1950s reading public that did not know or care about the World War II internment. Her work served to interest white America in the history of Japanese Americans and permitted subsequent Japanese-American writers, artists, and politicians to lobby for recognition and reparation.

Ann Beebe

Song, Cathy (1955–   )

Born to a Korean-American father and a Chinese-American mother in Honolulu, Cathy Song spent most of her life in Honolulu and now lives there with her husband and children. Song first demonstrated her talent at the age of 11 by writing a "spy novel," short stories with blond heroines, and imaginary interviews with movie stars. Continuing to write in high school, Song worked with poet John Unterecker at the University of Hawaii for two years and left for Wellesley College, where she earned a degree in English literature. Then she entered the master's program in creative writing at Boston University, receiving an M.A. degree in 1981. She later attended the Advanced Poetry Workshop conducted by Kathleen Spivak. In 1987, along with her husband, a physician, and their children, she returned to live in Hawaii to teach creative writing at the University of Hawaii while also working for Bamboo Ridge Press with other local writers.

Her first book-length manuscript, PICTURE BRIDE, was selected by poet Richard Hugo from among 625 manuscripts as the winner of the 1982 Yale Series of Younger Poets Award, one of the most prestigious literary awards for young poets. The manuscript was published by Yale University

in 1983 and was also nominated for that year's National Book Critics Circle Award. The success of her first book carried the young poet to national recognition, and other awards followed for her two successive books. Winning the Shelley Memorial Award, the Hawaii Award for Literature, and *Poetry* Magazine's Frederick Bock Prize, Song has established herself as a significant "canonical" writer in American literature. Her second volume of poems, *Frameless Windows, Squares of Light,* appeared in 1988 and her third collection, *School Figure,* in 1994. Her poems, mostly from *Picture Bride,* have been widely anthologized in influential works including *The Norton Anthology of American Literature, the Norton Anthology of Modern Poetry, The Heath Anthology of American Literature,* and *The Open Boat: Poems From Asian America.* The visibility of her poems has been a major breakthrough for Asian-American and Hawaiian poetry.

Critics have pointed out the highly visual characteristics of her poetry, its "organic" imagery, its connection of "the sensuous and the sensual," and the representations of the female body. Her poetry generally deals with Song's personal experiences in the roles of a child, sister, woman, wife, and mother, in relation to animals, people, and the land. Her inward exploration of her selfhood through various roles and her perceptions of the exterior world are filtered through the lens of her body.

Bibliography

Chen, Fu-jen. "Body and Female Subjectivity in Cathy Song's *Picture Bride.*" *Women's Studies: An Interdisciplinary Journal* 33, no. 5 (2004): 577–612.

Sumida, Stephen H. *And the View from the Shore: Literary Traditions of Hawaii.* Seattle: University of Washington Press, 1991.

Wallace, Patricia. "Divided Loyalties: Literal and Literary in the Poetry of Lorna Dee Cervantes, Cathy Song, and Rita Dove." *MELUS* 18, no. 3: 3–19.

Fu-jen Chen

Sugimoto, Etsu (Etsuko) I.   (1873–1950)

Author of several books including A DAUGHTER OF THE SAMURAI, which became a best seller in the

United States in the 1920s and has been translated into seven languages, Etsu Sugimoto was born to a prestigious samurai family in the Nagaoka domain in Echigo Province (present-day Niigata Prefecture). The character for "Etsu" stands for a "battle-ax," an unusual choice for a girl's name even in a samurai family. Her father, Heisuke Inagaki, was a former chief retainer of the Nagaoka domain. The rule of the Tokugawa Shogunate had just ended with the Meiji Restoration of 1868, and the samurai class had lost many privileges. In addition, the Nagaoka domain was recovering from the devastation resulting from its fierce battles against the new government's army during the Boshin war (1868). Etsu grew up under the guidance of her mother and great-grandmother ("Grandmother" in *A Daughter of the Samurai*). She received strict education as a member of the samurai class, in part because she was considered an heir after her elder brother ran away from home. She recited the verses from the Confucian classics while being ordered to keep an upright position throughout the lesson.

At age 12 she was engaged to Matsunosuke Sugimoto (Matsuo in *A Daughter*), her brother's friend living in the United States. To become a good wife, she continued her education in a Christian school. While at the school, she enjoyed reading English books, including the Bible and the poetry of Tennyson, and soon converted to Christianity. In 1898 she moved to the United States to marry Matsunosuke—then a merchant in Cincinnati whom she had never met. In Cincinnati the couple lived with the Wilsons—a distinguished local family who served as host to Etsu. In particular, she became friends with Florence Wilson, a collaborator in writing *A Daughter*. Etsu lived in Cincinnati for 12 years, during which time she gave birth to two daughters, Hanano and Chiyono. When she was traveling in Japan with her two daughters, she received the news that her husband had died of appendicitis. For a while she worked as a writer for a magazine for a Christian women's group in Tokyo (the experience curiously omitted in *A Daughter*). Worried about the education of her daughters, who were experiencing culture shock, however, she moved back to the United States, this time settling in New York in 1916. She was determined to make her living as a writer, and continued to submit articles despite many rejections. Eventually her writing was discovered by the editor and author Christopher Morley, who encouraged her to write "some little memories of her girlhood in Japan" for his newspaper column. The serialization of *A Daughter of the Samurai* in a magazine called *Asia* began in December 1923 and continued through 1924. Florence Wilson encouraged Etsu and edited her writing throughout the serialization. In 1925 it was published in book form by Doubleday, Page & Co. The publisher reported that the book was "the most continuously successful book of non-fiction on the Doubleday, Doran list" in 1932.

In 1927 she resigned from the teaching position at Columbia University—a post she had occupied since 1920, teaching Japanese-culture courses—and returned to Japan in order to conduct research for her new book. As Japan headed for war with China first and then with the United States in the 1930s, she continued to write for the American audience. She published "The Daughter of the Narikin" (1932), about a nouveau-riche in Japan; "A Daughter of the Nohfu" (1937), about peasant life in Niigata; and "Grandmother O Kyo" (1940), about the lives of the people during the Sino-Japanese War of 1937. Once the war was over in 1945, she was able to regain her friendships in the United States. In 1950 she died of liver cancer at the age of 76.

Shion Kono

Sui Sin Far   See FAR, SUI SIN.

Suitable Boy, A   Vikram Seth   (1993)

A daunting read at a hefty 1,325 pages, this winner of the WHSmith Literary Award and the Commonwealth Writer's Prize is a notable departure from the experimental, magical realist narrative style of VIKRAM SETH's contemporaries, such as Salman Rushdie. Instead, Seth embraces the laid-back unobtrusiveness of the classic realism of 19th-century novelists such as George Eliot, Charles Dickens, and Tolstoy. Indeed, *A Suitable Boy* outdoes the baggy monstrousness of most Victorian novels in its prodigious cast of characters, epic proportions, and historical sweep. The book is a veritable soap opera, peopled with a plethora of characters, most of whom get passing attention, and are rarely, except for the main ones who power the plot, developed beyond a sketch.

Set in the early 1950s, in newly postindependent India, the novel is imbued with the lingering idealism that inspired a whole generation of freedom fighters in their anticolonial campaign against the British. The small town of Brahmpur, where most of the action takes place, is located in the imaginary province of Purva Pradesh in North India. The narrative seems untroubled by the angst of postcolonial identity conflict and confusion arising from the long history of colonial rule by Britain in India or even the bloodbath that ensued in North India following the partition of the country after independence. And yet hitherto ignored conflicts of class, caste, religion, and gender linger just behind the scenes, only to surface when they are intertwined with such issues as the conflict over the land reform laws and the resettlement of large Hindu and Muslim populations dislocated following the partition of the country.

The novel combines satire and romance to great effect as it traces the fortunes of four families, the Mehras, Kapoors, Chatterjis and Khans. The complex train of events that constitutes the novel is set off when Rupa Mehra, the resourceful, widowed mother of Lata, declares to her daughter that "You too will marry a boy I choose." The main narrative framework, then, is anchored by the conflicting loves, lives, and contrasting personalities of the four young men who are presented as potential mates for Lata. The first, Mann Kapoor, who is one of the principal characters in the text, is the somewhat misguided, hopelessly romantic younger son of Mahesh Kapoor. Lata and Mann are connected to each other through their respective siblings, Savita and Pran, whose marriage opens the novel's narrative. The narrative only teases us momentarily with a possible relationship between them, before it follows more intimately Mann's obsession with the courtesan singer, Saaeda Bai, and through her a vanish-

ing world of courtly traditions and high culture. Kabir Durrani, the dashing college mate whom Lata first falls in love with, is considered unsuitable because he is Muslim. Amit Chatterji is the easy-going, talented young litterateur who is attracted to Lata, but she rejects the hyperactivity, insincere cosmopolitanism, and tiring linguistic prodigiousness of the Chatterjis. Haresh Khanna, who appears at first to be objectionable in his abruptness and apparent insensitivity, wins Lata over with his down-to-earth honesty, entrepreneurial drive, and integrity. It helps, too, that he is suitable in his caste and class affiliations, even if he is less than elegant for the sophisticated tastes of Lata's brother.

Seth has a keen eye for the comedy of manners, and his command over the English language is seen in the way he delineates characters and their social milieu through their use of language. A hilarious example of this wicked sense of humor is encapsulated in the Brahmpur University Poets Society meeting.

Despite its ambitious pan-Indian vision of secular inclusiveness, *A Suitable Boy* is determinedly bourgeois and North Indian in focus, limited in its regional and class interests. Despite its realist bent, the novel cannot resist becoming an allegorical narrative of the aims and aspirations of a young postcolonial nation that emulates a Eurocentric economic and social model in eschewing traditional identities, secular ideals, and the homegrown entrepreneurial energy of the Punjabi people. So Haresh Khanna, the man Lata chooses to marry, exemplifies the integrity and drive that modern India needs. He may be unfashionably stodgy and lack the cosmopolitan urbanity of Arun Mehra and the Chatterjis but is more admirable in his honesty and gruff warmth.

In arguing for the eventual disappearance of traditional caste- and religion-based identities, the novel affirms an unalloyed belief in meritocracy. Even the hapless Varun, Lata's marijuana-smoking younger brother, makes it to the Indian Administrative Service (IAS), the new elite of modern post-independence India, through a competitive exam. *A Suitable Boy* lauds the ethic of hard work and intelligence and offers a new vision of a bourgeoisie that is less pretentious, more salt-of-the-earth, but still buoyed by family connections.

Rajender Kaur

Suleri Goodyear, Sara   (1953–   )

Born in Karachi, Pakistan, Sara Suleri Goodyear is best known for her memoir *Meatless Days* (1989), which details her family's migrations between England and Pakistan, and her own immigration to the United States. It also relates the tragic deaths of her sister and her Welsh-born mother, who were both killed in hit-and-run accidents. In her second memoir, *Boys Will Be Boys* (2003), Suleri again chronicles her family's history, focusing this time on her father, the prominent political journalist Ziauddin Ahmed Suleri, whom his children nicknamed "Pip," short for "patriotic and preposterous." Suleri graduated from Kinnaird College in Lahore, Pakistan, in 1974 and received her M.A. from Punjab University in 1976 and her Ph.D. from Indiana University in Bloomington in 1983. She now lives with her husband in New Haven, Connecticut, teaching English literature at Yale University. Suleri has been instrumental in developing cultural criticism in Yale's curriculum and was a founding editor of the *Yale Journal of Criticism*. She has established herself as a leading scholar of postcolonial studies and is well known for her work to reconceptualize English literary history in a postcolonial context.

Meatless Days, which Suleri calls an "alternative history," focuses on the relationships among the women in her family. The different narratives are at once deeply personal and political because they intertwine the stories of her family with the traumatic history of Pakistan in a way that puts the private in dialogue with the historical. Suleri famously declares that "there are no women in the third world," a statement by which she introduces another major theme of her work: the inadequacy of social categories such as "minority," "woman," or "Asian American." Suleri regards these categories as dangerous in that they ignore specific historical and cultural contexts, so that the category of "women" used in the West is inadequate

for describing the experiences of women in the non-Western world. *Meatless Days* is not only a milestone in Pakistani English literature but also a classic in postcolonial literature; as such, it is taught widely.

Her second book, *The Rhetoric of English India*, traces the literary relationship between India and its former colonizer, England, and the effect colonialism has had on this relationship. Suleri writes about E. M. Forster, Rudyard Kipling, Edmund Burke, British women travel writers, as well as V. S. Naipaul and Salman Rushdie. She argues that colonial relationships should be understood as dialogic, not in terms of binaries of colonizer/colonized or dominant/other. Conceptualizing colonial and postcolonial processes as highly interrelational and constituted by mutual complicity and guilt, Suleri works to challenge the idea of rigid power relations of domination and subordination. In this complicated and controversial study, Suleri also criticizes postcolonial critics for romanticizing otherness in ways that threaten to re-inscribe what they themselves describe as Orientalism.

In *Boys Will be Boys: A Daughter's Elegy* (2003) Suleri reflects on her father's political life as a journalist and patriot, as well as on his private life as a father who demanded his children's utmost loyalty, as he read their diaries and interfered in their friendships. From the perspective of a daughter's remembrance, Suleri interweaves her father's story with that of her family, her childhood in Lahore, and her life in the United States. The book rings with the linguistic and cultural traces of her Pakistani childhood; the chapter titles are taken from Urdu verses, songs, and sayings, followed by Suleri's English translations. The book is not only a bicultural text but one that speaks to the importance of language in imagining personal as well as public life.

Bibliography

Bizzini, Silvia Caporale. "Sara Suleri's *Meatless Days* and Maxine Hong Kingston's *The Woman Warrior*: Writing, History and Self after Foucault." *Women: A Cultural Review* 7, no. 1 (Spring 1996): 55–65.

Rahman, Shazia. "Orientalism, Deconstruction, and Relationality: Sara Suleri's *Meatless Days*," *Literature Interpretation Theory* 15 (2004): 347–362.

Andrea Opitz

Suyemoto, Toyo   (1916–2003)

Born in Orville, California, to Japanese immigrant parents Mitsu Hyakusoku and Tsutomu Howard Suyemoto, Toyo was the first born of 11 children. When she reached college age, the family moved to Berkeley, where Toyo graduated with a bachelor's degree in English from the University of California. From 1942 to 1945 Toyo and her family, like most West Coast Japanese Americans, were forced to relocate to internment camps. First, they were interned at the Tanforan Race Track in California and later at the Topaz Relocation Camp in Utah. During the internment, Toyo and other college graduates set up a high school for the children of the camp, where she taught English and Latin. It was also at the Topaz camp in Utah that she first began to work as a librarian. After being released in 1945, Toyo worked at the Cincinnati Museum and later at the University of Cincinnati as a reference librarian. After the death of her son Kay at 16, Toyo earned an M.S. in Library Science from the University of Michigan. Between 1958 and 1987, she worked at the Ohio State University libraries. Toyo donated her writings and journals to the Suyemoto collection at the Ohio State University library. In the documentary film, *Life of Toyo Suyemoto Kawakami*, produced by Keith Kilty, Toyo Suyemoto discussed the difficulties she faced during internment, providing many examples of the racism she encountered as a Japanese American during World War II. Toyo died in her home in Columbus, Ohio, on December 30, 2003, at the age of 87.

Throughout her life, Toyo has been writing poetry using her maiden name, Toyo Suyemoto. Prior to World War II, she published poems in various Japanese-American newspapers on the West Coast. During internment, she belonged to the group of writers and artists who published the camp journals, *Trek* and *All Aboard*. After the war, her poetry

appeared in a number of journals and anthologies including the *Yale Review* and *Amerasia Journal*.

The central theme common to all of Suyemoto's works is the sense of loss. For Suyemoto, this sense is twofold. On the one hand, it refers to the "loss" of her identity—and her attempt to find her own unique voice as a second-generation Asian American. On the other hand, it refers to the "loss" of her sense of belonging, which resulted from her family being removed from its home and from one internment camp to another.

Suyemoto's best-known poems include "In Topaz," which was originally published in the camp journal *Trek* in the Topaz (Utah) internment camp in 1943, and "Camp Memories," which was composed in 1978. Juliana Chang, author of *Quiet Fire: A Historical Anthology of Asian American Poetry, 1892–1970*, describes Suyemoto's poems as "works of subtle beauty, which become powerfully poignant when the reader considers their place of authorship: a barren internment camp in the West where she and other Japanese-Americans were confined." Chang says Suyemoto's poems can be read as "metaphors for a barren lifestyle and hope for a fruitful spring" or as "allusions to Japanese-American agrarianism and its attempts to transform desert wastelands in the internment camps."

Bibliography
Chang, Juliana, ed. *Quiet Fire: A Historical Anthology of Asian American Poetry, 1892–1970*. New York: Asian American Writers' Workshop, 1996.

Monika Dix

Sze, Arthur   (1950–)

When he performs his work, Sze allows his hand to quietly measure out the rhythms and silences that shape his poetry. His poetry comes alive not in complex symbols that must be researched but in multivoiced dialogues and reflective silences that must be experienced.

Born in New York City, Sze is a second-generation Chinese American who early on saw poetry and science as complements to each other. As a young student at MIT, he soon found that his writing overtook his academic interest in science. Moving West, Sze graduated as a member of Phi Beta Kappa from the University of California, Berkeley, where he majored in creative writing. At Berkeley he immersed himself in Chinese language and literature and in such great T'ang-dynasty poets as Li Po, Tu Fu, and Wang Wei, feeling that through careful study he could best develop his own voice as a poet. Sze, however, insists he writes for neither an Asian nor an American aesthetic. Instead, he writes within and across the spaces of various cultures, discourses, and histories. His poetry incorporates his Chinese heritage, language, literature, and philosophies, but, rather than simply reproduce that heritage, Sze mediates it with his relationships to science and Native American culture.

To date, Sze has authored several volumes of poetry, including *Archipelago,* winner of the 1996 American Book Award in Poetry, *The Redshifting Web: Poems 1970–1998,* a finalist for the 1999 Lenore Marshall Poetry Prize, and *The Silk Dragon: Translations from the Chinese,* winner of the Western States Book Award in Translation. His poems have also appeared in numerous magazines, including *American Poetry Review, The Paris Review, Mother Jones, Conjunctions,* and *Bloomsbury Review.* Translations of Sze's work have been published in Italy and China. He has been honored with numerous awards including a Lannan Literary Award for Poetry, three Witter Bynner Foundation Poetry Fellowships and two Creative Writing Fellowships from the National Endowment for the Arts.

Sze's poetry largely derives from the associations he finds among classical Chinese poetry, quantum physics, the uniqueness of a very American landscape, and his immersion in Pueblo traditions. A speaker of Mandarin, Sze began translating poems in college and has worked at this craft at various times throughout his career. It was not until the publication of *The Silk Dragon* (2004), however, that Sze brought together the works that have influenced his own poetry. Although he acknowledges that any translation betrays its original in some way, Sze works methodically to capture not only the meaning and dynamic vision of the work

he translates but also its rhythmical flexibility, which varies dramatically from the stress patterns in English. He starts a translation by writing out the Chinese characters as the sounds and tones for a word, phrase, or cluster of words so he can sense the inner motion of the poem. He then revises the overall poem, changing initial translations to others that better fit the poem's context. By working carefully with the Chinese tones, Sze tries to capture not only the original poem's cadences but also its silences. The translation, like Sze's own poems, becomes a work of art that avoids teaching lessons or drawing conclusions.

Sze finds he enriches rather than complicates his poetry with a subtlety and emotional power that he draws from translating Chinese writers—classical to contemporary. From Asian poetry, Sze draws themes of oneness and multiplicity and precise imagery into the juxtaposed architecture of his writing. To this background he adds Buddhist and Native American art and culture, as well as his study of the French symbolists, Rimbaud, Yeats, and others. The union of past and present, the exotic with the everyday, and physics with lyricism creates a vivid, surrealist imagery that can surprise Sze's readers: Radios in Antarctica send messages to outer space; legislators vote by raising their feet, and Zen monks carry fax machines. Sze succinctly describes his method as one in which "you knock the / gyroscope off the axis of spinning, / so that one orientation in the world vanishes / and the others appear infinite" ("The Axis").

Conventional metaphor, sequential narrative, and logical connections among ideas do not play the central roles in Sze's work that they do in most Western poetry. Instead, Sze patterns his work with nonsymbolic imagery, fragmented sentences, multiple points in time, and collage, turning the reader into an "absorbing form" ("The Redshifting Web"). As the poet disappears behind the poem, readers are caught in a moment in time filled with unlikely associations. Some may want to believe that "The ecology of the Galapagos Islands / has nothing to do with a pair of scissors," but, in truth, "The world of the quark has everything to do / with a jaguar circling in the night" ("The Leaves of a Dream

Are the Leaves of an Onion"). A seemingly random set of images from nature, Asian writing, and quantum physics (as in "The String Diamond, 3": Deltoid spurge, / red wolf, / ocelot, / green-blossom pearlymussel, / razorback sucker, . . .") come together in the reader's mind to build tableaus and pose open-ended questions such as "In the mind, what never repeats? Or repeats endlessly?" Even "redshift" in the title of Sze's most successful collection, *The Redshifting Web*, ties the natural and poetic to the scientific in a conjectural fashion: Redshift is an astronomical phenomenon that occurs when galaxies move apart and their light shifts from the higher (blue) to the lower (red) end of the spectrum. To Sze, all things in the universe, including humans, are intricately connected in patterns of constant motion and change.

In the early 1990s, Sze settled in Pojoaque, New Mexico, with his wife, poet Carol Moldaw (*The Lighting Field, Chalkmarks on Stone*). He now directs the creative writing program at the Institute for American Indian Art in Santa Fe, New Mexico, gives lectures and poetry readings worldwide, and publishes his poetry and that of others from the Santa Fe Public Library Workshops and the Institute of American Indian Arts.

Bibliography

Sze, Arthur. *The Redshifting Web: Poems 1970–1998.* Port Townsend, Wash.: Copper Canyon Press, 1998.

———. *The Willow Wind: Translations From the Chinese and Poems.* Santa Fe, N.M.: Tooth of Time, 1972. Rev. ed., Santa Fe, N.M.: Tooth of Time, 1981.

Xiaojing, Zhou. "*The Redshifting Web:* Arthur Sze's Ecopoetics." In *Ecopoetry: A Critical Introduction,* edited by J. Scott Bryson, 179–187. Salt Lake City: University of Utah Press, 2002.

LynnDianne Beene

Sze, Mai-mai (1905–1987)

As an artist, Sze published a comprehensive study of Chinese painting called *The Tao of Painting* in 1946. An important writer in Chinese-American communities during the Sino-Japanese War, Sze wrote about the war and immigrant experiences. Crossing cultural boundaries, as the daughter of a Chinese ambassador, she also attempts to deconstruct the binary opposition between East and West.

Writing in the 1940s, when Western readers often expected exotic descriptions of the Orient, Sze described herself as a homeless cosmopolitan rather than a tour guide of Eastern exoticism. In her autobiography, *Echo of a Cry: A Story Which Began in China* (1945), she records her life as a rootless Chinese-American woman. Born in China, she was taken to England, cared for by an Irish nanny, sent to a private school in France, and then lived in New York. During a return visit to China for a birthday celebration, she felt disconnected from her Chinese heritage. Noticing an old baby photograph of herself on the wall, she realized how distant this part of her life had become. In the Western world, however, her feelings of displacement and exile were even worse. For instance, in the United States she was subjected to racial slurs. On a painting trip to France, she was viewed as a curiosity. Sze's diasporic experiences show how difficult it is to determine one's identity after so many relocations. She captures the profound loneliness and loss at the heart of the immigration experience.

During the Sino-Japanese War, Sze organized the first Chinese war relief campaign in the United States and lectured on China's war efforts across North America. Her antiwar sentiment is revealed in her novel, *Silent Children* (1948). Unlike early Chinese immigrant writers who wrote patriotic stories of the Sino-Japanese War to gain support for their mother nation, Sze does not show an urgent patriotism in this novel. Instead, in a surrealist setting, her narrative centers on a band of war orphans who struggle to survive near the outskirts of a nameless city and who work together for their future. Sze uses the homeless and miserable condition of the orphans not only to criticize the dehumanizing effects of war but also to reflect on the psychological conditions of diasporic subjects.

Bibliography

Amato, Jean. "Mai-mai Sze." *Asian American Autobiographers: A Bio-Bibliographical Critical Sourcebook,* edited by Emmanuel S. Nelson, 345–349. Westport, Conn.: Greenwood Press, 2000.

———. "Mai-mai Sze." *Asian American Novelists: A Bio-Bibliographical and Critical Sourcebook,* edited by Emmanuel S. Nelson, 357–359. Westport, Conn.: Greenwood Press, 2000.

Ling, Amy. *Between Worlds: Women Writers of Chinese Ancestry.* New York: Pergamon Press, 1990.

Su-lin Yu

Takei, George (1937–)

This Japanese-American actor, community activist, and writer was born on April 20, 1937, in Los Angeles, California. He is known primarily for playing Mr. Sulu (later Captain Sulu) in the original *Star Trek* television series and first six films, although his acting career includes participation in more than 30 movies and 100 television shows. Takei studied architecture at the University of California at Berkeley until a small part in a film convinced him that acting was the career he was meant for. He then transferred to UCLA to study theater arts, acting in various films and theater productions during those years. His first film was *Ice Palace,* starring Richard Burton, in 1959. He was cast by Gene Roddenberry in "Where No Man Has Gone Before," the second *Star Trek* pilot in 1966, which led to his becoming a regular when the series went into production. Because of his distinguished career, he received a star on Hollywood Boulevard's Walk of Fame in 1986, and he placed his signature and handprint in the forecourt of the landmark Grauman's Chinese Theater in Hollywood in 1991. Apart from his work in film, Takei has been active in politics and was a member of the board of directors of the Southern California Rapid Transit District from 1973 to 1984. President Clinton appointed him to the board of the Japan-United States Friendship Commission, on which he served two terms, and for which the emperor of Japan awarded him in 2004 the Order of the Rising Sun. Takei has played a vital role in Japanese-American community affairs, such as the East West Players, the nation's foremost Asian Pacific American theater, and has worked actively for decades with the Japanese American National Museum.

Takei's autobiography, *To the Stars* (1994), opens with his family's evacuation, along with more than 120,000 Japanese Americans to the internment camps at the outbreak of World War II. He spent years of his childhood at Camp Rohwer in Arkansas and at Tule Lake in northern California. This autobiography is one of a few that effectively chart the successful trajectory of a Japanese-American subject in the context of the changing historical and political circumstances of the United States in the last 60 years. Written chronologically and clearly, Takei's autobiography describes his growing sense of ethnic identity in the different contexts he occupied, as well as his determination to make the history of the Japanese in America part of the country's awareness of itself. Much of the text also describes his years working in Hollywood, which are of particular interest to the legions of *Star Trek* fans. Takei's first memory, as articulated in *To the Stars,* is the train journey to Rohwer, which his parents convinced their three young children was a vacation. The writer cleverly juxtaposes the child's perspective on this adventure with the adult's awareness of the gross injustice being enacted on American citizens by their own government. Years later, Takei looks back on this childhood experience as the impetus for his community work with Japanese Americans as well as for his representation of Sulu in *Star Trek*. As the first Japanese-American actor to work for a nationally broadcast and popular TV show, Takei was aware of his responsibility in making Asian Americans visible in American media and popular culture, as a crucial departure from traditionally stereotypical Hollywood representations of Asians as "buffoons, menials, or menaces." For him and other Japanese Americans who were interned, "Rohwer and Tule Lake were still not history"; his driving passion therefore has been to strive for personal and communal recovery through art and politics.

Rocío G. Davis

Tamagawa Eldridge, Kathleen
(1893–1979)

Kathleen Tamagawa was the product of an early interracial marriage. During the 1880s, her father, a Westernized Japanese, settled in Chicago and met his Anglo-Irish immigrant wife. The two fell in love and were married, although their union was delayed for several years by her family's opposition. After their wedding, the couple opened a short-lived business in Atlantic City, New Jersey, where Kathleen was born in December 1893. The family soon returned to Chicago, where Kathleen spent her childhood years. To her annoyance, she was regarded by friends and neighbors as Japanese and treated as a living "China doll." She thus welcomed the family's decision to move to Japan in 1906, assuming she could now be among her kind. Once in Japan, however, Kathleen felt even more foreign. Unable to identify or communicate with the Japanese, she felt herself without any "race, nationality, or home." The Tamagawa family ultimately settled in Western-style quarters in Yokohama's multiracial foreign colony, where Kathleen attended school. While in Yokohama she met men of different backgrounds but refused to add "an additional hyphen" to her identity by marrying

any of them. Instead, she deliberately selected an American diplomat, Frank R. Eldridge, as her husband because she perceived him (falsely, she later admitted) to be "ordinary."

Following her marriage in 1912, Kathleen returned to the United States with her husband. The Eldridges spent the succeeding years in Washington, D.C., and Tennessee, where they had four children. Frank worked for the U.S. Commerce Department and wrote several books on trade with Asia. Kathleen, distancing herself from her Japanese heritage, blended into white middle-class American life and motherhood.

In 1928 the Eldridges moved to the New York City area. Following the onset of the Great Depression, Kathleen took a part-time job as a librarian at Columbia University to help the family's finances. Her mother's death shortly afterward inspired Kathleen to analyze her ambivalent feelings about her mixed-race identity. She enrolled in a creative writing class at Columbia University and began a memoir. The first of the three installments of the work entitled *Holy Prayers in a Horse's Ear* appeared in October 1930 in *Asia*, a popular Asian affairs magazine. Its positive reception encouraged Kathleen to sign a book contract with the publishing firm of Ray Long and Richard Smith. In order to flesh out the manuscript, she added a section dealing with her 1927 trip to Asia and the letters from her mother describing the Tokyo earthquake of 1923.

Holy Prayers in a Horse's Ear, the first mainstream book by a nisei author, appeared in February 1932. In the work, Kathleen recounts her life in Japan and America as an "accident of nature." Although she dismisses racial difference as a trivial phenomenon and mocks as silly those who find meaning in it, she opposes interracial marriage as a source of grief and confusion (ironically, she did not perceive her own marriage as an interracial union). In an unusual ending, the author "disappears." Speaking in her husband's voice, she notes that the Japanese government has announced that, because she was not registered at the time of her birth, for official purposes she does not exist. She presents the statement as the apex of the absurdity that her mixed heritage engenders but simultaneously embraces it as a metaphor for her identity.

Holy Prayers attracted significant popular attention and went through several printings. Critics nationwide were divided in their appreciation of the work, both on stylistic grounds and in relation to the author's views on interracial marriage. Kathleen's publisher, gratified by the book's success, solicited her to write another, prompting her to work on a novel set in Japan. "A Fit in Japan," Kathleen's satirical tale set in Tokyo's foreign colony, which may have been an excerpt from the novel, appeared in a literary anthology in mid-1932. However, between her job and child-care responsibilities, Kathleen found it difficult to find time to write and abandoned the project. In 1934 the Eldridge family moved to Washington. After lecturing at George Washington University on her impressions of Japan, she began a book on Japanese culture. However, she lacked confidence and could not find the drive or time to work. Instead, she devoted the rest of her life to caring for her family. In the 1940s, Kathleen and her husband formed the Lenma society, a branch of the General Semantics Movement. In the late 1960s, she worked with the Washington Forum, a public affairs discussion group. *Holy Prayers,* long forgotten at the time of the author's death in 1979, has since been reclaimed as a significant text by both Asian-American and Hapa studies scholars.

Greg Robinson

Tan, Amy   (1952–)

Her first novel, *The JOY LUCK CLUB,* was published in 1989 and made into a major motion picture in 1993; thus Amy Tan began her distinguished career as a contemporary author who explores the complex relationship between mothers and daughters. She revisits the themes of familial and generational continuities and misunderstandings in each of her subsequent novels, including *The KITCHEN GOD'S WIFE* (1991), *The HUNDRED SECRET SENSES* (1995), and *The BONESETTER'S DAUGHTER* (2001). Compounding the intricacies inherent in each mother-daughter story is the additional factor of immigration: Each mother is a Chinese immigrant and each daughter is a first-generation American, both of whom must negotiate linguistic and cultural differences to understand and come to terms with the other.

Fueling each of these novels is the challenging relationship Tan experienced with her own mother, Daisy (Tu Ching) Tan, as well as the fascinating and heart-wrenching experiences of her mother and extended family, both in China and in the United States. Daisy and her husband, John Yuehhan Tan, settled in the San Francisco area in 1949, the year of the Communist takeover in China. What the Tans left behind in China, their daughter Amy would years later reinvent in fiction in the United States. Tan's maternal grandmother, Jing-mei, lived in exile with her daughter Daisy on an island off the coast of Shanghai because the widowed woman had been raped and forced to become a rich man's concubine. After Jing-mei gave birth to the man's son, a higher-ranking wife claimed the boy as her own, and Jing-mei ate a deadly amount of raw opium. Tan's grandmother's story became the basis for An-mei Hsu's narrative in *The Joy Luck Club* and also informs parts of her other novels. Nine-year-old Daisy, who had witnessed the suicide of her mother, was cared for by relatives and then entered an arranged marriage. Daisy endured years of physical and mental abuse, including rape and being forced to sign fake divorce papers with a gun to her head. She finally left this abusive marriage and three daughters, whom she was forced to give up upon her divorce. She was not reunited with them until 1978. Daisy's tragic story is told most fully—though in a fictionalized format—in *The Kitchen God's Wife* and, to a lesser degree, in other novels.

Amy Tan's mother had been a nurse in China, and her father was an electrical engineer, but both took on new careers in their new country. Her mother became a full-time homemaker and her father gave up a scholarship at the Massachusetts Institute of Technology to become a Baptist minister. Tan was raised in a household of conflicting religious opinions—overtly, they were Christians, but her mother never lost her strong belief in Chinese mysticism, often asking her daughter to channel ghosts or seeing foreboding signs in everyday occurrences. When Tan was 14, her father and older brother both died of brain tumors, and her mother decided to leave their bad luck behind by taking her and her younger brother to Switzerland in 1968, where she finished high school. The Tans returned to the San Francisco area the next year, and Tan studied first at Linfield College in Oregon, and then transferred to San Jose City College to be near her future husband, Louis DeMattei. Continuing her parents' tradition of new beginnings, Tan also changed her major from pre-med to a double major in English and linguistics. This irked her mother, who had wanted Tan to be a brain surgeon and a concert pianist in her spare time, and the two did not speak to each other for six months.

Tan graduated with a B.A. in English and linguistics in 1973 and a master's degree in linguistics in 1974 from San Jose State University, married DeMattei, a tax lawyer, and began work on a doctoral degree at the University of California. Tan decided to leave her doctoral program and worked as a language development specialist for developmentally disabled children for five years. Tan then moved into freelance business and technical writing, a very lucrative but unfulfilling venture. She produced work for major corporations, including AT&T and IBM. However, she became a workaholic and began therapy to organize her life, eventually working through her issues on her own with the help of creative writing. Her first short story, "Endgame," about a Chinese chess prodigy and her difficult mother, was the first creative effort that Tan worked on within a community of writers. She has since worked with a group of writers led by Molly Giles and attended writers' workshops. Through Giles, Tan met her literary agent and wrote the short stories that would become *The Joy Luck Club*. The book was selected as a finalist for the National Book Award for Fiction and the National Book Critics Circle Award. The novel stayed on the *New York Times* best-seller list for almost a year and has been translated into more than 20 languages. She has since published four more novels, *The Kitchen God's Wife* (1991), *The Hundred Secret Senses* (1995), and *The Bonesetter's Daughter* (2001), and *Saving Fish from Drowning* (2005). She also wrote a nonfiction book of personal essays, *The Opposite of Fate* (2003), and two children's books, *The Moon Lady* (1992) and *Sagwa, the Chinese Siamese Cat* (1994), which has been adapted into a cartoon series for children on PBS. She has also written numerous essays on literary and linguistic matters. Her work is both critically and popularly acclaimed.

In her novels, Tan treats themes of complex and multifaceted familial ties—most often between mother and daughter, but sometimes between other family members, as when she writes about sisters in *The Hundred Secret Senses*. She often employs various characters' voices to tell different parts of each story, and so her novels are layered with diverse interpretations of similar events in each character's life. The landscapes of the novels move from the United States to China and back again, and the time periods involved generally span several lifetimes, reaching from the present back to the pre–World War II era. Tan resists being labeled an ethnic writer, preferring to recognize her novels as "American" rather than representative of Chinese culture. Her characters' issues are the issues of all men and women, not only those who are born Chinese. Through each novel, Tan's connection to her mother's life story is evident, and her mother's gift for storytelling is indelibly preserved.

In her spare time, Tan travels and sings with the literary rock band Rock Bottom Remainders with fellow writers, including Stephen King and Dave Barry. The band performs at benefits that support children's literacy programs.

Bibliography
Huntley, E. D., ed. *Amy Tan: A Critical Companion*. Critical Companions to Popular Contemporary Writers. Westport, Conn.: Greenwood Press, 1998.

Vanessa Rasmussen

Tham, Hilary (Hilary Tham Goldberg) (1946–2005)

Poet, editor, and artist Hilary Tham Goldberg was born on August 20, 1946, in Kelang (or Klang), Malaysia, to Chinese immigrant parents. She authored nine books of poetry and one memoir under the name Hilary Tham, served as editor for a variety of publications, and was also a painter. Tham attended the University of Malaya and graduated with a B.A. in English. While in Malaysia, Tham married a Jewish-American Peace Corp volunteer, Joseph Goldberg, and converted to Judaism shortly thereafter. In 1971 the couple came to the United States, settling briefly in New Jersey before moving to Arlington, Virginia, in 1973. Tham passed away on June 24, 2005, in Arlington, from metastatic lung cancer.

Tham occupies a unique space within Asian-American and Asian diasporic culture as a Chinese-Malaysian writer with Judaic influences. Tham's family spoke Cantonese, but the diverse environment in Malaysia in which Tham grew up played an important role in her career. Tham's attendance at a convent school run by Irish nuns and a Catholic school run by Dominican monks exposed her to a wide range of cultures, languages, and literatures. At the urging of her prep school English teacher in Kuala Lumpur (a school where Tham was one of 12 females permitted to attend the otherwise all-male institution), Tham began to take writing seriously. After moving to the United States, Tham continued to write and also became active in her community. She chaired the Northern Virginia Coalition, which helped to resettle Vietnamese refugees; served as sisterhood president at her synagogue; participated in various poet-in-residence and artist-in-residence programs throughout northern Virginia; served as editor-in-chief of Word Works, a nonprofit poetry press; and served as poetry editor for *Potomac Review*, a biannual literary magazine. Tham was also the recipient of several awards. Her book *Bad Names for Women* (1989) won second prize in the 1988 Virginia Poetry Prizes and the 1990 Paterson Prize, and *Tin Mines and Concubines* (2005) received the Washington Writers Publishing House Prize. The Fall/Winter 2005–06 issue of *Potomac Review* contains a tribute to Tham.

Tham's characters and her own sense of self as articulated in her memoir offer perspectives from both Malaysian and American geopolitical contexts, often critiquing both. In addition to making transpacific crossings between Malaysia and America, Tham's work also moves beyond those reference points to the broader region of Southeast Asia, and Tham demonstrates a general concern for humanity regardless of geographical borders. Some critics view Tham's range of thematic interests as difficult to classify within Asian-American studies, but Tham's work can be said to demonstrate social concerns shared by many Asian-American writers—for instance, issues of race, sexuality, and what it means to be alien in a democratic America.

While the social concerns in Tham's work are significant, the aesthetic aspect of her writing is equally so. In her memoir *Lane with No Name: Memoirs and Poems of a Malaysian-Chinese Girlhood,* Tham remembers how the nursery rhymes and Cantonese proverbs her mother recounted would significantly shape Tham's own poetry. To Tham, the language found in both Cantonese proverbs and daily Cantonese speech was suggestively condensed and imagistic. Some critics trace the prominence of metaphors, images, and terse vocabulary found in her work to her childhood experiences with Cantonese. Tham also painted, and she viewed both literature and painting as capturing the rhythmic, emotive motions of an event. Her book *Men & Other Strange Myths: Poems and Art* (1994) blends poetry with her own drawings.

Perhaps Tham's interest in social issues and aesthetic form is most evident in her well-known character Mrs. Wei, whom some have called Tham's poetic alter ego. Mrs. Wei appears in many of Tham's poems, and in 2003 Tham collected her Mrs. Wei poems in *The Tao of Mrs. Wei*. A Chinese figure who has resided in both Malaysia and America, Mrs. Wei is a traditional mother who is also outspoken on politics. The titles of Tham's Mrs. Wei poems are simple, yet the often ironic form and content of those poems are packed with social meaning and critique. A selection of titles quickly demonstrates this point—"Mrs. Wei and the Modern Marriage," "Mrs. Wei and the Gay Poet," and "Mrs. Wei Meets the New Improved American Dream."

Tham's work remains understudied, though critics note that the turn toward transnational approaches to Asian-American studies could bring more attention to her work. Her literary treatment of U.S.–Southeast Asia relations and how they link to current interests in transnationalism and globalization are areas warranting further investigation.

Bibliography

Hashim, Ruzy Suliza, and Faridah Abdul Manaf. "Ties That Bind: A Comparative Study of Two Asian Women Memoirists." *Feminist Studies in English Literature* 10, no. 2 (Winter 2002): 189–208.

Lim, Shirley Geok-lin. Review of *Paper Boats* by Hilary Tham. *CALYX* (1990): 93–94.

Xiaojing, Zhou. "Hilary Tham." *Asian American Autobiographers: A Bio-Bibliographical Sourcebook,* edited by Guiyou Huang. Westport, Conn.: Greenwood Press, 2001.

Marguerite Nguyen

Thousand Pieces of Gold
Ruthanne Lum McCunn (1981)

Based on the life story of the courageous Lalu Nathoy (1853–1933), later known as Polly Bemis, the novel examines the double marginalization faced by women of color as the protagonist Lalu/Polly is subjected to oppression because of her gender and race.

As northern China suffers a two-year drought, bandit raids have surged in Lalu's village. During one bandit attack, Lalu's father reluctantly sells Lalu for two bags of seed. The bandit leader then sells Lalu to a brothel, which turns out to be a cover for a slave trade operation between a Chinese government official and American slave merchants. Lalu soon finds herself on a ship bound to San Francisco; only the dream of returning home with gold to support her family sustains her spirit.

Once in San Francisco, Lalu learns the harsh reality of her fate. The promise of gold has been fabricated by her buyer; instead, she finds herself stripped naked for a slave auction. Lalu is purchased by Hong King, who runs a saloon in the mining town of Warrens in Idaho. Hong King has hired a Chinese packer named Jim to bring Lalu

back to the mining camp. Lalu learns from Jim that she has been bought for the purpose of attracting customers. Jim promises Lalu that he will buy her freedom.

Lalu, renamed Polly by Hong King, once again has her dream of freedom dashed when another tragedy hits—Jim has been killed in an accident. Jim's death brings Polly and Charlie, Jim's friend, closer as he is now her only friend. Charlie devises a plan and wins Polly from Hong King in a poker game. Polly expresses to Charlie her desire to become an independent woman by establishing her own boardinghouse, but Charlie informs her that Chinese cannot own land in America. Charlie confesses his love for Polly and offers to help her by building a house for her under his name.

Having experienced many difficulties together, Polly, at age 31, and Charlie finally agree to marry. They build a ranch in Salmon Canyon and name it Polly Place. However, after a couple of peaceful decades in Salmon Canyon, another disaster strikes when Polly Place burns down and Charlie succumbs to his already weakened health. After Charlie's death, Polly moves back to Warrens for a short period of time, but she finally decides that her life belongs to the ranch that she and Charlie built. Polly moves back to Salmon Canyon and lives there until her death in 1933.

Ruthanne Lum McCunn skillfully juxtaposes Polly's experiences with those of other marginalized subjects to articulate the many forms of social injustice. For example, McCunn compares the Western custom of corseting to the Chinese practice of foot binding, exposing both as the tools of patriarchy to exert control over a woman's body.

McCunn also shows Polly traversing between cultures while questioning both. For instance, Polly uses the gardening techniques that she learned as a child from her father to plant her own garden in Salmon Canyon and uses herbal medicine to cure the children of Warrens. However, Polly also discards the Chinese traditional belief in luck and adopts the philosophy of American individualism. By combining the cultural beliefs and practices of both China and America, Polly has created a Chinese-American identity for herself despite the gender and racial oppressions that she has encountered.

Bibliography

Cheung, King-kok. "Self-Fulfilling Visions in *The Woman Warrior* and *Thousand Pieces of Gold.*" *Biography: An Interdisciplinary Quarterly* 13, no. 2 (Spring 1990): 143–153.

Terry, Patricia. "A Chinese Woman in the West: *Thousand Pieces of Gold* and the Revision of the Heroic Frontier." *Literature/Film Quarterly* 22, no. 4 (1994) 222–226.

Nan Ma

Through the Arc of the Rain Forest
Karen Tei Yamashita (1990)

In this debut novel by KAREN TEI YAMASHITA, characters of different talents and nationalities come together in Brazil: a three-armed American man called Tweep who runs a global plastic enterprise; a Japanese man named Kazumasa who has a satellite hovering over his head; and Brazilians Batista and Tania Aparecido, who use their ability to train carrier pigeons to mass-market their pigeons. In the background is a story of a relationship between humans and Mother Nature gone awry; however, Yamashita's satirical narrative and unusual configuration of characters and landscapes render her work different from other narratives about humans' relationship with nature. Her intricately interwoven cultural symbolisms of Japan, Latin America, and the United States produce a complex matrix of hybrid characters and cultures that challenges readers to question and probe established cultural norms.

Human beings and waste migrate to Brazil as nature orchestrates a global recycling system. The system channels industrial waste spewing from every artificial orifice on the Earth's surface through the Earth's mantle, ultimately siphoning the transformed material through the Earth's crust as a black magnetic substance in the heart of the Brazilian forest. With the arrival of the "Matacao," as the substance is called, it not only brings

forth new species of life whose habitat revolves around it but it also becomes a source of global business for Tweep, who advertises and sells the material as a new type of plastic that is more malleable and durable than any other plastic that has ever been made. Meanwhile, Kazumasa, accompanied by the satellite hovering over his head, travels from Japan to Brazil with the initial intention of contributing his skills to Brazil's railway industry only to discover his talents in winning the lottery. Tweep and his company, GGG Enterprise, form a business partnership with Kazumasa and his satellite; however, at the height of this thriving mix of humans' capitalistic drive and nature's power of adaptation and evolution, everything suddenly begins to disintegrate. A new strain of bacteria creates an epidemic and begins to destroy the Matacao. Even the mysterious satellite that hovers in front of Kazumasa's head also begins to fade away as it is discovered to have been made of the same material as the Matacao. Ultimately, with the destruction of the Matacao and the collapse of GGG Enterprise, the flow of miracle-seekers that gushed forth to pay homage to the Matacao disappears, and peace returns to the forests of Brazil. However, the narrator, who is indeed the remnants of Kazumasa's satellite, concludes that despite the return of peace, the forest "will never be the same again."

The manner in which Yamashita attempts to blur the representational boundaries among the United States, Japan, and Brazil through her depictions of hybrid characters and global commercialism seems to coax a dialogue for a critical reassessment of cultural diversity and its enabling capacity. Therefore, her depictions of an amiable coexistence among the multiracial characters who gather in Brazil seem to suggest her attempt to break away from Asian-American narratives centralized on Asian-American characters and to incorporate issues revolving around Latin America. According to Rachel Lee, Yamashita's text shows that "Asian Americans might widen the scope of their struggles and de-ethnicize their communal fidelities in order to fight for the poor and oppressed regardless of national origins" (*Bound-*

ary 2, 249). Hence, in *Through the Arc of the Rain Forest*, Yamashita may be attempting to widen her narrative scope to explore not just the relationship between East and West but also North and South.

Bibliography

Lee, Rachael. *The Americas of Asian American Literature.* Princeton, N.J.: Princeton University Press, 1999.

———. "Asian American Cultural Production in Asian-Pacific Perspective." *Boundary 2* 26, no. 2 (Summer 1999): 231–254.

Rody, Caroline. "Impossible Voices: Ethnic Postmodern Narration in Toni Morrison's *Jazz* and Karen Tei Yamashita's *Through the Arc of the Rain Forest.*" *Contemporary Literature* 41 (2000): 618–641.

Yamashita, Karen Tei. *Through the Arc of the Rain Forest.* Minneapolis, Minn.: Coffee House Press, 1990.

Eliko Kosaka

To Swim across the World
Frances Park and Ginger Park (2001)

In 1941 Sei-young and Heisook live at opposite ends of Korea under the colonial occupation of Japan. Sei-young is a young boy in southern Korea, unable to understand his father's drinking habits in the face of his family's poverty. In northern Korea, Heisook is the privileged daughter of a minister who bribes the Japanese to let him run his church. She lives comfortably under Japanese occupation until Changi, her older brother who rebels against the Japanese, enlightens her with the truth of their nation's humiliating subjugation. Her blistered hands from sewing socks for Japanese soldiers symbolize her premature departure from childhood at the age of 12. Heisook's older brother is drafted to fight for the Japanese army and her father flees to the south.

In the south, Sei-young suffers the loss of his father and beloved younger brother. After Japan loses the war and leaves Korea, Sei-young and Heisook find their lives even more complicated with the intrusion of Russian and American governments.

Heisook is forced to leave her mother in North Korea as she moves south to reunite with her father. Before the outbreak of the Korean War in 1950, Sei-young and Heisook meet in Seoul. Their subsequent marriage symbolizes a triumphant union, though the people around them are increasingly polarized before and after the Korean War. Their story ends in 1955 with their departure to the United States, which signifies a new beginning for them. Although a strong thread of Christian faith runs through both Sei-young's and Heisook's stories, they each question God's protection and sovereignty as death and violence descend upon their families under Japanese occupation. The end of the Korean War brings neither true peace nor unity of the nation, but Seiyoung and Heisook's marital union brings hope for a better future.

In this riveting story of tragedy, love, and nationalism, the Park sisters weave together their parents' histories to form one unifying tale of survival and to show the effect of a nation's unfortunate history on so many lives. It is a testimony of how faith could uphold families in the face of the most horrendous times of suffering. The story celebrates the perseverance of an entire nation still plagued by remembrances of war. Sei-young's name means "to swim across the world" according to his grandfather; it symbolizes Korea as a nation that extends its influence across oceans and borders.

Sarah Park

Trenka, Jane Jeong (1972–)

The Language of Blood: A Memoir (2003), Jane Jeong Trenka's first novel, is a memoir of her life as a Korean adoptee in the United States and her journeys back to Korea in search of her origin and birth family. Jane and her biological sister, Carol, formerly Kyong-Ah and Mi-Ja respectively, were born in Korea and adopted by a white couple in Minnesota. The couple raised Carol and Jane as though they were white children whose lives began not at their birth, but at the moment they stepped on American soil. Carol, the older daughter, adapted more easily into the homogenous town of Harlow, Minnesota. Jane, however, constantly questioned her place in the world; as a child, she worried that she might be "exchanged for a better girl" (23) if she misbehaved. As an adult, she went to Korea and lived with her birth mother, trying to put the disaggregated pieces of her life into place.

In addition to telling the story of the author's life, *The Language of Blood* questions the practice of transnational adoption. As a child, Trenka asked, "But why would anyone give away her children? Don't all mommies love their babies?" (22) Later, as an adult, her questions became more complex: "How can I weigh the loss of my language and culture against the freedom that America has to offer, the opportunity to have the same rights as a man? . . . How many educational opportunities must I mark on my tally sheet before I can say it was worth losing my mother?" (200–201).

Trenka employs screenplays, narrative, letters, and transcripts of telephone conversations to tell the story of her birth, adoption, and search for identity and family, reflecting the multiple layers and complexity of her experiences and relationships. Throughout the novel, she moves between the past and the present and includes her birth mother's letters and her own memories to reconstruct the fragmented versions and periods of her life. The nonlinear progression and multiple methods of her storytelling destabilize the reader, who is led into the complicated web of Trenka's life.

Trenka's memoir joins other Korean-American adoptee autobiographies, such as Katy Robinson's *A Single Square Picture* and Elizabeth Kim's *Ten Thousand Sorrows.* However, Trenka's memoir is different in that it more aggressively analyzes the romanticized view of transnational adoption, especially as she presents her relationship with her adoptive parents. Also, unlike most other adoptees, she received some communication from her birth mother early in her youth and was able to meet and spend time with her birth mother and siblings as an adult.

Bibliography

Trenka, Jane Jeong. *The Language of Blood: A Memoir.* St. Paul, Minn.: Borealis Books, 2003.

Sarah Park

Tripmaster Monkey
Maxine Hong Kingston (1989)

Tripmaster Monkey: His Fake Book is MAXINE HONG KINGSTON's only novel to date, and it is at once her most challenging and most unabashedly comedic book. Presenting several frantic days and nights in the life of Wittman Ah Sing, a University of California, Berkeley, graduate and aspiring playwright in the late 1960s, *Tripmaster Monkey* draws from sources as disparate as Western movies, Communist history, jazz, Shakespeare, Superman comics, Chinese folklore and opera, European poetry, and the Vietnam War. It tells the story of the beleaguered Wittman's attempts to mount an epic drama, starring all of his friends and fellow artists. This drama, he hopes, will bring a true knowledge of Chinese culture, beyond "sweet and sour pork and Charlie Chan movies," to American theater audiences and from thence to the entire nation.

Like the Monkey King, whose ancient Chinese legend gives the book its title, Wittman has a knack for getting into trouble. But his talent for quick invention keeps him from being captured by the forces that attempt to confine him, such as government offices, his draft board, and even his own family. Frustrated by the stereotypes of Asian people that stress humility, inscrutability, exotic cuisine, and mangled English, Wittman wanders through San Francisco over a long weekend, sketching out plans for his massive theatrical production.

Tripmaster Monkey's narrative style is episodic, recalling the performance style of oral folktales and "cliffhanger" serials; for example, the narrator says, "To see how he does it, go on to the next chapter." During the course of four frenzied days, which span roughly two-thirds of the book, Wittman crashes drunken parties, gets married to a Caucasian girl named Taña, searches for missing relatives in the Bay Area, and bluffs the San Francisco Unemployment Office into giving him financial assistance for six months while he writes his epic. The latter portion of the book presents that colossal stage production, capped by a final chapter in which Wittman speaks directly to his audience, cataloguing his frustrations and making clear his reasons for writing this play.

Wittman Ah Sing is not an immigrant. He is a fifth-generation American, as "American as [Beat writer Jack] Kerouac," and he conceives of his work as a distinctly American project; even his name is an echo of that quintessential American poet, Walt Whitman. Wittman does not plead for "understanding" from the dominant Caucasian culture in America. Like Kerouac, whose depiction of Chinese characters Wittman finds exceedingly insulting, he demands to be taken on his own terms, thus placing himself in a long line of American individualists, both real and fictional. A formidable blend of the "high" and "low" arts of two cultures, *Tripmaster Monkey* is a demanding but enormously playful and rewarding novel, which earned its author the 1989 PEN West Award in Fiction.

Bibliography

Kakutani, Michiko. Review of *Tripmaster Monkey, New York Times,* 14 April 1989, C30.

Royal, Derek Parker. "Literary Genre as Ethnic Resistance in Maxine Hong Kingston's *Tripmaster Monkey: His Fake Book.*" *MELUS* 29, no. 2 (Summer 2004): 151–156.

Schrieber, Le Ann. Review of *Tripmaster Monkey, New York Times,* 23 April 1989, sec. 7, p. 9.

Smith, Jeanne R. "Rethinking American Culture: Maxine Hong Kingston's Cross-Cultural *Tripmaster Monkey,*" *Modern Language Studies* 26, no. 4 (Fall 1996): 71–81.

Eric G. Waggoner

Tropic of Orange
Karen Tei Yamashita (1997)

Bouncing back and forth between Matzatlán, Mexico, and Los Angeles, California, *Tropic of Orange* tells a fantastic tale of migration between the two cities revolving around a Los Angeles traffic accident and an apocalyptic temporal/spatial anomaly caused by a mobile tropic of Cancer. The multiracial cast of characters—Mexican housekeeper Rafaela; her Singaporean husband, Bobby; Latin-American journalist Gabriel; Japanese-American news editor Emi; her homeless grandfather Manzanar; the 500-year-old Spaniard Arcangel; and African-American Vietnam veteran Buzzworm—by their very existence challenge and problematize common notions of ethnicity, as well as the significance and consequences of border crossing.

The story begins at a location on the tropic of Cancer, the small town of Mazatlán, Mexico, where space and time distortions begin to occur as the tropic of Cancer itself begins to migrate north when Rafaela and her son Sol smuggle an orange to which the tropic of Cancer is attached. Having been inadvertently involved in a conspiracy involving infant organs and poisoned oranges, Rafaela and Sol must flee from a mysterious pursuer, a mythical dark force that materializes out of Mexican legend. Eventually, they are able to cross the Mexican border safely and reach Los Angeles's Pacific Rim Auditorium, where they are reunited with Rafaela's husband, Bobby, at a wrestling match between Arcangel and SuperNAFTA. Here they witness Arcangel being defeated by his opponent, SuperNAFTA, who, clad in his titanium armor, unleashes a missile, penetrating the heart of Arcangel, and kills him. Occurring in parallel to these events is a large-scale traffic accident, which erupts on a Los Angeles freeway. The freeway suddenly becomes a converging point for the homeless, news media, and law enforcement, as well as the tropic of Cancer approaching from the South. A war erupts, and abandoned vehicles are suddenly reoccupied by vagabonds, half of whom are war veterans. Among the vagabonds is an insane Japanese-American ex-internee during World War II, Manzanar Murakami, who sees himself as a conductor of orchestral music out of the traffic sounds on the freeway. Journalist Gabriel goes to Mexico to follow a story about the stolen infant organs while Emi and Buzzworm remain on the highway to broadcast the catastrophic event. In the confusion, Emi is shot and killed by a sniper's bullet. While being lifted off in an emergency helicopter, Manzanar, with Emi's body in his arms, watches all of the stopped vehicles unleash their airbags in unison, which brings the freeway war to an abrupt stop.

In KAREN TEI YAMASHITA's works, lines and borders which serve to articulate cartographic, political, economical, as well as narrative contexts are further complicated by migration over these lines as well as the lines' and borders' own mobility and instability. Critic Alvina E. Quintana even asserts that Yamashita operates as a trickster because she writes "at the crossroads between worlds," to "resist and transform" (225). From a more contextual standpoint, Yamashita's satirical personification of NAFTA (North American Free Trade Agreement), her magic realism of conjuring a tangible tropic of Cancer, and naming the character of Manzanar after an actual internment camp that housed Japanese Americans during World War II are just a few examples of symbolism that create an ironical undertone suggesting a critical view of racial, economic, and political imbalances in the American continent.

Bibliography

Lee, Rachael "Asian American Cultural Production in Asian-Pacific Perspective." *Boundary 2* 26, no. 2 (Summer 1999): 231–254.

Quintana, Alvina E. "Performing Tricksters: Karen Tei Yamashita and Guillermo Gomez-Pena." *Amerasia Journal* 28, no. 2 (2002): 217–225.

Yamashita, Karen Tei. *Tropic of Orange.* Minneapolis, Minn.: Coffee House Press, 1997.

Eliko Kosaka

Truong, Monique   (1968–   )

Born in Saigon, Truong immigrated to the United States as a refugee at the age of six. Having graduated from Yale University and the Columbia University School of Law, Truong specialized in intellectual property before pursuing her writing career. Despite having grown up in America and, at her own admission, having a limited familiarity with Vietnamese history and culture, Truong nevertheless describes Vietnam as a place that constantly "tugs" at her, a country with which her identity will always be associated. In a piece for *Time International,* she refers to herself as being lost somewhere between countries: "The physical journey was completed long ago, but the emotional one is ongoing." If finding one's "home" is an emotional endeavor, then for Truong, such an act is marked by ambivalence rather than nostalgia. Truong writes of her feelings about the only memory she has of Vietnam: "If this useless violence is my history, a madness that lurks in my gene pool, a propensity that might again show itself, I am not eager to travel back to its—and my—place of origin." Conversely, if Truong hesitates to identify with a history of violence, America's involvements in war during her adulthood, as well as the ignorance and racism she experiences as a person of Asian descent, prevent her from feeling entirely "at home" in America.

It is perhaps not surprising, then, that Truong's debut novel, *The Book of Salt,* is about a man lost between countries. Binh, a gay Vietnamese chef, flees from his tyrannical father in Vietnam and finds employment in the house of Gertrude Stein and Alice B. Toklas in Paris during the 1930s. When "the Steins" choose to return to New York at the novel's end, Binh is forced to decide where his next home will be. But before Binh's decision is revealed, his narrative takes the reader through his life story, which includes interactions with historical figures, such as Paul Robeson and Ho Chi Minh. This, too, perhaps is reflective of Truong's goal; to include this lost man in the official history of the Lost Generation may grant the "lost" author, once a child of wartime, a means to fix herself in history without resorting to the boundaries of nation.

Truong is also coeditor of *Watermark: Vietnamese American Poetry and Prose.* She was awarded the Lannan Foundation Writing Residency in 2001. For *The Book of Salt,* Truong was awarded the American Library Association's Barbara Gittings Book Award in Literature, as well as the 2003 Bard Fiction Prize. Truong lives in Brooklyn, New York.

Catherine Fung

Tsiang, H. T. (Jiang Xizeng)   (1899–1971)

The poet, playwright, novelist, and actor H. T. Tsiang was born in Qi'an, a village in the district of Nantong, Jiangsu Province, in China. The son of a grain store worker and a maid—both of whom died young—Tsiang grew up in impoverished circumstances. A gifted student, Tsiang secured an education by winning scholarships to the Tongzhou Teachers' School in Jiangsu and Southeastern University in Nanjing, where he received a B.A. in political economy in 1925. Interested in revolutionary movements taking place not only in China but also in other parts of the world, Tsiang learned to read English-language newspapers by age 16. After graduating from college, he worked briefly for the Kuomintang (Nationalist Party), but his radical politics soon drew the ire of his party, which became increasingly conservative after the death of its leader, Sun Yat-sen, in 1925.

Fearful of persecution, Tsiang fled to the United States in 1926, enrolling at Stanford University in order to qualify for a student exemption to the Chinese Exclusion Acts. In California, he began his career as a writer who sought to inform American readers about Chinese politics and convince them to support a Chinese workers' revolution, which he envisioned as part of a worldwide revolution that included leftist movements in the United States. To this end, Tsiang founded and wrote for the bilingual periodical *Chinese Guide in America.* Repeatedly threatened by the Kuomintang-friendly Chinese-American community in California, Tsiang moved to New York in 1927.

While at Columbia University, Tsiang blossomed as a creative writer. Encouraged by his professors, Tsiang published poems about Chinese politics and Chinese-American workers in Communist periodicals such as *Daily Worker* and *New Masses.* In 1929 he self-published *Poems of the Chinese Revolution,* which met with some acclaim especially within leftist circles. Although Tsiang continued to write poems, even while detained at Ellis Island for possible deportation, he concentrated next on composing novels. The epistolary novel, *China Red* (1931), traces the effect of 1920s-era political upheavals on two lovers: a woman who bears witness in China and a man who experiences a political awakening while studying abroad in America. The collective novel, *Hanging on Union Square* (1935), follows several characters in Depression-era Manhattan, a class-stratified hell in which many suffer

and a privileged few engage in despicable extravagance. The proletarian novel *And China Has Hands* (1937) dramatizes the awakening of a laundryman and an aspiring actress from their dream of bourgeois success to an awareness of racism in America, as well as imperialism abroad.

In 1938 Tsiang turned to the stage, composing and acting in *China Marches On,* a play about a Chinese regiment's heroic defense of a tactically significant warehouse during the Japanese invasion of Shanghai in 1937. As is typical of Tsiang's style, he combined Chinese materials with forms that he encountered in the United States. *China Marches On* adapts the story of Hua Mulan—the legendary woman warrior who disguised herself as a man—by imagining her as one of the soldiers in this regiment. Tsiang couched this story, however, in the genre of the Living Newspaper, an experimental, documentary-like form of theatrical presentation developed by the Federal Theatre Project between 1935 and 1939. Tsiang continued to make a living in the world of drama, acting in films such as *Behind the Rising Sun* (1943) and *Ocean's Eleven* (1960). He also continued to write but never published anything else. He died in Los Angeles in 1971.

Contemporary reviewers consistently expressed amusement at Tsiang's quirky and apparently naäve characters, and they sometimes remarked condescendingly upon Tsiang's occasionally nonstandard word choice and syntax. Few caught Tsiang's sense of humor or understood his use of irony. In fact, Tsiang drew upon a wide range of literary sources, from the folktales of China to the plays of William Shakespeare to the rhythms of street protest in America. Hence, his talent for experimentation and combining literary forms equaled his commitment to radical political change.

Bibliography

Cheung, Floyd. "Tsiang's 'Chinaman, Laundryman.'" *Explicator* 61, no. 4 (2003): 226–229.
———, ed. *The Complete Works of H. T. Tsiang.* New York: Ironweed Press, 2005.
Lee, Julia H. "The Capitalist and Imperialist Critique in H. T. Tsiang's *And China Has Hands.*" In *Recovered Legacies: Authority and Identity in Early Asian*

American Literature, edited by Keith Lawrence and Floyd Cheung. Philadelphia: Temple University Press, 2005.

Floyd Cheung

Tsukiyama, Gail (?–)

The child of a Japanese father, native to Hawaii, and a Chinese mother, native to Hong Kong, Tsukiyama has been interested in exploring Asian and Asian-American themes from a multicultural perspective. Her novels have often had historical rather than contemporary settings, and she has demonstrated an equal appreciation of the exotic and the grimly mundane aspects of her characters' lives. Born in San Francisco, Tsukiyama completed a B.A. and an M.A. in English, with an emphasis on creative writing, from San Francisco State University, where she has subsequently taught creative writing. She has reviewed books for the *San Francisco Chronicle* and served as the book review editor for the *Waterbridge Review.*

Women of Silk (1991), Tsukiyama's first novel, is set in China at the beginning of the 20th century. A story of initiation and maturation, the novel focuses on a young woman named Pei who becomes a burden on her impoverished parents. She takes a job in a silk factory, where the hours are long and the work is both tedious and physically exhausting. Still, she not only achieves a level of independence through her work, but also finds among her coworkers a community of friends who become a sort of surrogate family.

The Samurai's Garden (1995), set primarily in Japan, features a male protagonist named Stephen, an aspiring painter and native of Hong Kong who is sent by his family to a Japanese coastal town to recover from tuberculosis. There, a man named Matsu nurses him physically and emotionally back to health. Stephen's recuperation is juxtaposed with the Japanese invasion of China proper and the deteriorating international situation.

In *Night of Many Dreams* (1998), Tsukiyama chronicles the escape of two sisters, with their mother and an aunt, from Japanese-occupied Hong Kong to Macao, as well as their return to Hong Kong at the end of the war. The novel also traces their lives over the next two decades as Hong Kong gradually develops into an economic dynamo. Interesting for its interplay between continuity and discontinuity, the narrative relates the sisters' steady progress toward maturation, but the war fragments their experience and complicates their sense of connection to Hong Kong.

Also set during the Japanese invasion of China, *The Language of Threads* (1999) is a sequel to *Women of Silk.* The main character, Pei, flees ahead of the Japanese forces to Hong Kong, where she finds a temporary sanctuary but feels dislocated.

In *Dreaming Water* (2002), Tsukiyama focuses on five women. Cate and her daughter, Hana, are coping with their grief at the death of Cate's husband and Hana's father. Worse yet, Hana is suffering from a terminal genetic disorder that causes her to age at an accelerated rate. Laura, one of Cate's childhood friends, re-enters her life along with her two daughters to help Cate and Hana come to terms with their difficult situation.

Martin Kich

Tuan, Alice (1963–)

Born in Seattle, Washington, Tuan is best known for her play *Last of the Suns* (1995). She is the daughter of Shin-Teh Tuan, a thermodynamics engineer, and Ada Li-Ching Tuan, a daycare-center owner. After her family moved to the San Fernando Valley area when she was five, Tuan attended Chatsworth High School in Chatsworth, California, and went on to earn her B.A. in economics from UCLA in 1987. Upon graduation, Tuan lived in Guangzhou, China, for a year, an experience that inspired her to earn an M.A. in Teaching English to Speakers of Other Languages (TESOL) at California State University, Los Angeles, in 1991. Her thesis was entitled "The Viability of Soap Operas as a Listening Comprehension Tool for Adult ESL Learners." According to Tuan, teaching English as a second language served as training for performing and "building language." Tuan found herself engaged in questions about language strategy and the "oddness of the English language, i.e. irregular verbs, silent letters." As Tuan continued to explore her interest in language, she wrote her first play, *Last of the Suns.* The play, first produced by Berkeley Repertory Theater in 1995, was later revived at Ma-Yi Theatre in New York City in 2003. After writing *Last of the Suns,* Tuan attended Brown University, where she earned an M.F.A. in Creative Writing in 1997, studying with playwright Paula Vogel and novelist Robert Coover. At Brown, Tuan wrote several plays: *Ikebana,* produced in Los Angeles at East West Players in 1996; *Some Asians,* produced at Perishable Theater in Providence, Rhode Island, in 1997; *mALL,* produced at Cypress College in 2000; and *Coastline,* a "virtual hypertext play" produced by Serious Play! in Northampton, Massachusetts, in 2004. Tuan's other important plays include two works produced off-Broadway: *Ajax (por nobody),* which premiered at the Flea Theater in 2001, and *The Roaring Girlie,* which premiered at the Foundry Theater in 2004. *Ajax,* which has echoes of Euripides' play *The Bacchae,* ironically does not refer to Sophocles' hero, but to the household cleanser by that name. The play explores the notion of sex as a recreational activity and centers on two women, Annette and Alma, who invite two men, Alexander and Jesse, to their home for an orgy. But rather than erotic titillation, the play is concerned with human relations, as Tuan critiques modern hedonism, along with its potential for emptiness and excess. *The Roaring Girlie,* a freewheeling adaptation of a 1611 comedy by Thomas Middleton and Thomas Dekker, centers on Mary Frith, a pickpocket who dresses like a man and is commonly known as Moll Cutpurse. Tuan uses contemporary language to reveal the original play's relevance to the present, with its critique of corruption and thirst for fame.

Tuan's most famous work is *Last of the Suns.* Inspired by the life of her own grandfather, who was a lieutenant general in Chiang Kai-shek's army, *Last of the Suns* takes place on General Sun's 100th birthday as he negotiates memories from the past and the burdens of contemporary family life. As the general is haunted by two mythical Chinese figures, Eight Pig and Monkey King, he thinks back to his days of power, fighting off Commu-

nism and enjoying his patriarchal supremacy over both his wife and his concubine. Another major character is Twila, a figure skater apparently based on Olympic silver and bronze medalist Michelle Kwan. Twila, after a disappointing televised performance where she falls several times, disappears for five years. Her return home becomes the catalyst for action in the play, as the rest of her family is forced to confront not only her disappearance, but also the buried family traumas of immigration, forced assimilation, and loss of their original culture. Twila's public failure as a figure skater allows Tuan to explore several issues of concern to the children of immigrants: the pressures placed on young Asian Americans by their parents, the inequalities based on gender in Chinese culture, and young women's internalization of their mothers' traumatic experiences of displacement.

Despite the various themes in her plays, Tuan's plays share a few commonalities. Tuan, for instance, tends to write with humor, even as she delves into serious dissections of human relations and politics. Tuan's reliance on puns, wordplay, and humorous situations lends a sense of irreverence to her playwriting. Thematically speaking, Tuan finds rich ground in the situation of women in the 20th and 21st centuries; she not only examines their limited agency but also the possibility of subverting gender roles. As part of a second-generation of Asian-American playwrights, Tuan develops characters who are not necessarily defined by their Asian background. They are "American" as much as they are "Asian," defining themselves in a way that acknowledges their status as U.S. citizens rather than foreigners. In terms of her use of language, Tuan's work evokes Absurdist Theater, especially Samuel Beckett and Eugene Ionesco, as well as the theater of contemporary British dramatist Caryl Churchill. Tuan's dialogue tends to be lyrical and poetic, relying sometimes on rhythmic non sequitur, and repetitive phrasing that echoes hip-hop and urban poetry jams. Aside from her work as a playwright, Tuan is also known as a teacher of writing. She has taught at the David Henry Hwang's Writers Institute in Los Angeles and at the Michener Center for Writers at the University of Texas, Austin. She lives in the Elysian Park/Echo Park section of Los Angeles.

Samuel Park

Turning Japanese: Memoirs of a Sansei
David Mura (1991)

Part memoir and part travelogue, *Turning Japanese: Memoirs of a Sansei* is DAVID MURA's extended analysis of his time in Japan. In 1984 Mura was awarded a U.S./Japan Creative Artist Exchange Program fellowship to stay in Japan for one year. Assimilated into the mainstream culture in America, identifying closely with European culture, having an antipathy to travel, and seeing little connection to the culture of Japan, Mura initially viewed the fellowship as an opportunity to write while studying contemporary Japanese art. The travel, however, effected him in ways he never anticipated, as chronicled in *Turning Japanese*.

While in Japan, Mura becomes a *Butoh* dance student under Kazuo Ono and studies the Noh theatre. He also meets members of the political left and participates in a major political demonstration. Possessing rudimentary skills in the Japanese language, Mura falls in with a small circle of friends through which Mura describes cultural differences in art, relationships, gender and sexuality. Mura discovers that many of the differences he has attributed to himself are legacies of his Japanese ancestry, yet he realizes that he is clearly very different from the Japanese.

This new knowledge of Japanese culture forces Mura to confront his own identity as a Japanese American whose family had assimilated. Like many nisei (second generation) families, they had repressed their Japanese heritage and silently bore the indignities of racism to prove their Americanness and gain acceptance into mainstream America in the years after internment. More specifically, Mura looks to his paternal grandfather, whom he knows primarily through the stories told by his aunt Ruth, as a role model of masculinity who did not entirely submit to the demands of racism. This grandfather, though deeply affected by internment,

never shunned his racial difference and eventually returned to Japan.

During a dinner honoring a visiting Italian critic, Mura realizes the culturally paternalizing attitudes of European scholars. As a foreigner and guest, the critic is treated deferentially, but this show of humility is mistaken by the guest as an open acknowledgment of his cultural superiority. This exchange makes Mura conscious of his position as an outsider to the European culture with which he had closely identified. To the West, Mura is always a cultural upstart, a mere curiosity rather than a serious contributor. From this, Mura realizes that he must write out of this sense of plurality and multiple identifications at the margins of European and American culture.

Turning Japanese won the Oakland PEN Josephine Miles Book Award and was listed among the *New York Times* Notable Books of the Year.

Bibliography

Franklin, Cynthia. "Turning Japanese/Returning to America: Problems of Gender, Class and Nation in David Mura's Use of Memoir." *Literature Interpretation Theory* 12 (2001): 235–265.

Mura, David. *Turning Japanese: Memoirs of a Sansei.* New York: Atlantic Monthly Press, 1991.

Taylor, Gordon O. "'The Country I Thought Was My Home': David Mura's *Turning Japanese* and Japanese-American Narrative Since World War II." *Connotations* 6 (1997): 283–309.

John Pinson

Tyau, Kathleen (1947–)

Kathleen Tyau, who is of Chinese-Hawaiian lineage, was born in California. She lived in Waikiki as a child, and when she was a teenager, moved with her family to Pearl City Heights, a suburb built in the sugarcane fields above Pearl Harbor. After graduating in 1965 from Saint Andrew's Priory, a private Catholic girls' school in Honolulu, Tyau moved to Portland, Oregon, to attend Lewis and Clark College. She received a B.A. in English from Lewis and Clark in 1969 and has lived in

Oregon ever since. After college she pursued several careers and interests including working as a hand-weaver, freelance journalist, and legal secretary. Nearly two decades after graduating from college, Tyau returned to literature and writing and found institutional and critical support for her work. She received fellowships from the National Endowment for the Arts, the Oregon Arts Commission, Literary Arts, and Fishtrap. She has taught creative writing and has been a guest lecturer and reader at numerous northwest colleges and universities. Tyau has published two books, both of which draw from Tyau's personal experiences and her family history, reflecting on Hawaii's postwar society.

Tyau's first book, *A Little Too Much Is Enough* (1995), is a series of vignettes about an extended Chinese-Hawaiian family living in post–World War II Oahu. The vignettes are loosely tied together through protagonist Mahealani (Mahi) Suzanne Wong's youthful experiences with eating, preparing, buying, and working with food. Whether Mahi is learning how to cook the perfect rice from her mother, or her extended family is ritualistically feasting on a banquet, food provides their everyday connection to one another and past family history, as well being the means through which Mahi and her family negotiate the difficult terrain of Hawaiian society for natives and Asian immigrants. In this way, food is not only a metaphor for the imperative to assimilate into Hawaiian and American culture but also a marker of class and race difference and a reminder of the enduring influence of the past on the present.

A Little Too Much Is Enough is innovative in that its 40-some stories are narrated by multiple characters and in different modes. Even though Mahi's growth remains at the center of the novel, there is no single perspective or a single character's voice to which the novel attempts to draw our attention. Tyau also uses different narrative modes, from dialogue to internalized monologue, which exemplifies the postmodern technique of showcasing different modes of being. Moreover, the novel's nonlinear narrative challenges any idealized notion of the protagonist's proper growth

and development. Critics have also pointed out that the narrative strategy is an attempt to portray the multivocality of the Chinese-Hawaiian community.

Several critics have criticized the novel's lack of coherence, some even arguing that it is more a collection of short stories than a novel. In interviews, however, Tyau has stated that she drew inspiration from Sandra Cisneros' novel *House on Mango Street*. She hopes that the stories, although nonlinear and at times disjointed, come together to tell a complex story of an extended immigrant and mixed-race family living in Hawaii. By featuring Mahi and her family's intergenerational and multiregional relationships in terms of the ritual of eating and preparing food, the novel shows how intimate and immediate the connections between these characters and places are.

Instead of a single dominant plotline or narrative development, the novel is structured around themes and ideas, several of which emerge as particularly predominant. In the first story, "Moon Baby," Mahi's mother, Anna, worries that Mahi's non-Anglicized name will limit her daughter's chances of success and acceptance on the mainland. In this story and others, the mainland represents a place where a "real American" success is possible. Another important theme throughout the vignettes is the coexistence of the past with the present. While this is implied by the novel's nonlinear narrative style, it is also explored specifically in several stories. For example, in "Red Paper," Mahi's father tells us how the ghost of his father-in-law shadows his everyday life.

Another predominant theme is that of a paradise lost. Hawaii's image as an idyllic and lush tropical paradise is countered by the difference in wealth and prestige between whites and Chinese-Hawaiians like Mahi's family. This is represented in several stories such as "All Lips," in which Mahi attempts to erase her "Hawaiian" lips from a school picture, and in "Fifty-Dollar Pineapple" and "Pick Up Your Pine," which show Mahi and her brother Buzzy engaged in brutal and dangerous work in the pineapple fields and canneries. Mahi's painful growth in Hawaii and her subsequent move to Oregon to go to college is perhaps the most poignant reminder of the paradise lost.

A Little Too Much Is Enough had its beginning in a writing class at Lewis and Clark College, in which she wrote a story on "How to Cook Rice." In interviews, Tyau said that she wrote the story for her family, specifically to memorialize the stories and experiences of her grandparents. While the novel is not an autobiography, nor can it be read as such, critics have noted how many of the characters in her novel are similar to, or draw inspiration from, several members of her family. The novel was generally well received by critics, and Tyau won a 1996 Pacific Northwest Bookseller's Association Award, in addition to being a finalist for the Oregon Book Award and Barnes and Noble first book award.

Tyau's second novel, *Makai,* was also well received and was a finalist for the 2000 Oregon Book Award. Unlike the first novel, *Makai* focuses on a friendship between two Chinese-Hawaiian women. Alice Lum is introverted and dependable, but her best friend Annabel Lee is outgoing and aggressive. As they both vie for the affection of Sammy Woo, who works for Annabel's father's Chinese restaurant, Annabel appears to be the winner at the beginning. Eventually, however, Sammy is attracted to Alice, and they soon get married and move to the island of Maui. Years later, Alice and Annabel meet again to confront the past. The novel not only sheds light on the psychology of Chinese-Hawaiian women but also on the cultural landscape of Hawaii.

Bibliography

See, Carolyn. "Heaven in Small Bites," *Washington Post,* 28 July 1995, sec. B p. 2.

Tyau, Kathleen. "Author's Notes." In *Growing Up Local: An Anthology of Poetry and Prose from Hawai'i,* edited by Eric Chock, James R. Harstad, Darrell H. Y. Lum and Bill Teeter. Honolulu: Bamboo Ridge Press, 1998.

Wilson, Rob. *Reimagining the American Pacific: From South Pacific to Bamboo Ridge and Beyond.* Durham, N.C.: Duke University Press, 2000.

Jinah Kim

Typical American Gish Jen (1991)

GISH JEN's first novel, *Typical American,* begins with Ralph Chang's journey in 1947 from a small town in China to New York City, where he enrolls in graduate school. The first chapter underscores the mythological status of America as a land of promise, opportunity, and dreams. Jen opens the novel with a simple phrase, "It's an American story," and ends the first chapter with a sharp contrast between the "dusty shops and rutted roads" of China and the "mighty bridges" of America where "the very air smelled of oil." Ralph has come for an education and hopes that the land of money and oil will transform him into a new man. When his big dreams collapse and he can no longer return to China due to the Communist takeover of his country, Ralph becomes despondent and feels caught between the two worlds, neither of which he can claim as his own. Just at his moment of greatest need, he meets his long-lost sister, Theresa, who immigrated to America before him. She introduces him to his future wife, Helen, who is also a Chinese immigrant.

Jen focuses the novel on the processes of assimilation for Ralph, Theresa, and Helen. Although the three seemingly harbor ill feelings toward Americans, they strive to follow the American rags-to-riches dream of being self-made and self-reliant. They criticize American culture and lifestyle: "typical American no-manners," "typical American unreliable," "typical American no-consideration-for-other-people," and "typical American wasteful." As the novel progresses, however, defining an "American" becomes complicated. Ralph, Helen, and Theresa become clichéd Americans: Ralph becomes obsessed with money, evades the INS and the IRS, opens his own fast-food restaurant ("Ralph's Chicken Palace") and buys a house in the suburbs; Helen partakes in a sexual affair in their own home with Ralph's friend and mentor, Grover Ding; and Theresa falls in love with a married man and American fashion.

Many aspects of the novel cohere with the most widely discussed themes of Asian-American literature, such as generational and cultural conflict, the consequences of Americanization, language barriers, and reciprocal learning between two cultures. However, Jen is quick to note that *Typical American* also exhibits themes such as sibling rivalry, family dynamics, individual limits, the conflict between religion and business, and shifting versions of the American dream. In an interview with *MELUS*, Jen discussed her hope that the novel would be recognized as more than Asian-American fiction: "I wanted to challenge ideas of what a 'typical American' looks like, to put forward the idea that the Changs are not less American than anyone else. . . . They wonder about their identity, they ask themselves who they are, who they're becoming. And therefore, they are American" (Matsukawa 115).

Bibliography

Huang, Betsy. "The Redefinition of the 'Typical Chinese' in Gish Jen's *Typical American*." *Hitting Critical Mass: A Journal of Asian American Cultural Criticism* 4, no. 2 (1997): 61–77.

Matsukawa, Yuko. "*MELUS* interview: Gish Jen." *MELUS* 18, no. 4 (1993–94): 111–120.

TuSmith, Bonnie. "Success Chinese American Style: Gish Jen's *Typical American*." *Proteus* 11, no. 2 (1994): 21–26.

Wang, Chih-Ming. "'An Onstage Costume Change': Modernity and Immigrant Experience in Gish Jen's *Typical American*." *NTU Studies in Language and Literature* 11 (2002): 71–96.

Xiaojing, Zhou. "Becoming Americans: Gish Jen's *Typical American*." In *The Immigrant Experience in North American Literature: Carving Out a Niche,* edited by Katherine B. Payant and Toby Rose, 151–163. Westport, Conn.: Greenwood Press, 1999.

Amy Lillian Manning

U

Uchida, Yoshiko (1922–1992)

Yoshiko Uchida was born in Alameda, California, and raised in San Francisco. Her father, Dwight Takashi Uchida, was a businessman and her mother, Iku, was a homemaker. At the age of 10, Yoshiko explored her creativity by drawing and writing stories. She and her family traveled often during the summers and, at the age of 12, she traveled to Japan for the first time. Besides speaking English, she became fluent in Japanese and also in French.

While living in Japan, she realized that she was not as comfortable in the Japanese atmosphere as she had hoped, nor was she completely comfortable living the American life. Her writing often reflects this theme of bicultural dilemma as she presents characters with a dual identity, struggling to find their place in society just as she did. Yoshiko was a constant witness to racism both in America and abroad. On December 7, 1941, the Japanese armed forces attacked a U.S. naval base at Pearl Harbor in Hawaii, sending a wave of radical racism throughout the United States. Yoshiko, along with tens of thousands of Japanese Americans, was relocated to an internment camp. She received her bachelor's degree in English, philosophy, and history from the University of California, Berkeley, but her diploma had to be sent by mail to her at the internment camp at the Tanforan Race Track. Her family was eventually moved to the Topaz internment camp in Utah, where they waited for their release. Her family and others that occupied the area lost homes, businesses, prized possessions, and family heirlooms, which were not returned to them even after they were freed.

Yoshiko spent her time teaching a second-grade class at the camp in Topaz. The conditions in the camp were terrible. She found comfort with her fellow internees who were also trying to divert their attention away from the poorly constructed shelters. In the camp she had the opportunity to observe and talk with other Japanese Americans about their views and opinions of the war and the disregard the United States had for American citizens of Japanese ancestry. These themes can be found throughout Yoshiko's stories, written with passion and concern for the people suffering in a country where they had hoped to find a home and a future.

Upon release in 1943 from Topaz, Yoshiko went to Northampton, Massachusetts, to study at Smith College for a master's degree in education. After graduating, she spent 1944 and 1945 teaching at the Frankford Friends' School in Philadelphia, Pennsylvania. Over the next two years, Yoshiko worked in various offices as a secretary to make ends meet. In 1949 she published her first book, *The Dancing Kettle and Other Japanese Folk Tales.* In 1951 she published her second book, *New Friends for Susan,* which was her only book that did not focus on the turmoil of Japanese-American citizens. During her two-year fellowship study in Japan, Yoshiko wrote *The Magic Listening Cap: More Folk Tales from Japan,* her second collection of Japanese folktales, and wrote articles for *Nippon Times* in Tokyo. After returning to the West Coast of the United States in 1955, she wrote a column entitled "Letters from San Francisco" for the magazine *Craft Horizons* published in New York.

Over the course of her career, Yoshiko was honored with numerous awards for her portrayal of her life as a Japanese American growing up in the troubling times of World War II. Her book *Journey to Topaz* (1971), based mainly on her experience in the relocation camp in Topaz, was selected as the American Library Association Notable Book in 1972. One of her most popular books, SAMURAI OF GOLD HILL (1972), was given the Commonwealth Club of California Medal for best juvenile book written by a Californian author. The novel *A JAR OF DREAMS* (1981) received another Commonwealth Club of California Medal in 1982. In 1983 another American Library Association Notable Book award was given to her book *The Best Bad Thing* (1983), the first sequel to *A Jar of Dreams.* In 1981 she received the Distinguished Service Award, given by the University of Oregon, for her dedication to educate American people about Japanese-American culture and the hardships that Japanese Americans have endured over the decades. In 1985 she received the Young Author's Hall of Fame Award from the San Mateo and San Francisco Reading Associations for her collection of books that benefit young readers.

Her collection of more than 30 books for young readers includes *The Promise Year* (1959); *The Sea of Gold and Other Tales from Japan* (1965); *In-Between Miya* (1967); *Journey Home* (1978); and PICTURE BRIDE (1988). Yoshiko's novel *Desert Exile* (1984) is for both young readers and adults. Her last book, *The Invisible Thread* (1991), is an autobiography written for young readers in which Uchida depicts her life in the interment camps and her years of devotion to educating the public about Japanese Americans through her books, articles, short stories, and poems. Throughout her career, Yoshiko utilized her own hardships as

templates by which to mark her literary characters who grow stronger through pain and distress. She relates these aspects to the younger audience in order to give them an insight into their country's history; in doing so, she uses fiction to make to keep history alive and believable. Yoshiko Uchida died in Berkeley, California, on June 21, 1992, at the age of 71.

Bibliography

Online Archive of California. "Uchida (Yoshiko) Photograph Collection: Biography." Available online. URL: content.oac.cdlib.org/ark:/13030/ft6k 4007pc;jsessionic=DdmXhJ9SO_hBAQiK?&que ry=icjoda%20photograph&brand=cac. Downloaded on October 19, 2006.

Zia, Helen and Susan B. Gall, eds. *Notable Asian Americans.* New York: Gale Research, 1995.

Anne Bahringer

Umrigar, Thrity (1961–)

Thrity Umrigar was born in Bombay and received her B.S. from Bombay University. After moving to the United States for graduate school in 1981, she received a Ph.D. from Kent State University. She has published two novels, *Bombay Time* (2001) and *The Space between Us* (2006), and a memoir, *First Darling of the Morning* (2004). In addition, she has published essays and journalistic pieces in the *Akron Beacon Journal, Washington Post,* and *Boston Globe.*

Umrigar's debut novel, *Bombay Time,* has received many laudatory reviews. Like BAPSI SIDHWA and Rohinton Mistry, Umrigar writes of the Parsi community, an ethnic minority in India that practices Zoroastrianism and traces its origins to Persia. The novel is set in a middle-class apartment complex in contemporary Bombay, and the residents of that building become the collective protagonist of the novel. The story centers on the wedding of the son of Jimmy Kanga. As the members of the community arrive at the wedding, the author gives us carefully nuanced portraits of the main characters: Kanga's economic success and his rootedness in the community; the Billimorias' marriage devolving from great romance to misery; the tragedy of Tehmi Engineer; and the betrayal of Soli Contractor. The novel emphasizes how a close-knit community supports individuals through their travails. It also demonstrates how an ethnic minority develops strategies for survival in a changing nation.

Umrigar's second novel, *The Space between Us,* examines the class divisions between Sera, a middle-class Parsi woman, and Bhima, her maid. Sera and Bhima develop a close relationship despite their economic differences because as women they suffer through betrayal, domestic violence, and tragic loss. But when Sera's son-in-law seduces Bhima's young granddaughter and gets her pregnant, their relationship unravels and both women have to choose between family and loyalty to a friend.

In *First Darling of the Morning,* Umrigar tells us of her upbringing in an extended middle-class family surrounded by a loving father, doting aunts, and a loving uncle. This loving family, however, is challenged by her mother's unbridled anger and verbal and physical violence toward her sister-in-law and daughter. Umrigar describes her survival in such an abusive relationship, the economic ups and downs endured by the family in their business, and the formative friendships in school and in the neighborhood. We learn of the tragic death of her uncle, her intellectual and political development, and her decision to leave India to escape her dysfunctional mother.

Umrigar explores the supportive role of families, the dysfunctionality within families, the preoccupation with class divisions in India, the postcolonial middle-class sensibilities, and the construction of masculinity and femininity in middle-class India, especially in the Parsi community. Umrigar's fiction is rooted in the Bombay of the 1960s to the 1980s, and the city becomes more than simply the setting of the novel. Through her portrayal of Bombay, we see the development of postcolonial urban India and the many divisions based on religion, language, class, and gender in this developing democratic nation.

Bibliography
Umrigar, Thrity. *Bombay Time.* New York: Picador, 2001.
———. *First Darling of the Morning.* New York: HarperCollins, 2004.
———. *The Space between Us.* New York: HarperCollins, 2006.

Nalini Iyer

Ung, Loung   (1970–   )

Born in Phnom Penh, Cambodia, Loung Ung was five years old when the communist Khmer Rouge force defeated the Lon Nol army and invaded Phnom Penh in 1975. Since her father, Sem Im Ung, was a military police captain in the Lon Nol government, Ung's family joined the rest of the city's population in a mass exodus from the capital to the countryside. The Ungs settled in the village of Bat Deng, where Ung's extended family lived. They were able to hide their past and work with local villagers and farmers until December 1976, when two Khmer Rouge cadres came to their hut and asked for their father's assistance in helping to push their oxcart out of a mud pool. This was the last time Ung saw her father alive. Deciding it was safer to separate the family, Ung's mother sent her children off to separate labor camps.

Ung lost her parents and two sisters before the Khmer Rouge regime fell in January 1979, when Vietnam invaded Cambodia. In 1980 Ung and some of her remaining siblings hid on a boat traveling from Vietnam to a refugee camp in Thailand. Five months later, they were resettled in Essex Junction, Vermont, through the sponsorship of a church organization. A therapist whom Ung consulted for post-traumatic stress disorder encouraged Ung to write her experiences in a diary, which ultimately led to her memoir. In 1993, after graduating with a degree in political science from St. Michael's College in Vermont, Ung began working at a domestic shelter in Maine. In 1995 she returned to Cambodia for the first time and was deeply moved by the deaths and injuries caused by land mines. Although accepted to Columbia

University, Ung postponed graduate school and became a spokesperson for the Campaign for a Landmine-Free World.

Published by HarperCollins in 2000, *First They Killed My Father: A Daughter of Cambodia Remembers* received several awards including the 2001 Asian Pacific American Award for Literature and the 2002 Books for a Better World Literary Awards. Ung's memoir was, however, received unfavorably by some Cambodian-American communities. Critic Sody Lay, for example, describes the memoir as a "sensationalization and over-dramatization of the Killing Fields" (173) and questions the authenticity of her narrative. Ung also received death threats from those who accused her, an ethnic Chinese-Khmer, of speaking on behalf of all Cambodians. Nevertheless, her memoir was published in 11 countries, translated into several languages including Khmer (Cambodia's official language), and adapted into plays.

First They Killed My Father is written in the present tense and from a child's point of view, creating a raw experience for the reader. Ung uses family photographs, refugee identification cards, and a family tree to authenticate her narrative. In writing this testimonial literature, the author uses her personal and family experiences to represent the collective experience of the Cambodian people under the Khmer Rouge regime. In the author's note, Ung writes, "Though these events constitute my experiences, my story mirrors that of millions of Cambodians." The theme of survivor's guilt is also prevalent in Ung's memoir, as the young Ung struggles with the fact that she survived, while others, like her sisters and parents, perished. Other topics include memory and trauma, writing and healing, oppression and resistance, literature and history, dehumanization and (de)evolution of self, gender and ethnicity, and the strength of family love.

Ung is probably the most popular Cambodian-American writer writing today. She has traveled extensively, giving public lectures on land mines, women's issues, racism, child soldiers, and her experiences under the Khmer Rouge regime. She has also made appearances on radio and television shows. In 2005 Ung published her second memoir, *Lucky Child: A Daughter of Cambodia Reunites with the Sister She Left Behind.*

Bibliography

Lay, Sody. "The Cambodian Tragedy: Its Writers and Representations." *Amerasia Journal* 27 (2001): 171–182.

Bunkong Tuon

Upadhyay, Samrat   (1964–)

Samrat Upadhyay is the first Nepal-born South Asian writer to gain prominence in the West. He came to the United States at the age of 21 and now teaches creative writing at Indiana University, Bloomington. His first book was a collection of short stories entitled *Arresting God in Kathmandu* (2001), which won a Whiting Award. His second book is a novel, *The Guru of Love* (2003), which became a *New York Times* Notable Book, *San Francisco Chronicle's* Best Book of the Year, and a finalist for the Kiriyama Prize. His third book is also a collection of short stories, *Royal Ghosts* (2006).

Upadhyay's primary preoccupation as a writer has been to foreground ordinary people's sex lives, proclivities, and fantasies. His first anthology, *Arresting God in Kathmandu,* consists of nine short stories, all of which explore very carefully how everyday people in Nepal experience their sexuality. For example, in "The Good Shopkeeper," he writes of how Pramod, who loses his job and struggles to find another, has to deal with Nepal's nepotistic, feudal, and emasculating business world. He ends up entering into an adulterous relationship with a woman of another class as a means of reasserting his masculinity. In "Deepak Misra's Secretary," he writes of the protagonist's struggles with his failed marriage to an American woman and his search for selfhood through a sexual relationship with his secretary. His stories are erotic, and they examine constructions of masculinity within contemporary Nepali society.

His novel *The Guru of Love* is an extensive treatment of the same themes as in his first anthology. His protagonist, Ramachandra, is an impoverished math teacher who is married to Goma, who comes from a well-connected family. They have two children, but Goma's family constantly criticizes Ramachandra for his lack of economic success. His wife does not echo their sentiments, but she does not stand up to her family, either. Ramachandra enters into a liaison with his student, Malathi, a young, single mother who is trying to graduate from high school. He finds his adulterous relationship liberating and exciting. However, his wife and children find out about his infidelities when Malathi encounters financial problems and becomes homeless. She moves in with Ramachandra and his wife at Goma's invitation. As the plot evolves, Goma leaves Ramachandra and lives with her parents; his daughter resents him for his infidelities; and Malathi returns to her first lover and the father of her child. All of this action takes place against the backdrop of Nepal's political turmoil, a disastrous and exploitative monarchy, and the Maoist insurgency against the monarchy.

Upadhyay is not necessarily a political writer, but his new collection, *Royal Ghosts*, downplays sexuality and focuses more on politics. His fiction is not thinly veiled political history; rather, it is about the sexual politics of a feudal society struggling with modernity. Upadhyay's work is also significant in that it refuses to romanticize or exoticize Nepali people; instead he shows how Nepali people live, think, and act in their everyday lives, and how some people use sexuality to resist authority or escape from hardship.

Bibliography

Upadhyay, Samrat. *Arresting God in Kathmandu.* Boston: Houghton Mifflin/Mariner, 2001.
———. *The Guru of Love.* Boston: Houghton Mifflin/Mariner, 2003.
———. *Royal Ghosts.* Boston: Houghton-Mifflin/Mariner, 2006.

Nalini Iyer

Uyehara, Denise   (?–)

Denise Uyehara grew up in the suburbs of Orange County in Southern California. Her parents, both scientists, restricted television viewing, and Uyehara developed her imagination as she dreamed of adventures and alternative worlds. She describes her performance and dramatic work as an exploration of "what it means to be an Asian American, a queer-identified bisexual, a woman, and a human being, not necessarily in that order." Her work also investigates issues of identity and belonging in terms of family and community. Her own family background is marked by her parents' personal experiences of the forced relocation of Japanese Americans to internment camps following the bombing of Pearl Harbor.

After her studies at the University of California, Irvine, where she majored in biology before graduating with a B.A. in Comparative Literature, Uyehara got involved in theater and performance art as a community activist. The Los Angeles Riots in 1992 and the terrorist attacks on September 11, 2001, provoked her to examine her responsibilities as an artist and her accountability as an American citizen. As both an artist and a citizen, Uyehara believes it is important to respond, to raise voices, and to demonstrate. Committed to performance as a powerful mode of narration, she makes innovative use of the voice and body to tell stories. She has returned as a guest instructor to the University of California, Irvine, to teach drama and performance in the Department of Asian Studies.

In her performances, Uyehara explores questions of stereotypes, sexual identities, memory, and nationalism. *Hello (Sex) Kitty: Mad Bitch on Wheels* juxtaposes Hello Kitty, the cute imported icon of Japanese *kawaii* culture with the queer gender identities of Kabuki. The Asian identities she performs in this piece include a young man finding it difficult to have sex and a lesbian stand-up comic. *Maps of City and Body* is an interdisciplinary solo performance that has been performed in Helsinki (1998), San Francisco (1998), Los Angeles (1999), and Tokyo (2001). The performance is motivated by memory: what has been lost and found, and how the body serves as a record. *Big Head* (2003) looks at what it means to pledge allegiance to a single nation in a multicultural country. She recalls the changes made in the Pledge of Allegiance since its beginning in 1892 and the irony of imprisoned Japanese Americans reciting that pledge in the internment camps during World War II. Uyehara then repositions herself as a young Muslim woman being considered for the position of editor-in-chief of a university newspaper. A young Japanese American wonders how the Muslim woman's religious beliefs will affect her ability to do the job. *Big Head* suggests that it is important for all who have experienced injustice to condemn racism and to support the people whose rights as citizens and human beings are denied.

Beverley Curran

Uyemoto, Holly   (1970–)

Born in Ithaca, New York, Uyemoto moved with her family to Kansas when she was seven years old, and again to California the following year. Like her paternal grandfather, who was a sumo wrestler and the black sheep of his family, Uyemoto demonstrated a similar defiance when she chose to quit school at the age of 15 to write her first novel. However, her parents supported her decision, and her ambition became a reality when she was 19 years old with the publication of her first novel, *Rebel without a Clue* (1989). She has since pursued higher education, studying at Wellesley College. Uyemoto's second novel, *GO,* was published in 1995.

Despite their drastically different subject matters, these two books are both coming-of-age novels. *Rebel without a Clue* is the story of two best friends, Thomas Bainbridge and Christian Delon (the 18-year-old narrator), who hang out together during the first summer after high school when Thomas Bainbridge, all-American model and superstar actor, confesses to his parents and his best friend that he has AIDS. Near the end of the novel, Christian discovers Thomas having sex with a girl who is uninformed about Thomas's AIDS. In denial of his responsibilities to his sexual partners, Thomas defends himself by saying that he is using condoms. This leads to the final scene, in which Thomas is headed to Oregon without Christian. Christian decides not to be witness to Thomas's final demise, either physically or morally: "I knew that for Thomas the sun would set into the bay

from Oregon too, but I didn't need to see it" (194). The double entendre of the last line implies that when Thomas dies, Christian will be leading a life of integrity elsewhere.

Uyemoto's next novel, *GO,* follows the maturation of Wilimena, a 21-year-old, third-generation Japanese-American female protagonist. Wilimena narrates her self-discovery through a series of family events, carefully considering the psychology of her various family members, and finding their personal motivations to be bound by the memory of their internment during World War II. While mental health, abortion, peer pressure, racial prejudice, cultural hybridity, and family are dominant themes of this second novel, the pivotal subject is the internment of Japanese Americans. Wilimena's mother, an overbearing perfectionist, and her relatives label Wilimena as different, but she sees herself as the ugly duckling to her perfect mother. According to her mother, Wilimena thinks and talks too much. Wilimena, however, is frustrated by the lack of family communication: Her family has too many taboo subjects, which, based on their degree of sensitivity, are either discussed in hushed tones or not at all. Impatient with the familial versions of events, which soften, reinvent or erase facts, Wilimena tells all: the gruesome death of her cousin Kiki, Uncle Sen's alcoholism and infidelity, Cousin Hope's common-law relationship and pregnancy with her boyfriend, the dysfunctional family dynamic, her own mental break, her abortion, and the internment of the family during World War II. Just as in the first novel, the protagonist of *GO* is so self-centered and immature as to allow, ironically, for clarity of vision and insight into the lives of other characters.

Both Christian and Wilimena are dynamic characters who mature by the end of their respective stories. As *Rebel without a Clue* progresses, Christian notes Thomas's physical deterioration and his observations imply a parallel moral demise: Thomas maintains the immoral self-centeredness of youth, while Christian matures. At the end of *GO,* Wilimena acknowledges that she is on a path away from the ignorant bliss of youth, toward the enlightened happiness of maturity: "I'm turning twenty one today. By Japanese methods,

I'm a little less than forty years away from my own happily ever after" (197). Having realized that she is part of the family, and more like them than different, Wilimena becomes more accepting of the family's failings.

A witty writer, Uyemoto has captured both the folly and wisdom of youth in a way that sheds new light on two socially and politically sensitive subjects of the 1980s and 1990s: AIDS and Japanese-American internment. Her writing is imbued with a drollness that adds intelligence and depth to her characters, whether they be white, upper-class Californian boys and their families, or a Japanese-American girl and her relatives. Humor also makes Uyemoto's sensitive subjects accessible to a diverse readership. She effectively introduces the illicit in a palatable, lighthearted way.

Bibliography

Massa, Suzanne Hotte. "Holly Uyemoto." *Asian American Novelists: A Bio-Bibliographical Critical Sourcebook,* edited by Emmanuel S. Nelson, 382–386. Westport, Conn.: Greenwood Press, 2000.

Uyemoto, Holly. "An Interview with Holly Uyemoto" by Scott Shepard. *Hitting Critical Mass: A Journal of Asian American Cultural Criticism* 4, no. 2 (Summer 1997): 111–124.

Sheena Wilson

V

Villa, José García (1908–1997)

José García Villa was born in Singalong, Manila, to Guía García and Dr. Simeón Villa, personal physician to revolutionary general Emilio Aguinaldo. Villa's complex relationship with his father symbolizes the generational tension between a father living in the past and a son eager to embrace the new American culture. Villa graduated from high school in 1925 and began taking college courses first as a pre-med and later as a pre-law major. Meanwhile, his interest in literature and art in general grew rapidly. In 1929 he was suspended from the University of the Philippines and fined by the Manila Court because of his series of obscene erotic poems called *Man Songs.* In the same year, however, he won a prize from the *Philippine Free Press* for his short story "Mir-i-Nisa." With the prize of 1,000 pesos, he immigrated to the United States, where he lived until his death.

In the United States, Villa attended the University of New Mexico, where he edited and published a literary magazine called *Clay.* Soon he began to collaborate with a number of young American writers. When his short-story collection, *Footnote to Youth. Short Stories,* was published in 1993, Edward J. O'Brien, in his introduction to the book, considered Villa as one of the half dozen important American short-story writers.

Considered a leading modernist American poet, Villa wrote many metaphysical but innovative poems. His "comma poems," in which he puts a comma after each word in order to force slow enunciation, and his attempts to build his own history through the creation of an imaginary homeland called Doveglion (dove, eagle, and lion) are examples of his innovative poetic experiments. The golden period of his poetic production, between his arrival in the United States in 1929 and his "retirement" from writing poetry in 1953, saw the publication of his poetry anthologies such as *Many Voices, poems* (1939), *Poems* (1941), *Have Come, Am Here* (1942), *Volume Two* (1949), and *Selected Poems and New* (1958). But in the mid-1950s García Villa gave up writing poems abruptly because, he argued, he did not wish to repeat himself.

Covadonga Lamar Prieto

Village Bride of Beverly Hills, The
Kavita Daswani (2004)

Kavita Daswani's first novel, *For Matrimonial Purposes,* had focused on the courtship experiences of a young Indo-American woman, Anju. This second novel of Daswani explores the life of Priya, an Indian bride who comes to Los Angeles following an arranged marriage. We follow Priya's story from the time her marriage is arranged to Sanjay to her arrival in California after the wedding. Priya finds that life in Los Angeles is not happy since she lives with her parents-in-law and her sister-in-law and is basically their unpaid cook and maid. When Priya does not have a baby within the first year of her marriage, her parents-in-law encourage her to find a job so she can contribute to the financial well-being of her family.

Priya gets a job as a receptionist in a Hollywood media firm and, due to a series of coincidences, gets to interview a major movie star for the entertainment magazine published by her company. Priya has the rare talent of getting celebrities to reveal their deepest feelings and also has discretion about how she uses this information in her writing. She experiences a meteoric rise in her career, but at home she has to keep her glamorous life a secret. Her husband and his parents are not supportive of what they see as a corrupt American lifestyle and insist that Priya dress in Indian clothes and give up a major career. Priya manages to keep her home life and her work separate from one another for a short while. When her secret becomes known to her family, she realizes that her situation is untenable, as her husband does not support her. She tricks him into marriage counseling, but his reaction to that experience compels her to leave the marriage. She returns to India an unhappy woman. However, her husband realizes his mistake, undergoes therapy, and returns to India to court his wife. This time he works hard to win her over, and Priya finds the romance that she has always been looking for.

As in her previous novel, Daswani produces engaging characters, and her novel is fast-paced. She returns to the themes of love, romance, cultural clash, and familial relationships in this novel. Her focus is not so much on a critique of cultural institutions as on creating a character who manages to find a middle ground between two vastly different cultural worlds.

Nalini Iyer

Volcano: A Memoir of Hawai'i
Garrett Hongo (1995)

GARRETT HONGO's *Volcano: A Memoir of Hawai'i* examines his own experiences to connect to his Japanese ancestry. A fourth-generation Japanese American, Hongo was in his thirties when he felt the internal pressure to seek out his roots. *Volcano* chronicles his first and subsequent journeys to the village where he was born. Having grown up in multicultural Los Angeles, Hongo felt a cultural dissociation from his Japanese ancestry. His family's silence on the subject of the Japanese relocation camps during World War II was especially frustrating to him. The book grew out of a need to discover his identity.

Reviewers of the book praise Hongo's beautiful descriptions of his birthplace near the Kilauea volcano. Hongo says that *Volcano* is written in the form of a Japanese *nikki*, a travel diary in the vein of Henry David Thoreau's *Walden*. In a review of the book, Mark Jarman says that Hongo's minute descriptions of the plants and geological formations of the area surrounding Kilauea, the world's most active volcano, frame an analogous comparison to the imagination's "geologic upheaval" in creating a homeland. Hongo's visits to his homeland place him in the midst of a family that has been disrupted for decades. The healing process begins as the poet reconstructs his past. Hongo attempts to recreate the island of his father and grandfather. His grandfather's nightly retelling of his arrest by FBI agents during World War II compels Hongo to remember and to pass on the stories of his own and his people's losses—those of land, possessions, and identity.

Volcano, then, becomes a story of a quest. Through the narratives and anecdotes of his relatives, Hongo goes beyond the confines of the immigrant memoir to forge an almost mythical account of a people who have kept their traditions alive. By listening to them in his many visits to his birthplace, Hongo internalizes this mythology and makes it his own, creating for himself an identity from which he has hitherto felt alienated and dispossessed.

Volcano is a travel book, a memoir, and a narrative of the poet's rebirth. In lyrical language that has been compared to Walt Whitman's for its use of repetition and lists of images, Hongo treats many of the themes that are present in his poetry. He recounts his confusion in school as he reads accounts of history that exclude the Japanese presence in America. It is not until he is an adult that he learns of the internment camps into which many Japanese Americans were forced. Hongo furiously vents his outrage not only against those who perpetrated the crimes but against those who have been silent about them. He rages against his textbooks, his teachers, and his family for not telling him about the events that shaped the lives of generations of Japanese Americans.

Bibliography

Evans, Alice. "A Vicious Kind of Tenderness: An Interview with Garrett Hongo." *Poets & Writers Magazine* (September–October 1992): 37–46.

Hongo, Garrett. *Volcano: A Memoir of Hawai'i.* New York: Alfred. A. Knopf, 1995.

Jarman, Mark. "The Volcano Inside." *The Southern Review* 32, no. 2 (April 1996): 337–343.

Patricia Kennedy Bostian

Wait for Me   An Na (2006)

Wait for Me, An Na's second novel, is a major breakthrough for Korean-American young adult literature. Na pushes the boundaries of conventional Korean-American adolescence in every way imaginable by portraying, among other issues, the facade of a model minority protagonist, her handicapped sister, sexually experienced teenagers, and the forbidden intimacy between a Korean American and a Mexican immigrant.

Mina Kang, a high school senior protagonist, and her little sister, Suna, spend the summer at their parents' dry cleaning business. Mrs. Kang, a Harvard-obsessed, overbearing Korean mother, pushes Mina to be close with Jonathan Kim, a Stanford-bound church friend. To stave off her mother, Mina needs to stay suspended in her web of lies about her academic standing and SAT courses, but as the summer goes on she finds it harder to keep her lies from unraveling.

Like most father characters in other Korean-American novels, (Ronyoung Kim's *Clay Walls* and An Na's *A Step from Heaven,* for example), Mr. Kang cannot provide for his family so he needs their help in running the dry cleaning business. When he is injured, they hire Ysrael, but Mina's mother watches him like a hawk, yelling at her husband, "You must keep your eyes on him. Some of these young Mexicans steal and then they disappear" (48). Mina and Suna run into Ysrael a few days later at the library and begin to hang out with him instead of studying. Mina envies his freedom and confesses that she is suffocating under her mother's pressure and expectations. He encourages her to live her own life, and she succumbs to him.

Suna also falls for Ysrael, but more as a little girl's first crush. She jealously watches her beloved sister and Ysrael grow closer, to the point where Mina decides to leave behind her family to follow him to San Francisco. Unable to bear the thought of losing both her sister and Ysrael, Suna takes matters into her own hands. For the first time, she has her own agency and purposefully sabotages her sister's plans.

Wait for Me is told primarily by Mina in the first person, but every alternate chapter is a brief aside from Suna's perspective in the third person. Through these private moments with Suna, readers will see her on her own terms, instead of through Mina's lens.

An Na has taken great care to flesh out some of the controversial issues facing Korean Americans today, yet she does so without stereotyping or generalizing. Though she places this prototypical Korean-American family in Southern California as the owners of a dry cleaning business, they struggle financially. Though the family attends church, Mina is not religious. Mrs. Kang is a prototypical, Harvard-obsessed Korean mother, but Mina does not live up to her mother's expectations; in fact, she outright defies them. By exploring the complexities inherent in Korean-American adolescence, and by resisting conventional definitions of what is Korean American, An Na suggests that perhaps Korean-American identity is not so easily boxed in.

Bibliography

Na, An. *Wait for Me.* New York: G. P. Putnam's Sons, 2006.

Sarah Park

Waiting   Ha Jin (1999)

The novel that established HA JIN as a major writer, *Waiting* is a tragicomic account of a curious but complicated relationship that takes place in northern China over a 20-year period, beginning in the early 1960s. More specifically, it depicts a love triangle among the protagonist, Lin Kong, and his two wives, Shuyu Liu and Manna Wu. For 18 years, Lin waits for his first wife, Shuyu, to agree to divorce him so that he may marry his lover, Manna; then after he finally succeeds in marrying Manna, he waits for the death of his second wife in order to return to the first. As Jin depicts Lin's travails, with the sensitivity and humor that have come to characterize his work, he masterfully illustrates how human desire and cultural traditions sometimes conspire to subvert people by giving them precisely what they thought they had been searching for.

Before the narrative opens, Lin has allowed his parents to persuade him to marry Shuyu in order that his sickly mother might have someone to take care of her. Lin is a physician at an army hospital in Muji City, a town far from his home, Goose Village. He is also a book lover, who owns an excellent library, with many textbooks in foreign languages and forbidden novels. In contrast, Shuyu is illiterate, looks considerably older than Lin, and even has bound feet. So despite her loyalty to him and his parents, Lin never has much of a married life with her. In fact, after she gives birth to their daughter, Hua, they never share a bed again. Also, even though he goes home to Goose Village for his 12-day vacation every year, he never brings Shuyu

to the hospital since he is embarrassed to be seen in public with her. It is while working at the hospital that Lin becomes involved with Manna, a former student of his who is now a nurse. Manna is educated, has a pleasant voice and slim figure, and is thus more attractive to Lin. Still, almost the moment they marry, after the seemingly interminable wait because of personal and cultural reasons, their love for each other seems to dissipate.

Waiting is a fictional meditation on the nature of love, desire, and social responsibility, especially toward one's immediate kin. Near the end of the novel, Jin has Lin Kong conclude that he is a "superfluous" or "useless" man. But this is clearly not the case. Rather, Lin is someone torn between his social obligations toward a homely traditional wife he respects and even admires and his desire for a mate closer to him intellectually but with whom he appears to have fewer affinities than he imagined. As is evident from his own ambivalence about divorce, Lin is caught between two cultures. However, it is not between China and the West, but between the new China and the old. *Waiting* won both the 1999 National Book Award and the 2000 PEN/Faulkner Award for Fiction, making it Ha Jin's most acclaimed work.

Bibliography

Moore, John Noell. "The Landscape of Divorce: When Worlds Collide." *English Journal,* 92, no. 2 (2002): 124–128.
Sturr, Robert D. "The Presence of Walt Whitman in Ha Jin's Writing." *Walt Whitman Quarterly Review* 20, no. 1 (2002): 1–18.

Jianwu Liu and Albert Braz

Wang, Ping (1957–)

Born in Shanghai, Wang grew up in a naval base on an island in the East China Sea. After three years of farming in a mountain village before the end of the Cultural Revolution in 1976, she attended Hangzhou Foreign Language School and received her B.A. in English from Beijing University in 1984. In the following year, Wang came to the United States to work on her M.A. in English at Long Island University. In 1999 she received her Ph.D. in comparative literature from New York University. After teaching in various writing workshops, she is now an associate professor at Macalester College, Minnesota. Besides writing fiction and poetry, Wang also introduced and translated contemporary Chinese poetry into English. She edited and cotranslated *New Generation: Poems from China Today* (1999), a collection of poems by 24 Chinese poets.

American Visa (1994), Wang's first book, is a collection of 11 related short stories featuring Seaweed's journey from a small island to a farming village in China and to New York. The eldest and seemingly least cherished daughter of four children, Seaweed is made to do all the housework by her harsh and abusive mother, whose talent for music and desire for beauty have to be buried during the Cultural Revolution. When Seaweed is sent to the countryside to be re-educated by farmers, she is relieved. Yet life there is no less torturous for Seaweed; in fact, it is even tragic for most of the women in the village. Ju, one of the women, drowns herself in defiance of an arranged marriage to a blind old man. Ju's mother, after the deaths of her first two husbands, abuse at the hands of the third, and the suicide of her daughter, also dies soon after. In the 1980s, Seaweed manages to come to America. However, the American dream, touted by an old woman at a book stand in New York subway station, turns out to be an illusion, as evidenced by Seaweed's encounters with the diseased, the deserted, and the lost in the city.

The title story, "American Visa," depicts the desperation and despair of Seaweed's two sisters in finding their way out of China. In the end, however, an American visa, as Seaweed's experience proves, does not guarantee a brighter future. In "Lotus," Seaweed links the obsolete foot-binding practice in China with modern high-heeled shoes and finds the latter, in effect, a contemporary equivalent. The binding of women, physically, emotionally, and spiritually, is a theme that is shared by all the stories in *American Visa*. Wang is at her best when detailing the life of ordinary people in China and reflecting on her protagonists' Chinese and American experiences with a balanced view.

Wang explores a similar theme in her novel, *Foreign Devil* (1996). Ni Bing, the protagonist, largely resembles Seaweed in character and experience. However, some elements of the plot, such as the secret of Ni Bing's birth and her love affair with a married man, make the novel a sensational and gripping read.

"Language, like woman / Look best when free, undressed," exclaims Wang in "Syntax," a poem in her first poetry collection, *Of Flesh and Spirit* (1998). The language in Wang's poems is direct and incisive. In a passionate and powerful way, Wang deals with her usual themes such as Chinese women's identity and experience and the journey of the Chinese to and within America. As is best exemplified by the title poem of her second collection, *The Magic Whip* (2003), Wang also experiments with the poetic form, making it a pastiche of verse, prose, and other nonconventional elements to produce an intense and disquieting effect.

In *Aching for Beauty: Footbinding in China* (2000), Wang adopts cross-cultural and interdisciplinary perspectives to examine the old practice of footbinding. She introduces various literary texts and oral accounts on footbinding from the Ming and Qing dynasties to the present, as well as linguistic, literary, and psychoanalytic theories from the West.

Wang's works have earned her a number of awards and fellowships including the Eugene M. Kayden Book Award in 2001 for the Best Book in the Humanities (for *Aching for Beauty*) and the Bush Artist Fellowship for Poetry in 2003.

Yan Ying

War Trash   Ha Jin   (2004)

Set largely in South Korean and U.S. POW camps during the Korean War of the early 1950s, *War Trash* is the first of HA JIN's works to take place outside mainland China. *War Trash* opens, and ends, in Atlanta, Georgia. While visiting his son and his family in the United Sates, 73-year-old Yu Yuan decides to write a memoir about his war experiences as a gift to his American grandchildren. As he relates his story, Yu is a junior officer in the Chinese army, who leaves his mother and fiancée to go to Korea as a member of the Chinese People's Volunteers. Due to poor leadership, his division suffers numerous casualties, and Yu and many of his comrades are captured and sent to POW camps. However, the conflict is not merely between the Chinese and their South Korean and American enemies. The Chinese prisoners themselves are bitterly divided between the Communists, who wish to be repatriated to mainland China, and the Nationalists, who want to be relocated to Taiwan, from where they intend to wrest power from the Communists.

Yu is neither a Communist nor a Nationalist, but, because of his knowledge of English, he becomes an interpreter for both groups. The Nationalists try to persuade, or compel, every POW to follow them to Taiwan. Given his desire to be reunited with his family, Yu deliberately keeps himself away from the Nationalists, even after they tattoo him with an anti-Communist slogan. But when he witnesses the brutal manner in which the Nationalists torture and kill the POWs who express a desire to go back to the mainland, Yu reluctantly announces that he too will go to Taiwan. However, during the screening, he tells the officers that he wants to return to the mainland and is transferred to a camp controlled by the Communists. Yu then attempts to gain the trust of the Communists by actively participating in operations against their American captors, in which the lives of many POWs are sacrificed for ideological reasons. Furthermore, he comes to question his decision to side with the Communists when he realizes that he is assigned to replace another POW on a dangerous mission because the other soldier is a party member. By the end of the narrative, Yu is repatriated to the mainland with other Chinese POWs, but they are condemned as traitors and punished by the Communists. In addition, his homecoming turns out to be anticlimactic, since his mother has died and his fiancée has left him.

Ultimately, *War Trash* is a fictional exploration of how an individual manages to survive in a "hellish place" in which human beings are treated as "war trash" by different ideological and national groups. Ha Jin's greatest achievement, though, is the way he is able to capture the reality of the Korean War in a novel.

Jianwu Liu and Albert Braz

Watanabe, Sylvia (1953–   )
Born on the island of Maui, Sylvia Watanabe is a third-generation Japanese-American writer of fiction, essays, and memoirs, and a professor of creative writing. Her collection of short stories, *Talking to the Dead* (1992), won the PEN Oakland Josephine Miles Award. She has also won a Pushcart Prize, an O. Henry Award and a National Endowments for the Arts fellowship. Along with Carol Bruchac, she has coedited two anthologies of Asian-American literature: *Home to Stay: Asian-American Women's Fiction* (1990), and *Into the Fire: Asian-American Prose* (1996).

Watanabe says that her extensive reading turned her to writing, which she found adventuresome. Though she initially wrote to record what she thought was the eradication of Hawaiian culture, she soon discovered that the traditions she deemed static were actually dynamic and evolving. Exposed to different cultures and religious traditions from the East and the West, she writes about the multicultural life of multiethnic people living in multigenerational households on the Hawaiian Islands. In her fiction she tries to imagine the private struggles of people as they encounter differences in culture.

The stories in *Talking to the Dead* explore the struggles of several generations of people in a Hawaiian village where the vast ocean is visible from almost every window. Against this expansive physical setting, which demands a gaze into the distance and occasionally a desire to escape, the rhythmic tug and pull of family ties and the tensions arising thereby are articulated and resolved. Within the family, there is a power struggle between the stabilizing forces of the older generations and the mobilizing forces of the younger generation with its capitalistic culture. Characters tie the stories together through their relationships, appearing and reappearing in different stories at different stages of their lives. The stories also interpret and make relevant older cultural beliefs. In the first story, "Anchorage," the curative power of the Prayer Lady is mentioned as a dubious medical option; but in the last story, "The Prayer Lady," her power is revealed to be more than just dubious superstition, for she is able to challenge and cajole sick people into abandoning depressive thoughts and return to good health.

The stories are all women-centered with the men occupying peripheral positions. Power struggles within the family between the young and the old persist with the older women dominating the younger ones. But in stories like "The Bishop's Wife," the young successfully challenge this domination. In the story, Missy effectively separates her own desires from her mother's ambitions for her, rejecting a prestigious scholarship in order to stay on the island. Yet when necessary, the younger women give the old their due as revealed by the ninth story, "Talking to the Dead," in which the ghost of an old woman known as Aunty Talking to the Dead returns to haunt her son, Clinton, who in his impatience for progress has forgotten to give her life a traditional closure. Only when Yuri, her apprentice in the traditional funeral business, gives her a proper cremation does Aunty put everything back in order. "Talking to the dead" means balancing the new ideas entering the island with the traditional wisdom of the old. As the old once indulged the romantic fantasies of the young, the young indulge the old by keeping alive the memory of their traditions. Only then can there be a balance between the old and the new and between the living and the dead.

Sukanya B. Senapati

Watkins, Yoko Kawashima   (1933–)

The child of a Japanese diplomat, Yoko Kawashima was born in Japan but spent most of her childhood in southern Manchuria and in the town of Nanam in northern Korea, then under Japanese control. She lived a comfortable middle-class life in her home in a bamboo grove in Nanam, attending school and learning about Japanese language and culture through extra lessons in calligraphy, floral arrangement, tea ceremony, and the like.

In her first autobiographical book for young adults, *So Far from the Bamboo Grove* (1986), Watkins tells the story of how she, her mother, and her older sister escaped from Korean Communists who stormed Nanam at the close of World War II in 1945, seeking retribution for Japan's long subjection of their country. Because Yoko's father was on diplomatic duty in Manchuria and her older brother, Hideyo, was working miles away, the mother and girls had to flee alone. Mother Kawashima, 16-year-old Ko, and 11-year-old Yoko make their way slowly toward Seoul—first by sneaking aboard a hospital train and later by foot. During the journey, Yoko is wounded in the chest and deafened in one ear by an explosion. The women experience hunger, many hardships, and narrowly avoid being killed on their way to Seoul. They eventually make their way to Japan on a refugee ship. They travel to Kyoto, where Yoko enrolls in the Sagano School for Girls and is relentlessly teased. Meanwhile, the mother journeys to northern Japan, only to find that her parents and in-laws have been killed in the war. The mother dies at the train station in Kyoto upon her return, leaving the two girls to fend for themselves. Living in wretched poverty, they await the return of their father and brother. A separate thread of the story explains how Hideyo is saved and fostered by a friendly Korean family before escaping to Japan to be reunited with his two sisters.

Watkins continues her life story in *My Brother, My Sister, and I* (1994), focusing on the first six years of her life as a refugee. Still living in poverty, the two teenaged girls and their older brother occupy a room in a warehouse. When the warehouse burns to the ground, Ko is badly injured while trying to save the family's heirlooms and documents. Hideyo and Yoko work hard to nurse their sister and pay her hospital bills over the next eight months. Meanwhile, the Kawashima children are accused of theft, arson, and a double murder that took place at their old warehouse home. They work with the police to find the real killers, and this book, too, ends with a reunion: Father Kawashima, who has been a POW, returns to them, only to be told that his wife died six years ago.

Watkins is also the author of *Tales from the Bamboo Grove* (1992), a collection of one Ainu and five Japanese folktales told around the dinner table when she was a child. In the foreword, she explains the context of each tale's telling. For example, "Monkey and Crab," in which the trickster monkey learns his lesson, was told her by her father when she complained about the school bully.

After graduating from Sagano, Yoko Kawashima took an intensive English course at a university and began working at a U.S. Air Force base, where she met her husband, Donald Watkins. The author now lives in Cape Cod with her husband and has four grown children. Major themes of Watkins's works include the importance of family bonds, commitment to preserving Japanese culture, and her earnest wish for peace.

Sandra S. Hughes

When My Sister Was Cleopatra Moon
Frances Park (2000)

Toggling chapters between the present and the past in FRANCES PARK's novel, readers are drawn into Cleo and Marcy Moon's turbulent lives. As teenagers, Cleo is sexy, wild, and fiercely independent, but Marcy is plain, studious, and obedient. Returning home after her first year of college, Cleo promises adolescent Marcy that the two of them will have a fabulous summer. Despite Cleo's wild lifestyle, Marcy begins to emulate her sister's clothing and makeup and even dates a boy who calls her "Miss Moonface." When he tries to force himself onto her, however, she realizes that she does not want to become her sister. The sisters' relationship falls apart as Marcy begins to distance herself from Cleo's destructive personality.

When the narrative moves to the present, Cleo's husband has just passed away, and she needs Marcy not for emotional support but to babysit her children while she attends a food show in New York City. Marcy is annoyed that Cleo could think about a food show in the midst of her husband's death and even neglect her children. Determined to "see Cleo for who she really is" (35), Marcy is convinced that Cleo is capable of having orchestrated his death. Concerned about the safety of the children, Marcy takes troubled teenager Luke and baby June to White Sky, the Native American community where she lives with Pablo, her partner. "Cactus Bear," the name of Marcy and Pablo's store, represents a transcendent moment of peace and triumph that signifies victory, but the real victory is the reconciliation of the sisters in the finale.

The perpetual absence and untimely death of Marcy and Cleo's father and their mother's inability to control her daughters in his absence cast a dark shadow on the family's pursuit of the American dream. In the same way that memories of the Korean War haunt their parents, memories of a troubled adolescence haunt Cleo and Marcy. With the father's death, the mother and Cleo splinter into their own worlds, leaving young Marcy "all alone in the world with no one to turn to" (152). In rescuing June and Luke from their mother, Marcy is actually inviting Cleo to rescue her from the solitude that stems from their past. The two stories weave together different time periods, bridging the past with the present and creating a new reality for the Moon sisters.

Bibliography
Park, Frances. *When My Sister Was Cleopatra Moon.* New York: Hyperion, 2000.

Sarah Park

When the Rainbow Goddess Wept
Cecilia Manguerra Brainard (1947–   )

Set in the Philippines in an idyllic atmosphere, this novel opens with vivid descriptions from the voice of the child-narrator Yvonne Macaraig, whose childhood will soon be marred by the brutality and violence of war. Yvonne's musings in the opening chapter illustrate the idyllic and peaceful town of Ubec, where she lives with her extended family. The distant rumblings and the constant talk of war among the adults foreshadow a war that will come to define the fate of Yvonne's whole family and, by extension, the Philippines.

As the war arrives in Ubec, the Macaraig family evacuates to the countryside, where Angeling, Yvonne's mother, gives birth to a stillborn son. CECILIA MANGUERRA BRAINARD's exquisite prose lends an air of authenticity to the everyday events in the lives of the protagonist, Yvonne, and her family in the jungle as they struggle to make it safely to the mountain to join the guerrilla movement against the Japanese. The stillborn baby is emblematic of the death and violence that haunt the characters struggling to reinvent their lives in the face of untold hardships.

Characters such as Nida (the subservient owner of Slapsy Maxie, a bar for American servicemen), Laydan, Bitong, Doc Menez, and Lolo Peping come to life in this starkly realistic yet beautifully passionate story of the coming of age of not just its child narrator but also a nation attempting to scratch out an identity for itself in the face of both Japanese aggression and American colonization. In a twist of fate, Nida, who with her husband, Max, longs to have a child, is raped by a Japanese soldier as she tries to protect and save a boatload of locals on their way to Tatayan, a safe haven for the guerrillas. Nida, always exuberant and filled with laughter, now weighs the consequences of having a bastard child. Brainard's eloquent prose also urges the reader to look closely at the nation of the Philippines, which in the 20th century has been "raped" by foreign powers and continues to be humiliated as it struggles to forge its own identity. Still, the strength and dignity of the nation are unmistakable as Yvonne's innocence reverberates with the echoes of a mythological history and epic tales injected into the narrative by the family's maid, Laydan, who embodies the deepest ideals and fortitude of her country. Her appearance, as depicted by Yvonne, is less than flattering: a leathery face and a large growth on the neck. Yet Laydan's quiet demeanor belies a beautiful and compassionate soul whose suffering mirrors all of the events surrounding her. Her quiet movements become a reassuring monotone for the readers as we follow her footsteps into the jungle, always careful and mindful of the people around her. It

is no accident that the chapter on "Women Warriors" becomes central to understanding the story as Brainard leads the reader to the very depths of what it means to fight. Women like Nida, Laydan, and Angeling not only fight the Japanese but also become the standard bearers and repositories of family, tradition, values, and culture.

When the Rainbow Goddess Wept depicts the epic struggle of a fledgling nation and its proud and dignified people to recover its history. It is also a life-affirming story of the will to live, love, and dream on one's own terms even in the face of insurmountable odds.

Ray Chandrasekara

Who's Irish?   Gish Jen (1999)

This first collection of short stories by GISH JEN comprises eight stories. The title story, one of Jen's most anthologized stories, is a first-person narrative written entirely in the Chinese-American dialect of an aging immigrant Chinese grandmother. In her sarcastic, humorous, and bitterly passive tone, the unnamed narrator complains about her Americanized daughter (Natalie), her lazy Irish-American son-in-law (John Shea), and their undisciplined daughter (Sophie). Although Sophie looks "brown" and Chinese, the grandmother grumbles, "already I see her nice Chinese side swallowed up by her wild Shea side" (6). Frequently wild, stubborn, and unmanageable, Sophie does not fit the model of the perfect, docile, and tractable Chinese girl. Readers soon realize, however, that the story is less about a wild toddler, and more about the grandmother's fear of assimilation and becoming "Americanized." After being kicked out of her daughter's home for mistreating Sophie, the grandmother moves in with her son-in-law's Irish mother, Bess. Slowly, the grandmother replaces her exclamations of "Did you ever see a Chinese girl act this way?" to a wistful remembrance of how Sophie used to kiss her on the nose: "I never see any other child kiss that way." Fittingly, the grandmother realizes that she should simply have seen a beautiful "child" in Sophie, rather than a "Chinese girl" who would not *act* Chinese. In the ironic, and perhaps superficial, ending, Bess dubs the grandmother a "permanent resident" of her house and an "honorary Irish" for her companionship while watching television.

"In the American Society," Jen's earliest story about the Chang family, eventually becomes the subject of her first novel, TYPICAL AMERICAN (1991), and her second novel, MONA IN THE PROMISED LAND (1996). "The Water Faucet Vision," which appeared in *Best American Short Stories* (1988) continues to develop the Chang family's story from the perspective of the eldest daughter, Callie. "Birthmates," chosen by John Updike for *Best American Short Stories of the Century,* is a third-person, humorous narrative about Art Woo, a divorced, paranoid computer salesman who finds himself being cared for by a young black woman after he is knocked unconscious in a random attack. "Duncan in China," a novella-length story, follows a Chinese-American man who travels to China in hopes of finding "the China of ineffable nobility and refinement." In the end, he finds himself disenchanted with his family, the politics, and culture. "Just Wait" is an omniscient narrative told through the perspective of Addie Lee, a pregnant Chinese-American woman whose impending birthing brings together her brothers and her fickle, estranged mother. In "Just Wait," Jen focuses on character development and the subtle play of family dynamics against cultural conflict. "Chin," the shortest and most tragic tale within the collection, depicts the disintegration of the Chin family in Yonkers, New York. Ma Chin eventually rescues herself and her daughter from the abusive husband, packs a bag, and leaves the house without anywhere for them to go. No one in the neighborhood rushes to rescue them even as they watch the pair stranded in the street. The collection of stories ends with "House, House, Home," another novella-length story narrated by an Asian student who divorces her very Western and eccentric husband, Sven, and begins a relationship with a Hawaiian man who helps her understand "how she had been wifed, how she had been fetishized, how she had been viewed as Orientalia" by her ex-husband.

Jen's short-story collection has garnered high praise for her ability to use short fiction as a sort of trial run for her longer works. Jen also frequently discusses the freedom and relaxation her stories offer her from the rigorous practice of novel writing. Rachel Lee writes that Jen focuses in her short fiction on the sense of home by depicting "the unsettling of home implied not only in literal leave-takings of members from households but also in reconfigurations of the family structure following intercultural pressures" (14).

Bibliography
Jen, Gish. *Who's Irish?* 1999. New York: Vintage Books, 2000.
Lee, Rachel. "Who's Chinese?" *Women's Review of Books* 19, no. 5 (2002): 13–14.
Perry, Rachel. Review of *Who's Irish?* by Gish Jen, *Mid-American Review* 20, nos. 1/2 (2000): 253–256.

Amy Lillian Manning

Wild Meat and the Bully Burgers
Lois-Ann Yamanaka (1961)

Wild Meat and the Bully Burgers, LOIS-ANN YAMANAKA's first novel, introduces three themes the author returns to in her later novels: legitimacy of self-definition, ethnic authenticity, and the difficulty of language acquisition.

Set in mid-1970s Hilo, Hawaii, the novel portrays the daily life of a working-class Asian-American family through the narration of daughter Lovey Nariyoshi. As Lovey comes of age, she tells us about her desire to be an all-American girl who speaks perfect English and looks like a Barbie doll. As a child, she wanted to be like Shirley Temple with her "perfect Blond ringlets and pink cheeks and pout lips" (3). As an adolescent, she envies the American beauty and sexuality in the movies. She also wants to be like the popular Asian-American girls at school who are able to fit in with mainstream, white American culture much more readily than Lovey can. While they shop at all the fashionable stores, live in nicer houses, and eat American food bought at the grocery store, Lovey must wear cheap-imitation clothes and eat whatever food her family hunts and grows. Desperately wanting to fit in and be a "model minority," Lovey feels overwhelming shame for her family's lifestyle.

The contrast between Lovey and her peers "reminds readers of the multiplicity and variation of Asian American identities in terms of class, geography, and ethnicity" (Ho 51). Even if Lovey cannot look white American, she at least wants to feel American and accepted. Throughout the novel, Lovey notices that all things white and light-colored in American popular culture are privileged: "Owning white items and eating white items, Lovey believes, will make her white by association, as her consumption of white food demonstrates her desire to literally eat her way into what she perceives as a more socially accepted identity" (Ho 57).

Yamanaka's debut novel received wide acclaim when it was published. Critics praised the novel's humor and Yamanaka's ability to write the Hawaiian Creole English (pidgin) dialect with accuracy and ease. Even as we laugh at Lovey's disastrous home perm, we share her disgust and sadness when her father slaughters a family cow that she and her sister had called Bully and treated like a pet. At the heart of the novel's humor and realism, Yamanaka shows her commitment to writing about the variety of Asian-American experiences in Hawaii.

Bibliography

Ho, Jennifer Ann. *Consumption and Identity in Asian American Coming-of-Age Novels.* New York: Routledge, 2005.

Amy Lillian Manning

Woman Warrior, The
Maxine Hong Kingston (1976)

MAXINE HONG KINGSTON's highly acclaimed first book, *The Woman Warrior: Memoirs of a Girlhood among Ghosts,* begins with a mother admonishing her daughter to keep silent: "'You must never tell anyone,' my mother said, 'what I am about to tell you.'" The story Brave Orchid then tells her daughter—who now relates it to her readers in direct violation of her mother's command—concerns Brave Orchid's sister-in-law, who was attacked by her townspeople in China for giving birth out of wedlock, and who afterward killed both herself and her child. In refusing to keep her family's secret, the narrator of *The Woman Warrior* reworks her aunt's tragic story and turns a cautionary tale against sexual impropriety into a powerful metaphor for the cultural silencing of women. This bold literary act—the reclaiming and rescuing of Chinese and Chinese-American women's stories from anonymity and enforced silence—is *The Woman Warrior*'s central project.

The notion of the "talk-story," the liberal blend of family narrative and folktale/myth through which Brave Orchid frequently tries to warn her daughters about the dangers of cultural transgression, is crucial to understanding the book's complicated narrative structure. Throughout *The Woman Warrior,* storytelling is shown to have been a tool for the perpetuation of women's subordinate status; legends, family anecdotes, jokes, and aphorisms passed down through generations frequently characterize women as weak and unintelligent. But by rewriting ancient stories and creating new ones, the narrator rejects those characterizations, demonstrating literature's potential to resist and subvert gender stereotypes.

Because the book freely combines autobiography and family narrative with fiction and folktale, *The Woman Warrior*'s many editions have listed its genre variously as "memoir," "fiction," "literature," and "nonfiction." While *The Woman Warrior* does not fit neatly into any single generic category, much of its dramatic power derives from Kingston's extensive use of her family's history to show how the silencing of women is accomplished and sustained through generations. In many ways the book's most memorable character, Brave Orchid is a strong-willed woman whose words and actions contradict the stereotype of the subservient Asian wife; aside from the narrator's, it is Brave Orchid's commanding voice we hear most frequently throughout the text. However, despite her insistence that her children grow to be independent,

Brave Orchid is equally determined that they will not become "Americanized" and thus lose touch with their Chinese heritage. The narrator and her brother and sisters therefore feel a constant tension between an America whose dominant racial culture they can never be a part of, and a China whose history they know only through harrowing stories of violence and the punishment of women who transgress social taboos.

The Woman Warrior is composed of five sections: "No Name Woman," "White Tigers," "Shaman," "At the Western Palace," and "A Song for a Barbarian Reed Pipe." Each is a blend of realistic and nonrealistic (or "fantastic") narrative styles, allowing Kingston to slip easily between the world of everyday experience and the worlds of memory, myth, or legend. Often the female characters in the present-day sections, set in 1970s California, find themselves haunted by ghosts or other ancient supernatural entities who threaten to render them powerless against oppressive forces. Conversely, "White Tigers," a retelling of the life of the legendary Chinese female warrior Fa Mu Lan told in the first person, is written in a spare, unsentimental style that lends a modern and contemporary feel to a very old tale of honor and retribution.

Each of the book's five sections tells the story of a central female character's struggle against cultural and domestic male dominance. Some of these characters, such as the narrator's suicidal aunt and Brave Orchid's sister Moon Orchid, are irreparably hurt or utterly destroyed by that struggle, although their tales survive as damning testimony to their destruction. Others, such as the narrator and Brave Orchid herself, succeed in resisting their oppressors, but only at tremendous costs to themselves and others.

In "A Song for a Barbarian Reed Pipe," for example, Brave Orchid proudly claims to have cut her daughter's tongue when she was a baby, in order to free up her tongue for speaking any of the world's languages. Instead, when the narrator enters public school she is afraid to speak aloud for the first year. In a harrowing scene late in the section, the young narrator, now in the sixth grade, corners another young, silent Chinese girl in the school bathroom. The narrator tortures the little girl for hours, yelling at her, pulling her hair and pinching her face until the girl weeps softly: "I could work her face around like dough. She stood still, and I did not want to look at her face anymore; I hated fragility." Seeing in this young girl a reminder of her own enforced silence, the narrator finishes her abuse with a menacing echo of her own mother's words which opened the book: "Don't you dare tell anyone I was bad to you." Silence and self-loathing are ingrained in the narrator until, as a young woman, she comes to understand the potential of writing to interrupt that cycle and help her fashion a new identity independent of her family and cultural stereotypes: "I continue to sort out what's just my childhood, just my imagination, just my family, just the village, just movies, just living."

The Woman Warrior won the National Book Critics Circle General Nonfiction Award in 1976, and was named one of the top 10 nonfiction books of the 1970s by *Time* magazine. It was followed by a companion volume, CHINA, MEN, in 1980.

Bibliography

Crafton, Lisa Plummer. "'We Are Going to Carve Revenge on Your Back': Language, Culture, and the Female Body in Kingston's *The Woman Warrior*," In *Women as Sites of Culture: Women's Roles in Cultural Formation from the Renaissance to the Twentieth Century,* edited by Susan Shifrin, 51–63. Aldershot, England: Ashgate, 2002.

"Staging *Woman Warrior:* Maxine Hong Kingston retells her 'talk-story,'" *Boston Globe,* 4 September 1994, Arts & Film, p. A1.

Wong, Sau-Ling Cynthia. *Maxine Hong Kingston's The Woman Warrior: A Casebook.* Casebooks in Contemporary Fiction Series. Oxford: Oxford University Press, 1999.

Woo, Eunjoo. "'The Beginning Is Hers, the Ending, Mine': Chinese American Mother/Daughter Conflict and Reconciliation in Maxine Hong Kingston's *The Woman Warrior*." *Studies in Modern Fiction* 9, no. 1 (Summer 2002): 297–314.

Eric G. Waggoner

Wong, Elizabeth (1958–)

Born in an industrial section of Los Angeles called Southgate and raised in Chinatown, Wong experienced a childhood full of hardship. Her father died when she was only five years old, and her mother was forced to work multiple jobs to support the two children. These difficult times led Wong to intense reading and studying. Her escape through books inspired Wong to learn more about a particular role model: Anna May Wong, the first Chinese-American actress. Through diligent study and a desire to escape the ghetto, Wong finished high school, received a bachelor's degree in journalism from the University of Southern California, and entered an M.F.A. program in playwriting at New York University.

Before her playwriting career began, Wong established a successful career in the 1980s as a television and newspaper journalist in Los Angeles, San Diego, and Hartford, Connecticut. Through the mid-1990s, Wong continued to contribute occasional opinion pieces to the *Los Angeles Times*, although her primary focus remained writing, producing, and directing her own plays. Her first play, *Letters to a Student Revolutionary* (1989), not only earned praise from audiences but also received the 1990 Playwright Forum Award from Theatre Works in Colorado Springs. In addition to *Letters*, Wong's most acclaimed plays include *Kimchee and Chitlins* (1990) and *China Doll* (1995). Wong also made history as a writer for *All-American Girl* (1994–95), the first all Asian-American cast television show, starring Margaret Cho.

Letters to a Student Revolutionary premiered at the Pan Asian Repertory Theatre in New York City. The play commemorates the 1989 Tiananmen Square massacre in Beijing. With minimal props and a bare stage, Wong's first play set a minimalist standard for most of her other plays. The play narrates the story of two friends: Bibi, an "all-American" teenage girl, and Karen, a girl in China. Their friendship begins when Bibi travels with her parents to China for a "back to your roots" family vacation. During their 10-year friendship, these two girls, Chinese and Chinese-American, share the idealistic visions and misconceptions each has of the other's culture and nation. Culminating with the 1989 massacre, the play ultimately underscores the characters' difficulty in defining American freedom and Chinese oppression given the gross misconceptions each has about the other's cultural reality.

China Doll and *Kimchee and Chitlins* also grapple with cultural issues such as race and prejudice. *China Doll,* Wong's most widely acclaimed play, creates a fictionalized life for the playwright's role model, Anna May Wong. *Kimchee and Chitlins* is a comedy that questions media involvement in the serious subject of the 1990 black boycott of Korean-owned stores in New York City.

In addition to Off-Broadway runs, Wong's plays have also been featured in prestigious national and international festivals in Los Angeles, New York, Tokyo, and Singapore. More recent plays, such as *The Happy Prince* (1997) and *Prometheus* (1999) have continued to garner praise for Wong's ability to see what is left unseen and unsaid in American culture. Wong views her writing as a form of social activism: "When responding to social issues, some people write letters and write editorials; I write a play."

Amy Lillian Manning

Wong, Jade Snow (1922–2006)

From the obscure position of fifth daughter of an immigrant family in San Francisco's Chinatown, Jade Snow Wong became a ceramics artist, travel agent, and author of two volumes of memoirs, including *Fifth Chinese Daughter* (1950), the first work by a female Chinese American to receive wide attention. Wong explained that she wrote the book to foster American understanding of Chinese culture; the U.S. State Department also saw its potential to educate Asians about America. In 1953 she toured many Asian countries to speak with people who had read her book in translation, and Wong recounts her travels in her second memoir, *No Chinese Stranger* (1975).

Fifth Chinese Daughter, although an autobiography, is written in the third person, in modest

Chinese fashion. The work illustrates Chinatown's characters, customs, and celebrations for Western readers, but more important, it chronicles Jade Snow's childhood and early adulthood, and her desire to be recognized as an individual and to bring honor to her family. At the heart of *Fifth Chinese Daughter* is Jade Snow's relationship with her father. Not outwardly affectionate, Daddy is an exacting disciplinarian absorbed in the work of his factory and community organizations. According to Chinese custom, his children must defer to elders, and sons are given priority over daughters; however, his conversion to Christianity leads him to believe that girls, too, should be educated. Patiently he tutors Jade Snow in Chinese, as he had taught her older sisters, and sends her to Chinese school once she is old enough to enroll.

In addition to Chinese school, Jade Snow attends public school, where she learns that she will often be forced to choose between American and Chinese ways. She is insulted by a classmate who calls her "Chinky, Chinky, Chinaman," but she also admires the tenderness and fairness of American families that she observes while working as a housekeeper. Throughout the book, Jade Snow tries to forge an identity that includes the best of both Chinese and American philosophies, and becomes a "critical spectator" of both her family and the outside world.

The memoir continues after her graduation from Mills College in 1942, when Jade Snow goes to work in the office of a shipyard to help the war effort. There, she wins an essay contest and is invited to christen a ship; the respect she gains in the Western sphere and in Chinatown also glorifies the Wongs. After leaving the shipyard, Jade Snow decides to become a writer and to support herself by making and selling pottery, renting space in the front window of a Chinatown shop. Although the Chinese laugh at her, the Westerners are intrigued, and the business thrives. One last triumph closes the memoir: Once the business is established, Daddy tells her that she has achieved just what he had hoped when he left China—greater freedom and individuality for his daughters. Jade Snow's success has been both public and private, bring-ing honor to her both in the Western world and in her family.

In 1950, shortly before the publication of *Fifth Chinese Daughter,* Jade Snow married Woodrow Ong. Together they raised four children, expanded Jade Snow's ceramics business, and became travel agents leading tours of Americans to Asia. Not long after President Richard Nixon's historic visit to Peking in 1972, the couple arranged their own trip to China, a journey chronicled in detail by *No Chinese Stranger.* Wong's earlier book made her a cultural ambassador from America to Asia, but in *No Chinese Stranger,* she brings Asia to America, giving Western readers an impartial look behind the bamboo curtain.

Bibliography

Bloom, Harold, ed. *Asian-American Women Writers.* Philadelphia: Chelsea House, 1997.

Lim, Shirley Geok-lin. "The Tradition of Chinese American Women's Life Stories: Thematics of Race and Gender in Jade Snow Wong's *Fifth Chinese Daughter* and Maxine Hong Kingston's *The Woman Warrior.*" *American Women's Autobiography: Fea(s)ts of Memory,* edited by Margo Culley, 252–267. Madison: University of Wisconsin Press, 1992.

Trudeau, Lawrence J., ed. *Asian American Literature: Reviews and Criticism of Works by American Writers of Asian Descent.* Detroit: Gale Research, 1999.

Jaime Cleland

Wong, Nanying Stella   (1914–2002)

Known to her friends as "Starla," Nanying Stella Wong was born in Oakland, California, the oldest of five daughters born to Chinese Americans whose California heritage dates back to the gold-rush era. Although both parents excelled in business, owning a Chinese herb store and a Chinese restaurant, her mother was a renowned stage actress who also appeared in many early motion pictures with her eldest infant daughter. This family background in the arts manifested itself in all of the children through their interest in painting and drawing, but it was Nanying who achieved recognition for her artistic promise. While attending Oakland's Technical High School, where teachers fostered her burgeoning talent, she won three third-place prizes in the National Scholastic Art Exhibition where her work competed against 7,000 others. When the curator of the Oakland Art Gallery, William Clapp, happened to eat at the Peacock Inn, the family restaurant, he became so impressed with Wong's work hanging on the walls that he helped her procure a scholarship to the California College of Arts and Crafts, where she learned watercolor painting. Although a gifted visual artist, Wong also desired to become a writer, so she simultaneously enrolled at the University of California, Berkeley, to study creative writing. For the next 70 years of her life, Wong attempted to fuse the art of painting with the art of writing to varying degrees of success.

Upon earning a B.A. from the University of California in 1933 and a B.F.A. from the College of Arts and Crafts in 1935, Wong attended graduate school at Cornell University. Although she lived in New York City for a short time designing costume jewelry for Helena Rubenstein, Wong moved back to the West Coast in 1940 to join the Bohemian community of Chinese-American artists and writers who were doing pioneering ethnic artwork in and around San Francisco's Montgomery block. Once here, she became a well-known Bay Area artist, exhibiting her work at the San Francisco Museum of Art, the Palace of Fine Arts at the Golden Gate Exposition, and the Pal Elder Gallery as well as having painted a mural for San Francisco's Fong Fong Bakery and Fountain.

A decade after her return to California, Wong's writing career took off. In the late 1940s, she began working on a novel that covered the lives of five generations of two different immigrant families, one Irish and the other Chinese, which allowed her to explore the clash of Eastern and Western ideas that occurred in central California during the late 19th and early 20th centuries. Shortly after beginning the book, she was awarded scholarships to conduct research in Dublin and to work on the novel at the Mexico City Writing Center, then run by California writer Margaret Shedd. At about the same time Wong developed an interest in bronze sculptures, so she traveled to southern China to research the subject and ended up transcribing the oral wedding songs of elderly women from the village of Toysun for her book's opening chapter, which depicts a Chinese wedding. Although her groundbreaking novel never appeared in print, Wong did publish her translations of the wedding songs in the Chinatown issue of the short-lived journal *Number*. This issue also included several drawings by her, including the cover art.

Because of the failed reception of her novel, Wong spent the rest of her writing career focusing on poetry, which found publication in a variety of magazines, books, and anthologies including *Bearing Dreams, Shaping Visions: Asian Pacific American Perspectives; Peace and Pieces: An Anthology of Contemporary American Poetry;* and *Ting, Anthology of World Poets.* As with the multicultural emphasis of her novel, Wong's poems rely heavily on family, history, and immigration issues to explore the ideological connections between East and West. During the late 1960s, she also became a political poet, writing, for example, "From One Delta to Another" to illustrate her concern for the destruction of the natural environment and "San Francisco–Saigon" to criticize American involvement in the Vietnam War.

Many of Wong's poems are thematically daring for their times, having been written before an audience existed for Asian-American writing. Aesthetically, they often rely upon the imagist theories of William Carlos Williams, with whom she corresponded briefly, and they are heavily influenced by her background in the visual arts. Wong's fusion of these two different art forms became an integral part of her artistic activities. She often reviewed Asian-American novels around the Bay Area by making sketches that illustrated their characters and plots, an example being Lin Yutang's *A Leaf in a Storm,* and she used drawings to accentuate readings of her own poetry, highlighting the artistic process of both.

Because she never published a volume of her own verse and since her poems remain scattered in journals, books, and anthologies of varying quality, Wong will be remembered more as a visual artist than as a poet. Toward the end of her life, she was honored with many career retrospectives including an exhibition of her watercolors at the Asian Resource Center in 1995 and another, posthumously, at the Chinese Historical Society of America Museum and Learning Center in 2002. She passed away on January 12, 2002, after a long bout with a stomach ailment.

Bibliography

Brown, Michael D. *Views from Asian California, 1920–1965,* 63. San Francisco: Michael Brown, 1992.

Holliday, Shawn. "Nanying Stella Wong (1914–   )." *Asian American Poets: A Bio-Bibliographical Critical Sourcebook,* edited by Guiyou Huang, 311–312. Westport, Conn.: Greenwood, 2002.

Hughes, Edan Milton. *Artists in California, 1786–1940,* 512. San Francisco: Hughes Publishing, 1986.

Poon, Irene. *Leading the Way: Asian American Artists of the Older Generation.* Wenham, Mass.: Gordon College, 2001.

Shawn Holliday

Wong, Nellie (1934–   )

Writer and radical activist Nellie Wong was born on September 12, 1934, in Oakland's Chinatown to new immigrant parents from China. She maintained close ties to the Bay Area throughout her life through her activism and service, as reflected in many of her poems featuring the Bay Area's people and history. Throughout World War II, Wong worked as a waitress in her family's Great China Restaurant in Oakland's Chinatown while also attending public schools. The internment of Japanese Americans during World War II influenced Wong's understanding of U.S. racism, a subject which she later addresses in her poetry. After graduating from Oakland High School in 1964, Wong began work as a secretary at the Bethlehem Steel Corporation, a job she held until 1982. Wong then worked as a senior analyst in the Office of Affirmative Action/Equal Opportunity at the University of San Francisco until her retirement in 1998. Wong's writing and activism stemmed directly from her working-class background and her working life, as well as from her family histories in Oakland and China. Her works address feminism for women of color, struggles against racism, workplace injustice, and the difficulties in forging a dual identity as writer and activist.

In the early 1970s, when she was in her mid 30s, Wong pursued studies in creative writing at San Francisco State University. Here she found women of color communities who supported her attempts to bridge writing and activism. Wong became involved with the Women Writers Union on campus, which was organized around issues of race, gender, and class. Wong also embraced radical socialist politics and joined Radical Women and the Freedom Socialist Party. MERLE WOO, with whom Wong formed a lasting friendship, Wong and several others founded Unbound Feet, a writing collective of Chinese-American women who read and lectured at California universities in the late 1970s and early 1980s. In many ways Wong and 1970s San Francisco proved to be a generative match for each other. Wong's writing and activism challenged the predominantly white and middle-class orientation of the women's rights movement while Wong furthered the cause of women's rights by demanding that race, class, and gender oppressions be seen as intersecting and overlapping.

Wong's first collection of poems, *Dreams in Harrison Railroad Park,* was published in 1977, followed by two other collections of poetry, *Death of Long Steam Lady* (1986) and *Stolen Moments* (1997). The themes and ideas captured in *Dreams in Harrison Railroad Park* are emblematic of Wong's anger at the racial injustice suffered by Asian Americans. Her poems paint assimilation as a racist compulsion that forces immigrants to reject the cultures of their homeland and to embrace the dominant culture. As such, these poems challenge the dominant conflation of white culture with American culture. Both angry and hopeful in tone, her poems paint a powerful need to uncover and recenter people of color, women, and working-class history. She also coedited *Voices of Color* (1999) with Yolanda Alaniz, as well as *Three Asian*

American Writers Speak Out on Feminism (2003) with Merle Woo and MITSUYE YAMADA. Her works were well received and Dreams in Harrison Railroad Park is the most successful release in Kelsey Street Press's history. Wong continued to find support for her creative output throughout the latter half of her life, and she remained committed to using her writing to further social justice. She used her success as a writer to bring awareness of the issues affecting women of color and Asian Americans, and to educate society about these communities' contributions to activism and social justice. In 1983, with Tillie Olsen as well as Alice Walker and other noted writers of color, Wong traveled to China on the first U.S. Women Writers Tour to China, sponsored by the US-China Peoples Friendship Association. She was also invited to read her poetry in China and Cuba. During the 1980s and 1990s, Wong keynoted at many national and regional conferences including Third World Women and Feminist Perspectives and the National Women's Studies Association Conferences. Wong has taught Women's Studies at the University of Minnesota and poetry writing at Mills College in Oakland, California.

Her work has appeared in more than 200 anthologies, and in 1996, her poem "Song of Farewell" was installed on a San Francisco F-Line Muni platform. Wong is featured in several film projects such as Art as Revolution (2003) and is the subject, along with fellow Asian-American activist and writer Yamada, of Mitsuye and Nellie, Asian American Poets (1981). In 1998 Wong donated her papers to California Ethnic and Multicultural Archives (CEMA) at the University of California, Santa Barbara.

Her insistence on the importance in bridging activism and writing, as well as her contributions to the study of race, gender, and class as intersecting oppressions, paved the way for future Asian-American writers, activists and thinkers. Her poetry and essays made visible the contributions by women of color to American history and highlighted the particular experiences of Asian-American women thus far ignored. Along with Cherrie Moraga, Gloria Anzaldua, and Angela Davis, Wong is an important member of what is now recognized as the Third World Women of Color Movement.

Bibliography

Madsen, Deborah, ed. Asian American Writers. Farmington Hills, Mich.: Thompson Gale, 2005.

Mohanty, Chandra Talpade, Ann Russo, Lourdes Torres, eds. Third World Women and the Politics of Feminism. Bloomington: Indiana University Press, 1991.

Wong, Nellie, and Mitsuye Yamada. Mitsuye & Nellie, Asian American Poets. Directed by Allie Light and Irving Saraf. 58 min. Women Make Movies, 1986. DVD/VHS.

Jinah Kim

Wong, Rita   (1968–   )

Rita Wong spent her childhood in Calgary with her Chinese immigrant parents, who owned a local grocery store. Trained in the fields of English, Asian studies, and archival studies, Wong has held a variety of jobs: an English instructor in Japan and China, a coordinator for the Alberta Network of Immigrant Women, and an archivist with the U'mista Cultural Centre in Alert Bay. Currently, Wong is pursuing a Ph.D. in English at Simon Fraser University.

One of the few openly bisexual Asian-American women poets in North America, Wong has contributed poetry and prose to journals such as Fireweed, Contemporary Verse 2, Kinesis, and Prairie Fire as well as to books such as The Other Woman: Women of Colour in Contemporary Canadian Literature and Hot and Bothered: Short Fiction on Lesbian Desire. Wong's most substantial work to date, however, is her collection of poetry, Monkeypuzzle (1998). Memories of the poet's formative years comprise the opening segment entitled "Memory Palate." As if to piece together an image of what it means to grow up Chinese Canadian, Wong portrays her dull childhood days in the corridors of her parents' Sunset Grocery Store, her ancestors who "live in the flicker of candle flames" (18), and the night sounds of mah-jongg. The second and most sizable chapter experiments with form by exploring the politics of language and power within the superstructure of transnational capitalism. In "Write about the Absence," the poet writes that

grammar is an invisible net in the air,
holding your
words in place. grammar, like wealth,
belongs in the hands of
the people who produce it. (29)

The collection's penultimate cluster of poems grapples with the sometimes uncomfortable yet beautifully complex in-between space of being marked as both Chinese and Canadian. The closing poems turn toward the body with a strong dose of the erotic as Wong gives voice to lesbian desire.

Monkeypuzzle has been widely reviewed in feminist, Asian-American, and leftist journals. Though one critic suggests that a few poems in the volume are prose pieces disguised as poems, most readers agree that Wong's writing is incisive and politically urgent in its discussion of sweatshop labor, mail-order brides, and discrimination against immigrants. Wong has received the Emerging Writers Award from the Asian Canadian Writers Workshop and was nominated for the Lambda Literary Award for poetry.

Bibliography

Wong, Rita. *Monkey puzzle.* Vancouver: Press Gang, 1998.

Mimi Iimuro Van Ausdall

Wong, Shawn   (1949–)

Both an advocate of Asian-American studies and a pioneer in defining Asian-American literature as a literary tradition, Wong belongs to the vanguard of Asian-American writers who began to publish in the 1970s. He, however, differs from most of his predecessors in his depiction of characters, situations, and sentiments that shatter the majority of white stereotypes of Asian America. Wong's distinctive style is marked by his preoccupation with the establishment of an Asian-American male identity and Asian-American aesthetics.

Born in Oakland, California, he was raised by an engineer father and an artist mother in Berkeley. After finishing his undergraduate study at the University of California, Berkeley, Wong started writing his first novel, *HOMEBASE,* under Kay Boyle's supervision at San Francisco State University, where he received an M.F.A. in creative writing in 1974. *Homebase* won both the 1980 Pacific Northwest Booksellers' Award and the Washington State Governor's Writers Day Award. This recognition was followed by a National Endowment for the Arts Creative Fellowship in 1981.

Wong's second novel, *AMERICAN KNEES,* is a humorous look at inter- and intraracial dating among Asian Americans. The novel was later adapted into a screenplay for Celestial Pictures. Wong has also published poetry, essays, and reviews in numerous periodicals and anthologies. He is the editor or coeditor of several influential anthologies of Asian-American literature including the widely acclaimed *Aiiieeeee! An Anthology of Asian American Writers* (1974) and *The Big Aiiieeee! The History of Chinese America and Japanese America in Literature* (1991). He also coedited a special issue of Asian-American prose work for *Yardbird Reader* (1975), and *Before Columbus Foundation Fiction/ Poetry Anthology: Selections from the American Book Awards, 1980–1990.* In 1996 Wong edited his own anthology, *Asian American Literature: A Brief Introduction and Anthology.* He is a recipient of a Rockefeller Foundation residency in Bellagio, Italy. Active in the Seattle arts community, Wong was featured in the 1997 PBS documentary "Shattering the Silences." He is at present a professor and chairman of the department of English at the University of Washington.

Bibliography

Chen, Chih-Ping. "Shawn Wong." In *Asian American Novelists: A Bio-Bibliographical Critical Sourcebook,* edited by Emmanuel S. Nelson, 391–397. Westport, Conn.: Greenwood Press, 2000.

Kim, Elaine H. "Shawn Hsu Wong." In *Asian American Literature: An Introduction to the Writings and Their Social Context,* 194–197. Philadelphia: Temple University Press, 1982.

Utenberger, Amy L, ed. *Who's Who among Asian Americans 1994–1995.* Detroit: Gale Research, 1994.

Su-lin Yu

Woo, Merle   (1941–)

As a leading member of the Radical Women and the Freedom Socialist Party, Merle Woo has dedicated her life to fighting for social justice. Committed to the group's ideals of genuine democracy and full equality for all, the Korean-Chinese-American activist has worked to preserve women's reproductive freedom, immigrant rights, and freedom of speech. In 1982, as part of a wide-scale attack on radicalism, affirmative action, and intellectual freedom during the Reagan years, Woo was dismissed from her position as lecturer of Asian American Studies at the University of California, Berkeley. While the university cited a new stipulation confining lecturers' appointments to four years, which Woo had exceeded, many of Woo's supporters saw the firing as directly related to Woo's radicalism, open lesbianism, feminism, and socialism. In a series of acclaimed court cases, Woo, with the support of the American Federation of Teachers, the National Lawyers Guild, the Merle Woo Defense Committee, and others, fought the university on the grounds of unfair labor practices and won. The four-year limit on lecturer appointments was struck down by the court, and Woo was granted a two-year visiting lecturer position and financial remuneration. She chose to forgo additional legal battles that might have secured the tenure-track appointment she had originally been promised; instead, she turned her attention to healing from the breast cancer with which she had just been diagnosed.

Woo's activism includes producing work in a variety of genres: nonfiction essays, performance art, and poetry. She has contributed to a number of Radical Women publications such as *Permanent Revolution in the U.S. Today,* which includes her essay "Lesbian and Gay Liberation: A Trotskyist Analysis," and *Three Asian American Writers Speak Out on Feminism,* which features several of Woo's dramatic monologues and poems that give voice to her ancestors. In the late seventies and early eighties, Woo, along with fellow radicals NELLIE WONG and Kitty Tsui, participated in an Asian-American feminist performance art group called "Unbound Feet Three." While much of the work that Woo completed with this group has remained unpublished to date, Woo's poetry has circulated widely in journals such as *Plexus, Haight-Ashbury Journal,* and in collections like *Breaking Silence, The Forbidden Stitch, Making Waves* and *My Lover Is a Woman.*

Among Woo's best-known works are her personal essay, "Letter to Ma," which appears in *This Bridge Called My Back,* and her collection of poems *Yellow Woman Speaks.* While Woo's letter is addressed to her mother, its audience is much broader, as Woo points to the similarities among Asian women's experiences of racism, sexism, and economic disadvantage and requests that yellow women and their allies unite to eliminate such injustices. *Yellow Woman Speaks,* originally released in 1986 and reprinted in 2003 with a handful of recent poems discussing trans-genderism and queer sexuality, approaches themes similar to those in "Letter to Ma": lesbian identity and sexuality, honoring ancestors, racial oppression, and feminism. While several poems from this book have been widely anthologized, they received little critical attention, a fact that Sunn Shelley Wong attributes to an academic dismissal of poetry that uses informal diction, democratic instead of difficult themes, and overtly oppositional politics. Slowly though, critics are turning an eye toward Woo's work, whose co-authored *Three Asian American Writers Speak Out on Feminism* was positively reviewed in *Iris* magazine upon the book's rerelease in 2003. Moreover, Professor Suzanne Juhasz has cited Woo's poem on lesbian sexuality, "Under a Full Moon" (previously published as "Untitled"), as exemplary of what she calls the "complimentary identification" of lesbian desire (156–158), that is, an identity that is based both on difference and sameness.

Bibliography

Huang, Su-ching. "Merle Woo." In *Asian-American Poets: A Bio-Bibliographical Critical Sourcebook,* edited by Guiyou Huang and Emmanuel S. Nelson, 323–330. Westport, Conn: Greenwood Press, 2002.

Juhasz, Suzanne. *A Desire for Women: Relational Psychoanalysis, Writing, and Relationships between Women,* 143–166. New Brunswick, N.J., and London: Rutgers University Press, 2003.

Sheffer, Jolie. Review of *3 Asian American Writers Speak Out on Feminism,* by Mitsuye Yamada, Merle Woo, and Nellie Wong. *Iris* 47 (2003): 91.

Wong, Sunn Shelley. "Sizing Up Asian American Poetry." In *A Resource Guide to Asian American Literature,* edited by Sau-ling Cynthia Wong and Stephen H. Sumida. 285–308. New York: Modern Language Association of America, 2001.

Mimi Iimuro Van Ausdall

Wooden Fish Songs
Ruthanne Lum McCunn (1995)

The story of Lue Gim Gong, the Chinese American whose innovative cross-pollination contributed millions to the citrus industry, is pieced together in this historical novel by RUTHANNE LUM MCCUNN through the narrations of three women who know him best: his mother, Sum Jui, his white American mentor, Miss Fanny Burlingame, and Miss Fanny's African-American servant Sheba. Even as a child growing up in southern China, Lue seems to have had a natural affinity with plants and animals. His curiosity has propelled him to question everything and experiment with new ways of gardening. At the age of 10, fascinated by the stories that his fourth uncle brought back from the "Gold Mountain" (America), Lue decides to come to America. Once in America, however, Lue soon becomes disappointed by the discrepancy between his uncle's stories and the harsh reality of everyday life. Lue joins a group of workers and moves to North Adams, Massachusetts, to work in a shoe factory. In North Adams, Lue meets Miss Fanny, who has volunteered through the local church to teach the newly arrived Chinese workers the English language and Christian doctrines. A friendship quickly develops between them, and Lue soon becomes a Christian.

Miss Fanny encourages Lue to pursue his interests in plants, gains permission for him to work in her father's garden, and finds books about plant improvement techniques for him. Lue diligently studies the works of Malthus and Darwin and begins to experiment with cross-planting in the Burlingame garden. In the meantime, he regularly sends money to China to help his family.

In the late 1870s, America falls into an economic depression and the country's anti-Chinese sentiment becomes strong. At the same time, Lue's village in China suffers a long drought, and his family faces starvation. With little work, Lue can barely make enough money to support himself. Miss Fanny convinces her father to hire Lue as their gardener, but Mr. Burlingame only provides Lue a minimal allowance. As Lue sinks into deep debt trying to send money to his family, Miss Fanny persuades him to put his family in God's hands. When Lue's nephew dies of starvation in China, both his village in China and his Chinese coworkers in America blame Lue's failure to provide for his family as the cause of his nephew's death. Lue decides to go back to China as a missionary, but he soon realizes that the liberal beliefs and scientific knowledge that he has gained in America are incompatible with traditional Chinese values. With Miss Fanny's help he returns to America, where he devotes his life to the development of a frost-resistant orange and the *Lim Gim Gong* orange.

In life, Lue Gim Gong was ostracized by the Chinese-American community and discriminated against by white society, As the epilogue of the novel shows, even after his death, Lue Gim Gong remained unrecognized. Throughout the novel, McCunn convincingly shows the alienation and sorrow that Lue Gim Gong experiences as a person living in between cultures. She also gives him his due recognition for his accomplishments.

Stylistically, because the three narrators of the novel come from different racial/ethnic and class backgrounds, together they are able to create a complex narrative about race, gender, and class constructions in both China and the United States in the late 19th and early 20th centuries. By intertwining the three voices, McCunn not only recovers Lue Gim Gong's contributions that have been scarcely acknowledged, but also skillfully exposes the unfair racial, and class hierarchies from which this lack of acknowledgment originates.

Nan Ma

Worra, Bryan Thao   (1973–   )

Poet Bryan Thao Worra was born Thao Somnouk Silosoth on January 1, 1973, in Vientiane, Laos, and moved to the United States in July of the same year. He attended the Rudolf Steiner School in Ann Arbor, Michigan, and Otterbein College.

Worra's poetry draws on Lao and Hmong culture, the experience of resettlement in the United States, and everyday life in the Midwest, often employing humor, and self-conscious meditations on its uses, to dismantle and play upon ethnic stereotypes and the racial politics of art. In "Anthology," Worra recites and ridicules the expectations encountered by Asian-American writers writing in "Eastern Voices for Western Coffeehouses," declaring "I will not write / of white rice / or shades of yellow." In "Secrets," he jokes about putting his life in danger by disclosing the "secret to good pad thai." "Going Bamboo" conversely parodies the romantic appropriation and solemn glamorization of multiculturalism by white artists: "She's written of her journey / on the path of the Tai Chi Sword . . . Sure, she's Irish and drives an SUV / but she's got as much right to write as you and I." A poem depicting an interview with an elder Hmong shaman who prefers to talk of professional wrestling is entitled "The Spirit Catches You, and You Get Bodyslammed."

In chapbooks such as *The Tuk-Tuk Diaries: My Dinner With Clusterbombs* (published in 2003) and *Touching Detonations,* Worra also explores the afterlife of war in Laos embodied by the continued threat of unexploded ordnance (UXO). His poems have appeared in the literary anthology *Bamboo among the Oaks* and periodicals including the *Paj Ntaub Voice Hmong Literary Journal, Defenestration,* and *Speakeasy,* among others. Worra lives in Saint Paul, Minnesota, where he has organized poetry readings and art exhibitions and worked with organizations including the Hmong American Institute for Learning the SatJaDham Lao Literary Project. His awards include a Minnesota Playwrights' Center Many Voices Award in 2002 and a Minnesota State Arts Board Cultural Collaboration Award (with Mali Kouanchao) in 2005. Worra makes many of his poems available on his Web site (members.aol.com/thaoworra) in the form of e-chapbooks.

Alex Feerst

Yamada, Mitsuye (May) (1923–)

While she has published less extensively than some of her contemporaries, Mitsuye Yamada is an important figure in Japanese-American literature, as she is noted for her political and feminist activism as well as for her poetry. Born on July 5, 1923, in Fukuoka, Japan, to parents who were legally U.S. residents living abroad, Mitsuye Yamada (then Mitsuye Yasutaka) immigrated to the United States in 1926 when her parents returned home to Seattle, Washington. She became a naturalized U.S. citizen in 1955.

In 1942, pursuant to Executive Order 9066, Mitsuye's family was incarcerated at Minidoka Relocation Center in Idaho, an experience that would serve as the primary subject of her first and most widely known book, *Camp Notes* (1976). After signing a statement renouncing loyalty to Japan, she was released along with her brother to attend the University of Cincinnati in 1944. She later transferred to New York University, where she received her B.A. in 1947, and went on to the University of Chicago's graduate school, obtaining her M.A. in 1953. While living in Chicago, she met Yoshikazu Yamada, an artist, scientist, and U.S. Army veteran who was then pursuing a Ph.D. in inorganic chemistry at Purdue.

Mitsuye and Yoshikazu were married in 1950, first living in Chicago and then in Brooklyn. In the mid-1960s the couple—by now with a daughter, Jeni, and two sons, Stephen and Kai, in tow—relocated to Southern California, where their second daughter, Hedi, was born. In California, Mitsuye Yamada began teaching literature and creative writing at several colleges and universities. From 1966 to 1969 she was an instructor at California State University, Fullerton; she later joined Cypress College in Orange County, California, first as an instructor, and later as an associate professor of English and coordinator of the Women's Program in 1976.

Yamada, whose father was a translator and poet, began writing after her release from Minidoka in an attempt to come to terms with that experience. *Camp Notes,* a cycle of poems about her family's incarceration, examines "visibility" and "invisibility" as two unavoidable states of being for Japanese Americans, particularly for women. As presented in *Camp Notes,* life in Minidoka is a constant struggle between wanting to be "seen" as American and wanting to remain "invisible," undetectable by camp administrators so as to avoid danger and harm.

In "Evacuation," the opening poem, a young girl is told to smile by a *Seattle Times* photographer as she boards the bus to Minidoka; the child's photo is later printed in the *Times* over the caption: "Note smiling faces / a lesson to Tokyo." In "The Question of Loyalty," Yamada suggests that the twin desires for visibility and invisibility are symptomatic of an enforced identity crisis among incarcerated Japanese Americans, recalling her mother asking, "If I sign this / What will I be? / I am doubly loyal / to my American children / also to my own people. / How can double mean nothing?" The cycle closes with the widely reprinted "Cincinnati," in which the narrator, eager to be at last "in a real city / where / no one knew me," is met on the street by a "hissing voice that said / dirty jap / warm spittle on my right cheek." Looking at her soiled reflection in a shop window, the narrator ruefully observes, "Everyone knew me." A second collection of fiction and poetry, *Desert Run,* was published in 1988, and Yamada edited or contributed to several literary collections throughout the 1980s and 1990s.

Besides being a poet and editor, Yamada is a lifelong advocate of women's and ethnic minorities' rights. She founded the Multi-Cultural Women Writers of Orange County, and has served as a board member for Amnesty International (U.S.A.) and the Pacific American Asian Center. With NELLIE WONG, she was the subject of the 1981 public television documentary *Mitsuye and Nellie: Asian American Poets* and appeared as one of the primary interviewees in Yunah Hong's 2001 documentary *Between the Lines: Asian American Women's Poetry.*

Bibliography

Usui, Masami. "A Language of Her Own in Mitsuye Yamada's Poetry and Stories." *Studies in Culture and the Humanities* 5, no. 3 (1996): 1–17.

Yamada, Mitsuye. "Invisibility Is an Unnatural Disaster: Reflections of an Asian-American Woman." In *This Bridge Called My Back: Writings by Radical Women of Color,* edited by Cherríe Moraga, and Gloria Anzaldúa, 35–40. New York: Kitchen Table Press, 1981.

———. "A *MELUS* Interview: Mitsuye Yamada," by Helen Jaskoski. *MELUS* 15 (1988): 97–108.

Yamada, Mitsuye, Merle Woo, and Nellie Wong. *Three Asian American Writers Speak Out on Feminism.* Seattle: Red Letter Press, 2003.

Eric G. Waggoner

Yamamoto, Hisaye (Hisaye Yamamoto DeSoto) (1921–)

Hisaye Yamamoto may well be one of the most widely anthologized authors in the United States, but she considers "housewife" as the term that would best describe her occupation (Cheung 5). Yamamoto was born in Redondo Beach, California, in 1921, a mere three years before the 1924 Asian Exclusion Act was passed, to Japanese immigrant parents from Kumamoto. She grew up speaking Japanese and, like many of her peers, only began learning English in kindergarten. As a student at Compton Junior College, she majored in French, Spanish, German, and Latin. During World War II, she and her family were interned in Poston, Arizona, where she wrote a series of works for the camp newspaper, *The Poston Chronicle.* Few of these works were fiction, but she did publish a serialized mystery titled "Death Rides the Rails to Poston" as well as a short piece called "Surely I Must Be Dreaming." More of her work during this time was in journalism, a field she would later return to during a three-year span, between 1945 and 1948, when she worked as a reporter for the *Los Angeles Tribune.* After adopting a son in 1948, she volunteered to work at a Catholic Worker rehabilitation farm in Staten Island from 1953 to 1955. She met and married Anthony DeSoto in 1955, and the family returned to Los Angeles, where Yamamoto and DeSoto had four additional children. She lives in Southern California.

Yamamoto began publishing in literary journals in 1948, the same year she adopted her son Paul, then 5 months old. She turned to full-time creative writing when she was awarded one of the initial John Hay Whitney Opportunity Fellowships in 1950. She spent that year (1950–51) writing, and in the following year, "Yoneko's Earthquake" was included in *Best American Short Stories of 1952.* Martha Foley's yearly "Distinctive Short Stories" list also featured a number of Yamamoto's stories: "Seventeen Syllables" made the list in 1949; both "The Brown House" and "Yoneko's Earthquake" in 1951; and "Epithalamium" in 1960.

Her creative works have been widely reprinted in both anthologies and periodicals. In 1986

Yamamoto was awarded the American Book Award for Lifetime Achievement from the Before Columbus Foundation. The now-out-of-print anthology of her short stories from Kitchen Table: Women of Color Press was published two years later and was honored with the Award for Literature from the Association of Asian American Studies. Rutgers University Press reprinted the collection, SEVENTEEN SYLLABLES AND OTHER STORIES, in 1998.

Bibliography

Cheung, King-Kok. Introduction. *Seventeen Syllables and Other Stories*, 3–16. New Brunswick, N.J.: Rutgers University Press, 1998.

Cheung, King-Kok, and Stan Yogi. *Asian American Literature: An Annotated Bibliography*. New York: Modern Language Association, 1988.

Anne N. Thalheimer

Yamanaka, Lois-Ann (1961–)

A third-generation Japanese American, Yamanaka was born on the Hawaiian island of Molokai and grew up with her parents and three younger sisters in Pahala, a small sugar plantation village on the big island of Hawaii. Although her mother and father held fairly normal jobs as a schoolteacher and a principal, her father also practiced a more earthly and eccentric occupation as a self-employed hunter and taxidermist. Living in a small house filled with dead stuffed animals both contrasted with and complemented living on a vast, wild, and lush island. Yamanaka's family lived off the land; they kept their own animals, grew their own produce, and hunted their own meat. She frequently accompanied her father on his hunting expeditions for wild boar, sheep, and sharks for eating and stuffing.

As a native Hawaiian, Yamanaka grew up outside the island's privileged white populations. Most immigrants from Asian countries, particularly from Japan and the Philippines, had come to the islands in the 1800s to work on the sugarcane and coffee plantations. Due to a history of settlement by European Christian missionaries and American capitalists, Hawaii's native Polynesian community and Asian immigrant workers became second-class citizens. The rift between white and "other" in Hawaii solidified with the ensuing industrialization, land development, and consumerism of the islands in the middle and late 20th century.

The racial and cultural clash surrounding Yamanaka during her childhood profoundly influenced her writing, career, and use of language. As a child, she suffered ridicule and criticism from white teachers and white classmates for her "pidgin" English, a Hawaiian dialect spoken by most Asian Americans in Hawaii. This dialect is the language of Yamanaka's fictive Asian-American characters in Hawaii, where almost all of her short stories and novels are set. Just as her characters fight against institutional discrimination within the educational system, Yamanaka began her career with this goal in mind. She studied education at the University of Hawaii, where she earned a B.Ed. (1983) and an M.Ed. (1987), and went on to teach "at-risk" students in predominantly Asian-American and economically suffering areas of Honolulu. Due to her own personal experiences of discrimination caused by institutional racism in Hawaii's public schools, Yamanaka could especially relate to her students and help them navigate the sharp divide between white and "other" in Hawaiian society.

Yamanaka's island life has also infused her writing career with sharp realism and cultural criticism. Her first book, *Saturday Night at the Pahala Theater* (1993), set a precedent in her later novels for the wide use of pidgin English and a visceral portrayal of growing up Asian-American in Hawaii. Structured as a collection of verse poetry, or vignettes, *Saturday Night at the Pahala Theater* drew attention for its treatment of racial stereotypes, sexual violence, and adolescent angst. Yamanaka's young characters are "prematurely exposed to a racist and sexist world which blinds and debilitates them. . . . The authority figures in the work perpetuate this dark world of fear and ignorance" (Shim 86). These themes continue with Yamanaka's following novels: WILD MEAT AND THE BULLY BURGERS (1996), BLU'S HANGING (1997), *Heads by Harry* (1999), *Name Me Nobody* (1999, young adult fiction), *Father of the Four Passages* (2002), and *Behold the Many* (2006).

Major themes of her novels include the absence of the mother and subsequent loneliness of childhood and adolescence; sexual violence and psychological trauma; children's difficulty with using and acquiring the necessary language to narrate experience; lack of self-control; the difficulty of sexual maturation and awareness; the challenge of establishing self-expression, self-control, and self-confidence; the importance of the natural environment and living with the land; and institutionalized discrimination. Of her writing, Yamanaka has said "I am devoted to telling stories the way I have experienced them—cultural identity and linguistic identity being skin and flesh to my body."

Her books have received widespread acclaim in newspapers, magazines, and literary circles. Following her first major award, the Pushcart Prize for Poetry in 1993 for *Saturday Night,* Yamanaka received several grants from the National Endowment for the Humanities, a Carnegie Foundation Grant, the Lannan Literary Award (1998), and the Asian American Literary Award (1998). These awards, however, have not been received without controversy. After Yamanaka received the National Book Award from the Association for Asian American Studies for *Saturday Night at the Pahala Theater,* the Filipino caucus protested that one of the poems in the collection presented a racist portrait of Filipinos. When she received the same award for *Wild Meat and the Bully Burgers* the following year, protests from the Filipino caucus forced the association to rescind the award. The controversy escalated for a third year when Yamanaka received an additional award for *Blu's Hanging,* which includes a male Filipino character who sexually molests a child. Yamanaka currently lives with her husband and son in Honolulu, where she has started an all-ages writing school called Na'au: A Place for Learning and Healing.

Bibliography

Chiu, Monica. *Filthy Fictions: Asian American Literature by Women.* Walnut Creek, Calif.: AltaMira Press, 2004.

Johnson, Sarah Anne. *Conversations with American Women Writers.* University of New England Press: Lebanon, N.H., 2004.

Lim, Shirley Geok-lin, Larry E. Smith, and Wimal Dissanayake. *Transnational Asia Pacific: Gender, Culture, and the Public Sphere.* Urbana: University of Illinois Press, 1999.

Parikh, Crystal. "Blue Hawaii: Asian Hawaiian Cultural Production and Racial Melancholia." *Journal of Asian American Studies* (October 2002): 199–216.

Shim, Rosalee. "Power in the Eye of the Beholder: A Close Reading of Lois-Ann Yamanaka's *Saturday Night at the Pahala Theater." Hitting Critical Mass: A Journal of Asian American Cultural Criticism* 3, no. 1 (1995): 85–91.

Amy Lillian Manning

Yamashita, Karen Tei   (1951–   )

Yamashita initially established herself as a short-story writer and playwright before she became widely recognized for her novels such as her debut work, THROUGH THE ARC OF THE RAIN FOREST (1990), which won her both the American Book Award in 1991 and the Janet Heidinger Kafka Award in 1992; her second novel, BRAZIL-MARU (1992); and her third novel, TROPIC OF ORANGE (1997). She also published *Circle K Cycles* (2001), a collection of essays and short stories. Praised by critics for her unique style and dynamic themes, Yamashita boldly challenges common notions about sociopolitical issues and experiments with narrative techniques.

Yamashita was born and raised in Oakland, California, until her family moved to Los Angeles, where she spent most of her childhood. Upon graduating from high school, she went on to Carleton College, where she studied English and Japanese. During her junior year, she spent a year abroad in Japan as an exchange student, studying at Waseda University. Following graduation from Carleton, she began studying Portuguese in an intensive language program, and in 1974 Yamashita was awarded the Thomas J. Watson Fellowship to conduct research on Japanese immigration to Brazil, which began as a two-year research project. However, she ended up staying in Brazil for nine years, during which time she met and married architect/artist Ronaldo Lopes de Oliveira, with whom she has two children. While in Brazil, she published short stories such as "The Bath" (1975), published in *Amerasia Journal,* "Tuscano" (1975) and "Asako no Miya" (1979), published in *Rafu Shimpo.* Her first play, *Omen: An American Kabuki,* was performed in 1978.

When she returned to Los Angeles with her family in 1984, she began working for KCET, a local public television station, and between work and family she continued to write. Among her plays are *Hiroshima Tropical* (1984), *Kusei: An Endangered Species* (1986), *Hannah Kusoh* (1989), *Tokyo Carmen vs. L.A. Carmen* (1990), *GiLAwrecks* (1992), and *Noh Bozos* (1993). Her 1990 short story, "The Orange," won the American-Japanese National Literary Award and was published in the *Los Angeles Times Magazine.*

Following the completion of her third novel, Yamashita was awarded another Thomas J. Watson fellowship, which allowed her to return to Japan for a second time, from 1997 to 1998. During her stay, she researched Brazilians living in Japan, which became the source for *Circle K Cycles.* Presently, Yamashita resides in Gardena, California, and continues to write, while teaching literature as an assistant professor at the University of California at Santa Cruz.

An effective reading of Yamashita's works may begin with an examination of her representations of borders and border-crossings. This theme is indeed also a key to understanding the author, who has resided in three countries: the United States, Japan, and Brazil. As a writer she often puzzles critics, who struggle to examine her writing within a strictly Asian-American context. Recently, however, Ryuta Imafuku has proposed that there is a new concept of geography in Yamashita's writing, a new cartographic concept that reflects the freedom of movement across the borders. These conscious efforts to redefine and reexamine national and cultural borders are demonstrated in Yamashita's texts, which, Douglas Sugano says, "describe a world with increasingly permeable political borders." In essence, Yamashita's works continue to contribute to the growing body of discourse that attempts to challenge and transcend restrictive, nation-centered boundaries that have existed for centuries.

Bibliography

Imafuku, Ryuta. "The Latitude of the Fiction Writer: A Dialogue." Available online. URL: http://www.cafecreole.net /archipelago/Karen_Dialogue.html. Accessed October 21, 2006.

Murashige, Michael S. "Karen Tei Yamashita: An Interview," *Amerasia Journal* 20, no. 3 (1994): 49–59.

Sugano, Douglas. "Karen Tei Yamashita." In *Asian American Novelists,* edited by Emanuel Nelson, 403–408. Westport, Conn.: Greenwood Press, 2000.

Eliko Kosaka

Yamate, Sandra S. (1959–)

Children's writer, editor, and publisher, Sandra Yamate is a fourth-generation Japanese American who lives and works in Chicago. She graduated from the University of Illinois and Harvard Law School. After focusing for 10 years on the legal defense of insurance, she founded in 1990 an independent children's press based in Chicago called Polychrome Publishing, whose slogan is "stories of color for a colorful world." The main purpose of this press is filling a problematic gap in the American book market, namely the lack of stories featuring children of Asian ancestry as the main characters. By doing so, the press aims to provide positive models that young readers can emulate, to eliminate stereotypical, exoticized representations, and to promote religious tolerance and cultural understanding in a truly multiethnic society.

Sandra Yamate wrote two books: *Ashok, by Any Other Name* (1992) and *Char Siu Bao Boy* (2000). The first volume tells the story of a boy who finds it difficult to come to terms with his Indian name, Ashok. He is ashamed of it since every schoolmate seems to mispronounce it. Ashok decides to adopt an American name, but at the end of the volume and after many humorous mishaps, he decides to go back to his real name, following a long talk with Mr. Fletcher, a teacher of African descent who tells him the story of his great-grandfather, who, coming from Africa as a slave, had been forced to give up his African name and, with it, his cultural heritage and identity.

Char Siu Bao Boy tells the story of Charlie, a Chinese-American boy who enjoys eating *char siu bao* (Chinese barbecued pork buns) and brings them to school every day for lunch. His friends find the looks of the buns disgusting, and they persuade Charlie to eat ordinary food such as sandwiches and hotdogs. He tries for a while, just to be accommodating, but one day he goes to school with a *char siu bao* for each of his friends and asks them to taste the soft buns. Every child seems to like *char siu bao*s and from that moment onward Charlie is requested to bring them every day and to share the Chinese delicacy with his classmates.

Sandra Yamate taught Asian-American literature at DePaul University in Chicago and is currently the director of the American Bar Association's Commission on Racial and Ethnic Diversity.

Elisabetta Marino

Yamauchi, Wakako   (1924–)

Yamauchi's parents, Yasaku Nakamura (father) and Hamako Machida Nakamura (mother), immigrated to the Imperial Valley before World War II. Born in Westmoreland, California, Yamauchi was the third of the Nakamuras' four children. Her parents worked as tenant farmers because of the Alien Land Law, which did not allow Japanese to own land. Her parents spoke only Japanese, and Yamauchi learned English at school. Her family subscribed to a Japanese paper, in which Japanese-American short story writer HISAYE YAMAMOTO published English columns using her pen name, Napoleon. Yamamoto's works were Yamauchi's favorite. After the Great Depression and the 1940 earthquake when her parents' lettuce farm failed, her parents gave up farming, moved to Oceanside, California, and started a boardinghouse for Japanese immigrants and migrant workers. At a cooperative of Japanese farmers called Kumamoto Mura, Yamauchi met Yamamoto on several occasions.

At the outbreak of World War II, just as the Nakamuras paid off their debt from their boardinghouse, Yamauchi, her three siblings, and her parents were interned in Poston, Arizona, and her father died in the internment camp. It was at the camp that she met Yamamoto again. Yamauchi started contributing her art works to the *Poston Chronicle,* a camp newspaper to which Yamamoto contributed stories. After spending 18 months in the camp, Yamauchi moved to Chicago to work at a candy factory and started to go to theaters. She spent a short period of time at the Writers Guild of America's Open Door Project and later took two correspondence courses in short story writing with the University of California at Berkeley. She married Chester Yamauchi in 1948 and had a daughter, Joy, in 1955.

Yamauchi started writing short stories in her mid-30s. After her mother's death, Yamauchi found her mother's diary, written in Japanese, which she could not read. She realized that, because she had not known about her mother's life, she wanted to leave something of herself to her daughter Joy. After her short story, "AND THE SOUL SHALL DANCE," was rejected by various publishers, she started taking writing courses and learned that she was not writing for a white audience. In the 1970s Yamamoto encouraged her to contribute "And the Soul Shall Dance" to an anthology, *Aiiieeeee!: An Anthology of Asian American Writers* (1974). Her story caught the attention of Mako, the artistic director of the East West Players in Los Angeles. He encouraged her to transform the story into a play and gave her the Rockefeller Foundation grant for playwright-in-residence. *And the Soul Shall Dance* was performed as a play in Washington, D.C., New York, Hawaii, and Seattle. It also won the Los Angeles Critics' Circle Award for best new play in 1977 and was broadcast on PBS in 1978.

Kyoko Amano

Yankee Dawg You Die
Philip Kan Gotanda (1988)

The best known of Gotanda's theatrical works, *Yankee Dawg You Die* premiered in 1988 at the

Berkeley Repertory Theatre and was restaged in 1989 by Playwrights Horizons in New York.

Despite their common grounds as struggling Asian-American actors in a white-dominated entertainment industry, the two protagonists of the play, Vincent Chang and Bradley Yamashita, represent two polarities of the Asian-American experience: assimilation and ethnic consciousness. Vincent is a seasoned veteran of the stage and film (with an Oscar nomination under his belt) who prides himself on never turning down a role, however demeaning and stereotypical. Although Vincent was his childhood idol, the young and idealistic Bradley nevertheless passionately clings to the conviction that "every time you do one of those demeaning roles, the only thing lost is your dignity."

During their brief initial encounter at a Hollywood Hills party, Bradley muses, "I think the two of us meeting is very important. The young and the old. We can learn from each other." The plot revolves around the friendship that blossoms between the two and the lessons that they inevitably learn from each other.

In Bradley, full of purposeful vitality and determination, Vincent sees himself 35 years ago when he first embarked on an acting career. In the end, Vincent turns down a lucrative but typecast role in a major motion picture in order to star in an ethnic-based independent film about a Japanese-American family. Bradley, born Shigeo Nakata, begins to embrace his ethnic identity, which he had consciously negated in his ongoing pursuit of the American dream. Bradley realizes that what strides current artists such as him have been able to make owe much to the personal dedication and sacrifices made by early pioneers such as Vincent. Ironically, Bradley accepts the very role that Vincent rejects, in the belated realization that, as exemplified in Vincent's past career, the Asian-American actor's uphill battle for recognition must necessarily be paved with negotiations and compromises of personal principles.

The primary structure of *Yankee Dawg You Die,* a series of elaborate colloquies between the two dramatis personae, is interlaced with dramatic monologues, dream sequences, and lively song/dance skits. The play is also intertextually rich with excerpts from past television, movie, and play scripts, some reenacted verbatim but others satirically modified.

The play closes with a fervent outcry, "Why can't you hear what I'm saying? Why can't you see me as I really am?" This may well be an apt battle cry for all Asian-American writers across different literary genres who must endure and negotiate the inequities of a still discrimination-ridden society to finally find their voices and, more important, have their voices heard.

Kihan Lee

Yau, John   (1950–)

John Yau was born in Lynn, Massachusetts, to a Chinese mother of the Shanghai aristocracy and a father who was the son of an English mother and a Chinese father. Yau's parents refused to teach him Chinese, so he felt isolated from the children of Boston's Chinatown; yet he did not fit into the white schools he attended, either, because of his mixed racial heritage. His works of poetry and prose often try to reconcile, or at least understand, the feelings of being neither entirely Chinese nor entirely American.

Yau moved to New York City in 1975 to study with poet/art critic John Ashbery. Under Ashbery's tutelage, Yau developed a career as a freelance art critic and began to experiment with ways of creating identity in his poetry without relying on autobiography. Along with writing many essays about obscure artists, Yau's early work as a poet incorporated both visual art techniques and references to artists and their works. One collection of these "painterly poems" is "The School of Johns," which appears in *Radiant Silhouette* (1998). With artists and photographers, Yau also collaborated on several volumes of poetry such as *Postcards from Trakl* (1994) with prints by Bill Jensen and *Berlin Diptychon* (1995) with photographs by Bill Barrette.

In *The Sleepless Night of Eugene Delacroix* (1980), Yau shows the influence of painters such as Jasper Johns and Andy Warhol, both of whom produced works in series. Like them, Yau frequently creates work through a series of discreet paragraphs or stanzas (for example "Postcards from Nebraska"). Johns was also an influence in *Corpse and Mirror* (1983), which was selected by Ashbery for the National Poetry Series. The title of the volume is a reference to a sequence of Johns's paintings. Later in his career, Yau published monographs on both Warhol and Johns and taught art and writing at various institutions.

Yau is quoted as saying that he is a "poet who is too postmodern for the modernists and too modern for the postmodernists." Yet his books such as *Forbidden Entries* (1996) and *My Symptoms* (1998) are most noted for their dismantling of the wall dividing fiction from poetry, a strong postmodern theme. His earliest volumes, *The Reading of an Ever-Changing Tale* (1977) and *Sometimes: Poems* (1979), also present prose poems that criticize imperialism and begin to establish Yau as a postmodern writer who refuses to maintain a persona as either a poet, a storyteller, or an art critic.

His writings blend elements from many different genres to examine Asian-American identity. In the Hollywood poems of *Forbidden Entries,* for instance, Yau explores the stereotypes that adversely affect Asian-American experiences in the American film industry. Two short-story collections continue Yau's treatment of the themes of identity. *Hawaiian Cowboys* (1995) is a more conventional collection of stories. *My Symptoms,* however, integrates prose and poetry.

A fiction anthology Yau edited in 1998, *Fetish,* collects commissioned pieces that explore dimensions of voyeurism. *Borrowed Love Poems* (2001) continues Yau's interests in painters and other artists. *My Heart Is That Eternal Rose Tattoo,* also appearing in 2001, returns to the prose poems found in *Radiant Silhouette* and *Forbidden Entries.*

Bibliography

Chang, Juliana. Review of *Forbidden Entries, MELUS* 23, no. 3 (Fall 1998): 226–228.

Morris, Daniel. "'Death and Disaster': John Yau's Painterly Poems." In *Remarkable Modernisms: Contemporary American Authors on Modern Art,* edited by Daniel Morris, 41–60. Amherst: University of Massachusetts Press, 2002.

Xiaojing, Zhou. "Postmodernism and Subversive Parody: John Yau's 'Genghis Chan: Private Eye' Series." *College Literature* 31, no. 1 (Winter 2004): 73–104.

Patricia Kennedy Bostian

Year in Van Nuys, A
Sandra Tsing Loh   (2001)

In her send-up of Peter Mayle's *A Year in Provence* (a memoir of pleasurable living in the French countryside), SANDRA TSING LOH tells a tale of downward mobility in a less-than-glamorous suburb of Los Angeles. *A Year in Van Nuys* is a fictionalized account of Loh's experience as a writer seeking fame and fortune—or at least a living wage—while coping with life in the San Fernando Valley. Loh's narrator is an artist in crisis. She has reached her mid-thirties, the brilliant novel has not materialized, and she lives in one of the most celebrity-obsessed regions of America. Frustrated by a three-year writer's block, she is depressed, self-absorbed, envious of others, and embarrassed by her misery. "My mouth widens, Roman mask-like, into a bitter howl. 'Why why why not me me me me me me me me me me?'" (31).

Loh's tone throughout this book is edgy and comical. Her narrator's low self-esteem becomes a vehicle for satire as she discusses the things that conspire to keep her unfulfilled: a tacky environment, a bossy and successful big sister, unappreciative editors, fatuous promoters, bubbly television executives, her lack of swingy hair, and the bags under her eyes. The good things, too, are presented sardonically. Her "Technicolor World of Futility" (86) does have its moments, as with the take-out chicken gobbled over the sink and the Valium that comes with laser eye-bag surgery. Her partner is wonderfully supportive or at least passionately nonconfrontational, and her therapist, who speaks of the human psyche in terms of labyrinths and cave paintings, "understands how, sometimes, the most creative thing about a Writer can *be* her Block" (28).

In *A Year in Van Nuys,* Loh perfects the art of the whine. Her persona, neurotic and hyper-attentive to her neurosis, seems both familiar and new. She is a caricature of the angst-ridden creator but a postmodern caricature, self-reflexive and self-dramatizing to an absurd degree. Her text is checkered with dashes, exclamation points, italics, boldface, CAPS, and strikethroughs (as though the writer were editing herself even as she ferments). Quirky drawings, charts, lists, and "manuscript" pages sometimes interrupt her narratives. (A photograph of Bert Lahr as the Cowardly Lion bears the label "The King of Eye Bags" [169].) In effect, Loh presents a series of short takes on the tragicomedy of suffering for one's art before one knows exactly what that art will be.

But the book does trace an emotional curve, a movement from despondency to acceptance. Though the titles of its "seasonal" subdivisions— "The Winter of Our Discontent," "Spring without Bending Your Knees," "Summer Where We Winter," and "Fall of Our Dearest Expectations"—give no hint of redemption, the "Fall" section tells of a fortunate fall. To drop a set of crippling expectations is not an easy task, but Loh's narrator manages to do so, grumping all the while. If her year in Van Nuys does not bring a significant change in her circumstances, it does bring a grudging sense of maturity. The "Sandra" who tells this tale finally comes to terms with an outworn identity and decides to move on: "And so, I step out of the cracked dead shell of my Youth, and older, yet oddly lighter, I set off" (232).

Bibliography

Loh, Sandra Tsing. *A Year in Van Nuys.* New York: Crown, 2001.

Janis Butler Holm

Year of Impossible Goodbyes
Sook Nyul Choi (1991)

In this autobiographical novel, SOOK NYUL CHOI's narrator is 10-year-old Sookan Bak, who lives in Pyungyang, North Korea, in the spring of 1945, near the end of World War II, and during the Japanese occupation of North Korea. Choi wrote the novel as an adult, yet she effectively conveys a child-like view of the arresting horror and abject misery that are the consequences of war. Choi skillfully establishes the novel's underlying theme of preserving cultural identity when the narrator, Sookan, begins her story by remembering the courage of her grandfather and his insistence on meditating outside, despite his fear of the Japanese soldiers: "It has been thirty-six years since I have meditated in the warmth of a spring sun. Today, the Japanese soldiers will not keep me inside" (2). Choi juxtaposes the simple courage of Sookan's grandfather with the peaceful quietude of his meditation and prayer beneath his favorite pine tree, a tree that a few pages later is cut down by Japanese soldiers.

As the novel progresses, Choi develops each character's desire to hold onto cultural practices that are the constant target of attack by Japanese soldiers. Choi's protagonist keenly combines the innocent observations of a child with a more profound introspection brought on by the extraordinary circumstances of war and military occupation. Within the narrative, Choi demonstrates the interconnectedness of all life, past and present, as the novel weaves together the lives of Sookan's family with the political events in the world around them. Sookan and her brother learn their family's history when their mother explains each precious photo in an old, charred wooden box. The experiences of Sookan's grandfather also become an important part of the drive to preserve their family's cultural identity. Just before her grandfather dies, he asks her to wash his feet with lemon oil. As the old man's feet are revealed to her, Sookan is shocked at their condition, which was caused by the torture her grandfather suffered while in prison for being a part of the Korean resistance: "I held his toes in my hands. My eyes filled with tears. I wished that I could comfort these poor toes" (44).

Through Sookan's eyes, Choi probes the psychological effects of war and adversity on children. Young Sookan must decide, as her mother is detained by Russian soldiers, if she can continue the journey alone without her. Choi tenderly exposes the emotional turmoil inside Sookan, who is forced to grow up fast and deal with adult situations in a war-ravaged country. Amazingly, despite the horrors of war and the separation from her mother, Choi's protagonist retains her childlike idealism and a belief in the forces of hope, courage, and family, as well as her belief in the honor and tradition of her Korean heritage. At the end of the novel, Sookan and her brother Inchun are reunited with their father and older brothers in Seoul. Their mother, who was able to escape the Russians, joins them six months later.

Though the novel was initially intended for young adults, it has enjoyed success across all age groups. The lyrical self-validation of young Sookan's suspenseful journey to freedom highlights the remarkable power of the human heart.

Bibliography

Choi, Sook Nyul. *Year of Impossible Goodbyes*. Boston: Houghton Mifflin, 1991.

Debbie Clare Olson

Year of the Dragon, The   Frank Chin (1981)

The Year of the Dragon shows the disintegration of a Chinese-American family in San Francisco's Chinatown. A travel agent and Chinatown tour guide, Fred Eng is the 40-year-old, unmarried son of Pa Eng. Throughout the play, Fred strives for recognition from his father by sacrificing his ambition to become a writer, leaving college to run the family tourism business, supporting his younger sister through college, nursing his father when he is ill, and caring for his younger brother. The father, however, never acknowledges the father-son relationship in public because he feels ashamed of his son. Refusing to recognize his son's individuality and adulthood, the father verbally abuses the son and slaps him repeatedly. Moreover, the father insults the son by refusing to introduce him in the presence of eminent Chinatown citizens and by asking his white son-in-law instead of his son to edit his mayoral speech during the Chinese New Year. The play ends with Fred's final futile attempt at asking his father for once to recognize him as an individual.

The Year of the Dragon was first staged in 1974 at the American Place Theatre in New York City and a year later videotaped by Public Broadcasting Service for its "PBS Theatre in America." Reviews of the play have been mixed. Early reviews of the play often condemned the play as incomprehensible. Later criticism, however, tended to appreciate FRANK CHIN's concerns with identity and manhood and his attempts to dispel stereotypes about Chinese Americans.

Fu-jen Chen

Yep, Laurence Michael   (1948–)

Laurence Yep, author of more than 60 books for children and young adults, was born in San Francisco, California. His father, Yep Gim Lew, moved to the United States from China when he was 10, while his mother, Franche Lee, was born in Ohio and raised in West Virginia. Yep was brought up in a predominantly African-American and Hispanic area of San Francisco, where his family owned a grocery store, and attended St. Mary's Grammar School, a Catholic mission aiming at converting Chinese Americans. He soon experienced feelings of alienation and isolation, as described in his 1991 autobiography entitled *The Lost Garden*. He also began to see his existence as an intricate puzzle that could only be described in writing. In his African-American neighborhood, he played the role of the "all-purpose Asian" who could play the part of a Japanese or Korean soldier, depending on which war game was played on the playground. At school, due to his limited proficiency in Chinese (at home his parents spoke only English), he was also regarded as an outsider who did not get the jokes that his Chinese-American friends used to tell in Chinese so as not to be understood by the nuns. As he writes in his autobiography, he was not particularly proud of his cultural heritage. When he was a child, he wanted to be as American as possible and he was, therefore, scolded by the old-timers. He nonetheless absorbed his "Chineseness" through his grandmother, Marie Lee, who later inspired the character of the Chinese grandmother Paw Paw in Yep's 1977 young-adult novel CHILD OF THE OWL.

In high school, he was faced for the first time with white American culture. When he was 18, his English teacher, Reverend John Becker (to whom

The Lost Garden is dedicated) encouraged him to write his first science fiction story, which he managed to sell for one penny a word to a magazine. He initially chose this genre because it best mirrored his own sense of estrangement. Yep studied journalism at Marquette University, Milwaukee, in 1966–68, and there he met Joanne Ryder, his future wife, who further encouraged him to write. He earned his B.A. in 1970 from the University of California, Santa Cruz, and his Ph.D. in 1975 from the State University of New York, Buffalo. Besides winning numerous awards and honors for his novels and short stories, Yep has taught creative writing and literature in several universities including San Jose City College and the University of California, Santa Barbara.

Many of Yep's books, written mostly for juvenile and young adult audiences, deal with Chinese-American cultural heritage. *Dragonwings* (1975), inspired by the life of the Chinese-American inventor and aviator Fung Joe Guey, tells the story of Moon Shadow, a child who, at the beginning of the 20th century, moves from China to San Francisco's Chinatown in order to join his father, whose dream is to build a flying machine. The novel explores the life of Chinese immigrants in America at the turn of the century, thus drawing a realistic portrait of their bachelors' society. *The Rainbow People* (1989) is a collection of 20 folktales originally narrated in the 1930s by Chinese immigrants in Oakland's Chinatown and retold by Yep. Most of the stories are set in China and are grouped into five sections (each one preceded by an introduction to the theme): Tricksters, Fools, Virtues and Vices, Chinese America, and Love. *Dragon's Gate* (1993) depicts the life of a young Chinese railroad worker who moves in the 1860s to California to join his father and uncle. Even though he feels alienated in the new land, he wants to learn as much as possible in order to take technology back to China and help release his country from the shackles of the Manchu invaders.

In 1995 Yep published *Hiroshima*, a children's book dealing with the nuclear bombing in Japan and its painful aftermath, as seen through the eyes of young Sachi. Two years later, he wrote another children's book, *The Dragon Prince,* a Chinese version of *The Beauty and the Beast,* in which a farmer is taken prisoner by a huge, golden dragon and is freed only when his youngest and most talented daughter named Seven agrees to marry the dragon. Seven is carried by the dragon to his kingdom beneath the sea, where he turns into a handsome prince. One of her sisters tries to murder her and take her place, but she is reunited with her husband eventually. In this story Yep reflects on the stereotypes about physical appearances that still affect children of Asian origin. In *The Imp That Ate My Homework* (1998), Yep tells the story of Jim, a U.S.–born child of Chinese descent whose teacher has given him the troublesome task of writing about his grandparents. With his grandmother dead, Jim has to write about Grandpop, who regularly scolds him for not being Chinese enough and for not being interested in the stories about life back in China. When Jim's homework gets eaten by a green Chinese imp, however, Jim and his grandpop team up to get rid of it.

Yep's recent volumes include *The Amah* (1999), in which a young girl has to face more responsibilities and misses her ballet practice when her mother begins to work as a nanny; *Dream Soul* (2000), set in West Virginia in 1927, describing cultural clashes between Chinese and Western festivities; and *Spring Pearl, the Last Flower* (2002), set in 1857 during the Opium War in China.

Yep's works help solve a critical problem in children's literature, namely the absence of books dealing with the history of Asian Americans and with the problems faced by children of Asian-Pacific heritage as they come to terms with their cultural identity and develop strategies to deal with biases and contradictions.

Bibliography

Johnson-Feelings, Dianne. *Presenting Laurence Yep.* New York: Twayne Publishers, 1995.

Kutzer, M. Daphne, ed. *Writers of Multicultural Fiction for Young Adults: A Bio-Critical Sourcebook.* Westport, Conn.: Greenwood Press, 1996.

Rochman, Hazel. *Against Borders: Promoting Books for a Multicultural World.* Chicago: American Library Association, 1993.

Elisabetta Marino

Yew, Chay   (1967–   )

Born and raised in Singapore, playwright and director Chay Yew came to America at the age of 16 to study at Pepperdine University in 1982. Thereafter, he went on to Boston University for a Master of Science degree. As director of the Mark Taper Forum's Asian Theatre Workshop in Los Angeles since 1995, resident director at Los Angeles's East West Players, and artistic director of Northwest Asian American Theatre in Seattle, Yew has received many awards and grants, becoming one of the most outstanding Asian Americans on the national and international stage. In 1995 *Asian Week* listed Yew among the 50 leading Asian Americans.

In his works, Yew attempts to move beyond embedded stereotypes of Asian Americans. Instead, he offers a theatre that poses questions about the complexities of Asian-Americans' struggles to negotiate their identities and to survive in America. A distinguishing characteristic of Yew's plays is the poetic, sensual language and witty diction found in the characters' dialogues and monologues that are often extended. His first play, *As If He Hears* (1988), was banned in Singapore because of its positive depiction of a homosexual character, which the government perceived as inappropriate to societal values. Yew's groundbreaking work, *Porcelain,* won London's 1992 prestigious Fridge Award for Best Play. *Porcelain* depicts a young British-Chinese man shooting his lover in a public restroom, unsettling expectations of the model minority myth, and bringing to bear the power politics of race, gender, and sex in interracial relationships. Breaking taboos in writing about sexuality and violence, *Porcelain* anticipates the reform in the British Sexual Offences (Amendment) Bill in 1994. *A Language of Their Own* premiered at the New York Shakespeare Festival and won Gay and Lesbian Alliance Against Defamation's Best Play of 1995. Set in Boston, this play depicts the intimacies of two Asian Americans and their break-up after one of them discovers he is HIV-positive. Significantly, this play crystallizes the human and social components of illness and relationships between patient and partners, dramatizing the implications of health and sickness.

The Hyphenated American (2002) is a collection of four plays. *Red* (1998) traces the journey of an Asian-American author in search of her father, who used to perform female roles in the Beijing Opera. *Wonderland* (1999) presents the conflicts and travails of an Asian-American family. *Scissors* (2000) sketches the intercultural affinities between two septuagenarians—an Asian and a Caucasian American—in 1929. *A Beautiful Country* (1998), first presented in Los Angeles, is a multimedia production in which aspects of citizenship, community, diaspora, and memory are examined. *A Beautiful Country* mobilizes the figure of an immigrant drag queen Miss Visa Denied to displace conventional modes of representation and to stage a tapestry of Asian-American immigrant history between 1871 and 1998.

Yew's works are never merely about sex or sexuality. Rather, they provoke us to critically rethink how race and the regulation of sexuality refract off notions of home and nation, racial and sexual identifications, and cultural and patriarchal anxieties. By focusing on transnational labor, cultural mobility, and the contradictory practices of Asian Americans, Yew raises questions about class, ethical choices, and complicity in global capitalism. Yew's earlier plays attend to themes of whiteness, cultural belonging, interiority, and sexuality; in recent plays, however, Yew seems to shift his focus to reconsidering the future of the gay community, establishing affiliations across color and gender lines, examining aging and poverty, and tracking Asian immigrant history in relation to the larger context of America. In *Question 27, Question 28* (2003), Yew documents the many constituencies and struggles of Japanese-American female internees of World War II by drawing on historical archives and interviews. In *A Distant Shore* (2005), a play set in a Southeast Asian rubber plantation in the 1920s, Yew undertakes the political project of remapping new geographies of characters and places. In *Home: Places Between Asia and America* (1998), his multicultural adaptation of Federico García Lorca's *The House of Bernarda Alba* (2000), Yew shows his ongoing interest in, and commitment to, carving out complicated characters, exploring the interface between the local and transnational, and narrating Asian-American stories to both Asian-American and non–Asian-American audiences.

Bibliography

Diehl, Heath A. "Beyond the Silk Road: Staging a Queer Asian America in Chay Yew's *Porcelain.*" *Studies in the Literary Imagination* 37, no. 1 (Spring 2004): 149–167.

Drukman, Steven. "Chay Yew: The Importance of Being Verbal." *American Theatre* 12, no. 9 (November 1995): 58–60.

Lim, January. "Father Knows Best: Reading Sexuality in Ang Lee's *The Wedding Banquet* and Chay Yew's *Porcelain.*" In *Reading Chinese Transnationalism: Society, Literature, Film,* edited by Philip Holden and Maria N. Ng, 143–160. Hong Kong: Hong Kong University Press, 2006.

Poole, Ralph. "Learning to Be Chinese: Postcolonial Mourning in Asian Drama in English." In *Race and Religion in Contemporary Theatre and Drama in English,* edited by Bernard Reitz, 109–117. Trier, Germany: Wissenschafflicher, 1999.

Román, David. "Los Angeles Intersections: Chay Yew." In *The Color of Theater: Race, Culture, and Contemporary Performance,* edited by Roberta Uno, 237–252. New York: Continuum, 2002.

January Lim

Yokohama, California   Toshio Mori   (1949)

Although originally planned for publication by Caxton Printers in 1942, *Yokohama, California*'s release date was indefinitely postponed after the Japanese attack on Pearl Harbor on December 7, 1941. In the ensuing seven years until its appearance, TOSHIO MORI had been incarcerated in Utah's Topaz Internment Camp for Japanese Americans and the small audience that once existed for such a book dried up due to the postwar era's political conservatism and anti-Japanese sentiment. Both the collection and its author languished in obscurity for three decades until the University of Washington Press republished *Yokohama, California* in 1985 due to academics' growing interest in reviving the progenitors of Asian-American literature.

The version of *Yokohama, California* that eventually appeared in 1949, however, differed from the original collection by two stories, "Tomorrow Is Coming, Children" and "Slant-Eyed Americans," which Caxton Printers added to soften postwar resentment and to influence its critical reception. These stories ended up changing the book's tone. Instead of presenting a series of innocuous vignettes based upon the daily lives of Japanese Americans in California's San Leandro, Mori's hometown, these two stories darken the collection by presenting the patriotism of Japanese Americans during World War II with no mention of the cruelties of camp life that exist as subtext. Even though the grandmother in "Tomorrow Is Coming, Children" is stuck inside an internment camp and the family in "Slant-Eyed Americans" have a son heading off to war, the negative historical conditions that destroyed so many lives never appear, creating a book that panders to its audience as much as it presents a realistic slice of Japanese-American life.

Upon its resurrection in the mid-1980s, however, many ethnic scholars noticed how *Yokohama, California* fit into both Japanese and American literary traditions, which made it an important text through which to discuss Japanese-American syncretism. Although Mori's minimalist writing style, anticlimactic plots, and single community setting derived from his love of Sherwood Anderson's *Winesburg, Ohio,* his major American literary influence, Lawson Inada notes that Mori's stories also fit into the ancient Japanese *shibai* tradition of folk drama and humorous skits. A story such as "The Eggs of the World" fits into this tradition by depicting a friendship that ends over a misunderstanding with a metaphorical egg. Similarly, Gayle K. Sato notes that many stories in Mori's cycle illustrate the Japanese cultural concept of *amae,* where an adult yearns to be loved without putting forth the work or effort to have his or her desires fulfilled by an explicit request. "The Woman Who Makes Swell Doughnuts," Mori's most anthologized story from the collection, illustrates *amae* by having its narrator travel throughout Yokohama solely to provide indulgent listening and complimentary flattery to community members, especially to the woman who makes "swell" doughnuts.

Yokohama, California is often credited as being the first collection of published short stories written by a Japanese American. While the book gained some notoriety because of this, it is deemed important today for providing a glimpse into the everyday prewar life of Japanese Americans. For this, along with Mori's creative fusion of Japanese and American literary traditions, *Yokohama, California* will be remembered and read.

Bibliography

Bedrosian, Margaret. "Toshio Mori's California Koans," *MELUS* 15, no. 2 (1988): 47–55.
Sato, Gayle K. "(Self) Indulgent Listening: Reading Cultural Difference in *Yokohama, California*," *Japanese Journal of American Studies* 11 (2000): 129–46.

Shawn Holliday

Yoo, David   (1974)

David Yoo grew up in Connecticut, which is the setting for his first novel, *Girls for Breakfast* (2005). He graduated from Skidmore College and attended a graduate program at the University of Colorado-Boulder. He currently lives in Boston, Massachusetts, but frequently returns to his childhood home to do "research," poring through yearbooks "to try to revive the dusty memories of being a teenager." In *Girls for Breakfast,* Yoo explores themes of insider/outsider, identity politics, sexuality and friendship through the lens of a teenage Korean-American boy growing up in an all-white town. In addressing how his own youth influenced his writing, Yoo says, "In my writing I tend to explore the negative moments from my life, the uncomfortable feelings that are perpetually bubbling under the surface. . . . Self-sabotage. Hatred. Self-loathing . . . I write because it's the one thing that makes me feel truly *alive*." Yoo's sister, Paula Yoo, is the author of the picture book *Sixteen Years in Sixteen Seconds: The Sammy Lee Story* (2005).

Girls for Breakfast follows Nick Park's coming-of-puberty from third grade until high school graduation. Nick's adolescence in Renfield Hills, the fifth-richest town in Connecticut, is a paradox; he has to climb to the top of his neighborhood to go home after school each day, yet he is perpetually stuck at the bottom of the social totem pole. He becomes curious about girls in the fourth grade when his friend shows him *Playboy*. Unable to detach himself from the magazines, Nick spends the rest of his youth obsessing over the different women in his life—his friends' moms, the bus driver, teachers, and all of the popular girls in school. Every so often he has real contact with a girl but he fouls up all these relationships. Nick's sole claim to popularity is his place on the soccer team with the jocks, but they do not accept him either. The boys make fun of him for being socially awkward and exclude him from their weekly class parties. Despite his social standing, which he squarely blames on his Korean ethnicity, Nick is, by senior prom, finally dating Maggie, one of the hottest girls in his class.

Girls for Breakfast is an important contribution because it speaks to Korean-American young men about peer pressure, sexuality, and identity for those growing up in all-white areas—topics rarely addressed anywhere. By rejecting his Korean ethnicity, Nick rejects his parents, their Korean church, food, and everything and everyone he associates with being Korean. However, since he is simultaneously outcast by the popular white kids at school, he is paralyzed between the two cultures. He finally creates his unique identity near the end of high school. Besides Sheri Cooper Sinykin's *The Buddy Trap,* John Son's *Finding My Hat,* and MARIE G. LEE'S *NECESSARY ROUGHNESS,* this novel is one of the few stories to reflect the realities of Korean-American males.

Sarah Park

Yun, Mia   (?–)

Born and raised in South Korea, Yun moved to the United States in 1981 to study creative writing at the City College of New York. Yun's appreciation of female legacies is a forceful theme in her writing as she explores women's relationships with their families and communities.

Yun's novels to date include *House of the Winds* (2000) and *Translation of Beauty* (2004). Her memory of standing in a cabbage patch during a sunny spring afternoon, blissful and secure with her mother, was Faulknerian in its power to inspire Yun's first novel. Readers first meet the girl narrator, Kyung-A, in this dreamlike setting in Korea. The novel chronicles the maturation of Kyung-A, who begins to understand Korean women's lives through listening to traditional myths, neighborhood women's talk, and family stories. Her mother, identified as Young Wife, weaves stories of magic to create a world of possibility and security for her children during the upheaval in the immediate aftermath of World War II. Young Wife's magical tales for Kyung-A are tempered, however, by the reality of women's suffering, which is revealed during other forms of female storytelling such as Young Wife's bitter conversations with her own mother. To avoid the forced prostitution of young Korean women by Japanese soldiers, Young Wife's mother had hastily arranged a marriage for Young Wife, who protested against spending her life with an unknown, older man. Ultimately her marriage fails to provide security for her and their children because he turns out to be a dreamer who pursues financially fruitless schemes.

The strong mother and dreamer father appear again as characters in the next novel, *Translations of Beauty*, this time as the parents of South Korean twin girls Inah and Yunah. When four-year-old Inah's face is tragically scarred, the family's pain and guilt force them to adopt the American dream in hopes of remaking their lives. If a woman's face truly determined her fortune in Korea, then Inah would never be accepted, so the family hoped that their sacrifice of moving to America would enable Inah to realize her potential by working hard. Reality confronts the family's dream, however, when Inah suddenly drops out of graduate school at Oxford University and backpacks to India. In an attempt to bridge familial and geographical distances, the twins' mother insists that Yunah find Inah and tour Italy with her. In Italy, Inah earnestly

studies the museum exhibits while Yunah studies her scarred sister juxtaposed against the glorious art and landscape. Then Yunah learns to see beyond what the guidebooks instruct and recognizes beauty in unexpected places and people. Since her conversations with Inah are tense and terse, Yunah communicates with her twin by writing letters. In the process, she realizes that her family has been using Inah's scar as an excuse for their own unfulfilled expectations of their sacrifices.

The power of writing and articulated agency are fruitful ways for thinking about Yun's novels. Yun intends for her novels to serve as bridges between the past and present and between individuals. Her stories present multiple voices of Korean and Korean-American women who defy silence and stereotyping. Both novels were first written in English, a foreign language for the author. Yun's use of English to express Korean memories and Korean-American experiences helps her to capture the bilingualism and dual vision of immigrants. It also points to the complexities wrought by the immigration experience.

Karen Li Miller

Yung, Wing (Rong Hong) (1828–1912)

The educator, reformer, and autobiographer Yung Wing was born in the village of Nanping, Guangdong Province in China. At the urging of his father, Yung attended Mrs. Gutzlaff's School in Macao and the Morrison Educational Society School in Hong Kong, where English was the language of instruction. Yung's father, a poor farmer, believed that such an education could lead to success in a changing world. In 1847 Yung came to America to continue his education, first at Monson Academy in Massachusetts and ultimately at Yale College, from which he graduated in 1854, becoming the first Chinese person to earn a bachelor's degree in the United States. Inspired by his own educational experiences, Yung resolved to reform China by making similar opportunities possible for other Chinese.

After returning to China in 1855, Yung spent several years as an interpreter and businessman, but he never relinquished his dream of reform. In 1863 Yung convinced Governor-General Zeng Guofan to underwrite the education of more than 100 Chinese boys in America who would eventually return to help reform China. Yung oversaw these students at the Chinese Educational Mission, based in Hartford, Connecticut. During these happy years, Yung married Mary Louise Kellogg, who bore him two sons, Morrison and Bartlett, but political circumstances on both sides of the Pacific were against him. As the result of increasing anti-Chinese sentiment in America and increasing skepticism among conservative officials in China about the value of such an education, the mission was recalled in 1881. Hence on this and other occasions, Yung's plans met with resistance and, sometimes, failure.

At the age of 74, Yung started to write *My Life in China and America.* The autobiography attempts to enhance his reputation, casting the best light on his successes and ignoring or explaining the reasons behind his failures. Like the autobiographies of Benjamin Franklin, Frederick Douglass, and Booker T. Washington, Yung's text presents a rags-to-riches rise made possible by hard work and education. Besides allying himself with this traditional strain in American autobiography, Yung borrows language from his contemporary Theodore Roosevelt to contest Roosevelt's own logic. In 1899 Roosevelt claimed that China deserved no respect because Chinese people were incapable of living what he called the "strenuous life." As a retort, Yung declares in his autobiography, "in a strenuous life one needs to be a dreamer in order to accomplish possibilities" (65). Indeed, Yung accentuates his strenuous experiences in his autobiography to counter Roosevelt's accusation, but he also articulates a dream of education made possible not only for the few but for everyone: "The time will soon come . . . when the people of China will be so educated and enlightened as to know what their rights are, public and private, and to have the moral courage to assert and defend them whenever they are invaded" (73).

Since the publication of Yung's book in 1909 and his death in 1912 in Hartford, both he and his book have received mixed reviews. Contemporary American reviewers respected Yung, and most recent Chinese scholars have valorized him as a pioneer in Chinese educational reform. In Asian-American literary criticism of the 1980s and 1990s, Yung's autobiography fared poorly, having been labeled assimilationist and inauthentic. More recently, scholars have put forth more balanced views that seek to place Yung's life and work in historical perspective. While critics will continue to argue about Yung's personal choices and literary purposes, his book remains significant in the history of Asian-American literature for its early date of publication, its adaptation of American autobiographical conventions, and its account of a remarkable, influential, and bicultural figure.

Bibliography

Cheung, Floyd. "Early Chinese American Autobiography: Reconsidering the Works of Yan Phou Lee and Yung Wing." *a/b: Auto/Biography Studies* 18 (2003): 45–61.

———. "Political Resistance, Cultural Appropriation, and the Performance of Manhood in Yung Wing's *My Life in China and America* (1909)." In *Form and Transformation in Asian American Literature,* edited by Zhou Xiaojing and Samina Najmi, 77–100. Seattle: University of Washington Press, 2003.

Harris, Paul William. "A Checkered Life: Yung Wing's American Education." *American Journal of Chinese Studies* 2 (1994): 87–107.

Lee, Bill Lann. "Yung Wing and the Americanization of China." *Amerasia Journal* 1 (1971): 25–32.

Ling, Amy. "Reading Her/stories against His/stories in Early Chinese American Literature." In *American Realism and the Canon,* edited by Tom Quirk and Gary Scharnhorst. Newark: University of Delaware Press, 1994. 69–86.

Yung, Wing. *My Life in China and America.* New York: Holt, 1909.

Floyd Cheung

BIBLIOGRAPHY OF MAJOR WORKS BY ASIAN-AMERICAN WRITERS

⌒⌒⌒

Compiled by Jina Lee

Abbasi, Talat. *Bitter Gourd and Other Stories.* Karachi: Oxford University Press, 2001.

Abdullah, Shaila. *Beyond the Cayenne Wall: Collection of Short Stories.* New York: iUniverse, 2005.

Abu-Jaber, Diane. *Arabian Jazz.* New York: Random House, 1995.

————. *Crescent.* New York: Norton, 2003.

————. *The Language of Baklava: A Memoir.* New York: Pantheon, 2005.

Adachi, Jiro. *The Island of Bicycle Dancers.* New York: St. Martin's Press, 2004.

Ai. *Cruelty.* Boston: Houghton Mifflin, 1973.

————. *Dread.* New York: Norton, 2003.

————. *Fate: New Poems.* Boston: Houghton Mifflin, 1991.

————. *Greed.* New York: Norton, 1993.

————. *Killing Floor.* Boston: Houghton Mifflin, 1979.

————. *Sin.* Boston: Houghton Mifflin, 1986.

————. *Vice: New And Selected Poems.* New York: Norton, 1999.

Alexander, Meena. *The Bird's Bright Ring.* Calcutta: Writers Workshop, 1976.

————. *Fault Lines.* New York: Feminist Press, 1993.

————. *House of a Thousand Doors.* Washington D.C.: Three Continents Press, 1988.

————. *I Root My Name.* Calcutta: United Writers, 1977.

————. *Illiterate Heart.* Evanston, Ill.: Triquarterly, 2002.

————. *In the Middle Earth.* New Delhi: Enact, 1977.

————. *Manhattan Music.* San Francisco: Mercury House, 1997.

————. *Nampally Road.* San Francisco: Mercury House, 1991.

————. *Night-scene, the Garden.* New York: Red Dust, 1991.

————. *Raw Silk.* Evanston, Ill.: Triquarterly, 2004.

————. *River and Bridge.* Toronto: TSAR, 1996.

————. *The Shock of Arrival: Reflections on Postcolonial Experience.* Boston: South End Press, 1996.

————. *Stone Roots.* New Delhi: Arnold Heinemann, 1980.

————. *The Storm: A Poem in Five Parts.* New York: Red Dust, 1989.

————. *Without Place.* Calcutta: Writers Workshop, 1977.

————. *Women in Romanticism: Mary Wollstonecraft, Dorothy Wordsworth, and Mary Shelley.* Savage, Md.: Barnes & Noble, 1989.

————, ed. *Indian Love Poems.* New York: Everyman's Library/ Knopf, 2005.

Ali, Agha Shahid. *The Beloved Witness: Selected Poems.* New York: Viking Penguin, 1992.

———. *Bone-Sculpture.* Calcutta: Writers Workshop, 1972.

———. *Call Me Ishmael Tonight.* New York: Norton, 2003.

———. *The Country without a Post Office.* New York: Norton, 1997.

———. *The Half-Inch Himalayas.* Middletown, Conn.: Wesleyan University Press, 1987.

———. *In Memory of Begum Akhtar and Other Poems.* Calcutta: Writers Workshop, 1979.

———. *A Nostalgist's Map of America: Poems.* New York: Norton, 1991.

———. *The Rebel's Silhouette: Selected Poems by Faiz Ahmed Faiz.* Translated by Agha Shahid Ali. Amherst: University of Massachusetts Press, 1995.

———. *Rooms Are Never Finished.* New York: Norton, 2001.

———. *A Walk through the Yellow Pages.* Tucson: SUN/gemini Press, 1987.

———, ed. *Ravishing DisUnities: Real Ghazals in English.* Middletown, Conn.: Wesleyan University Press, 2000.

Ali, Samina. *Madras on Rainy Days.* New York: Farrar, Straus and Giroux, 2004.

Aoki, Brenda Wong. *Mermaid Meat: A Piece for Symphony.* Excerpt. In *Extreme Exposure: An Anthology of Solo Performance Texts from the Twentieth Century,* edited by Jo Bonney, 270–271. New York: Theatre Communications Group, 2000.

———. *The Queen's Garden.* In *Contemporary Plays by Women of Color,* edited by Kathy A. Perkins and Roberta Uno, 14–31. New York: Routledge, 1996.

———. *Random Acts of Kindness.* Excerpt. In *Extreme Exposure: An Anthology of Solo Performance Texts from the Twentieth Century,* edited by Jo Bonney, 267–270. New York: Theatre Communications Group, 2000.

Bacho, Peter. *Cebu.* Seattle: University of Washington Press, 1991.

———. *Dark Blue Suit and Other Stories.* Seattle: University of Washington Press, 1997.

———. *Nelson's Run.* Holliston, Mass.: Willowgate Press, 2002.

Barroga, Jeannie. *Walls.* In *Unbroken Thread: An Anthology of Plays by Asian American Women,* edited by Roberta Uno, 201–60. Amherst: University of Massachusetts Press, 1993.

———. *Talk-Story.* In *But Still, Like Air, I'll Rise: New Asian American Plays,* edited by Velina Hasu Houston, 1–47. Philadelphia: Temple University Press, 1997.

Brainard, Cecilia Manguerra. *Acapulco at Sunset and Other Stories.* Manila: Anvil, 1995.

———. *Magdalena.* Austin, Tex.: Plain View Press, 2002.

———. *Philippine Women in America.* Quezon City, Philippines: New Day, 1991.

———. *Song of Yvonne.* Quezon City, Philippines: New Day, 1991.

———. *When the Rainbow Goddess Wept.* 1994. New York: Plume, 1995.

———. *Woman With Horns and Other Stories.* Quezon City, Philippines: New Day, 1987.

Bulosan, Carlos. *America Is in the Heart.* 1946. Seattle: University of Washington Press, 1973.

———. *Bulosan: An Introduction with Selections.* Edited by E. San Juan, Jr. Manila: National Book Store, 1983.

———. *Chorus for America: Six Philippine Poets.* Los Angeles: Wagon and Star, 1942.

———. *The Cry and the Dedication.* Edited by E. San Juan, Jr. Philadelphia: Temple University Press, 1995.

———. *If You Want to Know What We Are: A Carlos Bulosan Reader.* Edited by E. San Juan, Jr. Minneapolis: West End Press, 1983.

———. *The Laughter of My Father.* New York: Harcourt, 1944.

———. *Letter from America.* Prairie City, Ill.: J.A. Decker, 1942.

———. *Now You Are Still and Other Poems.* Manila: Kalikasan, 1990.

———. *On Becoming Filipino: Selected Writings of Carlos Bulosan.* Edited by E. San Juan, Jr. Philadelphia: Temple University Press, 1995.

———. *Sound of Falling Light: Letters in Exile.* Edited by Dolores S. Feria. Quezon City: University of the Philippines Press, 1960.

———. *The Voice of Bataan.* New York: Coward-McCann, 1943.

Cao, Lan. *Monkey Bridge.* New York: Penguin Books, 1997.

Carbo, Nick. *Andalusian Dawn.* Cincinnati: Cherry Grove Press, 2004.

———. *El Grupo McDonald's.* Chicago: Tia Chucha Press, 1995.

———. *Secret Asian Man.* Chicago: Tia Chucha Press, 2000.

Cha, Theresa Hak Kyung. *Dictée.* New York: Tanam, 1982.

Chai , May-Lee. *The Girl from Purple Mountain* (Co-author). New York: St. Martin's, 2004.

———. *Glamorous Asians.* Indianapolis: University of Indianapolis Press, 2004.

———. *My Lucky Face.* New York: Soho Press, 1997.

Chan, Jeffery Paul. *Eat Everything Before You Die: A Chinaman in the Counterculture.* Seattle: University of Washington Press, 2004.

Chin, Frank, Jeffery Paul Chan, Lawson Fusao Inada, and Shawn Wong, eds. *Aiiieeeee!: An Anthology of Chinese American and Japanese American Literature.* New York: Meridian, 1991.

Chan, Jeffery Paul, Frank Chin, Lawson Fusao Inada, and Shawn Wong, eds. *The Big Aiiieeeee!: An Anthology of Chinese American and Japanese American Literature.* New York: Penguin, 1991.

Chang, Diana. *Earth, Water, Light: Poems Celebrating the East End of Long Island.* Brentwood, N.Y.: Binham Wood Graphics, 1991.

———. *Eye to Eye.* New York: Harper and Row, 1974.

———. *The Frontiers of Love.* New York: Random House, 1956.

———. *The Horizon Is Definitely Speaking.* Port Jefferson, N.Y.: Backstreet Editions, 1982.

———. *The Only Game in Town.* New York: Signet, 1963.

———. *A Passion for Life.* New York: Random House, 1961.

———. *A Perfect Love.* New York: Grove, 1978.

———. *What Matisse Is After.* New York: Contact House, 1984.

———. *A Woman of Thirty.* New York: Random House, 1959.

Chang, Lan Samantha. *Hunger.* New York: Penguin, 1998.

———. *Inheritance.* New York: Norton, 2004.

Chang, Leonard. *Dispatches from the Cold.* Seattle: Black Heron Press, 1998.

———. *The Fruit 'n Food.* Seattle: Black Heron Press, 1996.

———. *Over the Shoulder.* New York: HarperCollins/Ecco, 2000.

———. *Underkill.* New York: St. Martin's Minotaur, 2003.

Chao, Patricia. *Mambo Peligroso.* New York: Harper-Collins, 2005.

———. *Monkey King.* New York: HarperCollins, 1997.

Cheng, Terrence. *Sons of Heaven.* New York: Harper-Collins, 2002.

Chin, Frank. *Born in the USA: A Story of Japanese America, 1889–1947.* New York: Rowman & Littlefield, 2002.

———. *Bulletproof Buddhists and Other Essays.* Honolulu: University of Hawaii Press, 1998.

———. *The Chickencoop Chinaman and the Year of the Dragon.* Seattle: University of Washington Press, 1981.

———. *The Chinaman Pacific and Frisco R. R. Co.* Minneapolis: Coffee House, 1988.

———. *Donald Duk.* Minneapolis: Coffee House, 1991.

———. *Gunga Din Highway.* St. Paul, Minn.: Coffee House Press, 1994.

Chin, Frank et al., eds. *Aiiieeeee!: An Anthology of Chinese American and Japanese American Literature.* New York: Meridian, 1991.

———. *The Big Aiiieeeee!: An Anthology of Chinese American and Japanese American Literature.* New York: Penguin, 1991.

Chin, Marilyn Mei Ling. *Dwarf Bamboo.* New York: Greenfield Review Press, 1987.

———. *The Phoenix Gone, the Terrace Empty.* Minneapolis: Milkweed Editions, 1994.

———. *Rhapsody in Plain Yellow.* New York: Norton, 2002.

Chiu, Christina. *Eating Disorder Survivors Tell Their Stories.* New York: Rosen, 1998.

———. *Lives of Notable Asian-Americans: Literature and Education.* New York: Chelsea House, 1995.

———. *Teen Guide to Staying Sober.* New York: Rosen, 1998.

———. *Troublemaker and Other Saints*. New York: Penguin, 2001.

Choi, Sook Nyul. *Echoes of the White Giraffe*. Boston: Houghton Mifflin, 1993.

———. *Gathering of Pearls*. Boston: Houghton Mifflin, 1994.

———. *Year of Impossible Goodbyes*. Boston: Houghton Mifflin, 1991.

Choi, Susan. *American Woman*. New York: HarperCollins, 2003.

———. *The Foreign Student*. New York: HarperCollins, 1998.

Chong, Denise. *The Concubine's Children*. New York: Penguin, 1996.

———. *The Girl in the Picture: The Story of Kim Phuc, the Photograph, and the Vietnam War*. New York: Viking, 1998.

Chong, Ping. *Kind Ness. Plays in Progress* 8.9 (1986): 1–43.

———. *Nuit Blanche*. In *Between Worlds: Contemporary Asian-American Plays,* edited by Misha Berson, 2–28. New York: Theatre Communications Group, 1990.

———. *Snow. Plays in Progress* 10, no. 9 (1988): 1–62.

Chu, Louis Hing. *Eat a Bowl of Tea*. Seattle: University of Washington Press, 1979.

Daswani, Kavita. *For Matrimonial Purposes*. New York: G. P. Putnam, 2003.

———. *The Village Bride of Beverly Hills*. New York: G. P. Putnam, 2004.

Dawesar, Abha. *Babyji*. New York: Anchor Books, 2005.

———. *Miniplanner*. San Francisco: Cleis Press, 2000.

Desani, Govindas Vishnudas. *All about H. Hatterr: A Gesture*. London: Aldor, 1948.

———. *All about H. Hatterr, Etc*. Rev. ed. New York: Farrar, Straus and Young, 1951.

———. *All about H. Hatterr: A Novel*. 2nd rev. ed. New York: Farrar, Straus and Giroux, 1970.

———. *All about H. Hatterr: A Novel*. 3rd rev. ed. New York: Lancer Books, 1972.

———. *All about H. Hatterr: A Novel*. 4th rev. ed. Preface by Anthony Burgess. Penguin Modern Classics series. London: Penguin, 1972. Reprint,

New Delhi: Arnold Heinemann, 1985. Reprint, Kingston, N.Y.: McPherson, 1986. Reprint, New Delhi: Penguin Books India, 1998.

———. *Hali: A Poetic Play*. Foreword by T. S. Eliot and E. M. Forster. London: Saturn Press, 1950. Reprint, Calcutta: Writers Workshop, 1967.

———. *Hali and Collected Stories*. Kingston, N.Y.: McPherson, 1991. [Includes *Hali* and 23 stories.]

Divakaruni, Chitra Banerjee. *Arranged Marriage*. New York: Doubleday, 1995.

———. *Dark Like the River*. Calcutta: Writers Workshop, 1987.

———. *Leaving Yuba City: New and Selected Poems*. New York: Doubleday, 1997.

———. *The Mistresses of Spices*. New York: Doubleday, 1997.

———. *Queen of Dreams*. Detroit: Thomson/Gale, 2004.

———. *The Reason for Nasturtiums*. Berkeley, Calif.: Berkeley Poets Workshop and Press, 1990.

———. *Sister of My Heart*. New York: Doubleday, 1999.

———. *The Unknown Errors of Our Lives*. New York: Doubleday, 2001.

———. *The Vine of Desire*. New York: Doubleday, 2002.

Eaton, Winnifred. *The Heart of Hyacinth*. New York: Harper, 1901.

———. *The Honorable Miss Moonlight*. New York: Harper, 1912.

———. *A Japanese Blossom*. New York: Harper, 1906.

———. *A Japanese Nightingale*. New York: Harper, 1901.

———. *The Love of Azalea*. New York: Dodd, Mead, 1904.

———. *Miss Numé of Japan: A Japanese-American Romance*. 1899. Reprint, Baltimore: Johns Hopkins University Press, 1999.

———. *Sunny-San*. New York: George H. Doran, 1922.

———. *Tama*. New York: Harper, 1910.

———. *The Wooing of Wisteria*. New York: Harper, 1902.

Far, Sui Sin (Edith Maude Eaton). *Mrs. Spring Fragrance and Other Writings*. Edited by Amy Ling and Annette White-Parks. Urbana: University of Illinois Press, 1995.

Fenkl, Heinz Insu. *Memories of My Ghost Brother.* New York: Dutton, 1996.

Fong-Torres, Ben. *Hickory Wind: The Life and Times of Gram Parsons.* Edited by Leslie Wells. New York: Simon & Schuster, 1991.

———. *The Hits Just Keep on Coming.* San Francisco: Backbeat Books, 1998.

———. *Rice Room: Growing up Chinese-American—From Number Two Son to Rock 'n' Roll.* New York: Penguin, 1994.

Fulbeck, Kip. *Paper Bullets: A Fictional Autobiography.* Seattle: University of Washington Press, 2001.

———. *Part-Asian, 100% Hapa.* San Francisco: Chronicle Books, 2006.

Furutani, Dale. *Death in Little Tokyo: A Ken Tanaka Mystery.* New York: St. Martin's Press, 1996.

Ganesan, Indira. *Inheritance.* New York: Knopf, 1998.

———. *Journey.* New York: Knopf, 1990.

Ghose, Zulfikar. *The Art of Creating Fiction.* London: Macmillan, 1991.

———. *Confessions of a Native Alien.* London: Routledge, 1965.

———. *The Contradictions.* London: Macmillan, 1966.

———. *Crump's Terms.* London: Macmillan, 1975.

———. *Don Bueno.* New York: Holt, 1984.

———. *The Fiction of Reality.* London: Macmillan, 1984.

———. *Figures of Enchantment.* New York: Harper-Collins, 1986.

———. *Hamlet, Prufrock and Language.* New York: St. Martin's Press, 1978.

———. *The Incredible Brazilian: The Beautiful Empire.* London: Macmillan, 1975.

———. *The Incredible Brazilian: A Different World.* London: Macmillan, 1978.

———. *The Incredible Brazilian: The Native.* London: Macmillan, 1972.

———. *Jets from Orange.* London: Macmillan, 1967.

———. *The Loss of India.* London: Routledge, 1964.

———. *A Memory of Asia.* Austin, Tex.: Curbstone, 1984.

———. *The Murder of Aziz Khan.* New York: John Day, 1969.

———. *A New History of Torments.* New York: Holt, 1982.

———. *Selected Poems.* Oxford: Oxford University Press, 1991.

———. *Shakespeare's Mortal Knowledge: A Reading of the Tragedies.* New York: St. Martin's Press, 1993.

———. *The Triple Mirror of the Self.* London: Bloomsbury, 1992.

———. *The Violent West.* London: Macmillan, 1972.

Gotanda, Philip Kan. *Yankee Dawg You Die.* New York: Dramatists Play Service, 1991. Reprinted in *New American Plays.* Introduction by Peter Filichia. Portsmouth, N.H.: Heinemann, 1992, 77–124; in *Fish Head Soup and Other Plays.* Introduced by Michael Omi. Seattle: University of Washington Press, 1995, 69–130; in *Playwrights of Color.* Edited by Meg Swanson and Robin Murray. Yarmouth, Me.: Intercultural Press, 1999, 129–57.

Hagedorn, Jessica. *Dogeaters.* New York: Pantheon, 1990.

———. *The Gangster of Love.* New York: Houghton Mifflin, 1996.

Hahn, Kimiko. *Air Pocket.* Brooklyn, N.Y.: Hanging Loose Press, 1989.

———. *The Artist's Daughter.* New York: Norton, 2004.

———. *Earshot.* Brooklyn, N.Y.: Hanging Loose Press, 1992.

———. *Mosquito and Ant.* New York: Norton, 1999.

———. *The Unbearable Heart.* New York: Kaya Productions, 1995.

Hammad, Suheir. *Born Palestinian, Born Black.* New York: Harlem River Press, 1996.

———. *Drops of this Story.* New York: Harlem River Press, 1996.

———. *Zaatar Diva.* New York: Cypher, 2006.

Han, Suyin (Rosalie Chou). *. . . . And the Rain My Drink.* Boston: Little, Brown, 1956.

———. *Destination Chungking, an Autobiography.* With Marian Manly. Boston: Little, Brown, 1942.

———. *Eldest Son: Zhou Enlai and the Making of Modern China, 1898–1976.* New York: Hill and Wang, 1994.

———. *The Morning Deluge: Mao Tse Tung and the Chinese Revolution, 1893–1954.* Boston: Little, Brown, 1972.

———. *My House Has Two Doors: China, Autobiography, History.* London: Jonathan Cape, 1980.

———. *Wind in the Tower: Mao Tse Tung and the Chinese Revolution, 1949–1976.* Boston: Little, Brown, 1976.

Hayslip, Phung Thi Le Ly. *Child of War, Woman of Peace.* With James Hayslip. New York: Doubleday, 1993.

———. *When Heaven and Earth Changed Places: A Vietnamese Woman's Journey from War to Peace.* With Jay Wurts. New York: Doubleday, 1989.

Hazo, Samuel John. *As they Sail.* Fayetteville: University of Arkansas Press, 1999.

———. *Blood Rights.* Pittsburgh: University of Pittsburgh Press, 1968.

———. *The Holy Surprise of Right Now.* Fayetteville: University of Arkansas Press, 1996.

———. *Just Once.* Pittsburgh: Autumn House Press, 2002.

———. *Stills.* New York: Simon and Schuster, 1989.

Him, Chanrithy. *When Broken Glass Floats: Growing Up Under the Khmer Rouge.* New York: Norton, 2000.

Hirahara, Naomi. *Gasa-Gasa Girl.* New York: Dell, 2005.

———. *Snakeskin Shamisen.* New York: Dell, 2006.

———. *Summer of the Big Bachi.* New York: Dell, 2004.

Ho, Minfong. *The Clay Marble.* New York: Farrar, Straus and Giroux, 1991.

———. *Rice Without Rain.* London: Deutsch, 1986.

———. *Sing to the Dawn.* New York: HarperCollins/ William Morrow, 1975.

Holthe, Tess Uriza. *When the Elephants Dance.* New York: Random House/Crown, 2002.

Hongo, Garrett. *The Buddha Bandits down Highway 99.* With Alan Chong Lau and Lawson Fusao Inada. Mountain View, Calif.: Buddhahead, 1978.

———. *The River of Heaven: Poems.* New York: Knopf, 1988.

———. *Volcano: A Memoir of Hawai'i.* New York: Knopf, 1995.

———. *Yellow Light: Poems.* Middletown, Conn.: Wesleyan University Press, 1982.

Hosokawa, Bill. *Colorado's Japanese Americans from 1886 to the Present.* Boulder: University Press of Colorado, 2005.

———. *Nisei: The Quiet Americans.* New York: William Morrow, 1969.

———. *Out of the Frying Pan: Reflections of a Japanese American.* Boulder: University Press of Colorado, 1989.

———. *Thirty-Five Years in the Frying Pan.* New York: McGraw-Hill, 1978.

———. *Thunder in the Rockies.* New York: William Morrow, 1976.

———. *The Two Worlds of Jim Yoshida* (with Jim Yoshida). New York: William Morrow, 1972.

Hosseini, Khaled. *The Kite Runner.* New York: Riverhead Books, 2003.

Houston, Jeanne Wakatsuki. *Farewell to Manzanar.* New York: Houghton Mifflin, 1973.

Houston, Velina Hasu. *Asa Ga Kimashita* (Morning has broken). In *The Politics of Life: Four Plays by Asian American Women,* edited by Velina Houston. Philadelphia: Temple University Press, 1993.

———. *Tea.* In *Unbroken Thread: An Anthology of Plays by Asian American Women,* edited by Roberta Uno, 155–200. Amherst: University of Massachusetts Press, 1993.

Huynh, Jade Ngoc Quang. *South Wind Changing.* Saint Paul, Minn.: Graywolf Press, 1994.

Hwang, Caroline. *In Full Bloom.* New York: Dutton, 2003.

Hwang, David Henry. *Family Devotions.* 1983. Reprinted in *Broken Promises: Four Plays.* New York: Avon, 1983, 101–68; in *FOB and Other Plays.* Foreword by Maxine Hong Kingston. New York: New American Library, 1990, 87–146; in *Trying to Find Chinatown: The Selected Plays.* New York: Theatre Communications Group, 2000, 89–150.

———. *F. O. B.* 1979. Reprinted in *FOB and Other Plays.* Foreword by Maxine Hong Kingston. New York: New American Library, 1990, 2–49; in *Trying to Find Chinatown: The Selected Plays.* New York: Theatre Communications Group, 2000, 1–51.

———. *Golden Child.* 1998. New York: Dramatists Play Service, 1999.

———. *M. Butterfly.* 1988. New York: Penguin, 1989.

Hyun, Peter. *In the New World. The Making of a Korean American.* Honolulu: University of Hawai'i Press, 1995.

———. *Man Sei! The Making of a Korean American.* Honolulu: University of Hawai'i Press, 1986.

Iizuka, Naomi. *36 Views.* Woodstock, N.Y.: Overlook Press, 2003.

Inada, Lawson Fusao. *Before the War: Poems As They Happened.* New York: Morrow, 1971.

———. *The Buddha Bandits down Highway 99.* With Garrett Hongo and Alan Chong Lau. Mountain View, Calif.: Buddhahead, 1978.

———. *Drawing the Line.* Minneapolis: Coffee House Press, 1997.

———. *Legends from Camp.* Minneapolis: Coffee House Press, 1992.

Inada, Fusao, et al., eds. *Aiiieeeee!: An Anthology of Chinese American and Japanese American Literature.* New York: Meridian, 1991.

———. *The Big Aiiieeeee!: An Anthology of Chinese American and Japanese American Literature.* New York: Penguin, 1991.

Ishigaki, Ayako. *Restless Waves: My Life in Two Worlds.* Feminist Press. New York: Feminist Press at CUNY, 2004.

Jaisohn, Philip. *Hansu's Journey.* Philadelphia: Philip Jaisohn and Co., 1921 or 1922.

———. *My Days in Korea and Other Essays.* Edited by Sun-pyo Hong. Seoul, Korea: Institute for Modern Korean Studies, Yonsei University, 1999.

Jen, Gish. *Love Wife.* New York: Knopf, 2004.

———. *Mona in the Promised Land.* New York: Vintage, 1996.

———. *Typical American.* Boston: Houghton Mifflin, 1991.

———. *Who's Irish?: Stories.* New York: Random House, 1999.

Jhabvala, Ruth Prawer. *Amrita.* New York: Norton, 1958. (First published as *To whom she will.* London: Allen and Unwin, 1955).

———. *A Backward Place.* New York: Norton, 1965.

———. *Esmond in India.* London: Allen and Unwin, 1958; New York: Norton, 1958.

———. *An Experience of India.* London: John Murray, 1972; New York: Norton, 1972.

———. *Get Ready for Battle.* London: John Murray, 1962; New York: Norton, 1963.

———. *Heat and Dust.* London: John Murray, 1975; New York: Harper and Row, 1976.

———. *The Householder.* London: John Murray, 1960; New York: Norton, 1960.

———. *How I Became a Holy Mother and Other Stories.* London: John Murray, 1976; New York: Harper and Row, 1976.

———. *In Search of Love and Beauty.* London: John Murray, 1983.

———. *Like Birds, Like Fishes and Other Stories.* London: John Murray, 1963; New York: Norton, 1964.

———. *The Nature of Passion.* London: Allen and Unwin, 1956; New York: Norton, 1957.

———. *A New Dominion.* London: John Murray, 1972. (Also published as *Travellers.* New York: Harper and Row, 1973).

———. *Out of India.* New York: Morrow, 1986.

———. *Poet and Dancer.* London: Penguin, 1994.

———. *Shards of Memory.* London: Murray, 1995.

———. *A Stronger Climate: Nine Short Stories.* London: John Murray, 1968.

———. *The Three Continents.* London: John Murray, 1987.

———. *To Whom She Will.* London: Allen and Unwin. 1955. (Published as *Amrita.* New York: Norton, 1958).

———. *Travellers.* New York: Harper and Row, 1973. (Published as *A New Dominion.* London: John Murray, 1972).

Jin, Ha. *The Bridegroom: Stories.* New York: Pantheon, 2000.

———. *The Crazed.* New York: Knopf, 2002.

———. *In the Pond.* Cambridge, Mass.: Zoland, 1998.

———. *Waiting.* New York: Pantheon, 1999.

———. *War Trash.* New York: Pantheon, 2004.

Joseph, Lawrence. *Before Our Eyes.* New York: Farrar, Straus and Giroux, 1993.

———. *Codes, Precepts, Biases, and Taboos: Poems 1973–1993.* New York: Farrar, Straus and Giroux, 2005.

———. *Curriculum Vitae.* Pittsburgh: University of Pittsburgh Press, 1988.

———. *Into It.* New York: Farrar. Straus and Giroux, 2005.

———. *Lawyerland: What Lawyers Talk About When They Talk About The Law.* New York: Penguin, 1997.

———. *Shouting At No One.* Pittsburgh: University of Pittsburgh Press, 1983.

Kadohata, Cynthia. *The Floating World.* New York: Viking Press, 1989.

———. *The Glass Mountains.* New York: ereads.com, 1999.

———. *In the Heart of the Valley of Love.* Berkeley: University of California Press, 1992.

———. *Kira-Kira.* New York: Atheneum, 2004.

Kaneko, Lonny. *Coming Home from Camp.* Waldron, Wash.: Brooding Heron, 1986.

———. "Nobody's Hero." In *Asian American Literature: A Brief Introduction and Anthology,* edited by Shawn Wong, 147–156. New York: Harper, 1996.

———. "The Shoyu Kid." In *The Big Aiiieeeee!: An Anthology of Chinese American and Japanese American Literature,* edited by Jeffery Paul Chan, Frank Chin, Lawson Fusao Inada, and Shawn Wong, 304–313. New York: Penguin, 1991.

Kang, Younghill. *East Goes West: The Making of an Oriental Yankee.* 1937. New York: Kaya Productions, 1997.

———. *The Grass Roof.* 1931. Chicago: Follett, 1966.

———. *The Happy Grove.* New York: Charles Scribner's Sons, 1933.

Keller, Nora Okja. *Comfort Woman.* New York: Viking, 1997.

———. *Fox Girl.* New York: Viking, 2002.

Keltner, Kim Wong. *Buddha Baby.* New York: HarperCollins, 2005.

———. *The Dim Sum of All Things.* New York: HarperCollins, 2004.

Kim, Myung Mi. *The Bounty.* Minneapolis: Chax Press, 1996.

———. *Commons.* Berkeley: University of California Press, 2002.

———. *Dura.* Los Angeles: Sun and Moon Press, 1999.

———. *Under Flag.* Berkeley: Kelsey St. Press, 1991.

Kim, Patti. *A Cab Called Reliable.* New York: St. Martin's Press, 1997.

Kim, Richard E. *The Innocent.* Boston: Houghton Mifflin, 1968.

———. *The Martyred.* New York: George Brazilier, 1964.

———. *Lost Names.* 1970. Los Angeles: University of California Press, 1998.

Kim, Ronyoung (Gloria Han). *Clay Walls.* 1986. Seattle: University of Washington Press, 1990.

Kim, Suki. *The Interpreter.* New York: Farrar, Straus and Giroux, 2003.

Kim, Yongik. *Blue in the Seed.* Boston: Brown and Company, 1964.

———. *The Shoes From Yang San Valley.* New York: Doubleday, 1971.

Kingston, Maxine Hong. *China Men.* 1980. New York: Vintage International, 1989.

———. *The Fifth Book of Peace.* New York: Knopf, 2003.

———. *Tripmaster Monkey: His Fake Book.* 1989. New York: Vintage International, 1990.

———. *The Woman Warrior: Memoirs of a Girlhood among Ghosts.* 1976. New York: Vintage International, 1989.

Kirchner, Bharti. *Darjeeling.* New York: St. Martin's Press, 2002.

———. *Pastries.* New York: St. Martin's Press, 2003

———. *Sharmila's Book.* New York: Dutton, 1999.

———. *Shiva Dancing.* New York: Dutton, 1998.

Kogawa, Joy. *Itsuka.* 1981. New York: Anchor Doubleday, 1994.

———. *Obasan.* 1992. New York: Anchor Doubleday, 1994.

Kuo, Alex. *Chinese Opera.* Hong Kong: Asia 2000, 1998.

———. *Lipstick and Other Stories.* Hong Kong: Asia 2000, 2001.

Lahiri, Jhumpa. *Interpreter of Maladies.* Boston: Houghton Mifflin, 1999.

———. *The Namesake.* Boston: Houghton Mifflin, 2003.

Lam, Andrew. *Perfume Dreams: Reflections on the Vietnamese Diaspora.* Berkeley: Heyday, 2005.

Lam, Andrew et al., eds. *Once Upon a Dream: The Vietnamese American Experience.* San Jose, Calif.: San Jose Mercury News, 1995.

Lau, Evelyn. *Choose Me: A Novella and Stories.* Toronto: Doubleday, 1999.

———. *Fresh Girls and Other Stories.* Toronto: HarperCollins, 1993.

———. *In the House of Slaves.* Toronto: Coach House Press, 1994.

———. *Inside Out: Reflections on a Life So Far.* Toronto: Doubleday, 2001.

———. *Oedipal Dreams.* Victoria, B.C.: Beach Holme, 1992.

———. *Other Women.* Toronto: Random House, 1995.

———. *Runaway, Diary of a Street Kid.* Toronto: HarperCollins, 1989.

———. *Treble.* Vancouver, B.C.: Polestar Book Publishers, 2005.

———. *You Are Not Who You Claim.* Victoria, B.C.: Porcepic Books, 1990.

Le Thi Diem Thuy. *The Gangster We Are Looking For.* New York: Knopf, 2003.

Lee, Chang-Rae. *Aloft.* New York: Penguin, 2004.

———. *Gesture Life.* New York: Riverhead, 1999.

———. *Native Speaker.* New York: Putnam/Riverhead, 1995.

Lee, C.Y. *The Flower Drum Song.* New York: Farrar, Straus and Cudahy, 1957.

Lee, Don. *Country of Origin.* New York: Norton, 2004.

———. *Yellow.* New York: Norton, 2001.

Lee, Gus. *Chasing Hepburn: A Memoir of Shanghai, Hollywood, and a Chinese Family's Fight for Freedom.* New York: Harmony Books, 2003.

———. *China Boy.* London: Robert Hale, 1992.

———. *Honor and Duty.* New York: Ivy Books, 1995.

———. *No Physical Evidence.* New York: Fawcett Columbine, 1998.

———. *Tiger's Tail.* New York: Knopf, 1996.

Lee, Helie. *In the Absence of Sun.* New York: Crown Publishing, 2002.

———. *Still Life with Rice.* New York: Simon and Schuster, 1996.

Lee, Li-Young. *The City in Which I Love You.* New York: BOA, 1990.

Lee, Marie G. *Finding My Voice.* New York: Houghton Mifflin, 1992.

———. *Necessary Roughness.* New York: HarperCollins, 1997.

———. *Saying Goodbye.* New York: Houghton Mifflin, 1994.

———. *Somebody's Daughter.* Boston: Beacon, 2005.

Lee, Mary Paik. *Quiet Odyssey: A Pioneer Korean Woman in America.* Edited by Sucheng Chan. Seattle: University of Washington Press, 1990.

Leong, Russell. *The Country of Dreams and Dust.* Minneapolis: West End Press, 1993.

———. *Phoenix Eyes and Other Stories.* Seattle: University of Washington Press, 2000.

Li, Ling-ai (Gladys). *Children of the Sun in Hawaii.* Lexington, Mass.: D. C. Heath and Company, 1944.

———. *Life Is for a Long Time: A Chinese Hawaiian Memoir.* New York: Hasting House, 1972.

Lim, Shirley Geok-lin. *Among the White Moon Faces: An Asian-American Memoir of Homelands.* New York: Feminist Press, 1996.

———. *Crossing the Peninsula and Other Poems.* Kuala Lumpur, Malaysia: Heinemann Writing in Asia Series, 1980.

Liu, Aimee E. *Cold Mountain.* New York: Warner Books, 1998.

———. *Face.* New York: Warner Books, 1994.

———. *Flash House.* New York: Warner Books, 2003.

———. *Solitaire.* New York: Harper and Row, 1979.

Loh, Sandra Tsing. *Depth Takes a Holiday.* New York: Riverhead Books, 1996.

———. *A Year in Van Nuys.* New York: Crown Publishing, 2001.

Loh, Vyvyane. *Breaking the Tongue.* New York: Norton, 2004.

Lord, Bette Bao. *Eight Moon.* New York: Harper and Row, 1964.

———. *Legacies: A Chinese Mosaic.* New York: Knopf, 1990.

———. *The Middle Heart.* New York: Knopf, 1996.

———. *Spring Moon.* New York: Harper and Row, 1981.

———. *The Year of the Boar and Jackie Robinson.* New York: HarperCollins, 1984.

Louie, David Wong. *The Barbarians are Coming.* New York: Putnam, 2000.

———. *Pangs of Love.* New York: Knopf, 1991.

Lum, Darrell H. Y. "Encountering Sorrow." In *The Quietest Singing,* edited by Darrell H.Y Lum, Joseph Stanton, and Estelle Enoki, 134–156. Honolulu: Bamboo Ridge Press, 2000.

———. *Sun: Short Stories and Drama.* Honolulu. Bamboo Ridge Press, 1980.

———. *Pass On, No Pass Back.* Honolulu: Bamboo Ridge Press, 1990.

Mah, Adeline Yen. *Chinese Cinderella.* New York: Delacorte, 1999.

———. *Falling Leaves: The True Story of an Unwanted Chinese Daughter.* New York: John Wiley, 1998.

———. *A Thousand Pieces of Gold: A Memoir of China's Past through Its Proverbs.* New York: HarperCollins, 2002.

———. *Watching the Tree: A Chinese Daughter Reflects on Happiness, Tradition, and Spiritual Wisdom.* New York: Broadway Books, 2001.

Maki, John M. *Government and Politics in Japan: The Road to Democracy.* New York: Praeger, 1964.

———. *Japanese Militarism: Its Cause and Cure.* New York: Knopf, 1945.

Massey, Sujata. *The Bride's Kimono.* New York: HarperCollins, 2001.

———. *The Floating Girl.* New York: HarperCollins, 1999.

———. *The Flower Master.* New York: HarperCollins, 2000.

———. *The Pearl Diver.* New York: HarperCollins, 2004.

———. *The Salaryman's Wife.* New York: HarperCollins, 1997.

———. *The Samurai's Daughter.* New York: HarperCollins, 2003.

———. *The Typhoon Lover.* New York: HarperCollins, 2006.

———. *Zen Attitude.* New York: HarperCollins, 1998.

Matsueda, Pat. *The Fish Catcher.* Honolulu: Petronium Press, 1985.

———. *Stray.* Honolulu: El León and Manoa Books, 2006.

———. *X.* Honolulu: Communica Press, 1983.

Matsuoka, Takashi. *Autumn Bridge.* New York: Bantam Doubleday Dell, 2004.

———. *Clouds of Sparrows.* New York: Bantam Doubleday Dell, 2002.

McCunn, RuthAnne Lum. *The Moon Pear.* Boston: Beacon Press, 2000.

———. *Thousand Pieces of Gold: A Biographical Novel.* Boston: Beacon Press, 1988.

———. *Wooden Fish Songs.* New York: Penguin, 1996.

Meer, Ameena. *Bombay Talkie.* New York: High Risk Book, 1994.

Mehta, Ved Parkash. *Daddyji.* New York: Farrar, Strauss and Giroux, 1971.

———. *Face to Face.* Boston: Atlantic–Little, Brown, 1957.

———. *The Ledge Between the Streams.* New York: Norton, 1984.

———. *Mamaji.* New York: Oxford University Press, 1979.

Min, Anchee. *Becoming Madame Mao.* New York: Houghton Mifflin, 2000.

———. *Red Azalea.* New York: Pantheon, 1994.

Mirikitani, Janice. *Awake in the River.* San Francisco: Isthmus Press, 1978.

———. *Shedding Silence: Poetry and Prose.* Berkeley, Calif.: Celestial Arts, 1987.

———. *We, the Dangerous: New and Selected Poems.* London: Virago, 1995. Reprint, Berkeley, Calif.: Celestial Arts, 1995.

Mochizuki, Ken. *Baseball Saved Us.* New York: Lee and Low, 1993.

———. *Beacon Hill Boys.* New York: Scholastic, 2002.

———. *Heroes.* New York: Lee and Low, 1995.

———. *Passage to Freedom: The Sugihara Story.* New York: Lee and Low, 1997.

Mohanraj, Mary Anne. *Bodies in Motion.* New York: HarperCollins, 2005.

Mori, Kyoko. *Polite Lies: On Being A Woman Caught Between Cultures.* New York: Henry Holt, 1997.

———. *Stone Field, True Arrow.* New York: Henry Holt, 2000.

Mori, Toshio. *Yokohama, California.* 1949. Seattle: University of Washington Press, 1985.

Mukerji, Dhan Gopal. *Bunny, Hound and Clown.* New York: E. P. Dutton, 1931.

———. *Hari the Jungle Lad.* New York: E. P. Dutton, 1924.

———. *Kari the Elephant.* New York: E. P. Dutton, 1922.

Mukherjee, Bharati. *Jasmine.* New York: Viking Penguin, 1989.

———. *The Middleman and Other Stories.* New York: Viking Penguin, 1988.

Mura, David. *Turning Japanese: Memoirs of a Sansei.* Boston: Atlantic Monthly Press, 1991.

Murayama, Milton. *All I Asking for is My Body.* 1975. Honolulu: University of Hawai'i Press, 1988.

———. "I'll Crack Your Head Kotsun." *Arizona Quarterly* 15, no. 2 (1959): 137–149.

Na, An. *A Step From Heaven.* Honesdale, Pa.: Boyds Mills Press, 2001.

———. *Wait for Me.* New York: Penguin, 2006.

Narayan, Kirin. *Love, Stars, and All That.* New York: Washington Square Press, 1994.

———. *Mondays on the Dark Night of the Moon: Himalayan Foothills Folktales.* New York: Oxford University Press, 1997.

———. *Storytellers, Saints and Scoundrels: Folk Narrative in Hindu Religious Teaching.* Philadelphia: University of Pennsylvania Press, 1989.

Narita, Jude. *Coming Into Passion/Song for a Sansei.* Ms. 345. Roberta Uno Asian Women Playwrights Scripts Collection 1924–1992, W. E. B. DuBois Library. Amherst: University of Massachusetts Press, 1985.

Ng, Fae Myenne. *Bone.* New York: Hyperion, 1993.

Ngor, Haing. *Haing Ngor: a Cambodian Odyssey.* With Roger Warner. New York: McMillan, 1987.

Nieh, Hualing. *Mulberry and Peach: Two Women of China.* New York: The Feminist Press, 1998.

Nigam, Sanjay. *The Non-Resident Indian and Other Stories.* New Delhi: Penguin India, 1996.

———. *The Snake Charmer.* New York: William Morrow, 1998.

———. *Transplanted Man.* New York: HarperCollins, 2002.

Nishikawa, Lane. *The Gate of Heaven.* With Victor Talmadge. In *Asian American Drama: 9 Plays from the Multiethnic Landscape,* edited by Brian Nelson, 161–208. New York: Applause, 1997.

Noguchi, Yone. *The American Diary of a Japanese Girl.* New York: Frederick A. Stokes Company, 1902.

———. *From the Eastern Sea.* New York: Mitchell Kennerley, 1910.

———. *Selected English Writings of Yone Noguchi: An East-West Literary Assimilation.* Edited by Yoshinobu Hakutani. London: Associated University Press. Vol. 1, *Poetry,* 1990; Vol. 2, *Prose,* 1992.

———. *The Story of Yone Noguchi, Told by Himself.* Philadelphia : G. W. Jacobs Co., 1915.

Nunes, Susan. *To Find the Way.* Honolulu: University of Hawaii Press, 1992.

———. *The Last Dragon.* New York: Clarion Books, 1995.

———. *A Small Obligation and Other Stories in Hilo.* No. 16, Bamboo Ridge Series. Honolulu: Bamboo Ridge Press, 1982.

Nye, Naomi Shihab. *19 Varieties of Gazelle.* New York: HarperCollins, 2002.

———. *Habibi.* New York: Simon and Schuster, 1997.

Oeur, U Sam. *Sacred Vows.* Translated by Ken McCullough. Minneapolis: Coffee House Press, 1998.

Okada, John. *No-No Boy.* Seattle: University of Washington Press, 1976.

Okita, Dwight. *Crossing with the Light.* Chicago: Tia Chucha Press, 1992.

———. *The Rainy Season.* In *Asian American Drama: 9 Plays from the Multiethnic Landscape.* Edited by Brian Nelson, 209–262. New York: Applause, 1997.

Okubo, Mine. *Citizen 13660.* New York: Columbia University Press, 1946.

Ondaatje, (Philip) Michael. *Anil's Ghost.* New York: Knopf, 2000.

———. *The Collected Works of Billy the Kid: Left Handed Poems.* New York: Norton, 1970.

———. *The English Patient.* New York: Knopf, 1992.

Ong, Han. *The Disinherited.* New York: Farrar, Straus and Giroux, 2004.

———. *Fixer Chao.* New York: Picador, 2001.

Otsuka, Julie. *When the Emperor was Divine.* New York: Knopf, 2002.

Oyabe, Jenichiro. *A Japanese Robinson Crusoe.* Boston & Chicago: Pilgrim Press, 1898.

Ozeki, Ruth. *All Over Creation.* New York: Viking, 2003.

———. *My Year of Meats.* New York: Viking, 1998.

Pak, Gary. *Children of a Fireland.* Honolulu: University of Hawaii Press, 2004.

———. *A Ricepaper Airplane.* Honolulu: University of Hawaii Press, 1997.

———. *The Watcher of Waipuna and Other Stories.* Honolulu: Bamboo Ridge, 1992.

Pak, Ty. *Cry, Korea, Cry.* New York: Woodhouse, 1999.

———. *Guilt Payment.* Honolulu: Bamboo Ridge, 1983.

———. *Moonbay.* New York: Woodhouse, 1999.

Park, Frances. *Good-bye, 382 Shin Dang Dong.* Illustrated by Yangsook Choi. Washington, D.C.: National Geographic, 2002.

———. *When My Sister Was Cleopatra Moon.* New York: Miramax, 2001.

Park, Frances, and Ginger Park. *My Freedom Trip: A Child's Escape from North Korea.* Illustrated by Debra Reid Jenkins. Honesdale, Pa.: Boyd Mills Press, 1998.

———. *The Royal Bee.* Illustrated by Christopher Zhong-Yuan Zhang. Honesdale, Pa.: Boyd Mills Press, 2000.

———. *To Swim Across the World.* New York: Hyperion, 2001.

Park, Linda Sue. *Archer's Quest.* New York: Clarion, 2006.

———. *Bee-bim Bop.* New York: Clarion, 2005.

———. *The Firekeeper's Son.* New York: Clarion, 2004.

———. *The Kite Fighters.* New York: Clarion, 2000.

———. *Mung-Mung.* Watertown, Mass.: Charlesbridge Publishing, 2004.

———. *Project Mulberry.* New York: Clarion, 2005.

———. *Seesaw Girl.* Illustrated by Jean and Mousien Tseng. New York: Clarion, 1999.

———. *A Single Shard.* New York: Clarion, 2001.

———. *When My Name Was Keoko.* New York: Clarion, 2002.

Park, No-Young. *Chinaman's Chance.* 1940. 3rd & rev. ed. Boston: Meador Publishing, 1948.

———. *Making a New China.* Boston: Stratford Co., 1929.

———. *An Oriental View of American Civilization.* Boston: Hale, Cushman, & Hunt, 1934.

———. *Retreat of the West: The White Man's Adventure in Eastern Asia.* Boston: Meador Publishing, 1937.

———. *The White Man's Peace: An Oriental View of Our Attempts at Making World Peace.* Boston: Meador Publishing, 1948.

Phan, Aimee. *We Should Never Meet.* New York: St. Martin's, 2004.

Pittalwala, Iqbal. *Dear Paramount Pictures.* Dallas, Tex.: Southern Methodist University Press, 2002.

Qiu, Xiaolong. *Death of a Red Heroine.* New York: Soho Press, 2000.

———. *A Loyal Character Dancer.* New York: Soho Press, 2002.

———. *When Red is Black.* New York: Soho Press, 2004.

Rachlin, Nahid. *Foreigner.* New York: Norton, 1978.

———. *The Heart's Desire.* San Francisco: City Lights Press, 1995.

———. *Jumping Over Fire,* San Francisco: City Lights Press, 2006.

———. *Married to a Stranger.* San Francisco: City Lights Press, 1983.

———. *Veils: Short Stories.* San Francisco: City Lights Press, 1992.

Rahman, Imad. *I Dream of Microwaves.* New York: Farrar, Straus and Giroux, 2004.

Rao, Raja. *The Cat and Shakespeare.* New York: Macmillan, 1965.

———. *The Chessmaster and His Moves.* New Delhi: Vision Books, 1988.

———. *Comrade Kirillov.* New Delhi: Orient, 1976.

———. *The Cow of the Barricades, and other Stories.* Madras: Oxford University Press, 1947.

———. *The Ganga Ghat.* New Delhi: Vision Books, 1989.

———. *Kanthapura.* New York: New Directions, 1963.

———. *The Policeman and the Rose.* Delhi: Oxford University Press, 1978.

———. *The Serpent and the Rope.* London: John Murray, 1960.

Rizzuto, Rahna Reiko. *Why She Left Us.* New York: HarperCollins, 1999.

Rno, Sung. *Cleveland Raining.* In *But Still, Like Air, I'll Rise: New Asian American Plays,* edited by Velina Hasu Houston, 227–270. Philadelphia: Temple University Press, 1997.

———. *wAve.* Alexandria, Va.: Alexander Street Press, 2003.

Rosca, Ninotchka. *Bitter Country and Other Stories.* Quezon City, Philippines: Malaya Books, 1970.

———. *Endgame: The Fall of Marcos.* New York: Franklin Watts, 1987.

———. *The Monsoon Collection.* Santa Lucia and New York: University of Queensland Press, 1983.

———. *State of War.* New York: Norton, 1988.

———. *Twice Blessed.* New York: Norton, 1992.

Rowland, Laura Joh. *The Assassin's Touch.* New York: St. Martin's Minotaur, 2005.

———. *The Pillow Book of Lady Wisteria.* New York: St. Martin's Minotaur, 2002.

———. *Shinju.* New York: Random House, 1994.

———. *The Way of the Traitor.* New York: Villard Books, 1997.

Ryan, Teresa Le Yung. *Love Made of Heart.* New York: Kensington, 2002.

Saiki, Patsy Sumie. *Early Japanese Immigrants in Hawaii: The First Hundred Years.* Honolulu: Japanese Cultural Center of Hawaii, 1993.

———. *Ganbare! An Example of Japanese Spirit.* Honolulu: Kisaku, Inc., 1981.

———. *Japanese Women in Hawaii: The First 100 Years.* Honolulu: Kisaku, Inc., 1985.

———. *Sanchie, A Daughter of Hawaii.* Honolulu: Kisaku, Inc., 1977.

Sakamoto, Edward. *In the Alley. Kuma Kahua Plays.* Edited by Dennis Carroll. Honolulu: University of Hawai'i Press, 1983.

———. *Aloha Las Vegas and Other Plays.* Honolulu: University of Hawai'i Press, 2000.

———. *Hawai'I No Ka Oi: The Kamiya Family Trilogy.* Honolulu: University of Hawai'i Press, 1995.

Sakamoto, Kerri. *The Electrical Field.* Toronto: Knopf, 1998.

———. *One Hundred Million Hearts.* Toronto: Knopf Canada, 2003.

Santos, Bienvenido N. *The Praying Man.* Quezon City, Philippines: New Day, 1982.

———. *Scent of Apple: A Collection of Short Stories.* Seattle: University of Washington Press, 1979.

———. *Villa Magdalena: A Novel.* 1965. Quezon City, Philippines: New Day, 1999.

———. *The Volcano.* 1965. Quezon City, Philippines: New Day, 1986.

See, Lisa Lenine. *Dragon Bones.* New York: Random House, 2003.

———. *Flower Net.* New York: HarperCollins, 1997.

———. *Greetings from Southern California.* Portland, Oreg.: Graphic Arts Center, 1988.

———. *The Interior.* New York: HarperCollins, 1999.

———. *Lotus Land.* New York: Coward-McCann, 1983.

———. *On Gold Mountain: The One Hundred Year Odyssey of My Chinese-American Family.* 1995. Reprint, New York: Vintage, 1996.

———. *One Hundred Ten Shanghai Road.* New York: McGraw-Hill, 1986.

Seth, Vikram. *All You Who Sleep Tonight.* New York: Knopf, 1990.

———. *Arion and the Dolphin.* New York: Dutton, 1994.

———. *Beastly Tales from Here to There.* New Delhi: Viking, 1992.

———. *The Golden Gate.* New York: Random House, 1986.

———. *From Heaven Lake: Travels Through Sinkiang and Tibet.* London: Chatto and Windus, 1985.

———. *The Humble Administrator's Garden.* Manchester: Carcenet Press, 1985.

———. *Mappings.* Calcutta: Writers Workshop, 1980.

———. *A Suitable Boy.* New York: HarperCollins, 1993.

————. *Three Chinese Poets: Translation of Poems by Wang Wei, Li Bai, and Du Fu.* New York: HarperCollins, 1992.

Sidhwa, Bapsi. *An American Brat.* New Delhi: Penguin India, 1993.

————. *The Bride.* New York: St. Martin's, 1983.

————. *Cracking India.* Minneapolis: Milkweed Editions, 1991.

————. *The Crow-Eaters.* Minneapolis: Milkweed Editions, 1992.

Son, Diana. *R.A.W. ('Cause I'm a Woman).* In *Contemporary Plays by Women of Color: An Anthology,* edited by Kathy A. Perkins and Roberta Uno, 290–296. New York: Routledge, 1996.

————. *Stop Kiss.* Woodstock, New York: Overlook Press, 1999.

Sone, Monica. *Nisei Daughter.* New York: Little, Brown, 1953.

Song, Cathy. *Frameless Windows, Squares of Light.* New York: Norton, 1988.

————. *Picture Bride.* New Haven, Conn.: Yale University Press, 1983.

————. *School Figures.* Pittsburgh: University of Pittsburgh Press, 1994.

Sugimoto, Etsu Inagaki. *A Daughter of the Narikin.* New York: Doubleday, 1932.

————. *A Daughter of the Nohful.* New York: Doubleday, 1935.

————. *A Daughter of a Samurai.* New York: Doubleday, 1925.

————. *Grandmother O Kyo.* New York: Doubleday, 1940.

Suleri, Sara. *Boys Will Be Boys: A Daughter's Elegy.* Chicago: University of Chicago Press, 2003.

————. *Meatless Days.* Chicago: University of Chicago Press, 1989.

————. *The Rhetoric of English India.* Chicago: University of Chicago Press, 1992.

Suyemoto, Toyo. "Camp Memories: Rough and Broken Shards." In *Japanese Americans: From Relocation to Redress.* Rev. ed., edited by Roger Daniels, Sandra C. Taylor, and Harry H. L. Kitano, 27–30. Seattle: University of Washington Press, 1991.

————. "In Tropaz." *Quiet Fire: A Historical Anthology of Asian American Poetry, 1892–1970.* Edited by Juliana Chang. New York: Asian American Writers' Workshop, 1996.

Sze, Arthur. *Archipelago.* Port Townsend, Wash.: Copper Canyon Press, 1995.

————. *The Redshifting Web: Poems 1970–1998.* Port Townsend, Wash.: Copper Canyon Press, 1998.

————. *The Silk Dragon: Translations from the Chinese.* Port Townsend, Wash.: Copper Canyon Press, 2001.

————. *The Willow Wind: Translations From the Chinese and Poems.* 1972. Rev. ed. Santa Fe, N.Mex.: Tooth of Time, 1981.

Sze, Mai-Mai. *Echo of a Cry: A Story Which Began in China.* New York: Harcourt, Brace, 1945.

————. *Silent Children.* New York: Harcourt, Brace, 1948.

Takei, George. *To the Stars: An Autobiography of George Takei, Star Trek's Mr. Sulu.* New York: Pocket Books, 1994.

Tamagawa, Kathleen. *Holy Prayers in a Horse's Ear.* New York: Ray Long and Richard R. Smith, 1932.

Tan, Amy. *The Bonesetter's Daughter.* New York: Putnam, 2001.

————. *The Chinese Siamese Cat.* New York: Macmillan, 1994.

————. *The Hundred Secret Senses.* New York: Putnam, 1995.

————. *The Joy Luck Club.* New York: Putnam, 1989.

————. *The Kitchen God's Wife.* New York: Putnam, 1991.

————. *The Moon Lady.* New York: Macmillan, 1992.

————. *The Opposite of Fate.* New York: Putnam, 2003.

————. *Saving Fish from Drowning.* New York: Putnam, 2005.

Tham, Hilary. *Bad Names for Women.* Washington, D.C.: Word Works, 1989.

————. *Lane with No Name: Memoirs and Poems of a Malaysian-Chinese Girlhood.* Boulder, Colo., London: A Three Continents Book/ Lynne Reinner Publishers, 1997.

————. *Men & Other Strange Myths: Poems and Art.* Colorado Springs, Colo.: Three Continents Press, 1994.

———. *Tao of Mrs. Wei.* Washington, D.C.: Word Works, 2003.

———. *Tin Mines and Concubines.* Washington, D.C.: Washington Writers' Publishing House, 2005.

Trenka, Jane Jeong. *The Language of Blood: a Memoir.* Saint Paul, Minn.: Graywolf Press, 2003.

Truong, Monique. *The Book of Salt.* Boston: Houghton Mifflin, 2003.

Tsiang, H. T. *The Complete Works of H. T. Tsiang.* Edited by Floyd Cheung. New York: Ironweed Press, 2005.

Tsukiyama, Gail. *Dreaming Water.* New York: St. Martin's Press, 2002.

———. *The Language of Threads.* New York: St. Martin's Press, 1999.

———. *Night of Many Dreams.* New York: St. Martin's Press, 1998

———. *The Samurai's Garden.* New York: St. Martin's Press, 1994.

———. *Women of the Silk.* New York: St. Martin's Press, 1991.

Tuan, Alice. *Last of the Suns.* Ms. 345. Roberta Uno Asian Women Playwrights Scripts Collection 1924–1992, W. E. B. DuBois Library, University of Massachusetts, Amherst; also at the Joyce Ketay Agency, New York City, 1995.

———. *Some Asians.* In *Perishable Theatre's 5th Annual Women's Playwriting Festival,* 20–31. Seattle: Rain City Projects, 1997.

Tyau, Kathleen. *A Little Too Much Is Enough.* New York: Farrar, Straus and Giroux, 1995.

———. *Makai.* New York: Farrar, Straus and Giroux, 1999.

Uchida, Yoshiko. *The Best Bad Thing.* New York: Atheneum, 1983.

———. *The Dancing Kettle and Other Japanese Folk Tales.* San Diego, Calif.: Harcourt Brace, 1949.

———. *Desert Exile.* 1982. Seattle: University of Washington Press, 1984.

———. *In-Between Miya.* New York: Scribner, 1967.

———. *The Invisible Thread.* New York: Simon and Schuster, 1991.

———. *Jar of Dreams.* 1981. Boston: Houghton Mifflin, 1995.

———. *Journey Home.* New York: Atheneum, 1978.

———. *Journey to Topaz.* New York: Scribner, 1971.

———. *The Magic Listening Cap: More Folk Tales from Japan.* 1955. Berkeley, Calif.: Creative Arts Book Co., 1987.

———. *New Friends for Susan.* New York: Scribner, 1951.

———. *Picture Bride.* 1987. Seattle: University of Washington Press, 1997.

———. *The Promise Year.* San Diego, Calif.: Harcourt Brace, 1959.

———. *Samurai of Gold Hill.* New York: Scribner, 1972.

Umrigar, Thrity. *Bombay Time.* New York: Picador, 2001.

———. *First Darling of the Morning.* New York: HarperCollins, 2004.

———. *The Space Between Us.* New York: HarperCollins, 2006.

Ung, Loung. *First They Killed My Father: a Daughter of Cambodia Remembers.* New York: HarperCollins, 2000.

———. *Lucky Child: A Daughter of Cambodia Reunites with the Sister She Left Behind.* New York: HarperCollins, 2005.

Upadhyay, Samrat. *Arresting God in Kathmandu.* Boston: Houghton Mifflin/Mariner, 2001.

———. *The Guru of Love.* Boston: Houghton Mifflin/Mariner, 2003.

———. *Royal Ghosts.* Boston: Houghton Mifflin/Mariner, 2006.

Uyehara, Denise. *Hello (Sex) Kitty: Mad Bitch on Wheels.* In *O Solo Homo: The New Queer Performance,* edited by Holly Hughes and David Roman, 377–409. New York: Grove, 1998.

———. *Maps of City and Body and Other Tales.* New York: Kaya Publications, 2001.

Uyemoto, Holly. *Rebel Without a Clue.* New York: Crown, 1989.

———. *Go.* New York: Dutton, 1995.

Villa, Jose Garcia. *Footnote to Youth: Short Stories.* New York: Scribner, 1993.

———. *Have Come, Am Here.* New York: Viking, 1942.

———. *Many Voices.* Manila: Philippine Book Guild, 1939.

———. *Mir-i-Nisa.* Manila: Alberto S. Florentino, 1966.

———. *Poems by Doveglion.* Manila: Philippine Writers' League, 1941.

———. *Selected Poems and New.* New York: McDowell, Obolensky, 1958.

———. *Selected Stories of Jose Garcia Villa.* Manila: Alberto S. Florentino, 1962.

———. *Volume Two.* New York: New Directions, 1949.

Wang, Ping. *Aching for Beauty: Footbinding in China.* Minneapolis: University of Minnesota Press, 2000.

———. *American Visa.* Minneapolis: Coffee House Press, 1994.

———. *Of Flesh and Spirit.* Minneapolis: Coffee House Press, 1998.

———. *Foreign Devil.* Minneapolis: Coffee House Press, 1996.

———. *The Magic Whip.* Minneapolis: Coffee House Press, 2003.

———. *New Generation: Poems from China Today.* Brooklyn, N.Y.: Hanging Loose Press, 1999.

Watanabe, Sylvia A. *Home to Stay: Asian-American Women's Fiction* (Co-editor). Greenfield Center. N.Y.: Greenfield Review, 1990.

———. *Into the Fire: Asian-American Prose* (editor). Greenfield Center, N.Y.: Greenfield Review, 1996.

———. *Talking to the Dead.* New York: Doubleday, 1992.

Watkins, Yoko Kawashima. *So Far from the Bamboo Grove.* New York: Puffin Books, 1986.

———. *My Brother, My Sister, and I.* New York: Aladdin Paperbacks, 1996.

———. *Tales from the Bamboo Grove.* New York: Simon and Schuster, 1992.

Wong, Elizabeth. *China Dolls (The Imagined Life of an American Actress).* In *Contemporary Plays by Women of Color: An Anthology,* edited by Kathy A. Perkins and Robert Uno, 310–316. New York: Routledge, 1996.

———. *Kimchee and Chitlins.* In *But Still, Like Air, I'll Rise: New Asian American Plays,* edited by Velina Hasu Houston, 395–450. Philadelphia: Temple University Press, 1997.

———. *Letters to a Student Revolutionary.* In *Unbroken Thread: An Anthology of Plays by Asian American Women,* edited by Roberto Uno, 261–

308. Amherst: University of Massachusetts Press, 1993.

Wong, Jade Snow. *Fifth Chinese Daughter.* 1945. Seattle: University of Washington Press, 1989.

———. *No Chinese Stranger.* New York: Harper and Row, 1975.

Wong, Nanying Stella. "From One Delta to Another." In *Bearing Dreams, Shaping Visions: Asian Pacific American Perspectives, Peace and Pieces: An Anthology of Contemporary American Poetry,* edited by Linda A. Revilla, Gail M. Nomura, Shawn Wong, and Shirley Hune, 127–128. Pullman: Washington State University Press, 1993.

Wong, Nellie. *Dreams in Harrison Railroad Park.* San Francisco: Kelsey St. Press, 1977.

———. *Death of Long Steam Lady.* Los Angeles: West End Press. 1986.

———. *Stolen Moments.* A Crimson Edge Chapbook. Goshen, Conn.: Chicory Blue Press, 1997.

Wong, Rita. *Monkeypuzzle.* Vancouver, B.C.: Press Gang, 1998.

Wong, Shawn. *American Knees.* New York: I. Reed Books, 1979.

———. *Homebase.* New York: Simon and Schuster, 1995.

———. *Yardbird Reader* (Co-editor). Berkeley, Calif.: Yardbird Publishing Cooperative, 1975.

Wong, Shawn, ed. *Asian American Literature: A Brief Introduction and Anthology.* New York: HarperCollins, 1996.

Wong, Shawn, et al., eds. *Aiiieeeee!: An Anthology of Chinese American and Japanese American Literature.* New York: Meridian, 1991.

———. *The Big Aiiieeeee!: An Anthology of Chinese American and Japanese American Literature.* New York: Penguin, 1991.

Woo, Merle. "Letter to Ma." In *This Bridge Called My Back.* 2nd ed., edited by Cherrie Moraga and Gloria Anzaldua, 13–23. Latham, N.Y.: Kitchen Table/Women of Color Press, 1986.

———. *Yellow Woman Speaks: Selected Poems.* Seattle: Radical Women Publications, 1986 and 2003.

Yamada, Mitsuye (May). *Camp Notes.* San Lorenzo, Calif.: Shameless Hussy Press, 1976.

———. *Desert Run.* Latham, N.Y.: Kitchen Table/Women of Color Press, 1988.

Yamamoto, Hisaye (Desoto). *Seventeen Syllables and Other Stories.* Latham, N.Y.: Kitchen Table: Women of Color Press, 1988.

———. *Seventeen Syllables: Hisaye Yamamoto.* Edited by King-kok Cheung. Women Writers: Texts and Contexts Series. New Brunswick, N.J.: Rutgers University Press, 1994.

Yamanaka, Lois-Ann. *Behold the Many.* New York: Farrar, Straus and Giroux, 2006.

———. *Blu's Hanging.* New York: Farrar, Straus and Giroux, 1997.

———. *Father of the Four Passages.* New York: Farrar, Straus and Giroux, 2002.

———. *Heads by Harry.* New York: Farrar, Straus and Giroux, 1999.

———. *Name Me Nobody.* New York: Hyperion, 1999.

———. *Saturday Night at the Pahala Theater.* Honolulu: Bamboo Ridge, 1993.

———. *Wild Meat and the Bully Burgers.* New York: Farrar, Straus and Giroux, 1996.

Yamashita, Karen Tei. *Brazil Maru.* Minneapolis: Coffee House Press, 1992.

———. *Circle K Cycles.* Minneapolis: Coffee House Press, 2001.

———. *Through the Arc of the Rain Forest.* Minneapolis: Coffee House Press, 1990.

———. *Tropic of Orange.* Minneapolis: Coffee House Press, 1997.

Yamate, Sandra. *Ashok, by Any Other Name.* Chicago: Polychrome, 1992.

———. *Char Siu Bao Boy.* Chicago: Polychrome, 1991.

Yamauchi, Wakako. *And the Soul Shall Dance.* In *West Coast Plays, 11–12,* edited by Rick Foster, 117–164. Berkeley: California Theatre Council, 1982.

———. *The Chairman's Wife.* In *The Politics of Life: Four Plays by Asian American Women,* edited by Velina Hasu Houston, 101–149. Philadelphia: Temple University Press, 1993.

———. *The Music Lessons. Unbroken Thread: An Anthology of Plays by Asian American Women,* edited by Robert Uno, 53–104. Amherst: University of Massachusetts Press, 1993.

———. *12-1-A.* In *The Politics of Life: Four Plays by Asian American Women,* edited by Velina Hasu Houston, 213–260. Philadelphia: Temple University Press, 1993.

Yau, John. *Berlin Diptychon* (with Bill Barrette). New York: Timken Publishers, 1995.

———. *Corpse And Mirror.* New York: Henry Holt, 1983.

———. *Forbidden Entries.* Santa Rosa, Calif.: Black Sparrow Press, 1996.

———. *Hawaiian Cowboys.* Santa Rosa, Calif.: Black Sparrow Press, 1995.

———. *My Symptoms.* Santa Rosa, Calif.: Black Sparrow Press, 1998.

———. *Radiant Silhouette.* Santa Rosa, Calif.: Black Sparrow Press, 1998.

———. *The Reading of an Ever-Changing Tale.* Clinton, N.Y.: Nobodaddy Press, 1977.

———. *The Sleepless Night of Eugene Delacroix.* Brooklyn, N.Y.: Release Press, 1980.

———. *Sometimes: Poems.* Gardiner, Me.: Tilbury House, 1979.

Yep, Laurence. *The Amah.* New York: Putnam, 1999.

———. *Child of the Owl.* New York: Harper and Row, 1977.

———. *The Dragon Prince.* New York: HarperCollins, 1996.

———. *Dragon's Gate.* New York: HarperCollins, 1993.

———. *Dragonwings.* New York: Harper and Row, 1975.

———. *Dream Soul.* New York: HarperCollins, 2000.

———. *Hirohima.* New York: Scholastic, 1995.

———. *The Imp That Ate My Homework.* New York: HarperCollins, 1998.

———. *The Lost Garden.* New York: Simon and Schuster, 1991.

———. *The Rainbow People.* New York: Harper and Row, 1989.

———. *Spring Pearl, the Last Flower* Middleton, Wis.: Pleasant Company, 2002.

Yew, Chay. *Porcelain and A Language of Their Own: Two Plays.* New York: Grove, 1997.

———. *The Hyphenated American.* New York: Grove, 2002.

Yoo, David. *Girls for Breakfast.* New York: Random House, 2005.

Yun, Mia. *House of the Winds.* New York: Penguin, 2000.

———. *Translation of Beauty.* New York: Atria, 2004.

Yung, Wing. *My Life in China and America.* New York: Holt, 1909.

BIBLIOGRAPHY OF SECONDARY SOURCES

Agarwal, Priya. *Passage from India: Post-1965 Indian Immigrants and Their Children – Conflicts, Concerns and Solutions.* Palos Verdes, Calif.: Yuvati Publications, 1991.

Aguilar-San Juan, Karin, ed. *The State of Asian America: Activism and Resistance in the 1990s.* Boston: South End Press, 1994.

Chang, Juliana, ed. *Quiet fire: A Historical Anthology of Asian American Poetry, 1892–1970.* Philadelphia: Temple University Press, 1996.

Chen, Tina. *Double Agency: Acts of Impersonation in Asian American Literature and Culture.* Palo Alto, Calif.: Stanford University Press, 2005.

Cheung, King-Kok. *Articulate Silences: Hisaye Yamamoto, Maxine Hong Kingston, Joy Kigawa.* Ithaca, N.Y.: Cornell University Press, 1993.

———. *An Interethnic Companion to Asian American Literature.* New York: Cambridge University Press, 1996.

Cheung, King-kok, and Stan Yogi. *Asian American Literature: An Annotated Bibliography.* New York: MLA, 1988.

Chin, Frank, Jeffery Chan, Lawson Inada, and Shawn Wong, eds. *Aiiieeeee! An Anthology of Asian-American Writers.* Washington, D.C.: Howard University Press, 1974.

Chow, Claire S. *Leaving Deep Water: the Lives of Asian American Women at the Crossroads of Two Cultures.* New York: Dutton, 1998.

Dasgupta, Shamita Das. *A Patchwork Shawl: Chronicles of South Asian Women in America.* New Brunswick, N.J.: Rutgers University Press, 1998.

Eng, David L., and Alice Y. Hom. *Q & A: Queer in Asian America.* Philadelphia: Temple University Press, 1998.

Galang, M. Evelina, ed. *Screaming Monkeys: Critiques of Asian American Images.* Minneapolis: Coffee House Press, 2003.

Hsu, Kai-yu, and Helen Palubinskas. *Asian-American Authors.* Boston: Houghton, 1972.

Huang, Guiyou, ed. *Asian American Autobiographers: A Bio-Bibliographical Critical Sourcebook.* Westport, Conn.: Greenwood Press, 2001.

———. *Asian American Poets: A Bio-Bibliographical Critical Sourcebook.* Westport, Conn.: Greenwood Press, 2002.

———. *Asian American Short Story Writers: An A to Z Guide.* Westport, Conn.: Greenwood Press, 2003.

Kim, Elaine H. *Asian American Literature: An Introduction to the Writings and Their Social Context.* Philadelphia: Temple University Press, 1982.

Leonard, George J., ed. *The Asian Pacific American Heritage: A Companion to Literature and Arts.* New York: Garland, 1999.

Li, David Leiwei. *Imagining the Nation: Asian American Literature and Cultural Consent.* Palo Alto, Calif.: Stanford University Press, 2000.

Lim, Shirley Geok-lin, and Amy Ling, eds. *Reading the Literatures of Asian America.* Philadelphia: Temple University Press, 1992.

Ling, Jinqi. *Narrating Nationalisms: Ideology and Form in Asian American Literature.* Oxford: Oxford University Press, 1998.

Liu, Miles Xian. *Asian American Playwrights: A Bio-Bibliographical Critical Sourcebook.* Westport, Conn.: Greenwood Press, 2002.

Lowe, Lisa. *Immigrant Acts: On Asian American Cultural Politics.* Durham, N.C.: Duke University Press, 1996.

Lye, Colleen. *America's Asia: Racial Form and American Literature, 1882–1945.* Princeton, N.J.: Princeton University Press, 2004.

Ma, Sheng-mei. *Immigrant Subjectivities in Asian American and Asian Diaspora Literatures.* Albany: State University of New York Press, 1998.

Nelson, Emmanuel S., ed. *Asian American Novelists: A Bio-Bibliographical Critical Sourcebook.* Westport, Conn.: Greenwood Press, 2000.

———, ed. *Reworlding: The Literature of the Indian Diaspora.* Westport, Conn.: Greenwood Press, 1992.

———, ed. *Writers of the Indian Diaspora: A Bio-Bibliographical Critical Sourcebook.* Westport, Conn.: Greenwood Press, 1993.

Shah, Sonia, ed. *Dragon Ladies: Asian American Feminists Breath Fire.* Boston: South End Press, 1997.

Srikanth, Rajini. *World Next Door: South Asian American Literature and the Idea of America.* Philadelphia: Temple University Press, 2006.

Takaki, Ronald. *Strangers from a Different Shore: A History of Asian Americans.* New York: Penguin, 1989.

Ty, Eleanor, and Donald C. Goellnicht. *Asian North American Identities: Beyond the Hyphen.* Bloomington: Indiana University Press, 2004.

Wong, Mitali P., and Zia Hasan. *The Fiction of South Asians in North America and the Caribbean: A Critical Study of English-Language Works Since 1950.* Jefferson, N.C.: McFarland & Co., 2004.

Wong, Sau-ling Cynthia. *Reading Asian American Literature: From Necessity to Extravagance.* Princeton, N.J.: Princeton University Press, 1993.

Wong, Shawn, ed. *Asian American Literature: A Brief Introduction and Anthology.* New York: HarperCollins, 1997.

Zhou, Xiaojing, and Samina Najmi, eds. *Form and Transformation in Asian American Literature.* Seattle: University of Washington Press, 2005.

LIST OF
CONTRIBUTORS

Kyoko Amano, University of Indianapolis

Alissa Appel, University of Rochester

Suzanne Arakawa, Claremont Graduate University

Mimi S. Van Ausdall, University of Iowa

Anne Bahringer, University of Wisconsin at Milwaukee

Ann Beebe, University of Texas at Tyler

LynnDianne Beene, University of New Mexico

Patricia Kennedy Bostian, Central Piedmont Community College

Albert Braz, University of Alberta

Heejung Cha, Indiana University of Pennsylvania

Ray W. Chandrasekara, Albany College of Pharmacy

Fu-jen Chen, National Sun Yat-Sen University, Taiwan

Floyd Cheung, Smith College

Peggy Cho, Kyung Hee University, Korea

Katharine Chubbuck, Princeton University

Hyeyurn Chung, Korea University

Jaime Cleland, Graduate Center of the City University of New York

Beverley Curran, Aichi Shukutoku University at Nagoya, Japan

Rocío G. Davis, University of Navarra, Spain

Nandini Dhar, University of Texas at Austin

Monika Dix, SOAS, University of London

M. Vizcaya Echano, University of Bristol, U.K.

Melissa Gabot Fabros, University of California at Berkeley

Mary Fakler, State University of New York, College at New Paltz

Kate Falvey, New York City College of Technology/CUNY

Alex Feerst, Macalester College

James Fleming, University of Florida

Anne Marie Fowler, Keiser College

Bennett Fu, Concordia University, Canada

Catherine Fung, University of California at Davis

Julie Goodspeed-Chadwick, Ball State University

Dana Hansen, Humber College, Toronto

Fayeza Hasanat, University of Central Florida

Susanna Hoeness-Krupsaw, University of Southern Indiana

Shawn Holliday, Alice Lloyd College

Janis Butler Holm, Ohio University

Sandra S. Hughes, Western Kentucky University

Rachel Ihara, Graduate Center of the City University of New York

Nalini Iyer, Seattle University

Rajender Kaur, William Patterson University

Hyunjoo Ki, Kyonggi University, Korea

Martin Kich, Wright State University, Lake Campus

Jinah Kim, University of California at San Diego

Michelle Har Kim, University of Southern California

Izabella Kimak, Maria Curie-Sklodowska University in Lublin, Poland

Shion Kono, Sophia University, Japan

Eliko Kosaka, University of Tokyo

Joel Kuortti, University of Joensuu, Finland

Paul Lai, University of St. Thomas, Minnesota

Gui-woo Lee, Seoul Women's University, Korea

Hellen Lee-Keller, California State University at Sacramento

Jina Lee, Rider University

Kihan Lee, Myong Ji University, Korea

SuMee Lee, Korea University, Korea

January Lim, University of Alberta

Jeehyun Lim, University of Pennsylvania

Jianwu Liu, University of Alberta

Nan Ma, University of California at Riverside

Leo Mahoney, Mohave Community College

J. Edward Mallot, Rhodes College

Amy Lillian Manning, University of New Hampshire

Elisabetta Marino, University of Rome "Tor Vergata"

Janet Melo-Thaiss, York University

Matthew L. Miller, University of South Carolina, Aiken

Akhila Naik, Rider University

Hanh Nguyen, University of Florida

Marguerite Bich Nguyen, University of California at Berkeley

Seiwoong Oh, Rider University

Debbie Olson, Oklahoma State University

Andrea Opitz, University of Washington

Kevin De Ornellas, University of Ulster

Alice Otano, University of Navarra, Spain

Samuel Park, Columbia College, Chicago

Sarah Park, University of Illinois at Urbana-Champaign

Linda Pierce, University of Southern Mississippi

John Pinson, University of California at Riverside

Tina Powell, Fordham University

Covadonga Lamar Prieto, Universidad de Oviedo

Vanessa Rasmussen, Temple University

Greg Robinson, Université du Québec à Montréal

Asma Sayed, University of Alberta, Canada

Zohra Saed, Graduate Center of the City University of New York

Sukanya B. Senapati, Abraham Baldwin Agricultural College

Jeff Shantz, York University, Toronto, Canada

Jinbhum Shin, Songho College, Korea

Jeanne Sokolowski, Indiana University, Bloomington

Valerie Solar, University of California at Riverside

Anne N. Thalheimer, independent scholar

Bunkong Tuon, University of Massachusetts

Kirsten Twelbeck, Free University of Berlin

Manuela Vastolo, University of Naples, Italy

Eric Waggoner, West Virginia Wesleyan College

Tamara Wagner, Nanyang Technological University, Singapore

Zach Weir, Miami University

Sheena Wilson, University of Alberta

Yan Ying-Clifton, Ningbo University, China

Su-lin Yu, National Cheng Kung University, Taiwan

INDEX

◦◦◦

Note: Page numbers in **boldface** indicate main entries.

A

I